P9-EGL-423

THE WALL STREET JOURNAL.

THE WALL STREET JOURNAL.

The story of Dow Jones & the nation's business newspaper

LLOYD WENDT

RAND McNALLY & COMPANY
Chicago New York San Francisco

PERMISSIONS The author gratefully acknowledges permission to quote from the following publications:

The Age of Keynes by Robert Lekachman, copyright © 1966. Reprinted by permission of the publisher, Random House, Inc.

Everybody's Guide to the Stock Market by Harold M. Finley, copyright © 1956. Published by Henry Regnery Company. Reprinted by permission of the author.

Fortune, "The Story The Wall Street Journal Won't Print," by Carol J. Loomis (August 1971). Copyright © 1971 Time Inc. All rights reserved. Reprinted by permission of the publisher.

Harper's, "The Wall Street Journal Woos the Eggheads," by John Brooks (March 1959). Copyright © 1959. Reprinted by permission of the author.

Panic on Wall Street by Robert Sobel. Copyright © 1968. Reprinted by permission of the publisher, The Macmillan Company.

A Pride of Prejudices by Vermont Royster. Copyright © 1967. Published by Alfred A. Knopf. Reprinted by permission of the author.

A Proud Profession by William F. Kerby. Copyright © 1981. Published by Dow Jones-Irwin, Inc. Reprinted by permission of the author.

PICTURE CREDITS Except where otherwise noted, all photographs and other illustrations are from the Dow Jones Archives.

Library of Congress Cataloging in Publication Data
Wendt, Lloyd.
The Wall Street Journal.

Bibliography: p.
Includes index.
1. Dow, Jones & Co.—History. 2. Wall Street Journal —History. I. Title.
HG4910.W37 338.7′61071471 82-5341
ISBN 0-528-81116-9 AACR2

Printed in the United States of America
First printing, 1982

Contents

THE WALL STREET JOURNAL.

Prologue

In late March 1644 the Dutch West India Company at New Amsterdam concluded that too many cows and too many Indians were wandering at large on Manhattan Island, so a fence was decreed built: "Resolved, that a fence shall be made, beginning at the Great Bouewery, and extending to Emanuel's plantation, and all are to repair thither on Monday 4th April, with tools to build a fence." The resulting barricade was mostly a slight earthen embankment studded with uprooted tree trunks, but it caused the cows to munch their way homeward each sunset along a path that someday would be called Broad Street.

By springtime 1653 Governor Peter Stuyvesant concluded that the British, at war with the Netherlands as usual, were about to attack, and he assumed they would come by land. Stuyvesant decreed that the fence across the southern tip of Manhattan should become a fortification. The citizens were summoned to dig a ditch, a moat 5 feet deep and 10 to 12 feet wide, to extend from the east river to the north river. Carpenters were instructed to prepare needed stakes and rails, soldiers and servants of the Company "without exception" were to work on the fort by raising a wall 12 feet high, and they were to build gun platforms and carriages. Farmers were to haul turn, sawyers were to saw timbers.

The resultant wall had a gate, Watergate, at what later would be Wall and Pearl streets. The gate was shut at sundown, and entry to the town after that hour was forbidden "on pain of death." But the British didn't attack by land. They came by sea in 1664, anchoring off Coney Island just below the Narrows, and captured the settlement without firing a shot. Later the British burned and destroyed the wall. In 1704 Abraham de Peyster ceded a part of his property along Wall Street as a site for the New York City Hall, which was completed that year and later became the first capitol of the United States, the setting for George Washington's inauguration as president in 1789.

The first Congress met in City Hall, renamed Federal Hall, on Wall Street in 1789 and 1790. It assumed the debts of the several colonies and of the new government, issuing about $80 million in government notes, which were offered to the general public. This created an immediate and exciting market in securities sold by bankers, merchants, and auctioneers becoming active in Wall Street. These and other stocks and bonds—as well as orders for commodities and shipping, and warehouse receipts—were put up for sale and were bought by the traders who gathered each day under the buttonwood (sycamore) tree at 68–70 Wall Street.

In March 1792 *Loudon's Register*, a New York newspaper also called the *Diary*, carried this advertisement: "The stock exchange office is opened at No. 22 Wall Street for the accommodation of dealers in stock, and in which Public Sales will be held daily at noon as usual in rotation by A. L. Bleecker & Sons; J. Pintard, McEvers & Barclay; Cortlandt & Ferrers; and Jay & Sutton."

Loudon's reported on March 23, 1792: "A meeting was held at the Corres Hotel on Wed. last, March 21st, of the merchants and dealers in stocks, when they came to the resolution that on and after the 21st of April next they will not attend any sale of stocks at Public Auction, and also appointed a committee to provide a proper room for them to assemble in, and to report such regulation relative to the mode of transacting their business, as in their opinion may be proper."

This effort to regulate and order business in Wall Street would be unending and only partly successful. Generally, the traders were attempting to protect themselves and their commissions rather than the public. There was fierce competition, and various groups formed in an effort to dominate trading. Mostly the traders continued to meet in the street, though meetings were held with some regularity in the Tontine Coffee House, built in 1793 at the corner of Wall and Water streets, after it had been chartered as a Merchants' Exchange that same year. The Exchange had 203 members, but many renegades continued their street auctions in competition. In 1827 a new Merchants' Exchange building was erected at Wall and Hanover streets to serve the New York Stock and Exchange Board. This Board had organized in 1817, and on January 26, 1819, it had passed a rule that, when effective, helped to create the need for a new Wall Street industry—that of reporting hard-to-get financial news. Said the Board's resolution, "It is mutually understood that the members of this Board do not communicate to persons out-doors what members of this Board are purchasers or sellers of stocks at this Board, or what members offer to purchase or to sell."

Since the orders were far from effective in the beginning, the development of professional stock reporting proceeded slowly. However, there were specialized writers of financial and mercantile letters in Wall Street, as elsewhere, almost from the beginning. The merchants of Babylon and Carthage, Venice and London, had such letter-writers for hundreds of years; they were in fact the forerunners of the newspaper. Banks and financial and insurance houses, especially the Rothschilds and Lloyd's of London, developed their own communication networks. All persons and companies involved in stocks, bonds, banking, or the movement of goods (or money representing goods) needed fast, accurate information and were willing to pay for it. The purveyors of such information had to have unusual access, extensive knowledge and dependability, and the capability to act swiftly.

Following the War of 1812, as American commerce improved, the West was opened to development that would supersede the fur-trade barter era, and vast amounts of government bonds were available for sale as a result of the cost of the war and the authorization of interior improvements such as river and harbor development. New York's Wall Street boomed. The city's population had grown to 175,000 by 1827, and that was only the beginning. Waves of immigration struck Manhattan Island, markets opened, and railroads were built until 20 lines served New York, connecting ocean steamers and packet boats with a vast interior network. In 1830 the first railroad stock, the Mohawk and Hudson, was traded. New railroads would be added within a few years—New York Central, Erie, Harlem Central, Hudson River, Michigan Southern, Prairie du Chien, Fort Wayne, and Rock Island.

Even in 1840, however, the boardrooms of the New York Stock and Exchange Board were of a modest sort. The Merchants' Exchange at Wall and Water streets had been gutted by fire in 1835, and until it was rebuilt in 1842, the Board had several different locations. "The very room in which millions in stock were sold was once only a hay loft," says a city directory of the period. There was a rival organization even more poorly accommodated, though it called itself "The Bourse" after the Paris Bourse, organized in 1726. It met outdoors.

There was a constant promulgation of rules by the organization calling itself the Stock and Exchange Board: "No fictitious sales or contracts shall be made at the Board," and "Any member leaving the Room during the calling of stocks, without Permission of the president, shall be fined 25 centes." The penalty seemed small, but a member failing to attend a meeting could be fined only 6 cents. Presumably, the culprit leaving the room, if he was not answering a call of nature, was about to divulge information to an unauthorized person, thus incurring the greater penalty.

In 1856 there were two daily calls, or auctions, of stocks—in the morning and in the afternoon, evidently by rival groups. One such group for a time called the stocks in a basement room at 23 William Street, dubbed the "Coal Hole." In his well-documented history of the New York Stock Exchange, Francis L. Eames, president of the Exchange from 1894 to 1898, notes that the newspapers were reporting both the "sales of the Coal Hole" and "sales of the Public Stock Board" by 1862. On January 29, 1863, the New York Stock and Exchange Board changed its name to the New York Stock Exchange and raised the initiation fee to $3,000 (except for a clerk who had served a member for three years, who could be admitted for $1,500). The Exchange had finally matured. Also, some of the open-air traders decided to change their ways. "As business increased in 1861–62," wrote Eames, "the influential elderly men were naturally unfitted for transacting business in the street and they formed in 1864 the Open Board of Brokers."

On December 9, 1865, the Stock Exchange moved from its meeting place in Lord's Court (where it had met since 1857) to a new four-story building at 10–12 Broad Street, which had been constructed for it by the New York Stock Exchange Building Company. The New York Stock Exchange and the Open Board consolidated on May 8, 1869, under the name of the former. There were now 1,060 members. Even so, there were still free-lance calls in the evenings in a parlor of the Fifth Avenue Hotel, and various specialized exchanges developed, the most notable being the New York Gold Exchange.

The firms specializing in reporting Wall Street news had also developed so that hundreds of messengers sped about the streets of lower Manhattan carrying their news bulletins to increasing numbers of subscribers.

It was the Gold Exchange that first instituted a specialized wire reporting system in Wall Street. Dr. S. S. Laws, a former gold broker and onetime student of physics at Princeton University, in 1867 modified a telegraph instrument to impress electrical impulses on a moving tape, recording the fluctuations of the gold market. The following year Laws set up his sending equipment in the Gold Exchange and acquired a few subscribers among the brokerage offices. The machine was cumbersome and costly since it required several wires and an attendant at the receiving end, but it worked.

Later, Bostonian E. A. Callahan also developed a variation of the printing telegraph to report the gold market. His machine moved the receiving tape by an electric motor that emitted a clicking sound, so it was called a "stock ticker." Thomas Edison studied the machine in Boston. Arriving in New York to try his fortune, Edison visited a telegrapher friend, who was operating the Laws system, when the equipment broke down. Dr. Laws was frantic because none of his maintenance people were able to make repairs. Edison, however, succeeded where Laws's experts failed, and Laws gave him a job. The young man stayed on to invent an electromagnetic stock ticker eventually placed on the market. The newspapers reported in connection with the emergency caused by the breakdown that Dr. Laws earned $300,000 a year for the services of his reporting system.

In a few years Dr. Laws had a rival in the ticker business. John Kiernan, who had employed dozens of boy runners to carry his special reports on the markets since Civil War days, installed Edison's stock tickers as a supplemental service. The tickers carried only the reports of sales, not the details provided in Kiernan's memos, which were written by hand on "thin sheets" and carried by messengers to clients whenever news events justified. Kiernan insisted that his clients now required both of his services, and they appeared to agree.

The Kiernan News Agency distributed news, quotations, and occasional gossip of particular interest to the New York business people who were intimately involved in the activities of the New York Stock Exchange, the Gold Exchange, banks, business in general, and some of the trading conducted outside the regularly organized group, sometimes at night when regular exchanges were closed. The subscribers to Kiernan's service expected informed news speedily, especially earnings statements, which would affect the market. Despite the new stock tickers, the business depended basically on the boy messengers who delivered the thin-sheet bulletins.

Kiernan hired reporters to cover the stock exchanges who could obtain the earnings statements early, who knew traders, callers, brokers, and customers, and who could provide relatively accurate reports on the condition of the markets and the latest transactions at any time. This material had to be copied swiftly and accurately by an editor, who used a stylus to impress the sandwich books of tissue and carbon papers so that up to 24 copies of a bulletin or series of bulletins could be inscribed simultaneously.

Three of the young men hired by Kiernan decided, after working for him for a time, to start a financial news agency of their own—Charlie Dow, Eddie Jones, and Charles Bergstresser. No one knows the exact day when tall, courtly, black-bearded Charles Henry Dow and his partner, Edward Davis Jones, hunkered down on random crates and boxes in a small basement office at 15 Wall Street to start their financial news company. It was sometime in November 1882. The two men almost immediately realized they needed Charles Bergstresser's abilities and his financial contribution, but the name Dow, Jones & Bergstresser didn't sound just right. So the partners agreed to call their firm Dow, Jones & Company.

Chapter 1

Charlie Dow, Eddie Jones

Charles Henry Dow was born in a snug little farmhouse on the windy ridge of Ekonk Hill in the town of Sterling, Connecticut, near the Rhode Island line, on November 6, 1851. There was a post office on Ekonk Hill then, a few miles from the present village of Oneco. The acres tilled by the boy's father, Charles, and his grandfather Asa have since become the site of a prosperous dairy farm, and the farmhouse has grown to 15 rooms. The small, white Congregational church still stands nearby. It bears a plaque memorializing Charles Dow, founder of *The Wall Street Journal,* placed there by the Sterling Historical Society in 1971.

Ekonk Hill, natives say, got its name from the mournful cry of Canadian geese wintering in the cedar swamps below the ridge, which extends for several miles. Their "Ekonk, Ekonk!" can be heard on gray November days. Dow's ancestors arrived in the area during colonial times. They were descended from Henry Dow, who came from Ormsby, England, to Watertown, Massachusetts, in 1637. An early Ebenezar Dow settled in Voluntown, and when the town of Sterling was created by division in 1794, his farm was on the north side of the new town line. Great-grandfather Ebenezar Dow helped to found the Sterling-Voluntown Congregational Church, built on land deeded by John Gallup, another pioneer in the area. The town line, as well as the Windham county line, ran through the church's center.

Dows were prominent in the secluded rural

community. Members of the Congregational Church met in Ebenezar's home before the church was built. A Benjamin Dow was one of the early Sterling town officials, and Samuel T. Dow, who built the house in which Charles Henry Dow was born, was Ekonk Hill postmaster in 1857. That was the year Charles Dow, Sr., died, when his son was 6 years old. Two other children of the Dows died earlier. Charles Henry entered the one-room school at Ekonk Hill, learned to read and write, absorbed the rural virtues, and grew tall and lean. At 16, he left his widowed mother, Harriet Allen Dow, who was in comfortable circumstances, to take a job as an apprentice printer and reporter on a weekly newspaper (probably the *Windham County Transcript,* which served the area).

Precisely how young Dow got his first newspaper job isn't known. When Dow died in December 1902, *The Wall Street Journal* said that "the record of his early years before full manhood, and of his experiences previous to settling in New York would, if set down, read like a romance." The paper evidently referred to Dow's career from the time he departed from Connecticut to work on city newspapers. Dow himself once said that he had held some 20 jobs before he found a compatible life in journalism. Whatever may have been his boyhood experiences, Dow never forgot his mother and the neighbors at Ekonk Hill. According to Ruth Gallup and her sisters, descendants of John Gallup, who were still living near Dow's birthplace in 1982, Charles Dow "generously endowed" the Congregational Church (which became the Church of Christ in 1981) and the family plot in Cedar Swamp Cemetery, where his father, brothers, and mother are buried. Charles Dow himself rests in Providence, Rhode Island. Sterling is proud of its illustrious son. Mathias P. Harpin, town historian, who led the group that honored Dow with a memorial plaque, summarized Sterling's feeling as he glanced down the crossroads running from Ekonk Hill. "Well," said Harpin, "he took the right branch."

Charles Henry Dow was a tall, thin, dark-eyed lad, laconic and aloof, when he went to work in about 1869 for Samuel W. Bowles, the brilliant and acerbic editor who had made his *Springfield* (Massachusetts) *Republican* a nationally known daily newspaper. Dow became a reporter and part-time printer. He rose rapidly during his first years at the *Republican.* Early in 1872 Samuel Bowles divided the printing and newspaper publishing business, forcing a reorganization of the company, as a result of strife among his associates. Two of Bowles's partners departed to acquire the rival *Springfield Union.* Charlie Dow declined an invitation to join them, a decision doubtlessly appreciated by Bowles. Young Dow, just past 20, was listed in the Springfield City Directory of 1872–73 as assistant editor of the *Springfield Republican,* a job he continued to hold for the next two years.

It was a period of bad political experiences for Samuel Bowles, who aspired to even greater recognition as a mover and shaker of the Republican party, and Charlie Dow evidently learned about politics from them. During the summer of 1872 Bowles joined with Horace White, editor of the *Chicago Tribune,* Henry Watterson of the *Louisville Courier-Journal,* and Murat Halstead of the *Cincinnati Commercial* to form a group called the Quadrilateral to push the presidential candidacy of a liberal to oppose President Ulysses S. Grant for the Republican nomination. Bowles's own dark-horse candidate was Senator Charles Francis Adams of Massachusetts. In a convention of Liberal Republicans in Cincinnati, Adams appeared to be winning at one point, but the Quadrilateral was outmaneuvered. The convention bolted and nominated Horace Greeley, the eccentric editor of the *New York Tribune,* for president by a vote of 318 to Adams's 292. The Greeley campaign was a disaster. President Grant was reelected by a margin of 763,000 votes. Assistant Editor Dow, witnessing the humiliation of Samuel Bowles, vowed never to forget what he learned about politics that summer and fall. Never in his years as editor of *The Wall Street Journal* did Charles Dow endorse a candidate for president of the United States, nor has the newspaper he helped found done so since, except to recommend a vote for Herbert Hoover in 1928.

Dow's association with Bowles was useful in many positive ways, as the young man acknowledged in later years. According to George W. Bishop, Jr., a biographer of Dow, Bowles was among the first editors to demand that a reporter "put it all in the first sentence" of a news story—a practice of including the "who, what, when, where, and why" that was widely used in journalism during the next century. Bowles, however, obdurately refused to adopt another tactic that Dow and others endorsed in the ensuing years—that of printing corrections when the newspaper was proved wrong. There was a single exception, according to James Melvin Lee in his *History of American Journalism.* Confronted by a man who had been reported dead in the *Springfield Republican* and who demanded a correction for obvious reasons, Bowles reportedly replied, "We cannot print a correction, but as your case demands some attention, we will bring you back to life by printing your name in our birth column."

"By sheer determination, perseverance and unremitting toil, Mr. Dow earned the undisguised respect and even admiration of that rather tart but discerning editor [Bowles]," *The Wall Street Journal* said in 1902 in its obituary of Charles Dow. But Dow departed Springfield in 1875 for Providence, Rhode Island, where he became night editor of the *Press and Star,* and then joined the *Providence Journal,* edited by George W. Danielson. "His manner of joining the [*Providence*] *Journal* was characteristic," wrote John W. Barney, an associate there whom Dow later brought to New York. "He wasn't satisfied with the other paper and he called on Mr. Danielson to show him his string of articles, told him what he received for it, and asked for a chance to work. Mr. Danielson said he had nothing for Dow to do. Mr. Dow said he didn't need to give him anything to do; that he knew news and wanted only to go out and get it for the *Journal*. From that time until he went to New York he was a strong feature of the *Journal*."

Dow's early contributions to the *Providence Journal* cannot be followed because reporters and even editors usually did not get by-lines at the time. According to Barney, "His work left its impress . . . particularly in the line of careful, painstaking research, in the development of articles of historical value and of more than ephemeral life, and as a precursor of the special articles and the correspondence which have come to occupy so large a space in the papers of today. . . . He would get together a page article, broken into sections by double heads [headlines], of great historical value, and his less important daily contributions were all along the most original lines."

One article definitely written by Dow (it carried his name when it was later reprinted as a book) was about steamboats and appeared in the *Providence Journal* on April 23, 1877. It traced the history of steam navigation on Long Island Sound and Narragansett Bay from 1792 to 1877 and included observations on transportation in general, packet lines, stagecoaches, and some of the early railroads. Bishop notes that Dow was especially interested in the economic aspects of the rival transportation systems, the struggles of the packet boats against the steamboats, and finally the successful challenge of the steamer lines that had combined with the railroads to the steamship companies lacking rail connections. This might have been the beginning of Dow's keen interest in transportation as economic news of major importance, culminating in his strong emphasis on railroad news in *The Wall Street Journal*. In evaluating Dow's work, in 1902 Thomas F. Woodlock, his associate and successor as editor, described Dow's campaign for railroad regulation and responsibility as among his best achievements.

Another *Providence Journal* report written by Charles Dow and reprinted as a book is a history of Newport, Rhode Island, "Newport: The City by the Sea." It appeared in the *Journal* on May 22, 1879. Again, Dow demonstrated his determined research abilities, carrying his history back to the days of the Norsemen. He also showed his appreciation of the economic forces effective in the development of communities and regions.

These articles and others locally established Dow's reputation as a historian. They led to his being invited to accompany a group of eastern financiers bound for Leadville, Colorado, a mining camp that didn't have a single house in 1877 but was a thriving boomtown of 18,000 when Dow arrived there in May 1879. A tremendous silver strike near Leadville, creating the famous Little Pittsburgh mine in May 1878, had excited the country. U.S. Senator Jerome Bonaparte Chaffee, promoter of mining interests, Colorado for statehood, and his own ambition to dominate the Republican party, acquired an interest in the Little Pittsburgh and evidently organized the group that invited young Dow and his newspaper to participate. John Barney, describing Dow's assignment, wrote: "He was selected by people identified with the management of the properties as the best equipped to write informingly about them, and on their request to the editor of the *Providence Journal,* he was assigned to this work. Association on that trip with men of prominence in the financial world revealed to Mr. Dow a field for his efforts in financial journalism in which he could attain an importance and usefulness not to be hoped for in ordinary newspaper work."

The group from the East was particularly interested in Camp Bird, which had been discovered by three Irish laborers, the Gallagher brothers, who, according to Dow's first story, "in a fortnight advanced from penury to undreamed-of wealth." The Gallaghers had come to Leadville as laborers so impoverished that they were refused credit for "a few loaves of bread." Exactly how the Gallaghers were grubstaked, or financed, Dow did not explain, but he asserted that they were paid $250,000 for their share of Camp Bird. He drew on their experience to describe the prospecting experience of those who had good luck: "Everywhere the men dug, they came to silver ore. Men sprang from poverty to affluence in an hour. It was entirely a new thing. The experienced miner, the skilled mineralogist, looked at the indications and saw nothing. The ignorant laborer dug his post-hole and emerged to daylight a millionaire. Then the experts cast away their science, and the California miners boasted their acumen, and each dug their holes in the side of Bald Mountain and they, too, became millionaires."

As Dow continued to report in the ensuing days, he demonstrated that he was learning a lot about the mining industry. His first Leadville stories were filled with fascinating accounts of poor men's luck and the struggle of the rich to get into the action. Levi Z. Leiter, a partner of Marshall Field in Chicago, for example, paid William H. Stevens and Alvinus B. Wood, prospectors, $40,000 for a half interest in "The Iron Mine" and shared in the $15 million the mine produced in two years. Dow detailed the story of Lieutenant Governor Horace Tabor, who grubstaked George Hook and August Rische, thereby gaining from his $17 investment a one-third interest in the Little Pittsburgh, which in November 1878 was combined with other mines into a stock company with a capitalization of $20 million.

Dow wrote general articles on the mining industry in Leadville and on mining economics as well as stories of individual quick fortunes, describing the problems of mining and the not infrequent failures. About the sponsors of the expedition, who had invited him, he wrote: "There were, at the time in New York, a number of wealthy gentlemen who recognized the fact that mining was destined to be of great importance for the next few years. They recognized the other fact that if people could be persuaded to look upon mining as they did any other business; could be induced to buy mining property only after such investigation as they would apply to any other proposed purchase; could be convinced that a mine which they knew to be valuable would be honestly and intelligently managed, there would be strong demand for mining securities."

In a subsequent article he discussed those who should and should not go to Leadville: "There have come to Leadville hundreds of men who had no money, no recommendations, no trade, no mining skill, no muscular strength, no gumption, no brains. They failed. Had they possessed a single one of the essentials named, they might have succeeded. Whiskey and gambling have about as unfortunate effects on men at Leadville as elsewhere."

Dow wrote also of the ordinary men. "The oldest inhabitant of Leadville came here in May, 1877. He came on foot by the way of Mosquito Pass and slept the first night behind a log. He was George Albert Harris. Harris found silver and used the profits to build Leadville's first hotel, in 19 days. It was ten feet wide, twelve feet long and a story and a half high. The first floor served as dining-room, office, kitchen, baggage room and parlor, etc., and the attic was the lodging room. It accommodated eight sleepers at a time in three sections of eight hours each, and the new hotel was full continually. As soon as one set of slumberers awoke, another set took the bunks."

Charlie Dow soon concluded that Leadville and silver mining were not for him, and his nights on the town in gambling saloons and dance houses simply confirmed his determination to go back East. His report on the evils of Leadville was brief. He watched the gamblers and greenhorns in games of high poker, faro, chuck-a-luck, and lansquenet, a game in which the player gambled against all comers, the house taking a cut. The player sometimes won big, but more often went broke.

Dow noted that one of the biggest saloons in town was named "The Little Church on the Corner." It offered "Denver prices, two drinks for 25 cents." He wrote little of the dance houses except to comment, "The ladies are few, good clothes are not prominent, the line of men extends from the ticket office into the street. The charge to men for dancing is 50 cents a set. The women, of course, are those who have descended to the very foot of the soiled ladder. The majority have neither youth nor beauty to recommend them." There were also, he noted, better houses. "They are numerous, luxurious and well patronized. The inmates are attractive in appearance and are treated with all the respect that could be afforded anybody. Not a few mining camps bear the names of these young women. Some have exerted a very powerful influence upon the affairs of the city. Some are celebrated for deeds of kindness. Some have married and appear to be model wives. Whenever one of the dance house girls has died, her virtues have been chronicled in the newspapers, and her friends have given her remains a gorgeous funeral. Theories which seem all right in Providence do not apply at all in Leadville, and a reflective mind gets a good deal befogged upon the subject of absolute right and absolute wrong."

On July 10, 1879, Charles Dow's final Leadville letter appeared in the *Providence Journal.* It described the last gathering of the little group in Leadville after the weeks spent visiting mining camps and examining the mining industry. The delegates were eager to return home. "Be it ever so humble there's no place like Fifth Avenue," Dow quoted one of the members of the "Little Pittsburgh excursion party" as saying as he prepared to down a beer at the farewell party. Senator Chaffee, his enormous head covered with glistening white curls, his cheeks ruddy after exposure in the wilds, paid special attention to the young newspaperman and invited Dow to visit the senator's New York home on Fifty-second Street, where he expected to be in residence that winter. Dow promised, but the meeting was prevented by Chaffee's long illness. Tabor wanted Dow to remember him; he expected to become a United States senator from Colorado, like Chaffee, and in fact he soon did.

Dow didn't say so, but it could be inferred from his final story that he was saying goodbye to Providence. He had, in fact, decided to go to New York. He regarded himself as expert in journalism, having learned from two masters, Bowles and Danielson. He had studied the problems and opportunities in transportation and mining, and found that neither appealed to him over newspapering. He realized his forte as a writer was in researching and analyzing rather than daily reportage, but he did not know of any newspaper that would pay a man well, if at all, for such writing. He got in touch with his friend Eddie Jones, who had become editor of the *Sunday Dispatch* in Providence, but Jones by no means encouraged Dow's return; he said he was thinking of a job in New York, so the two agreed to join forces there.

In New York Charlie Dow turned to financial-news reporting. His articles on Leadville had attracted some attention and he had a recommendation from Senator Chaffee, so he had no trouble getting a job late in 1879 as a writer on mining stocks with the *New York Mail and Express,* owned by Cyrus W. Field, who had laid the telegraph cable across the floor of the Atlantic. In later years *The Wall Street Journal* described Dow's "financial editorials" in the *Mail and Express* as the "first examples of real financial criticism in the daily press."

But Dow didn't remain long with Cyrus Field. Within months he had departed to take a job as an editor with John Kiernan, the operator of the Kiernan News Agency at 2 Broad Street. Kiernan was said to have been known to every top banker in Wall Street, including J. Pierpont Morgan, reportedly Kiernan's friend. Kiernan had gone into New York politics and was a state senator. He also was a partner in Albert Frank and Company, an advertising agency that *The Wall Street Journal* would say in later years "had a virtual monopoly on New York financial, marine and insurance patronage."

Dow, now known in the trade as an expert in mining shares, was one of the writing editors at Kiernan's. He had married Lucy M. Russell in 1881 and resided with her and her daughter by a previous marriage on East Fifty-sixth Street, an affluent area near the Fifty-ninth Street woods bordering the city. Whether his mining knowledge was of much benefit in his new job is doubtful, for Kiernan's bulletins generally were entirely confined to crisp news developments and factual statements. Few clients at the time were looking for financial guidance from a messenger service.

Charles Dow, however, thought that a kind of daily news report would be welcome and would earn the company extra revenue. The added reading material could enable the clients to pass along useful information to their customers, Dow told Kiernan. But Kiernan, an extroverted man who was busy with his politics and advertising interests, wasn't really interested. Kiernan simply wanted Dow to provide good, readable news copy in a hurry, and if he possessed extra energy, he could go out to solicit new clients.

For a time, Dow, always an agreeable man, appeared reconciled to his dull life as a news-bulletin writer and editor. He was cheered when Kiernan allowed him to employ his old *Providence Journal* friend, Eddie Jones, who had popped up in New York mumbling furtively about debts and problems with his wife. Jones, a tall, lean, red-haired man with smiling blue eyes and a dimpled chin, had always appealed to the introverted Dow, and he fitted smoothly into the Kiernan organization. Eddie covered the New York Stock Exchange, quickly becoming a favorite with traders, bankers, and customers. He was fond of the bar at the Windsor Hotel on Fifth Avenue and Forty-sixth Street, sometimes called the "All-Night Wall Street," where much Wall Street news could be gathered, and when Jones was required in the office at times to help manage the crew boys, he appeared promptly and did a good job.

Jones, in fact, did all things well. There were hints from time to time that he continued to be too friendly with the bottle, but he always appeared sober on the job. His wife, Jeanette Conkling Jones, joined him in New York. He increasingly managed the office as Kiernan's business grew, and he listened politely when Charlie Dow would outline the possibilities for improving the Kiernan services. Jones, it turned out, had ideas also, and gradually the two began to consider the possibility of going into the reporting service for themselves. There was a problem, though. They had no capital, and while Dow had saved a little money and both were well paid, it wasn't likely that Eddie Jones would accomplish more than the payment of his debts in the foreseeable future.

It was probably at this point that Dow sought the advice and perhaps the aid of at least one man, Collis Huntington, who helped to build the Union Pacific. Huntington had a home on Fifth Avenue but was only modestly active in Wall Street, which may have been another reason Dow sought him out. Dow could get advice without depending on someone with major interests in the Street, such as James R. Keene, a special friend of Jones, who was noted as a manipulator of stocks, sometimes driving them down as a bear or up as a bull, depending on the clients or pool he represented. Huntington's advice was a positive "Go ahead."

If Charles Dow was concerned about Eddie Jones's fast friends, he repressed his worries. After all, the spectacular operators in Wall Street made news, and it was necessary to have access to them. Dow knew Jones to be brilliant as well as personable. Born in Worcester, Massachusetts, on October 7, 1856, Jones had entered Brown University with the class of 1877, but dropped out in his junior year because he preferred being a newspaperman. While a student, he had served as a drama critic for the *Providence Journal*, receiving only extra tickets and dinner money for his efforts most of the time; when he was offered a full-time job as a reporter and critic along with an opportunity to invest his senior-year tuition in the paper, he speedily accepted the offer.

Jones's family had some wealth, believed in education, and wasn't entirely pleased that Edward wanted to quit school; his brother was a graduate of Brown and his sister attended Wellesley College. His family finally concurred in Jones's choice of a career but sought to encourage him to get a better job than reporting. So the young man, some time after Dow took his job in New York, proposed to Editor Danielson of the *Journal* that they start a financial-news page with Jones as editor. Danielson rejected the idea. Jones tried other Providence jobs, lost the money he invested in the *Journal*, and took up drinking with some of his newspaper and theater friends.

There was no doubt, however, about Jones's ability in the financial-news business. He could read and understand a financial report faster than anyone Dow knew, including himself. His specialty was railroad-earnings reports; Jones could find hidden meanings and mistakes in them when no one else could, and he didn't hesitate to expose them. Jones was a first-rate financial journalist, and he was fond of Dow and admired him. He even thought he could get some money from his family in Providence to help them get started after Dow vetoed his proposal to discuss the idea with Jim Keene.

Dow and Jones spent much of their free time talking about plans for the future. The country began to prosper as the long depression following the panic of 1873 appeared to be over. Railroads and river and harbor improvements had opened the West after the Civil War, making the products of farms and mines available for export. The United States had a favorable balance of trade, and New York banks were increasingly powerful. Interest in Wall Street's markets was growing, attracting agents of the big financial houses in Europe and the daring adventurers in finance from Chicago and San Francisco who hoped to find fortunes there. The reputable brokers were joining the bankers and speculators as men of wealth and distinction. They created large offices and required support services such as Kiernan provided, so there would always be room for newcomers in the field. These affluent traders were able to live uptown in Manhattan or on the cool Brooklyn Heights, easily accessible via the Wall Street ferry. Dow and Jones talked with enthusiasm about the future. New areas of market interest were constantly developing. Both men considered themselves expert in railroads, Dow also knew the mining field, and Jones was looking into communications. Cyrus Field had made a fortune from the telegraph, and Western Union had erected one of the huge new buildings in lower Manhattan. Bell's telephone was being exhibited, while Thomas Edison had opened his new electric-power station on Pearl Street, providing lights to the very area served by Kiernan's messengers. All around them sprang tall business buildings, such as the Equitable, the first in New York to have an elevator, and the New York Evening Post Building, ten stories high. Insurance, newspapers, mining, railroads, and the new telephone exchange, which began operations in 1878 and was rapidly expanding, would all offer new opportunities for investment and the expansion of Wall Street.

Dow was less excitable than Jones, but he also was enthusiastic about the new investment opportunities and wrote in one of their early bulletins, "The industrial market is destined to be the great speculative market of the United States." Now, in 1882, New York had a population of 1,300,000. It was served by 20 railroads and scores of shipping lines along the piers lining the Hudson and East rivers. Thousands rode to their jobs in lower Manhattan via the hundreds of horse-drawn carriages, railway cars, and elevated trains. The new Brooklyn Bridge was soon to be opened, affording added access to lower Manhattan. The prosperity immediately ahead seemed almost palpable. Dow and Jones could feel it, and they were determined to share it; all that was required was nerve and a little capital. They thought that they complemented each other well. Jones could write succinctly and with authority, exactly the style required for the bulletins, and he could manage the boys. Dow liked to write the deep study projects he did so well, the thoughtful analyses for which the Kiernan service had no space or time but which Jones agreed would enhance the bulletins. Jones, in fact, was an innovator at heart, open to all suggestions.

Sometimes Charles Milford Bergstresser, a new Kiernan employee, would join Dow and Jones in their talks, and sometimes they would guardedly discuss their business plans in his presence. Bergstresser was immediately interested, but Dow and Jones were sure they couldn't split profits three ways. Jones good-naturedly bullied the small, excitable Bergstresser, calling him "Buggy," and wouldn't even consider him as an employee until Buggy's news items from the Drexel, Morgan & Company banking house changed his mind. Jones himself was good at making friends—a new one, for instance, was William Rockefeller, of the Ohio Standard Oil family, who had just bought a seat on the New York Stock Exchange and given Jones an order for the Kiernan service—but even Jones had never talked with J. Pierpont Morgan. They could use Buggy as a reporter once they were under way. A newcomer, he knew Wall Street better than many veterans, Jones had to concede, but he could not manage messenger boys, and neither could the quiet, studious Dow; Jones would have to handle that himself.

Bergstresser was short, stocky, pugnacious, and always appeared to stare malevolently through his thick-lensed glasses, yet he won the confidence and friendship of men who were sources of news. He had an ability to make men talk. Bergstresser, like Jones himself, was a college man, graduated from Lafayette College in Easton, Pennsylvania, in 1881, and Dow was especially impressed by this fact. Bergstresser told them something about his family, which warmed Dow to him. He was a farm boy, too, one of 11 children reared in an old stone farmhouse in the Lykens Valley of Pennsylvania. He had earned his way through school, partly with his shorthand. Bergstresser also was intensely frugal. He had worked in New York fewer than 18 months, but he let Dow know that he had saved some money and was prepared to invest it.

Dow and Jones made their decision. They were going to start a reporting firm that sent out stock-market news via boy messengers, and they would include in their manifold reports stock-market analyses and the kind of gossip Jones could gather at the All-Night Wall Street at the Windsor Hotel, as well as the usual news of the Street. They admitted they needed Bergstresser, not only for his skills but for the capital he could contribute, along with the subscribers he could bring in.

So the deal at last was made—after Dow and Jones opened their office at 15 Wall Street, a small unpainted room at the bottom of some wooden steps past Henry Danielson's soda-water establishment. The office was dreary, but it was close to the New York Stock Exchange. If Bergstresser was disappointed by what he saw, he hid it, and Jones affably told him that he and Dow had agreed to take him on as a silent partner. Their secret agreement, made in November 1882, included the division of responsibility. Bergstresser was to open the office in the morning and prepare the first manifold sheets, a digest of late news events of the previous day termed "A Summary of Private Wires," and a summary of the London market, which opened ahead of New

York. Jones would cover the night meetings, generally at the Windsor Hotel, for exclusive stories to be carried in the second bulletin; then Jones would be in charge of the office during the day. All three men would call on scores of banks, brokerage offices, and the various exchanges. They would seek news as well as clients for their service. Dow, the tall, stooped young man who reminded both Jones and Bergstresser of a college professor, would also undertake to analyze companies and industries, because all three agreed that such in-depth studies, which no competitor was even attempting, should become part of their service. Generations later, Robert Sobel, historian of Wall Street, would call Dow "the most famous analyst in the history of the Street."

Chapter 2

The Wall Street Journal Is Born

On the morning of June 6, 1884, John G. Gerrity, freshly graduated from high school and just past his sixteenth birthday, paid his nickel fare to the conductor of the Ninth Avenue horsecar and started downtown to claim the Dow Jones messenger job his parents had arranged through Charles M. Bergstresser. Young Gerrity was scrubbed and shined and in excellent spirits. He did not know Bergstresser, described to him as a "Pennsylvania Dutchman, short and stocky, with a pointed beard," but he was sure he would recognize him when he saw him. Gerrity was a bit afraid of downtown New York, however, and he didn't really know what to expect in his new job. Yet he had to go to work, and Wall Street ought to be as good a place as any. He got off at Trinity Church to look for No. 15 Wall Street.

John Gerrity was not much impressed with the building at No. 15. It seemed out of keeping among the grand structures of the insurance companies and banks in the area. "It was a little, ramshackle place, two stories high, next door to the Stock Exchange," Gerrity wrote to the editors of *The Wall Street Journal* 64 years later.

> I had been told to go to the basement, behind the soda counter. There was a narrow, dark passageway to the rear and I thought I might be in the wrong place, but then I saw Mr. Bergstresser himself coming out, and he took me back and introduced me to Mr. Jones.
>
> As we entered, my mind flashed back to my reader at school, which contained an excerpt from Dick-

ens' *Nicholas Nickleby* recording the first time Squeers brought Nicholas into school: "At first Nicholas saw nothing at all. By degrees, however, the place resolved itself into a bare hole with a few forms, a detached desk for Squeers. . . ." This, indeed, was a small dark room (light on all day) without any attempt at painted walls or a floor covering. On one side of the room a little space was walled off by a few plain pine boards and gave privacy of a sort to two desks, one for Mr. Dow and the other for an assistant. Mr. Jones' desk was at the far end. If Mr. Bergstresser had a desk I never knew where it was. The center of the room was taken up by copywriters. We boys—well, we were just there.

Gerrity got the job as a messenger at $5 a week, a fantastic amount for a schoolboy just graduated. Shop and factory boys and girls in New York were rarely paid more than $3.50 a week, and men in unskilled jobs considered themselves fortunate if they could earn $6 a week for six ten-hour days. The Dow Jones job would be a rigorous one, Edward Jones told Gerrity. "Mr. Jones—very tall and very slim—wore a long, flowing red moustache and sat, or rather reclined, in a lean-back chair with his feet up on the desk the entire day, and from that position he dictated to the writers."

Jones was relaxed and affable as he explained the job to Gerrity, but when a runner dashed down the steps and someone shouted, "Earnings! Earnings!" and the boys took up the chant, Jones became a different man. His feet crashed to the floor and he leaped from the chair, angrily assailing the arriving messenger, who was late. Then Jones accepted some pages of notes from the cringing fellow. He dictated a few lines and divided the notes between himself and another writer, then began to ply his stylus to a pad of thin sheets.

Jones and his assistant, a Mr. Henderson, soon completed their bulletins, whereupon Mr. Jones shouted, "Boy! Boy!" in a loud voice, and a half dozen messengers descended upon him to receive the memos Jones and Henderson had just completed. Meantime, other messengers were arriving, some heading toward a water faucet and basin at the rear to wash their grubby hands.

In a space of minutes Jones had broken the tension, written a bulletin, dictated another to Henderson, and each had got his manifold originals and several duplicate copies on the way. So, as he stood near Jones's desk, Gerrity had observed more than 100 bulletins processed, 24 at a time. Then Jones relaxed into his chair again, put his immaculately shod feet on the desk, continued to outline to Gerrity what his duties would be, and supplied him with a list of customers.

Gerrity could go to work immediately, Jones indicated. The first thing he should do was clean his nails and wash his hands. The boy later learned that his benefactor, Bergstresser, used Jones's desk when he came in at 7 o'clock in the morning to open the Dow Jones office and to write and dispatch the first bulletin. When Jones arrived, Bergstresser would depart for his rounds on Broad and Wall streets. Jones frequently covered news at night and then conferred with Dow at the latter's home about the next day's schedule.

It wasn't until several days later that Gerrity realized there was another man on the premises. That man, he knew, was Charles Dow, whose office area had been closed off by the pine boards so that he had privacy. At last Gerrity saw the senior member of the firm. "Mr. Dow was over six feet tall," he wrote. "He must have weighed 200 pounds [Dow weighed 210 at that time], but he wasn't fat. He was rather stooped. He had jet black hair and a full beard."

Dow's glance at the boy was impersonal yet not unfriendly. He spoke a few words with Jones, then returned to his office. "We boys thought of him as part of the business, and we passed by his cubby hole without paying him any attention," Gerrity wrote.

Mr. Jones was considered the boss, and he conducted himself as a good boss should. He received the news, he wrote it or dictated it, and he summoned the boys and sent them on their way. He also disciplined them or complimented them in a general way, and each week he paid them. Jones had a system of fines and punishments that he would threaten to invoke if the boys misbehaved, as a company of lads ages 14 to 16 was certain to do, but no one ever remembered a fine actually being imposed when payday arrived. Jones would more likely punish a boy by giving him extra duties, such as making up the thin sheets and carbon books or cleaning up the office.

Now and then—quite frequently, in fact—Mr. Jones would rise from his recumbent position for angry outbursts of profanity, picturesque and effective. No one in the office appeared to know exactly what had set Jones off; he simply appeared a bit nervous at times. But when a crisis arose, Jones was calmer than anyone except Mr. Dow, and even Dow appeared to wait diffidently for instructions from Jones on such occasions. A shout from Jones when an outsider reported the rumor of an important story brought Dow from his office and Bergstresser on the run if he happened to be anywhere near. "Mr. Bergstresser and Mr. James King were the chief news gatherers," Gerrity wrote to the editors in 1948. "But any other person could bring in a story they heard, and Mr. Jones would send either Mr. Bergstresser or Mr. King to verify it."

If Bergstresser was somewhere on Broad or Wall streets, one or more of the boys would be sent to find him. Bergstresser was supposed to be on certain stations at certain times, and his absence from these posts would be sure to trigger Jones's rage. At such times Jones really cussed.

So it was regularly said around Wall Street that Eddie Jones ran Dow, Jones & Company, and the boys liked it that way. "He knew all of us," Gerrity recalled. "He called each of us by name and he tried to keep some kind of order, which wasn't easy among a dozen boys." But the boys were extremely responsible and responsive most of the time. They carried out Jones's injunction to always be on the lookout for news and new customers.

James King had joined the company as a printer in 1884, and he also served as a reporter. There evidently was another bulletin writer added because the total editorial force that year was said to number six. Each bulletin, or manifold, writer now had a group of boys attached to him. Each boy serviced 8 to 12 customers and was responsible for assembling the supplies of books with tissues and carbons.

Despite generally depressed economic conditions, New York's Wall Street continued to grow in wealth and influence, passing Boston's State Street as a financial center. In November 1883, the firm expanded its activities to include a *Customers' Afternoon News Letter,* a venture made possible by its early reputation for competent coverage and accurate reporting. The *Afternoon News Letter,* a summary of the day's bulletins, provided a brisk resumé of the day's market developments, and occasionally included a brief but penetrating analysis of any swing in the stock market and sometimes even a prescient hint or two of financial things to come, usually contributed by Charles Dow.

Initially, the *Afternoon News Letter* was inscribed on the thin sheets with an agate stylus, a burnishing tool first used by bookbinders and adopted by Jones for his stencils. Dow and Bergstresser helped Jones with the thin sheets as the subscriber list passed 125. But on a day in May 1884 there was high excitement when a new, costly piece of equipment was moved into the gloomy little shop behind the soda fountain. It was a cylinder press, a small, hand-cranked machine adopting part of the principle of the Richard Hoe high-speed rotary press that was revolutionizing the daily newspaper business. The press acquired by Dow Jones, however, had no refined, stereotyped plates that could be locked onto the press cylinder. Instead, the rotary press had slots in the cylinder that enabled the printer to insert 16 lines of type. Thus, when the cylinder was turned by hand, the type would transfer ink to a small sheet of newsprint hand-fed into the press. These printed bulletins were limited in size—5 × 9 inches, somewhat smaller than the handwritten thin sheets—but the day of the stylus or agate stencil was over. More customers could now be given better, easier-to-read service in less time.

One of the first big stories distributed by the Dow Jones news-bulletin service and the *Afternoon News Letter* involved the failure on May 6, 1884, of the New York Stock Exchange firm of Grant and Ward, in which former President Ulysses S. Grant was a partner—a circumstance that made an otherwise minor incident big news. The Dow Jones 12:30 P.M. bulletin reported: "The Marine Bank, corner of Pearl and Water streets, closed its doors this morning. James D. Fish is its president. The suspension of the bank is attributed to James D. Fish's real estate speculations. The immediate cause of the suspension of the Marine Bank is said to be a balance of $500,000 due the Clearing House [an association of New York banks] this morning. The bank did a shipping and produce business. James D. Fish was a senior partner in Grant and Ward. A member of the firm says they will have to announce their suspension from the Stock Exchange."

This bulletin was followed by two other items:

> President Baldwin of the Fourth National Bank says "the Marine Bank suspension is a very small thunder shower."
>
> Mr. Jay Gould has just said, "I do not consider the failure of the Marine Bank as a matter of much importance. The market has declined more on the strength of it being a bank than on account of the amount involved. I think that the general situation has begun to improve, and earnings of our roads [railroads] are increasing. . . . People I meet say that business is better. I think we have seen the worst of it [the panic]."

However, the Dow Jones closing bulletin on May 6 said that one of Jay Gould's railroads, Union Pacific, had been sold heavily and that the market broke badly. There had already been thousands of bank closings across the country during the year, and Wall Street was understandably nervous. The opening of Union Pacific at 56 3/4 the following day signified trouble. The opening Dow Jones bulletin on May 7, probably Bergstresser's work, said, "This is almost panicky." Later bulletins that day, however, were calm, and concluded, "The suspension of Grant and Ward, tragically bringing in the name of ex-President Ulysses S. Grant, one of the partners, had little effect upon the market."

A week later, May 14, the Dow Jones bulletin began by recording the events of the previous night at the Windsor Hotel. The report, undoubtedly supplied by Jones, chronicled the beginning of a New York bank panic, detailing specifically the problems of the Second National Bank:

> The Windsor was crowded last night. Bulls and bears were nervous until it was announced that any trouble in the Second National Bank had been completely fixed up by Mr. Amos R. Eno, and that the firm of A. Dyett & Co. was not seriously involved.
>
> President Randolph of the Continental Bank said at 9:45, "I think there is no doubt that Dyett & Co. will have deposited sufficient money to meet all checks by 10 o'clock."

The bulletin went on to note that London quotations of American stocks prior to the opening of the New York Stock Exchange showed sharp breaks, and then resumed its own reports of that morning's activity in Wall Street:

10 A.M. Wm. Heath & Co. will make clearance and settlement for Dyett & Co.

10:25 A.M. The suspension of Nelson Robinson & Co. has been announced.

10:30 A.M. O. M. Bogart & Co., the large private dealers, announce their suspension.

President Hatch of the Stock Exchange announced from the rostrum that the Second National Bank is perfectly solvent and is worthy of all confidence.

10:35 A.M. The suspension of J. C. Williams, 30 Broad Street, is announced.

10:40 A.M. Hatch & Foote have announced their suspension. The rumors that Peters, Wetmore & Schenck were in any trouble are absolutely false.

10:45 A.M. The Metropolitan Bank has just closed its doors and checks are being cashed as presented.

11:10 A.M. The Metropolitan Bank has refused to pay out any more money, but the doors are not closed.

The bulletins appeared as 16-line takes, the capacity of the new hand-cranked press, but they provided a smooth narrative of the crisis as they appeared at the rate of two or more editions an hour throughout the day. The boys dashed down the steps, washed their hands as in the days when they handled the thin sheets, and awaited the cry, "Boy! Boy!" when the press was operating. Jones now dictated directly to James King, the printer setting the type.

As the day wore on, the Dow Jones bulletins turned a bit optimistic.

The president of the Fourth National Bank says that the street talk about his bank is nonsense.

11:50 A.M. The Gallatin National Bank has $1,100,000 in cash in its vaults, the best answer to "any rumors."

12:30 P.M. Directors of the Metropolitan Bank are in session, but no decision has been reached in regard to resumption.

President Hatch of the Exchange says that there has been informal talk about closing the Exchange, but it did not appear that the situation warranted closing.

1:45 P.M. Donnell, Lawson & Simpson failed.

The Phoenix Bank has $135 for every $100 liabilities. The largest depositors know this and are not disturbing deposits.

2:00 P.M. Williard, Chapin, Van Emburgh and Gould brokers are buying the list.

We understand that the Clearing House has taken action similar to that in 1873, when the bank decided to stand by each partner.

2:30 P.M. Hotchkiss, Burnham & Co. have announced their suspension.

Money loaning 1 percent per day.

On May 15 the Dow Jones bulletins continued to reflect Wall Street confidence as Dow, Jones, and Bergstresser circulated among the bankers and brokerage houses and sent in their reports to King, who was in temporary charge of the bulletin service. An eleven o'clock bulletin stated that the

Metropolitan Bank was about to reopen, as it did at noon after its president, George I. Seney, resigned. The panic was definitely over. However, there were 10,968 bank failures recorded in the United States that year. Former President Grant, impoverished and in a state of shock, was driven to writing his memoirs in order to survive.

"Large shorts covered yesterday, and in a good many instances went long to cover the market," said the *News Letter* of May 15, 1884, which survives in the Dow Jones archives. Shorts, also known as bears, were stock-market traders who expected the market to go down and who sold borrowed stock that they could replace at low cost if they were right, thus making a profit. But if they turned out to be wrong, they would need to cover, or go long, before the market went higher. (Bulls, on the other hand, bought and held stock in expectation of the market rising.) Another item noted that "Mr. Gould [Jay Gould, the noted capitalist and speculator] bought and sold, apparently keeping his account about even." What Gould did was important. On March 13, 1884, when the market fell alarmingly, Gould demonstrated his faith in the financial future of America by calling in reporters to exhibit the stock holdings he had on hand in his "tin box." They included $23 million worth of Western Union bonds, $12 million worth of Missouri Pacific, $6 million worth of Manhattan Elevated, and $2 million in bonds of Wabash preferred. Gould offered to produce $30 million more, but the doubters were convinced.

The best of the *Afternoon News Letter* was the frequent leading item frankly titled "Morning Gossip." Jones, a gregarious man who could tell a good story, brought in many of the "Gossip" tidbits, especially those originating at the Windsor Hotel's All-Night Wall Street. Said the May 15 *Letter,* "Windsor thronged last night. It was known that the investigating committee was at work for the Metropolitan Bank, and everyone agreed that the market today would depend a good deal upon whether the bank would be able to resume or not."

The *Afternoon News Letter* updated that "Morning Gossip" report, of course. The two following bulletins appeared on the same thin sheet, relieving the suspense: "9 A.M.—Cashier McGourkey, of the Metropolitan Bank, says, 'We shall resume at 12 o'clock' "; and, "Notice has been posted on the doors of the Metropolitan Bank, signed by Mr. Scriba, Bank Examiner, that the bank will resume business at 12 o'clock today." The second bulletin was brought in by a messenger boy alerted by Jones to be on the watch for such things; in fact, it was one of the Dow Jones–trained boys who had brought in a report of the Metropolitan Bank closing in the first place (he had not been able to get into the bank to deliver one of the bulletins). From the beginning, Dow Jones took pride in the fact that it trained its own people and taught them well; in those early days it wasn't unusual for an employee to rise from messenger boy to part-time reporter. Throughout the paper's history many of its executives started their careers as editorial workers on the *Journal* or the wire services.

On July 3, 1884, Dow, Jones & Company began to publish the average closing prices of representative active stocks, a list of ten railroads and two industrials for a beginning. This list, consisting of stocks Dow had determined from his studies to be significantly reflective of market trends, would be expanded and revised in subsequent years and would be used almost universally as the Dow Jones Averages.

Early in 1885 the company began to print its *Afternoon News Letter* at 71 Broad Street on a press that enabled it to increase the size of the publication to two pages, 10 1/2 × 15 1/2 inches, each carrying two columns of type, the precursor of *The Wall Street Journal.* The little cylinder press remained at 15 Wall Street and continued to grind out news bulletins on a half-hour and later a ten-minute schedule. Thus the company began the functional divisions of its work with the *Afternoon News Letter* and the bulletins intended for special clients. Although the *Letter* was initially intended to help brokers prepare their letters to their customers, it ultimately appealed to the general public. Each developing service complemented the other.

The messenger boys and other early Dow Jones employees eventually learned that Mr. Dow was not always in his little pine-board office as Gerrity initially assumed. Like Bergstresser and Jones, Dow also had duties on the outside. Thomas F. Woodlock, Dow's close associate and his successor as editor of *The Wall Street Journal,* described Dow's work in 1892: "Mr. Dow attended to stock market news and he wrote stock market gossip. He was well and favorably known in the brokerage houses. Mr. Dow could make more out of a single sentence or a single fact than anyone I knew." Woodlock declared that Edward Jones "had a special facility for editing the news and devising assignments. He was also the first 'corporation analyst' on Wall Street." Bergstresser circulated in search of statements and interviews and would track down important visitors in town for possible interviews, Woodlock said.

Jones preferred to work outside, mostly at night and especially when there were meetings at the Windsor Hotel. The Windsor was described in New York City guidebooks of the period as "the most elegant and costly hotel in the world" and was a favorite retreat of successful operators in Wall Street. However, "adventurers" from Chicago such as Philip D. Armour, a flamboyant trader of his time, and John W. "Bet-a-Million" Gates, the noted gambler and market speculator, preferred the Waldorf-Astoria.

The Windsor wasn't far from Dow's home on East 56th Street. When Jones had covered the news at the Windsor, he would walk to Dow's apartment to discuss plans for the next day's bulletins. Both Dow and Jones also sought out potential clients for the bulletin service, Woodlock said. He described the partners and Bergstresser in appearance and temperament. Dow was a tall, slightly stooping man with a grave air and the "measured speech of a college professor." Jones was "tall and ruddy, swift in his motions, high strung as a race horse, tempestuous in manner and speech, with a mind quick as lightning, and a nose for news." Bergstresser, short and stocky with a thick, black beard, "had a fine memory, a capacity for penetrating recesses where no other reporter could gain access." Bergstresser was especially valuable because he had once been a shorthand reporter, Woodlock said. "He knew absolutely everyone in the financial district. No one ever asserted that Bergstresser had ever misquoted him. . . . Jones used to say that Bergstresser could make a wooden Indian talk, and tell the truth!"

The only thing the partners had in common was business, Woodlock said. Jones referred to Dow as a "Connecticut Yankee" and to himself as a "New England Baptist." Bergstresser, coming from Lykens Valley, was, of course, a "Pennsylvania Dutchman." Like everyone else who commented on Dow, Woodlock praised the man for his humility and mildness. "He worked noiselessly, never raised his voice, and habitually practiced that rhetorical figure which Englishmen use so generally, known as meiosis," or expressive understatement. Bergstresser worked more in Dow's fashion, Woodlock remembered. The three teamed perfectly and rarely disagreed. One exception, however, occurred when Jones was away and Dow and Bergstresser determined on a course Jones had previously opposed. "When Jones heard of it, he exploded like a dynamite cartridge, . . . but the quarrel was quickly over because Dow refused to get angry," Woodlock wrote. "He said it took him 24 hours to get angry, and then he stayed that way."

Charles Dow got little credit from Woodlock or anyone else for another of his main concerns—maintaining the financial stability of Dow, Jones & Company. Since the company paid $1 a week more to the boys than the Kiernan News Agency did, invested in the cylinder press, and later rented the press facilities at 71 Broad Street, Dow Jones had to carefully husband its cash flow to remain in business. It had no revenue from a ticker service as Kiernan did, chiefly because Dow concluded that such printing telegraph machines were relatively unreliable; besides, Dr. Laws had the best service in town, and it would be futile for a young company to attempt to compete with him. There is some evidence that Dow reluctantly permitted an experiment with an early news ticker, a cumbersome device seemingly operated by a 96-pound weight on the principle of a grandfather clock, as well as by telegraph wires, but Dow, Jones & Company did not go into the news-ticker service until 1897, when it obtained rights to manufacture its own machine.

Dow rarely talked about business or his personal life except to say that Dow, Jones & Company never at any time received outside financial help from anyone. Historians who probed into company affairs in later years had to take Dow's word for it, since none of the partners retained written records that have been found. The company, a joint-stock association, was not incorporated until 1930. There was no capitalization for the purchase of heavy equipment or for extensive inventory. The boys were paid in cash, and presumably the partners drew agreed-upon amounts for expenses and salary, dividing profits on a monthly basis, as was customary in most partnership businesses until well past 1900. In any event, there are no Dow, Jones & Company records extant prior to 1900.

If there was anything Edward Jones liked better than running the Dow Jones office in a time of crisis, it was being on the street. As the staff expanded, Jones seized more and more opportunities to go out in search of news and to renew acquaintanceships that brought him tips by telephone and messenger. A *Wall Street Journal* columnist in later years recalled his special friends, James Keene, William Rockefeller, Lansing Lamont of Jesup & Lamont, John H. Davis, and Cyrus Townsend Brady, all men prominent in Wall Street. On meeting Rockefeller, said the columnist, Jones was greeted warmly and asked, "Edward, would it mean anything to you to get a little advance Standard Oil news?" Jones beamed, said the writer, and exclaimed, "Kind sir, would you dare say that again?" Rockefeller replied, "Here's something I jotted down for you, if you care to use it. Only, please, keep your authority confidential!"

On another occasion, recalled by Thomas Woodlock, things were less pleasant. Jones sought out Philip Armour, the Chicago trader, while the latter was attempting to corner St. Paul railroad stock. He found Armour in the Green and Bateman brokerage offices. "Your friends are saying I misquoted you," Jones began angrily.

"What's that?" the surprised Armour demanded.

"Your friends say I misquoted you," Jones repeated, "and that you repudiate me." Jones was red-faced and furious. Armour didn't wish to fight. "What's a little fuss?" he responded mildly.

"And just what do you say?" Jones insisted.

"I say that Dow Jones is nobody's goat."

No one was sure just what the men were implying to one another, but Jones was mollified. He indicated that he would have a further bulletin on Armour's financial affairs.

"Shake," said Armour. "And if you shoot out another bulletin saying I say just what you said I said, say that I meant it, and that I say for you that St. Paul is the best. Jones, I like you—it's great to meet a Man!"

Armour later told other newspapermen, according to Woodlock, "That

Jones gets the first grip on more facts that are facts than all the rest of Wall Street put together, but he's a headstrong chap; when I offered him a hundred dollars a day to be my secretary, he just laughed and told me to come uptown and dine with him and Bill Wheeler [Armour's archrival], that Yale baseball fellow that's doing the sharpshooting against my St. Paul."

Other brokers and traders offered jobs to Jones, Woodlock noted, among them Jim Keene and Addison Clammack, the "Big Bear" noted for his raids that drove down the stocks in which he had gone short. But not until 1899 would Jones be lured into the brokerage business, at which time he joined Keene after a brief stint with another firm.

Due to the lack of personal records left by Dow, Jones, and Bergstresser, Dow's reason for becoming a member of the New York Stock Exchange, on Christmas Eve, 1885, presents something of a mystery. Possibly, the editor-to-be of *The Wall Street Journal,* intent on studies that would lead him to formulate what would later be called the Dow Theory, simply wanted to know more about the workings of the market. The records of the New York Stock Exchange show him as a member of Goodbody, Glynn & Dow from December 24, 1885, to April 30, 1891.

William Peter Hamilton, later an editor of *The Wall Street Journal,* in his book on the Dow Theory, *The Stock Market Barometer,* tells a story of Dow's formal association with the market: "It came about in a rather curious way. The late Robert Goodbody, an Irishman, a Quaker, and an honor to Wall Street, came over from Dublin to America. As the New York Stock Exchange requires that every member shall be an American citizen, Charles H. Dow became his partner. During the time necessary for Robert Goodbody to naturalize, Dow held a seat in the Stock Exchange and executed orders on the floor. When Goodbody became an American citizen Dow withdrew from the Exchange and returned to his more congenial newspaper work."

Dow evidently had an additional reason, a family relationship, for his close association with Goodbody: his stepdaughter was married to William Woodcock Goodbody, Robert's younger brother. Not even the launching of *The Wall Street Journal* in the summer of 1889 with Dow, Jones & Company as publisher caused Dow to give up his New York Stock Exchange seat. He promptly withdrew, however, once Robert Goodbody received his naturalization papers and thus was able to organize Robert Goodbody & Company on April 30, 1891. Apparently, Dow's primary purpose in joining the Stock Exchange, risking accusations of conflict of interest, was to help a friend through his naturalization period. Editor Hamilton, in discussing Dow's stock-market experience, said that Dow traded infrequently and on a small scale, though he did make trades on the floor.

In 1887 Dow, Jones & Company became associated with another editor who pioneered in the news agency business and was an extensive owner of stocks. He was Clarence W. Barron, a former *Boston Transcript* financial writer who had established the Boston News Bureau, a reporting service like Dow Jones for brokers, and published a newspaper called the *Boston News Bureau*. Barron telegraphed news items to New York for the Dow Jones *Afternoon News Letter* and received Wall Street news in return. Additionally, in 1887 Dow Jones obtained the services of the Exchange Telegraph Company of London, which supplied news of the London markets and some European financial coverage. Dow Jones also began to receive free-lance business reports from correspondents in Washington, Philadelphia, Chicago, and other cities.

On Monday, July 8, 1889, the first *Wall Street Journal* appeared, an afternoon business newspaper of four pages, 15 1/2 by 20 3/4 inches, set in four columns of 16 picas each, the outside columns carrying the subscription terms and advertising. The publisher was Dow, Jones & Company, 26 Broad Street, the address of the new company printing office, where a large, rebuilt press had been installed. The price was 2 cents a copy or $5 a year. It would be delivered by carrier without charge to "subscribers of our regular news service." Reduced rates were offered to bankers and brokers, and the advertising rate was announced as 20 cents a line.

In creating *The Wall Street Journal,* Dow Jones made use of the logistics it had been developing for its news-bulletin service and *Afternoon News Letter.* Company lore credits Bergstresser with naming the paper *The Wall Street Journal,* a claim he evidently registered at home since it was supported in letters written by his daughter, Ethel, in later years. The somewhat parochial name, representing the tiny community along seven city blocks, provided no geographical limitation for the editors of *The Wall Street Journal.* They laid claim to circulation territory extending from Montreal to Washington, D.C., on the very first day of issue. The paper also made clear on page one and in a page-two statement (similar to the prospectus used by many newspapers to set forth a compact for their readers) that it would not only circulate widely but search the United States, Canada, and Europe for its news. The paper was to be published daily, except Sunday and Stock Exchange holidays, at 3:15 P.M., immediately after the markets closed. It promised readers to provide facts, not opinions.

The lead article was a recapitulation of the average movement of stock prices. "The bull market of 1885 began July 2, with the average price of 12 active stocks 61.49. The rise culminated May 18, 1887, with the same twelve stocks selling at 93.27. Prices gradually declined for about a year, reaching the next extreme low point April 2, 1888, the 12 stocks selling at 75.28." Significant trends in the market fluctuations of the stocks then followed, and the stocks were named: St. Paul, Lake Shore, Northwest, New York Central, Lackawanna, Delaware & Hudson, Northern Pacific preferred, Western Union, Union Pacific, Pacific Mail, Missouri Pacific, and Louisville and Nashville. All but Western Union and Pacific Mail were railroad stocks and all had been carefully selected by Charles Dow. The list had appeared first in the *Afternoon News Letter* July 3, 1884, and Dow considered it still representative. In a second article on the market, the *Journal* suggested that "there is some reason for believing that operators identified with the bear party sent early orders to London to depress Americans in that market as a preparation for the opening here. These orders were faithfully executed, and London at 9:30 was quoted as opening weak and as having become very weak."

If *The Wall Street Journal* wished to signal its readers that it was acquainted with the methods used by market manipulators, whether bears or bulls, it couldn't have chosen a more dramatic example of what traders could accomplish. They were frequently caught selling to one another, of course, to raise or drive down prices, but the London operation took greater power and skill, plus capital for high cable costs.

The London houses responded by selling in the early hours of the day, but a lack of buyers developed as soon as prices were off as much as one point. It was sufficient to start the attack in Wall Street. The bear drive slackened about eleven o'clock, the paper reported, "but there was no general rally." Favorable railroad news from Chicago later provided resistance to the bears and demonstrated that Charles Dow was right in basing his averages chiefly on railroad stocks; generally, as rails went, so went the market.

The *Journal's* Boston report was slightly optimistic: "The week opens with a decidedly firmer feeling in the money market. Money between banks continues in sharp demand, 5 and 6% being readily paid for loans this A.M. It is possible that money will be brought over from New York to-night." The report from Philadelphia was somewhat negative: "The special feature of the Philadelphia market to-day was some heavy liquidation in Reading by bull houses—some 7,000 shares being sold at 22 3/4. . . . Outside of this the market is dull and traders are not inclined to do much until the situation is cleared." The *Journal* editors soon discovered that the Reading Railroad was under a pool (a group of traders secretly joining to push the prices up or down) manipulation, one that would preoccupy the paper in the months ahead.

The most bullish report of the day came from the *Journal's* Chicago correspondent: "Chicago special—It is stated on excellent authority that the Western presidents are getting positive orders from New York and Boston banking houses to settle the Western troubles [a railroad rate war] at the meeting to-morrow. Some sort of plan to take care of C.,B.&N. [Chicago, Burlington & Northern] will be considered, and it is believed that if

C.,B.&N. can be controled, a general settlement can be effected."

The *Journal* would continue to be intensely interested in railroad news and analysis, giving nearly half its attention to the subject. The railroads were reorganizing and demonstrating that they could make money when they were properly managed. The West, opened to traffic via land and water and provided with steel plows and McCormick reapers, was shipping grain, pork, and beef in vast quantities not only to the East Coast but to Europe as well. The railroads and their coal mines fueled the eastern prosperity, and New York and Wall Street especially prospered as the demand for capital and manufactured products increased.

That the *Journal* editors intended to make some kind of appeal to more general interests was indicated by a small item among the bank and railroad reports in column three concerning a boxing match: "Cincinnati—It is reported here from a reliable source that Sullivan and Kilrain were fighting at 11:45 A.M. The contest was a long one and Sullivan was having the best of it and was sure to won [sic]." Later in the same column: "Bulletin, New Orleans, says the fight took place near Richburg. On account of there being no communication with the place particulars won't be had until the return of the train, which is due at 2 P.M." (Whether the *Journal* told its readers the result of the fight probably will never be known, for the original file of the paper, now at the Yale University Library, includes only fragments of the July 9 issue, none of them carrying the Sullivan-Kilrain result.) Some of the other 15 New York daily newspapers did publish reports of the championship boxing match held at Richburg, Mississippi, a few miles from New Orleans and outside the State of Louisiana, where prize fighting was illegal. The great John L. Sullivan defeated Jake Kilrain in the seventy-fifth round when the challenger's seconds threw in the sponge after Kilrain was badly battered.

Column three of *The Wall Street Journal* on July 8 closed with the summary of that day's New York market: "Total—Listed 244,188; unlisted 88,056."

Among the first advertisers to appear in the paper on page one were 12 banks and brokerage firms, including McIntosh & Mygatt, Denver brokers; a railway equipment company based in New York; the Central Railroad Company of New Jersey and the Aspen Mining & Smelting Company announcing dividends; and the Chicago publishing firm Rand, McNally & Company, announcing its line of railroad maps, "which for correctness and fulness of detail and general quality, surpass all others."

On page two, Dow, Jones & Company disclosed further details of its plan for the *Journal* and its other services.

> Its object is to give fully and fairly the daily news attending the fluctuation in prices of stocks and bonds and some classes of commodities. It will aim steadily at

> being a paper of news, and not a paper of opinions. It will give a good deal of news not found in other publications, and it will present in the market article, its news, its tables and its advertisements, a faithful picture of the rapidly shifting panorama of the Street.
>
> We believe that such a paper will be of use to operators, bankers, and capitalists who can find in its columns essential statistics compiled so that their pith and bearing can be readily remembered; also the events which have moved or are moving prices, together with the draft of opinion in the Street. Our bond table is unique in that it gives the yield as well as the price, and enables the investor to observe the return on one issue compared with another, without laboriously consulting tables of investments.

The paper said it would be an excellent advertising medium because of its Wall Street circulation and "because its early hour of issue enables it to reach subscribers in an entire tier of cities extending from Montreal to Washington, and west to Buffalo and Pittsburgh, early on the morning after issue. This puts the out-of-town trader in a better position as far as information is concerned than the New York speculator who depends for financial news upon the city morning papers; hence our large out-of-town circulation. Furthermore, the make-up of the *Journal* puts every advertiser in a preferred position next to reading matter." It was true, of course, that a paper published at 3:15 P.M. could get farther from New York than one issued at midnight, and it would have an equal amount of market news except, perhaps, for what was happening at the Windsor Hotel's All-Night Wall Street.

No statistics on the circulation of the *Journal,* inside or outside the city, were provided until 1904, however, when the total circulation was said to have averaged 11,957 the prior year. In the beginning it was about 1,500, but advertisers flocked in, filling the outside columns of front and back pages immediately. During its first year the *Journal* also had its first full-page advertisement, which appeared on October 19, an announcement of a plan for the reorganization of the Atchison, Topeka and Santa Fe Railroad.

Dow, Jones & Company included in its prospectus a statement of its other operations. Printed news bulletins would continue to be delivered from 9 A.M. to 3 P.M. "on an average of every eight minutes," a doubling of the number of editions. "This service, begun in November 1882, has grown until we include among our customers nearly all the large operators and active commission houses in the Street. The number of persons employed in the work has risen from six to about fifty, and our means for rapid reproduction of news has evolved from the slow, indistinct manifolding process to clear type with a press which gives 200 or more copies a minute." The price of the service was now $20 a month.

The *Journal* and the Dow Jones bulletin service could call upon vast facilities in the coverage of news, the paper said. "We have a private wire to Boston, and telegraphic connections through the Postal Telegraph Co. with

Washington, Philadelphia and Chicago, which insure promptest transmission of inquiries and news. Our London correspondents, the Exchange Telegraph Co., has its employees in every considerable town in Europe." Also, Dow Jones had correspondents in Chicago, Washington, St. Louis, Pittsburgh, Philadelphia, Albany, Boston, and elsewhere, the paper said.

Newspapers in New York and some other eastern cities greeted *The Wall Street Journal* with warm welcome, most suggesting that the excellent reputation of Dow, Jones & Company insured that *The Wall Street Journal* also would be successful. "As its name implies, it is devoted to Wall Street interests; and it undoubtedly will serve them with the enterprise its managers always display," commented the *New York Commercial Bulletin*. The *New York Sun* sniffed a bit, but came through with praise also: "While frequently open to criticism, the [Dow Jones] service has been appreciated by Wall Street, and with fewer 'opinions' in the form of 'special dispatches' there ought to be little doubt of the success of the enlarged circular."

The *Daily Financial News,* a competitor, said of the *Journal,* "It will be eagerly sought after by the large class who purchase the regular evening papers for the comparatively brief financial intelligence imparted." The *Philadelphia Press* commented: "[It] is bright and new as might be expected. The firm in question have for years been collectors of news which they sent out through the day, and they are a most enterprising firm with reliable connections in all parts of the world." But the *New York Daily Indicator* declared crushingly, "[It] might properly be called the 'Wall Street Rehash,' it being made up of the previously issued news (?) items of Dow, Jones & Co., flanked by columns of dead-headed advertising, with a portion of the *Daily Indicator's* bond tables as a guarantor of usefulness." There were more who praised the *Journal,* among them the *Baltimore Sun:* "[It] contains a lot of financial news and items of interest to the railroad and financial community"; and the *Boston Post:* "Judging from the first issue, it looks like a paper that is here to stay." The *Journal* published such commentary, good and bad, and kept reprinting it in the weeks ahead, together with its prospectus.

The new paper attempted to follow through on its initial report on the railroad situation in the West. It carried no editorials, but it printed on page two of its July 12 issue a summary of the railroads' statement about their rates under the headline "It Is Not True That the Railroad Trunk Lines Have Agreed to Pro-rate with the Western Roads." Then, beneath the story asserting that all the western roads were trying to lower all rates to meet northern competition, the *Journal* had a second headline, "What the Facts Are," followed by its "special" story:

> We wired Chicago early this morning for the facts about the meeting of Western presidents. He (our correspondent) replies: "At the meeting yesterday it was unanimously agreed, C.,B.&N. assenting, to ignore the long and short haul

> clauses of the Interstate law on Northwestern traffic, and meet the competition of water routes and Canadian roads through business, while holding local rates up. Only the details of this agreement remain now to be worked out by the Western Freight Association. If this plan can be carried out, railroad officials generally agree that it solves the rate problem in the Northwest. The *Inter-Ocean* [a Chicago daily] says: 'The settlement of the Northwestern situation takes away all danger from the St. Paul roads.' "

The Wall Street Journal didn't have formal editorials in its early years but got the equivalent from the pen of Charles H. Dow by a strange route. On July 20 it began publishing a biweekly column called "Various Opinions," contributed by brokerage firms and consisting mostly of excerpts from their customer-service letters. The column continued for months; the leading contributor, taking almost a column of space, was Goodbody, Glynn & Dow. The first such column, unsigned by an individual but almost certainly written by Charles Dow, attributed the railroad maneuvers in Chicago to part of a scheme to extinguish the Chicago, Burlington & Northern in the process of establishing a railway trust. It concluded, "The rumors of the purchase of C.,B.&N. to get it out of the way as a disturbing factor have been revived in several forms this week. First it was Northwest that had bought; then a combination of Grange [Western] roads, and then the old story of consolidation with C.,B.&Q. [Chicago, Burlington & Quincy] was revived. C.,B.&Q. people having always owned C.,B.&N. we suppose someday it will be nominally, as well as realistically, made part of the system; but the conquest of Holland by the Dutch would make as much change in European politics as the absorption of C.,B.&N. by C.,B.&Q."

In addition to the Dow-authored brokerage letter providing publicity for Goodbody, Glynn & Dow, that firm also bought advertisements in the paper that frequently appeared immediately adjacent to the opinion column. Whatever might have been Dow's purpose in starting the "Various Opinions" column, it evoked no local comment concerning possible conflict of interest on the part of one of the *Journal's* owners, though it might have helped to cause the paper moderate annoyance in Philadelphia. There, in the course of the formation of the Reading pool to manipulate Reading Railroad stock, a man named R. K. Dow was said to be joining forces with the Drexels of Philadelphia and J. P. Morgan of New York. *The Wall Street Journal* complained, "The *Philadelphia Ledger* has devoted nearly half a column to the abuse of us under the mistaken idea that Mr. R. K. Dow was a member of our firm."

By July 31 the paper showed that it was responsive to the attitudes of its readers. "We publish what the bond houses and the customers say they want," said the *Journal,* boasting that it printed "nearly all the bonds listed on the New York Stock Exchange." It also began the publication of "London arbitrage stocks" to serve speculators who engaged in the arcane practice of simultaneously purchasing and selling stocks in different places (in this case, London and New York), depending on a slight monetary difference in stock prices and the time differential to earn a profit. It also added a list of the New York theater attractions, "Theatres Tonight."

In November, Dow, Jones & Company announced, "We have added to our plant a Hoe two-revolution press" that would take printing up to 31 1/2 × 50 1/2 inches. It invited those who had "large work" to check with the company for job prices. The paper published its first travel advertisements, from an agent promising to supply lists of the best hotels in Florida at Jacksonville, Sanford, Orlando, and Tampa, as well as hotels in Havana, Cuba. On December 24, 1889, there appeared what may be the shortest *Wall Street Journal* market report in its history: "The market today was of a purely holiday character with fractional change on both sides and few features. Money was 6 @ 10%."

The year 1889 had been a good one for Dow, Jones, Bergstresser, and the newborn *Wall Street Journal.* Despite frequent depressions and panics in the decade closing, the country was relatively prosperous, having paid off many of its Civil War debts and obligations incurred in Europe for its rapid railroad expansion and other commercial growth in the West.

In November 1890 the company moved its offices to 41 Broad Street. Thomas Woodlock described the equipment as he saw it two years later:

> The plant, consisting of three Mergenthaler linotypes, one old-fashioned flatbed press, a couple of hand-driven rotary presses for the news slips [the bulletins being issued every eight minutes for messenger delivery during market hours], and a couple of presses for the printing of broker's market letters, was assembled on a single floor in an old building at 41 Broad Street. Power was furnished by an antiquated Babcock & Wilcox engine in the cellar.
>
> The messenger boys who delivered the news slips were also lodged on the same floor. Light was furnished by gas. At the back of the building was a cozy little cubbyhole with one old-fashioned walnut desk of probably 1860 vintage and three chairs. This was the firm's private room; here "conferences" were daily held at the close of business. We produced the daily bulletin news service, the matter which furnished the meat of *The Wall Street Journal* each afternoon at the close of business and circulated some 1,500 copies a day.

Woodlock evidently referred to the circulation of the news bulletins. The circulation of the paper was small, but it was growing and would pass 11,000 in 1902. The news-bulletin service had increased its monthly rate from $15 to $20 and thus would be grossing $300,000 a year. *The Wall Street Journal* received more advertising than it could print in the outside columns on pages one and four, and soon the advertisements were allowed to encroach into editorial areas.

There was no explanation for the financing of the new equipment, all of it secondhand, with the exception of a new Chambers folder added shortly after the first of the year. Dow said flatly some time later that *The Wall Street Journal* had no outside help, which wouldn't, of course, preclude bank loans. Since the newspapers praising *The Wall Street Journal* almost unanimously referred to Dow, Jones & Company as the most reliable and best-known of the New York news agencies, it is probable that the improvements and expansions were paid for by ordinary financing and from cash flow. There were no frills. The new quarters didn't even have electric lights, as did the premises at 26 Broad Street.

Chapter 3

Edward Jones Departs

The Wall Street Journal was published six days a week—stock-exchange holidays excepted—and Dow, Jones & Company news bulletins were issued even more frequently, on an average of every eight minutes from 9 A.M. until the market closed in the afternoon. Dow Jones was meeting fierce competition, not so much from Kiernan, who was preoccupied with politics, but from the aggressive *Wall Street News,* which did not intend to allow the newcomers a bigger foothold in the New York market. Unlike Kiernan and the Wall Street News Agency, Dow Jones did not operate a telegraph ticker service until 1897, and so had to combat its rivals by means of intensive coverage of the news, swift and sure messenger service, and complete dependability. The five editorial men in charge of the paper—Dow, Jones, and Bergstresser, along with Thomas F. Woodlock and Frank Phelps, who joined the staff in the late 1880s—did triple duty in the editorial, advertising, and circulation departments until 1892, when Charles Dow brought in an old friend, John W. Barney from the *Providence Journal,* to assist them in the business phase of Dow Jones affairs. Barney was soon named business manager of *The Wall Street Journal.*

The small staff was able to get out both the newspaper and the bulletins because of dedication to work—the three partners frequently met in Dow's home for business discussions after nighttime assignments, and all worked 12-hour days, according to Woodlock.

It wasn't long before the partners improved their news-exchange arrangement with Clarence Barron, the proprietor of the Boston News Bureau, by using some of the special reports from his newspaper, also called the *Boston News Bureau.* Barron began publication of his financial newspaper in 1887, two years before the advent of *The Wall Street Journal.* He was a vigorous practitioner of colorful personal journalism and his dispatches enlivened the pages of the *Journal.* In return, he received more staid dispatches, but these included the *Journal*'s superb railroad reports and analyses and its highly dependable reports on the New York Stock Exchange, the Curb Exchange, and the gold and commodity markets. Thus Barron and Dow Jones reinforced one another so that each soon dominated its home market—Dow Jones in Wall Street, Barron in Boston's State Street. Barron, always aggressive, invaded Philadelphia to establish the *Financial Journal* there in 1896, and again he exchanged dispatches with *The Wall Street Journal.*

Edward Jones continued to edit the news-bulletin service and, in effect, was managing editor of the *Journal.* Woodlock and Phelps covered Wall Street with Bergstresser. Dow spent only part of his time in the office, since he was at the same time in charge of Goodbody, Glynn & Dow and also held a seat on the New York Stock Exchange. Yet Dow, according to Woodlock, wrote much of the *Journal,* his work coming much closer to opinion than the initial prospectus had proposed. Many of his articles were editorials, although they were not so designated. Jones continued to report on the night meetings in the Windsor and Fifth Avenue hotels, in addition to developing and writing news provided throughout the day by his tipsters.

Every afternoon when the paper was going to press, the five young men would gather to discuss the day's work and to allocate the nighttime chores. In winter, Woodlock remembered, they frequently had to wear their overcoats in the office: vibrations from the press were likely to shake hot coals off the stove grates and onto the floor, so the fire was put out until the pressrun was finished. Woodlock and Phelps, as hired hands, had the night to themselves, and Bergstresser, who had early morning duties, escaped late assignments most of the time. Jones was the after-dark reporter, and Dow wrote his columns at night at home. The three original partners left no records, no letters, no memoirs. But Tom Woodlock, who rose rapidly in the company and eventually became the owner of ten shares of Dow Jones stock, published his recollections in the *Journal* in later years, after serving as editor and, in effect, chief executive officer. Woodlock credited Jones with greater acuity than the others in news editing and regarded Charles Dow as the scholar and theorist of the group, while Bergstresser, Woodlock felt, was the best reporter of the three.

Generally, the work of the five editors and two dozen or so boys went smoothly, especially after Dow returned full-time to the paper when Goodbody took charge of his brokerage firm. Sometime following the arrival of Woodlock, Phelps, and Barney, probably after the spring of 1893, Dow, Jones & Company hired its first female employee, Louise Egan. Miss Egan was expert on the typewriter and telephone, which the company acquired that year, Woodlock said. She could take dictation directly on the typewriter, and she could take dictated news bulletins from the telephone. In addition, Woodlock noted, the presence of a lady inhibited Jones's profanity. "Miss Egan, up to her marriage and retirement from the staff, took all the copy that Dow and Jones and Bergstresser produced," Woodlock wrote. "She was a remarkably rapid operator."

During the early 1890s, *The Wall Street Journal* kept a tenacious grip on two leading stories dealing with events that helped trigger the panic of 1893—the fate of the Philadelphia & Reading Railroad and the increasing drain on the government's gold reserve. The editors of the *Journal* blamed the country's economic troubles mainly on the Sherman Silver Purchase Act of July 14, 1890, and the overcapitalization of the railroads and some other large industries. The Sherman Silver Purchase Act required the purchase of 4,500,000 ounces of silver a month by the United States Treasury. The act was supported, naturally, by silver-mining interests and by debtor farmers in the South and West. Since the Treasury paid for the silver by issuing new currency, debtors foresaw an inflation that would let them pay off their debts with a cheaper currency. Bankers and businessmen in the East as well as foreign investors foresaw the same thing and were appalled. Foreigners were so concerned about the future of American money that they became much less willing to hold dollars. Their withdrawal of investments from the United States was reflected in an outflow of gold, the only means for settling international obligations. Ironically, the outflow of gold offset the issuance of new silver currency so that deflationary pressures continued.

A financial crisis was temporarily averted by a bumper wheat crop in 1891, which increased farm exports. This brought back some European gold, especially since, the *Journal* reported, there were massive crop failures abroad. Despite the improvement in export trade, *The Wall Street Journal* in December 1892 estimated that $89 million in gold had been shipped abroad during the year, and that the $100 million in the Treasury gold reserve—the minimum required by law to back the American dollar—was in danger. On December 15 Edward Jones sent a reporter to interview his close friend Jim Keene on the economic situation. Keene's statement was featured on page one the following day:

> Mr. James R. Keene said last night:
>
> There seems to be some apprehension about money. It suddenly became quite stringent on Thursday and today it showed the same features. Why this is I cannot understand. . . . There evidently has been an attempt by interested people to

> create a sentiment which would tend to increase the interest rate; and there is some plausibility in the argument that we are sending away gold. This in itself would not disturb the public mind, if it was not adroitly associated with the danger of the silver question, which seems to be always with us.
>
> I think the present gold export is legitimate. It means that we have been importing (goods) heavily. The internal trade of the United States has never been more prosperous; nor the people so able to buy, and for the matter of that, so willing.
>
> The silver question is the one that doubtlessly causes much anxiety, but the real danger is not half as great as it is pictured by some of the gentlemen who are in charge of our financial institutions.

Having made his thrust at Morgan and others, Keene took up the Sherman Silver Purchase Act: "There are few people in this portion of the country who do not deplore the existence of the Sherman Law. . . . Personally, I would be delighted to see the Sherman Act, vicious as it undoubtedly is, repealed."

The Wall Street Journal's attack on the silver legislation was under way and would not cease until repeal of the purchase clause on November 1, 1893. The panic of 1893 was widely blamed on the silver purchases, but it resulted chiefly from reactions to the purchases. Fears of inflation weakened confidence in the currency and in the banks. But many bank loans and many banks that would have prospered if prices had been rising or stable suffered in the actual deflation that occurred.

On January 3, 1893, the *Journal* reached J. P. Morgan, the dour banker who in the past had wanted no part of Keene. Keene was castigated by many as a stock manipulator because he formed pools, groups of speculators interested in driving specific stocks up or down. (Some of the group might sell short; that is, sell stocks they had merely borrowed. Big, dramatic sales of a stock by some of the pool operators could start a stock downward, then other members of the group might buy at the lower prices, replacing the stock sold short.) Morgan had called Keene a freebooter, an interesting choice of language considering Morgan had named his own famous yacht the *Corsair*. When the *Journal*'s writer, probably Bergstresser, called on him, the financier found himself in public agreement with Keene, possibly for the first time. Said Morgan in the *Journal* of January 4, "I am unqualifiedly opposed to the present Sherman silver law."

On February 15, 1893, the *Journal* reported that the government's gold reserve was in genuine trouble. The Treasury was required by law to maintain a reserve of $100 million. The surplus over that amount had dropped to $982,410 and appeared to be going down fast. Said the paper's lead story, "The president of the largest [of the] national banks, who was one of the first to exchange certificates at the subtreasury for legal tender, says: 'I do not think the banks will give any more gold to the Treasury.' " In its commentary the *Journal* said, "We are informed that it is practically certain that three millions of gold will be exported Saturday." And farther down it noted that J. P. Morgan was in Washington "to confer with the government. . . . The other bankers say they have left the matter with Mr. Morgan."

The *Journal* reported on February 17: "The President is hopeful that an emergency necessitating the sale of bonds will not arise, at least that it can be avoided until after the 4th of March." Treasury Secretary John G. Carlisle was quoted as saying that the Treasury was about to receive $8 million in "free gold." The *Journal* said that exceptionally heavy tax receipts (evidently from the healthy domestic trade Keene had described) would help the gold situation, which "shows a slight improvement."

The problems of the Philadelphia & Reading Railroad, which the *Journal* followed assiduously, were symptomatic of those of the country. America had experienced a boom as the West was opened after the Civil War, and railroad construction led the way, with mining, especially of gold and silver, close behind. The United States had become an exporting nation and had been able to accumulate gold as well as produce it. But, by 1893, the currency needs of the expanding economy exceeded the reserves of gold. Grover Cleveland, the Democrat elected president in 1892 with Wall Street support, believed fervently in the gold standard and was determined to defend it. The developing West wanted more money in circulation and demanded a bimetallism policy of gold plus free coinage of silver. The new rising industrialists, led by the railroad builders, required enormous supplies of capital, which could be raised rapidly by stock auctions, such as that at the New York Stock Exchange.

Some of the entrepreneurs building the railroads and creating business trusts had become buccaneers seeking to control entire sectors of the economy. They were prepared to crush a competitor or to smash an enterprise for the sake of quick gain and cumulative power. The bears of Wall Street were accused of being such men, among them James Keene and Addison Clammack, close friends of Edward Jones. *The Wall Street Journal* charged Keene and Clammack with leading a raid on the stock of the Reading Railroad. The report was undoubtedly true, and details probably were supplied to Jones by Keene and Clammack themselves. Reading stock was ripe for attack. President McLeod of the Philadelphia & Reading had sought to invade New England to build a railroad there in competition with the Morgan-dominated lines, and had been repulsed by Morgan forces, suffering heavy losses.

On February 20, the Dow Jones News Service told its clients that Reading directors were meeting that day in Philadelphia, adding: "It is feared that receivership is the only way out." Later that day *The Wall Street Journal* carried the story. The petition for receivership of the Reading was filed the same afternoon. Financial historians would write that the collapse of the

Reading in February and the National Cordage Company on May 4 triggered the Wall Street phase of the panic of 1893. The *Journal* on February 24 blamed Keene and Clammack for Reading's troubles, but also attributed the jittery market to shortage of currency in circulation as a result of depleted gold reserves. "Gold shipments were large and the Treasury's stock of gold, excluding the $100,000,000 reserve, which is a fetish, had fallen to the lowest point since the resumption of specie payments. . . . The money market remains very hard."

Gold was being withdrawn by London and other banks. The American dollar, it was estimated, was worth only 55 cents in gold. On March 4, 1893, the day of Cleveland's inauguration, the *Journal* had given page-one prominence to a special report which suggested that President Cleveland would solve Treasury problems by selling U.S. gold-backed bonds abroad: "We are informed upon excellent authority that the incoming Executive are in treaty with a foreign firm of world-wide influence through their correspondents here for an issue of bonds abroad. We are satisfied with the correctness of the statement. . . . We are also in a position to announce that an offer has been made to the Treasury by an institution here for five million 4% bonds . . . to be paid for in gold."

Such a move by President Cleveland, who had been a member of a Wall Street law firm and was close to leaders there, would without doubt have diminished the gold drain by strengthening United States credit. Congress, however, adjourned without taking any action to shore up the economy, the forces being divided between the gold hard-liners and the rebels from the West advocating free silver coinage at the rate of 16 ounces of silver having the value of one ounce of gold. Meantime, economic depression spread through the country. Before it would end, railroad firms controlling 30,000 miles of track would fail, more than 600 banks close, and other commercial failures total over 15,000. The price of silver dropped from 80 cents in May to 65 cents on July 1, and the government's gold reserves fell to $95,485,413.

In May there were rumors that President Cleveland would call a special session of Congress to deal with the monetary problem, but the *Journal* acted to squelch them. It simply telephoned Grover Cleveland's office. "We asked the office of the President," the paper said on May 31, "and we are told that there is no truth to the rumors the President will call a special session now. He is opposed to a special session prior to September. There will be no special session prior to that time, if then." Throughout July the rumor resurfaced, causing ripples in the stock market, and each time the *Journal* denied it. But it dropped the phrase "if then" after saying there would be no special session until September.

On July 26 the rumor again floated, but the stock market crashed. Prices fell throughout the list. It was a bankers' panic rather than a general malaise, analysts pointed out, since the public was not generally in the market at that time. Nevertheless, the shock was severe on Wall Street and other financial centers, and the gold-depletion crisis that menaced the entire economy loomed closer. Alexander Dana Noyes, a financial writer for the *New York Post* at the time, summarized the situation in his memoirs: "Large gold exports continued, the consequent tumbling of the gold reserve behind the currency in April brought that fund 5 percent below the statutory $100 million. Five months after inauguration day, July 26, 1893, came financial panic. . . . Wall Street and its patrons had gone mad. There was hopeless gloom, each sound of the telephone meant fresh news of disaster. A half dozen railroads fell from $50 to $15 a share." In Boston the Harvard University historian and author Henry Adams declared, "Boston is suddenly old and haggard. I feel I will find myself a beggar." Noyes visited his bank in New York and was allowed to draw from his account only $25 at a time "for personal and household expenses."

The following day stocks rallied slightly. *The Wall Street Journal* covered the meeting of financial operators at the Windsor on the night of July 27, and its report the next morning was optimistic. "The feeling last night was distinctly better. Money worked easier and there was an idea that anticipation of interest by the government and by big corporations were [sic] not only creating a supply of funds, but was having an effect upon public confidence." The paper stated that the heavy selling on the 26th occurred because the shorts realized they were in a precarious position. The paper implied that the bears drove prices down to enable themselves to cover their short position, a tactic possible when such experts as Keene and Clammack were dominating the maneuvers. "Something led Mr. Keene and Mr. Clammack to buy a large amount of stock [on the 27th]," the *Journal* said. "Some thought it was early information in regard to the meeting of Congress. Others credited the action to the probability of gold imports. The undisputed fact was that they bought, and a large following bought, too, materially reducing the short interest at the close."

On July 28, the *Journal* spoke of a "strong rally" in the market, explaining that London investors had bought between 60,000 and 80,000 shares. But the rally was brief, prices continued to fall, and President Cleveland summoned Congress to an early special session, contrary to the latest predictions of the *Journal*. The President appeared before a joint session on August 8 to call for repeal of the Sherman Silver Purchase Act. The *Journal* published the news in its lead column on page one, quoting the President: "I earnestly recommend the prompt repeal of the provisions of the Act passed July 14, 1890, authorizing the purchase of silver bullion, and other legislation that may put beyond all doubt or mistake the intention and ability of the Government to fulfill its pecuniary obligations in money universally recognized by all civilized countries."

The *Journal* proprietors were wrong in predicting that the session would not occur before September, but the President's speech endorsed the silver and gold position the paper had taken. Although the Sherman Silver Purchase Act was repealed November 1, silver men would not support measures intended to increase the supply of gold to the Treasury. On January 15, 1894, a $50 million Treasury bond offering was authorized, but since there was no provision for redemption in gold, the bonds did not return expected revenues. Disaffection in the country continued. The McKinley protective tariff, passed in 1890, tended to strip the Treasury of money as revenues from import tariffs almost ceased. This result, forecast by foes of a high tariff, including the *Journal*, was called the true cause of the panic by some economists. Not only was the government denied proceeds that would have accrued from normal import taxes, but goods from abroad failed to enter the country under the unusually high protective tariff. Thus consumers, including businesses requiring European machine tools and other essentials, were forced to pay higher prices. The Wilson-Gorman tariff, passed in July 1894, only partly corrected the mischief. Meantime, Congress continued its defiance of President Cleveland by failing to authorize a government bond issue that could be redeemed in gold.

The proprietors of *The Wall Street Journal* clearly believed that the Cleveland administration would be able to solve the economic problems, since they announced that summer an expansion program that demonstrated their own confidence in the economic future. They had purchased a new Hoe "Perfect" press that was being built for installation in the new company headquarters at 42–44 Broad Street. It would be a rotary press using the stereotype process by which a flatbed of type could be converted to curved metal plates, which locked onto the press to ink rolls of newsprint. Woodlock, recalling the move to 44 Broad Street in his memoirs, noted that "there was a considerable increase in population also," a reference to added employees. Brief notices in the paper heralded the new press facility and invited printing contracts. The company said it had close to 100 employees, which, of course, would have included the messenger boys; but without doubt Dow, Jones & Company and *The Wall Street Journal* were prospering and growing. So many advertisers sought admission to the paper's columns that John Barney, the business manager, reduced the type size and still found it necessary to run six columns of advertising on page one, leaving a mere single column of 16 picas for news or editorial comment.

During January 1895 *The Wall Street Journal* published rumors that the gold crisis would finally end by precisely those means it had announced so confidently on March 4, 1893. The government would enhance American credit by issuing gold-backed bonds that would interest a great foreign banking house. The *Journal*'s story of almost two years before had stated, "The . . . Executive are in treaty with a foreign firm of world-wide influence through their correspondents here for an issue of bonds abroad." It had taken a long time for Congress to become convinced that, in President Cleveland's words, the government would have to "fulfill its pecuniary obligations in money universally recognized by all civilized countries"—money backed by gold. On the 28th Cleveland sent his message to Congress, saying in part, "The only way left open to the Government for procuring gold is by the issue and sale of its bonds," bonds to be redeemed in gold.

First, the government had to obtain the gold, and the procedure proved to be that suggested in *The Wall Street Journal* report in March 1893. On January 29, according to John K. Winkler, the Morgan biographer, Treasury Secretary Carlisle sent his chief assistant, William E. Curtis, to call upon August Belmont in the banker's New York home. He handed Belmont a series of cablegrams. They indicated that the powerful House of Rothschild in London, the financier of governments abroad, had been approached by American emissaries to buy U.S. bonds. The Rothschilds, Curtis reminded Belmont, would not touch U.S. government bonds unless payable in gold, and gold alone. Belmont, of course, already knew the Rothschild position; he was their American representative. Curtis was there to receive guidance. "Why don't you see Morgan, perhaps he can suggest something," Belmont told Curtis, according to Winkler.

J. Pierpont Morgan had received his own cables from the House of Rothschild in which joint action on the American gold problem had been proposed. Belmont called upon Morgan, and they had discussed the problem. Morgan wasn't sure they could get enough gold together to meet the government's desperate need. When a survey indicated they could, Morgan proposed the terms. He and Belmont would take 30-year 4-percent bonds at a price equivalent to 104 1/2. Years previously government 4-percent gold-backed bonds brought 111 on the market, but now that the bonds lacking gold support were not moving at any price, the Rothschilds demanded that they be redeemable in gold.

On February 8, 1895, *The Wall Street Journal* reported that J. P. Morgan was in Washington "to meet with Secretary Carlisle." The paper noted that Morgan had arrived the day before and that Belmont, scheduled to attend the meeting also, had not appeared. The report was correct but incomplete. Belmont had been delayed by a storm, and Morgan had met, not only with Carlisle, but with President Cleveland and other members of his cabinet. There had been a run on the Treasury; only $9 million in gold remained in the subtreasury in New York. At the meeting in President Cleveland's study, according to Winkler, Morgan began by telling Cleveland, "Mr. President, the Secretary of the Treasury knows of a check outstanding for $12 million. If this is presented today, it's all over." Carlisle nodded in confirmation. Having thus established the gravity of the emergency, Morgan proposed his plan. Morgan and Belmont, backed by the Rothschilds, would buy the government bonds with gold, thus stabilizing the Treasury gold reserve. Since the bonds would pay high interest and initially be purchased at a discount, the banks would profit when the bond prices rose, as was certain to happen when news of the gold-redemption clause and of the support of the world's leading banking house got out. The *Journal* caught some of the details in its final February 8 edition:

> Washington special—The President in his message says:
>
> Because of continued anxiety at lack of Congressional action, the Treasury must issue bonds.
>
> He recommends $62,400,000 to be sold to yield 3-3/4 percent.
>
> Half of the issue has been taken abroad.
>
> Washington special—Present loan promises, President says, better results than any here-to-fore made. The sixty-two millions, added to what there is already in the Treasury, will make whole gold reserve.

The bonds, the story said, would be redeemed in gold.

The terms of the settlement predicted by the *Journal* had been largely met, except that the net interest rate was 3 3/4 percent rather than the 4 percent the paper had forecast in March 1893. The long delay would prove expensive to the government.

On February 9 the *Journal* reported angry congressional reaction to the President's message and the Morgan plan. The silver men who had opposed gold-backed bonds were greatly enraged. But the Wall Street reaction was favorable, and the *Journal* said that the press generally approved. Modestly, it did not mention that it had forecast the bond-sale plan:

> It is understood that the syndicate which has sold 3,500,000 ounces of gold coin to the Government includes, besides Messrs. Morgan and Belmont, several banks in this city, among others the Chase National, the Park National, the City National, the National Bank of Commerce, the Hanover National and the American Exchange National. . . .
>
> Washington dispatches generally indicate that the present syndicate has an understanding with the Government by which it will have preference in the event of a repetition of the operation becoming necessary.
>
> Bankers in this city and the newspapers editorially commend the President's action and the placing of the responsibility for the onerous terms, on which the loan was made, on Congress. . . .
>
> The President's recommendation that 3% old bonds be authorized within the next ten days to replace the 4% bonds sold will be taken up by the Ways and Means Committee of the House today. It is possible that a bill might be reported by the House, but the Senate would not permit such a bill to pass in ten days. The

silver men are greatly enraged at the President's demonstration of the cost of the silver folly.

Who had provided the essence of the proposal to *The Wall Street Journal* 22 months previously? August Belmont? J. P. Morgan? The paper in 1893 had said flatly that the "Executive" was instituting the action. Possibly a Treasury leak had been authorized by President Cleveland, and the response of the silver senators had caused him to delay. But there also remains to be considered the interesting coincidence that Charles Dow, as president of Goodbody, Glynn & Dow, maintained offices adjacent to the Drexel Building at the southeast corner of Broad and Wall streets, the Morgan headquarters. Dow and Morgan had been neighbors, and, despite the fact that Dow criticized Morgan in later years, there were some on Wall Street who said the two men had been friends.

The run on gold was ended. Some $18 million in gold was taken from ships in New York harbor and redeposited in the United States subtreasury. By July 8, 1895, the gold reserve totaled $107,571,230. The Morgan-Belmont bonds sold at 124 late in the summer, and J. P. Morgan had become the most powerful man in Wall Street. According to Winkler, Drexel and Morgan made a profit of $5 million on the deal.

On February 27, 1897, the *Journal* announced another expansion which demonstrated that the company was by no means concentrating inordinate attention on the newspaper and printing phases of its business. Dow, Jones & Company was going into the telegraph-ticker service using a new broad-tape ticker developed by Dow Jones in conjunction with the Printing Telegraph Company, and it had leased a plant from that company to manufacture the newly developed ticker.

For some time before 1897, three organizations had offered financial news to Wall Street via stock-market tickers, the paper explained. One used the system developed by Dr. Laws and perfected by Thomas A. Edison, the widely known narrow-tape ticker seen in many brokerage offices. Another system had been developed by E. A. Callahan in Boston, and it, too, had been modified by Edison, who later was granted his own patent. This system was used by C. W. Barron in Boston and by a small firm in New York. John Kiernan, the pioneer news agency, "provided the wide ticker service which became the standard method of distributing such news as the service developed." This meant it carried news bulletins rather than market listings only.

When Kiernan retired in 1896, Dow, Jones & Company had arranged with the Printing Telegraph Company, which manufactured the Joy stock-market tickers, to take over its operations and the machines it leased to

Kiernan. In 1897 Dow Jones was ready to start its own telegraphic news service, using Joy machines modified to its specifications. For a time the company worked with the owners of the Printing Telegraph Company, George Couch and Ben Tyler. Eventually, Dow, Jones & Company acquired ownership of the manufacturing facilities as well as the machines that produced broad-tape reports equal in size to the printed bulletins distributed by the Dow Jones messengers rather than the narrow tapes of competitive machines.

The *Journal* anticipated that customers would want both the ticker and the messenger bulletins:

> We believe that the competition in business among brokers resulting from the instantaneous use of private telephones and private wires will make it to the advantage of very many houses to take both services—the ticker service for private wire use and short quick matter, the printed slips for general use of the customers.
>
> Our facilities for gathering news have been strengthened in various ways as a result of this acquisition, and we trust that our service in the good times coming will increase in interest and value. We have been in business a little more than 15 years and have seen the number of our customers increase twenty fold. We now have 100 persons on our payroll, and our issue of news matter, which began as 800 words, now runs from 20,000 to 25,000 words a day.
>
> Ten years ago we revolutionized the news business in Wall Street by developing a way of using printed bulletins instead of the manifold. We believe that our present move of an express service for "rush" with full printed slips in addition will prove an important departure.

The company continued to offer its messenger delivery service of printed bulletins until after World War II.

The paper then described the ticker to be used. The combined services—ticker, bulletins, and *The Wall Street Journal*—would cost subscribers $30 a month. Later, when Dow, Jones & Company took over full manufacturing rights, business manager Joseph Cashman was placed in charge of the manufacturing operations.

The *Journal* took another important news-gathering step in 1897 when it opened its Washington bureau with Jesse M. Sarvis as bureau chief. The bureau not only provided vital news to both the newspaper and the Dow Jones ticker service, a function of the entire news staff, but it also became a kind of graduate school for future editors of the paper. In later years, many of the *Journal*'s top editors were men who had served the paper in the Washington bureau.

On November 14, 1898, the *Journal* announced that it would publish a morning edition as well as an evening one, fixing the subscription price for both issues at $8 a year. Subscribers to the ticker service would receive both morning and evening editions without charge.

> *The Wall Street Journal* will henceforth have a morning as well as an evening edition. The evening *Journal* dates back to 1883 [the year the *Afternoon News Letter* started]. It was first issued as a summary of our news service, then in 1889 as a financial newspaper, enlarged to its present form in 1892.
>
> The evening *Journal* has had a steady growth in circulation, especially outside the city, from the outset. It has been hampered, however, by the necessity of going to press at 3:15 P.M., an hour too early to enable us to give a good quotation service, and there have been difficulties in the arrangement of matter that could not be overcome.
>
> The morning edition will enable us to make a better paper, one which we hope will make friends. . . .We have had many years of experience in this work. We have facilities for doing it well and we have a strong desire that the *Journal*, like our News Service, may be found to be intelligent, accurate, unbiased and worthy of the confidence of those who take it.

The new edition was well received, the circulation, morning and evening, rising above 10,000 the following year. Advertising became so plentiful that some pre-Christmas issues ran 70 percent paid linage on page one. New general consumer-advertising clients were added, among them Wanamaker's Department Store, the Philadelphia-based company that had acquired the famed A. T. Stewart store in New York. Wanamaker became a leading account in the *Journal*. One of the new advertisers was a builder at Bensonhurst-by-the-Sea, who offered a 15-room Victorian house on five lots with steam heat and modern plumbing at $11,000. The *Journal* advertised its own wire service: "Quick as a Flash! We give quotations, telegrams, cables and all kinds of news affecting the markets / Page printers are the latest electric device / News carried by electricity printed by electricity / Arranged on a page easily read and filed / No banker or broker can well afford to be without our Financial News Service. / Dow, Jones & Co. / 44 Broad St." The Dow Jones telephone number was One Broad.

And there was another modest advertising card—for the Boston News Bureau, C. W. Barron, Manager, Boston, and C. W. Barron, Manager, New York, soliciting advertising linage. Barron probably was also keeping close watch on his friends at the *Journal*, since his New York office was in the Edison Building at 44 Broad Street, the Dow Jones headquarters.

On January 9, 1899, without public warning, the following appeared in two columns on page one of *The Wall Street Journal:*

> NOTICE
>
> The firm of Dow, Jones & Co. is this day dissolved by mutual consent, Mr. Edward D. Jones retiring.
>
> Charles H. Dow
> Edward D. Jones
> Charles M. Bergstresser
> Thomas F. Woodlock

The business of Dow, Jones & Co. will be continued by the undersigned under the name of Dow, Jones & Co., and the undersigned assume all assets and liabilities of the old firm.

Charles H. Dow
Charles M. Bergstresser
Thomas F. Woodlock
Frank M. Brady

The undersigned has associated himself with Messrs. T. J. Taylor & Co., 30 Broad Street, where he will place at the disposal of his friends such experience and knowledge of railroad and industrial properties as he has acquired during his interest in this business since its formation in 1882.

January 7, 1899 Edward D. Jones

The *Journal* made no attempt to explain the departure of Edward Jones in January 1899, nor does any written record survive to indicate the probable difficulties within the firm. Dow and Jones were not yet among the most publicized names in American life. Both men and Bergstresser, their partner, were reclusive in their business lives, and Dow and Bergstresser in their personal lives as well. Their own activities were not recorded in the *Journal* or anywhere else. Dow was ill at the time Jones departed, and within four years he would die. There would be no photograph at that time; the paper had none. Other newspapers would cover the death of Dow in just two paragraphs, the demise of Jones in 1920 in one paragraph, and Bergstresser's death in a notice in 1923. The three men had the obscurity they appeared to crave in their lifetimes and in death. It remained for the media of the future to make Dow and Jones household words.

Obviously, there were difficulties in the Dow Jones offices in the last decade of the century, problems that led Jones to sell his stock. Their nature could be inferred from changes in *The Wall Street Journal,* which began shortly after Jones's departure and steadily continued. Also, Tom Woodlock, destined to succeed Dow as editor, disclosed some hints of the growing intramural clashes when he wrote about his own experiences in later years. A key to the problem of the fraying relationship of Dow and Jones after their years of close association lay in the essential contrast of their natures, Woodlock believed. "In every particular they were diverse types."

Jones, an emotional, explosive man, had calmed down somewhat after his many years in the stressful job as boss of the news-gathering operations for the *Journal,* the ticker, and the bulletin services. But there would be occasional, fierce eruptions as Jones exploded angrily in the evident belief that Dow and Bergstresser were in alliance against him. Jones had some reason for such an inference, according to Woodlock, who recalled the 1899 events years after the three partners were dead. Dow and Bergstresser considered Jones the weak member of the company, Woodlock said. Despite his valiant work in a demanding job over a number of years, his partners constantly feared that Jones would fail them, probably because they disapproved of his friends and recalled his drinking problems of an earlier time. It was Bergstresser initially who had been rejected and called "Buggy" by Jones in front of the messenger boys. But Dow had married Mrs. Lucy Russell, and she introduced his partner Bergstresser to her cousin, Helen Russell. They were married in North Branford, Connecticut, in 1889. Thereafter the Dows and the Bergstressers were together often, and this familiar relationship sometimes became evident in the office. Jones was left out.

At some point, management of the messenger boys was turned over to Bergstresser. Dow and Bergstresser evidently intended to relieve Jones of this duty to allow him more time for news gathering, but the move was misunderstood by both Jones and the boys. Bergstresser was tenth in a family of 11 children and knew something about getting along with youngsters, but his Dutch-Scottish ancestry showed in his stubborn, frugal ways. He demanded maximum production from the boys but was slow to respond with praise, which Jones had handed out lavishly, or with money. One of the young men, Charles M. Price, recalled that in 1898, "after Bergstresser became the inner office man, handling the news and the boys," he asked for a $2 raise and was refused. Bergstresser told him he was doing good work, but patience was required. In his next pay envelope, Price found a 50-cent raise. He stormed into Bergstresser's office, pounded the desk, and flung back the 50 cents. "You need this worse than I do; I'll go elsewhere," he told Bergstresser. Then Dow or Jones intervened and Price got his increase.

The Price incident indicates that Jones actually had been supplanted by Bergstresser a year before he left the company. Beyond doubt Jones had for a long time been dissatisfied with pay conditions at Dow Jones. In 1900, the first year for which company records are available, each partner received $7,500 plus $1.20 a share in annual dividends, and the amount may have been lower in 1899. Even in his later years, Jones continued to love the good life of Wall Street. He enjoyed friends such as Jim Keene, the spectacular Wall Street pool operator who, according to William Peter Hamilton, "made the market" in United States Steel and Anaconda copper; Phil Armour, the Chicagoan who tried to corner wheat; the Astors, rich in New York real estate; and Stanford White, the architect and playboy. They were Jones's special cronies, big spenders in the Gay Nineties crowd. Jones enjoyed their company at Delmonico's, Sherry's, or Moriarty's after he had covered night meetings of the Wall Street people still gathering at the Fifth Avenue Hotel, the Windsor, or the elegant new St. Regis to make deals and news.

There were no more partners' meetings at Charles Dow's apartment. The Dows had moved to Brooklyn, where they lived modestly and somewhat obscurely because of Dow's ill health and also by his preference. Jones himself was neither a Jim Fiske traveling about with a bevy of pretty women, nor a Bet-a-Million Gates gambling at Canfield's or in a Waldorf-Astoria suite for high stakes. Jones was merely on the fringe of the fast crowd, always welcome but not always able to pick up the check. He lived within his moderate income in a quiet Upper East Side apartment with his wife, Jeannette, but he was rarely home before morning. Scandal never attached to him, as it did to many of his friends. But Jones was discontented. He agreed to increased advertising in the paper until page one often had six columns of ads to one of editorial, usually Dow's column. He may even have pushed for extra advertising revenues because the overload on page one ended (until the advent of a new owner) shortly after Jones departed. It is doubtful that Jones alone could have instituted the policy of packing page one with non-editorial content, but he did not successfully resist it, and someone did when Jones was no longer with the paper. However the revenues were earned, Dow insisted they should be used to improve the product rather than for the enrichment of the owners.

The Dow Jones stock was closely held, and Jones may have been dissatisfied by his inability to add to his holdings even if their dividends were not great. The number of shares he acquired is not on record, but Dow is believed to have had more than 50 percent before he and Bergstresser bought Jones's interest, which gave Dow 3,630 shares and Bergstresser 850, so the holdings of Jones could not have been large. Since the dividends paid were only 10 cents a month in 1900, perhaps an even more important factor in the conflict is the likelihood that Jones was upset by the attitude of his partners and possibly felt that he did more than his share of the work.

Also, Dow, at least by implication, disapproved of Jones's life-style. The high-living Wall Street crowd and the new real-estate millionaires who were among Jones's friends, especially those said to be gambling at Canfield's and Moriarty's, were anathema to the somber, serious-minded Dow. He increasingly felt that Wall Street had to be protected from charges by preachers, politicians, and the popular press that it and the stock exchange were really a gambling institution. The excesses of the big spenders, who built magnificent mansions along Fifth Avenue, gave extravagant parties and lavish balls, and ostentatiously displayed their wealth in elegant restaurants, were giving Wall Street a bad name, Dow believed. He wrote more and more in defense of Wall Street, including even bears and pool operators, who, he admitted reluctantly, were also necessary to maintain an orderly market. But Dow's defensive articles evidently irked Jones, since it was his friends who by implication appeared to be those most needing protection from criticism.

So Jones left, first to join the brokerage firm of Talbot Taylor, James Keene's son-in-law, and then, according to the *New York Times,* to become one of the brokers associated with Keene himself. Keene was about to enter his most successful period, making the market for United States Steel for Morgan and his steel-industry associates, Judge Elbert Gary and Henry Clay Frick, and then acquiring J. P. Morgan as his special client in the Northern Pacific battle. With Keene, Jones must have finally found the excitement, companionship, and money he required. Jones, for instance, was a member of the Taylor establishment when Keene made his son-in-law's firm the headquarters for his Northern Pacific corner operations in 1901, and probably transferred to Jim Keene at that time.

When Dow, whose health began to fail a short time after Jones left the company, died in his Brooklyn home on December 4, 1902, Jones sent the *Journal* an appreciation of his former associate, indicating that their parting had not left a residue of bitterness.

Chapter 4

Charles Dow's Final Days

Shortly after the departure of Edward Jones, the character of *The Wall Street Journal* showed a subtle change, though typography remained the same. There were now fewer advertisements on page one. There was a reduction in such recycled material as the excerpts from other newspapers, attention was paid to culture in addition to the theater, and theater news was expanded. Books were reviewed in an "Among the Books" column; lectures were reprinted. A major change was in the paper's approach to matters of opinion. Several editorials appeared, mostly commenting on railroad problems. The paper invited participation by readers, urging them to send in their questions about stock-market situations, promising personal replies if a stamped, self-addressed envelope was enclosed. Early in the spring, Dow, Jones & Company published Thomas F. Woodlock's book on railroad economics, *One Ton Mile,* publicizing the book and its writer, who was praised as the *Journal*'s expert on railroads. The success of the venture led Dow, Jones & Company to offer for sale through its offices and by mail the Wall Street Library, a series of books edited by Samuel Armstrong Nelson that would later present the works of other *Journal* writers, including Dow himself after his death.

Two days after Jones left the paper, the *Journal* ran the equivalent of an editorial, appearing under the page-two masthead, the usual position for editorials in other newspapers:

> The market is resolving itself into a problem of

> whether the public is going to carry the advance along irrespective of the efforts of those who feel a reaction is needed. It is certain that quite strong efforts have been made in the past few days to check the over-trading. These efforts have made a change in the character of the speculation, but they have not reduced the volume of business. People who have taken profits in one group of stocks, after watching the market for an hour or two, have bought something else. . . . The market has ceased to be professional. The public is the great force, and when the public exerts its power for or against prices, it has been repeatedly found useless for any group of men to turn the tide. The question is whether the public will continue in the present frame of mind and whether there is anything in sight likely to exert a general influence upon public buying.

The statement was mild, but it further indicated a decision on the part of Dow to seek a wider readership for *The Wall Street Journal* rather than limit its appeal to professionals and insiders. On March 9, 1899, the paper spelled out its relationship with its readers: "When we founded *The Wall Street Journal* as successor to our *Summary* established in 1884 [the *Customers' Afternoon News Letter,* actually begun in 1883], we supplied a relatively small circle of readers. While the *Journal* was recognized from the first as the best daily financial newspaper published and as occupying a unique position, it was also looked upon more or less as a 'class' newspaper of necessarily limited circulation. Its growth was therefore somewhat slow." The paper then disclosed that it was ordering a new press to accommodate its expected circulation growth "to provide once and for all for any requirements that may arise." It said its circulation totaled 10,000 and again indicated an intention to broaden its public appeal:

> It is a source of much gratification to us to find our *Journal* so well appreciated. Our Wall Street news service has been since its inception eighteen years ago admittedly the standard of accuracy, reliability, promptness and independence. We think we may fairly say that the "Street" has always so regarded it. We have endeavored to place *The Wall Street Journal* in a position similar, among newspapers, to that occupied by our news service—that is, in all things first, and in many things alone. The public to which *The Wall Street Journal* appeals is nothing if not discerning, and, in the support that we have received, we think we can see proof that we have succeeded in our efforts.
>
> We hope and expect to improve the *Journal* as time goes on, but we intend that it shall always keep the two great characteristics which have placed it in a class by itself, viz.: accuracy and independence.

On April 21, 1899, the "Review and Outlook" column of commentary began, written by Charles Dow. He used it to educate the general reader in the ways of the stock and bond markets. Dow spoke repeatedly of the long-range changes that should be followed in the market; patience was the prime prerequisite for the investor in stocks. He indicated that a bull market might extend over four years while a bear market might be slightly shorter. "The time involved in these turns," Dow wrote, "is determined by natural causes. The cause is that the stock market reflects general conditions, and it takes several years for such a change for the better or for the worse to work its way through the community, so that the mass of people are either optimistic or pessimistic in their views. Some people foresee changes in the situation much quicker than others, but it takes a change of opinion on the part of millions of people to produce a well-defined sentiment throughout the country."

The first serious scholar to study Dow's market theories as they developed from that 1899 column was William Peter Hamilton. Hamilton joined the paper in 1899 and would become editorial-page editor of the *Journal.* He had reported on the markets in London and Johannesburg, South Africa, as well as in New York. Hamilton is credited by George W. Bishop, Jr., author of *Charles H. Dow and the Dow Theory* and *Charles H. Dow: Economist,* and by Harold M. Finley, author of *Everybody's Guide to the Stock Market,* with establishing and popularizing the so-called Dow Theory. Hamilton's book on the subject, *The Stock Market Barometer,* published in 1922, sold out seven editions. Scores of books have been written since on the Dow Theory; millions of references to it and the Dow Jones Averages have appeared in the financial and popular press and have been heard on radio and television; thousands of "Dow Theory" letters on the stock market have been sold by specialists. Yet Dow himself never made claim to a theory of the market except by implication.

The first person to recognize the value of Dow's work as a guide to investors was Samuel Nelson, publisher of Nelson's Wall Street Library. He selected Charles Dow's editorials on the stock market for a book in his library series, *The ABC of Stock Speculation,* published in 1903. It was Nelson, according to Bishop, who first used the phrase "Dow Theory" to describe Dow's work. Hamilton, however, established the Dow Theory among schools of economic thought as well as among the financial community, according to author Finley. Hamilton's essays appeared as editorials in *The Wall Street Journal* and in *Barron's Financial Weekly,* as well as in his frequently cited book. Hamilton quoted Dow extensively, including Dow's picturesque exposition of his concept of stock-market action that appeared in the *Journal* on January 31, 1901:

> A person watching the tide coming in and who wishes to know the exact spot which marks the high tide, sets a stick in the sand at the points reached by the incoming waves until the stick reaches a position where the waves do not come up to it, and finally recede enough to show that the tide has turned.
>
> This method holds good in watching and determining the flood tide of the stock market. The average of twenty stocks is the peg which marks the height of the waves. The price-waves, like those of the sea, do not recede at once from the

top. The force which moves them checks the inflow gradually and time elapses before it can be told with certainty whether the tide has been seen or not.

The Dow Jones Averages were the creation of Charles Dow, first appearing in the *Customers' Afternoon News Letter* July 3, 1884. He revised his list from 11 to 20 representative stocks in 1886 and then to 30 on May 18, 1887, explaining that readers had attacked his lists as being too narrow. He pointed out, however, that each list, whether of 11 or 20 or 30 representative stocks, after comparison over a period of a year, showed the same rise and fall for the market. This was the beginning of the famous averages, which Dow revised 12 years after their initial appearance. William S. McSherry, manager of news department services for *The Wall Street Journal*, has provided in his preface to an anniversary book of the Averages published in 1972 one of the best and most succinct analyses of this oldest and best-known stock-market barometer:

> Dow did not use a weighted mean or make adjustments of any nature. He simply added the closing price of stocks in his average and divided the total by the number of companies included in the list. As an historian as well as a journalist, Dow found the use of chart and statistics useful and in his editorials advised traders to keep various records on individual stocks as well as the full list. There is no evidence Dow looked upon the averages as containing anything more than an indication of the statistical nature of the stock market as a whole.
>
> The first average compiled in 1884 was a mixed bag. It contained nine railroads and two industrials. Dow found it desirable to include "active" stocks in his compilation. And, it wasn't easy to find them. A quarter-million shares traded was the average day's activity on the Big Board, mostly in railroads.
>
> Industrials were new and speculative. They had no past for comparative purposes. Despite this, Dow clearly foresaw the role industrial companies would play in the economic life of the nation. He, therefore, continued to work toward compilation of an industrial average. It took 12 years of additions, deletions and substitutions before Dow, on May 26, 1896, came up with a list consisting entirely of industrial stocks. The list included:
>
> American Cotton Oil
> American Sugar
> American Tobacco
> Chicago Gas
> Distilling & Cattle Feeding
> General Electric
> Laclede Gas
> National Lead
> North American
> Tennessee Coal & Iron
> U.S. Leather, pfd.
> U.S. Rubber

The new list was published occasionally until October 7, 1896, at which time daily publication began. "It is generally considered that the present Dow Jones industrial and railroad (transportation) averages had their inception on this date," McSherry wrote. "The famous averages are now circulated not only by the Dow Jones News Service, but by Associated Press, United

Press International, and other news agencies by arrangement with Dow Jones. There are other industrial lists, including the AP's own industrials, the New York Stock Exchange averages, the *New York Times* industrials, and Standard and Poor's industrials. The Dow Jones Averages now include 65 stocks, with utilities added in 1929. The divisor is changed from time to time to adjust for stock splits and thus maintain historical continuity." McSherry admitted that the public is frequently confused by the Dow Jones Averages. "The confusion springs from the fact that the 'averages' aren't really averages anymore," he wrote. "They were in the beginning. Usage still so labels them. But, though they are useful measures of the stock market's overall movement, the numbers in them should not be mistaken for dollars-per-share prices of stocks."

Charles Dow used his averages to advance his theory of market behavior in his series of editorials beginning April 21, 1899. But not until Hamilton's book appeared in 1922 did the Dow Theory become really well known. "Dow's theory is fundamentally simple," Hamilton said, and then used 300 or so pages to demonstrate his contention. Half a century later, Paul Blustein, in an article on stock-market analysis in the January 12, 1981, *Journal,* provided a truly simple and succinct explanation: "The Dow theory holds [that] if peaks in the charts of the Dow Jones Industrial Average keep getting higher and troughs also keep getting higher, then prices are trending upward in a bull market. If things are the other way around, prices are headed down in a bear market."

Blustein's explanation does not include aspects of market-behavior confirmation used by Hamilton and later students of the theory, but the essentials are there. Hamilton was especially impressed by the fact that Dow, in his first article in *The Wall Street Journal* in April 1899, forecast the bull markets of the early 1900s. Later *Wall Street Journal* editors, however, have emphasized that the Dow Theory was developed by Dow as a means of reviewing market history, not of forecasting market behavior. Harold Finley, citing the Dow editorials, agrees. "As Mr. Dow and later exponents of his 'theory' repeatedly pointed out, many people expect too much of it," Finley wrote. "It was never meant to be a system of specific buy and sell recommendations. In all, dozens of books have been written about the Dow theory. Many stock-market advisory services have claimed to use it as a basis for their forecasts, and several prominent financial journals have regularly carried a column discussing it in relation to the current market picture. Its popularity has both risen and fallen, but even its severest critics have utilized some of its ideas as a starting point for their own philosophies."

In more recent years Dow Jones & Company executives and *Journal* editors regard the Dow Theory as primarily of historical interest. However, the Dow Jones Averages are treated as important financial news in both *The*

Wall Street Journal and *Barron's* magazine, and also by the Dow Jones News Services. The averages also appear daily in hundreds of other newspapers and on radio and television broadcasts by agreement with Dow Jones & Company. Although a number of competing market averages and indices have been created over the years, the system devised by Charles Dow remains by far the most popular and widely followed of all stock-market measurements.

One of the changes in *Wall Street Journal* policy predated the retirement of Jones: the newsstand price had gone to 3 cents. The size of the paper soon after was increased to eight pages, at a cost far exceeding any additional revenues from circulation. Advertising no longer crowded out news and commentary on page one. Soon, however, the improved product and extra selling activity brought in new, varied advertising accounts intended to appeal to a general, though affluent and elitist, reader. On a typical day in April 1899, advertising ranged from the usual brokerage houses, banks, and insurance companies of previous days to Pomeroy's champagne and offerings of pianos, oriental rugs, cigars, golf balls, gifts for women, office furniture, typewriters, men's shoes and shirts, diamonds, and silver. The faithful Wanamaker Department Store increased its use of *Journal* space.

Other publications also sought the paper's presumably wealthy readers, among them *Official Golf Guide* and *Rider & Driver* magazines. Rich New Yorkers were mad about horses, Kate Simon would write in her *Fifth Avenue: A Very Social History*. "They valued their horses more than their women." New York newspapers, especially the *World,* began to advertise their circulation figures in *The Wall Street Journal,* expecting to reach the city's opinion-makers in the advertising community. *The Wall Street Journal* also advertised itself as "The Largest Financial Newspaper in America. It is receiving complimentary notice from prominent men. Tell your friends about it." On December 6, 1899, the *Journal* published its largest consumer advertisement to date—five columns from Charles L. Seabury & Company, New York, offering sailboats and steam and naphtha yachts. The paper had previously published full-page announcements from banks, mining companies, and insurance firms, but they were formal statements rather than efforts to sell products.

The bull market was under way in 1900, as Dow had predicted. There was relative labor peace, and Wall Street was only mildly disturbed that young Theodore Roosevelt, known to hold some views critical of big business, accepted the Republican vice-presidential nomination after vowing he would not. Even with Roosevelt as a handicap, William McKinley was inexpressibly better, in Wall Street's view, than William Jennings Bryan. The *Journal* comforted its readers on November 2, 1900, by pointing out that should Bryan win office, he could not do immediate harm to the country, thanks to a new law. "Suppose Mr. Bryan to have been chosen President and to have selected next February a silver man as Secretary of the Treasury," said the paper, committing to print the unspeakable. "Long before then, holders of legal tenders would have employed them in drawing gold from the Treasury, and the new Secretary, in the most unfavorable event, would be confronted with a rapidly decreasing gold reserve." And why should such a catastrophe give anyone comfort? Because, said the *Journal,* the new Gold Standard Act of March 1900 would be triggered, gold bonds would be issued, and they would be paid from the government's general funds. The lessons of 1893 had been learned.

The *Journal*'s readers, however, did not have to confront that awesome alternative. The paper was highly pleased with the triumph of McKinley and Roosevelt, saying on November 8:

> The election proved to be a victory for sound money, for business stability and for the policy of expansion. There are those who would regard its magnitude as further evidence of what has seemed to be a leading and protecting power in the affairs of this country in the last four years. Others will regard it as further proof of the sober good sense of the common people.
>
> The most important outcome of the election is the re-establishment of confidence; confidence that the weighing, measuring and testing of the power of money in use will not be impaired; confidence that business and corporate interests will not be overthrown in an attempt to destroy the evils connected with expansion, will not be made the excuse for national disgrace; confidence, in short, that measures which are on the whole sound and wise will prevail and that the country will not suffer the comprehensive evils embraced in the term "Bryanism."

On February 8, 1901, the paper took up conditions in the steel industry, saying, "The steel situation continues to be the most vital factor in the general market." Eastern big steel, as represented by Andrew Carnegie and Henry C. Frick, was in the opinion of many on Wall Street being menaced by John W. Gates of Chicago and his associates, among them Judge Elbert Gary, who had put together a combination of steel companies strong enough to challenge Carnegie's Pittsburgh group. Eastern steel men under Frick, once an employee of Carnegie, came to Morgan to seek his aid in stabilizing the industry as he had helped to stabilize the railroads. They wanted Morgan somehow to induce Carnegie to stop his price-cutting. It turned out that Morgan had been thinking along that same line, and, as usual, he sought a shortcut to the solution.

Carnegie was especially well situated to produce steel for less money than his scattered opponents. But the Gates-Gary group had demonstrated the capacity to put together a string of plants in the Midwest that could readily reach northern ores controlled by John D. Rockefeller and James J. Hill. Hill was an ally of Morgan, and Rockefeller was ready to deal. What Morgan needed, however, was an associate who knew something about steel production. John W. Gates, whom Morgan detested for his crude ways, could not be considered. At one brief meeting arranged by Judge Gary between Morgan and Gates, the dour, domineering banker, known for his exploits with women, upbraided Gates for his public gambling. "Well, Mr. Morgan, what I do is no worse than what you do behind closed doors," Gates is reported to have said. "That, Mr. Gates," growled Morgan, "is what doors are for."

On March 3, 1901, the Morgan forces made public the plans for an enormous steel combination to be called United States Steel Corporation. Morgan had arranged to buy out the Carnegie interests! The new firm's capitalization made it the largest corporation ever organized up to that time—$510 million of preferred, $508 million of common, $303 million of bonds—and the world's first billion-dollar corporation. Judge Gary, former head of the John Gates steel interests, was to direct the management of the giant; Charles M. Schwab, a Carnegie man, would be in charge of manufacture. The following companies, in addition to Carnegie, were among those acquired: National Steel, American Steel Hoop, American Sheet Steel, National Tube, Federal Steel, American Steel & Wire, and Rockefeller's Lake Superior Consolidated Iron Mines. Gary, John Gates's protégé, was in; John W. Gates was out.

The newspapers generally called the great corporation a trust, but *The Wall Street Journal* did not agree. It even questioned whether the huge combination actually had all the resources required to be a powerful, prosperous company. But United States Steel was to become a potent force in the great banking and industrial complex J. P. Morgan was creating.

For years the big operators in Wall Street had dreamed of cornering a major stock, but none had been able to pull it off. When such a corner finally transpired in the spring of 1901, it was entirely by accident. The paralyzing panic that resulted, said *The Wall Street Journal,* proved that even the canniest and most experienced Wall Street traders could not always control the forces they set in motion.

The Northern Pacific corner began as a struggle among the most powerful of the bankers and railroad builders, including J. P. Morgan, Jacob Schiff, James J. Hill, and E. H. Harriman, for control of the new transcontinental railroad lines being put together by Hill and Morgan. These two men led one combination of interest, and Schiff and Harriman another. After the panic of 1893, most of the nation's railroads were in trouble, and Harriman, a railroad man, and Schiff, head of Kuhn, Loeb & Co., the second most powerful investment house on Wall Street after the House of Morgan, joined forces to take over three western roads in the hands of receivers: the Union Pacific, the Southern Pacific, and the Santa Fe. At the same time, Hill, backed by Morgan, was putting together his own western railroad system, to include Hill's Great Northern and Northern Pacific lines.

Rivals Hill and Harriman were the railroad men, and they knew that their railroads would not be complete without a line through Chicago. Such a road was the C.,B.&Q. (Chicago, Burlington & Quincy), known as the Burlington. Both, through their financial allies, began buying C.,B.&Q. stock in the spring of 1900. First it appeared that Harriman would win, since by June 6 he had acquired 69,800 of the 200,000 shares required for control. By July 25, however, Harriman and Schiff could buy no more than 80,300 shares. They realized that Morgan and Hill were among those holding the remaining stock through their Northern Pacific interest. Thus Northern Pacific would gain a terminal in Chicago, where it could link up with the New York Central, controlled by J. P. Morgan.

Harriman had been shut out. He appealed to Hill for opportunity to participate in controlling the Burlington so that his Union Pacific could enter Chicago, but Hill refused. Harriman then determined to get the Chicago access he needed indirectly, by purchasing control of Hill's own railroad, the Northern Pacific. He could only do this by going as quietly as possible into the open market to acquire the needed shares. Harriman's steady acquisition of Northern Pacific of course gradually pushed up the price, but Harriman could afford it, since he was selling Burlington stock back to Morgan and Hill at nearly $200 a share.

The Wall Street Journal first took note of the developing allure of Northern Pacific in an item published April 2, 1901, under the apt title "Combinations Make Combinations." At that time the paper said that the Morgan-Hill interest had obtained control of the Burlington. "Hence headway has been made in the project toward an alliance between Northern Pacific and Burlington. Should this alliance be consummated . . . there would be nominally a Hill-Morgan transcontinental route."

That bit of intelligence should have sent *Journal* readers scurrying to acquire any stock available in either Northern Pacific or Burlington. But by April 20, Morgan and Hill, through their Northern Pacific interests, had purchased 96 percent of the Burlington stock, paying as much as $200 a share, and Harriman was driving up the price of Northern Pacific shares but could find little more to buy. Nevertheless, Schiff and Harriman had been able to acquire $14 million worth of Northern Pacific shares before Morgan and Hill realized what was happening. Their brokers simply assumed that Morgan and Hill would want to reap some of the handsome profits available as the Northern Pacific shares kept climbing, and consequently had sold some of their clients' Northern Pacific stock!

Morgan was in seclusion in France, visiting a countess, it was said. Hill, suspecting that Harriman and Schiff were doing the buying, rushed to New York by chartered train to take charge of a counterattack. On May 3 he walked into Schiff's office at Kuhn, Loeb to see if he was responsible for the action. Schiff admitted that he was, and when Hill began to make threats, he was informed that Harriman and Schiff had bought 370,000 shares of Northern Pacific common and 420,000 of preferred, worth $79 million at par. Schiff and Harriman believed that they now controlled Northern Pacific, which in turn could control Burlington. And they did have control, except for one factor. The directors of Northern Pacific could recall the preferred, which would destroy the Harriman leverage, leaving him short in common. The move was legally possible, though the cost would be great. When Harriman perceived this possibility, he determined to get the remaining available 30,000 to 40,000 shares of Northern Pacific common to insure control under any circumstances. But now Hill was alerted. According to one Morgan biographer, he frantically cabled Morgan, who didn't wish to interrupt his dalliance with a new beauty and therefore couldn't be reached at once.

On May 6, 1901, *The Wall Street Journal* again dealt with the Burlington–Northern Pacific development in an editorial:

> We have more than once pointed out that the purchase of the Burlington by the Northern Pacific and the Great Northern changed the balance of railway power in the West and made new hostilities or new alliances inevitable. . . . The past ten days have shown that peace instead of war is to prevail, and that the plan at the moment is for a new combination of interests. Union Pacific, Burlington and St. Paul will come under one general policy. How this will be brought about is not yet clear. . . .
>
> The great strength in Northern Pacific implies that another step has been taken. It is possible that the Union Pacific–Northwest party may have been large buyers in Northern Pacific in order to create a community of interest in that section. If it should transpire that the Morgan-Hill interest is a large owner of Union Pacific, there might be a good offset in the fact that Union Pacific people were large owners of Northern Pacific.

The *Journal* had the ingredients of the plot, though not precisely in the right order. Considering that Hill and Morgan themselves had been caught off guard, permitting some of their own Northern Pacific stock to be sold, the *Journal* was very much up on the game. By Monday, J. P. Morgan had been reached, and he recognized that it was time for rapid, decisive action. Consequently, he suppressed his repugnance for James R. Keene and ordered Keene and his brokers, representing him and Hill, to go into the market and buy Northern Pacific.

Keene, a former cowboy, mule skinner, and newspaper editor, was probably the ablest pool operator in Wall Street. Known as the Silver Fox of Wall Street because of his impeccable manners and dress, Keene had managed the copper pool for the Rockefeller interests and knew how to get action in a hurry. He used the office of Talbot Taylor, Edward Jones's partner, as his command post, and organized his brokers and traders, probably Jones among them, for the attack. Keene was to acquire 150,000 shares of Northern Pacific. He sent his forces under Harry Content, "prince of the brokers," onto the floor of the New York Stock Exchange with his own telephone operator and floor manager at the trading post to make sure nothing went wrong. The final battle for control of Northern Pacific was on. The shares jumped $40 within a few hours. The immediate result, wrote John Winkler in his biography of J. P. Morgan, was the "swiftest and most paralyzing financial paroxysm the country has ever known." The Wall Street bears were beginning to realize they could not buy enough Northern Pacific stock to replace the borrowed shares they had been selling. Call money (short-term, on-demand loans to brokers) was unobtainable. There was terrorizing panic.

There were three days of furious trading, and by May 9, *The Wall Street Journal* declared that Northern Pacific had demolished the shorts. "It is singular that this stock should have played an important part in railway affairs at three periods so widely separated as 1873, 1884 and 1901. Twice Northern Pacific has brought ruin to those who were long of the stock, and now it has brought very heavy losses to those who were short. Northern Pacific pulled down the house of Jay Cooke & Company and defeated the ambitions of Mr. [Henry] Villard who earlier had helped to organize the railroad. Where the burden of loss will finally rest this time remains to be seen."

As the Wall Street day developed, there was no doubt of it—Northern Pacific was cornered. Shorts were unable to cover, even at $1,000 a share. A few share owners in the public sector who had not sold earlier sold at the day's high prices, but the Harriman-Schiff and Morgan-Hill factions held onto what they had. In his memoirs, Alexander Dana Noyes, The *New York Times* financial editor, described what followed: "All other stocks broke violently, declines of 50 percent or more occurring in many of the soundest shares. It was admitted afterward that on the books of the lending banks and on the basis of the day's low prices for collateral pledged against stock exchange loans, a good part of Wall Street was technically insolvent."

Later Morgan, Hill, and Harriman realized that their battle had destroyed many innocent people. In partial atonement, they permitted the shorts to settle for $150 a share, the *Journal* said on May 11. "The conflict was wanton," Winkler wrote. "These men trampled ruthlessly upon the rights of the public, bankrupted thousands, depressed values by the hundreds of millions. . . . They fed the hatred that millions of Americans already entertained for the Captains of Industry and all they stood for."

The Wall Street Journal undertook to explain what had happened and to excuse the participants who, after all, had played by the existing rules and had shown mercy to the vanquished bears. Said the paper on May 13: "The Northern Pacific corner was unintentional and was regretted by those who were most influential in bringing it about. Control of the Northern Pacific is likely to be involved in uncertainty for some time. Both parties claim control, which means there are questions which have yet to be adjusted. The probabilities are there will be adjustment by agreement, but it may not come for a little time."

There was an adjustment. In the settlement, J. P. Morgan was allowed to choose the board of Northern Securities, the holding company for Northern Pacific, and he included Harriman and Hill. It was merely a game for money and power among the tycoons, and the little people who got in the way, either innocently or because they ignorantly sold short in a greedy wish to quickly reap big profits, were crushed. There were a few, of course, who bought Northern Pacific early in April and sold it at $1,000 a share. The episode was understood and excused in Wall Street, but there was much public outcry.

However, Wall Street and the bankers could by no means rely on *The Wall Street Journal* always to understand, forgive, and support the establishment. The following May 1902, when John Mitchell, president of the United Mine Workers, led 140,000 of his men out on strike against the anthracite coal industry, the *Journal*'s editorials showed comprehension of the strikers' position and called for arbitration. In addition, when the mine owners asserted that they had vast supplies of coal ready for shipment, the *Journal* disputed the claim. On July 16 the paper said its position was in favor of neither the owners nor the strikers. It denied that the union had a right to a closed shop throughout the industry, as it claimed, but again defended the union's right to strike. "A combination of labor is just as legal and just and moral as a combination of capital," the paper said. "But, just as a combination of capital becomes illegal when it seeks to stifle free competition, so a combination of labor becomes illegal and immoral when it undertakes to deprive free labor of its right to sell its services on whatever terms and conditions it sees fit."

Woodlock, in his recollection of the strike, wrote: "Mr. Dow, who wrote the Review and Outlook column, developed a very strong opinion on the strike against the side of the coal operators and wrote several editorials which attracted much attention. These were, in fact, the first strictly editorial utterances of *The Wall Street Journal*, and they had a curious sequel. One Saturday afternoon there came into Mr. Dow's office three men. One was Mr. Walter

Weyl, afterwards well known in the economic field. They announced themselves as advisory counsel for Mr. John Mitchell, head of the anthracite miners' union, and said they had observed the course of *The Wall Street Journal* on the strike. They wished the paper to undertake the preparation of statistics for the side of the miners. Naturally, this could not be done."

The *Journal* urged Theodore Roosevelt, who had become president after the assassination of William McKinley in September 1901, to take action to end the strike. Like Charles Dow, Roosevelt was unimpressed by the statement of George F. Baer, president of Philadelphia & Reading Coal and Iron Company, the spokesman for the anthracite mine owners, who had said on July 17, "The rights and interests of the laboring man will be protected and cared for not by the labor agitators, but by the Christian men to whom God . . . has given control of the property interests of this country." The President intervened to arbitrate the strike and settled it by means of his Anthracite Coal Commission, which awarded the miners a 10 percent wage increase while denying recognition to Mitchell's union.

The surviving minute books of Dow, Jones & Company date back to 1900, and they record the rapid rise in the company of Thomas F. Woodlock, the *Journal*'s railroad expert. On February 14, 1900, Charles H. Dow was again elected president of the company; C. M. Bergstresser, secretary; and Thomas F. Woodlock, treasurer. The nominations were made by Bergstresser, who moved also that the company purchase 220 shares of stock from Dow at $12.50 a share. These shares were then offered to 25 employees of the company. Woodlock purchased ten shares; Louise Egan, the first female employee of Dow, Jones & Company, bought three. The firm was not incorporated. The owners signed "Articles of Agreement and Association of Dow, Jones & Company, a joint stock company."

Thomas Woodlock, the new treasurer, was born in Dublin, Ireland, and educated at Beaumont College and London University. He served as a clerk in a London brokerage firm before joining his father and brother in the London stock-exchange firm of Woodlock Brothers. But Woodlock, a highly literate young man who read Euripides and Aristophanes in the original, a marveling associate noted, yearned to become a writer. He engaged in economic reporting on a free-lance basis in London, then came to New York in 1892 and promptly found a job with *The Wall Street Journal*.

In 1900 Charles Dow was in ill health, and Bergstresser's desire to travel resulted in Woodlock's acting as managing editor, assuming duties relinquished by Jones. These duties had been shared by the two partners for a time. On March 14, on Bergstresser's motion, it was voted that the "general policy of the company in its published matter and whenever it bears upon specified corporations or individuals shall be conservative, impartial, and yet not unfriendly and that this policy shall prevail except when departed from with the knowledge and concurrence of at least three members of the board." The purpose of the instruction remains something of a mystery since there was no evident discord among the owners at the time. Possibly the rules were for the guidance of Woodlock, regarded as a youngster by Dow and Bergstresser, when he should be in full charge. Also, Dow and Bergstresser may have been preparing for the planned sale of a large interest in Dow, Jones & Company to an outsider. Woodlock was not given a title beyond that of treasurer, but, again on Bergstresser's motion, it was voted that each officer would be paid a salary of $7,500 a year, and Woodlock had become a Dow Jones officer. Dow devoted himself to writing his "Review and Outlook" column, and Bergstresser began his travels, searching for relatives and ancestors in Europe. He found half a village of Bergstressers and their kin in Malchin, Germany. "All fine Protestants," he told his daughter in a letter.

Woodlock acquired a talented assistant, William Peter Hamilton, a staff newcomer who was born in Scotland and, like Woodlock, had worked in the London stock market. Hamilton also had been employed by the *Pall Mall Gazette* in London. He served as a war correspondent in South Africa, having arrived there as a member of the British Auxiliary Forces, Royal Engineers. Hamilton indicated that he had some market experience with the Paris Bourse and the stock market in Johannesburg. He joined *The Wall Street Journal* in 1899. As assistant to Woodlock, he recalled, he wrote "more than 200 editorials" for the paper before he became editor of the editorial page in 1908.

The financial affairs of Dow, Jones & Company were evidently in reasonably good order, for a monthly dividend of ten cents a share was voted on April 7, 1900, and continued at that rate each month thereafter. Charles Dow continued to write editorials for the paper well into the latter part of 1902, and Bergstresser traveled. Externally, nothing at *The Wall Street Journal* appeared changed, but there was a major change in mid-March 1902.

On March 13, it was noted in the minutes that "Charles H. Dow tendered his resignation as a Director and President. On motion of Charles M. Bergstresser, same was accepted. Moved by C. M. Bergstresser, seconded by T. F. Woodlock, that J. W. Barney be elected as Director in place of C. H. Dow. Motion carried. . . . Moved by T. F. Woodlock, seconded by J. W. Barney, that the Association receive the resignation of Mr. Dow with much regret and that there be entered upon the minutes of the Board of Directors an expression of the same. Mr. Bergstresser referred in feeling terms of the long and most valuable services rendered by Mr. Dow from the foundation of the business of which he was to so large an extent a creator. The motion was adopted by unanimous vote." Barney, of course, was John Barney, the business manager.

That same day Dow entered a notation in the minute book: "In accordance with the Articles of Association of Dow, Jones & Co., I, as the holder of 3,410 shares of stock of said association, do hereby give my written consent to my sale of the good will, assets and property of the said association . . . and also my consent to the dissolving of the association."

Charles Dow had approached a potential purchaser of Dow, Jones & Company—Clarence Walker Barron, owner of the Boston News Bureau agency and its newspaper of the same name, which duplicated the Dow Jones services in the State Street business community of Boston. Barron also owned the Philadelphia News Bureau and the *Philadelphia Financial Journal.* A dynamic, fast-talking pundit well known throughout New England as the founder of financial journalism, he had exchanged news dispatches with the Dow Jones proprietors since before *The Wall Street Journal* appeared. Barron's succinct, decisive writing style was admired by the more deliberative and philosophic Dow, who evidently believed that C. W. Barron (as he signed himself) would devote his total talents to *The Wall Street Journal* should he become the principal owner. Barron, known also for his gargantuan appetite, was five foot five and weighed over 300 pounds. He lived in regal style at the Waldorf-Astoria when he was in New York and was assumed to have wealth. But in fact, Barron was losing in Philadelphia or spending on high living in New York most of the money he made in Boston.

Barron had established his New York advertising office in the old Edison Building at 44 Broad Street and had been a neighbor and good advertiser himself in *The Wall Street Journal.* He was eager to purchase control of Dow, Jones & Company, but he lacked the needed funds and evidently did not care to seek bank loans for the purpose. Instead, he induced the owners to accept his personal notes, 63 in all, plus a limited amount of cash. Most, if not all of this cash payment of $2,500, according to William P. Tidwell, Barron's secretary, was provided by Barron's wife, Mrs. Jessie Waldron Barron. Some of Tidwell's recollections are clearly unreliable, but he was a man to whom Barron confided his personal as well as business affairs, so the report of Mrs. Barron's contribution may be accurate. Barron, a boarder with Mrs. Barron in Boston for 14 years before he married her in 1900, found among her possessions some supposedly worthless mining stocks left her by her late husband, Samuel Waldron, Tidwell said, and sold them for $2,500. Whether or not she provided any funds, Mrs. Barron did acquire nearly 90 percent of the Dow Jones stock.

When Barron arrived in New York to close the deal, he informed Dow and Bergstresser that he was giving all the Dow, Jones & Company stock he could acquire to Mrs. Barron. She would represent him on the board of directors. He would provide guidance through Mrs. Barron, and he assured Dow and Bergstresser that she had the requisite wisdom and experience. In letters to two of his stepgranddaughters, Martha Endicott and Mary Bancroft, Barron wrote, "Grandmother's wisdom has made me what I am." He evidently convinced Dow and Bergstresser of Jessie's competence, especially after he offered them contracts to remain with the company at least during a transition period. Barron met with the Dow Jones directors late in March 1902 and did not attend another directors' meeting for almost ten years.

On March 31, the stock transfers were recorded in the minutes: 10 shares from Dow; 3,400 shares from his wife, Lucy; 10 shares from Bergstresser; 571 from his wife, Helen; and 1,875 shares from Woodlock, who evidently had been gathering shares from other employees. Then Dow and Bergstresser resigned their directorships. (Many owners of stocks at the time "judgment-proofed" themselves by putting their company ownerships in their wives' name. Thus, should the company lose a lawsuit for damages, only the company and its assets would be risked, since the wife owned no other tangible property. This was not Barron's reason in the purchase of Dow, Jones & Company, however. Mrs. Barron, it later developed, owned their summer home at Cohasset, near Boston, and other property.)

There was no public announcement of any sort concerning the sale of Dow, Jones & Company to Clarence W. Barron. The only evidence of change in *The Wall Street Journal* itself was the listing of four names in the editorial-page masthead on March 14, 1902:

The Wall Street Journal
Published by Dow, Jones & Co.

Charles H. Dow
Charles M. Bergstresser
Thomas F. Woodlock
J. W. Barney, Business Manager

Never before had any names of company or *Journal* officials been published in the masthead since the paper was founded in 1889. And finally the names appeared when none of those listed owned a single share of stock! There was no explanation. It was reported in later years that Barron paid $130,000 for Dow, Jones & Company, including *The Wall Street Journal*. A fragment in the Dow Jones archives, which appears to be part of the official record, indicates that to be the agreed selling price.

On December 4, 1902, the *Brooklyn Daily Eagle* announced the death of Charles H. Dow, 51 years old, in his home in Brooklyn Heights. It attributed death to a heart attack and indicated that he had informed his stepdaughter, Mrs. William Goodbody in Ireland, of his serious illness, since the paper said that she and her husband were already on their way to America and that funeral services would be delayed until her arrival. *The Wall Street Journal* published the news of Dow's death on December 5, turning the rules, the printer's tribute in which the thin metal column rules printed black lines of mourning. The *Journal* published an editorial from the *Boston News Bureau* paying tribute to Charles Dow and brief statements from several Wall Street leaders. The most eloquent appreciation came from Edward D. Jones:

> May I offer a brief tribute to the memory of your senior partner with whom I worked as an editor 28 years ago in Providence, R.I., and whose partner I was in Dow, Jones & Co. until three years ago. He was always a ceaseless searcher for facts and the best way to tell and distribute them. He was a tower of strength in early struggles to force reluctant railroad managers to furnish reports which tell something to protect the speculating public from swindlers in and out of Wall Street and to praise where praise was due. His honesty was rugged, his industry was prodigious, his integrity unsullied and his home life ideal. Financial journalism loses one of its most honest exponents, his family mourns a devoted, loving son, husband and father, and Wall Street parts with a most conscientious, forceful and able critic. I do not think that his place can be filled.

The Wall Street Journal did not speak editorially of Charles Dow, in keeping with its custom of avoiding obituaries and reports of deaths. There had been two notable exceptions: the death of Queen Victoria in 1901 had been reported by special bulletin; and when Collis P. Huntington, the capitalist and Union Pacific railroad builder, died in his Adirondack fishing camp August 14, 1900, *The Wall Street Journal* published not only a news account but also Huntington's portrait, the first halftone reproduction to appear in the paper and the only one to be used in the news columns until nearly a decade later, when photographs were occasionally used. No picture of Charles Dow appeared, however. The man who was praised for his modesty as well as other qualities had not provided his own newspaper with a photograph.

The exceptional display of Huntington's picture at the time of his death was not explained to the public or to *The Wall Street Journal* staff at the time, a further example of Dow's reticence. The explanation did not become known until 26 years later, when an account of the founding of Dow, Jones & Company provided by Barron appeared in *Barron's* magazine after the death of Barron. Dow evidently told Barron the story, perhaps at the time Barron bought the company. According to Barron, Charles Dow had visited Huntington in 1882 to discuss his plan for founding a news agency. "I see the opportunity, but I fear that Mr. Jones and I may not know enough about the stock market to succeed with a news agency," Dow told Huntington, who had become a temporary resident of New York. "Go ahead," replied Huntington. "Nobody knows anything about the stock market."

The *Boston News Bureau* tribute, undoubtedly inspired by C. W. Barron, provided other bits of news about Dow's final days. He had made a recent trip to Europe and visited his stepdaughter in Ireland. He also planned to cease all work for the *Journal* "within a few weeks." Charles Dow's name remained in the page-two masthead through December 17. On the 18th Charles M. Bergstresser, Thomas F. Woodlock, and J. W. Barney were the names remaining.

Chapter 5

Jessie Barron and Her Editors

It did not take some executives of Dow, Jones & Company long to learn that while Clarence Walker Barron was not taking direct charge of the company or *The Wall Street Journal,* he had a most effective representative on the New York scene in the person of his wife, Mrs. Jessie Waldron Barron. Mrs. Barron, four years older than her husband, who was 46 at the time, was a handsome, capable, and sometimes formidable woman. She owned all the Dow Jones stock her husband had purchased, nearly 90 percent of the available shares. Consequently, her presence on the board of directors did not constitute mere symbolism. Mrs. Barron coolly and graciously informed the board members that she intended to learn as much as she could, present suggestions from her husband, and provide a few recommendations of her own. The officers and directors paid her polite attention almost from the beginning, though Charles Bergstresser, who kept the minutes of the 1902 meetings in his own hand, persisted in writing Mrs. Barron's first name as "Jennie."

As Barron freely conceded, Mrs. Barron had long provided guidance to her husband in his development of the leading financial newspaper in New England, the *Boston News Bureau.* She had known Barron for many years prior to their marriage, since the day he became a star boarder at her select boarding house in Boston in 1886. A widow, born Jessie Marie Barteaux in Annapolis, Nova Scotia, Jessie Waldron was successfully rearing her two daughters, Jane and Martha Waldron, when C. W. Barron began taking his meals at her home. He remained, becoming a most impressive advertisement for her table. Barron not only was fond of her cooking, but appreciated her sage counsel. When he found time to propose marriage in 1900, he also agreed to adopt Jessie's daughters. By 1902, when Dow approached him with his offer to sell Dow Jones, Barron was a successful and respected Boston businessman, though some of his constituency in the State Street financial community regarded him as brash and overly aggressive. Despite his early career as a financial reporter for the staid *Boston Transcript* ("There are three reporters waiting, sir, and a gentleman from the *Transcript,*" ran an old Boston newspaper joke), C. W. Barron, five feet five and as thick as he was tall, one acquaintance said, was considered somewhat gross and flamboyant by some of his Beacon Street neighbors.

Over the years Mrs. Waldron, whose husband died in 1882, had won tentative admission to Boston society for daughters Martha and Jane by her proper conduct as a working widow and her good works in the city's hospitals and among the poor. Shortly after the Barrons moved into the splendid mansion at 334 Beacon Street, they had the privilege of announcing the engagement of Martha to H. Wendell Endicott, eldest son of a leading Boston industrial family, who was destined to take over the family shoe-manufacturing business. Jane would marry Hugh Bancroft, of an equally patrician Cambridge family, a few years later.

So Mrs. Jessie Barron came to the Dow Jones board of directors with considerable business knowledge and some social experience in the rigorous Back Bay environment. Inevitably, in later years, when C. W. Barron's secretaries recollected their experiences under their demanding, testy employer, they recalled that his wife showed them consideration and that Barron himself thoroughly respected her and doted on his stepdaughters and later his grandchildren. When Barron, after a day in New York and an evening dictating on the night train to Boston, wanted to continue working with his faithful secretary, Louis M. Atherton, Mrs. Barron would always stop them at eleven o'clock, Atherton remembered gratefully. "She knew it would be my last chance to get the trolley home," Atherton told his wife.

Mrs. Jessie Barron in the spring of 1902 was a trimly plump, matronly woman, firm and decisive in manner, respectful of the opinions of others, and quietly confident in her knowledge of the business. So she easily assumed her almost unique role as a female Wall Street executive. She and her husband shared his suite in the Waldorf-Astoria on Fifth Avenue, and Jessie was regularly on hand for the weekly board meetings and for consultation with her editors and executives as required.

Jessie Barron dressed in the conservative style of her time, arriving impressively for the board meetings at 44 Broad Street in a fashionable brougham, almost regal in her voluminous tailored suits and her vast picture hats studded with glittering pins, her black-kid-gloved hands clasping a black purse or a furled umbrella as she sat rather stiffly looking straight ahead until William, her driver, prepared to hand her to the curb. Then she alighted gracefully, showing just a flash of high-buttoned black shoes as she continued to look firmly ahead while heading for the 44 Broad Street doorway, impervious to the stares of the men on the sidewalks or the clerks and messengers inside. Not since the misses Victoria Woodhull and Tennessee Claflin operated their brokerage office at 44 Broad Street some years before had there been such a vision of feminine grandeur in the financial district.

Mrs. Barron was usually escorted by Treasurer Tom Woodlock into the modest Dow Jones offices, which also served as the boardroom. Inside, she seated herself, nodded to Bergstresser, who asserted his independence by remaining seated in her presence, and then to Woodlock, who would signal his working associates to take their seats around the table. After a comment or two on the New York weather and the whereabouts of her husband, Mrs. Barron would be ready for the proceedings to begin. Mrs. Barron wore her hair in the pompadour style popularized by Mrs. William Astor, the doyenne of New York society, when she occupied her box at the Metropolitan Opera House. The new Dow Jones director had all the dignity of that grand old lady but was less imperious. She spoke softly, smiled rarely, and appraised her fellow board members and the reporting business staff men carefully and coolly through gold-rimmed pince-nez. Jessie Barron obviously was a consummate, no-nonsense businesswoman.

The directors knew, of course, that Mrs. Barron in effect owned the entire company, but initially they were not especially impressed. Mrs. Dow and Mrs. Bergstresser held the majority of their husbands' stock and never once appeared in the company offices. But all soon learned that Mrs. Barron's situation was different; most company personnel called into the directors' meetings realized that Mrs. Barron meant it when, at the outset, she indicated that she not only owned control of the company but she intended to exercise control. She was considerate and gracious in explaining her position, too much so, perhaps, since not all who heard her, especially Bergstresser, understood at once that she meant business. But Bergstresser was soon off on his travels, and Woodlock understood. After he wrote Clarence Barron congratulating him on the purchase, promising the new owner his full cooperation, and received no reply, Tom Woodlock discovered for himself that C. W. Barron did not own a single share. Barron did not come down to 44 Broad Street with his wife, and he was rarely if ever seen in the Dow Jones offices during the nearly ten years his wife was on the board, though he visited his advertising office in the same building as often as once a week when he was in the country.

C. W. Barron, in fact, was something of a mystery man to *The Wall Street*

Journal in those first years. After a brief flurry of format changes following his purchase of the company, moves that Barron presumably directed in a barrage of memoranda as he did in later years, the *Journal* settled into patterns decreed by Tom Woodlock. There were brighter headlines and profiles of businessmen, businesses, and entire industries. The news stories and editorials were crisp and readable, and the paper upgraded its coverage in Washington by sending Frank Phelps there as the paper's first Washington correspondent, to assist John Boyle, successor to Sarvis as bureau chief. Barron's wishes, so far as the board was concerned, were made known by Mrs. Barron. He requested an assistant to manage his New York advertising office and was given Harry W. Doremus from the advertising department. Barron incorporated his advertising agency as Doremus & Company, though Doremus owned no part of it and left for another agency after two years. Meantime, Doremus & Company grew profitable under Barron's part-time management and supplied much of the linage published in *The Wall Street Journal* as well as in his Boston and Philadelphia publications.

There developed smoldering resentment at the *Journal,* and eventually outright revolt, as Jessie Barron took over. Mrs. Barron, after all, had undertaken to supervise the affairs of a relatively well-known pioneer New York company in the complex, arcane area of financial-news reporting at a time when women were considered by many men and even some women to be congenitally unable to handle their own financial affairs. In fact, in some states they were legally prevented from doing so if they were married.

The first *Journal* executive to be totally won over to Jessie was the erudite and thoroughly capable editor, Thomas Woodlock. Since Bergstresser was angrily absent most of the time, Woodlock, with Mrs. Barron's full support, took over the day-to-day operations of *The Wall Street Journal* and then the Dow Jones ticker service, though John W. Barney was elected president of the company on March 17, 1904.

Meantime, the *Journal* continued to change in appearance until it completely lost the somewhat dowdy look of most financial newspapers of that day, especially the *Boston News Bureau* and the *Philadelphia Financial Journal*. The label headlines of *The Wall Street Journal* had been brightened immediately following Barron's purchase of the paper, but they were still labels. Now Woodlock used the neat banks of headlines characteristic of the *New York World* and other papers competing for general circulation, headlines that told a story and sought to advertise the news. The body type was reduced from 9 point leaded (having space between the lines of type) to 7 point, a smaller, compact type often unleaded (without space) that was a bit harder on the reader's eyes but provided more accommodation for news and advertising. There was a further increase in the use of profiles, columns, and reviews. The paper became attractive, exciting, and lively, especially in cultural areas. Some of C. W. Barron's articles in the *Boston News Bureau,* representing the one area of its superiority over New York, were picked up and reprinted by Woodlock.

Woodlock, despite his excellent education and his wide experience, could not match Barron as a vivid financial writer, but he was a knowledgeable editor and had two excellent assistants in William Peter Hamilton and Sereno Stansbury Pratt, the latter experienced in both financial and political reporting. Pratt, born in New York, began his career with the *Advertiser* in St. Albans, Vermont, moved to the *Montpelier Argus and Patriot,* where he was a political writer, and then joined the staff of the *Daily Commercial Bulletin* in New York in 1878. From his New York base, Pratt also wrote special articles for leading dailies around the country. He came to *The Wall Street Journal* as an associate editor in 1903. In Woodlock, Hamilton, and Pratt, the *Journal* had three of the most capable financial writers and editors in New York, and the pages of the paper reflected that fact. Only Alexander Dana Noyes, who had moved from the *Post* to the *New York Times,* could equal them.

C. W. Barron habitually intruded into the affairs of others, especially members of his family, even when he was not invited. But there is considerable evidence that Barron did not directly control *The Wall Street Journal* until he formally took over in 1912. It is true, however, that the *Journal* adopted Barron's slogan from the *Boston News Bureau,* "The truth in its proper use," and ran it daily in its editorial-page masthead. The paper in 1904 began giving its employees an Easter bonus rather than a Christmas bonus, a Barron eccentricity attributed to his Swedenborgian faith, and, at some point, news employees were required to turn in scrapbooks of their work for evaluation, another Barron contribution. Qualifying workers would receive gold stars. However, the minutes of the Dow Jones board meetings from 1902 through 1911 indicate that Mrs. Barron made decisions in emergency situations, often decisions of grave consequence, without pausing to consult her absent husband or her lawyers.

Evidently C. W. Barron did not concentrate on *The Wall Street Journal* while it flourished under his wife's supervision. Circulation rose, and dividends in subsequent years provided Mrs. Barron with handsome revenues that her husband was able to use in paying off his 63 notes. So long as things went well, Barron was satisfied. In the record he kept of his activities, Barron noted on November 14, 1904: "At Windsor hotel after addressing the Dow Jones & Company employees, met Charles M. Schwab. He talked with Woodlock, Otis, Bergstresser and myself." There are numerous entries concerning New York engagements and dinners he and Mrs. Barron attended, but no other mention of an appearance at Dow, Jones & Company until 1911.

One of Barron's rare direct interventions in *Journal* operations occurred in May 1905 when he hired a staff member, Walter P. Barclay of Toronto, at

$10 a week. At the time, Barron wasn't even sure who was managing editor under Woodlock. "You can hand this to Mr. Woodlock, who is in charge there, or Mr. Keys or Mr. Edwards," Barron wrote Barclay. "Mr. Woodlock is the editor-in-chief, Mr. Edwards will probably be managing news editor, and Mr. Keys will probably take you in charge." Barron then suggested that if "Professor Mavor," evidently of Toronto, knew one or two other young men "of pleasing address who desire to grasp the financial situation . . . in the graduating class," they should be invited to come to New York also. They, too, would be hired at $10 a week. Barron conceded in his letter that an earlier Mavor recommendation did not work out. But Barclay did well. In time he became managing editor of the *Journal*, remaining in that position until Barron replaced him with Kenneth C. Hogate in 1923.

By 1903 the slogan of the *Journal* had become "The Newspaper for the Investor," and in 1904 the previous year's circulation average—a healthy 11,957—appeared daily on the front page. This was the first time the paper published its circulation totals. While they were not audited, they were accepted as reliable since advertising linage continued to increase.

Despite such indication of prosperity, there was evidence of management strife. Some of the men continued to resent the dominance of Mrs. Barron, and Thomas Woodlock, who had joined forces with her almost from the beginning, became engaged in a power struggle with John Barney. Barney by 1904 had acquired 838 shares of stock, and in March of that year he was elected president of Dow Jones. Woodlock held 828 shares, and F. A. Russell, publisher of a small newspaper for the provisions markets, owned 10 shares, which he may have obtained from the Russell family, into which both Dow and Bergstresser had married. The contest between Barney and Woodlock came to a head at a board meeting early in 1905, when Woodlock won a stunning victory. On February 14, Barney, evidently obeying an order, introduced a highly unusual resolution that made Barney as president completely superfluous: "Resolved, That Thomas F. Woodlock be hereby appointed editor-in-chief and that *The Wall Street Journal* and Dow, Jones & Co. news services, both ticker and bulletin, be subject to his absolute direction and control; no advertisement will appear in *The Wall Street Journal* nor will there be any news or editorial presentation therein to which he objects;—and no changes among the employees of Dow, Jones & Co. shall be made to which the editor-in-chief objects."

There was an even stranger policy decision by the board on March 8. It authorized editorial employees of *The Wall Street Journal* to solicit advertising: "Any news gatherer desiring to enter the list for the gathering in of financial advertising will notify Mr. Woodlock or any other director of the company of his intention to secure for Doremus & Co. an advertising contract and will submit in writing indicating the line of advertising he thinks he can influence in the direction of Dow, Jones & Co. or of Doremus & Co., and, upon permission being given, he will take up this line of work without interference with his regular newswork."

On March 23, 1905, Barney resigned as president, although he continued to serve as a director. Bergstresser, whose name continued to appear in the editorial masthead, was in Europe. He dispatched violent protests to Woodlock when he heard of the board decisions, but, for a time, nothing happened.

The counting room and its logistical ally, the advertising department of *The Wall Street Journal,* and, in fact, the whole of Dow, Jones & Company had seemingly been swallowed up by Woodlock, the English-trained journalist who had taken the lead in accepting the rule of Jessie Barron. Quality continued to improve, advertising linage increased, and the paper was strong in its support of President Theodore Roosevelt, who launched his campaign against trusts shortly after succeeding the martyred President McKinley. When Roosevelt was elected on his own in November 1904, Woodlock wrote, "It was manly steadfastness of principle that yesterday won for Theodore Roosevelt such popular endorsement as was never before given by a free people. Against such a frank, fearless, honest personality, capital and combination [the railroad combination] beat as vainly as break the waves upon rock-ribbed shores." Woodlock backed the President in his assaults on the beef and tobacco trusts and in his indictment of Standard Oil and the actions against Northern Securities, formed by J. Pierpont Morgan and James J. Hill. President Roosevelt and the government were successful in all of those actions.

Editor-in-Chief Woodlock appeared to have the best of all possible worlds—editorial freedom and control of advertising quality and personnel. Yet Charles Bergstresser's written protests at last prevailed when he demanded that his name be dropped from the paper if management policies were not changed. Woodlock, astonishingly, offered to resign when he presented Bergstresser's protest to the board of directors, i.e., Mrs. Jessie Barron.

Mrs. Barron responded promptly. "Tell Mr. Bergstresser," she told Woodlock, "that he is under contract for two more months. Until that time his name will continue to remain in the paper." She accepted with regret the resignation of Woodlock and induced him to stay on for two more months. On September 24, 1905, the editorial-page masthead carried the names of Charles M. Bergstresser, Thomas F. Woodlock, and Sereno S. Pratt, with business manager Charles Otis's name in smaller type. On September 25, all names were gone and there was an announcement: "It is with regret the publishers announce that Mr. Thomas F. Woodlock retires from the editorship of *The Wall Street Journal* to enter other business. He will carry the best wishes of all his associates for his future success. Mr. Sereno S. Pratt, who was associated with Mr. Woodlock, becomes editorial head of the paper."

In October 1905 Charles Otis was elected president of Dow, Jones & Company, and F. A. Russell was named to the board of directors. Otis, formerly the assistant manager of the *Boston News Bureau,* evidently had been sent to New York by Barron in an effort to solve the management problem at Dow Jones. He was born in Yarmouth Port, Massachusetts, and attended business and shorthand schools in Boston before joining Barron. He served briefly as business manager of *The Wall Street Journal* before his elevation to president of Dow, Jones & Company.

No names appeared in the editorial box of the paper until after the November 10 board meeting, when Mrs. Jessie Barron and Sereno Pratt were reelected directors. John D. Lane and Hugh Bancroft were added to the board. Young Bancroft, a Boston lawyer with patrician antecedents and a Back Bay social position, was eventually to join the Barron family by his marriage to Jane Waldron Barron.

While it was evident that C. W. Barron was introducing members of his own team into the Dow Jones lineup, it nevertheless remained clear that Mrs. Barron continued to possess power as well as votes in New York. Bancroft, in fact, was her choice. In addition to receiving stock dividends of $2 a share in 1906 and 1907, Mrs. Barron was voted a special dividend of $10,000. This amount was increased to $42,000 in 1908, when the total regular dividends were $100,000. In 1909 the regular dividends paid out totaled $120,000, but no specials were recorded for Mrs. Barron. By 1910, however, the regular dividends had fallen to $35,000, and in 1911 there were none.

As editor of *The Wall Street Journal,* beginning in late 1905, Sereno S. Pratt closely followed Woodlock's editorial policies. The *Journal* continued its enthusiasm for President Theodore Roosevelt, who had greatly alarmed most of America's upper classes with his famous, thundering speech against the "malefactors of great wealth" and who then set out to prove he meant what he said. When the President began his tour of the Southeast to defend his administration in October 1907, the *Journal* restated its approval of his utterances and policies, saying on October 3: "To the charge that his policy is creating a 'dangerous' centralization of power, the President points to the fact that a great centralization of power already exists in the immense aggregations of corporate capital controlled by a few men, and he argues that the chief economic question of today is to provide a sovereign for those corporations. The trusts and combinations have grown so colossal as to overshadow the power of single states. Many of them became practically the masters of states, and the people found themselves virtually powerless in their hands. There was only one way possible to deal with this condition and that was by invoking the power of the Federal Government."

On October 5 the *Journal* backed President Roosevelt's conservation program as outlined in his Memphis speech. "The main outlines of the masterly program are not new," the paper conceded.

> They have been urged in public and private for years by a struggling minority of leaders in thought and action. But hitherto they lay as scattered ideas gaining strength but slowly in popular faith. Now they are crystallized into a unit which makes their support a self-evident duty of every citizen. . . .
>
> Specifically, the President urges as a national duty the improvements of our thousands of miles of inland navigation, the irrigation of our arid lands, the reclamation of our lowlands, the conservation of our forests and soils, the utilization of our water powers, and the purification of our streams as the foremost problems in the economic policy of the country. . . . The glory of this program lies in the purpose that gives it force. It is not in the creation of material goods nor in the conservation of natural resources alone that this idea gets its dynamic quality of stirring action. It is in the fact that all these powers and responsibilities are for the welfare and the happiness of the people, for the evolution of a better type of American citizenship, for the utilization by the individual of our institutions and our national resources in realizing the ideals of national life.

Then, on October 12, the *Journal* warned Wall Street that it had better mend its business ways. "The Wall Street man looks out upon the country and sees many suspicious, indignant and angry faces turned toward him. Each successive disclosure of financial wrongdoing increases the popular lack of confidence in Wall Street methods and Wall Street securities." The head of a corporation must not abuse his power, the *Journal* said; the lawyer must not permit himself to become the tool of the unprincipled manipulator. "The editor must not make use of his columns to pervert the public judgment."

The Wall Street Journal would reemphasize the latter theme repeatedly in the ensuing weeks as the country was swept into another financial crisis, a banking panic in which J. Pierpont Morgan would again be called upon for help and would play the role of a benevolent dictator, while Roosevelt abruptly reversed his trust-busting course. The *Journal* editors found themselves required to practice under difficult conditions the high principles they preached.

On October 16, 1907, the *Journal* expressed an uneasiness about the declining stock market and general business conditions. Money was in short supply. Gold reserves backing the American dollar were being depleted despite the fact that the United States had become a major exporting nation following the panic of 1893. Gold was in short supply worldwide, since the capital needed for expansion of industries exceeded the productive capacities of the mines, and governments squandered their reserves in wars (the Boer War and the Russo-Japanese War cost England, Russia, and Japan a total of almost $3 billion). Demands for new capital in America doubled between 1900 and 1907, the United States Steel requirement in 1901 alone totalling $1.4 billion. Wall Street raised much of the capital required in the United States as the Dow Jones Industrial Average rose from a low of 46 in 1904 to 96 in 1907. During this three-year period American business vastly expanded, and enormous trusts were created. From January 7, 1907, to November 15, the average fell 45 percent, wiping out three years of advance.

President Roosevelt had told Congress on December 3, 1906, that the country "continued to enjoy unprecedented prosperity," but Jacob Schiff, James J. Hill, and others had warned that there was trouble ahead because of the currency shortage. They proved it the hard way early in 1907 as they sought to sell long-term bonds to refinance their debts. The bonds could not be sold, and the stock market faltered. In the beginning, *The Wall Street Journal* attributed the trouble to the bears. "There is nothing intrinsically wrong in selling short," the paper said, but it added that a prolonged bear situation could wreck an otherwise healthy economy: "Bear talk . . . takes no account of values, dividend yield nor earning capacity. It says the public has lost faith and confidence. Apparently, a bear position in the market is taken to justify efforts to bring about the very collapse in trade which would be necessary in order to further profits on the bear side." It was reversal of the paper's earlier view of bear activity.

Three days later, the *Journal* said that a distinction should be drawn between current stock-market declines and prior recessions. "There is enormous business, but it is hampered by lack of money, or rather credit," the paper explained. There were other factors. President Roosevelt had begun his biggest trust-busting case. Powerful Standard Oil of New Jersey had been fined $29,250,000 for illegal acceptance of rebates, and actions against other corporations were pending. There was fear in Wall Street. Westinghouse could sell only a third of a common-stock issue of 100,000 shares offered at $50 a share, and New York and Boston were unable to sell their bonds. Banking institutions were in trouble. Some bankers sought to recoup by gambling in western copper mines. Mercantile National Bank of New York fell under the control of copper speculators Frederick Augustus Heinze and Charles W. Morse, who used the bank's assets to purchase control of the Knickerbocker Trust Company. When the New York Clearing House discovered that bank funds were, in effect, being used to gamble in copper, it forced the resignation of the Mercantile National Bank directors. *The Wall Street Journal* praised the Clearing House for its decision to withhold funds from Mercantile, but the action exposed the banking scandal as Heinze and

Morse were among those forced out. On October 10, copper shares plummeted. Wall Street knew that Mercantile was the "linchpin" in the Heinze and Morse combine, wrote Robert Sobel, the historian of Wall Street, and it knew that Mercantile owned Knickerbocker Trust. There was a run on both institutions, and the 1907 bank panic was under way. Again the New York bankers called to J. Pierpont Morgan for aid. The aging, weary banker was in Richmond, Virginia, attending a religious retreat, and he was suffering from a cold. But he heard the Macedonian cry and on October 17 he boarded his private car for New York.

At the beginning of the Wall Street troubles, C. W. Barron was in his Waldorf-Astoria suite, keeping in touch with his friends in the banks, brokerage houses, and his papers, and, according to his own private report, with President Theodore Roosevelt. Just how much and how directly Barron participated in the financial crisis and the policies of the *Journal* at that time is known only from a letter he wrote a friend: "Foreseeing coming trouble I maintained a close watch in 1906 and 1907 to see that my policies of news conduct were not violated [at any of the three papers in Boston, Philadelphia, and New York]. For a long time these efforts left me only a few hours of sleep, and night after night I would read all the papers and reports until two or three o'clock and then be up at seven A.M. or before." Barron was also worried about his heavy commitment in the stock market, mostly on margin. He could keep up payments on his notes to Dow Jones creditors only with difficulty. Just how Barron kept in touch with the Dow Jones executives is not recorded. But he had his secretary Atherton with him, to whom he regularly dictated scores of notes a day. Some undoubtedly went to the *Journal*. Also, Barron liked to use the telephone. And he undoubtedly visited his Doremus & Company offices, which were in the same building occupied by Dow Jones.

The Wall Street Journal continued to point out that the banking disaster overtaking the city had resulted from excessive speculation in the copper market by some of the bankers. It lectured New York Clearing House on its public relations. It must avoid the appearance of panic in the crisis. It also was to take constructive steps, said the paper. "It has another duty and that is the duty of a conservative publicity in this time. There is a way of publishing legitimate news of a crisis without adding to the excitement and distress. This is a duty which is imposed not only upon the bankers themselves, but upon the newspapers. It is a question whether the situation has been handled with entire wisdom so far."

The bankers had no intention of trusting the newspapers. All possible measures were taken to preserve secrecy, a policy which J. P. Morgan, of course, endorsed. He stayed at the home of his son-in-law, Herbert Satterlee, took some of his meals at his favorite club, the Union, then on Fifth Avenue at Fifty-first Street, and met with the bankers in his library. The newspapermen camped outside the library, but Morgan evaded them, using the Union Club brougham drawn by a white horse when it was imperative to travel. This stratagem was quickly discovered, yet Morgan still refused to answer questions. One reason, he confided to Satterlee, was because he didn't know the answers. He did suggest that people should leave their money in the banks, advice that failed to stop the ruinous runs. The tellers paid out as deliberately as possible, but the disaster grew. By October 23 there was no money to be had on Wall Street, and the market plunged. Interest rates had soared to 150 percent. Reported the *Journal:* "October 23 will pass into the history of Wall Street as one of its memorable days. Not since the panic of 1884 has Wall Street witnessed the picturesque spectacle that was presented yesterday. The panic of 1893 was much more severe than that of 1884, but it was devoid of the intense excitement and the big crowds which gathered during the earlier crisis."

There was terror in Wall Street, Morgan's biographer John Winkler wrote. So many angry, frightened crowds gathered in front of the Stock Exchange and before banks and trust companies that mounted police were called out. Panic was spreading, threatening to paralyze the business community. Yet this time there was hope because government and businessmen were attempting to work together. The paper praised Secretary of the Treasury George A. B. Cortelyou, who represented President Roosevelt,

> for sitting calmly all day in the office of the subtreasury assuring all callers that he would do everything which the powers of a Secretary permitted him to do for the protection of the financial situation. . . . He was equally impressive because he represented the power of the President. [The President, the paper noted, was bear-hunting in Louisiana.]
>
> Scarcely less impressive than this was the spectacle of J. Pierpont Morgan in his office directly opposite the subtreasury representing the power of private capital directed for the relief of the financial situation. Mr. Morgan represented confidence. It is significant how in time of strain Wall Street turned to Mr. Morgan as the only individual in private life who seemed to have the prestige and the ability to lead it out of danger.

The *Journal* thought that the worst was over, and so did President Roosevelt, who wrote to Cortelyou, "I congratulate also those conservative and substantial businessmen who in the crisis have acted with such wisdom and public spirit."

But the panic was not over. Morgan still did not have a solution, and as he smoked and played solitaire, his favorite game, in the library, he listened to advisers, rejecting their plan for the issuance of Clearing House certificates to be used to end the bank runs and to restart the stock market, because he hoped to find a better way. On Thursday the 24th, John D. Rockefeller called upon the Union Trust Company, a bank near failing, with $10 million for deposit. Then, according to Satterlee, Rockefeller visited Morgan at the latter's office to offer further help. Morgan saw a way to move. R. H. Thomas, president of the New York Stock Exchange, arrived shortly afterward to say that he would have to close down.

"What time do you usually close it?" Morgan asked calmly.

"Three o'clock."

"It must not close one minute before that hour today," Morgan said, according to Satterlee. Morgan sent for the bankers, who reached his office at two o'clock. He told them that unless $25 million was provided within the next quarter of an hour, he feared 50 firms would go under. Cold-eyed James Stillman, president of the National City Bank and banker to Rockefeller, promised $5 million on loan to the Exchange before closing time. Morgan nodded. Stillman had heard from Rockefeller. There was now a chance to win. Morgan called the roll of bankers. When one man hesitated, Morgan glared at him as he chewed his cigar and waited. The banker grew pale and made his pledge. Within minutes Morgan had $27 million pledged. He ordered the news to be communicated to three traders on the floor of the New York Stock Exchange who had been chosen to make the announcement. Soon there was cheering in the Exchange.

The terror in Wall Street had ended and, wrote Winkler, "over night Morgan had become a towering, heroic figure." But problems were far from solved. Although London banks were induced to pledge millions in gold shipments, New York banks provided more cash, and the Clearing House certificates were issued in lieu of money, the city of New York was nearly bankrupt; school teachers were going unpaid. James Stillman's bank still had gold, and Morgan summoned the banker to meet with city officials in his library. The meeting lasted through the night; when it ended, Stillman had reluctantly agreed to participate in the purchase of $30 million in municipal bonds. The Morgan bank, as in the earlier subscription, took its share.

Morgan had gone sleepless for hours, except for his fitful naps as the conferences went on about him, but he was not ready to relax. He knew that United States Steel, the company he had helped to organize, desperately wanted control of Tennessee Coal, Iron & Railway Company, an acquisition that would virtually give United States Steel the monopoly Roosevelt was determined to prevent. Morgan summoned Judge Gary, now president of United States Steel, and explained his plan. Major New York banks and a leading brokerage firm might go down yet if Tennessee Coal & Iron could not make good its loans, Morgan claimed. That would restart the panic. Let

United States Steel buy the ailing company it so eagerly desired for its huge coal and iron deposits. Let Tennessee Coal & Iron then pay off its debts. Judge Gary's eyes gleamed, but then his shoulders sagged and his jaw went slack. "We can't do it, Mr. Morgan, not without consulting President Roosevelt."

Roosevelt not long before had publicly excoriated Wall Street bankers before newsmen at Washington's famed Gridiron dinner, and some thought his myopic glare had been fixed on J. P. Morgan, but Morgan now was willing to seek Roosevelt's aid. "Order a special train," Morgan said. Gary could obtain only a locomotive, tender, and Pullman coach in the middle of the night, but that got him and his associate Henry Frick to Washington. President Roosevelt felt compelled to approve the deal and to take the heat.

When it was over, *The Wall Street Journal* on November 7 again paid its respects to J. Pierpont Morgan and called upon him to render yet another service:

> Now Mr. Morgan having performed this service has it within his power to go still further and make to Wall Street and the country a contribution greater than any other financier has made since the days of Alexander Hamilton. His name is already written in the history of American finance in large letters; but he has the opportunity to put himself among the number of the few immortals, if he will follow up the service which he has already performed by taking the lead in the establishment of certain mighty financial reforms.
>
> Already in the financing of the panic something has been done in this direction. Most notable of all has been the elimination from Clearing House banking exponents of sensational and speculative finance. Something more is now needed. It is one thing to face and beat down a great panic, but it is a still higher thing to effect such changes and devise such methods as will make other panics less common and less dangerous.
>
> Mr. Morgan's prestige and authority are now so great that any stand which he may take in behalf of financial reform can be put through, whereas at some later period it might be impossible even for him to do much in that direction. We want in this country some system of emergency circulation to be issued either under the authority of the Secretary of the Treasury or of some representative banking institution like a Federal Clearing House or a central bank. We need a union of the banks and trust companies in the Clearing House under satisfactory arrangements as to reserves, and with the publication of a bank statement which should be comprehensive, giving to the public a faithful picture of money market conditions. We need a better regulation of the call money market so as to prevent the extravagant fluctuations of interest. We need such changes in stock exchange methods of clearances as shall make the inevitable and legitimate speculation of Wall Street less burdensome upon the money market. We need to eliminate the abuses of banking competition, and especially to put the practice of payment of interest upon deposits, particularly those of reserve institutions, on a saner and safer basis. We need also to consider the desirability of increasing the rates of Wall

> Street margins, and also to look into the subject of drawing some proper distinction between cash deposits and check deposits, cash payments and check payments.
>
> These and other banking reforms are vital for the future progress of the country. Now is the time for some strong leader like Mr. Morgan to undertake them.

The paper was in effect calling for some kind of federal reserve plan, an idea that, according to Satterlee, J. P. Morgan began considering shortly after the panic. On November 22 *The Wall Street Journal* again urged a "central bank, an emergency circulation, and other plans of inducing elasticity in the currency. . . . [This] will not prevent panics, but certainly a well-devised scheme by which money circulation could be increased in times of stringency or crisis would serve to make the interest rates more stable and prevent the worst aspect of uncontrolled panic."

United States Senator Nelson W. Aldrich was thinking along similar lines. He worked with Morgan and other financiers to devise the Aldrich-Vreeland Act, creating the National Monetary Commission to provide for "emergency currency in times of stringency," an act which became law May 30, 1908.

But, as the *Journal* frequently observed, it usually took a long time for needed legislation to be obtained, even after many warnings and crises, whereas the executive branch of the government sometimes was immediately responsive to need. Not until December 23, 1913, five years and more than a dozen *Wall Street Journal* editorials later, was the Federal Reserve System created by the Owen-Glass Act.

Wrote Clarence Barron to a friend after the events of October and November 1907, "As trouble approached I told President Theodore Roosevelt that it would take $500 million to stop the panic. Later I footed up the total relief from Washington, London and the New York banks and it was just $520 million. . . . Nobody will ever know how hard I worked through many channels to keep the Wall Street fire from spreading. When the crisis was over I went home [to Beacon Street, Boston] and slept for a very long time, and it took nearly a year to recover my nervous energy." Barron's secretary Atherton, who was required to keep a bag packed for instant travel at any time, confided to his wife that he would be in town for a while. "Mr. Barron is ill, and his doctor says he won't be traveling for months," Atherton told her. Barron was quite ill. Also, he had lost heavily in the market during the panic and was required to seek delays in paying off his Dow Jones notes. For the next several months, when there were office problems demanding Barron's attention, Atherton would be called to the mansion on Beacon Street, where Mrs. Barron would consult her husband and then dictate his decisions and answers.

During the period of his illness and slow convalescence, Clarence and Jessie Barron were comforted by the fact that their capable son-in-law was increasingly taking over the responsibilities of the company. They had hoped that Hugh Bancroft might become the successor to their leadership when they lured the young man from his law practice in Boston in 1906 and he proceeded to fall in love with their daughter Jane. Hugh and Jane were married in 1907, and Hugh was made secretary of both the Boston News Bureau and Dow, Jones & Company. When Jessie Barron felt it necessary to spend an increasing amount of time with her ailing husband in Boston in 1908, young Bancroft allocated more of his time to Dow Jones and *The Wall Street Journal*.

Bancroft was all any proud parents could want in a son-in-law. He was six feet four, handsome, reserved, and so gracious to everyone that it was said he even said hello to the elevator operator when he entered a strange building. He was the epitome of the proper Bostonian, the rugged, tweedy, slow-smiling type to be found in cigarette and automobile advertisements in *The Wall Street Journal* and in popular magazine illustrations. But Bancroft didn't smoke and preferred walking and biking to driving a car.

Hugh Bancroft could trace his ancestry to John Bancroft, who, with his wife, Jane, settled in Lynn, Massachusetts, in 1632. His father, William Bancroft, was a lawyer, mayor of Cambridge for 12 years, overseer of Harvard University, and chairman of the board of the Boston Elevated Railway. Hugh graduated from Harvard at the age of 17. He then studied civil engineering at Harvard's Lawrence Scientific School, receiving his Master of Arts degree in 1898. He entered Harvard University Law School the following year, earning his degree in 1901, and was admitted to the Massachusetts bar that same year. As a Harvard undergraduate, Bancroft rowed number 6 on the Harvard crew and was a member of Delta Upsilon fraternity and the Hasty Pudding Club.

Bancroft joined his father's law firm, Stone, Ballinger & Bancroft. He was named assistant district attorney in 1902 and served through 1906, when he was elected district attorney of Middlesex County. His first wife, Mary, died in 1903. Bancroft was reluctant to give up his law and political career, but he was very much in love with Jane, and the Barrons were persuasive. By 1908, when Clarence Barron was seriously ill and deeply depressed, Bancroft agreed to concentrate on the Barron interests, including Dow Jones in New York, and Mrs. Barron promised to settle 25 percent of her Dow Jones holdings on Jane and Hugh.

In addition to serving the *Boston News Bureau* and Dow Jones with his legal and administrative talents, Hugh Bancroft also did some reporting in Boston and proved himself an able writer of special articles. His series on inheritance-tax laws, published in the *Boston News Bureau* in 1911, later appeared in book form, edited by A. W. Blakemore and published by Houghton Mifflin Company, Cambridge. It sold out several editions.

After Barron had recovered his health as much as his eating practices would permit and had engaged in some trips abroad in search of special articles for his publications, he became increasingly aware of problems at *The Wall Street Journal.* Circulation, advertising, and profits had declined. Barron became unhappy with Charles Otis's performance, and he quarreled with Bancroft so bitterly that the young man refused to speak to his father-in-law; they communicated by notes dictated to Atherton, according to Arthur Lissner, another of Barron's later secretaries. Barron became further enraged when he learned that Bancroft was determined to quit to become chairman of the Boston Port Authority late in 1911. After all, said Bancroft, at last speaking to Barron again, it was the kind of work for which he had been trained, and journalism was not. Barron had to act. He went to the Dow Jones offices in New York and clashed with President Charles Otis. Otis, Barron told Jessie, would have to go.

On March 26, 1912, the Dow Jones board authorized the transfer of one share of stock from W. A. Edwards, a Dow Jones reporter, to C. W. Barron. It also accepted the resignation of Sereno S. Pratt as a director and elected C. W. Barron in Pratt's place. Three days later, at a special meeting of the directors, Charles Otis resigned as president, though he continued as a director. Then C. W. Barron was elected president. President Barron at once turned to former President Otis. "You will remain a director at the pleasure of the president," he said coldly. Meanwhile, Bancroft's quarrel with Barron had been patched up by Mrs. Barron, and Bancroft was made treasurer.

Dow, Jones & Company and *The Wall Street Journal* were entering upon two decades of change, new excitement, and unprecedented prosperity under the redoubtable C. W. Barron.

Chapter 6

C. W. Barron Takes Charge

"I was born July 2, 1855, in the old north end of Boston on Cross Street in a stone house whose front was covered with green vine growing from the smallest kind of a front garden." Thus Clarence Walker Barron began his autobiography in 1927, the year before his death. Barron did not get far; too many other interests diverted him. His mother's accouchement occurred in the home of Mr. and Mrs. Clarence Walker, and the boy lived with the Walkers for the first years of his life. His parents were poor, their cottage small. His father, Henry Barron, had come to Boston from the family farm at Sterling, Massachusetts, and had gone into the teamster and drayage business on the Boston docks.

The family's paternal ancestor in America was said to be Ellis Barron, who came from Waterford County, Ireland, in 1640. His mother, Elana Noyes, was born in Unity, Maine, and through his mother—whose grandparents were Amos and Ann Lane Carver of Freeport, Maine—Clarence Barron would claim to be a descendent of John Carver, first governor of Plymouth Colony. Barron's parents lived in Charlestown, a small community adjacent to Boston and later part of the city. Evidently the home lacked room for the new infant along with three brothers and a sister, so Clarence lived with the Walkers until his frail health worried his mother, and she arranged for him to go to the farm home of her good friend, Sarah Hapgood, and her husband, Robert. Clarence credited Sarah with teaching him to read and to love books. When he returned to the home of his family in Charlestown at age 7, he possessed the rugged good health of a farm boy, some knowledge of history, and a voracious appetite. He attended Prescott Grammar School, took any odd jobs he could find, and was always hungry.

"My earliest recollections . . ." Barron wrote, "are of a vine-covered stone house [the Walkers'], with many household feline pets that nestled in sofas and chairs and atop of the family clock. . . . In those days the north end of Boston with its narrow streets were well crowded with horse-drawn vehicles and farmer boys from the country who were seeking their fortunes in the city. I loved the wharves, the granite blocks, and all the life that swung around the Boston Customs House and the crowded market streets."

Barron wrote also that he remembered the early days of the Civil War, for he held to his mother's skirts as she discussed slavery in her doorway, and he recalled "the soldiers marching, my father holding me high in his arms on a wagon to view the face of Abraham Lincoln." Then he recollected the days of working, two or more jobs at a time when he could find them, and his endless endeavors to get enough to eat. Although he lived in Charlestown with his parents, young Barron was given permission to attend the English High School in Boston, where he was an excellent student. With his friends he explored the waterfront and Bunker and Breed hills, examining the grass-grown entrenchments dug there in 1775. Barron could lecture to them on the subject because Sarah Hapgood's lessons took well and he was an intensive reader, especially of American history. Barron was fiercely patriotic throughout his life, which he attributed to those early excursions that also, he said, built up his legs for the arduous job of running after news. Such early development eventually helped Barron to support his 330 pounds of weight in later years, suggested Arthur Pound and Samuel Taylor Moore in their preface to the two volumes of his work, *They Told Barron* and *More They Told Barron*, which they edited.

Barron remembered that his favorite boyhood hobby was drawing maps on bristol board. "I made my own tools and colors, smoothing down and bending a flour-barrel hoop to mark my curved lines of latitude or longitude." Thus began his passion for travel, which he gloriously indulged in later years, together with his love of food. Barron also yearned to write. He began studying stenography on his own, believing this might help him to get a job on a newspaper. He became friendly with J. M. Yerrington, a court reporter, who taught him and offered to find him a job. However, Barron preferred to look on his own since Yerrington had no connections in the newspaper business. Barron would insist throughout his life that stenography, more than any other single skill, was responsible for his success. "I believe it is a great mistake to give the shorthand field over to girls," he wrote. "I think it is the best training for young men in practical life, far ahead of Greek or Latin. . . . I have followed the practice in my different offices of employing the best stenographers available and developing them into newspapermen. Many of them have graduated or fallen into banking fields and the way of wealth."

Barron got his first job with the *Boston Daily News*, and his shorthand skills enabled him to distinguish himself almost immediately. In 1875 the Social Science Association staged a debate between Wendell Phillips, the fiery orator and social reformer, and William Lloyd Garrison, the aging abolitionist. Rival reporters wrote only a paragraph or two, but Barron, who was fascinated by the discussion of financial reform, took down almost every word, most of them uttered by Phillips. The *News* printed his full story, "Wendell Phillips on Finance," and, according to Pound and Moore, sold out the entire edition. Barron was determined to write on financial subjects thereafter. He got a job with the *Boston Transcript* when he was just past 20, covering general news. *Transcript* editors boasted publicly that their newspaper reached the "50,000 best minds of Boston," and they evidently concluded that none of them delved into the tawdry affairs of the marketplace, for they had no financial section. But young Barron eventually changed their minds.

"I used to write up commercial features for the *Transcript*," he remembered, "finding my own problem and solving it." He offered his stories to his editors, and they were printed. One concerned the port of Boston. Barron had analyzed the port receipts and discovered that the Port Authority was losing $1 million on "through shipments," foreign imports that went West by railroad without paying a transit fee. Barron's article was reprinted by the Boston Board of Trade. There was no change in the port rules, but the young reporter was flattered by the interest shown and decided he must become a full-time financial writer, the specialty ignored by the *Transcript* and all the other Boston newspapers.

"One day I reported to my superiors," Barron wrote in the fragmented beginning of his incomplete autobiography, "that it was absurd to give the quotations of Boston securities and every transaction, yet never give the news under the fluctuations; that I believed there was a news item every day in State Street [Boston's financial street] that might be picked up. I was asked to annex that to my daily duties. I said, 'Give me my whole time.' My request was granted. . . . I thus established the financial section of the paper. The result was unexpected. The *Transcript* was already taken by everyone; yet in a few weeks the *Transcript* circulation increased fifteen per cent."

Barron's recollection was accurate. Years later the *Transcript* said, "He was first to define the need for financial journalism. . . . We are happy to recall that Clarence W. Barron was the *Transcript's* first financial editor. He gave our own financial department its inception." A report to which Barron always referred with special pride was one that he said first called the attention of the general public to the commercial possibilities of Alexander Graham Bell's telephone. Bell had given the first public demonstration of his invention before the Boston chapter of the American Academy of Arts and Sciences on May 10, 1876. The Bell Telephone Company was formed July 9, 1877. Barron wrote his special article on the telephone service later that year and predicted its potential importance:

> The rapidity with which Professor Bell's telephone is coming into practical use is truly astonishing. Scarcely do his public exhibitions cease, when the little black box begins vibrating in almost every city on the continent. But probably the most extended use yet made of this wonderful invention is by the Telephone Dispatch Company of this city. The company . . . has been in quiet operation for about four weeks, and now has telephonic connections with about a hundred mercantile houses, mostly in the dry goods quarter of the city, and with every express office.
>
> The principal business of this company thus far is the transmission of orders for express service but it is prepared to do all kinds of work now performed by the District Telegraph Company—such as furnishing messenger and police service, carriages, etc. . . . The telephones are located at the expense of the company, the user paying $3 to $5 a month, and having express messages transmitted without charge. Before long, connections will be made with hotels and residences.

Charles Glidden, a telephone company official at the time, admired Barron's report, which he acclaimed as complete and accurate. The two men became lifelong friends.

In January 1887 Barron resigned from the *Transcript*. He had decided that Boston could use an hourly news service covering the activity of the Boston and New York stock markets. He was aware of the work of Dow, Jones, and Bergstresser in New York and planned to emulate them by acquiring a small press to print news bulletins that messengers would deliver. Barron, unlike the Dow, Jones & Company proprietors, kept a careful record of his business beginnings. In his diary he estimated that 100 subscribers at $30 a month would pay for the bulletin service he planned, and he decided that he might be able to sell a summary of the day's news at 5 cents a copy to possibly 5,000 buyers and subscribers, the latter to pay $1 a month or receive a copy free if they took his bulletin service. An early January entry in his diary said: "Studied all day on News Bureau plans. I think I am finding my use and great is my joy." And another entry: "I propose to organize news in the interest of Boston and fear no rival." And then: "Am now seeking subscribers, eight in the first day, 10 the next, then seven and nine, total 34 the first week."

Barron was sure he could succeed, but some time elapsed before he had office space and a three-month credit arrangement for his printing needs. "Was 32 years old yesterday and now have 86 subscribers—outlook glorious," he wrote on July 3. On July 25, 1887, his diary stated: "Put out 26 separate bulletins each five inches by nine inches, delivered promptly by the boys." Exactly 40 years later, Barron attended a birthday celebration for his company where it was mentioned that his newspaper, the *Boston News Bureau*, had begun publication on July 25. Barron did not correct the error. Actually, the Boston News Bureau Company, distributor of printed bulletins and later the operator of ticker service in Boston, started on the 25th, but the first issue of the *Boston News Bureau*, a newspaper, appeared on July 27. On that day Volume 1, Number 1 came off the press, naming C. W. Barron as manager. It was printed on one sheet, two columns of type on the front and one column on the back, and consisted entirely of reprints of the day's bulletins. There was no advertising. His printers were Nathan Sayer & Son, on the floor above his own little office.

Thus Barron preceded Dow, Jones & Company into the newspaper business, as he did with his telegraph stock-market ticker service. He was able in the beginning to charge his customers $1 a day for his bulletin services, a level Dow Jones did not attain until later. Barron was an excellent reporter and editor, and Dow, Jones & Company readily agreed to exchange news dispatches with him. By December Barron noted in his diary: "Am working long hours; am killing myself but am closing my best year ever in business and mental broadening. Now have 125 bulletin subscribers but am neglecting my church and spiritual aims—must organize and economize my time for leisure."

Young Barron continued to believe that the requirements of his customers came ahead of his own needs. It was his duty, he said, to give his clients fast, accurate news reports as did Dow, Jones & Company, an organization he publicly praised and sought to equal in the bulletin business. However, since he was the sole proprietor and had a summary newspaper besides, he worked himself thin, so that his nickname among friends at the time was Skinny. It was necessary for Clarence Barron to supervise all phases of his service at all times. He was a slave to his work, and he dramatically proved his devotion to business in the Great Blizzard of March 1888, scrambling over the shingles and icy tin roofing of Boston rooftops to restring his wires while his local rivals were forced to close down their services. When the telegraph wires between New York and Boston were pulled down by ice and the trains stopped running, shutting off all New York reports, Barron found a simple but expensive solution: He ordered the New York stock-market reports from London via Cyrus Field's Atlantic cable. Thus, when the other Boston services did reopen, Barron alone had the full New York report, which they were unable to obtain for some days.

Barron's Boston news service prospered rapidly. He was no longer the nimble messenger and reporter described by Pound and Moore when he finally proposed marriage to Mrs. Jessie Waldron, owner of a rooming and boarding house, early in 1900, but a prosperous, corpulent 44-year-old businessman. William L. Moise, a Wall Street banker and broker who wrote a Barron manuscript biography, said that family records indicate an illness caused young Barron to become addicted to food. Or perhaps it was the excellence of Mrs. Waldron's cooking, which Barron had enjoyed since he first lodged with her in 1886. Moise also wrote that Barron finally was impelled toward matrimony when Mrs. Waldron confided that she was considering the proposal of another man. Louis Atherton and Edward Stein, Barron's secretaries, told Arthur Lissner, a later secretary, that Barron had said he proposed marriage because he was fond of Jessie's two daughters, Jane and Martha, as well as their mother, and he needed a hostess in the new, grand Back Bay mansion he had arranged to buy in 1900 after acquiring an equally elegant summer home at nearby Cohasset. Barron also told the young men that he worked too hard all his life to ever have thoughts of sex. The wedding to Mrs. Waldron took place at Cohasset on June 21, 1900, and was reported by the Boston papers as an important social event. The secretaries remembered Jessie Barron as a kind and considerate woman to whom Barron appeared devoted and from whom he accepted advice when he would listen to no one else.

But Clarence Barron was clearly more infatuated with power, money, and food than with Jessie. There was no doubt that he doted on his adopted daughters, and he loved the home comforts Jessie and the girls provided, especially after Jane and Martha married well and the grandchildren arrived. Barron was a tiger in the office and a lamb at home, his biographers agreed. He was courtly and flattering to women generally, and most were fond of him. He also was brilliant, a winner of prizes for scholarship in school and an avid reader of materials relevant to his business. The Boston papers appeared eager throughout his life to interview him and to praise him as a writer and editor. Yet, though he grew up in Boston amid the flowering of New England culture, he was little touched by the literary and scholarly sides of Boston life. Moise noted that Barron was "devoted to the works of Horatio Alger since he was seven." Alger's portrayal of virtue rewarded and hard work appreciated did not begin until the appearance of *Ragged Dick* in 1867, when Barron was 12 and had written his prize essay at school on railroad economics, an accomplishment also recorded by Moise. While C. W. Barron read neither Henry nor William James, Boston's illustrious sons of his time, his mind was undoubtedly several cuts above Horatio Alger. His instincts, however, were those of Ragged Dick. Ida M. Tarbell, the muckraker who wrote exposés of such money-makers as John D. Rockefeller, lunched with Barron in later years and was said to have exclaimed to friends, "That man is a glutton, for food and money!" And C. W. Barron was a glutton for work, as the staff of *The Wall Street Journal* would discover in 1912.

In 1877 Barron joined the Church of the New Jerusalem, a Boston congregation subscribing to the doctrines of Emanuel Swedenborg, the son of a bishop of the Swedish Lutheran church and former chaplain to the court of Charles XI. Possibly Barron did read the work of one of the James family, Henry, Sr., who wrote a book published in Boston, *The Secret of Swedenborg*. ("He kept it," wrote a disdainful Boston reviewer.) Swedenborg, a Swedish government engineer, in the mid-eighteenth century wrote 32 theological books after receiving a revelation from God, who, he said, had chosen Swedenborg to "explain to men the spiritual sense of the Scriptures." Barron became a firm believer, read all of Swedenborg's books, carried a copy of Swedenborg and one of the Bible, each wrapped in a silk handkerchief, when he traveled, and proselytized for his faith, winning a notable convert, Madame Amelita Galli-Curci, the famed opera singer, in 1917. Ten years later, according to Barron's notebook, when he lunched with her in Florida, the divine diva told him that she had read all 32 books Barron had sent her and that Swedenborg had enriched her life. Barron helped to finance an American edition of Swedenborg's works, attended services of the church when he was in Boston, and donated $27,000 to a new church building in 1927.

Barron, despite his religious convictions, or perhaps because of them, was a man who would not tolerate failure. He was foul-tempered when things went wrong, intolerant of inept and thick-witted minions, often cruel even to close associates. Although he truly loved and admired his wife, Jessie, for her good, common sense, not even Jessie would be allowed to drag Dow, Jones & Company and *The Wall Street Journal* through the desponding slough of red ink that Barron saw immediately ahead as he pored over the company accounts in his Boston mansion late in 1911. There was no special reason for the financial difficulties that Barron would discover when he made increasingly frequent trips to New York early in 1912, other than general incompetency for which those in charge would have to accept the blame.

It was true that Barron had known some failure himself, though he was not a man to admit it. There was his investment debacle of 1907. His invasion of Philadelphia had been a major error, which he insisted had kept down competition for his other companies, one of which he did not yet own when he established the Philadelphia paper. His *Boston News Bureau* was, of course, a great success. The New York paper, which did well in the immediate years after acquisition in 1902, had slumped ever since Charles Otis went down from Boston in 1905 to take over, following the departure of

Bergstresser, Barney, and Woodlock. Barron conveniently forgot that he had sent Otis down himself. As for dispatching Hugh Bancroft later, Jessie was certainly to be blamed. Bancroft turned out to be an insolent puppy at times, Barron once told him, and now, in late 1911, he was a deserter to the Boston Port Authority. Bancroft's help had been only minimal from the start, Barron angrily concluded. Still, he forgave Bancroft after fiercely attacking him, and his sedate son-in-law reluctantly agreed to continue as legal adviser and secretary to both the Boston and New York companies while he built the new Boston dry-dock and harbor facilities.

Finally, there was no help for it—C. W. Barron at long last concluded that he personally would have to take over Dow, Jones & Company and *The Wall Street Journal*. He obtained a single share of stock from W. A. Edwards, and Jessie's cooperation.

When Clarence Barron stormed into the editorial office of *The Wall Street Journal* in March 1912 following his election to the presidency of Dow, Jones & Company, he sent a shock of terror through the staff. Moise, who talked with workers under Barron, described the scene, or perhaps another like it, since Barron repeated it often: "He was portly, with dancing blue eyes and a full white beard. He strode into the room, kicking over waste baskets and whacking his cane on a desk to attract attention. He berated them all for their sins and mistakes and told them he intended to straighten them out, at once. They could obey him or they could get out."

The rotund, fierce publisher thereafter was teacher and taskmaster to the staff. His anger and sarcasm could wilt a man, yet even after a humiliating tongue-lashing, a beaten employee would be likely to praise Barron. "He was only trying to make a man of me," more than one said. Barron's avowed purpose was "to break the colt so he can be trained." He never fired a man, Moise noted, though he harassed some into quitting or into nervous breakdowns. Pound and Moore in their brief biographical sketch agreed that "never—absolutely never—did C. W. B. dismiss anyone from his employ. Partly this was sheer kindness of heart; partly the realization that the time he had put in training them to do the job would be lost if the recipient went elsewhere." They also noted that "C. W. B. was no easy boss. . . . It was part of his policy, as a boss, to 'ride' his men until they were broken to suit him. He considered this a part of his duty toward them no less than toward his properties and the public which both the men and the papers were expected to serve."

The quaking workers at *The Wall Street Journal* would learn in time that Barron's fiercest intimidation of a man might be followed by kindness, even a gift or a raise, especially if the victim summoned sufficient courage to threaten to quit. But at the start of Barron's personal reign in 1912, there was no discernible instant response to his leadership. The staff seemed temporarily paralyzed. Not only was the benign if tough demeanor of Mrs. Barron missing, but there was no Thomas Woodlock on hand. The improved headlines introduced under Woodlock had become dull and dowdy, and, for a time in 1912, they remained so. There was no restored glitter in the reportorial prose, either. Yet, slowly, the demoralized staff members regrouped; they caught Barron's message that financial news should be written simply and clearly so that all could read and understand. None could match the dramatic flair Barron himself used to make his reports fascinating to readers, but the paper once again sharpened its headlines and brightened its text. The announcement of new management, appearing on March 30, 1912, was restrained:

> C. W. Barron has been elected President of Dow, Jones & Co. and *The Wall Street Journal*, succeeding Charles Otis who has resigned to assume his active management of the Forest and Stream Publishing Company which he has acquired.
>
> Hugh Bancroft has been elected Secretary, and Joseph Cashman, Treasurer and Business Manager.
>
> Maurice L. Farrell has been chosen Managing News Editor.
>
> F. Medley Scovil, formerly with the New York business office of the Boston News Bureau, becomes president of Doremus & Co., the advertising agency department of Dow, Jones & Co., Ernest Mayglothing continuing as manager.

One unflappable executive at the *Journal* who was not at all disturbed by Barron's theatrics on the day he invaded the editorial department was Hamilton, editor of the editorial page since Sereno Pratt resigned in 1908. He may not have witnessed the scene, but Hamilton always got on well with Barron and reported favorably on him in later years. "He was the most astonishing worker I ever saw," Hamilton wrote. "He would begin a conversation with me while carrying on business with two secretaries and attending to two telephones. He would never get one of those threads of interest entangled with the others. He would put down one subject and resume his discussion with me exactly at the point he had left it a few minutes before. In the gathering of news he was utterly indifferent to the criticisms of others, and for that reason no one was big enough to snub him. . . . He interfered little, if at all, in the conduct of the editorial page."

Hamilton's editorials continued their urbane and placid ways. On March 30 the "Review and Outlook" praised former President Theodore Roosevelt, as the paper had done so often over the years: "Mr. Roosevelt, in dignified retirement, has before him greatest opportunities for usefulness. He may set our politicians a lesson in detachment and reserve, much needed since Grover Cleveland's death. His great abilities as a writer, and the benefit of experience vouchsafed to few, admirably equip him for the trusted counseling emeritus of his country, when once this foolish frenzy has passed away."

Rarely had a Hamilton editorial been so wrong. The "foolish frenzy," Roosevelt's quarrel with Taft, did not pass away; there was no dignified retirement. After big-game hunting in Africa, Teddy Roosevelt came home to attack President Taft, who was carrying out most Roosevelt policies effectively and much to the satisfaction of *The Wall Street Journal*. When Roosevelt stampeded his loyalists and the country's populists and progressives into backing his third-party candidacy (the Bull Moose campaign) in 1912, Democrat Woodrow Wilson was the beneficiary, and the *Journal* was not pleased.

Clarence Barron had more immediate concerns than the problems of the American presidency, though both Theodore Roosevelt and William Howard Taft were his friends and called upon him for advice about financial matters. By early June he had caused the news staff to restore the headline crispness characteristic of the Woodlock era, and the fruits of one of his talks with Hamilton were discernible in the editorial pages, as elsewhere, by summer, when the *Journal* began to comment more upon European problems than it had previously. Barron traveled widely in Europe and would soon establish himself not only as *The Wall Street Journal's* expert on foreign affairs but as one of the country's outstanding writers in that area. On October 3 the leading editorial foresaw danger in Europe. The gravity of the threat to peace in the Balkans could not be underrated, the *Journal* said. "The danger spot of Europe lies in the Balkan peninsula. It is no surprise that Montenegro, Servia and Bulgaria . . . are seeking to establish a dominant position for themselves in a region which, almost as much as Belgium ever was, has been the cockpit of Europe." The paper predicted that Austria, Germany, and Russia would clash should tension continue.

The following day the *Journal* castigated the *New York Herald* for asserting that "if the Balkan situation were to eventuate in war, European investors would be heavy buyers of our securities." "Of course," said the *Journal* acidly, "this is only the *New York Herald*. But there is considerable danger in second-rate thinking for second-rate minds, when the preponderance of second-rate minds is considered. . . . If there is a war in the Near East we may make up our minds that it will not mean one penny of investment to the American market which would not come here in any case, while it will involve the liquidation of American securities held abroad. . . . War is a waste, and one country cannot dissipate its savings in gunpowder smoke without hurting all the rest of us. In modern conditions of easy communication and international exchange, the misfortune of one is the misfortune of all."

This mean thrust at the *New York Herald*, a frequent advertiser in *The Wall Street Journal*, read refreshingly like C. W. Barron, though the editorial's numerous references to historical evidence of war's destructive effects on world economy more likely reflected the thinking and erudition of Hamilton.

As Barron sought to improve the financial situation of Dow, Jones & Company, he must have been well satisfied with the condition of the country generally. America was in an excellent economic situation, President Taft was eminently satisfactory to the *Journal*, and the Supreme Court upheld the dissolution of such trusts as Standard Oil and American Tobacco Company. (The Court also sustained the corporation-tax provisions of the Payne-Aldrich Tariff Act of 1909 as the *Journal* all along had predicted it would, though it did not approve.) Former President Roosevelt, of course, would indicate he might run for president again in 1912, despite the rather enduring goodbye he had received from the *Journal*. But politics still wasn't the paper's biggest problem in 1911 and 1912. It continued to be the decline in circulation and advertising, and difficulties caused by a lack of a proper franchise for the news-bulletin ticker service. Hugh Bancroft soon solved the latter problem by forming a subsidiary communications company.

Since no audited circulation records were kept, it wasn't possible to state precisely what the circulation of the *Journal* was in the spring of 1912 (estimated at slightly more than 7,500), but the paper had long since stopped posting the proud circulation average, always above 11,000, in its page-one flag. The diminished advertising—mostly banks and stock-exchange members remained—could easily be accommodated in the outside columns of pages one and eight, and in three columns of page five, the first page of the second section. The attempt to have editorial personnel sell advertising, begun shortly before Bergstresser and Woodlock departed, had been a disaster. Whether initiated by Barron, Mrs. Barron, or someone else, the blame fell on Harry Doremus, spurring his departure to join another advertising agency. By 1913 Doremus & Company, without Harry, was again doing well as the agency for all the Barron publications, probably under the personal direction of Barron, an excellent if erratic salesman.

Clarence Barron was a highly complex man. His grandchildren, who adored him, insisted that he looked and acted like Santa Claus, which precisely described his appearance and behavior toward them. He could be enormously charming to children, women, and men he wished to impress. Seated, he resembled a handsome member of royalty with his regal beard and bearing, a portly autocrat filled with benign dignity. When he walked about with quick, careful steps, he appeared more of a Humpty-Dumpty, his vast girth giving him an elliptical appearance, his limbs seeming too frail for his enormous body. Nevertheless, Barron emanated a warm, radiant personality when he chose. When Barron fixed his protruding, darting blue eyes on an individual he selected for his firm attention, he demonstrated such intelligent concern and empathy that the flattered subject generally responded with more intimate and sometimes secret information than he ever had intended to disclose. Barron won favor when he desired it. He had no shame about his gluttony and overweight condition, though he sometimes wryly condemned his vice and its consequences in letters to his granddaughters. Many women and men, including President Coolidge in later years, were genuinely fond of Clarence Barron. Charles Glidden, an admirer of Barron's, remained the editor's friend throughout his lifetime. It was Glidden, an automobile fanatic who was one of the first men to drive a motorcar from the Atlantic to the Pacific strictly for pleasure, who prompted Barron's great interest in the auto industry while it was young. Barron, said Glidden, had a "compelling analytical mind."

The Wall Street Journal took only a desultory interest in the three-way campaign for the presidency in 1912, adhering to Charles Dow's policy of avoiding a commitment. When Woodrow Wilson received 435 electoral votes to 88 for Theodore Roosevelt and 8 for William Howard Taft, the *Journal* declared President-elect Wilson to be "a conservative" and looked confidently to the future. "No man can predict, with any degree of certainty, what will happen in 1913," the paper had said on October 26, a week before the voting. "All that can be said at present is that nothing seems more remote than a panic in 1913. Our banking condition is strong, our crops promise to be the most valuable to the farmer that ever have been raised, our mining industry is flourishing, our manufacturies are running overtime, and every man who wants work can find employment at good wages." After the election, the paper stated that business leaders approved of Wilson and branded as false a report that Wall Street would "create panic" to show its displeasure at the Democratic victory. Then, on December 18, it took cognizance of the investigation of Wall Street by the House Committee on Banking and Currency under Chairman Arsene P. Pujo of Louisiana and warned the committee that it had better not trigger retaliation from Wall Street.

"One of the dangers of popular government is that too much weight is given to emotion, and too little to reasoned conviction," the paper said. "Freedom or liberty, as interpreted by the Pujos, is the power of the majority to coerce the minority. But Mr. Pujo and his friends have not repealed the *habeas corpus* act—yet." The committee was allegedly forcing reluctant New York bankers, including J. P. Morgan and George F. Baker, to testify about Wall Street manipulations and the concentration of banking power. The committee finally published a report stating that "existing banking and credit practices create a growing concentration of control of money and credit in the hands of a comparatively few men." The *Journal* had been saying the same thing since the panic of 1893, while calling for a Federal Reserve banking system, but it took exception to a portion of the committee report asserting that a "monopoly" of New York bankers controlled the New York Stock Exchange. The paper stated that there were 727 members of the Exchange, and fewer than a dozen were large banks, which it listed. "It will be observed then that the alleged monopoly does not exist," said the *Journal*, ignoring the possibility that the Morgan bank alone had greater power than several hundred brokerage houses. But the Pujo committee findings were soon forgotten.

When the Federal Reserve Act, also known as the Glass-Owen Act, was being debated, *The Wall Street Journal* published a map, one of its first, showing the proposed 12 Federal Reserve districts. It angrily charged that the districts had been gerrymandered to achieve the goodwill of certain politicians. Such tactics were perhaps required to accomplish passage of the Federal Reserve Act in December 1913. President Wilson signed the measure into law on December 23. For weeks C. W. Barron had been preparing his series of articles on the Federal Reserve, which would brilliantly support and analyze the law and the banking reforms being provided. The series, later sold as a book, opened impressively in *The Wall Street Journal* on January 10, 1914: "Next to the Declaration of Independence and the Constitution of the United States, the Federal Reserve Act, signed by President Wilson on December 23, 1913 may be the most important measure ever placed before the people of this country. Upon its wise administration depends the good or ill of a hundred million people and as a nation we shall probably live under it, not only for the 20 years named in the act, but, with amendments found necessary from time to time, for many generations."

Barron, in a preface to the series, recognizing the complexity of his problem, sought to establish a rapport with his readers, including the lay public unacquainted with the arcane craft of banking and generally hostile to bankers. "The miraculous thing about its creation," he wrote of the Federal Reserve Act, "is that it sprang forth in a few hours before the Christmas holiday from a Congress that understood little of currency and less of banking and a Chief Executive and a Cabinet that never made any pretense to a clear understanding of financial principles. Yet a Congress composed of financial experts with an administration and Cabinet composed of leading bankers, probably would not have composed so good a bill. Bankers are not generally progressive or even open-minded. The line of safety must be their rule of procedure and all changes they naturally regard with suspicion."

Having thus elicited a neutral, if not favorable, attitude on the part of his readers, Barron recited the history of the long campaign for banking reform, especially since the great panics of 1893 and 1907, when *The Wall Street Journal* had repeatedly called for a national reserve banking system. He then began, in the simple way he had long recommended to his staff writers, the explanation of the principles:

> The new United States Banking Law is named the Federal Reserve Act. According as the Federal Reserve Board thereunder acts it will be a reserve or a credit expansion act, the results of which no man can foresee. It is not rhetoric to say that the nations of the earth are watching that reservoir of one-fifth of the world's gold money which is in the United States and which may readily be tapped off if the Federal Reserve Act becomes a Federal inflation act.
>
> The purpose of this legislation, however it may work out under wise administration, is to cheapen money and smooth out the rise and fall of its availability for business purposes. . . .
>
> If the Federal Reserve Board in its membership is of the desired quality and character, it could be the most unpopular board that ever sat in Washington. It will turn deaf ears to all political and sectional considerations. The greater the clamor for easy money and credit, the tighter it will hold the reserves. It will keep a watchful eye on every section to see that banking facilities for cornering potatoes in Maine, cotton in Texas, lumber in Oregon, corn in Illinois, wheat in Kansas or stocks in New York are not furnished by any part of the reserve system. It will be watchful over extravagant imports and will know the causes for the rise and fall in prices and will lend a hand in checking the over-extension of credit to any area or industry.
>
> One of the great instruments of our financial independence will be the Federal Reserve Act if rightly administered, because it gives the Federal Reserve Board power to unshackle commerce and make the freest use of credit by transfers. To this end, our commercial manufacturing and distributing interests should welcome the establishment of the regional reserve banks and their branches so that the Government may minimize the expense and time of financial transfers and collections.

Barron's series continued to appear in the *Journal* as well as in his Boston and Philadelphia publications through April 16. Journalists, financiers, and politicians at once recognized that C. W. Barron had brought financial-news reporting to a peak of excellence. It was expository and analytical writing with wide appeal. It explained clearly and simply the significance of a major news event in language authoritative yet easily understandable by all. *The Wall Street Journal* had an unmatched writing star. Barron's fame became national and international as he went on to write other series on complex economic matters. These articles included interviews with Czar Nicholas II of Russia on Russian financial problems and Kaiser Wilhelm of Germany on Germany's financial future. Nearly every political leader, potentate, and financial giant would sit for C. W. Barron's word portraits and analyses for his *Wall Street Journal* and associated publications in the following decade and a half. Newspapermen and magazine writers in turn interviewed Barron wherever he traveled, those in Boston often turning out en masse when he returned from a journey in search of news. Barron never forgot the lessons learned in his interviews, or those he taught in his Federal Reserve series. In articles on world finance after World War I, he insisted that the weapon that really enabled America to effectively help the Allied powers win the conflict and then go on to aid in Europe's rehabilitation was the United States Federal Reserve System, which helped to make the American economy strong.

In addition to Barron's book on the Federal Reserve, published by his own Boston News Bureau, other books based on his *Wall Street Journal* articles were released by leading Boston and New York trade publishers in the years immediately following. Houghton Mifflin Company, Boston and New York, issued *The Audacious War* in 1915, followed by *The Mexican Problem* in 1917 and *War Finance* in 1919. In 1920 Harper & Brothers published *A World Remaking or Peace Finance*, and in 1930 and 1931 Harper & Brothers issued *They Told Barron* and *More They Told Barron*, his edited notes and writings. The selections in *They Told Barron* had previously appeared as a series under that title in *The Saturday Evening Post*. So great was Barron's fame by the 1920s that the president and directors of the Illinois Merchants Trust Company in Chicago, completing their new bank building in the city's Loop, asked Barron to provide two of the eight epigrams on finance chosen to be lettered in gold on the bank walls. The other thinkers included Francis Bacon, Cicero, Junius, Lord Leverhulme, Sir Edward H. Holden, and Hartley Withers, the last two being distinguished British financiers and economists. Barron's contributions:

> All Progress of Men and Nations Is Based Upon the Sacredness of Contracts.
>
> C. W. Barron
>
> The Wealth of Nations Is Not in Prices But Production and Reserves In Store and In Service.
>
> C. W. Barron

Throughout 1913 *The Wall Street Journal*, like President Wilson, believed in "watchful waiting" for the Mexican crisis to be solved, but it disapproved of President Wilson's November 4 ultimatum to Provisional President Victoriano Huerta to resign. Huerta's revolution had cost American lives and property, but the *Journal*, after reviewing the American reasons for intervention in Cuba in 1898, which it said had been justified, declared on November 7 that "no such conditions obtain today in the Mexican crisis. Instead of a popular clamor for war, there is strong sentiment against it. Indeed, the absence of excitement shows that as a whole the country does not consider armed intervention a near possibility. Except for a small minority of the American press, there is no demand for intervention." If the United States was not prepared to use force, it should not issue ultimatums, the paper added. President Huerta, nevertheless, was forced to make way for President Venustiano Carranza in July 1914.

Other events soon attracted the attention of the American people and momentarily devastated the world of Wall Street and the *Journal*. On June 28, 1914, Archduke Franz Ferdinand, heir to the Austrian throne, was killed by a Serb nationalist at Sarajevo. Austria declared war on Serbia on July 28, Russia mobilized the following day, and on July 30 the New York Stock Exchange closed at the final bell to avoid panic, an action made official at an early meeting of board members on July 31. It would remain closed through November. The London Stock Exchange shut down for the first time in its history on July 31, and in New York the directors of the Exchange decreed that stock prices would be fixed indefinitely as of July 30, 1914. By August 4 France and England were at war with Germany, which had invaded Belgium. "The closing of the Exchange was a necessary decision," wrote Robert Sobel in his history *The Great Bull Market*. If the New York Stock Exchange had remained open, he explained, "all the bears in the world would have congregated there to sell." *The Wall Street Journal* approved the order and said that it would not report the activities of the curb traders who gathered at 55 New Street each day to conduct an auction of stocks. On August 12, according to Sobel, the Stock Exchange members decided to try to regulate the outlaw market in New Street by opening trading on a limited basis at the Clearing House. The effort was only partly successful, United States Steel and Anaconda Copper selling at ten points under the July 30 listing. In November, the Exchange resumed trading, but still on a limited basis.

In October 1914, three months after the start of the war in Europe, C. W. Barron took dinner with an old friend from England, Sir George Fish, British banker and economist, and decided that he should go immediately to Europe to report the financial aspects of the conflict. His dispatches from abroad in the next three months were printed in *The Wall Street Journal* and his other financial publications and republished in book form as *The Audacious War*.

When the war began, *The Wall Street Journal*, like the nation, had sought to remain neutral. Barron, in fact, had appeared almost pro-German in September 1913 when he interviewed Kaiser Wilhelm of Germany. "Germany will not seek war but for defense against all powers she will always be prepared," Barron wrote. "Her banking system, her commercial tariffs and scientific educational plan have made Germany strong and the military establishment is an essential part of the whole. You can put her banking system first because it is the magnet around which her commerce and industry move in a steady swing to world-wide conquest."

In 1914, however, Barron foresaw the probable destruction of the German dream of an empire in the Middle East. "Few people," he wrote, "have comprehended the relation of this war to the greatest commercial prizes in the world: the shore of the Mediterranean, Asia Minor, Bagdad with its great Bagdad Railroad headed for the Persian Gulf, Mesopotamia with its great oil fields as a source of power and money and all the lands between the Mediterranean, the Indian Ocean and Asia." After the war President Wilson, too, would describe it as primarily a commercial struggle.

Barron proved also that he was a good war correspondent with a sense of strategy and logistics. "When Germany's conquering heroes came through Belgium, the war was thought to be a battle of human beings rather than fortifications. Now it is a war of machines. Submarines, aeroplanes and motor vehicles are three elements of warfare never before put to test, and the greatest of these so far is the gasoline powered motor vehicle. By this alone Germany may be defeated." Barron referred evidently to the British break through German lines with engine-powered tanks. He was at the front at the time. "This is not an audacious war on the part of the Allies. For them it is a defensive war in which Germans are the attackers and will be the heaviest losers. On the part of Germany it is an audacious war and its very audacity has astounded the whole world. Germany never meant to war against the world collectively. That was the accident of her bad diplomacy." The paragraph provided the title for his book.

Barron returned with "Lessons for the United States to Learn from This War," which he listed: (1) Nations can no longer be isolated units; the whole world is interested in maintaining peace. (2) If the burden of the peace is to be borne by England, she must have a growing empire to support the expense. (3) The United States will learn the value of wealth in national defense. Instead of trying to pull down the wealth of individuals and corporations, the country should recognize that savings and accretions of wealth are for the ultimate benefit of all.

Barron anticipated by more than a generation the one-world idea. "Today all social problems are merged in the greater problem of national existence," he concluded. "Alliances and a larger nationality become national necessities. Man comes into a larger citizenship—a citizen of the whole world. There is, there can be no other solution, no other universal peace. From this war must follow a world federation and international citizenship."

The *Journal*, of course, supported Barron's reports editorially. It detailed what it regarded as tactical mistakes by the seemingly victorious ground forces of the Central Powers and concluded, "In spite of victories and valor, and contrary to that superficial opinion which fails to grasp underlying realities, it can be said that never in the course of the war has the German military situation looked more desperate."

On January 3, 1915, the *Journal* explained its reasons for refusing to publish the quotations of the New Street curb market "right under our window." Stating that the *Journal* had been requested many times to furnish the quotations "in order that financial people might have a complete record," the paper said: "It is true that these quotations in part represented actual transfer of securities where cash was paid over for stocks; but to recognize the existence of this market even at the present time, is to establish a dangerous precedent. . . . The quotations that were made in New Street were no more legitimate quotations than the quotations that were made in Belgium, where people with securities in their pockets, and fleeing from war and starvation, sold them for cash at 30 to 40 per cent discount. . . . Neither in Belgium nor in New Street was there a free, fair or open market."

The paper pointed out that it was, of course, cognizant of the proceedings in New Street from the beginning, for the shouts of the sellers could be heard in its newsroom. "They were of some slight, general news worth, but in no way constituted a legitimate or quotable market. . . . In the interest of public safety, and as a defensive war measure for the protection of the general credit, and for no other reason, would *The Wall Street Journal* refuse to give its subscribers the full details of everything transpiring at the circumference as well as the center of finance."

On January 5, 1915, the *Journal* reported that the London Stock Exchange would reopen on a restricted basis. It hailed the move and observed that "probably no German observer, in his own heart, believes now in the possibility of sweeping to victory so blindly supposed to be within the gift of the irresistible war machine. Sporadic raids upon the British coasts, or even by means of airships upon interior cities, will not disturb the controlling fact in international trade—that Britannia still rules the waves, and can well afford to sacrifice an occasional warship to do so."

The *Journal* also praised the American Federal Reserve Act for contributing to stability. "The country has good reason to be thankful to the new banking system. There is here, admittedly, the possibility of inflation as well as of regulation. But such a possibility . . . ceases to be formidable." *The Wall Street Journal* cheerfully made its contribution to stability by withholding information it regarded as illegal and damaging to the general economic welfare until April 1, 1915, when all trading restrictions were lifted. The paper made no attempt to match the country's general-circulation papers in covering the war, but restricted its reports to economic, financial, and business news. Now Wall Street and the paper were about to benefit from the Great Bull Market, which would continue until 1923, outlasting Charles Dow's prescribed cycle by nearly five years.

President Wilson won the 1916 election largely because "he kept us out of war." America had prospered while England, France, and Belgium fought against Germany and her allies. American farmers never had it better, and factories boomed as orders for war supplies came in and the availability of European goods diminished. Wall Street banks helped to finance the European war and new industrial growth at home, the House of Morgan acting as a clearinghouse for British and French war loans. Thousands of Americans subscribed to British and French war bonds. Some were in the treasury of Dow, Jones & Company, recommended evidently by C. W. Barron.

German undersea attacks on neutral shipping, however, German intrigues in Mexico directed against the United States (which was having trouble with its southern neighbor), and an effective Allied propaganda campaign had turned most Americans against Germany. An important catalyst was a German submarine's sinking of the liner *Lusitania* without warning in May 1915, taking nearly 1,200 lives, 128 of them American. President Wilson had protested the German submarine campaign, and in many cities, Americans marched in preparedness demonstrations. By late 1916, most newspapers, including *The Wall Street Journal*, voiced Americans' desire for an end to Wilson's neutrality policy. When the President asked Congress for authority to arm merchant ships against submarine attackers, the *Journal* replied on February 27th: "Nothing that has occurred since the inauguration of the remorseless submarine campaign amounts to an 'overt act' in his eyes. He therefore has brought forward another phrase which does not represent any advance in the assertion of American rights. This is 'armed neutrality.'

"American ships are blockaded in American ports, and if Congress does not choose to authorize the granting of convoys or the arming of such ships, the German blockade will continue to be disgraceful." On the next day, in another editorial on the subject, the paper concluded, "Mr. Wilson is not asking for the power to do something. He is asking for an excuse to do nothing, and calling it 'armed neutrality.'"

America was moving toward war. C. W. Barron returned home to write a series of articles on American unpreparedness and the government's blunders in financing a preparedness program. "There is only one way to fight this war and that is to conserve and build up capital and bank reserves for every year the war lasts and at least three years thereafter," he wrote early in April as President Wilson issued a call for a joint session of Congress. "Tax the income of the individual after he gets it," Barron advised, "thus beginning the mobilization of the people's money with which any successful war must be fought."

Congress responded to President Wilson's request for a declaration of war on Germany by highly favorable margins, the Senate voting 82 to 6 for such a declaration on April 4 and the House concurring 373 to 50 on April 6, Good

Friday. C. W. Barron was widely in demand as a speaker on his front-line experiences in Europe and on the financial aspects of war, and was interviewed by other newspapers. Late in April the *Boston Sunday Post* provided a generous display of the kind of Barronisms the public was receiving. Said the headlines over the three-column interview, "Big Business Will Put / Patriotism Above Dollars / C. W. Barron Says Man in the Bank / With Man in the Trench Will Bet His / All There Is a God. / Financial World Awaits Guidance from Washington / No Exploiting War for Profit / Steel, Copper and Leather Already in Line to Help." And, said the *Boston Post* in an editorial aside, "There is no person in America closer to the soul of Big Business than the publisher of the *Boston News Bureau*."

Barron went about the country urging the need for unity of the people and Big Business if the war was to be won. By fall he had concluded that his evangelism was successful, for the *Journal* said on October 1:

> Depressing as it may be to the politician who has made capital out of assaults on capital, the war is rapidly bringing about not merely a truce, but a permanent peace between hitherto unenlightened public opinion and the great business interests of the country. The old attacks, in Congress and on the stump, upon capital fall flat or are received with open ridicule. The war, in fact, has revealed much that was hidden from the eyes of the easily deluded voter.
>
> When the man on a salary or the small farmer or the industrious artisan, the minister, the doctor or the lawyer see men who have been held up to them as examples of greed and selfishness, giving of their uttermost to the public good without hope of reward, they have to be an object lesson which the simplest mind may comprehend. It is true that before this country entered the war large profits were made in a strictly limited number of activities. But since the war, with few ignoble exceptions not in any way related to "big business," even this has been sacrificed. The captains of industry have placed all they have . . . at the service of their country.

In the summer of 1917 the *Journal* did not foresee an early peace. It scoffed at Henry Ford, who sent his "peace ship," *Oscar II*, to Europe loaded with idealists who thought they could talk an end to the war. On November 23 the paper said: "There is but one road to peace and that is over the German trenches. All other paths suggested end nowhere, where they do not clearly lead to future wars and the permanent endorsement of the German proposition that might makes right." The *Journal* had no doubt of the ultimate victory. "The German war machine still is powerful when it is flung against demoralized and unarmed troops. But it is increasingly unable to cope with forces like those arrayed against it on the western front. There it is outguessed, outgeneraled and outgunned."

Chapter 7

The Triumphs of C. W. Barron

The American economy soared during the war years, despite tight government controls, as factories and farms met the challenge of Allied requirements and the logistical needs of U.S. forces. *The Wall Street Journal* criticized Wilson and the government for moving too slowly before the declaration of war on April 6, 1917, and for too strict control of finance and industry thereafter. Yet, led by the personal expressions of C. W. Barron, its president, editor, and leading writer, the *Journal* became an ardent supporter of the war effort in editorials, news columns, and the purchase of war bonds, both American and those issued by England and France.

From 1915 through 1918, Barron spent much of his time in Europe, on speaking tours in the United States, or in Boston with Jessie, who was in ill health (she died in May 1918). The New York staff of Dow Jones and *The Wall Street Journal* was directed by Hugh Bancroft, who returned to Barron's employ after successfully completing his Boston Port Authority project. Joseph Cashman became the general manager of Dow Jones, though his official title was treasurer, and Hamilton continued as editor of the editorial page. Walter Barclay, the college graduate from Toronto hired by Barron for $10 a week in 1905, became managing editor after Lockwood Barr, who had succeeded Maurice Farrell. Hamilton was in effect executive editor of the paper. He was assisted by Sherwin Badger, a young *Journal* writer who married Bancroft's daughter, Mary, and who was moving up fast.

The management team was under the personal direction of Barron when he was in New York. When he was not, he bombarded it with telephone calls and ceaseless memoranda dictated to Atherton and the new secretary drafted from the *Journal*, Edward M. Stein. By 1915 the format of the paper had been completely reorganized and the editorial area again departmentalized according to the nature of the news: Stock Market, Bond Market, Public Utilities, Metals and Mining, Money and Exchange, Crops and Commerce, and European Notes, the last received by cable. During the war new groupings were included covering war industries and government rulings and directives. The stock quotations were in larger, clearer type. The daily stock averages were expanded to include 12 industrials and 20 railroads.

There was a new look in graphics, with halftone reproduction of photographs, graphs, bar charts, and war maps illustrating financial reports and the meager war news the paper published. There were new special columns, among them "Wall Street Straws," a melange of financial-area gossip; "Washington Notes" from that bureau; and a humor feature of verses and quips called "Pepper and Salt." The paper frequently printed cartoons culled from other publications. It designated a skilled reporter, James Metcalf, to review Broadway plays on a regular basis; another named Holland wrote a highly competent stock-market analysis each day. On Saturdays there were extensive reviews of books that would especially interest businessmen.

More dramatic than the editorial fare—except for C. W. Barron's articles on the economic aspects of the war, which received special prominence—were the advertising changes. The *Journal's* customary clients, the banks, brokerage firms, and manufacturers (the last wishing to be remembered for their consumer products although they had turned to war production), were joined by two new, flourishing producers of consumer goods, the automobile and cigarette makers. Their copy was prepared by skilled advertising agencies that demonstrated their concept of *The Wall Street Journal* market by the tone and appearance of the special ads they created. Handsome, middle-aged men and elegant women appeared in the *Journal* advertisements. They were shown against backgrounds symbolizing wealth, culture, and leisure. "Ask them at the Polo Match," urged the large Fatima cigarette ads showing young Wall Street types astride their charging ponies, mallets swinging. "Let Fatima smokers tell you." "At Yale and Harvard Fatima leads," the ads proclaimed. Or a distinguished and obviously successful man, mature and poised in white tie and tails in the Metropolitan Opera lounge, looked out confidently at his peers in *The Wall Street Journal* world, his Fatima smoke a delicate wisp, the advertising legend discreetly commenting, "For every man who enjoys fine tobacco, perfectly blended, Fatima. Nothing else will do." The Fatima man puffed a cigarette among the costliest town cars at the New York Auto Show, but his beautiful female companion did not—only a few daring women smoked. Fatimas were priced at 25 cents, while most cigarettes cost between 11 and 20 cents a package. "But, taste the difference!"

Much drearier than the cigarette advertisements and Christmastime ads offering gems, furs, and perfumes with the assistance of svelte, flat-chested young women of the John Held, Jr., school of beauty then in vogue were the enormously practical and profitable automotive displays. Automobile marketers at the time desired only to announce the price and power of their products in *The Wall Street Journal*. Such advertisements were illustrated with simple catalog art, usually spread over an entire page, and sometimes even two pages. All manufacturers were represented in the *Journal*, with one exception: the Ford Motor Company. Generally, the makers displayed their most expensive models in the *Journal*, and one reason Henry Ford was not represented, it was said, was that he sold his cars to the "little man." Among the makes to be found: Jordan, "astounding new price, $2,250—Compare Jordan on these points with any car built—appearance—comfort—performance—economy—detail—finish—body construction—balance—tire equipment—springs and velvet shackles—service record"; Willys-Knight, "with sleeve valve motor," $1,895; Marmon, $3,985, "the famous Marmon 34"; the Franklin, "air-cooled, 20 miles to the gallon, 12,500 miles to the set of tires," price not stated; the Moon Six-585 Petite Touring Sedan, $2,585; Packard touring, $2,975, sedan, $3,975; Studebaker, $1,125 for the roadster to $2,959 for the six-passenger sedan; Hudson six, $1,550. Overland, assuming some little people did read *The Wall Street Journal*, advertised its Overland touring at $750, sedan, $1,145. These and others were in the daily issues and were assembled in January for the *Journal's* annual auto-show edition that ran as many as 28 pages and marked the opening of the annual exhibition at the Grand Central Palace.

Joseph Cashman, a Princeton University graduate who had risen to general manager and manager of production, was chiefly responsible for advertising linage, aided by F. Medley Scovil and his Doremus & Company staff. Shortly after the war, the *Journal* initiated a special classified section of display advertisements soliciting personnel for executive positions and highly skilled jobs, an innovation that would become a top revenue-earner for the paper and would be adopted by general newspapers.

In the closing months of 1918 and the war, C. W. Barron worked with frenzied energy to bring to the *Journal* and his Boston and Philadelphia papers the best wisdom he could find in America and in Europe on aspects of war and peace problems and their possible solutions. His efforts were increasingly successful because world financial leaders were so eager to be interviewed by him. Barron's skill as a researcher, interviewer, and writer was such that he could complete two major series a year, each sufficient in scope and depth to find a place on a major book publisher's list, while also contributing assorted editorials and columns to his papers and engaging in management decisions. A series on Mexico ran early in 1918 and was published as a book that autumn at the same time his ambitious series "War Finance" was appearing in the *Journal*. Later, "War Finance" also appeared as a book.

His most successful series, however, may have been "Mexican Petroleum, Why It Is a Great Peace Stock," which discussed oil production and the American energy problem. The series linked the U.S. automobile industry and the future of the farmer to fossil-fuel energy, and Barron urged the United States to conserve its own oil supplies and ensure the availability of Mexican oil. In the course of this series, Barron departed from his previous policy of criticizing Henry Ford to praise him as one industrialist who could see into the future.

> The ambition of Henry Ford is a gasolene tractor within reach of the farmer. Success here will mean more for the world than all gasolene motor development to date. . . . It would solve the labor problem on the farm; enable the individual farmer to hold broad acres, by quick cultivation and crops quickly stored. The result of such prosperity would be great stores of food, steadying prices for the world.
>
> The farm power, the food power, the sea power, the world power, cry out for gasolene and fuel oil. The Pennsylvania and Indiana oil fields are failing. California is exhausting pocket after pocket. The great oil area of the world today stretches from Kansas to Tehuantepec. The lightest oil is at both these extreme points. The appearance is that the great central reservoirs are in the Mexican field.
>
> Their conservation is a world-wide necessity. Their protection is the duty of both nations.

C. W. Barron was generations ahead of his time. While he did not foresee the oil resources of the Arabian peninsula (nor perhaps the use of oil in the manufacture of agricultural fertilizer, which would be required when the horse vanished from the farms), Barron understood something of energy problems and energy opportunities well before most economists, businessmen, and politicians. He also foresaw the role of the American farm in world economy and that of gasoline motors in remaking America. The readers of *The Wall Street Journal* evidently sensed in Barron a man whose knowledge was broad and sure. The circulation of Barron's publications increased, though only the *Journal* in New York made advertising gains.

In August 1918, Barron again set off for Europe to write still another series, this time entitled "Peace Finance." The outlook for peace seemed good. The German retreat from France was under way, and the United States was at last ready to throw more than a million troops against the enemy.

While Barron was away on his frequent and extended trips, *The Wall Street Journal* staff continued to be busy with service innovations and other special articles and series. Early in 1918 the paper published an in-depth report on United States Steel, covering the company's operations from its beginning on April 1, 1901, to December 31, 1917, which it said was the "most complete tabulation of United States Steel ever published. No shareholder, banker or broker should be without a copy." It became the first of an unending series of similar company profiles. The *Journal* estimated United States Steel's worth at $525,383,487 in 1917, compared with the $138,110,545 in resources the company had when it was organized. The paper also published a series of articles on the production of new airplane motors and predicted that America would eventually lead the world in motorcar and airplane production.

Shortly after Wall Street stocks bounded and sales totaled 752,000 shares on October 1, following the collapse of Bulgaria, one of the Central Powers, the *Journal* published a special series on "Wall Street's War." The articles taunted critics who, the editors asserted, had said it was the fault of financial powers in New York that the United States entered the war. "Our once noisy pro-Germans once coined that phrase, 'Wall Street's War,'" the *Journal* said on October 23 in the first article of the series. "It was the cry of subsidized lecturers and subsidized printing presses. They were to makc such a tumult that no American would dare to stand up and say America's true place was in the ranks of the nations fighting valiantly to pen up the Hun horror." The articles valiantly defended Wall Street's patriotism and contributions to the war effort. "Billions invested [by Wall Street] in Liberty bonds, hundreds of millions poured from never closed pockets into the Red Cross, Belgian relief and other humanitarian efforts, millions mobilized for the war efforts, and men contributed as well as dollars."

Barron's "War Finance" series continued running in the *Journal* while he was in Europe and even after the Armistice on November 11, 1918. "Who won the war?" Barron asked rhetorically on December 19; his answer was not precisely that of most chauvinistic Americans, who asserted that the United States alone was responsible. "England," wrote Barron, "because she swept the seas. France, because she stayed the Hun. Russia, because she divided the Hun forces and thus saved France from early destruction. Italy, because she assisted in the break-up of Austria. And, lastly, the United States, because when everything was hanging in the balance, and the Hun was within fifty miles of Paris, we swept the line from Belleau Wood through Chateau Thierry on to Metz and in five months crowned the Allies as victors. Yet, over and above all, the women won the war. Five million women made good the places of six million men England enlisted. The women of France sustained the men of France, and the Red Cross sustained the women."

Barron's series included interviews with exiled German leaders who spoke of the problem of rebuilding Germany, and Barron predicted that the United States would ultimately be called upon to supply that nation with the funds needed for reconstruction if the Allies persisted in their demands for maximum reparations. He credited the Federal Reserve System with providing America with the financial strength to help save Europe but pointed out that American money could not be expected to accomplish Europe's reconstruction. Inflation, at home and abroad, would be the great postwar danger, the editor declared.

Readers of the *Journal* demanded to know when they could purchase "War Finance" in book form. It appeared early in 1919. His "Peace Finance" series, which won even greater attention in Wall Street, was published as a book by Harper & Brothers in March 1920. The latter series, similar in format to "War Finance," was based on discussions with financial leaders in London and Paris, though most articles were datelined "From the Roof of the World in Switzerland" in the *Journal's* promotional advertising. Barron's notes record talks with British Foreign Secretary Arthur Balfour; Lord Leverhulme, founder of Lever Brothers; Lord Pirrie of Belfast, a leading shipbuilder; Georg Brandes, "the most important man in Europe," according to Barron, and once an adviser to French Premier Clemenceau until the two broke; Claude Grahame-White, pioneer in British aviation; Sir George Paish, English economist and adviser to the chancellor of the exchequer; and Colonel Edward M. House and Bernard Baruch, advisers to President Wilson.

In "Peace Finance," Barron warned Wall Street and Americans generally that they should forget big profits to be made in the reconstruction of Europe and demanded that the U.S. government get out of shipbuilding, electric power (at Muscle Shoals, Alabama), railroads, and other wartime industrial activities as soon as possible. Europeans would need loans, he said, but they would repair their cities and industries themselves because they were no more than one-fourth damaged and they were not built with steel, American-style. "Reconstruction conferences are humbug," Barron wrote. He saw great opportunities for American business and industry in consumer products that both factories and farmers could provide if the government would remove its controls. They could supply a worldwide demand, and they would create jobs for the returning servicemen. Barron again warned that America should be prepared to make loans to the fallen enemy, Germany, if reparation demands were to be met by that country.

"England was the great sufferer by the war," Barron wrote, "but not by her human losses—more than three million casualties with a million dead—nor yet by her financial war burden that is expected to stand at between 35 and 40 billion dollars." Nor, Barron added, from the great German bombing raids. "The 843 bombs dropped in England in 108 raids . . . chipped the Thames embankment, killed 1,413 people and injured 3,407 more and made a map of London look like a peppered paper target . . . but they will leave no visible scar."

"Not German bombs but war wages and war prices have made here volcanic eruptions," said Barron's article from London in March 1919. The British problem, he declared, could be summed up in one word: "Transportation, the power to fetch and carry, to come and go. That sceptre of power, that lance of civilization has been struck down, and it may take more than one Lloyd George [the British prime minister] to set it up again." Barron predicted that Lloyd George would not succeed and that Japan would seize the leadership in world shipbuilding if the American government did not unfetter the shipbuilders. And he did not rule out a speedy German recovery that also could challenge England:

"Germany stands, armed *cap-a-pie* with all her industrial organization and manufactured and stolen machinery, ready to snatch up the commercial prize before Britain can reorganize in transport and rebuild in ships. . . . The United States, forced by war necessities, is building tonnage faster than Great Britain. And the United States must build quickly for herself and not for the world, because England can not alone restore the world's tonnage within a reasonable time." Yet Barron was optimistic for England. "Don't think for a moment that England can be put out of the game in competition, for even at construction cost slightly greater than Japan and the United States, England, with her coal bunkers around the world, her millions of profits from marine insurance, her experience in the multitudinous things that go with ship building and ship sailing would still be in the running and hold the post of advantage."

However, Barron saw socialism threatening England and sure to destroy that nation's power of recovery if it spread. "The government is selling bread at 15 to 20 per cent less than cost. Local tramways are maintained at taxpayers' expense. Rents cannot be increased upon the people and the government promise to provide 300,000 needed new homes has now risen to a million for new houses which only the government can build unless rents are doubled." Barron's gloomier forecast for England turned out to be the most accurate, though another world war would intervene before socialist planning would bring the British economy down.

In January 1919 Barron supplemented his European articles with discussions of Wall Street problems and his own solutions, rather than reporting on the views of European leaders. His "Wall Street Sermons" ran daily when he was in the country and in good health. Mortal sin, in Barron's lexicon, was inflation. The gospel was the credo of the Federal Reserve System as conceived by Congress in 1913, but its managers were by no means beyond criticism. Said his first "Sermon": "When the Federal Reserve System was created, care was taken to divorce it from Wall Street and the Eastern monetary centers. It was never dreamed when the power was taken from Wall Street and put into the Treasury building in Washington that the U.S. Treasury would become the greatest spender and the greatest borrower in the world." Barron demanded the liberation of the Federal Reserve from "government control." "When liberated from government (i.e., political) control, the Federal Reserve was justified in advancing its rate to function as a Reserve bank. It was not justified in advancing rates to force deflation. . . . If the system was created to take panics out of the money markets, it should function in a manner so as not to be a creator of alarms or of chills and fever in business. It is not the function of the bank to regulate the commerce of the country nor the prices of anything except excessive or dangerous money rates. The Reserve Board, however, (now) sets up as a regulator of values. In time the board will find that this is not its function but is beyond its power."

President Wilson, meantime, had presented his Covenant of the League of Nations at the third plenary session of the Peace Conference at Versailles on February 14, 1919. *The Wall Street Journal* editorialists were ready to be tough on Germany but were skeptical about the League. Said the paper on April 12, "If the Peace Conference will give the world a league which is a league and not an altruistic debating society, the United States of America, which is not quite the same thing as President Wilson, will be well content. No league can exist to any useful effect without the United States, and this country cannot enter a league without consent of the United States Senate." The Senate did not accept the League of Nations. President Wilson, after his fortieth speech in support of the Treaty of Versailles embracing the League, collapsed aboard his special train on September 26, 1919, and his campaign for the League was ended. The Senate failed to give the treaty its two-thirds majority.

In June 1919, as the Barron peace-inflation articles were concluded, the *Journal* stated editorially its optimism for a successful solution to the problems of inflation. It expected the Federal Reserve to create a favorable climate for investment in an American industry that was making a rapid conversion to a peacetime economy, and it even assumed that organized labor would cooperate in helping to make American industry and production competitive and profitable in world markets. Earlier, on January 24, 1919, the paper had declared its basic economic position: "Is not the very foundation of our Government—the open secret of the greatness of this country—the unlimited opportunity for the individual, for his energy, his enterprise, and his savings? If we want unlimited improvement—and we shall always want that—we must give unlimited rewards. . . . So, far from concentrating wealth in a few hands, on any honest comparison of national wealth, the

Wall Street, 1870, looking west toward Trinity Church. Charles Dow, Edward Jones, and Charles Bergstresser worked at the Kiernan News Agency (at left) before forming their own financial-news service in 1882.
(The New-York Historical Society, New York City)

The founders of Dow, Jones & Company (clockwise from top left): Edward Jones, Charles Dow, and Charles Bergstresser. In 1884 Dow first published a list of stock averages that would become world famous as the Dow Jones Averages. The professorial, retiring Dow sometimes disapproved of Jones, an excitable, gregarious man who liked the high living of the Gay Nineties. Jones was also a superb writer and editor, but left Dow Jones in 1899 for a brokerage firm. Bergstresser was especially effective in gaining the confidence of leading financiers. "He could make a wooden Indian talk," said Jones, "and tell the truth!"

THE WALL STREET JOURNAL.

VOL. 1.—NO. 1. NEW YORK, MONDAY, JULY 8, 1889. PRICE TWO CENTS.

THE WALL STREET JOURNAL

PUBLISHED daily, except Sundays and Stock Exchange holidays, at 3.15 P.M.

SUBSCRIPTION Price, $5.00 per annum. Delivered by carrier without charge, to subscribers of our regular news service. Reduced rates to bankers and brokers taking a number of copies for mailing. Postage charged on copies ordered for mailing abroad. All subscriptions payable in advance.

ADVERTISEMENTS 20 cents per line. Special rates to advertisers taking space for one, three, six or twelve months. Advertisements may be changed as often as desired without charge.

DOW, JONES & CO.,
26 BROAD STREET,
NEW YORK.

DOMINICK & DICKERMAN,
Bankers and Brokers,
74 BROADWAY AND 9 NEW STREET,

W. G. DOMINICK,
W. B. DICKERMAN,
A. DOMINICK,
G. F. DOMINICK.

Denver 6s and 7s

MC INTOSH & MYGATT,
BANKERS,
DENVER, COLORADO
FRANCIS L. HINE, AGENT

DECKER,
HOWELL
& CO.
Bankers and Brokers,
Nos. 44 & 46 BROADWAY,
NEW YORK.

CHICAGO NEW YORK
S. A. KEAN & CO.
Bankers,
115 BROADWAY.

List of High Grade Municipal Bonds on application.

WE FURNISH MAPS

SURPASS ALL OTHERS

WE ALSO PREPARE AND PRINT

RAND, McNALLY & CO.
323 BROADWAY, N. Y.

Spencer Trask & Co.
BANKERS AND BROKERS,
Nos. 16 & 18 Broad Street, New York.
Albany, N. Y. Providence, R. I. Saratoga.
Transact a General Banking Business.

Average Movement of Prices.

The bull market of 1885 began July 2, with the average price of 12 active stocks 61.49.

The rise culminated May 18, 1887, with the same twelve stocks selling at 93.27.

Prices gradually declined for about a year, reaching the next extreme low point April 2, 1888, the 12 stocks selling at 75.28. The movement since then, counting from one turning point to another, follows:

Last low point	Apr. 2, 1888,	75.28
Rallied to	May 1, "	83.54
Declined to	June 13, "	77.12
Rallied to	Aug. 8, "	85.95
Declined to	Aug. 18, "	83.78
Rallied to	Oct. 1, "	88.10
Declined to	Dec. 5, "	81.88
Rallied to	Feb. 18, 1889,	87.72
Declined to	Mar. 18, "	83.59
Rallied to	June 12, "	91.38
Closed Sat. night	July 6, "	87.71

The Market To-Day.

There is some reason for believing that operators identified with the bear party sent early orders to London to depress Americans in that market as a preparation for the opening here. These orders were faithfully executed, and London at 9.30 was quoted as opening weak and as having become very weak. Prices, however, were only a little below New York closing figures.

London houses were, however, sellers at the opening, and there developed a decided lack of buyers. Lake Shore furnished an illustration. It opened at 101⅜ and was then offered down an eighth at a time to 101 where the next sale was made. This temper started a rush to sell out, during the first hour, prices generally went off from ¼ to 1%. In St. Paul Mr. Randolph had a large selling order; in Union Pacific Mr. Savin made the lowest prices. Reading was sold by Oppenheim & Co., by Mr. Burras and Mr. Wheeler, and Northwest went down on sales by Davis Johnson. Traders made most of the transactions in Atchison although there was evidence of some support when the other market was weakest. The Trust Stocks were not a feature, although weakening in sympathy and on the execution of stop orders.

The drive ended about 11 o'clock and the market had little but there was no general rally. There was a single item of favorable news from Chicago to the effect that New York bankers were exerting a strong influence upon the railway managers in favor of peace. It was said also that a plan would be presented at the Chicago meeting to-morrow for taking care of Burlington & Northern.

The long expected Jersey Central dividend was declared at noon and proved a gratifying disappointment to those who have been expecting a four or five per cent. rate. The directors voted to pay a quarterly dividend of 1½%. No statement was made public, but the conservative management of Jersey Central is evidence that so high a rate would not have then made if the way to maintaining it had not seemed reasonably clear. Jersey Central profited by the Lehigh and Reading strikes last year, but without them was able in the first five months of the year to increase its net earnings $15,870 over those for the same time in 1888.

The news that the bankers syndicate was again exerting pressure upon the railroad managers quickened the disposition of traders to take profits on the short side and apparently led some of the larger bears to endeavor to lessen their following. The result was a decided rally carrying prices up ⅛@⅜% with New England and the Trust stocks leading.

Boston Money Market.

Boston special—The week opens with a decidly firmer feeling in the money market. Money between banks continues in sharp demand 5 and 6% being readily paid for loans this a. m. It is possible that money will be brought over from New York to-night. It is claimed by some that from this time on the clearing house rate will stand 4% at least. The firmness of clearing house money is reflected on the outside.

The banks are not loaning on call to-day less than 6% except in the case of very favored borrowers. Business on time loans is at very low ebb and rates are nominal at 4 or 5%. Very little paper will be offered until rates become more settled.

Philadelphia Market To-day.

Philadelphia special, 2.30—The special feature of Philadelphia market to-day was some heavy liquidation in Reading by bull houses—some 7,000 shares being sold at 22⅜. It was all well taken by New York and good houses here. Outside of this market is dull and traders are not inclined to do much until the situation is cleared.

Washington special. The Treasury accepted $35,800 at 106¼.

Produce Exchange, 2.15.—Wheat firmer on the late cables and some reports of crop damage. 3 loads milling; no exports. Corn quiet; 24 loads export.

Mr. Duncan A. MacTavish, of the British Bank of North America, died this morning aged 72.

Pittsburgh special—Oil brokers here are thoroughly sick of dealing in futures, as it has knocked business out entirely, and a movement was started on the Exchange to-day to get a conference of exchanges and have the amendment on that point rescinded. It seems likely to be carried.

Philadelphia special—Bank statement reserve decreased $367,030.

The Baltimore American puts up a bulletin that there is a rumor to effect that Kilrain has won and Sullivan's backers are holding the wire to hedge on bets.

Clearings Last Week.

Boston special—The Post's table of clearings shows gross exchanges of 41 cities for the week ending July 6, 1889, $1,127,114,523, against $883,993,314 last year, an inc. of 27.5%. Outside of New York the inc. is 14.2%. New York inc. 37.3%. Boston 27.9, Philadelphia 6.8, St. Louis 33.6, San Francisco 18, Cincinnati 7.2, Kansas City 27.5, New Orleans 3.1, St. Paul 2, Omaha 39.5, Minneapolis 15.2, Detroit 2, Denver 70.5, Peoria 12.7, Indianapolis 3.9, Ft. Worth 90.3, Wichita 48.4, Chicago dec. 5%. Milwaukee 1.6, Duluth 44.6 and Topeka 4.9.

For the month of June exchanges of 40 cities show an increase of 22.2%. Outside of New York increase 9.3%. New York increase 30.3%, Boston 18.8%, Philadelphia 12.1%, Chicago 0.1%, St. Louis 18.9%, San Francisco 2.7%, Kansas City 0.4%, St. Paul 2.1%, Omaha 20.8%, Denver 26.6%, Peoria 23.8%, Ft. Worth 47%, Topeka 18.4%. Duluth decrease 45.5%.

For 6 months gross exchanges of 40 cities show an increase of 15.8%. Outside of New York increase 11.9%. New York increase 18.2%, Boston 11.6%, Philadelphia 15.9%, Chicago 7.8%, St. Louis 8.5%, San Francisco 1.9%, Kansas City 11.3%, Omaha 19.5%, Denver 38.9%, Peoria 17.3%, Duluth 13.6%, Ft. Worth 31.8%, Topeka 31.4%.

Bankers Exerting Their Power.

Chicago special—It is stated on excellent authority that the Western presidents are getting positive orders from New York and Boston banking houses to settle the Western troubles at the meeting to-morrow. Some sort of plan to take care of C., B. & N. will be considered, and it is believed that if C., B. & N. can be controled, a general settlement will be effected.

Sales of stocks from 12 to 1—Listed 47,426; unlisted 5,454. Total, listed 194,408 unlisted 27,866.

12.40 p. m.—Slayback sold Union Pacific down.

The first bale of cotton from the South was sold at auction in front of the Cotton Exchange to-day and was bought by Henry Clews & Co. at 16¼.

Press, Cincinnati—It is reported here from a reliable source that Sullivan and Kilrain were fighting at 11.45 a.m. The contest was a long one and Sullivan was having the best of it and was sure to won.

1.35—Van Emburgh sold 2,000 Missouri Pacific.

The Position of Alton.

Chicago special—Vice President McMullin says: Alton is not inclined to reduce rates for the sake of reducing them or to injure the business of its competitors. We have stock, etc., from Missouri River for the reason that we think these rates too high and that the best interests of roads at the Missouri River will be subserved by the small reductions which we desire to put into effect. The fact is that since the roads began to charge live stock shipments on the basis of weight instead of carloads it has cost $65 to $75 per car from Kansas City to Chicago, whereas the old rate was $50 to $60. We reduced the passenger rate to meet the competition of scalpers who were selling tickets via other lines at a reduced rate.

Chicago special to Jones, Kennett & Hopkins—Local securities: Chicago City R'y 59@60, Chicago Pass. R'y 107½ asked, Diamond Match Co. 150@151, North Chicago Street R'y 122½ asked, West Chicago Street R'y 100@100½, Gaslight 5s 97½@97¾. Consumers 5s 96 asked.

Jersey Central Dividend.

Jersey Central has declared a dividend of 1½% for the quarter ending June 30, payable Aug. 1, 1889. Books close July 15. This dividend is declared with expectation of its continuance, in accordance with the statement in the annual report on page 11.

Bulletin, New Orleans, says fight took place near Richburg. On account of there being no communication with the place particulars won't be had till the return of the train, which is due at 2 p.m.

The Aspen Mining and Smelting Co. has declared the 9th regular monthly dividend of 20 cents per share to stockholders of record, payable on and after July 12th at office. Transfer books close July 10th and reopen July 15th.

2 p.m.—Slayback, Kirkner and other traders made the rally.

Boston special—Atchison officials say that in their opinion the stock is unassessable. In case of reorganization, however, stockholders would undoubtedly be willing to contribute rather than permit a foreclosure. Advices from Director C. K. Halliday, Topeka, Kan., say that the crop prospects of that State are better than ever before known. The wheat crop will be twice that of last year and the oat crop three times as great. Corn in the southern part of the State is already from 4 to 6 feet high, and commencing to tassel out. President Strong also confirms the report. There is little question but that Kansas will have a tremendous business this year and the future of Atchison depends on the rates it gets for carrying. The winter wheat crop has already commenced to move in some sections and will be moving freely by August.

Wheeling & Lake Erie has declared the regular quarterly dividend of 1%, payable Aug. 15. Books close Aug. 1 and reopen Aug. 16.

Boston special—Bank statement shows a decrease of $418,148 in the reserve.

2.10 p. m.—Kirkner bought 1,000 St. Paul and Tappin bid it up.

Philadelphia special—The Insurance Company of North America declares a semi-annual dividend of 7½%, payable on demand.

Boston special—The Boston & Albany is understood to be negotiating for the sale of its large granite building at Springfield and the early removal of the offices established there to this city. The Connecticut River Railroad Co. is it is said disposed to buy the block. The Boston & Albany Co.'s asking price is $150,000, a figure much below the original cost of construction.

Sales of stocks from 1 to 2—Listed 43,777; unlisted 3,336. Total—Listed 244,186; unlisted 88,066.

W. HOWARD GILDER,
J. C. KAHRER, Members N. Y. Stock Exchange
T. H. POWERS FARR.

GILDER, FARR & CO.
Bankers and Brokers
31 & 33 BROAD STREET,
NEW YORK.

Stocks and Bonds Bought and Sold on Commission.
DEALERS IN INVESTMENT SECURITIES.

OFFICE OF THE ASPEN MINING & SMELTING COMPANY,
No. 54 Wall St.,
NEW YORK, July 8th, 1889.

The 9th regular monthly dividend of twenty cents per share has this day been declared on the stock of this Company (200,000 shares) payable at the office of the Company on and after the 12th day of July to stockholders of record. Transfer books will close Wednesday, July 10th, at 3 o'clock p. m. and reopen Monday, July 15th, at 10 o'clock a. m.

J. L. TILTON, Secretary.

CENTRAL RAILROAD CO. OF NEW JERSEY
119 Liberty Street.
NEW YORK, July 8, 1889.

A dividend of one and a half per cent. has this day been declared, payable August 1st prox., for the quarter ending June 30th ulto. The transfer books will close on Monday, the 15th inst., and open on Friday, August 2d.

By order of the board.
J. W. WATSON,
Treasurer.

Toledo, Ann Arbor and
North Michigan Bonds
ON CADILLAC EXTENSION.
FOR SALE BY
CHARLES M. WHITNEY & CO
Bankers,
96 BROADWAY.

J. H. STERLING & CO.
Stock Brokers,
SPECIAL ATTENTION TO TRUST STOCKS.
30 Broad Street, New York.

HORACE L. HOTCHKISS & CO.
Bankers and Brokers,
34 & 36 WALL STREET, NEW YORK

J. W. OGDEN & CO
Bankers and Brokers
No. 4 Equitable Building, New York City.
DIRECT PRIVATE WIRES CHICAGO AND BOSTON.

New York Equipment Co.
RAILWAY EQUIPMENT,
10 WALL STREET, NEW YORK

PURNELL, HAGAMAN & CO.
Bankers and Brokers,
104 BROADWAY, NEW YORK
Stocks, Bonds, Grain, Provisions and Petroleum Bought and Sold for Cash or on Margins.
BRANCH OFFICES:

W. S. LAWSON & CO.
Bankers and Brokers,
49 Exchange Place | 24 Exchange Place
New York | Boston

Page one of the first *Wall Street Journal,* issued July 8, 1889. A year's subscription was offered for $5. Circulation at the time was estimated at 1,500; by 1982, daily circulation surpassed 2 million, the highest in the United States.

Opposite page: Dynamic Boston publisher and celebrated financial writer Clarence W. Barron (top left) bought control of Dow Jones in 1902. His wife, Jessie (top right), ruled the boardroom for ten years until C. W. stepped in. Her daughter Jane (bottom left) later became the principal Dow Jones stockholder. In 1907 Jane married Hugh Bancroft (bottom right), blue-blooded Harvard man, lawyer, and engineer who succeeded Barron as Dow Jones president after Barron's death in 1928.
Above: The building at 42–44 Broad Street, where the company moved its headquarters in 1894.

Right: Thomas Woodlock, the British-educated editor of *The Wall Street Journal* who joined the company in the days of Dow and Jones. He ran the paper under Jessie Barron until 1905, when he resigned in a dispute over editorial and business policy, but returned in 1928 to serve as an editor and columnist. **Below:** William Peter Hamilton, like Woodlock, was an erudite, able editor. He is credited with fusing Dow's writings on market economics into the famed Dow Theory. Hamilton continued to edit the *Journal* until the last days of his life in 1929.

Opposite page: The social triumph of C. W. Barron's lifetime—the visit of President Calvin Coolidge and his wife, Grace, at Barron's Cohasset summer home in 1925. Apparently even the ebullient Barron, shown here in his favorite commodore's uniform and flanked by his famous guests, couldn't coax a smile from Silent Cal. Taking the President on a tour of his dairy farm, the proud publisher boasted about his imported Guernsey bull. "Some bull!" is reported to have been Coolidge's response.

Above: Kenneth C. Hogate, whom Barron thought of as the son he never had and whom he groomed as his successor. Hogate rose rapidly and followed Bancroft as president in 1933. **Right:** William Henry Grimes, Pulitzer Prize winner and the *Journal*'s resident curmudgeon, ran the editorial page for 17 years and wrote some of the paper's most famous editorials.

rewards were its greatest and wisest distributors." The *Journal* was discussing the railroad business primarily, but it said that the American motor, airplane, and farm-tractor businesses would need the profit incentive to meet worldwide challenges and opportunities. And, in another editorial, it predicted that organized labor leaders would prove receptive to its ideas: "While, naturally, the great employers of labor read what is written in these columns, it is probably not so generally known that the more enlightened labor leaders welcome such discussion upon facts before them, and are by no means inaccessible to argument. Both sides are seeking, with more or less clarity, what is essential, if high wages, together with high standard of comfort (which is not necessarily the same thing), are to be maintained."

The year 1920 was to build to a high plateau for Barron and *The Wall Street Journal*. His directors voted him a salary of $60,000 a year plus $20,000 expenses, a reflection of the growth of circulation to more than 20,000, excellent advertising returns, and good profits. The plaudits for Barron's work were impressive, including a letter from Dr. Charles W. Eliot, president emeritus of Harvard University and editor of the Harvard Classics, or Dr. Eliot's Five-Foot Book Shelf, the repository of printed culture in thousands of American homes. Dr. Eliot had written from Cambridge: "Dear Mr. Barron, I have been reading with interest your articles on War Finance. Your style is always vivid and often somewhat jolting, like a corduroy road; but your sentiments and opinions always commend themselves to my judgment."

B. C. Forbes, the New York editor of *Forbes*, the prestigious financial magazine, called upon Barron for an interview and quoted him as saying: "We produce 60% of the world's cotton, 62% of the copper, 50% of its iron and steel, 85% of the automobiles, 45% of the grain, 75% of the agricultural machinery, 70% of the telephone apparatus, 85% of the typewriters and 50% of the ships. We lack only intelligent direction from Washington of the country's supply of gold, money and credit. Our Federal Reserve System could and should make more credit available to legitimate business and still have a percentage of gold reserves available larger than England or any other country."

"Mr. Barron," wrote B. C. Forbes, his leading rival as a financial writer and editor, "is the foremost financial editor in the world."

Without doubt, C. W. Barron was the *Journal's* glittering performer in print and in person among his peers in the financial world. He also was its cantankerous, demanding boss, capable of occasional viciousness, especially when he was in extended contact with Hugh Bancroft. He and Bancroft continued to quarrel whenever the two were together in New York or Boston, the two cities where Bancroft was required to divide his time. The reason may have been, as biographer William Moise and some of Barron's secretaries have suggested, the terms of Mrs. Jessie Barron's will. Barron had no objection to the provision giving "one-half of the stock which I own in Dow, Jones & Company, a joint stock association, and one-half of the stock which I own in the Wall Street Building Company, a corporation, to my daughter, Jane W. W. Bancroft" (her other daughter, Martha, had died in 1916). But then the will went on to Item 2: "I give and bequeath one-half of the stock [which again was legally described] to my son-in-law, Hugh Bancroft, in trust, to pay the income thereafter to my husband, Clarence W. Barron, for his life, and upon his death to hold said stocks or any portion thereof, and to invest and re-invest the proceeds thereof at his discretion, holding such proceeds upon the same trust." The trust was to continue until the youngest surviving grandchild reached the age of 25. Thus Bancroft could wield power so long as his wife concurred, and their relationship was close and enduring, but Bancroft's very consideration for the situation of his father-in-law evidently irked the older man.

Barron could beat down Hugh Bancroft, and he punished him by insisting on having Jane Bancroft and his grandchildren (who were, with one exception, Hugh's children) close around him whenever possible, especially after the deaths of his stepdaughter Martha and his wife, Jessie. When Barron decided to take a vacation, he would invite Jane and the children, including Mary Bancroft, Hugh's daughter by his first wife, and little Martha Endicott, to Florida or even to Europe while ordering Bancroft to stay home to tend the shop. Hugh inevitably stayed on the job as instructed, but Barron had to tolerate his presence at Cohasset since Bancroft also owned a summer home there in addition to his Boston home not far from Barron's.

When Barron traveled, he did it in style and with ample retinue. On vacations this included his stepdaughter, grandchildren, two secretaries, a male nurse, and the staff of his Beacon Street and Cohasset homes. The New Haven railroad on at least one occasion put on an extra coach when Barron arrived with his family, secretaries, servants, and 60 pieces of luggage. Barron was fond of automobile travel, but only occasionally for recreation, as when he accompanied his old friend Charles Glidden, who had driven and ferried an automobile around the world. Usually the business trips by car were short, with the editor and publisher accompanied by Baldwin, his chauffeur, Mikkleborg, his Swedish male nurse, and a secretary. Mikkleborg carried a urinal as part of Barron's health paraphernalia to provide for Barron's relief when they were in transit. The results were carefully noted, and there was jubilation if they totaled seven fluid ounces, according to secretary Raymond O'Brien.

Barron's summer home at Cohasset continued to be his favorite refuge after the death of Jessie, though he sometimes retreated for total seclusion to his nearby dairy farm, where the manager and a staff of 30 cared for the Barron herds and milk and delivery facilities. The Cohasset summer house that Barron bought in anticipation of his marriage to Jessie was in her name when she died, and she willed it to Mrs. Jane Bancroft with the provision that her husband could reside in it during his lifetime. Barron owned the family dairy farm, which constantly lost money and which Barron somewhat maliciously willed to Bancroft. But Cohasset was, in effect, neutral ground for Barron and Bancroft most of the time.

Barron's Back Bay mansion at 334 Beacon Street, Boston ("on the water side," he always said in mentioning it), was a turreted castle enclosing 26 rooms. It was built in 1871 and reconstructed by Cram and Hoodhue, leading church architects, who installed the library and elevator, in 1902. It was said that Barron had 18 telephones in the house, placed at strategic places, such as Barron's bathroom, and scattered about for the household staff. Barron continued to prefer Boston over New York. He felt almost as secure in his Back Bay mansion as he did at Cohasset. In Boston or at Cohasset he could royally indulge in his favorite activities—bridge, yachting (he was commodore of the Cohasset Yacht Club), fishing, motoring, and, above all, eating. Josie, his favorite cook, knew his preference in foods; he especially loved lobster, Boston scrod, and vegetables heavily laced with butter, according to Moise. His secretaries constantly bought Page and Shaw chocolates and salted nuts, which were at Barron's table for all meals except breakfast. Barron did not go hungry at breakfast, however. Secretary Edward Stein described one morning meal that included—at one sitting—juice, stewed fruit, oatmeal, ham and eggs, fish, beefsteak, fried potatoes, hot rolls and butter, and coffee with cream from Barron's own Guernsey herd.

Barron was a voluptuary not only at the table but also in his bath, where, with the water at exactly 104 degrees, he dictated many mornings attended by his secretary and his nurse and masseur, Mikkleborg. Barron also dictated while at stool, a duty his secretaries especially detested. Wherever he might be, Barron dictated memoranda, letters, notes for his autobiography, notes for his articles, and articles themselves. He spoke rapidly and crisply so that sometimes two secretaries worked simultaneously to insure that nothing would be missed. According to Moise, he received visitors while in his bath, "but only on business." When he dressed, Mikkleborg made sure his pants were buttoned properly and tied his shoes, shoes Barron himself had not seen in years.

Despite his eccentricities, his outbursts of temper, his contempt for slow-thinking people, and his frequent ill health as a result of intemperate eating, Barron got on well with his staff most of the time and was as decisive and forceful in the management of his properties as he was in his writing. Exceptions were his holdings in Philadelphia, the Philadelphia News Bureau and the *Philadelphia Financial Journal*, which generally were in financial difficulties requiring credit infusions from Boston or New York. Dow, Jones & Company and *The Wall Street Journal* especially prospered during the post-war bull market, which began in August 1921. Barron was much at home in Wall Street despite his preference for Boston. He was the leading defender and advocate of the establishment, an adviser to Wall Street and the government when Republicans were in power, and also Wall Street's most effective critic. Barron demanded total loyalty and integrity from his staff and did not hesitate to denounce deceit and fraud wherever he found it. One of his exposé series, published in the *Boston News Bureau*, resulted in a major libel suit in July 1920, though it was actually triggered by a Barron interview in the *Boston Post* on July 26. "Ponzi Sues C. W. Barron For $5,000,000," said a headline in the *Boston Herald* on July 30. Charles "Bellboy" Ponzi, a Boston speculator and confidence man who claimed to be a former hotel executive but who the evidence showed to have advanced only as far as bellboy, evidently did not read Barron's financial newspaper, but he saw the charges Barron leveled at him in the *Post*:

> Last night the *Post* asked C. W. Barron, publisher of the *Boston News Bureau* and recognized internationally among the foremost financial authorities of the world, to give an opinion of Ponzi's operations. Mr. Barron said, "No man of wide financial or investment experience would look twice at a proposition to take his money upon a simple promise to pay it back with 50 per cent increase in 90 days which means a 200 per cent annual rate. According to the facts thus far gathered the whole transaction looks to me like an immoral one. Exchanges under international agreements are legitimate but it is illegitimate for people to make use of the postal regulations between governments to make money at the expense of somebody's government. [Ponzi used purloined investments to buy international postal union coupons, taking advantage of favorable exchange rates.]
>
> "Right under the eyes of government court officials, Mr. Ponzi has been paying out U.S. money to one line of depositors from deposits made by a succeeding line. It is time for responsible officials to act in the Ponzi matter. Our government and our laws to protect the poor are being brought into contempt."

In an era when uninsured newspaper publishers sought to avoid libel suits and even put their publishing properties in their wives' names to protect their personal fortunes, Barron had deliberately attacked Ponzi in a way to attract legal action to himself. Ponzi, Barron's own paper said, was making a fortune by selling Florida land described as being "near" Jacksonville, though it was 65 miles distant, and then made more money by pretending to let fellow Italians in on his Florida land deals by taking their funds on an oral promise to pay the kind of profits Barron described. Ponzi paid back some of the money with high interest from funds eagerly pushed on him by hardworking countrymen who read little English and probably never saw the *Boston News Bureau*. But, evidently, they did read the *Boston Post*, and Ponzi could not ignore Barron's challenge.

Barron's attack, both in the *Boston News Bureau* and the *Post*, also prodded law officials into action. On August 23 they arrested Charles Ponzi, who was found to have a background in confidence games. He was convicted after a series of trials, sentenced to seven and a half years in prison on state and federal charges, and deported to Italy. Shortly before the outbreak of World War II, Ponzi emigrated to Rio de Janeiro, where he died in poverty in 1949. His libel action against Barron was dismissed without trial.

In the summer of 1920 Barron also began his personal involvement in national politics, a sequence of experiences that, he said, gave him his greatest satisfaction. In the spring he had been invited to the home of H. B. Endicott, the New England industrialist who founded the Endicott-Johnson Company. He was father of Barron's son-in-law H. Wendell Endicott and the grandfather of little Martha Endicott. Governor Calvin Coolidge of Massachusetts and his wife, Grace, were also guests. The garrulous C. W. Barron and taciturn Calvin Coolidge chatted at dinner and then engaged in a protracted conversation about finance and politics when the men adjourned for liqueur and cigars. Barron and Coolidge became friends that night. Barron was fascinated by the governor and immediately began urging him for national office in his newspapers. Barron rode the Republican delegate train to the national convention in Chicago, June 8–12, which nominated Warren G. Harding of Ohio for president and Coolidge for vice-president.

Barron sent back favorable reports on the nominations and personally campaigned for Harding and Coolidge, though he did not call for endorsement of the Republican ticket in *The Wall Street Journal*. For the first time, however, the paper came close to ignoring Charles Dow's policy of no national political endorsements. The *Journal* predicted victory for the Republicans, who won by a popular vote of 16,152,200 to 9,147,353 for the Democrats, James M. Cox of Ohio, the presidential nominee, and Franklin D. Roosevelt of New York for vice-president.

Despite his satisfaction with the political situation and the personal recognition he received, Barron was not satisfied with the progress his companies were making. He was past 65, his health was not good, and he began to worry about his successor, though he had no intention of retiring. Hugh Bancroft, he thought, was good enough in his way, especially when a man with legal training was required, but Bancroft was not a newspaperman and Barron, in any event, tended to distrust an executive who was "overeducated." Barron felt he needed a reliable newsman he could train. Walter Barclay, the Canadian who had become managing editor, wouldn't do. Barron told Barclay to look for a good man to train as his successor. Barclay, assuming probably that he would get a promotion, promised to look hard.

Barron was also unhappy over one of his continuing problems—his relations, or lack of relations, with Henry Ford. He had criticized Ford's peace-ship venture during the war and also Ford's negative attitude toward Wall Street and the New York bankers, as evidenced by his refusal to make Ford Motors stock available to the public. Ford needed Wall Street and the investment public, Barron believed, and his *Wall Street Journal* definitely could use Ford Motor Company advertising. And Barron was annoyed that, among all the world's tycoons, he had never interviewed Henry Ford, the man most people asked him about when he traveled in Europe. Barron had written favorably of Ford in his Mexican petroleum series; he knew that Ford was one of the most significant of American industrialists. He told Barclay he wanted an overture made to Ford that would bring him an interview appointment. In the spring of 1921, Barclay produced an extensive profile of the Ford Motor Company, one of a series on the automotive industry. It appeared while Barron was in New York so it may have been approved by him, but the article was unsigned and definitely was not written by Barron, nor did it in any way help his campaign to win the favor of Henry Ford. Said the *Journal's* headline over the story, "Ford Riches Curtailed by Lack of Wisdom / Immense Income Went into Uneconomic Expansion of Business / Fortune Tied Up in Enterprise."

Mostly, in 1921, the *Journal* was involved in its favorite activities, the defense of Wall Street against detractors and attacks on socialists. "Wall Street has been under incessant investigation since 1905," said the paper on March 14. "There has hardly been a day when some committee to investigate at least part of it has not been in existence. By these investigations it has been related to matters with which it has no connection." It then named the Lockwood committee of the New York State Senate as the current violator of fair play and said, "The senators who speak of the way the public is being robbed by wash sales and bucket shops know nothing about the stock exchanges." (Wash sales, wherein one broker pretends to buy stock from another, thereby falsely increasing the price, were known to the New York Stock Exchange as early as 1848 but had been barred by the Stock Exchange for more than 50 years. Bucket shops posted stock prices on blackboards, enabling the public to gamble on whether the prices would rise or fall. Frequently the numbers chalked on the boards had no relation to real activity in the stock market, and they never were actual quotations from the Exchange. Such shops in New York and other cities were usually operated by saloonkeepers and professional gamblers and criminals.)

The *Journal* blamed the "Hearst Press" for the latest assault on Wall Street by the New York legislature. On May 10, 1921, it openly attacked the *New York American*, an occasional advertiser in the *Journal*, for perpetrating its own kind of fiction—publishing stock reports it claimed to be its own but which were taken from the Dow Jones Averages, the *Journal* charged, "averages which have been the standard for comparison for a quarter of a century." Lawyer Hugh Bancroft consulted company attorneys and established a procedure for licensing the use of official Dow Jones Averages, a system that continued to be used.

In the same editorial, the paper defended the Dow Theory, replying to a reader who complained that he assumed a bull market was to prevail on Wall Street on the basis of a *Journal* Dow Theory editorial. He had followed the Theory but had not made any money, he wrote. The paper replied that the reader did not understand the editorial, which had merely asked the question "Is there a foundation for a bull market?" on March 30. The editorial, probably written by Hamilton, the paper's Dow Theory expert at the time, said that the Dow Theory was never intended to guide gambling in the market but was merely a barometer. Thereafter, *The Wall Street Journal* abjured discussions of the Dow Theory except to reiterate that it was not a system for gambling in the market.

Early in 1921 Barron and Bancroft again entered upon a truce, and Bancroft contributed one of his most profitable and enduring ideas for Dow, Jones & Company. Why not seize upon C. W. Barron's fame to establish a new financial weekly magazine to be called *Barron's*? Such a magazine could be edited by the staffs of Barron's newspapers; it could use idle press time in either New York or Boston; all the logistics could be provided by existing personnel and resources.

Barron modestly opposed the use of his own name for such a publication but pronounced Bancroft's proposal an act of genius. Planning would be required and a budget would be needed, yet there was no doubt that Dow, Jones & Company and the *Boston News Bureau* could handle the challenge. Bancroft was told to go ahead with the planning.

Chapter 8

Barron Finds a Successor

At first, launching *Barron's, The National Business and Financial Weekly*—the name first chosen for the new C. W. Barron publication—was a bit like initiating a Sunday edition of *The Wall Street Journal* or the *Boston News Bureau*, projects briefly considered as Hugh Bancroft's proposal was being studied. Despite Barron's objection, which may have been more affected than genuine, his name was quickly chosen for the venture; his family, including even the grandchildren, voted for it. The beauty of Bancroft's idea entranced Barron, restoring his confidence in his son-in-law: Not only would *Barron's* showcase the financial editor who had been termed the world's greatest by none other than B. C. Forbes, but it would present Harry Nelson of the *Boston News Bureau* as "The Trader," the name by which Nelson was widely known in New England. Barron also was certain he could attract world-renowned financial writers in London, Paris, and Berlin to write for the magazine at relatively little cost. All other expenses, except those for newsprint and overtime for the printers, would be borne initially by the *Journal* and *News Bureau* budgets. The *Boston News Bureau* press would be used, and the publication offices would be in the Bureau's building at 30 Kilby Street, Boston; the news and advertising departments would be housed with Dow, Jones & Company and Doremus & Company, 44 Broad Street, New York. All operations would be financed from cash flow.

Bancroft basked again in his father-in-law's regard, though their restored good relationship did not cause Barron to call off his search for an editorial successor. *Barron's, The National Financial Weekly*, the name finally chosen, would be published every Monday using the Boston press on Saturday. It would follow the format of the *Boston News Bureau*, which was that of a magazine, but a better grade of magazine paper would be used. Advertising would, of course, be accepted through Doremus & Company; the subscription price would be $10 a year; and the publication would sell for 20 cents on the newsstands. The motto of *Barron's* was provided by Barron himself: "The application of money to practical ends." The scope of *Barron's* would be well beyond Wall Street, covering the international financial world, and Barron himself would write on international economic problems. There would be elaborate Dow Jones charts, however, and William Peter Hamilton, editorial-page editor of *The Wall Street Journal*, was directed by Bancroft to prepare a series of articles on the Dow Jones Averages and the Dow Theory for early issues. Hamilton also would serve as executive editor of *Barron's*.

Many Wall Street investment counselors would have considered the spring of 1921 an especially inappropriate time for the launching of any major financial venture, especially one relating to the money markets. After a flourishing bull market following the war—a period in which the United States retooled, captured an increasing share of the European export market, and became increasingly a creditor nation—the country and Wall Street went into a severe if temporary economic recession. Wage cuts were being announced by many large industries, and unemployment, estimated at more than 4 million by the U.S. Department of Labor, was the worst since the 1907 panic. But Barron regarded such conditions as a challenge, especially when he learned that Bancroft and Cashman could finance *Barron's* without new capital. "What we want is confidence," Barron told Bancroft as they prepared the promotional statement to announce the new magazine; "A fresh financial publication based on sound sources of information and policy should be a helpful factor in assuring a return of confidence in a world of business." Bancroft included the precise words in the initial announcement. He also provided his own slogan, "*Barron's*, the new National Financial Weekly for those who read for profit." The first issue was scheduled for May 9.

C. W. Barron was off again for Europe in April. He wished to obtain the articles required for early issues of the new magazine plus magazine contributors and correspondents for the *Journal*. He was also eager to gain acceptance for his own solution to the German reparations problem. If Germany did not pay reparations, France would not pay its war debts, and Barron feared the entire economic order of the western world might collapse. His solution was a relatively simple one. The Allied Powers, including the United States, would allow Germany to issue bonds free of income tax in the countries where purchased. It was an idea that would be adopted for the sale of municipal bonds in the United States, but Barron's international plan would require agreement among several nations, including Germany itself. That his proposal was not warmly welcomed even in Washington did not in any way discourage the always optimistic editor.

He had talked with Vice-President Calvin Coolidge, Secretary of State Charles Evans Hughes, Eliot Wadsworth, assistant secretary of the treasury, and Senator Henry Cabot Lodge of Massachusetts about his idea for tax-free bonds, Barron noted in his diary. None gave him real encouragement, though all were interested. Said Secretary Hughes, "At present in the United States the temper of the people would by no means stand for aid to Germany on the basis of tax free bonds." Senator Lodge was more negative: "What Germany must do is repudiate her internal debt." And Barron said he replied, "Not repudiate, but set aside. There is no necessity for destroying the hope of the people that they may ultimately pay themselves."

He did not record the comment of Coolidge, but the vice-president took him to see President Harding. Barron was convinced that the government wanted him to sound out European leaders on his plan. He agreed that he would not publicize what he was doing until after discussions were complete.

Upon arriving in London, Barron first turned his attention to articles for *Barron's* magazine. Various British editors agreed to become contributors, but they would not be available for the first issues. Barron knew that he could easily provide what was required himself, and he alerted Herbert N. Casson, London correspondent of the *Journal*, to the need. It was agreed that Casson would write on the activities of the Fabian Society, a group of socialists, and the radicals in postwar British economic affairs while Barron would, of course, discuss war debts and reparations.

On publication day, May 9, 1921, *The Wall Street Journal* and Barron's papers in Boston and Philadelphia handled the total job of promoting *Barron's*. They did their work well, for the vendors in all three cities sold out. Said the *Journal's* advertisement the morning of the 9th:

> Out Today—*Barron's, The National Financial Weekly*.
>
> Edited by C. W. Barron of *The Wall Street Journal—Boston News Bureau—Philadelphia News Bureau*. [William Peter Hamilton, the executive editor, received no billing.] "European Unsettlements," first of a characteristic series written by Mr. Barron from Paris, London and Berlin. In this series Mr. Barron gets to the heart of the reparations problems.
>
> "British Soviet Smashed," written by Herbert N. Casson from London.
>
> Other features—"Frisco Bonds," "The Steel Stocks," "Union Pacific's Recovery," "An Inside View of Wall Street," "Investment Suggestions."

Barron's was well received in Wall Street, Boston's State Street, and Washington, but the mail-subscription appeal fell short of expectations. So a six-month trial subscription price at $1 was proffered instead of the $10 annual subscription rate first announced, and the offer continued throughout the year. But *Barron's* magazine had no trouble attracting advertising, gaining enough to keep the publication in the black almost from the beginning. Within a few weeks the format was improved and the second issue provided brighter, selling headlines. Barron's own article in the May 16 issue asked in its opening, "Is Germany deliberately ruining itself to cheat the Allies? . . . What has been the result of Wall Street's speculation in marks?" It ran under the sensational headline "Is Germany Committing Suicide?" Later William Peter Hamilton's long series on the Dow Theory, "Forecasting a Bull Market, Dow's Theory Applied to the Recovery after 1917," got similar treatment.

When the first issue of *Barron's* appeared in Boston and New York, C. W. Barron was in Paris, a houseguest of Sir Basil Zaharoff, whom he described in his notebook as the "richest and most powerful man in Europe." Under an agreement with friends in Washington, Barron could not report on his discussions with Sir Basil and various British and German leaders since they concerned his reparations plan. Sir Basil, who "bought ships right and sold them right," Barron said in an interview published later, had no interest in his reparations idea. Nor did Horace Finaly, managing director of the Banque de Paris et des Pays-Bas, who told the editor, "As to an international loan tax-free, that is a political question and I try to keep within my own sphere as a banker."

Barron refused to quit. He had secret meetings with Germans in Berlin and with Austrians in Vienna. "The altruistic character of his campaign," wrote Pound and Moore, "is more marked because he renounced at the outset all publicity regarding his conferences with foreign statesmen. . . . The desire of those statesmen for no public discussion in advance was scrupulously observed." Not until after the death of Barron seven years later was the full scope of his 1921 spring mission to Europe revealed.

Barron returned to America discouraged and in ill health. He at last realized that his reparations plan was dead. Possibly he began to understand that he was out of touch with public opinion in both Europe and the United States. For several months he appeared to abandon his interest in international financial problems and turned his attention to his own company and to Wall Street. His notebook records interviews on American financial and political affairs and talks about President Harding, including gossip and the possibility that the President could be blackmailed. "The President likes girls," Barron noted. He also recorded Harding's visits to "the little red house," which in Washington was referred to as "the little green house"—it was of red brick and had green trim. Harding drank and played poker there. With each of Barron's notes on Harding's scandalous behavior was the observation "Coolidge knows nothing of this." A later entry concerned Coolidge's conduct once he became president: "He always cleared his desk in the morning and then was ready to receive visitors. On one of these occasions when there had been whisperings and conspiracies well known to Coolidge as to how he should be shoved aside, . . . a member of Congress called and said, 'I suppose you are very busy.' President Coolidge quietly responded, 'Well, not particularly; but there are those who are.' "

At some point in 1921, Barron decided to step up his search for the young man who could be trained to succeed him as editor of *The Wall Street Journal* and also for someone to effect a truce and a peace with Henry Ford. It turned out that the discovery of one man helped to solve both problems. Barclay, instructed some months previously to find a successor and to pave the way for a Barron interview with Henry Ford, discovered a newspaperman who had interviewed Ford and was a rising young editor on the *Detroit News*. He was Kenneth Craven Hogate, a husky fellow of 24 who came from a newspaper family in Indiana. K. C. Hogate was called Casey by his friends. He was six feet two and carried his 300 pounds more gracefully than did Barron, who at the time had pared down to 297 but was still grotesquely fat at five feet five. Barron was scheduled to reenter the Kellogg sanitarium at Battle Creek, Michigan, that had been recommended to him by the oil man he had met in Mexico, Edward L. Doheny. Barclay told Barron he had found a potential Detroit bureau man in Casey Hogate, and he suggested that Barron might want to meet him on the trip to Battle Creek.

Barron and Hogate dined in Detroit, a meal that must have been memorable since Hogate was almost the equal of the *Journal* editor as a trencherman, but neither ever provided the details of their feast. Barron was enchanted with the young Detroit newsman, who had indeed interviewed Henry Ford and was as soft-spoken and diffident as Barron was brash and abrasive. Barron offered Hogate a job as Detroit bureau man, keeping in mind Barclay's suggestion that he had better go a cut above the *Journal's* customary salary scale. Barron was so impressed with Hogate that when he returned to New York after his sanitarium stay, he told Barclay, "He seemed like he could be my son."

Casey Hogate was born into the newspaper business in Danville, Indiana, on July 27, 1897. His father was Julian Depew Hogate, owner and editor of a weekly newspaper, the *Hendricks County Republican*. His mother was Atta Craven Hogate, of a pioneer Indiana family. Young Hogate learned the newspaper business country-style, working for his father while he attended public school and during summer vacations when he was in college. At DePauw University in Greencastle, Indiana, Hogate was a brilliant student, graduating with Phi Beta Kappa honors in 1918 after completing his college work in three and a half years. He was also editor of the college paper.

Army doctors rejected him when he applied for service in 1918, and Hogate took a job with the *Cleveland News Leader*. Within a short time he learned of a better job on the *Detroit News*, applied, and got it. Somehow Hogate, a strapping man, gave Malcolm W. Bingay, the *News* editor who hired him, the impression that he was much older than his 21 years, Bingay recalled years later. "He didn't mention that his eleven years of experience were mostly those during the years he was in grade school and high school," Bingay wrote.

Young Hogate swiftly proved his ability on the Detroit job. After brief service as a reporter, he became a copy editor under Bingay, who reluctantly let him go to Barron when the New York editor personally appealed to him. "After Mr. Barron told me that if he ever had a son he would have looked like Casey, how could I refuse?" Bingay asked. Barron used the emotional approach with Hogate as well, but he also had a practical argument. "Detroit is going to be the automobile capital of the world," Barron told his prospective employee. "It will be our most important bureau after Washington."

"I took the job," Casey Hogate recalled, "because it seemed to me that *The Wall Street Journal* was handling history."

Walter Barclay had concluded almost from the beginning that Casey Hogate was going to become managing editor of *The Wall Street Journal* as fast as he could be prepared for the responsibility. Barclay assured Barron that he would do everything possible to help. Casey was summoned to New York in 1922 and was soon made assistant managing editor. In August 1922 Barron wrote Hogate from Boston: "The way you are driving along and running so many things at once, the best way for us to keep closer is for you to work as I do—jump on the one o'clock train to Boston with your stenographer, fill him up with dictation, dine with me at Cohasset while he pounds away on the typewriter. Then you and I can have several hours of talk and you can return to New York the next day."

Barron wrote regularly to Hogate, giving him advice and encouragement. "You must keep your eyes on the markets at all times—wheat, coffee, cotton, bonds, stocks, money and foreign exchange. Underlying every one of these markets is a news story and every day you will find a big story under at least one of them." And, on another occasion: "Now, what I want you and Barclay to do in unison, with his experience and your quick perception and force, is hold the senior staff together so that they will not overwork and will find time to train others to do their work. What we want is not more men but every man more knowledgeable and efficient in his field—two or three times as many facts in every news column."

Barron, as one Dow Jones executive pointed out in later years, was not an executive; he was a boss. He could best get maximum effort from his personnel on a man-to-man basis. Hogate could motivate the staff, though he would have difficulty in mobilizing it from time to time, partly because of his own uncertainty about his goals and partly because some *Journal* staffers adamantly resisted change. Barron sought to guide the group with his maxims, and in 1922 published a booklet, *Confidential—News Rules for Six Cities*. Characteristically, he did not explain the title, which possibly contemplated an expansion of his publishing empire beyond the five institutions he named—*Barron's*, Dow Jones, the *Boston News Bureau*, the Philadelphia News Bureau, and *The Wall Street Journal*—though he may simply have intended his booklet for the three offices in New York, Boston, and Philadelphia, plus the bureaus in Washington, Detroit, and Chicago. The booklet listed 14 of Barron's rules of good journalism plus 20 more in a supplement.

"The soul of all writing," said Rule I, "and that which makes its force, use and beauty, is the animation of the writer to serve the reader. Never write from the standpoint of yourself, but always from the standpoint of the reader. Economize his time and crowd the most important facts and determining factors into the smallest possible compass that will carry the truth to his brain." Said Rule II: "The first rule of practice in financial journalism is thorough and full connection. A man should know as far as possible every official and every director in the company he is studying. . . . In brief, he should be an encyclopedia of statistics, history, policies and of prospects."

Barron was instructing his men in his own writing and research methods, which were acknowledged to be the best in the financial-reporting world of his day. Barron's "news rules" did not enjoy wide dissemination, and not merely because they were labeled confidential. Most of Barron's manual was replete with the truisms and platitudes he so adroitly mixed in his own work with unmatched skill. "If we are live wires," he wrote, "we can so project financial truth that it will at times illumine the path of the investor. We should not usurp his prerogative of selecting, guessing or predicting, but should steadily seek to illuminate his forward path." Barron's counsel, however, had value for reporters and writers generally, especially the injunction to which he gave an entire page of his booklet, "Close the switch on all doubtful words that might sidetrack the mind of the reader."

Late in 1922 Walter Barclay cleared the way for Hogate to be named managing editor by offering to return to his old job as the head of the paper's bond department, a detail not made public at the time. Barron took immediate advantage of the offer, and Casey Hogate was formally appointed, though no public announcement was made. (Commenting after his death in 1947 on Hogate's career, a career that made him chairman and chief executive of Dow Jones & Company, the *Journal* reported the circumstances of Hogate's fast rise: "Mr. Barclay cheerfully relinquished the managing editorship to Mr. Hogate and not only remained a loyal subordinate, but his warm personal friend as well.") On January 25 Hogate wrote to Barron indicating he had asked permission to provide raises to some members of the staff as his first action in the new job. "That 'cheap talent' to which you refer got on *The*

Wall Street Journal because it has been the policy of the paper to hire those who would work cheaply. . . . Since you have permitted me to take up improved compensation for our best men, I trust you will be free in letting my role be known with the consistent passing of all such matters through my hands.

"I have hired the best men to improve *The Wall Street Journal* which will require new type and rearrangement of space. It will actually result in economy of paper by getting all that is worthwhile into fewer pages into more readable form."

The appointment of Hogate as managing editor was not announced to the staff until January 1923. Hogate at the time was not yet 26 years old, and he had been with the paper less than two years.

While Barron gave his personal attention to the training of Casey Hogate as his successor, he maintained his interest in European affairs. He determined that *The Wall Street Journal* should cover the Genoa economic conference planned by the Allied Powers for the summer of 1922 and nominated himself for the job. His notebook indicates that Barron was astonished to learn that the United States did not intend to participate in the conference in any way. In Washington, his friend Vice-President Coolidge met him in his suite at the New Willard Hotel and explained that the United States could not participate in the conference because France refused to attend if German reparations were to be discussed. Coolidge said, according to Barron's notes: "That of course barred us out since we cannot discuss foreign indebtedness without discussing reparations. The trouble is France. She treats what Germany owes to her as a reality; what she owes to us as not a reality. . . . We want to help in the European situation, but the trouble is France. It will take time for the French people to become enlightened."

Barron concluded from his discussions in Washington that the government would be pleased if he attended the Genoa conference, not only to report to his papers, but also to provide his impressions to the State Department. He sent back long and costly cables that appeared in *The Wall Street Journal* and *Barron's*, and he later had discussions not only with State Department representatives but with the British as well. "The trip to Genoa was part of Barron's long campaign to educate American businessmen in world affairs with his belief that eventually there must be greater business between America and Europe," wrote biographer William Moise in his unpublished manuscript. He also believed it was his duty as a patriot to do what he could for the government. "This is the thirteenth conference and there is no definite plan of debate or decision," Barron wrote in an early dispatch. "The problem at Washington was the open door for China and here it is the open door for Russia. . . . Russia enters this conference as the stalking highwayman of Europe. In place of bread to trade for implements of agriculture and machinery it brings the spectre of famine and starvation. But it stands defiant, ready not to listen but to propose."

Barron was depressed by the Genoa conference, plagued by bickering and maneuver. He said that England was taking an overly liberal attitude toward Russia since she hoped to import grain from the Russians as she had done in the past. There were many problems, Barron wrote, but no decisions. He felt that a restored Germany was needed as a bulwark against the Russian Communists, but his dispatches showed that he by no means forgave the Germans.

> Germany has played two games in violation of the Ten Commandments. She coveted her neighbor's house and attempted to take it and when beaten back by her neighbor's friends and allies she has plotted how somebody other than herself should pay the bill.
>
> She has turned to her printing presses for something called money which has gradually become nothing but a fraud. . . . Part of Germany's planned machinations was the use of depreciating marks to build railroads and docks and houses and factories and to pad her government payrolls in order that nothing might be left over for reparations. But her new factories and buildings will be as ashes on her tongue when her people cry for bread, the stones in her streets rise up as masses riot and break windows.

Barron returned to the United States, discouraged by his failure to even make a dent in the German reparations problem and perhaps disillusioned by the attitudes of all the governments represented at Genoa. He would thereafter concentrate on American interests and would war against socialism and the kind of inflation he had witnessed in Germany. Nevertheless, he believed fervently in the benefits of foreign experience for newspapermen, and on February 24, 1923, he wrote his protégé Hogate, to whom he had formally given the title of associate editor and the added assignment of assistant to the president: "Under your new title . . . I must make you useful. One thing I want is for you to be stimulated by foreign travel and by news development from such travel."

The Wall Street Journal under Bancroft and Hogate was doing well. Advertising again had increased, and the format changes Hogate proposed to Barron enabled the paper to increase both advertising and news content slightly without added newsprint cost. The American automobile industry was now leading the world, as Barron had predicted it would, and the newspaper was benefiting from increased automotive advertising. Early in 1923 the paper reported that six motor companies made 83 percent of the 2,681,000 motorcars sold in the United States in 1922: Ford, General Motors, and an amalgamation of companies consisting of Dodge, Willys-Overland, Nash-

Hudson-Essex, and Maxwell-Chambers. All but Ford, the leader, advertised in *The Wall Street Journal*, and Barron could no longer assume that Ford was not in his newspaper because Ford sought only the lower end of the market. Determined to correct the situation, Barron again urged Hogate to arrange the long-promised meeting with Ford.

Meantime, Hogate was making progress with his own campaign to create the image of a national business newspaper for the *Journal*, as had been done for *Barron's* magazine. Barron again was the magic ingredient. Hogate published Barron's creed for the *Journal* in the pages of the paper and in a promotional bulletin issued early in 1923:

> In *The Wall Street Journal* I have sought to create a service. I have striven for a creation so founded in principles that it can live as a service—live so long as it abides in the laws of that service.
>
> I believe there is no higher service from government, from society, from journalism than the protection and upbuilding of the savings of the people.
>
> Savings in the United States may become investments, when guided by financial knowledge, more readily than in any other country in the world.
>
> Wall Street steadily improves and increases its service to the whole country by reflecting the true position of American and world investments.
>
> *The Wall Street Journal* must stand for the best that is in Wall Street and reflect that which is best in United States finance.
>
> Its motto is "The truth in its proper use."

Elsewhere in the booklet, the editors said: "*The Wall Street Journal* is in truth a national newspaper. It is as much interested in reporting crop conditions in the Northwest as in stock prices in New York; it is as much interested in general business in the South as in foreign exchange fluctuations; in fact, it is more interested in reporting business of most localities than are newspapers in that locality."

The lance thus thrust into the local press, however, was swiftly and gently withdrawn. "*The Wall Street Journal* contains, of course, a vastly more comprehensive chronicle of the business and financial news of the day than is possible for the financial departments of the large general newspapers. But the value of *The Wall Street Journal* is measured not so much by this complete daily chronicle of current business news as it is by the interpretative treatment of the information presented."

Fortunately for the *Journal* and Dow, Jones & Company, most of the daily newspapers accepted, approved, and even applauded this concept of the *Journal's* role in American journalism. "*The Wall Street Journal*," said the paper in another advertisement, "is a national daily newspaper of vital interest to every businessman. *The Wall Street Journal* is one of the most widely quoted newspapers in the world. It publishes the facts first." At the time, the *Journal's* only direct competitor was the *Wall Street News*, a daily financial publication and ticker service that Dow Jones editors used to measure the accomplishments of their own staff and that was known to the reporters and the ticker-service operators as Tammany. There was also the *Wall Street Chronicle*, called by the *Journal* a "brazen promotion sheet."

Early in 1923, before Barron's return from Genoa, the *Journal* had launched a new attack on government regulation of business and called for the abolition of all such programs left from the war era. The country was generally prosperous, wages were rising, United States Steel and other industrial powers were following Henry Ford in instituting an eight-hour day for labor, and crippling strikes had ended. But the *Journal* was disturbed by government interference, for Barron feared government control as an inevitable prelude to the socialism he felt was menacing Europe. Railroad-passenger traffic would be entirely in government hands in the United States within half a century, but passenger trains were still plentiful in 1923. On the day the editorial appeared, the *Journal* reported on page two that railroad-freight traffic was doing well despite regulation: "Remarkably heavy freight traffic continues." Freight-car loadings in 1922 had exceeded those in 1921 in every month, but 1921, of course, was a depression year when more than 50,000 businesses failed.

C. W. Barron was pleased with the progress of his paper as the business boom resumed. Hamilton at long last was expressing Barron's editorial thoughts well. Hogate was bringing a new concept of a national business newspaper to the *Journal*. Bancroft was talking about a total reorganization of the company with a view toward improving efficiency and providing for continuity under the inheritance-tax laws. All was going well in New York and Boston, and Barron allowed himself two vacation trips in 1923: one to Florida, which would become his favorite recreational area, and another to the Mediterranean, which, of course, he turned into a news-gathering trip. He was fascinated by the discovery of the tomb of King Tutankhamen in Egypt in 1922, and he wished to visit Palestine. Barron wrote several thousand words on the wonders of the Egyptian archaeological discoveries, which he cabled to New York. He also sent a short cable about the inability of the Egyptians to form a cabinet. The brief political story was printed in the *Journal*, but not a line on King Tut appeared. The editors decided it was far too prolix and not a suitable subject for *The Wall Street Journal*.

When Barron returned to America and discovered the omission of his King Tut story, he was furious until he heard the explanation offered by George Shea, one of the news editors, who blamed the foreign cable company that handled the dispatch. The cable, said Shea, was hopelessly garbled and unusable, a statement partly true. "You did quite right, Shea," the mollified Barron told his editor. "Don't pay that cable company one red cent, and don't give them any more of our business." It took Shea several weeks to cover the cost of the cable in his accounts, and, fortunately, for a number of years the paper had no occasion to send news from Egypt by cable.

C. W. Barron continued to be intensely interested in the nation's energy situation, which to him meant oil development. America was making automobiles faster than it could build good roads on which to drive them. The farmers were beginning to use tractors, as Barron had forecast in his Mexico series, and in 1923 he printed a further prediction that "in ten years the Diesel will take over the world," referring to diesel engines in ships, and that "there will be no coal fired ships on the oceans." Barron's fascination with the oil industry led him to his major journalistic mistake, though it harmed him more with historians than with his peers. In April 1922 Barron dined with his friend Lord Cowdray, the British engineer who had become the "oil king of Mexico," at the Reform Club in London. Cowdray praised Barron's acquaintance Edward Doheny as the outstanding oil man in the United States. Back home that year there were ugly rumors concerning a group of Barron's friends, including Doheny, who were said to be involved in an oil-lease scandal involving U.S. Navy oil-reserve lands at Teapot Dome, Wyoming, and Elk Hills, California. When Doheny denied that he had approached Albert B. Fall, secretary of the interior in President Harding's cabinet, in an attempt to get a Teapot Dome oil lease, as alleged in the rumors, Barron believed him.

On June 30, 1924, Doheny, Fall, and Harry F. Sinclair, another oil producer, were indicted for bribery and conspiracy to defraud the government in the Elk Hills and Teapot Dome leases. Barron published several stories seeking to prove Doheny innocent, and his notebooks record 22 interviews with Doheny on the subject over a period of years. In his *Journal* stories, Barron insisted that only three American oil companies could have undertaken the pumping of the Teapot Dome and Elk Hills reserves, and he declared that two of them, Standard Oil of Indiana and Cities Service Company, refused to bid. He quoted Robert W. Stewart, chairman of Standard Oil of Indiana, as declaring, "It was a fool affair and Teapot Dome is not worth a dime." Barron asserted that Doheny was actually performing a public service by making his bid for Navy oil since he offered in return the use of his oil-storage facilities at Pearl Harbor, Hawaii.

Doheny and Sinclair were acquitted in 1924 of charges of offering a bribe to Fall. Fall, however, who had resigned in 1923 from the cabinet, was found guilty in 1929 of taking bribes and sentenced to a year in prison. Doheny told Barron he had known Albert Fall as a rancher in New Mexico. When Doheny learned that Fall, who had just become secretary of the interior, was in financial trouble, he offered him a personal loan. Barron believed the story, and evidently the jury did also. To his death Barron insisted that Doheny was not only innocent but a public benefactor. On board a train on April 27, 1927, he discussed the Doheny case with Henry L. Doherty, president of Cities Service, and Doheny's lawyer, F. R. Kellogg, and told them, "I have tried to get Doheny . . . to come into conference with me in Washington . . . so that I might say to him [before the congressional investigating committee, evidently], 'Doheny, you are a patriot, always fighting for your country and for the defense of the Pacific Coast.' " What his companions had to say about this display of friendship and naiveté, Barron's notebook did not record.

Barron's friend Doheny had recommended the Battle Creek sanitarium operated by Dr. John Harvey Kellogg to him in 1920, and over the years Barron made 31 trips to the San, staying from a few days to as long as four weeks. When he arrived for a brief visit on February 1, 1923, Barron recorded Dr. Kellogg's comment to him: "You are short-breathed and your lips are blue and you must take time to pull the fat away from your heart or you will find yourself still further pinched in."

The big, continuing news story of the early 1920s was the burgeoning economy, reflected in the booming stock market and symbolized by Florida land speculation. The nation seemed to be realizing Barron's often expressed conviction that every working American should become an investor and thereby have a stake in the national affluence. Most middle-class Americans, it appeared, were buying stocks, Florida land, or western farms. The craze for investment would ultimately extend to those who had been content in the past to gamble on the races or in the bucket shops. Extra dividends were firing the stock market in late 1923 after prolonged raids by the bears. Barron and Hogate, in their *Wall Street Journal*, were striving to guide the public into the ways of wise investment, urging all who bought in Wall Street to buy their shares to keep and not for mere speculation. They were fighting a continuing war against the Wall Street bears, especially Jesse Livermore, known as the "Boy Plunger of Wall Street." Livermore, like Barron, was from Boston and the two men detested one another.

Casey Hogate was having his problems with the management of the *Journal* and the direction of his editorial staff; these problems were not diminished by the convictions and enthusiasms of his mercurial boss. C. W. Barron hated Jesse Livermore and all he stood for, and sought every opportunity to attack the notorious bear. Hogate approved the campaign against bears—reversing a policy dating back to the days of Charles Dow—but he deplored the use of the paper's columns in a personal vendetta. Hogate also privately disapproved of Barron's conducting a campaign to clear Doheny in the pages of the *Journal*. Then too, Hogate's editors sometimes behaved erratically, though with good intent. A few days after the *Journal* had castigated Livermore for his bear activities and had accused him of rigging Piggly Wiggly stock, first driving it down and then pushing it back up with vast profits to an inner few—a charge supported by Clarence Saunders, former president of Piggly Wiggly—a thoughtless editor quoted Livermore in the paper on the business outlook as if he were a respectable person.

Hogate was determined to establish a consistent, responsible editorial posture, critical of Wall Street when necessary, and free from influence and personal bias. It was a policy Barron himself frequently enunciated, but also a policy he sometimes forgot. In time the wisdom of Hogate's approach would be recognized and approved by Wall Street, and he would be named to a special board to recommend New York Stock Exchange reforms. But in the beginning some members of the *Journal* staff sought to undercut him by going directly to Barron himself. Barron, of course, supported his heir apparent. "Hogate and I go over all such matters together and find agreement on what is the right thing," Barron said.

Barron had learned many lessons about Wall Street and economics since taking over in New York, and his determination to end the onslaughts of the bears was genuine. Said Pound and Moore in their commentary on Barron's career: "[A] conclusion of the aging Barron, frequently mentioned in the notes, is that the Stock Exchange should limit short selling of standard securities. In one who believed in open trade and no interference with business, this may seem an inconsistency; but it reflects, not only a congenital optimism, but also his growing conviction that the investing public of America, now become the chief investment bloc in the world, needed protection from the buccaneers of Wall Street. Barron was the personal friend of the buccaneers. . . . Those who loved Barron for his weaknesses, as well as for his strength, perceive that he suffered through excess of loyalty to his friends."

Barron regarded Casey Hogate as a son, possibly the man he himself might have been were it not for his flaws. Bancroft he would bully and browbeat and sometimes treat with contempt until he drove his son-in-law, as he did so many others, to the edge of a nervous breakdown. Hogate he generally, but not always, treated with respect. Casey Hogate was Barron's exact opposite, according to those who knew both men well. Hogate was patient, kindly, affable, slow in speech, and slow to anger. He accepted the burdens of all who sought his help and uncomplainingly endured thoughtless slights and indignities from Barron since he was aware that Barron did love him. Bancroft, on the other hand, could never be sure about his relationship with his domineering father-in-law. To Barron's credit, he gave young Hogate enough authority, finally, to begin the long, difficult task of correcting the drifting course of *The Wall Street Journal*, which, despite statements about its national goals, still identified itself with a more parochial constituency.

In the fall of 1923 Barron resumed the campaign to win Henry Ford's friendship for *The Wall Street Journal* and Wall Street itself. Barron would write his own series of articles on the American automobile industry. He began with Studebaker at South Bend, Indiana, the first article of the series appearing October 31, and established his general thesis: "The automobile business in this country has forged so quickly to the front that few people realize that transportation as an investment base has shifted from rails to motors. National legislation, government control, politics and labor unions have crushed rail transportation, representing twenty billions of investment, down to about twelve billions in market value, or about one-third of their duplication cost at today's prices for labor and materials."

On November 23 Barron at last called on Ford in Dearborn, Michigan, accompanied by Phil S. Hanna, the *Journal's* Detroit bureau man, and Barron's secretary, Raymond O'Brien. The pudgy, aging editor and publisher got along well with lean but also aging Henry Ford, who was worried at the time about his wife's illness. Barron opened by supporting his paper's position that Ford had made a big mistake in not going public with stock in Ford Motors. "I tell my friends that such was the demand on the Ford works for expansion, that while he was the richest man in the world, he also was the poorest." That evidently took care of the *Journal's* story two years previously that claimed Henry Ford didn't know how to run his own business. Barron, who had criticized the Ford peace ship in wartime, now suggested that Ford ought to try for the Bok peace prize, the American award of $100,000 created that very year by E. W. Bok, editor of *The Ladies' Home Journal*. Ford turned to W. J. Cameron, editor of Ford's *Dearborn Independent*, who was also present at the interview, telling him, "We ought to try for that." If they did, they lost, for a Dr. C. A. Livermore won the Bok prize in 1924.

On May 22, 1924, Barron had his second interview with Ford, resulting in an extensive article, part of the series on the motor industry that had begun with Studebaker. Barron's admiration for Ford increased as their friendship warmed. Ford talked frankly with Barron for hours about his business, about Wall Street, and about world affairs. "His face has grown more beautiful and his smile even more kindly," Barron wrote. He was back October 28, 1924, for a third interview.

"Mr. Ford sees no saturation point for automobiles—they are making 7,500 a day and will be up to 10,000 a day in three months," Barron reported in his first story. " 'My mother died when I was 13 but she taught me the principles of service,' Mr. Ford told me. 'You are right in your creed, Mr. Barron, that service is the only basis for happiness, mutual service.' "

It was not Barron's usual interview. He wrote of Ford rather than his business. "Ford lives mostly in the factory, passing in and out and no one ever knows where to find him. He repeated that he writes no letters—only ten last year, all to children. He said, 'Conferences will kill a man.' On sales he said, 'The way to increase sales is by reducing prices, not by advancing them.' In the plant he said, 'I can tell by intuition from the sound of a machine the language the people speak who built it—whether it is French, German or English.' "

As 1924 was ending Barron himself was interviewed back in Boston. The *Boston Post* was most interested in his work procedures and methods of interviewing such men as Henry Ford, Sir Basil Zarahoff, and the German Kaiser of prewar days. "He is never without two small notebooks in which he records stenographic reports of words and thoughts," the paper explained.

The *Boston Traveler* wanted to know "What is the outlook for 1925?" The answer filled several columns, opening with Barron's respects to the Vermonter in the White House, President Calvin Coolidge. (President Warren Harding had died suddenly in San Francisco on August 2, 1923, and Calvin Coolidge, whom Barron admired more than any other living political leader, became president on August 3.) "The fundamental fact under the United States today is the strength of the government at Washington," Barron said. He made clear that he was speaking of a man, not Congress or a body of law.

> We have had a good deal of sloppiness in the government in the last 50 years and for the first time in a generation we now have a firm hand on the helm and a man that stands for plain speaking and fundamental principles in national security and defense.
>
> Since President Coolidge delivered his masterful message to Congress the outlook for business for 1924 has steadily improved. There is a more confident tone for business. . . . I hesitate to go on record concerning 1924 because my opinion is so distinctly different from so many people with whom I come into close contact. I can see nothing but a very good outlook for 1924 politically, financially and economically. . . . Most people have had their eyes too much on Germany and Europe. They would do well to take a small globe into their hands and to spin it to see what a relatively small spot Europe is. We forget expanding India. We read reports of disasters in Japan and revolutions in China; but nobody reports to us day by day business with these countries.
>
> The whole world is going forward, increasing its labor and production, and labor in its manifold forms is the basis of all wealth.

Then he added, "[But] there is no benefit in prophecy or prediction either to the maker or the hearer. Most people want other people to do their thinking and to give them the result, whereas they should consider the factors in every situation, get all the information they can, and do some thinking on their own account."

Chapter 9

The Happy Last Days of Barron

Wall Street's bull market charged on. *The Wall Street Journal* prospered, its circulation estimated at an average 22,228 copies in the early months of 1924. C. W. Barron felt secure with Casey Hogate in charge of the news department in New York and with President Calvin Coolidge in Washington. In addition to commuting to Europe even more frequently, he began a series of long sojourns in Palm Beach, Florida, which he designated the Winter Wall Street, and in the Kellogg sanitarium in Battle Creek, Michigan, his refuge when his health troubled him. Barron was fascinated with Florida and the Florida real-estate boom, which raged in the early 1920s like one of the tropical hurricanes that would help to end it in the fall of 1928. The Florida madness sucked up middle-class investors from all over America in a frenzy of buying and selling, creating instant fortunes for speculators not only in once solid communities but in the palmetto wilderness and alligator swamps where "choice" lots turned out to be under water.

Barron reported the land boom without making recommendations to his readers. But early in 1925, writing one of his "Wall Street Sermons" for the *Journal*, he did give his blessing to the Wall Street stock markets and lesser stock markets of the country while reiterating his opposition to selling short for speculative gain: "It is a bad influence. This is the wrong frame of mind towards one's country and fellow man. The bears think that they are very bright and can see further ahead than other fellows, but I think they are digging their own graves."

Warning that "in none of my publications is it permitted to predict that prices are going up or going down," Barron said that from the facts gathered by his publications at a cost of more than $1 million a year, he was able to conclude: "The truth is that the investment stocks of the country were never so cheap as today. I would have no hesitancy, if I were quitting business, in buying stocks in our leading companies and going off to Europe for a long rest without the slightest concern."

Barron's assessment of the market was at the time an accurate one. Years later economists would judge that stock prices in 1925 were in line with the prospects of American business and industry. "Until the beginning of 1928," wrote John Kenneth Galbraith in his excellent book, *The Great Crash of 1929*, "even a man of conservative mind could believe that the prices of common stock were catching up with the increase in corporation earnings, the prospect for further business, the peace and tranquility of the times, and the certainty that the Administration then firmly in power in Washington would take no more than necessary of any earnings in taxes." Robert Sobel, in his equally fine *Panic on Wall Street*, listed a half dozen leading university economists who as late as 1929 publicly predicted higher stock prices and no depression.

Although Barron was away from New York much of the time in 1924, he paid close attention not only to Wall Street but to the American political scene. President Coolidge invited him for an overnight stay at the White House, where he received a warmer welcome than he did at his own Washington bureau. Barron's reception at the bureau was invariably the same, veterans there remembered. The offices were on the second floor of the old press building, up a narrow stairway. There John Boyle, the *Journal's* Washington correspondent since 1892, was still titular chief during Barron's day, though Boyle for years—despite Prohibition, which he and the *Journal* had opposed from the beginning—had largely limited his intake of foods to alcohol, beginning each day with a hearty breakfast of it. Thus, whenever Barron appeared, Boyle could not negotiate the steps down, a feat he reserved for quitting time in the late afternoon, and Barron, of course, could not possibly climb them.

Barron would order his chauffeur to park his limousine under the bureau windows. "Boyle, Boyle!" he would shout, "Come down here!" Boyle always managed to stagger respectfully to the window and would yell back, "You come up." There was an inevitable standoff, Barron finally shouting instructions about the bureau and Boyle acknowledging having heard. Charlie Sterner, for 50 years the bureau office manager, said that in all this time he did not recall a single face-to-face conversation between Boyle and Barron.

Barron and the *Journal* loyally supported President Coolidge and the Republican administration. Despite his poor health, Barron attended the Republican convention in June 1924, which nominated Coolidge for president on the first ballot and chose Charles G. Dawes, the Chicago banker, as his running mate. During the fall campaign, Barron traveled about the country, sending back reports on the outlook for the Republican ticket, which he pronounced excellent. He summarized his findings in an interview with the *Boston Herald*, which the *Journal* reprinted on election day, November 4. "I have just returned from the West, and I see no reason for modifying my early estimate of a ten million plurality for Coolidge and Dawes. I listened to young Bob La Follette [son of Senator Robert M. La Follette of Wisconsin, the Progressive Party candidate for president] for over an hour, and I am astonished that either he or his father should attempt to put over the fallacies and misrepresentation they present. They urge people to think, but they do not appeal to thinkers."

In an editorial that morning, *The Wall Street Journal* urged all registered citizens to vote, stopping just short of recommending by name a vote for Coolidge over the Democrat, John W. Davis of West Virginia: "This is no time for experiments, for the Presidency is no job for ignorant self-sufficiency and noisy pretense. Even to say a candidate is honest is no sufficient reason for giving him your vote. The normal condition of the American citizen is that he is honest. He must be steadfast, capable, trustworthy, intelligent, cautious, courageous, a man of integrity far beyond mere material honesty."

President Coolidge and Charles Gates Dawes received 15,725,016 of the popular votes to 8,385,586 for Davis and 4,822,856 for La Follette. This was far below Barron's predicted plurality, but was a landslide nevertheless, providing 382 electoral votes for the Republicans to 136 for the Democrats and 13 for the Progressives. The *Journal* was well satisfied, saying editorially on November 6: "An unshaken confidence in the reelection of Calvin Coolidge, shown in the financial center of the United States, has been amply justified by the results of the presidential election. . . . Probably the first thing our President did this morning was to sit down at his desk and take a hand in the business of the day. Let us all do likewise."

Under the Coolidge editorial were more words of praise for another good though more recent friend of *The Wall Street Journal*. "When Henry Ford comes to be adequately understood, it is likely that the secret of his amazing career will be found to be less in the ordinary conception of genius than in the unparalleled freedom of his mind and spirit. Almost all men, even when they consciously endeavor to give imagination a free reign, are hampered by perceptions which they like to dignify by the name of principles. Henry Ford never had any difficulty in discarding familiar ideas, whether they happened to be other men's or his own."

And a few days later, on December 15, there were laudatory words for a man the *Journal* once considered one of the enemy—Samuel Gompers, president of the American Federation of Labor, who died in Mexico, where he was attending the inauguration of President Calles. According to the *Journal*, "Samuel Gompers' social and economic conceptions were sounder and clearer than many of his public utterances would give one to understand. He did at times take wholly indefensible positions, as when he asserted that labor unions were under no obligation to protect the public from the evils of jurisdictional warfare between unions. . . . As an executive of the general union alliance, however, he put his foot uncompromisingly upon all the more reckless varieties of communism. This newspaper has more than once dissented sharply from his ideas, but it is not to be doubted that he served his generation sincerely and ably, according to his lights."

Few visitors to Florida were more enthusiastic about the state than C. W. Barron. He loved the climate, the seascapes and sunsets, the fishing, the serene living on the houseboat *Edna B.*, which he regularly chartered, the bridge games, the gathering of the wealthy and mighty at Miami, Palm Beach, Coral Gables, Tampa, and Sarasota. Barron liked to say that he discovered Florida. And few who wrote about Florida knew more of its history, its statistics, and its potential. Barron promoted the scenery, the climate, the recreational opportunities, and the natural resources, including the potential for expanding citrus groves, truck farms, phosphate mining, and light industry. Between 1924 and his final illness in 1928, Barron wrote more than 20 major articles on Florida for *The Wall Street Journal* and *Barron's*. The *Journal's* special sections on Florida, begun in 1902, grew to 32 pages, greater even than its annual auto sections. Florida was a nationally absorbing story, and Barron made the most of it. "The Florida boom," wrote economist Galbraith 30 years later, "was the first indication of the mood of the twenties and the conviction that God intended the American middle class to be rich. But that this mood survived the Florida collapse is still more remarkable."

The hurricanes of September 1926 and 1928, which devastated many areas of south Florida, would eventually burst the Florida bubble, but, as Barron and the *Journal* pointed out, they could not destroy the Florida dream of the average American. The 1926 hurricane, which swept the Miami area, killing 392, did not check the boom. The worst of the storms struck Palm Beach, Barron's favorite retreat, the night of September 16, 1928, and moved inland. An estimated 1,850 persons lost their lives when Lake Okeechobee burst its dikes and inundated a wide area. Barron detailed some of the damage in his report to the *Journal*: "Of 9,000 buildings in the new city of

Hollywood, 2,000 were destroyed, Key Biscayne was a wreck, and of 60,000 coconut palms planted, 40,000 were uprooted, but now they have planted 120,000 more." The second storm smashed the Florida boom. Barron, like his drama critic James Metcalf at the New Haven opening of a Broadway show, was in effect covering the out-of-town tryout of Wall Street's forthcoming big event.

Barron did not buy Florida land or property himself. He rented his homes there, preferring to move about to enjoy the whole of the state. "There are three great reasons for believing in Florida," he wrote: "January, February and March." And Barron could always find important businessmen and millionaires, even in remotest Florida. "There is Winter Haven with 102 lakes in a radius of five miles and the Mountain Lake Club of millionaires' homes at Lake Wales," he wrote. "Everywhere is the color of flower and vine—three shades of bougainvilleas, the flame vine, and others." But Barron, like most of the millionaires, preferred Palm Beach (the Winter Wall Street), Miami, Coral Gables, and the West Coast fishing areas as he sought to demonstrate that Florida, a palpable dream for suddenly mobile and relatively rich middle-class America, would endure despite financial crash and devastating storms. "The wealth and income of Florida are in the air; the economic base, from mines and agriculture, are yet to come," Barron wrote in March 1925. "The biggest crop in Florida is northern tourists. The attraction is the likelihood of life extension from perpetual sunshine and flowers. . . . Florida fights death and taxes and lives by the sky."

Barron's Florida reports, written when he was well past 70, exemplified the qualities of his journalism, which could convey the kind of peculiarly American excitement that prevailed when a new frontier was found. He portrayed the Florida state of mind, representing the new American philosophy, in quick, deft words and by example. "The wealthy Mrs. Potter Palmer [of Chicago] came to Sarasota twenty-five years ago and bought all the property she wanted for two to five dollars an acre," Barron recalled. Later in 1925 the property along the water couldn't be had for $500 a front foot. He detailed the experience of Mrs. Horace E. Dodge, who paid $80,000 in 1924 for East Coast oceanfront property and was thought mad by her friends. But Mrs. Dodge sold it to developers for $1.5 million in 1925. The developers failed, and Mrs. Dodge recovered the property and sold it again for $600,000.

Barron especially loved Miami and Miami Beach. "Here are two majestic cities, heaven descended or hell bent, who can say? Approaching Miami from the water, one beholds a new Manhattan Island with Battery Park and a dozen skyscrapers—the creation of a year—It is all enchantingly wonderful as your ship glides between cities of skyscrapers and you view Venetian islands where the delicate tracery of Australian pines vie with varieties of palms and brightly blooming shrubs. . . . The city docks are crowded with ships unloading cargoes. . . . Less margin is required now to speculate in Florida land than to buy stocks in Wall Street. . . . The rise of Miami, Miami Beach and Coral Gables has no precedent on this planet." Speculators were in fact buying Florida land at ten cents on a dollar, sometimes after first borrowing the ten cents. They bought land as others in the North were buying shares of stock, without investigation or question, since they were buying not a parcel of land but the right to sell it to someone else at a profit.

Barron wrote not only of Florida when he was based there, but conducted general interviews, filled his notebooks, and composed his "Wall Street Sermons" at the Winter Wall Street. Early in 1925 he warned in a "Sermon" about Wall Street speculation:

> This may be a Wall Street year but already there are signs of financial unpreparedness. Millions of dollars are moving into Wall Street backed by little experience in markets and stock values. Markets are great educators if only people will stop, look and listen but too often they stop and run away without listening. As Benjamin Franklin said, "The best investment is in the tools of one's own trade." Or, to quote a famous English banker, "It is your losses that ought to make you smart."
>
> Never was it more important than today that the American businessman watch the financial chronicles. This is the year of financial expansion and recovery in values with renewed confidence in government and the field looks clear ahead. The present is a time of fruitage in valuations rather than the creation of new values.

Barron's somewhat mild and biblical suggestion that the market was possibly seeing its high may have been missed by most of his readers, and actually the main Wall Street boom was just beginning.

The *Journal* editor and president was especially happy in Florida during the winter of 1927–28. He had again chartered the luxurious houseboat *Edna B.* and had with him not only his stepdaughter and her children but also his special New York friend Mrs. Eames, a patron of the theater and the arts who often gave parties for Barron and her theatrical friends in her suite in the Marguery Hotel on Park Avenue and to whom Barron reported his day's experiences when they were in New York. Barron wrote of his friendship with Mrs. Eames in letters to his granddaughters, and he confided to Mr. and Mrs. Hogate and to the Bancrofts that he planned to marry her, according to biographer William Moise. They objected, Moise wrote, on grounds that Barron was too old and in ill health. They were correct in the latter instance at least; Barron would not live out the year. He continued to write about his beloved Florida in the spring of 1928, suggesting that every American who could afford it would be heading to the vacation paradise sometime.

During the months C. W. Barron was away in Europe, Florida, and Battle Creek, Bancroft and Hogate were completing the restructuring of *The Wall Street Journal*, carrying it to a stated circulation high of 27,925 in 1925. Casey Hogate constantly sought new ideas to improve the paper. Columns appeared and disappeared. Like Henry Ford, Casey did not hesitate to abandon an idea that didn't seem to work well, even if it was his own. To James Metcalf's theater reviews were added "Tips on the Theater," mini-reviews providing a daily guide to Broadway: "*Abie's Irish Rose*, a laughable low comedy dealing with Hebro-Hibernian social life in New York; *Listening In*—mediocre mystery play; *Romeo and Juliet*—Miss Ethel Barrymore's rather matronly Juliet and Miss Hopkins' eccentric editing of the classic; *Rain*—Keep away if you love missionaries, otherwise a strong drama of the Pacific isles with excellent work by Miss Jeanne Eagles." Twenty-five plays were listed each week.

Hogate evidently was not satisfied with his recourse to smaller type, since he restored the 8-point body type, but the paper ran 16 pages most days and up to 24 on others, so Hogate was getting the room he required for editorial material. He devoted between four columns and a full page to answering letters from readers, created new columns, such as "In and Out of Banks," "Insurance Stocks," and a Barclay column on the bond market, and assigned onetime copyboy and now star reporter Oliver Gingold to write two columns, "Heard on the Street" and "Abreast of the Market." Gingold had arrived from London on November 8, 1900, in the days of Thomas Woodlock, bearing a letter from a Woodlock friend, and was immediately given a job at the age of 15. He served the *Journal* for 65 years, ran a $2,500 loan into a $3 million fortune in the stock market, and was sought by Wall Street brokers for advice on the market. For a number of years Gingold was chairman of the company profit-sharing fund and guided its investment policy. He also acted as an investment advisor to widows of *Wall Street Journal* retirees. He was credited with inventing the phrase "blue chip" for top, old-line stocks. Early in 1924 Hogate introduced a new column, "Mirror on Washington," to provide better use of dispatches from his Washington bureau. The prevalence of varied, short items in the paper demonstrated Hogate's desire to broaden the scope of *The Wall Street Journal*, which he and Barron thought should serve a national constituency.

Hogate's relationship with Barron continued to be excellent—Moise describes it as a "perfect link"—but Barron's relations with Bancroft were deteriorating again. Nevertheless, Bancroft was "family," and he, Jane, and the children were present for the great social triumph of Barron's lifetime, the visit of President and Mrs. Coolidge with their staff in the summer of 1925. "The presidential yacht steamed into Cohasset harbor bringing the Coolidges for luncheon with Mr. Barron in recognition of their friendship and the strong support of the Barron publications in the Coolidge elections," wrote

Moise, who interviewed those present. "All members of the Barron family were on hand and the President was escorted on a visit to the Oaks Dairy Farm. After listening to CWB extolling the prowess of his imported Guernsey bull, the President's response is reported to have been, 'Some bull!' " The group then posed for a photograph, Barron standing proudly in his Cohasset Yacht Club commodore's uniform between Mrs. Coolidge and the President.

The Wall Street Journal was having an excellent advertising year, and late that summer Hugh Bancroft decided to recognize the men primarily responsible. On October 1, 1925, Paul B. Howard was named director of advertising and E. B. Ross was appointed advertising manager. Their names were added to the masthead of the paper where those of C. W. Barron, Hugh Bancroft, and Joseph Cashman had appeared in each issue for several years. It was the first time in the history of the paper that advertising men were so publicized. They deserved the honor: In January of 1924 and again in 1925 the *Journal* had some of its biggest auto sections, 26 pages. During the period, some of the country's major newspapers had been persuaded to use the *Journal* for their promotional advertising, and the full-page displays of the New York papers appeared more frequently as they were joined by out-of-town publications, including those of Chicago, Los Angeles, St. Louis, San Francisco, and Washington.

After a leisurely train trip through the West and South, Barron was briefly at Cohasset and then went off to Paris for a rest, to write articles on the European economic situation, and to submit to interviews with the foreign press. In New York the paper continued to do well. The street sale price had been increased to 7 cents, subscriptions to $18 a year. Hogate had increased the size of his news staff and was introducing a series of articles on new American industries. The first, on the communications industry, was written by Ray B. Prescott, who told the story of the Radio Corporation of America, which a few months later became one of Wall Street's glamour stocks.

Barron arrived back in New York two days before Christmas, and rumors of his rage subdued the staff through the remainder of the holiday season. Exactly what happened was not disclosed, but Bancroft and Barron had clashed again, and on January 1, 1926, the names of Bancroft, Cashman, Howard, and Ross disappeared from the *Journal's* masthead, that of C. W. Barron, President, alone remaining. No name other than Barron's would again appear during his lifetime. Casey Hogate's name had never been included on the masthead, and that omission may have triggered Barron's ire, though a more immediate offense seems more likely. Hogate, in any case, never had the problems his associates had with Barron, except when the Dow Jones president demanded that Casey provide a list of all employees buying stock on margin, including the amount of their loans. Hogate flatly refused, offering his resignation when Barron persisted. Hogate pointed out that employees had been involved in the stock market since the founding of the company. Barron sulked at Cohasset, and Mrs. Hogate, a frequent visitor there, went to tell Barron that her husband definitely intended to quit. Barron gave in. Early in 1926 Barron made K. C. Hogate a vice-president and general manager of Dow Jones.

Hogate also continued to act as executive editor of the *Journal*. When one of the editors wrote the president asking for a raise, Barron answered, "My policy is to have all of the editorial and reporter staff completely under Mr. K. C. Hogate. I give him general policy directions and, although I communicate directly with any of the men, salaries are in his hands. Therefore, I advise you to present your case to Hogate."

In August, Barron learned that a new automobile Casey Hogate had given his wife, Anna, had been wrecked when struck by a drunk driver. Mrs. Hogate, blameless, had been injured. Barron sent a note to the Dow Jones treasurer saying, "There will be a demand on you for about $3,000 from Hogate for an automobile. You can charge it to extra salary as I consider that he is underpaid on the contract that he himself proposed."

The best way to insure Barron's continuing criticism and enduring enmity, it appeared, was to be a male member of his family by marriage. Barron fought not only with Hugh Bancroft, despite Bancroft's continuing contributions to Barron's empire, but also with his other stepson-in-law, H. Wendell Endicott. Young Endicott, husband of the late Martha Waldron Barron and father of Martha (to whom Barron would leave his Back Bay home on his death), had become president of the family enterprise, Endicott-Johnson Company, one of the largest New England firms, and considered himself too busy to share his time with Barron. Nevertheless, Endicott agreed to serve as a Dow Jones director, and for a decade he faithfully attended the meetings and loyally presented most of Barron's resolutions. On January 25, 1924, however, Endicott resigned in anger, giving up his two shares of stock, which he had purchased from Sereno Pratt on April 2, 1912, to Jane Bancroft. There was no explanation of his action, but evidently Endicott refused to accept further badgering.

Endicott could resign from the board of Dow Jones, but Hugh Bancroft felt compelled to go on. He and Cashman continued to work for *The Wall Street Journal* after the banishment of their names from the masthead, and circulation, advertising, revenues, and profits continued to improve. Bancroft was pleased with the progress made by the *Journal* and by *Barron's* magazine; Hamilton, executive editor of the magazine, as well as editorial-page editor of the *Journal*, was responsive to his suggestions. It was Bancroft, Hamilton wrote, who suggested his highly successful series on the Dow Theory for the financial weekly, and he also initiated a series on inheritance-tax problems. Hogate, who appeared to get on well with everybody, moved ahead with his *Journal* improvements, emphasizing graphics in 1926. The *Journal* was spiced with cartoons from American and British newspapers and magazines, and halftone photos were again used. The paper's artist, John Major, was authorized to sketch on a daily basis and began to include scenes from the Lower East Side tenement area, which, the *Journal* explained, "is only a stone's throw from Trinity church," Wall Street's landmark, if not guardian. Hogate employed two new foreign correspondents, Sanford Griffith in London and Charles R. Hargrove in Paris. Over-the-counter market quotations were added, and out-of-town markets were expanded, including reports daily from Boston, Chicago, Philadelphia, Cleveland, Detroit, San Francisco, Baltimore, Cincinnati, St. Louis, and Pittsburgh. Hogate was moving on the objective he had discussed with Barron, a national daily business newspaper.

During 1926 Dow, Jones & Company received its first Ford Motor Company advertisement, an ad so small it probably was not authorized in Detroit. It was an announcement card one column wide by seven inches deep advertising the facilities of a garage the company owned in New York. But Ford's newest competitor, Durant Motors, bought space liberally to promote its new Star Four, a sports roadster being offered at a price the "little man" could afford, $495. It was, said the ad, the "largest car at its price, the lowest priced car of its size." There were other motor newcomers to the *Journal* pages—Elcar, Gardner, Hupmobile, Nash, Paige, Peerless, Reo, Studebaker's Erskine, and Velia. The *Journal* also carried extensive advertisements for other "big-ticket" consumer products, cabinet radios and electric refrigerators.

In June 1927 Barron was in Chicago, where his epigrams had been chiseled into the wall of the new Loop bank of the Illinois Merchants Trust Company. The *Chicago Daily News* sent a reporter to the Blackstone Hotel to interview Barron on the outlook for the rest of the year; he was asked to "summarize the financial situation." Barron replied by reviewing a *Wall Street Journal* editorial on credit, which had appeared the previous March 13: "This is not the age of Capital but the age of Credit. There is good evidence that China, two thousand years ago, had some of our modern banking practices, including checks and perhaps an elementary form of the bill of exchange. Credit must have been a part of the business systems of Venice and Genoa, or for the matter of fact, Carthage fifteen centuries earlier."

America, Barron told the *News*—and *Journal* readers also, when his own paper reprinted the interview—had gone beyond the ancients when it developed its Federal Reserve System. "Now the United States is the financial Atlas of the world. We now have a perfect reflection of the operation of the Federal Reserve Act. It gives credit where credit is due, and where no credit is properly due there can be declines and reorganizations without any effect upon the general situation. . . . As I pointed out several years ago, the effect of the Federal Reserve Act is to put us on a London basis, where 'rails' may advance and 'rubbers' decline, and there may be no relation between the two in the stock market. We now have a strong market for rails in this country, a weak market for rubbers, and every motor stock is standing on its own basis."

The *Daily News* reporter pressed for something specific on motors. "Everybody in the world is interested in American motors," Barron replied. "We are expanding our foreign trade in this field despite all the efforts of Germany and England and France to keep down the impact of American motors. The Studebaker gets out a new Erskine [a light model car] and surprises itself that one half the Erskines, as fast as it can manufacture them, go to Europe. But really the keynote of the motor field is with Henry Ford."

Henry Ford, Barron continued, had been doing some thinking and had concluded that he no longer would try to give the American people what he knew they ought to have, but would give them what they wanted, "a car with a gearshift and a more artistic hood." Barron was referring to Ford's announcement of his Model A after having celebrated the sale of the fifteen-millionth Model T Ford on May 26, 1927. Earlier in the year the *Journal* had predicted a new, six-cylinder model to be called the "Edison Six"; obviously, the paper was slightly off the mark. It also had said on February 8 that Henry Ford at last had made friends with Wall Street, a report supplied by its editor, who had become one of Henry Ford's friends.

Barron, sharing a box of Page and Shaw chocolates with the *News* reporter, chattered on in his staccato delivery, summarizing the financial situation as requested. "General Motors has advanced until it now sells 1,200,000 motorcars a year. It will take months to determine Mr. Ford's future position. He has got a struggle before him such as no man before him ever had in history. He is one man against organized finance, organized engineering and organized merchandising."

"Isn't there a saturation point for motors?" asked the reporter.

"There is no such thing as a saturation point for any serviceable thing," Barron replied crisply. "There is no such thing as a saturation point for men and women on this planet; there is no such thing as a saturation point for human service, and the motorcar is the greatest element in modern human service, for it is under all transportation, social order and progress."

"What is the keynote for 1927?" the dazzled reporter asked.

"Full employment for labor at good wages," Barron replied instantly. "The Saturday night payroll was never larger, and it is the Saturday night payroll that limits purchasing power; and don't forget that more than 90 per cent of what labor produces, labor consumes."

On August 2, President Coolidge, summering in the Black Hills of South

Dakota, made his famous announcement (understandable in New England if not the rest of the country), "I do not choose to run." A few days later, General Motors announced a stock split, two for one, and the market value of the doubled 8,700,000 shares shot up $5 a share. On August 15 *The Wall Street Journal* called to its readers' attention the fact that the split added no real value whatever to any General Motors stock: "All that the directors decided was that in the future the equity of common stockholders should be represented by 17,400,000 tokens instead of 8,700,000 tokens." The explanation was simple and clear, but the public was paying more attention to C. W. Barron's words of high confidence than to the *Journal's* editorial urging caution.

After surveying the public and politicians, *The Wall Street Journal* on September 20 provided comfort for those who feared that Calvin Coolidge really did not intend to run again: "Politically, everything is developing in the direction of the drafting of President Coolidge for another term. Among other things, Wall Street is well informed on history, and gives the records most patient analysis. It knows that no Republican candidate can win unless he carries the fifty-five electoral votes of the State of New York. He might lose with them, but he cannot win without them. . . . With the single exception of Coolidge, no candidate in sight can carry New York against Governor Smith, not even Charles E. Hughes."

The editorial, of course, was dead wrong; Herbert Hoover also could carry New York, but the *Journal* would remain loyal to the reluctant if not adamant Coolidge until the party convention in Kansas City, a position dictated by C. W. Barron himself. Barron and the *Journal* were not wrong, however, in their equally persistent support of the Federal Reserve System as the foundation of American financial strength. On October 18 the paper again editorialized in favor of the Federal Reserve, adding to the more than 100 such statements it had made since the law was enacted, but this one was almost jocular, saying that since the Federal Reserve Act became law in a Democratic administration, although it was almost entirely a Republican creation, the Democrats ought to claim it. The autonomy of the 12 district Federal Reserve banks, the paper implied, was in effect a powerful states' rights system consonant with the Democratic philosophy and strong enough to override a powerful central bank when necessary. The South, said the *Journal*, with so much to conserve, ought to back Republicans rather than "go chasing after colossal failures, public ownership and government interference with business. It need not tie itself up with every half-baked Socialist scheme presented for public approval. . . . All this is suggested in perfectly good nature. Wall Street has no prejudices. It likes the man whom it can trust, as, for instance, Mr. Coolidge. It merely wonders why the Democratic Party does not develop the courage of its own convictions."

The editorial presented William Peter Hamilton at his whimsical best, but the South did not get the message until 1980. The quality of the *Journal's* editorials somewhat deteriorated thereafter, as both Hamilton and Barron found themselves in declining health and each took long vacations. In December 1927 Barron again chartered the *Edna B.* and went off to Florida for most of the winter. Hamilton departed on the *Aquitania* on January 7, 1928, leaving the following statement with his paper: "I believe that conditions in America are fundamentally sound, business is good, and there is little cause for uneasiness. The mere fact that the banks are loaning plentifully in support of stock market operations is an indication that a healthy condition exists, and in itself should forestall any serious thought of a prolonged bear market."

The nation's motor-manufacturing executives attending the New York auto show were in agreement. "Manufacturers predict the greatest replacement market for automobiles in history," wrote the *Journal* auto editor, Edward Stein, who had been freed from service as Barron's secretary after eight years and three unaccepted resignations. "The trend toward more than one car to a family is another important sales factor." He quoted Alfred P. Sloan, Jr., president of General Motors, who said, "I feel quite certain it [1928] will be greater than 1927, it will be greater than any other previous year."

On January 10 the *Journal*, which had strongly opposed Prohibition from the beginning and thus felt compelled to laud the utterances of Governor Alfred E. Smith of New York on that subject from time to time, now disclosed how it really felt about Smith as it reviewed his annual message to the state legislature. "Not only did the Governor slip from his usual high level of intelligence in his attack on Prohibition, but, to put it as kindly as possible, lack of time has prevented the Governor from making the study of the question [of developing electrical energy] which would have excluded misleading statements from his message." Smith's sin, of course, was supporting government ownership of power plants.

The *Journal* itself soon embarked on an all-out fight against Al Smith for any position in government, and especially the job of president he was said to covet. On January 14 it applauded President Coolidge for saying he saw no need for unfavorable comment on brokers' loans. "Last year commercial loans were practically at a standstill," the paper explained. "In fact there was an actual decrease. The banks helped the economy of the country in 1927 by investing $811,133,000 in Wall Street and making loans on stocks and bonds totaling $836,708,000." By extending such credit, said the *Journal*, banks helped to insure the value of all securities listed on the New York Stock Exchange in 1927 at about $86 billion, $12 billion greater than in 1926. And, it added, "The present volume of the $4,432,907,000 of Stock Exchange brokers' loans is less than five per cent of these listings."

There was upbeat news in the same issue that had no immediate relationship to the stock market. "In Schenectady Friday, radio television leaped the barrier between the laboratory and the home in the first demonstration of television broadcasting arranged by Radio Corporation of America and General Electric Co. At three different points in the city, including the home of E. W. Allen, vice president of General Electric Co., engineers, scientists and others, standing before the first home television sets ever to be demonstrated, saw moving images and heard voices of a man and a woman transmitted from the research laboratories several miles away." It was not the first demonstration of television, the paper said, but it was the most dramatic. Yet no home television was foreseen soon. Radio broadcasting alone sufficiently interested the public to make "Radio" one of the exciting Wall Street stocks.

The week before, on January 8, *The Wall Street Journal* demonstrated its own interest in communications. It obtained London market reports, the kind Bergstresser had cadged from telegraph operators for the Dow Jones bulletins in 1882, via a transatlantic telephone connection with London. Griffith, the London bureau man, and Hogate arranged the demonstration, with Griffith providing the report to an unnamed *Journal* editor. "He reported the market active and steady with oils a feature," the paper said. "There was a lot of static."

Barron did not write for the paper again until late in January. His health was relatively good, but he was busy entertaining his friends, including Mrs. Eames, and his grandchildren; fishing; and collecting money from wealthy acquaintances for his favorite charity, the Coolidge Fund for the Clarke Institute for the Deaf. Barron had established this fund in honor of Mrs. Grace Coolidge, a former teacher at the Institute, and donated $130,000 that year. He raised $2 million that spring. One of his luncheons was with Treasury Secretary Andrew Mellon, one of America's richest men, who pleased Barron by quoting from one of his recent "Wall Street Sermons."

Barron attended the Republican convention in Kansas City on June 12–15, still hoping that Coolidge would be nominated. "The convention is first and last for Hoover if we can't get Coolidge," he wrote at the beginning of the convention. Editorially, the paper said the same day, "Taken by and large, Mr. Hoover is satisfying rather than exciting. He is perhaps the most efficient man, from the standpoint of public business, Washington has seen for many years. . . . It is complained that Mr. Hoover is not much of a politician. There are not many competent politicians, although Mr. Coolidge is one and Mr. Dawes is another. Each one of them has had all the abuse that could possibly be heaped upon Hoover. He will get that abuse anyway."

Herbert Clark Hoover, secretary of commerce in the Coolidge administration, was nominated on the first ballot, and Senator Charles Curtis of Kansas became his running mate. On June 26 the Democrats met at Houston and named Alfred E. Smith of New York and Senator Joseph T. Robinson of Arkansas as their candidates. The only thing against Hoover, the *Journal* noted with resignation, was his attitude on Prohibition. It predicted his election in November and his reelection in 1932 "unless somebody with courage and conviction runs on repeal of the Volstead law [the act that provided for enforcement of Prohibition]." The paper ruled out Smith regardless of his position on the Volstead law. "Governor Smith is committed to a program of government ownership," it said.

The next day the *Journal* admitted that its Republican bias did not square with its anti-Prohibition stand. It had denounced the Volstead Act consistently, called for repeal of the Prohibition amendment, and astonished even fervent Wets on June 3, 1921, by asserting that Prohibition had made criminals more efficient by keeping liquor from them. It had castigated the Anti-Saloon League for playing politics as crassly as Tammany Hall. Now the paper repeated its charges against the League: "Senators and Congressmen are browbeaten and cowered. They are told that repeal must not even be considered, that even discussion is disloyal. . . . We have imposed upon us a clerical rule of the most ignorant and intolerant kind."

The *Journal* said that the Republican party ought to be the party of freedom but was not so long as it tolerated bigotry. "Prohibition is the greatest issue today. . . . You cannot ameliorate a cesspool by sowing the surface with forget-me-nots and daisies." Nevertheless, it did not again mention Prohibition during the course of the campaign.

On July 4 the *Journal* denounced the Democratic platform, although it also insisted that the platform really wasn't of much consequence since Governor Smith would not be bound by it. "The distinguished Sacham of Tammany Hall knows far too much about corruption, in spite of his personal honesty, to waste his breath on Teapot Dome," the paper declared, referring to the platform's criticism of that Republican scandal. "It is noteworthy that the Democratic platform has nothing to say about currency. It is a curious omission from the historic party of inflation." The Democratic position on the tariff could not be called a straddle, the editorial sneered, "rather it is flop."

The newspapers of the country could read and quote what *The Wall Street Journal* had to say about the campaign, but they also sought out C. W. Barron for his personal views. The *Boston Herald* found him home at Cohasset in August and questioned him about Hoover. The *Journal* reprinted his reply: "Today the economist and statesman concerns himself with measures promoting material progress. No modern economist has better stated our problems of national progress than has Herbert Hoover."

In September Barron was back in the San, the Kellogg hospital in Battle Creek. It was his thirty-first visit, an extended stay for the regimen prescribed by Dr. John Harvey Kellogg: rest, exercise, massage, fresh air, baths, a pleasant social atmosphere, and a diet that omitted meat and fish and emphasized grains, fresh vegetables, and fruits, with nuts for protein, plus healthful liquids. Barron was extremely fond of Dr. Kellogg and had induced Kellogg to look into the possibility of establishing a winter clinic in Florida. Each time he saw Barron, Dr. Kellogg pleaded with him to get his weight down, and once Barron did, he said in a letter to Mary Bancroft, Hugh's daughter, "from 330 to 297 . . . but I will never get down to 250. . . . I fear I love chocolates too much."

Barron frequently smuggled his favorite Page and Shaw chocolates into the hospital, and he also slipped out for meals. His masseur, Mikkleborg, was partner to such surreptitious eating excursions. Barron was fond of Dr. John, but he hated the wheat and corn flakes that had made the sanitarium famous, recording in his notebook that they were invented when a cook dropped her rolling pin into a plate of the San's mush, which he hated even more. The drying batter flaked off, and "presto, corn flakes were born."

Each day Barron dictated to his secretary, William P. Tidwell, saw members of his family, and chatted with Mrs. Eames, who had taken a suite at the San to be near her friend. Casey Hogate came out to Battle Creek to consult with Barron and to report on the progress of the political campaign. Barron agreed that the election of Hoover was imperative, and Hogate was authorized to instruct Hamilton to call for a vote for Hoover by name, the first time Charles Dow's injunction against a presidential endorsement would be ignored.

Florida was struck by another storm on September 22, 1928, and Dr. Kellogg told Barron he was going to hold up his plans for a clinic at Clearwater for a while. Then Dr. Kellogg got down to the reason for his visit. Barron this time would have to obey his orders implicitly or he could not hope to get well. "I warned you years ago," Dr. Kellogg said, "that diabetes, kidney trouble, or something would get you if you did not reduce weight and correct your living and you are caught in the liver. You will feel better in a few weeks, and then your danger will be that you will forget what you have been through and what you are liable for. . . . You have had a very narrow escape and will probably never again have a full healthy liver but you have got a piece of it left and can build back, so with care you may live fifteen or twenty years." It was the final entry in Barron's notebook.

Late in the afternoon of October 2, C. W. Barron dictated to Tidwell and then signed some letters after asking, "What is the news? Are there any messages?" He indicated that he wished to nap after dinner, and at 7:30 P.M. he died in his sleep. He had observed his seventy-third birthday in July. *The New York Times*, publishing the story and Barron's portrait on page one plus two inside columns, included an Associated Press dispatch that said of the editor and Dow Jones president, "To a large extent he initiated the system of financial journalism in vogue today." On October 4 the *Times* in an editorial-page column paid its own tribute: "Barron took sides aggressively. . . . In the main his attitude was governed by a belief in the country's longer financial future and by sympathy with financial undertaking based on such belief. This view of things was apt to color his judgment of purely speculative movements; one of his hobbies was that some means ought to be discovered to restrain the activities of 'bear sellers' on the stock exchange. In the rapid dissemination of financial and speculative news, he was one of the pioneers."

The *New York Post* provided a tribute that would have especially pleased the feisty editor: "Clarence Walker Barron did for financial journalism what James Gordon Bennett did for general news. [Bennett, editor of the *New York Herald* in the Civil War period, is credited by journalism historians with developing enduring new methods of news coverage.] In 1887 he found the reporting of finance a matter of rumor and editorial opinion. Like Bennett, he separated the news from the chaos and concentrated upon its collection and delivery. *The Wall Street Journal's* coverage of the prices of the actual markets, the sheer facts of finance, is his monument today. Barron was one of the most picturesque figures that the starry skies of Wall Street ever produced." The *Saturday Evening Post* would state nearly two years later that "C. W. Barron was the father of financial journalism."

President and Mrs. Coolidge led the nation in honoring Clarence Walker Barron. The Coolidge telegram to Mrs. Bancroft and her family said in part, "It [Barron's death] will be a severe blow to business and philanthropic interests he has served so ably and unselfishly. . . . To me it is a personal loss as I valued his friendship and his counsel. Mrs. Coolidge joins me in heartfelt sympathy for you and your family." On October 4 *The Wall Street Journal* printed pages of tributes telegraphed and cabled from all over the world and reminiscences covering Barron's early days in New York by William Peter Hamilton, Casey Hogate, and other members of the staff. An especially warm appreciation came from former editor Thomas Woodlock, who left the paper in 1905 and who in 1928 was a member of the Interstate Commerce Commission in Washington. Several months later, on his retirement from the Commission, Woodlock would accept Bancroft and Hogate's invitation to return to the staff of the *Journal* as a special writer. Messages also were printed from Andrew W. Mellon, secretary of the treasury; Thomas W. Lamont of the House of Morgan; Charles M. Schwab, one of the founders of United States Steel; and Sir Basil Zaharoff. The *Boston Transcript* tribute, also reprinted, recalled: "His first important editorial position in Boston was the editorship of the financial department of the *Transcript*."

The funeral services were held October 5 in Trinity Church, Boston, since the Swedenborgian Church of the New Jerusalem, where Barron worshiped when he was in Boston, was being rebuilt, partly with a gift of $27,000 from Barron. His pastor, the Reverend H. Clinton Hay, officiated. Massachusetts Governor Alvan Tufts Fuller ordered the flags of the state house to be flown at half-mast during the time of the services.

On November 24 *The New York Times* provided details of C. W. Barron's will, which had been probated in Philadelphia. He left an estate of $1,575,000, said the paper, the bulk of it to Mrs. Jane Bancroft, his adopted daughter, who in 1918 had received with her children the majority of shares in Dow, Jones & Company from her mother. Barron's will named Hugh Bancroft and H. Wendell Endicott executors of trust funds of $100,000 each for grandchildren Jane, Jessie, and Hugh Bancroft, Jr.; Martha Endicott received his Beacon Street home in Boston. Barron's four brothers, Henry S., Frank E., George A., and Amos N., received $5,000 each, and the balance of his estate was to go to Mary Bancroft Badger.

Mary Bancroft actually received little from her stepgrandfather's fortune, but she did not suffer. She had divorced Badger (who, nevertheless, was given a job by her father as a writer) and married a Swiss businessman. In 1978, when she was 75, *Parade* magazine called Mary Bancroft "one of the world's most fascinating women." She was a confidante of Carl Jung, the famed analytical psychologist; Allen Dulles of the Office of Strategic Services, the United States intelligence service in World War II; and Henry R. Luce, a founder of *Time* and *Life* magazines; and she was the successful author of two novels. C. W. Barron would have loved it all.

Chapter 10

Bancroft and Hogate Take Over

> At a meeting of the Board of Directors of Dow, Jones & Company October 6, 1928 there were present Mrs. Bancroft, Mr. Bancroft and Mr. Hogate. Hugh Bancroft was elected to President in place of Clarence W. Barron, deceased.
>
> It was voted that Kenneth C. Hogate, Vice President, should thereafter be designated Vice President and General Manager with authority to sign checks on the various depositories of the Company and with authority to have access to the safe deposit vault of the Company, in company with other authorized officers.

Thus J. C. Hoskins began the official post-Barron chronicle of the company affairs after he had been named acting secretary, succeeding Bancroft, who had been elected president. Hoskins was also named treasurer. W. E. Jacoby was appointed auditor, replacing Hoskins, and Thomas J. Conlon was made assistant treasurer. Hogate, who had been vice-president and general manager under Barron, now became "an authorized officer" empowered to sign checks. The new secretary recorded that all 8,380 shares of the joint-stock association were represented by the three directors or by proxy. A 1928 dividend rate of $47 per share was approved.

On October 9 Hugh Bancroft's name and title of president appeared in *The Wall Street Journal* masthead, replacing that of C. W. Barron. As had

Barron's name, Bancroft's now stood alone. On page one of the paper appeared a statement:

> Ownership of Dow, Jones & Company, publishers of *The Wall Street Journal*, remains where it had been for many years. It is entirely in the hands of Mr. Barron's immediate family, who have long been and are actively engaged in the business.
>
> Directors of Dow, Jones & Co. are Jane W. W. Bancroft [Mrs. Hugh Bancroft], Hugh Bancroft and Kenneth C. Hogate; Vice President & General Manager . . . Kenneth C. Hogate; Secretary and Treasurer . . . J. C. Hoskins.
>
> I have been associated with Mr. Barron as his partner in the management of Dow, Jones & Co. and affiliated organizations for twenty years.
>
> Dow, Jones & Co. and *The Wall Street Journal* will continue their policy of national aggressiveness and independence under the same ownership and practically the same management as heretofore.
>
> Hugh Bancroft

Bancroft's name was set in 18-point type, somewhat larger than had been used previously by any Dow Jones chief executive in official announcements. The tall and tweedy Harvard graduate, engineer and lawyer by training, reluctant journalist by marriage, and longtime associate of the flamboyant Clarence Barron, was at long last firmly in control. He was proudly supported by his wife, Jane Waldron Bancroft, who owned all the stock except for that in trust for her children and sister Martha's daughter under the trusteeship of Hugh. He was backed loyally by Casey Hogate, general manager, and ailing editor William Peter Hamilton. Because of Hamilton's failing health, resulting in his death on December 9, 1929, Hogate often acted as editor of the editorial page while also serving as executive editor. Barron had urged that Hogate be given a chance to acquire Dow Jones stock, and within the year he had several hundred shares.

When Bancroft declared in his page-one statement that Dow Jones and the *Journal* would "continue their policy of national aggressiveness and independence," he was expressing his determination to carry out a plan that he and Hogate had discussed with Barron over several months—the establishment of a West Coast edition of *The Wall Street Journal* as the first physical move toward the creation of a truly national financial newspaper. Also, Bancroft was determined to restructure Dow, Jones & Company to bring under central control the various subsidiaries acquired under Barron's direction and to provide for additional managerial participation in the ownership while continuing family dominance. Bancroft ruled the Boston News Bureau, the Philadelphia News Bureau, and the *Journal*, as had Barron, but he believed a corporate entity was needed to replace the outmoded joint-stock association to enable Dow, Jones & Company to expand and to issue additional shares.

Bancroft's respect for Casey Hogate matched Barron's. He allowed his bulky deputy a free hand with *The Wall Street Journal* and the Dow Jones news services, while he sought to solve the financial problems of the Philadelphia and Boston companies. First, the directors authorized a loan of $185,000 to the Philadelphia News Bureau; a loan of $100,000 to the Boston News Bureau would follow a few months later. Barron had spent money freely in his final years, refusing to heed Bancroft's warnings. The Boston and Philadelphia managers had given Barron access to the cash drawers whenever he demanded it. According to William Tidwell, Barron's chief secretary in the 1920s, his boss had maintained this prodigal attitude ever since he learned that his wife, Jessie, had willed all her Dow Jones stock to her daughter and grandchildren and none to him. Pound and Moore, editors of *They Told Barron*, estimated that Barron spent half a million dollars a year, mostly drawn from the cash flow of his various companies, during the final years of his life. Such behavior may have been the real source of the constant friction between Barron and Bancroft. Following Barron's death, it was discovered that he had willed his dairy farm, which Bancroft insisted Barron couldn't afford, to his son-in-law as a grim postmortem jest. The tension between Barron and his son-in-law may have contributed to Bancroft's ill health, which threatened to cut short his tenure as the new Dow Jones chief executive; he hurried to get the company in order.

The officials of *The Wall Street Journal* scrupulously executed the editorial mandates of C. W. Barron during his last days and in the transition period after his death, emphasizing his perennial market bullishness while attempting to warn readers that stock-market prices were dangerously high. The paper also supported Herbert Hoover for president. On October 2, the day of Barron's death, the *Journal* rhetorically asked, "What is the Market Saying?" and answered that it was demanding the election of Hoover, which by then the *Journal* assumed was certain. The editorial also warned cautiously against speculation: "Not every market sign is favorable as students will readily recognize. For two years past the stock market has tended to contract in the activity of stocks following secondary reactions and to expand in the number of popular issues when those reactions are recovered and new highs in a long bull market are made. In the Industrial group, which monopolizes so much of the trading, it might be said that the front of the advance is more widespread and therefore conceivably vulnerable."

The editorial was, of course, unsigned, but Hamilton evidently was at work; it was the kind of language he used. He clarified his somewhat obscure warning by suggesting that there was the prospect of a business downturn, noting that the textile and building industries were showing weakness.

Hamilton and the *Journal* were less murky in discussing Al Smith's campaign for president on October 9: "Never did a candidate for public office make himself so cheap, give himself away so completely, as Alfred E. Smith in his speech at Sedalia, Mo. He devoted most of it to ridicule of economy in government. . . . The business people of the country know what economy means. Waste meant the squandering of millions in the last Democratic administration in Washington. Economy [under President Coolidge] has meant the reduction of the national debt by a third and the establishment of government efficiency at greatly reduced cost. . . . It is not merely true that Smith has reached his limit; he is going back."

On November 1 *The Wall Street Journal* carried out an order of the dying Barron to do what it never before had done, endorse a presidential candidate by name: "That a financial newspaper should be independent goes without saying. *The Wall Street Journal* has criticized the tariff more than it ever praised it. It has opposed the Eighteenth amendment. It regards the plea that labor is more efficient under Prohibition as a thoroughly immoral argument for chattel slavery. Nevertheless it advises its readers to vote for Hoover, as the soundest proposition for those with a financial stake in the country." Equally important, the paper said, was the issue of socialism. "The attitudes of the two candidates on State Socialism, a phrase which Mr. Smith ignorantly misunderstood, is of vital importance to finance. A financial newspaper which did not recognize the bearing of political and social problems would be like a doctor treating abrasions of the skin and ignoring the broken leg underneath them."

The socialism charge irked Democratic National Chairman John J. Raskob. But Raskob's protests were ignored, and the paper sought to offset his influence among its readers by publishing a copyrighted article by Henry Ford, which began, "I am asked by *The Wall Street Journal* to give my reasons for my support of Herbert Hoover for president of the United States." Ford's entente with the *Journal*, engendered by Barron as one of his final acts, was complete. Ford was available for frequent interviews, and Ford Motor Company and its subsidiaries had become regular advertisers in the paper.

There was no *Wall Street Journal* on November 7 since the stock exchanges were closed on election day. On November 8 the paper saluted Herbert Hoover's landslide victory with admirable restraint, noting that the popular vote of 21,392,190 for Hoover and Curtis to 15,016,443 for Smith and Robinson would translate into 444 of the 531 electoral college votes. Hoover carried New York, as the paper had said he must do to win, by more than 100,000 votes. When Democrat Franklin D. Roosevelt was confirmed as New York's governor by a narrow margin, Casey Hogate wryly told his associates to expect news of neighborhood fights. He had just bought a 300-acre farm in Dutchess County, where Governor-elect Roosevelt also had a country place. The two men became friends despite their political differences.

A Hoover "victory boom" sent the stock market soaring immediately after the election. On November 16 a record 6,641,250 shares changed hands. The market had gained from 5 to 15 points since the election. The public was buying heavily on margin, and the rate for call money (money lent by bankers to brokers that could be "called"—i.e., demand could be made for full payment—at any time) rose to 12 percent. When the *New York World* criticized the high rate, *The Wall Street Journal* denounced the paper as an "amateur in financial criticism, unable to get its facts straight." Call money at 12 percent over the end of the year was no great wonder, the *Journal* said. "Stocks sold in 1928 would have represented the cashing in of large profits on which income surtax would have been paid." Thus traders actually saved money by borrowing at 12 percent to retain their stocks. "In what way," the *Journal* asked querulously, "is the *New York World*, as representative of a large and fretful class, injured by strength in the stock market? Why need any of us be resentful because other people had made money? The money was not taken out of some unfortunate person's pocket and it can be conceded that some of the profits are paper profits. A bear of stock cannot make money unless somebody else loses; a bull of stock shares in general appreciation."

Throughout 1928 money had been pouring into New York from most of the world's financial centers either to buy shares or to participate in rising interest rates obtainable for brokers' loans financing the sale of stocks on margin. "A great river of gold," economist John Kenneth Galbraith called it 25 years later, flowing from London, Montreal, Shanghai, and Hong Kong. Not since the Dutch tulip craze of 1634–37 or the South Seas Bubble of the early eighteenth century had unrestrained speculation received such widespread support. While the public invested and gambled in stocks, great corporations, observing that vast profits could be made in the call-money market, supplied funds from their surplus accounts to bankers and brokers rather than investing in plants and inventory. Galbraith described the procedure in *The Great Crash of 1929*: "Banks supply funds to brokers, brokers to customers, and the collateral [the stocks purchased on margins of as little as 10 percent] goes back to the banks in a smooth and all but automatic flow." But, Galbraith noted, if the value of the collateral securities should fall and thus lower the protection they provided for the loan, there could be a call from the broker for added margin. If more margin was not forthcoming, the stocks could be sold at market prices to repay the loan. Robert Sobel, in his history of America's financial disasters, described the attitude of the suppliers of call money: "The corporations, realizing 20 per cent could be had in the call-money market, began to look at their cash surpluses and expansion programs in a new light. . . . Why buy bonds at 5 per cent or invest in a new plant which might return 10 per cent, when it would be much easier to lend money to margin buyers at 20 per cent?"

On December 6, 1928, as millions of happy Americans riding the crest of an unprecedented wave of prosperity prepared for a record holiday shopping season, there was a series of rude shocks in Wall Street, like the rumbles forecasting an earthquake. The Herbert Hoover boomlet, which it was said had disturbed the President-elect when he returned from a victory cruise to South America, had struck shoals. After rising more than 200 points in four years, the Dow Jones industrials fell ten points in a day. Two days later, in a front-page editorial, *The Wall Street Journal* summarized what it perceived as an ominous situation and urged an end to speculation:

> When the stock market has advanced to heights undreamed, over a period of more than four years, showing individual advances measurable in the hundreds with an average advance of over two hundred points in the Industrials of the Dow-Jones averages and seventy points in the Railroads, a decline, on a weighted average, of ten points in a single day may not be so formidable as it looks.
>
> With this premise it can still be said that Thursday's break in the stock market conveyed a warning. It says much for intrinsic strength that the market did not get out of hand even with a large public margin account open. Traders have grown used to wide fluctuations even if for a time they have all been one way. For the sensible observer the comment would be not that the decline was severe but rather that it should have been so long delayed. Everybody speculates nowadays and it is [a] matter of many years' experience that everybody's judgment is not so good as somebody's.
>
> There is obviously, and has been for some time past, an enormous amount of money in the country available for speculation, even irrespective of the New York call money market. We are still in a period of high prosperity, perhaps somewhat unevenly distributed, and with high wages considerably more general.
>
> It may be that the rich are growing richer, as the Socialists say, but it is certain that they are not growing richer at the expense of the poor. . . . The average income compares favorably with the true cost of living.
>
> But admitting all this latent strength in the general situation it is time to call a halt in speculative activities because of their unsettling effect when they have extended out of Wall Street into every considerable town or city in the country. . . . It is not everybody who is built for successful speculation but it takes a check in a great bull market to disclose that important fact.

The warning was a mild one and obviously was not directed at the "everybody" said by the *Journal* to have been infected with speculation fever. Actually, in 1928, fewer than 500,000 Americans were involved in the stock markets on an extended margin basis from among a population of 120 million, according to some economists. Later, economic historian Harold U. Faulkner estimated that 1 million were involved, and the *New York Times* reported that 2 million Americans owned securities in 1929, perhaps half that number on margin. Those gambling on margin were fewer than 1 percent of the population, but they mostly represented wealthy opinion leaders who were firmly optimistic. In 1928 they had seen Chrysler go from 63 to 132, General Electric from 136 to 221, and Allied Chemical & Dye to 250 from 154. Despite the fact that Radio Corporation of America, the darling of the bulls, fell an appalling 72 points during the brief December relapse (it previously had gone from 85 to 420, though it never paid a dividend), the general trader refused to be frightened by one small, faltering step of the bull market. *Journal* subscribers had enjoyed pleasant reading for an entire year, including such items as Montgomery Ward 117 to 440, Wright Aeronautics 69 to 289, and Du Pont 310 to 525. They were not about to be guided by the doubts and quibbles of the "Review and Outlook" editorials. The total number of shares traded on the New York Stock Exchange in 1928 was a record-breaking 920,550,032, compared with the prior record of 576,990,875. Unquestionably, a new record would again be set in 1929.

During the final week of 1928 it was rumored that President-elect Hoover might take some action on speculation following his inauguration, but Hoover remained silent, and the Federal Reserve rate stayed at 5 percent, with call money at 12. Alexander Dana Noyes, the financial editor of the *New York Times*, credited by some historians with forecasting a crash as early as 1928, was not all that sure in his report on the stock market published in the *Times* on January 1, 1929, though he, like William Peter Hamilton, urged caution. "Conservative judgment has only past experience to guide it," Noyes wrote, but that experience showed that "speculators always ignored high money rates, thus attracting abnormal supplies of funds into the market," funds that, he declared dourly, "inevitably fail the speculator in time of need." While Noyes implied trouble ahead, he was no more convincing than Hamilton. "Conservative prophets," he concluded, "seem yet too puzzled over the events of 1928 to make categorical predictions."

In February, as outgoing President Coolidge declared that the country was sound and stocks were cheap, Chairman Roy Young of the Federal Reserve Board in Washington cautioned bankers about the increase in supplies of call money, stating on February 14 after secret meetings of the Board that the Federal Reserve rate might go up from 5 to 6 percent. There were angry outcries in Wall Street, but the *Journal* said merely that the Federal Reserve Board should take action without making threats. Hoover was inaugurated on March 4. On March 26 the market again fell, this time an intra-day low of 15 points, as 8,246,740 shares changed hands. Charles E. Mitchell, robust and cocksure president of the powerful National City Bank and a director of the New York Federal Reserve Bank, led a Wall Street revolt against any Washington restraints. Mitchell announced that he intended to make $25 million available to the Wall Street community through the call-money market. "We feel that we have an obligation which is paramount to any Federal Reserve warning, or anything else, to avert any dangerous crisis in the money market," Mitchell declared.

Mitchell's effrontery was not challenged by *The Wall Street Journal*, though the paper would say later that his attitude was not that of the other officials of the New York Federal Reserve Bank. In Washington, Senator Carter Glass of Virginia called for Mitchell's resignation from the New York Federal Reserve Bank Board and demanded an investigation of the stock market and the easy-money policy of New York bankers. President Hoover summoned executives of the New York Stock Exchange for a discussion of the problems but took no action after he was advised that the New York Stock Exchange was subject to New York State and not federal regulation. Governor Franklin D. Roosevelt, however, also failed to act. *The Wall Street Journal* saw the problem easing and was undisturbed by government inactivity. It noted that bankers already were somewhat limiting the supply of call money. "It is true that banks are extending $296 million less to brokers directly than before the Federal Reserve Board issued its warning," the paper said, "but the fact that bank loans to brokers have been reduced is of little significance since such loans are only a small part of bank credit being extended on securities." At the same time, the *Journal* again warned that securities were overpriced in the context of long-term investment.

> The stock market is functioning normally when it gives free play to the efforts of those who are seeking highest prices for securities which investors can afford to pay. The idea that even speculators may logically ignore the long-term investment value of securities, though rather widely prevalent of late, of course, has no sound basis. One speculator may sell to another, but the ultimate disposition of stocks can only be to those who are willing to keep them. Any movement which carries prices beyond their investment level automatically cuts its own ground from under itself.
>
> Any question as to the right of the banking authorities to interfere with market activities then, becomes one of motive power behind the price movement. If prices are rising because intrinsic values are rising, traders in stocks are legitimately entitled to use credit in their intermediate processes of distribution. But if the prices are rising after the line of investment value, present and prospective, has been passed it can only be because more and more credit is being pumped into the loan account. To continue such a process after the ultimate market upon which all floating supplies of stocks are to be disposed of has been closed would obviously be foolhardy.

The *Journal* did not join Senator Glass in calling for the resignation of Mitchell from the New York Federal Reserve Bank. But Mitchell did eventually resign after pumping his $25 million into Wall Street to help finance call loans, which were earning interest at 16 percent. Said a brief note in the paper on April 12: "Approximately $25,000,000 loans were called by banks around noon, and later an additional $10,000,000 were called. New funds came into the market in the afternoon, however, more than compensating for withdrawals." It was Congress, not the press, that would expose Mitchell's machinations in the 1929 stock market at public hearings in 1933. At that time, he outraged the public by admitting he had arranged a "sale" of his National City Bank stock to his wife to support a net loss of $2,800,000 for income-tax purposes and had procured bank loans of $2,400,000 at no interest whatever to enable him to invest in the market, loans less than 5 percent repaid when he testified.

The Wall Street Journal did not excuse irresponsible conduct when it learned of it, however. It sometimes criticized big business, taking on the Ford Motor Company in March 1929, when Ford's Canadian subsidiary split its stock 20 to 1 shortly after W. R. Campbell, a Ford vice-president, had warned the public when the stock sold at $675 a share on the New York curb market that "our financial position does not warrant the assumption that we can earn dividends on a valuation of this kind." Following the split, the stock soared to an equivalent of $1,150 a share and closed above $1,000 a share. "Is this Henry Ford's conception of justice to stock sellers and buyers or merely Mr. Campbell's idea of it?" the *Journal* demanded. "Did Mr. Campbell know whereof he spoke when he said that the directors had never considered a possible new issue of stock, or is he excluded from the confidence of the directors?" The editorial pointed out that the company would soon report itself in the red by $3,700,000 on its 1928 operations. "A change in the company's situation in two months would be amazing," it concluded.

The *Journal* also attacked the critics of Wall Street and the general business community, including critics within business: "Now that both the Administration and opposition forces have had their ample say about unemployment, one thing is essential for the restoration of prosperity. That is for business to stop pawing itself over to find out how sick it is. If it ceases this morbid performance, it will have the right to ask outsiders to abandon their daily clinics over it."

Hugh Bancroft, the diffident, long-suffering chief executive of Dow, Jones & Company, was eager to prove to the world what he had demonstrated so often to the unappreciative Clarence Barron—that he knew how to move the company into higher levels of efficiency and profitability, to unify it, and to bring it into the era of modern business practices. Though he had become president of a company that was the largest financial-news organization in the world, he nevertheless was keenly aware that its structure was obsolete and anachronistic. While Dow, Jones & Company had grown up under those who could pontificate on the American and international economic order, some of its executives lacked knowledge or deep appreciation of current business philosophy or technique, Bancroft believed. Barron's policy of hiring $10-a-week stenographers who would learn the business from existing staff perpetuated faults and weaknesses. True, there were all sorts of unschooled geniuses who were building American business and industry, such as Thomas Edison, Henry Ford, and John Raskob, the new ruling bull in Wall Street. The *Journal* had done well in its way under Dow and Barron and currently had an ex-stenographer inventive genius of its own, Joseph Ackell, whom Casey Hogate had discovered and put to work in the company's production department. Casey himself, of course, was a college man; Barron could be credited for that. But the company was ingrown, Bancroft said; it was a conglomeration of scattered little fiefdoms; it was incapable of orderly expansion and could not hope to perpetuate itself if it remained an outmoded stock association.

There were 21 independent companies and business entities in the Barron complex, most of them created by Bancroft under Barron's orders. The system worked after a fashion so long as Barron was alive, though both the Philadelphia and Boston companies were near bankruptcy after meeting Barron's extensive demands for money for personal expenses over a period of years. Some of the subsidiary firms had been formed under Bancroft's direction to solve specific legal problems or to launch new activities. The Telegraph News Company was among the first, organized shortly after the Barrons acquired Dow, Jones & Company, when Bancroft discovered that the Dow Jones news-ticker service was operating without a required City of New York franchise. He hastened to obtain one through the new company. The Wall Street Building Company was formed to acquire the building at 44 Broad Street from the General Electric Company, and Bancroft later used the property as security for expansion loans. The Russell Telegraph Company, a ticker service operated north of Thirtieth Street, was another Dow Jones subsidiary. Doremus & Company was incorporated as a successor to Barron's advertising service in New York, and Barron's Publishing Company owned *Barron's, The National Financial Weekly*. There were several news-ticker companies outside New York: Illinois Telegraph News Company; Dow, Jones & Company of Michigan; Dow, Jones & Company of the Potomac; and Dow, Jones & Company of Ohio among them. Thus in 1929 Bancroft inherited lordship over a number of little baronies that he was required to service with news and direction from New York but which at first he could not adequately control. The rates most subscribers paid for Dow Jones and *Wall Street Journal* services were minimal, and the Boston and Philadelphia operations would probably require further subsidy.

What was needed, Bancroft told his wife, was a holding company that could provide central direction for all the subsidiaries. The problem was not an easy one, Bancroft acknowledged, but he could depend on Hogate, the one college man C. W. Barron had picked, a man who shared his own concerns about the problems and challenges of the future. Jane also was fond of Hogate and she strongly supported her husband. She and Hugh continued to control almost all the stock, but they arranged to make a block of 800 shares available to Hogate. Jane was aware that her husband's health problems made him want to provide for a line of succession under family control as soon as possible. In Jane's opinion there could hardly be a better man for this reorganization than Hugh Bancroft, who wrote the book on inheritance-tax problems and was the company's most experienced executive, especially in his outside contacts with the business community. Barron and Dow had been excellent reporters on the world of business and finance; Bancroft was a participant in it. He had proved himself in New England as a business administrator by directing the Boston Port Authority in its successful public-works projects. He was president of Dow, Jones & Company and the Boston and Philadelphia news bureaus, and he was publisher of *Barron's* as Barron had been; in addition, Bancroft was director of the Atlantic National Bank of Boston, the Cohasset National Bank, Counselors' Securities Trust Company, Chain and General Equities, Inc., and the Chain Store Investment Corporation. He was intelligently active in all his jobs and directorships.

Early in 1929 Bancroft arranged a salary and bonus agreement for himself and Hogate, a rather simple transaction since the two principals and Mrs. Bancroft were the only Dow Jones directors. The two men were to receive annual salaries of $60,000 each plus a yearly bonus of 5 percent of net profit up to $750,000, an arrangement that would continue until readjusted or abrogated. Under this arrangement Bancroft and Hogate divided a bonus of $37,500; just how the bonus was split is not indicated in the company minutes, but it was probably divided equally. The total represented relatively modest compensation for the two senior executives, since Dow, Jones & Company's net profit in 1929 would reach a whopping $1,843,799. The Hugh Bancroft family income would, of course, be based on share ownership as well as Hugh's salary and bonus; Mrs. Jane Bancroft's holdings and the trusts for her three children—Jane, Jessie, and Hugh, Jr.—and for Martha Endicott then consisted of 8,371 of a total 8,380 shares, prior to the allocation of shares to Hogate. The 1929 dividends would total $92 a share, including $20 extra declared in January.

As executive editor and general manager of *The Wall Street Journal*, Casey Hogate reorganized and coordinated the news-ticker and bulletin-messenger services so far as he could under the existing structure pending legal reorganization. Hogate named Joseph J. Ackell, director of manufacturing, in charge of those services, with H. C. "Deac" Hendee, formerly of the Washington bureau, as his assistant. Hogate chose well. Ackell, born in Brooklyn in 1906, had joined Dow, Jones & Company as a stenographer in the advertising department in 1925. He later served as secretary to business managers Joseph Cashman and J. C. Hoskins. As director of manufacturing, Ackell spent as much time as he could possibly spare improving and overseeing the repair of communications equipment, working at odd hours in a windowless "experiment room" in a company plant on Forty-seventh Street. By late 1929 Ackell had developed a new high-speed news ticker capable of receiving up to 60 words a minute and so reliable it would come to be known as the Iron Horse to the news-ticker service employees.

When Hogate put Ackell in charge of the ticker and bulletin services, Ackell let it be known that none of the independent offices was going to remain that way for long, and he obtained quick compliance with his directives when the local managers learned they would never receive the new fast tickers otherwise. Within the year Ackell had consolidated the management of the 24 ticker offices from Boston to Los Angeles, though Montreal with its French-speaking manager maintained its autonomy. Bancroft and Hogate were well pleased.

Like Bancroft, Casey Hogate continued to find much to be done toward immediate reorganization and improvement without awaiting a master plan for restructuring the company. Hogate undertook the expansion of the news content of the *Journal* and the brightening of its presentation. He sought experienced journalists and bright young college graduates in his effort to build a staff fully qualified for the national effort ahead. In 1923 Hogate hired William Henry Grimes, who had been financial-news editor of United Press in New York, as a writer and editor who would eventually take over as bureau chief in Washington from the aging and ailing John Boyle. Grimes, born in Bellevue, Ohio, on March 7, 1892, had organized the Washington bureau of United Press after working on Cleveland dailies while he was a student at Case Western Reserve University. In 1926 Grimes became the *Journal's* Washington bureau chief and was authorized to increase his staff from three to five.

Hogate had problems expanding his New York staff. Bancroft was accustomed to paying Barron's low rates for talent and Hogate was not seeking apprentices or stenographers. Consequently he was cheered when, in May 1929, a personable young man he had met months before at DePauw University, his alma mater, wrote seeking a job. He was Bernard Kilgore, editor of the *DePauw*, the student newspaper, and a graduating senior. Kilgore hoped to obtain a scholarship to the Columbia University School of Journalism and wondered if he also could be considered for work at *The Wall Street Journal*.

Hogate sent an encouraging reply, and when Kilgore's application to Columbia was not accepted, Hogate happily invited him to join the *Journal* staff in September at an unprecedented starting salary of $40 a week. Once again, Hogate prevailed over the counting room, as he had when he induced Barron to improve the starting pay scale in 1923.

However, Hogate's New York staff problems were far from resolved by employment of inexperienced college graduates. William Peter Hamilton, the brilliant English journalist who had joined the staff in 1899 and became editorial-page editor in 1908, obviously could not continue in his job much longer. Despite ill health, he was writing editorials for the *Journal* as well as *Barron's*, but Hogate had taken over the supervisory editorial-page duties in addition to his responsibilities as Dow Jones general manager and executive editor of *The Wall Street Journal*. Following the death of Hamilton in December 1929, Frederick A. Korsmeyer, born in Decatur, Illinois, August 4, 1877, assumed the editorial writing duties. He had joined the staff as railroad editor in December 1907 after working on the *New York Commercial* and various western dailies. Bancroft undertook to ease Hogate's personnel problems by inviting back to the paper his former son-in-law, Sherwin Badger, who had departed the *Journal* for the banking business after Mary Bancroft divorced him. Early in 1929 Badger was one of the by-line writers (under Hogate's policy of more by-lines in the *Journal*) and also a Hogate assistant. Badger became editor of *Barron's* magazine after Hamilton's death.

Casey Hogate was a busy man, and his wife complained that she rarely saw him. In addition to his *Wall Street Journal* duties, which kept him reading proofs in his office late at night, as Joe Ackell's superior he was responsible for all ticker-maintenance services and for the manufacturing ventures. Hogate participated in Bancroft's planning activities as a member of the new executive planning committee, which also included Ackell. There were trips around the country to look into the condition of the various Dow Jones news-ticker offices and news bureaus, including a visit to the West Coast. The ticker services, despite Ackell's threats, provided only sketchy inventories, and Hogate and Bancroft could find no cost-accounting procedures in place among any divisions of the company. Hogate was instructed to correct such misfeasances.

By summer 1929 Bancroft had made himself president of all the major Dow Jones subsidiaries, and the organization plans for the Pacific Coast edition of *The Wall Street Journal* were completed. As Hugh Bancroft marked his fiftieth birthday with his family at Cohasset on September 13, all appeared well. The Pacific Coast edition announcements were in type for publication the following day.

It was the summer of great content. America was prosperous. The nation's automobile industry led the world and was chief contributor to the burgeoning American economy. The country was behind in shipbuilding orders, as C. W. Barron had forecast, and coal mining was not going well, but there was an urban construction boom that especially flourished in New York City. It resulted in new skyscrapers racing to supplant the Woolworth Building, which, at 792 feet, had been the world's tallest building since 1913. The Manhattan skyline changed spectacularly as the Wall Street Building, a near neighbor of Dow, Jones & Company, was first to win the race at 927 feet. But this record did not last long. William Van Allen, architect of the Chrysler Building, symbolized the competitive spirit of the era's builders when he secretly designed an inner steel tower for the building, which was thrust up in the last phase of construction after the final height of the Wall Street Building was learned. This maneuver made the Chrysler Building 1,046 feet tall instead of the initially planned 925 and gave it the title for two years, until the Empire State Building topped the skyline at 1,250 feet. However, such accomplishments did not keep the construction industry's collapse from leading the way to economic disaster after the 1929 crash. But in 1929 this frenzied activity dramatized the feeling of New York and Wall Street that the rich would go on getting richer while the poor got poorer, as Van and Schenck would tell Broadway in song. Nevertheless, New Yorkers were intensely happy; they "danced in a champagne haze on the rooftop of the world," F. Scott Fitzgerald wrote, and even the narrator of *The Great Gatsby* was a Wall Street man.

John Raskob, General Motors executive, Democratic national chairman, and evangelical leader of the financial bulls, wrote an article for the August *Ladies' Home Journal* stating the Wall Street thesis: "Everybody Ought to Be Rich." And millions were beginning to think they were rich, as the great American middle class and skilled laborers finally began to obtain benefits previously reserved for the affluent. They bought automobiles, radios, refrigerators, household electrical appliances that took the place of the servants enjoyed by the very rich, comfortable davenports, Grand Rapids furniture, phonographs, and player pianos. They purchased multicolored lampshades imitating those created by Louis Comfort Tiffany, who popularized this brilliant facet of art nouveau in America. Competition from Europe had returned, but American industry was protected to an extent by the Fordney-McCumber Tariff of 1922 and by England's return to the gold standard, which pegged the pound at $4.86 and priced many British products out of the American market.

Few Americans paid attention to *The Wall Street Journal's* suggestion that they buy stocks to keep. Speculative trading was the order of the day. Owning Liberty bonds during the war had taught many ordinary investors to be comfortable with investment in securities rather than in more tangible goods, and they soon learned to gamble in bonds and shares and debentures, which were to be held only briefly on borrowed margin money. People liked to talk as if they were committed in Wall Street even if they were not, and it was becoming a mark of distinction to be seen with a copy of *The Wall Street Journal* or *Barron's* magazine. American farm products continued to bring in gold from abroad, and the interest rates on call money attracted capital from around the world. It appeared that prosperity had come to stay, that prices of stock would endlessly climb, and that most Americans could participate in the boundless prosperity. When Arthur Brisbane, leading columnist of the Hearst newspapers, dared to declare that call money at 10 percent was too high, *The Wall Street Journal* sharply admonished him, saying, "Even in general newspapers accurate knowledge is required for discussing most things. Why is it that any ignoramus can talk about Wall Street?" *Harper's* magazine, however, thought that a high order of intelligence was not characteristic of such discussion that summer and commented, "Investing has become a children's crusade, not an adventure for a few hard-boned knights; a place for the butcher, the barber and the candlestick maker."

On May 8 the *Journal* scolded the Federal Reserve Board severely for refusing to raise the rediscount rate, as recommended by the directors of the New York Federal Reserve Bank, but nevertheless making threats to do so. "What keeps the Federal Reserve from recognizing the futility of terrorist statements and inconsistent policies?" it asked.

> Why not try its most direct weapon, the bank rate, to accomplish its avowed ends? It is an open secret that the directorate of the New York bank has repeatedly voted for an increase in the rate only to be turned down by Washington. A similar recommendation has been made by the Washington Advisory Council.
>
> Why will not the board follow the advice of practical men of affairs? Can it believe that its own policy, a failure for more than a year, is the mildest method of reducing the outstanding volume of Federal Reserve credit? . . . What has our sound country to fear from legitimate credit control, enforced by a high bank rate? Or for that matter, what has Wall Street to fear when its margins are the highest in history?
>
> To hurt business is bad enough in all conscience. To hurt it without correcting alleged evils is worse than stupid. Positive action, however easily it could have been avoided, is preferable to the present policy of terrorism and unsettlement. Such action may be the most effective, yet mildest, method of correction. It may prove the final demonstration of whether stock transactions and prices are based upon savings and sound values, or upon speculation enthusiasm based upon borrowed money.

Economists in later years, Milton and Rose Friedman and Harold Faulkner among them, attributed the continuing Wall Street boom and the ensuing disaster in part to the easy-money policy of the Washington Federal Reserve Board, which rejected the warnings of the New York Federal Reserve Bank. "The . . . Federal Reserve System was to blame for the mistaken monetary policy that converted a recession into a catastrophic depression," wrote the Friedmans in their 1980 book, *Free to Choose: A Personal Statement*. Instead, they added, Hoover was blamed. In his memoirs, Hoover called the Washington Federal Board members "mediocrities." "The Federal Reserve Board, in those times, was a body of startling incompetence," Galbraith later agreed.

Wall Street, of course, was pleased when the Federal Reserve Board lowered the discount rate from 4 to 3½ percent early in 1927. Bankers and brokers made a profit on call money loaned as margin for as little as 5 percent so long as the Federal Reserve prime rate was 3½. When the price of call money rose to 20 percent and money was withheld from plant improvement and construction by corporations preferring to loan money at high rates, it was too late for the Federal Reserve rate, finally lifted to 6 percent, to provide any restraint upon speculators, bankers, or business. The *Journal's* scolding of the Federal Reserve Board in May 1929 had had no more effect than its previous reprimands. The Wall Street brokers and bankers were getting rich, and speculators, envisioning a 100 percent rise in stock prices within the year, were little concerned about the level of interest rates on their margin loans.

Those investing in the stock markets, however, were not the only ones exploiting easy credit. While the speculators in Wall Street were putting down as little as 10 percent, as the Florida land speculators had earlier, American consumers were also enjoying the credit boom and were caught up in proliferating installment-purchase plans, patterned after plans developed by Raskob for the automobile industry, which "contributed almost as much to the growth of the industry as the self-starter," wrote Jonathan Daniels in his book on the period, *The Time Between the Wars*. In time, the country was chin-deep in credit buying, not only of automobiles but also of radios, phonographs, furniture, and refrigerators, as Wall Street popularized its profitable invention, the investment trust. On May 25, General Motors, Ford's powerful new competitor, aided by Raskob's credit innovation, reported its greatest earnings in history: during the quarter ending March 31, 1929, its net profit totaled $61,910,987.

John Raskob, the former stenographer of Pierre du Pont who had induced E. I. du Pont de Nemours & Company to buy control of General Motors and install him as an influential executive, had moved his offices into Wall Street, where he became the high priest of the American dollar worshipers. Following Raskob to New York were other automobile tycoons, such as Walter P.

Chrysler, William C. Durant, and the Fisher Brothers, all firebreathing stock-market bulls. *The Wall Street Journal* sometimes referred to the group as the "western invasion." In his *Ladies' Home Journal* article, Raskob not only insisted that everyone ought to be rich, but he also explained precisely how they could accomplish it. All that was needed, Raskob wrote, was to save $15 a month for investment in common stocks, which in 20 years would be worth $80,000. Raskob also proposed a poor man's investment trust that would pyramid profits so that an investment of $200 in carefully selected stocks could be worth $500 within months. "From anyone else," wrote Sobel, "at a different time, the scheme would have been ridiculed. But this was 1929, and the writer was John Raskob; by September, plans were afoot to put the program into operation." The *Literary Digest* called Raskob's idea the "greatest vision of Wall Street's greatest mind."

Scores of investment trusts had been springing up for some months, in fact. Many had hole-in-the-wall offices with a desk, a chair, and a telephone. Others were mammoth companies organized by powerful banks and brokers. All were prepared to put together stock portfolios for the investor and to provide him with leverage, whereby a minimum amount of money mixed with credit could share interest in maximum holdings of stock. Some of the investment trusts quickly grew to tremendous size. One, United Founders, cited by Galbraith, suffered a net loss in assets of $301,385,504 by 1935. In 1929 its stock sold at $75 a share. By 1935 the price of the stock had dropped to less than 75 cents a share.

In the summer and early fall of 1929, few readers accepted *The Wall Street Journal's* counsel on investment for keeps as opposed to stock speculation. That included the editors of *Barron's, The National Financial Weekly* who, in an editorial on September 9, chastised Roger Babson, economist, educator, theologian, and forecaster, for saying before his annual National Business Conference in Wellesley, Massachusetts, that the stock market was headed for disaster. "Sooner or later a crash is coming," Babson declared, "and it may be terrific." Babson insisted that what had happened to the Florida land boom would happen to Wall Street. He predicted a 60- to 80-point drop in the Dow Jones Averages and said, "Factories will shut down . . . men will be thrown out of work . . . the vicious circle will go into full swing and the result will be a serious business depression."

Barron's scornfully called Babson the Sage of Wellesley and pointed out that Babson had made the same prediction at least twice previously during 1928, as indeed he had, though less emphatically. No one aware of Babson's "notorious inaccuracy" in past statements would pay any attention to him,

Barron's asserted. It was one of William Peter Hamilton's last editorials as editor of *Barron's*; he died on December 9 and was succeeded by Sherwin Badger.

Bancroft and Hogate evidently were quite convinced that the Wall Street boom and the nation's financial good health were not going to end in the near future. They moved ahead with their plans to establish the Pacific Coast edition, which was announced in the *Journal* on September 14:

> Dow, Jones & Co., publishers of *The Wall Street Journal*, take pleasure in announcing the PACIFIC COAST EDITION of THE WALL STREET JOURNAL, to be published on the Pacific Coast.
>
> This newspaper, which will begin publication in October, brings to the Pacific Coast a complete daily journal of finance and business employing the full national and international resources of the foremost financial news gathering and distributing organization in the world.
>
> THE PACIFIC COAST EDITION of THE WALL STREET JOURNAL will present daily all of the important Eastern and National financial news together with full coverage of western news. It will contain outstanding analyses of companies and the study of security values regularly appearing in *The Wall Street Journal* . . . exclusive features for which *The Wall Street Journal* is widely noted.

Bancroft and Hogate selected the staff for the new publication from Dow, Jones & Company despite a lack of staff depth. Carl P. Miller, West Coast advertising representative of Dow, Jones & Company, was named president and Deac Hendee, who had worked for the *Journal* in Washington and New York as a reporter and subeditor, was named editor.

The *Journal's* promotional advertisements heralding its West Coast edition continued to appear through September and into October. On October 14, the paper indicated that publication of the new edition was imminent: "Look for its first appearance this week. . . . [It] will provide the essence of last-minute news of finance and business, gathered through a private telegraph system embracing 93 cities of United States and Canada."

The new edition came off the press in San Francisco on October 21, just eight days before the bottom fell out of the stock market.

Chapter 11

Panic in Wall Street

After a euphoric 1929 Labor Day the stock market seemingly confirmed an era of good fortune for the peaceful, prospering nation by spurting to a new high on Tuesday, September 3. The Dow Jones Industrial Average stood at 381.17. United States Steel, a faltering leader during the summer, had recovered to 262. General Electric was at 396, more than triple its price of 18 months before. On Labor Day, radio station WJZ in New York telephoned the famed seer Evangeline Adams for her stock-market forecast. "The Dow Jones could climb to Heaven," said Adams, who claimed J. Pierpont Morgan, steel man Charles Schwab, and film star Mary Pickford among her clients. The market's rise on the 3rd made Evangeline appear infallible to her followers. Thousands subscribed to her financial newsletter and hundreds clamored to pay her $20 for personal counsel about the future of the New York stock market.

The Wall Street Journal ignored Evangeline Adams and would continue to do so, but it was pleased with the post–Labor Day trading on the various exchanges. "The forward movement of the main body of stocks was vigorously resumed in the early dealings," the paper reported on Wednesday. "While irregularity cropped out from time to time during the day, due to profit-taking attracted by the character of recent gains, the main upward trend was well sustained throughout the session. Bullish enthusiasm was sustained by the return of United States Steel to leadership in the industrial division." It was to be the high point of the Great Bull Market and the beginning of the end of a fantastic economic epoch.

There had been signs that summer that the speculators and investors chose to ignore. In August, the Federal Reserve Board at long last raised the discount rate to 6 percent, as *The Wall Street Journal* had long insisted it should. But the Board had acted too late, the paper said on August 12 after the deed was finally done; building starts had begun to decline, the consumer spending rate slackened, wholesale commodity prices decreased, and employment dropped after steadily rising through June. These signals were ignored by the bankers and speculators. Brokers' loans soon after Labor Day passed $6 billion. Clarence Hatry, an American-styled English speculator with many Wall Street ties, went bankrupt. It was feared that his failure in the coin-operated-machine and automatic-photography businesses—with losses of $60 million to investors—might discourage the American public about the profit potential of new investment ventures. Jesse Livermore, temporarily a leading Wall Street bull, said in New York that Hatry's failure had nothing to do with American market conditions. The securities markets plunged abroad but faltered only momentarily in America. Hatry was indicted and ultimately sentenced to nine years in prison for the defrauding of investors.

Following a break in prices on the New York Stock Exchange and a quick recovery on October 3, *The Wall Street Journal* found the future to be bright in its assessment on October 7. "Confidence regarding the immediate position of the market was greatly strengthened by recoveries which took place in Steel, American Can, Westinghouse, and the other leaders in the last few minutes of Friday's trading," the paper said. It denied rumors that Arthur Cutten, the Canadian expatriate and former Chicago bookkeeper who was supplanting John Raskob as leader of the bulls, had become a bear. "Mr. Cutten said no relaxation of the national prosperity is in sight, and expressed the opinion that the market structure could support brokers' loans from $10 billion to $12 billion."

The *Journal* also quoted the ubiquitous Charles E. Mitchell of National City Bank as he was about to embark home from Germany: "I see no reason for the end-of-year slump some are predicting. The markets are now in a generally healthy condition." And, of course, Professor Irving Fisher of Yale, economist and monetary reformer, was available for comment: "I expect to see the stock market a good deal higher than it is today within a few months. . . . There may be a recession on stock prices, but not anything in the nature of a crash."

These comments apparently were in response to the widely publicized forebodings of Roger Babson, the Sage of Wellesley, Massachusetts, which continued to circulate. On October 15 *The Wall Street Journal* renewed its criticism of the speculative frenzy in Wall Street, this time targeting on the popular investment trusts. Nearly 800 such investment companies had arisen and, while some were well managed, 751 were destined to go down in the course of the depression after the market debacle of October 1929. Noting the "bewildering variety of securities of investment trusts, trading corporations and holding companies which have been issued to investors of late," the *Journal* cautiously proposed that "it may be doubted whether purchasers of these wares have always examined them as carefully as they should. It is a little more than ordinarily important that the principle of *caveat emptor* be borne in mind when considering for investment the stocks of corporations, differing as widely in purpose and structure as these do, from familiar investments in the past as well as from one another."

But, generally, the *Journal* continued strong in defense of Wall Street, reserving mostly for itself the right of criticism, saying typically as late as September 13 that "Wall Street asks no favors but only to be left alone in its business of protecting those thrifty millions for whom it is trustee." When on October 16 the New York Investment Bankers Association expressed doubts about the future of "public service stocks" and stated that most issues "are selling far above their intrinsic value," the *Journal* said with some asperity that the Association should be more careful in its generalizing and declared that its report was already outdated when issued. On Friday, October 18, the market broke again, with blue chips, as Oliver J. Gingold, the paper's leading market analyst, called them, such as United States Steel, General Electric, and Westinghouse, down ten points or more in the day and a half of Friday-Saturday trading. Gingold wrote that bears led by Jesse Livermore (who had switched sides again) were responsible and predicted that Arthur Cutten and other leaders of the bulls wouldn't allow prices to slide much further. *The Wall Street Journal* continued optimistic in its editorials and pronounced itself pleased that Andrew Mellon, secretary of the treasury, had disclosed that he would remain in the cabinet at least until 1933: "Optimism again prevails. . . . [Mr. Mellon's] announcement did more to restore confidence than anything else."

But on October 21 William Peter Hamilton, editor of the *Journal's* editorial page and of *Barron's* magazine, decided that the time had come for another general warning on the speculative situation in the country. Three times previously, on January 7, 1927; June 25, 1928; and July 30, 1928, Hamilton had written in *The Wall Street Journal* that the Dow Theory, which he helped to define in his book on the subject, strongly indicated the termination of the long bull market. Like Alexander Noyes, the financial editor of the *New York Times*, Hamilton had warned in vain, but he tried once again, more emphatically this time, printing his editorial, entitled "A Turn in the Tide," on the editor's page of *Barron's*. Hamilton wrote:

> There is an interesting development in the price movement, as shown by the two Dow-Jones averages since the industrial high of 381.17 on September 3, and the railroad high of 189.11 on the same date. In a month, or down to October 4, the industrials had declined 56 points, and the railroads, which have normally a much smaller range of fluctuation, had lost over 20 points from the high of the year.
>
> Of course, 56 points represents a severe secondary decline in what has been a bull market for six years, remembering always that we are dealing with very high figures. Even then, with the industrial average in the neighborhood of 80, the equivalent would be an 11-point decline. Does the movement of the market indicate little more than this? In the successive rallies it will be noticed that the first brought the industrials back to 372.39, the second to 355.95 and the third, on October 10, to 352.86, or each one lower than the last.
>
> On Charles H. Dow's method of construing the barometrical indication, that would be a distinctly bearish warning, not indicating necessarily a change in the main market trend, but calling attention to the importance of future movements.

Hamilton then indicated the further bearish implications in the week of October 10–17 and continued:

> If, however, the market broke again, after a failure to pass the old highs, and the decline carried the price of the industrials below 325.17 and the railroads below 168.26, the bearish indication would be strong, and might well represent something more than a secondary reaction, however severe. It has often been said in these studies of the price movement that the barometer never indicates duration. There was a genuine bear market in 1923, but it lasted only eight months. One good reason for not taking the present indications too seriously is that they have been recorded in an unusually short space of time. The severest reaction from the high point of the year had just one month's duration. In view of the nation-wide character of the speculation, this seems a dangerously short period to infer anything like a complete reverse in public sentiment.

In effect, Hamilton was saying that the warning signs which had foretold a bear market of eight months' duration were present, but he did not expect the speculating and investing public to pay much attention to them. His position was unfortunately quite correct, though the additional confirmation of a bear market was not long in coming. Stocks fell on October 21 when sales totaled 6,091,870, the third biggest volume in the history of the New York Stock Exchange, but again there was a rally in the final minutes. Said Professor Fisher, "It is a shaking out of the lunatic fringe." On Tuesday, Charles E. Mitchell, arriving home from Europe, laid a cold hand on the hot speculative brow by declaring, "The decline has gone too far." Then, after taking the pulse, Mitchell added cheerfully that the patient was "fundamentally sound." On October 21, J. I. Case, a speculative stock, had fallen 100 points since its high of 350 on October 7, but United States Steel was down only 8 in that interval, Westinghouse down 14, and American Telephone & Telegraph down 9, while Adams Express actually gained 6 points.

The *Journal* observed the day previously in a market column: "There is a vast amount of money awaiting investment. Thousands of traders and investors have been waiting for an opportunity to buy stocks on just such a break as has occurred over the last several weeks, and this buying, in time, will change the trend of the market." The prices did rise on Tuesday, but on Wednesday even Adams Express, one of the best managed of the investment trusts, went down $96 a share. The break of 20.6 points in the Dow Jones Industrial Average set a new record for decline in the last hour of the day, the *Journal* reported. The stock-market quotation tickers had gone an hour and 44 minutes late during the hectic day. "The breaks," said the paper in its market report, "were exceptionally wide." London was an especially heavy seller of stocks, a reaction to the disclosure of Hatry's defalcations, and stocks broke also on the Paris Bourse. The *Journal's* market columnist attributed the New York decline to the actions of "professional bears."

On October 24, a Thursday, the market opened almost serenely. It was the calm before the first major shock of a quake following the rumbled warnings deep down. When the opening gong sounded on the floor of the New York Stock Exchange at 10 A.M., there was an extraordinarily heavy offering of stocks but not much action, since there were no bulls around to buy. Yet, within minutes, some traders had been authorized to snap up exceptional bargains, and before the hour closed, sales were the heaviest in the history of the Exchange; the *Journal* reported a total of 1,600,000 shares traded. Toward noon that day, Hogate met with his *Journal* editors and decided that the October 21st warning by Hamilton which had appeared in *Barron's* and had been carried by the Dow Jones news-ticker service, should be reprinted with emendations in the following morning's *Wall Street Journal*. It became one of the newspaper's most memorable editorials.

By one o'clock the carnage on the New York Stock Exchange had become general. There were losses from 5 to 50 points. As the news sped around Wall Street and the nation, the curious and morbid began gathering in Wall Street. The crowd outside was silent, fearful, wondering, but the visitors admitted to the Exchange gallery became unruly. "On the floor of the Exchange," wrote historian Robert Sobel years later, "brokers were too busy filling orders to ponder the meaning of the crash. . . . [Those in] the visitors' gallery overlooking the floor . . . screamed as they noted the large declines; others wept, or looked upon the tumult as though it was the end of the world. At 11 A.M. the gallery was closed, to keep the hysterical and the morbid from the scene. Later on, it was learned that more than $9.5 billion in paper values had been wiped out in the first two hours of trading."

It was a day of panic that destroyed many Wall Street bulls and would be known as Black Thursday. When it ended, 12,894,650 shares had changed hands, a record far exceeding the previous high of 8,246,700 shares sold on March 26, 1929. "With the whole list crumbling under the weight of urgent offerings, the whole market was in a demoralized state around noon," said the *Journal's* lead account on the 25th. Toward noon, veteran Wall Street bankers, recalling the actions of J. P. Morgan in the 1907 panic, gathered by invitation at the offices of J. P. Morgan & Company, 23 Wall Street, where Thomas W. Lamont, senior Morgan partner, acted as chairman of a meeting in the absence of Jack Morgan, son of J. P., who was in Europe. Among the bankers present were Charles Mitchell, Albert H. Wiggin of Chase National, William Potter of Guaranty Trust, Seward Posser of Bankers Trust, and George F. Baker, Jr., of First National, men who together controlled assets totaling more than $6 billion. "All were determined to use these assets to reverse the course of securities prices and send them upward again," Sobel wrote. Arthur M. Schlesinger, Jr., recording the scene in *The Age of Roosevelt*, noted that each banker had been authorized to contribute $40 million to a fund to be used to support the market. All present had incentive and each was heavily involved in Wall Street, personally and in his capacity as an investment banker. Richard Whitney, a broker and vice-president of the New York Stock Exchange, was authorized in the absence of Edward Simmons, the Exchange president, who was out of town, to take the news of the rescue mission by the "big boys" to the floor of the Exchange and to the world.

Whitney was the top representative of the Exchange on the floor that day, yet he was little noticed in the turmoil as he sought out a trader at the United States Steel post and asked its price. Specialists in various stocks were stationed at the trading positions, which had telephone connections where clerks recorded trades and fed information into the Exchange communication system and thence to the stock market's ticker-quotation service. Whitney was informed that the stock had last sold at 205, but subsequent bids were at 193½. The handsome broker then called out an order for 25,000 shares of United States Steel at 205, a signal to all who heard him that the powers in Wall Street were supporting the market. Cheering swept the floor of the Exchange as Whitney moved to other posts to make other bids. Buying support appeared, the "organized support" so often referred to when *The Wall Street Journal* described market rallies. The bankers' coup was successful. Some stocks that had fallen as much as 20 points at noon recovered by the close, United States Steel closing at 206. Whitney never did buy the 25,000 shares (some said 10,000) for which he bid, according to Schlesinger, but the "gesture of bidding was enough."

The Black Thursday panic hadn't seemed too bad in retrospect to Wall Street veterans, wrote historian Sobel. Most other historians and economists have agreed. The ticker-quotation service had run late throughout the day and did not complete its dismal record of events until after seven o'clock that evening, at which time it became clear that Wall Street had seen worse days, though more than 19 million shares had been traded on the Big Board and the Curb Exchange. Wall Street brokerage-house staffs worked most of the night attempting to account for the day's business. *The Wall Street Journal* went to press that night with partial reprint of the *Barron's* editorial by Hamilton, plus an added observation:

> There are people trading in Wall Street and many over the country who have never seen a real bear market, as for instance that which began in October, 1919 and lasted for two years, or that from 1912 to 1914 which predicted the Great War if the world had been able to interpret the signs. The big bull market was confirmed by six years of prosperity and if the stock market takes another direction there will be contraction of business later although on present indications only in moderate volume.
>
> Some time ago it was said in a *Wall Street Journal* editorial that if the stock market was compelled to deflate as politicians seemed earnestly to wish, they would shortly after experience a deflation elsewhere which would be much less to their liking.

With that ominous prediction the editorial closed. The following day 6 million shares were traded in relative calm, and on Saturday the *Journal* concluded that the market had merely purged itself during the prior week, an occasional requirement for good health, it said. "The condition is actual and large numbers of people are compelled to sell stocks for anything they will bring," the paper admitted about the injured margin traders. "The downward movement," it added, "being assisted by active traders on the floor whose short covering frequently accounts for the rally in the last half hour. . . . When to this is added an enormous volume of stock held not only in Wall Street but all over the country on borrowed money, which does not carry itself in dividends even at a reasonable money rate like 6 percent, the vulnerability of the market is readily seen. . . . So far as the barometer of the Dow-Jones average is concerned it has been clear since last Wednesday that the major movement of the market has turned downward. The market will find itself, for Wall Street does its own liquidation and always with a remarkable absence of anything like a financial catastrophe."

Thus the implied threat of the editorial on the 25th was removed, the paper concluding Saturday that general economic conditions did not appear to foreshadow a recession such as had been experienced in 1923. The *Journal* also reported that President Hoover had reiterated his belief that the country was sound, stating in his Friday press conference in Washington: "The fundamental business of the country, that is, production and distribution of commodities, is on a sound and prosperous basis."

Also on October 26, Dow, Jones & Company called the attention of *Wall Street Journal* readers to its accomplishments in covering the panic on Black Thursday by means of its news-ticker service. It published a three-column advertisement, which said:

> Thursday's / Stock Quotations were / VITAL . . . DOW JONES TICKERS / Flashed Floor Prices Every Ten Minutes . . .
>
> Thursday the Dow Jones Electric Page News Tickers were privileged to give their brokerage-houses and other subscribers the news of the stock prices which were prevailing on the floors of the New York Stock Exchange and the New York Curb Exchange.
>
> Approximately every 10 minutes, Dow Jones Tickers flashed the up-to-the-minute prices of a score or more of the leading stocks. Since they were the vital news of the day, Dow Jones featured the presentation of timely stock prices. The Dow Jones Electric Page News Tickers are strictly financial news distributors. They do not ordinarily feature the distribution of quotations. Their function is to present the news of finance—the news which often influences security values. When stock prices themselves become the most important news, the Dow Jones Tickers serve, as always, the first need of subscribers.

The company concluded its advertisement by proclaiming Dow, Jones & Company as the "world's leading financial news reporting agency. It employs by far the greatest financial news reporting staff in existence. It distributes its news over the largest of financial news ticker systems. In rising or declining markets, Dow Jones service is equally important."

Dow, Jones & Company was, in fact, entering its greatest, though brief, era of expansion in earnings since it was founded in November 1882, despite the stock-market panic and the threat of depression immediately ahead. The circulation of *The Wall Street Journal* would rise to a new high of 52,047 in 1930, when Dow Jones dividends would stand at $92 a share, a figure matched only by 1929 dividends; the renovation of the company's building at 42–44 Broad Street would get under way; the news-ticker service and news-bureau services would expand; and only the Philadelphia News Bureau and the new Pacific Coast edition among all the company's enterprises would fail to show signs of forward movement.

Nevertheless, in Wall Street itself the weeks immediately ahead were to be bleak ones. Not even the pronouncement by President Hoover that the country was sound nor the observation by English economists John Maynard Keynes and Josiah Stamp that the recent decline and fall of stock prices might prove salubrious for the American economy afforded Wall Street much comfort. That weekend, however, the country's financial writers and economists were almost sanguine about the future. Alexander Noyes noted in the *Times* that this time, unlike during the 1907 and other financial panics, there were no bank and business failures. The financial community, said the

Times, now "felt secure in the knowledge that the most powerful banks in the country stood ready to prevent recurrence [of panic]." Some preachers on Sunday asserted that Wall Street was reaping the whirlwind it richly deserved for past sins, but generally the country was not in a vindictive mood.

On Monday, many brokerage houses and investment banks ran advertisements in *The Wall Street Journal* and the general press urging investors to snap up the bargains available in the stock market before it was too late. On Tuesday, October 29, the *New York Times* said that the "investor who purchases securities at this time with the discrimination that as always is a condition of prudent investing may do so with utmost confidence." That same morning *The Wall Street Journal* stated its opinion that the panic of the prior week was not nearly as bad as some in the past, asserting that only overextended margin buyers had been hurt:

> It was a panic, a purely stock market panic, of a new brand. Everyone seems to agree that it was due to the fact that prices of some stocks were selling beyond respective intrinsic values and a correction has taken place in a number of stocks that show declines ranging from 50 to more than 100 points. . . . The slump was due to the market itself. . . . The storm left no wreckage except the marginal traders forced to sell at a loss. Mr. Baker, Mr. Morgan, Mr. Mellon and Mr. Rockefeller, and others who held stocks outright, stand just where they were before the break. The income is the same. They have lost a few tail feathers but in time they will grow again, longer and more luxurious than the old ones that were lost in what financial writers like to call a debacle.

Such was the *Journal's* cheerful attitude on the morning of October 29, which would become known as Black Tuesday. And such was the general optimism following the remarkable recovery from Black Thursday, with the Wall Street bankers leading the way, that the disastrous Monday market the day before did not appear to discourage the financial community. Volume on Monday had been far less than the prior Thursday—only 9.5 million shares traded as compared with 13 million—but on Monday prices had fallen further than in the entire week before. United States Steel, the bellwether, had dropped 18 points on Monday, a moderate loss compared with General Electric or American Telephone & Telegraph, both down 48. There had been two more secret meetings of the bankers on Monday, but no rescue mission from 23 Wall Street appeared on the floor of the New York Stock Exchange, and there was no recovery. On Monday United States Steel, for which Richard Whitney had bid 205 the previous Thursday, fell to 169 and rallied to 174 at closing. Westinghouse, which stood at 286 on the glorious September 3 not long past, was down 34 points.

The bankers' meeting at Morgan's on the 28th did not end until 6:30 P.M., when a spokesman said that the outlook was hopeful. It was made clear that the bankers did not intend to support the total market, but they had plans for stopping some leaks. There was not to be a further effort to protect gains such as had been successfully executed on Thursday. Thomas Lamont, it was said, had now declared that the goal of the bankers was to "watch for air holes."

On the 29th, as the opening gong sounded, the New York Stock Exchange was overwhelmed with sell orders. Enormous blocks of securities were up for sale "at the market." The margin calls of Monday continued throughout the day, and margin buyers were wiped out as their stocks fell below the loan values and their brokers sold them out, when they could find buyers. In many cases, there were no buyers whatsoever. As other markets opened across the country, the selling wave spread. "Liquidations took place in all parts of the country, and by every class of speculator," wrote Sobel in describing the panic. Said Galbraith, "The air holes, which the bankers were to close, opened wide." There were some buyers of stocks in large volume as the bargains became compellingly attractive, among them Joseph Kennedy and Floyd Odlum. "They were millionaires in 1929; by 1933, they were worth tens of millions," Sobel observed. There were others buying, such as John D. Rockefeller and his associates, *The Wall Street Journal* would learn. A record 16,410,030 shares were sold to somebody on the New York Stock Exchange, though millions of shares of stock offered had no takers.

According to Frederick Lewis Allen in his record of the period, *Only Yesterday*, at some point during the frenetic trading a messenger boy got the idea of bidding $1 a share for a small block of securities, did so, and got them. It was probably an apocryphal story, as were reports of brokers and investors leaping from skyscraper windows or committing other forms of suicide immediately after the October stock-market crash. Coroners' records for the New York metropolitan area for October and November 1929 actually show fewer suicides than had occurred in October–November 1928.

But Black Tuesday, October 29, was a debacle even though individual percentage declines of many stocks were less than on Monday and the prior Thursday. It had become clear that the liquidation of the securities markets was going far beyond the mere elimination of recent paper profits, though few then foresaw that within weeks all of the gains of the long bull market would be wiped out. On Wednesday, October 30, the opening market report in *The Wall Street Journal* was somber: "Yesterday's market was in many respects the most extraordinary in the history of the Stock Exchange. With margins drastically impaired by the convulsive declines . . . wholesale liquidation of accounts proved necessary. Transactions were swollen to proportions that had no parallel in the Exchange annals."

(Three years later on October 31, 1932, the *Journal* would provide revised statistics of the day: "Sales on the Exchange totaled 16,410,000 shares, the record for all time. There were approximately 15,000 miles of ticker tape used. There were 891 issues traded. Total sales for General Motors amounted to 960,000 shares, the record for any one stock. Sales on the New York Curb market totaled 7,096,300 shares, the record for all time." On the day the *Journal* printed the statistics, it recorded 359,000 shares traded in the two-hour Saturday session of the New York Stock Exchange, October 29, the third anniversary of Black Tuesday.)

Yet the *Journal* was far from dismayed by the behavior of the market in October 1929. It angrily answered critics, especially those in Congress who declared that the exchanges themselves and their procedures were greatly at fault, and it joyfully published news of a constructive nature about the market. One such story concerned the buying activities of John D. Rockefeller, Sr., and his son. "Exceeded in importance only by the cessation of the hysterical wave of selling securities and the general buying movement which developed Wednesday," said the paper on Thursday, "was an unprecedented piece of news on stock market conditions from his home in Pocantico Hills. The elder Rockefeller told the world that he and his son for some days had been purchasing sound common stocks and were continuing to do so." The *Journal* repeated in an editorial its assertion that the Black Tuesday selling was hysterical and said, "There is no doubt that the banking group felt much more hopeful about conditions." However, the New York Exchange was open only briefly on Thursday, when it closed until Monday to permit the overburdened exchanges to regroup and the hysteria rife among traders to subside.

In a November 1 editorial the *Journal* analyzed the significance of the Rockefeller move. "When so sound a judge as John D. Rockefeller, Sr., buys common stocks, he buys on values," the editorial began. "He looks for appreciation over a period of years and the yield of the investment after a time which may see wild fluctuations in the market. . . . Great purchasers on value, like Mr. Rockefeller, never get the bottom of the market or anything like it. They are not calling the turn, but it is a fair inference, from Mr. Rockefeller's statement, that he was not buying stocks when the average price of industrials was 100 points higher."

In *Barron's* magazine, Harry Nelson, writing as The Trader, commented, "From now on the stock market will sell 'ex-psychology.' The public has suffered the biggest speculative losses since 1920. A generation unfamiliar with the phenomenon of a liquidating market will hereafter pay less attention to the stock ticker, curtail its trading activities, and, when recovered from the shock, will probably be ready to study values again."

During the next several weeks the *Journal* frequently insisted that nothing was wrong with stock-marketing procedures that the New York Stock Exchange could not itself correct. When an investigation of the Exchange was urged on Governor Franklin Roosevelt by members of the New York legislature, the paper angrily demanded that the Exchange be given an opportunity to make its own recommendations for reforms, if any, and it specifically departed from the C. W. Barron stand against short selling. Said the paper on January 4, 1930:

> As for short selling either of securities or commodities, experience older than this country proves that it is a valuable adjunct of a wide, free market, ordinarily tending to prevent extremes of fluctuation. Selling for future delivery no more destroys values than buying on margin makes them. Stock Exchange authorities, notably those of the New York institution, bring most short operations under scrutiny just as they supervise the positions of the member firms on the long side. In protecting the public from irregular or abusive practices, they also protect themselves.
>
> No business man will easily believe that any form of state or federal regulation can be devised which will work more efficaciously to this end than the self-interest of the exchanges.

Several years would elapse before the New York Stock Exchange authorized its own study of abuses. Meantime, as the paper pointed out early in 1930, the Exchange firms would be preoccupied with the "work of clearing up the debris of the October collapse." In December the stock market moved cautiously upward, with the Dow Jones Industrial Average at 250, considerably above the panic low of 198.69 of November 13, 1929. On February 10 the paper said in an editorial, "Based on the well known Dow theory . . . the stock market has said definitely that the worst of the current industrial recession has passed."

As Wall Street began to sift through the wreckage of the crash, it was found that not everything had gone down. While automobile stocks lost heavily, with General Motors declining 40 points in the year and Nash Motors 55, American Telephone & Telegraph gained 30, J. I. Case 22, and Air Reduction 26. By early 1930 Robert Sobel noted, "Wall Street entered a subdued bull market." The Harvard Economic Society, which had been pessimistic during the summer, declared in November 1929 that the Wall Street crash "is not the precursor of business depression," and Professor Fisher in his book issued in 1930, *The Stock Market Crash and After*, continued to insist that stocks were still a good investment.

No one paid much attention to Professor Fisher any more, wrote Galbraith in his history of the crash. But Roger Babson, the Sage of Wellesley, who had predicted the crash in forthright terms, had become the new folk hero, recognized even in lower Manhattan. Wall Street's own hero was George Harrison, new governor of the New York Federal Reserve Bank, who caused the bank to buy up $370 million short-term notes while lowering the rediscount rate on new money loaned to 4½ percent by mid-November and

3½ percent by the following March. This action helped carry the market into a modest recovery until May 1930, when there was a further break.

The reason for the crash and the following depression was never sharply defined by the *Journal* nor by most contemporary economists. Market analyst Harold M. Finley, while recognizing the Dow Theory as a historical device and not a prognosticator, has suggested that William Peter Hamilton might have sought to explain the crash in terms of the theory if he had not been gravely ill in November. "The Dow's services to devotees in 1929 was similar to that on many occasions," Finley said. "Those thoroughly familiar with market wisdom set forth by Dow and Hamilton were certainly aware of the warning signals of serious trouble both at the 1929 top and in the early stages of the greatest crash in New York Stock Exchange history."

Finley, like Roger Babson a former theologian as well as a market analyst and investment counselor, called Hamilton's "Turn in the Tide" editorial "one of the most famous . . . in financial history. . . . It is unfortunate that Mr. Hamilton died on December 9, so soon after the panic that we do not know whether he would have remained bearish throughout the great bear market of 1929–32." Actually, Hamilton had continued working on his editorials until a week before his death, but not with his previous acumen and verve.

In December, Babson, the summer pessimist, was calling upon Congress to adjourn "until business confidence is restored," and he demanded that President Hoover be given full powers to prevent a possible depression. *The Wall Street Journal* found itself in agreement with the Sage of Wellesley, and Badger, the new editor of *Barron's*, arranged for Babson to write a series of articles for the magazine. Babson also launched a stock-market advisory letter, which he advertised regularly in *Barron's* and *The Wall Street Journal*. Frederick A. Korsmeyer, an editorial writer who had worked on Nebraska newspapers and the *New York Commercial* before coming to the *Journal* in 1907, took over Hamilton's writing duties, but Hogate himself remained in charge of the editorial page. Korsmeyer continued as an editorial writer for the paper until his retirement on January 1, 1954.

On December 17, 1929, Bancroft and Hogate, noting the growing prospects of a full market recovery and the *Journal's* increasing circulation, began an aggressive advertising campaign to establish *The Wall Street Journal* as "America's National Newspaper." The campaign was launched with a full-page advertisement in the *Journal*, which stated that the paper, with the advent of its Pacific Coast edition, had already earned the title of national business daily:

> A number of British newspapers are read daily from one end to the other of England. Some of these newspapers operate widely separated publishing plants to insure national circulations.

> But in this country, only one newspaper has ever found it practical to publish in more than one city. Only one single newspaper medium offers a truly national circulation reaching, simultaneously, the great centers of the country, from coast to coast.
>
> This newspaper is *The Wall Street Journal*.
>
> Now printed daily on the Atlantic and on the Pacific seaboards, *The Wall Street Journals* reach *on the same day of publication* 64 of the chief business centers in 22 states. These are the centers of the states in which reside 65% of the population of the United States, who pay 80% of all the income tax annually collected by the Federal Government.
>
> Within 48 hours, *The Wall Street Journals* are being read in all communities in the 48 states where business or investments command attention.

The advertisement summarized the hopes of President Bancroft and Editor-General Manager Hogate of *The Wall Street Journal* in New York, but the prospect it presented was somewhat overstated. The Pacific Coast edition was quite unlike the New York edition. The *Journal* had no facilities for producing basically identical editions on both coasts and would not have for a number of years. While summarized *Wall Street Journal* news was being sent to the editors in San Francisco by telegraph in December 1929, most of the "essence" of the New York edition described in previous advertisements was sent by mail. Little was published "simultaneously" and some not at all. The editor and publisher of the San Francisco edition felt themselves compelled by the principles of good journalism and practical logistics to publish their own version of a West Coast *Wall Street Journal*. A prime ingredient of all news, it was widely believed at the time, was propinquity; the nearness and timeliness of an event greatly increased its interest and usually its value. C. W. Barron had demonstrated to editors and readers that *The Wall Street Journal* was different, that financial and economic news from Europe could at times be more significant and interesting than New York or Boston business reports. However, this lesson did not impress those in charge of the Pacific Coast edition; indeed, they had little choice but to emphasize coverage of West Coast market and business news because of the lack of adequate dispatches from New York. At best these consisted of skeletal telegraph reports from the Dow Jones news ticker and *Journal* articles for the New York edition, which were mailed and arrived days late.

Hogate did his best to round up a competent staff for the new edition. Deac Hendee had been sent from the home office to serve as editor of the Pacific Coast edition, and Charles N. Stabler was managing editor. In December 1929 the young recruit in whom Hogate had such confidence, Bernard "Barney" Kilgore, was assigned to the San Francisco news staff after a few months' experience in New York. He soon was made news editor and in turn recruited Robert Bottorff, also a DePauw graduate, who would rise fast in the *Journal* organization. But Hendee and his staff had neither the means nor the desire to duplicate the format and content of the *Journal's* New York edition. Nor did the Pacific Coast edition soon change. Some 14 years later Barney Kilgore, back in San Francisco to study the West Coast problems after achieving notable editorial improvement in the parent edition in New York, reported to Hogate that the Pacific Coast edition was "out of gear with the New York edition. We are, in effect, publishing two distinct papers rather than two editions of one newspaper."

As the year ended, President Hoover, in public statements at least, was numbered among the economic optimists, although in November he had assembled leaders of business and labor in Washington to warn them that the country was in grave economic danger. Also in November he told the nation's press at its Gridiron Club banquet that his own seeming serenity following the October crash had been partly dissemblance to check further panic. "Fear, alarm, pessimism and hesitation swept through the country, which, if unchecked, would have precipitated absolute panic through the business world with untold misery in its wake," the President said. "Its acute dangers were far greater than we are able to disclose at the present time."

Harris Gaylord Warren, in his *Herbert Hoover and the Great Depression*, said that Hoover was quite specific about the dangers in the series of "secret" meetings with the country's leaders beginning November 21, 1929. "Hoover told the industrialists that the crisis went deeper than the market crash, that a severe depression had arrived which would see world-wide economic distress aggravated by the dislocations of the World War." Warren noted, however, that economists who were critics of Hoover called the sessions "scout meetings." Yet they resulted in a pledge by the industrialists not to cut wages and one by labor leaders to seek to prevent strikes, the latter bitterly attacked by the American Communist Party as a betrayal of organized labor.

The Wall Street Journal did not waver in its support of Hoover. "Among the risks of office which President Hoover courageously accepts is that of diagnosing the country's business situation," the paper said. "The White House statement [on the economy] was a justifiable reply to loose talk in Congress about the 'worst economic conditions ever known.' "

Hugh Bancroft and his associates had no doubt that the nation's securities markets would be restored and that the economy generally was in good health as they moved ahead early in 1930 with plans for a parallel expansion of facilities and the consolidation of control that Bancroft had long contemplated. He told his Boston attorneys to proceed with the legal preparations required for incorporation of Dow, Jones & Company in New York and the turnover of part of its assets—as well as the assets of the various subsidiaries owned by the Jessie Barron and C. W. Barron trusts—to a general holding trust. Bancroft also instructed architects to study the problem of a replacement for the Dow Jones headquarters at 44 Broad Street, the eight-story Edison Building once considered a skyscraper in lower Manhattan that the company had purchased in 1910. He advised Hogate and Ackell to move full speed ahead on the development of the Pacific Coast edition of *The Wall Street Journal* and the new high-speed news tickers.

Joe Ackell continued experiments with the news tickers and new automatic mailroom equipment throughout 1930 while Casey Hogate continued his experiments with the typography and content of *The Wall Street Journal*. In some ways Hogate appeared for a time to be returning to the Charles Dow era. Type was again smaller, news was well organized, and he had induced Thomas F. Woodlock, former editor, to return as associate editor after being away almost 25 years. Perhaps the Bancrofts influenced Hogate in this direction, since Woodlock had been a firm supporter of Mrs. Jessie Barron and had edited the paper effectively under her supervision. Possibly Hogate saw Woodlock as the writer who could replace C. W. Barron. He moved the "Review and Outlook" column from page one and established it on page eight to create a true editorial page for the *Journal*. Woodlock's essays then replaced the editorial column on page one. He was a skilled, graceful writer, but his commentaries lacked the dramatic flair of a C. W. Barron.

The *Journal* also gained some new, interesting columns, such as those written by Oliver J. Gingold, Richard E. Edmonson, and Henry Alloway. Space for letters to the editor was doubled. There were a review of sports events and a gossip column called "Wall Street Straws." The paper was neat, tight, and well organized, but the style of the Barron days was missing. Nevertheless, under Edward M. Stein, the former Barron secretary and *Journal* automobile editor who became circulation manager, circulation increased to 52,047 copies in May 1930, a new all-time high.

On June 1 the *Journal* boosted its circulation to more than 56,000 by acquiring a longtime rival, the *Wall Street News*. Circulation totals for both newspapers at the time were estimated, and no one could be sure how much duplicate circulation was acquired by the absorption of the *News*, but Stein's 56,000 estimate of total circulation indicated an overnight gain of about 4,000. The acquisition was a satisfying accomplishment. The *Journal* editors and writers for years had referred to the *News* and its publisher, the New York News Bureau, as "Tammany," evidently equating its relative power and ruthlessness with that of the paper's prime political enemy, New York's Tammany Hall political machine. The *Wall Street News* was small but highly respected, and the *Journal* kept the name in its editorial-page masthead through the following decade.

On December 3, 1930, Hugh Bancroft took the final steps he had long planned toward creation of a trust to consolidate the scattered holdings of the Barron financial-journalism empire. With his Boston attorneys he created the Financial Press Companies of America under the laws of the state of Massachusetts to be a holding company for Dow, Jones & Company, *The Wall Street Journal*, other properties owned by Mrs. Jane W. W. Bancroft, and the trust created in the will of Mrs. Jessie Barron for her grandchildren. Since Bancroft controlled the Jessie Barron stocks as trustee, he and his wife, Jane, cast all the votes. Dow, Jones & Company had been incorporated under New York law on November 21, 1930, as successor to the joint-stock association formed in 1900 by Charles Dow and his associates, which in turn had replaced the Dow, Jones, and Bergstresser partnership. Jane Bancroft, Hugh Bancroft, and K. C. Hogate held the first directors' meeting of Dow, Jones & Company, Inc., at 44 Broad Street on December 3. They elected Hugh Bancroft president, K. C. Hogate vice-president, and J. C. Hoskins secretary and treasurer.

The directors then voted as directors of the Financial Press Companies of America and elected Hugh Bancroft president. The other trust officers named are not indicated in the minutes available, but the further proceedings are detailed: "Dow, Jones & Company, a joint stock association formed under the laws of the State of New York in 1900, with the consent of all the stockholders, hereby offers to sell, assign and transfer to Dow Jones & Company, Inc., immediately after the close of business on the 31st day of December, 1930, all of its property, assets and business situated and/or operated in the State of New York (with the exception of certain securities, mortgages, cash, bills receivable, rights and other properties hereinafter specified), including *The Wall Street Journal* in all places and territories."

Long lists of properties included and excluded followed. Essentially, as of January 2, 1931, Dow Jones & Company, Inc., would retain facilities, money, and resources to publish *The Wall Street Journal* and most other publications once owned by C. W. and Jessie Barron. Exceptions were the Boston properties, including *Barron's* magazine, and some of the news-ticker services outside New York.

Under the Financial Press Companies of America trust agreement, Hugh Bancroft was authorized to acquire for the trust all outstanding shares of Dow Jones & Company and "to issue 160,000 shares of this Trust of the par value of $5 each to the transferrers of the said shares in Dow Jones & Company." The value of Dow Jones & Company, Inc., was indicated to be about $1 million. "Mr. and Mrs. Bancroft thereupon transferred to this trust 8,380 shares of Dow Jones & Company above referred," the record continued, "and Mr. Bancroft, on behalf of this trust, received and receipted for the same." Hogate obviously had not at that point purchased the 800 shares of Dow Jones he had been promised earlier, but he and Mrs. Hogate would in time become large stockholders. Initially, however, 108,000 of the trust shares were issued to Jane Bancroft and 52,000 to Hugh Bancroft as trustee. The principal office of the Financial Press Companies of America was 30 Kilby Street, Boston. Subsequent meetings of the board were held in Boston and Cohasset as well as New York.

As trustee under the will of Jessie M. Barron, Bancroft individually became a shareholder, director and/or officer in the Boston News Bureau company; Dow Jones & Company, Inc.; Dow, Jones & Company of Ohio; Dow, Jones & Company of Michigan; Dow, Jones & Company of the Potomac; Barron's Publishing Company; Dow, Jones & Co., Ltd. (Canada); Dow, Jones & Co., Ltd. (California); Illinois Telegraph News Company; Telegraph News Company (Missouri); Financial Printers, Inc. (New York); The Wall Street Journal Building Company (New York); and Doremus & Company (New York). Provision was made for employees to purchase stock. Later the record would show that the Martha Endicott Gannett Trust owned 13,000 shares of the new trust; Mrs. Anna Hogate, wife of K. C. Hogate, owned 8,000; Thomas Woodlock 500; Cy Kissane, managing editor, 600; Edward M. Stein, circulation manager, 1,760; and C. E. Robbins, a *Journal* newsman who would later become Chicago bureau manager, 150 shares.

On January 1, 1931, *The Wall Street Journal* was again optimistic and even relatively satisfied with 1930. "Wall Street brought 1930 to a close with an expectancy of better things in the air," the paper said. "Taking into consideration drastic adjustment of security values, and the tremendous reductions in brokers' loans, it was felt that the vast bulk of necessary deflation had been accomplished." Plans for the partial demolition of the Dow Jones building at 44 Broad Street and construction of expanded facilities at the same location could now proceed since a new permanent building on West Thirtieth Street would be ready by spring to house a printing plant and some of the news-ticker operating and support equipment. The venerable Broad Street building had long since grown too small for Dow Jones & Company, which had moved some production activities into a leased building on Forty-seventh Street.

Bancroft retained Lockwood, Green Engineers, Inc., as the architects and A. L. Hartridge Company as the builders. He let contracts to Richard Hoe & Company of New York and London for a five-unit Hoe press with a capacity of 80 pages, printed and folded at a rate of 25,000 copies an hour or 40 pages at 50,000 an hour. Provision was made in the plans for underground storage, loading docks, space for Ackell's automatic mailing machines, and a cooling system that would pump ice water through the building, a system that was never noticeably effective. There would be offices for all the ventures of the

Financial Press Companies of America and Dow Jones & Company, with printing, news-ticker, and manufacturing activities in the new Thirtieth Street plant. Before construction could begin, temporary quarters for the news and business staffs of Dow Jones, *The Wall Street Journal*, and *Barron's* would be required, and these were leased at 130 Cedar Street.

The move to 130 Cedar Street was smoothly made in August 1931 over a weekend, when the *Journal* was not being readied for the presses. Bancroft had made sure that the new five-story printing plant and news-ticker center at 453–57 West Thirtieth Street were prepared for total operations before the company quit 44 Broad Street. The demolition of the downtown building began in September, and the new structure was ready for occupancy April 1, 1932, ahead of schedule.

The year 1931 was another satisfactory one for Dow Jones, *The Wall Street Journal*, and other properties under Bancroft's control. The Financial Press Companies of America paid a dividend of $3.50 on each of 380,000 shares. Circulation remained strong except on the West Coast. But the country was moving into deep economic depression. President Hoover was about to propose his Reconstruction Finance Corporation to help industry and thus provide jobs for the millions of unemployed. Industrial production was down by 50 percent, farm prices 40 percent. Many of the stocks offered on Wall Street had sunk to 10 percent of their 1929 highs. Bancroft's building activities helped deplete his reserves, advertising declined, and the new Financial Press Companies of America would soon find itself in financial difficulties.

Chapter 12

The *Journal* and the New Deal

As the Dow Jones Industrial Average plummeted from its 1929 high of 381.17 to a low of 41.22 in the summer of 1932, Bancroft and Hogate struggled with the financial problems of the company while *The Wall Street Journal* fought the critics of Wall Street. They were numerous and vituperative. "Wall Street was exceptionally well endowed with enemies," observed historian John Kenneth Galbraith. The *Journal* was quite alone on the ramparts of public opinion, warding off odious accusations, canards, and some criticisms it later conceded were justified. The paper sustained losses in circulation and advertising. Wall Street had become a hated name, and the paper suffered along with the brokers and bankers, as Bernard Kilgore, the young recruit to the staff in 1929, ruefully observed. In later years, as general manager, he even asked whether the *Journal* should consider changing that part of its name which engulfed it after every panic in the general opprobrium.

The bad economic conditions affecting all publications were thus exceptionally difficult for *The Wall Street Journal* in 1932. Financial advertising, a mainstay since the newspaper's beginning, did not merely diminish, one executive observed—it almost disappeared. Circulation fell to half its prior high of 56,000. The financial panic had wounded the wealthy more than the general public, especially those who ignored the *Journal's* frequent admonitions to buy securities for keeps and not on extended margin. Many such unfortunates lost interest in the market. Sherwin Badger, editor of

Barron's magazine in the early 1930s, wrote of that dreary period: "The market was stagnant. The selection of news dealing with specific securities was difficult because there was so little news our readers really wanted to know."

Advertising was down to the point where the *Journal* sometimes accepted hotel scrip in payment, using such due bills to pay some employee expense accounts. The nation's corporations were short of money and were forced to retrench. Fewer manufacturers bought institutional advertising; there were fewer announcements of new security issues, fewer unveilings of new buildings and plants, and fewer new ventures publicized with large display advertisements such as appeared in the paper frequently in the boom days. Industrial production had declined from $38 billion in 1929 to $17.5 billion in 1932. No new skyscrapers were planned, and some announced plans were rescinded as private construction for the nation dropped from $7.5 billion to $1.5 billion. The new Dow Jones building was one of the last in the area as the Depression finally came to lower Manhattan, even after Wall Street appeared to revive in early 1930.

Casey Hogate did his best to enliven the pages of *The Wall Street Journal* with new, light columns, short features, and typographical brighteners, but he had to work with a limited budget and a curtailed staff. Even so, a Berlin office was opened with an anonymous correspondent, and Burton Crane sent dispatches from Tokyo. Thomas F. Woodlock in his page-one column and Frederick Korsmeyer on the inside editorial page attempted to explain why the country was in a depression and why President Hoover ought not to be blamed, though bureaucrats in the government did not escape censure. Henry Alloway, in his "By-the-Bye" column on the editorial page, sought to demonstrate to readers that there remained a bright side of life.

During the early Depression years, the *Journal* was preoccupied with the problem of German reparations and their effect on the world economy. In June 1931, after President Hoover proposed a year-long moratorium on all reparations and intergovernmental debts, the paper praised his action. "At long last Washington has publicly acknowledged the realization that the whole world is in this ditch together and that the United States cannot climb out alone. In a discreetly short and simple statement, Mr. Hoover has faced himself, his administration and his country toward the controlling facts in the world situation. The position of Germany is the heart of the matter." The *Journal* foresaw "strong indications of joint action leading to financial aid of a temporary nature to Germany." Hoover's plan was almost immediately adopted and later extended.

On June 19 the paper engaged in another of its frequent editorial jousts with the British political economist John Maynard Keynes, then lecturing in

New York. But this time the *Journal* and Keynes were in at least partial agreement. "Prof. Keynes by no means exaggerates the seriousness of universal indebtedness in its relationship to falling, or fallen, commodity prices," it said. "Security markets are registering the consequent loss of much former capital value, though possibly there has been an exaggeration there. Prof. Keynes admits the liquidation is the normal consequence of an era of great construction on an inflated price level, but protests that we do not have to accept that tendency 'fatalistically.' " However, the paper could not refrain from a final slap at the distinguished visitor. "More pertinent is the question whether we have to accept it in fact, whatever state of mind it engenders."

The *Journal* was highly optimistic about America's future as England embarked on a course the paper called one of the most significant for world economics in recent times—departure from the gold standard—on September 21, 1931. Said the paper on the 23rd: "Without question, the Gold Standard Amendment Act has created for America a great new opportunity. It is logical to suppose that for an indefinite time the world will look upon this country as the principal safe repository of banking and investment funds. Such at least will be its theory."

Whether the world would act upon that theory, the *Journal* said, depended upon America. First, America must restore confidence in herself. "A leader lacking in self-confidence is a contradiction in terms, an absurdity. Monday's decision of the New York Stock Exchange to remain open, to take the effects of London's gold suspension on the chin, was a splendid acceptance of the responsibility that goes with place and power." In a separate article, Woodlock explained the British action. It had been forced to leave gold because of pressure on its reserves. But, said Woodlock, there was no pressure on the United States to go off the gold standard. "If we were to go off gold it would be by deliberate and voluntary action and not from pressure," Woodlock declared. "Why should we do this? Only one possible purpose appears, and that is plain 'inflation' designed to advance the price of commodities and to reduce the value of debts."

In December 1931 President Hoover's proposals toward solving depression problems were weighed by the *Journal* editorialist and found to be on the plus side. The *Journal*, in discussing the President's annual message of December 9, 1931, approved his plan for the Reconstruction Finance Corporation (RFC), his encouragement of railroad consolidation, and his suggestion for modifying antitrust laws "so that natural resource industries may check the ruinous competition that now demoralizes them and their employees." These proposals were excellent, the paper said, but there was also much to deplore in Hoover's message to Congress; the President appeared inadequate to the task ahead:

> The reaction of the financial community was that of disappointment tempered by the afterthought that no great expectations of practical helpfulness to industry or finance had been widely entertained. The message was in fact disappointing, but not so much in matter as in its manner. This betrays Mr. Hoover as a man whose mental vision is apt to become focused on what he wishes to see.
>
> Thus, in a time of unsettlement, he opens his address to the new Congress with a long dissertation upon the manifold blessings which the country is enjoying. This is reminiscent of the Hoover of 1929. On the tariff, respecting which he might have displayed a sadly needed leadership in new ideas, he only reaffirms his faith in the one-legged Tariff Commission to protect the Ship of State in the world-wide economic hurricane. He proposes taxation which shall close the gap between Treasury income and outgo in the fiscal year to end June 30, 1933. This is a staggering program, but the President gives Congress no intimation of how he thinks it might be carried out.

Later, on December 23, the *Journal* praised two specific actions by President Hoover and his advisers. It congratulated the President's Organization for Unemployment Relief for "condemning all pending schemes for financing the return of prosperity with billions of government bonds," saying, "The Government cannot create new capital out of thin air." And it blessed once more the President's RFC plan for infusing government capital into business and industry: "The Reconstruction Finance Corporation, which Congress could set up in six hours, is infinitely preferable to mere schemes to gull the staggering taxpayer for casual and light-hearted spending. The institution could begin almost immediately to warm up chilled purchasing and employment power of hundreds, perhaps thousands, of industrial and transportation units already well organized with their labor supply about them, waiting for the blessing of a familiar job at home."

In the spring of 1932 the RFC got under way. In March the government began distributing 85 million bushels of wheat and 250 million pounds of cotton to aid needy persons and to expend farm surplus as the nation bumped along its economic bottom. Farm income had dropped from $4.1 billion in 1930 to $3.2 billion in 1931, and it would go down to $1.9 billion in 1932, a decline of more than 50 percent. Some citizens—those with jobs—appeared well off momentarily as prices fell in the stores. In the Piggly Wiggly self-service chain, prime rib could be had for 35 cents a pound, eggs were 25 cents a dozen, bread 11 cents a loaf, and coffee 24 cents a pound. In clothing stores, men could buy suits made from wool for $29 and good leather shoes at $4 a pair. Commodity prices were low, but not everybody could buy as unemployment rose and wages fell. The average family income, around $2,300 in 1929, dropped to less than $1,600 in 1932. By 1933 an estimated 13 million Americans were out of work.

Casey Hogate, the friendly bear of a man who knew and liked everybody, led *The Wall Street Journal* along a tenuous editorial path those difficult Depression days. The paper remained firmly Republican without subscribing fully to the policies of the Hoover administration. It was considerate of the Democrats, especially those who opposed Prohibition, as the *Journal* did. It liked Alfred E. Smith, the defeated Democratic candidate for president, for his honesty and his anti-Prohibition stand, but it strongly opposed the public ownership ideas of such liberal Democrats as Smith.

Although the *Journal* defended Wall Street against numerous and rancorous critics, it was frequently critical of Wall Street bankers and brokers and the New York Stock Exchange. Hogate, who had been acting as chief executive officer of Dow Jones ever since Bancroft retired because of illness in 1932 (though Bancroft's name remained in the masthead until his death), carried his heavy burdens cheerfully, so far as his associates knew, but his wife, Anna, complained that he was overworking dreadfully. If there was any dissatisfaction with him at the office, it was that Hogate didn't confide enough and that he didn't define his goals.

Some said Casey Hogate was a shy, friendly man who never raised his voice. Those who knew him best insisted that he was never shy. "He was a very outgoing, hearty person," William Kerby, a later Dow Jones president, recalled. "Attending a function with Casey, or even walking down Wall Street with him, was the equivalent of being in the company of a great celebrity. People would rush up to him to greet him and to shake his hand. He knew everyone, great and small." But Casey was somewhat aloof among strangers at times and he never permitted any personal relationships to influence the columns of the *Journal*. One good friend was New York Governor Franklin D. Roosevelt. Hogate was fond of Roosevelt, but *The Wall Street Journal* was cool to Roosevelt the politician.

Lowell Thomas, the journalist and commentator and a friend of both, remembered that Roosevelt and Hogate got together frequently for friendly discussion in New York City and in Dutchess County. But Hogate let his staff know that he and Roosevelt did not often agree on anything in politics. Hogate and the paper did approve of Roosevelt's attitude toward the New York Stock Exchange. *The Wall Street Journal* wanted the Exchange to reform itself, to impose tighter discipline upon its members so that neither the government in Washington nor the statehouse in Albany could prescribe rules. Roosevelt agreed and refused to press for yet another New York State investigation of the Stock Exchange, though it was within his power to do so. The *Journal* praised him for this but did not warm up when there was increasing talk of Franklin D. Roosevelt as the Democratic nominee for president.

At the same time the paper grew more critical of President Hoover. It praised former Governor Smith for telling a Washington audience that America should extend, perhaps for 20 years, the international debt moratorium Hoover had initiated the year previously. "Whatever its faults in detail," the paper said, "the Smith declaration challenges the Republicans and Democrats alike, in and out of office, to recognize the patent fact that war debts and reparations are the one and only point at which so much as a beginning can be made in re-ordering a disordered world. Neither war debts nor reparations, though they were some day collectible in full, could ever make good the damage now being worked by efforts to preserve them."

Yet as it became apparent early in 1932 that Roosevelt would seek the presidential nomination, the paper made it clear that it would stand with Hoover, saying in an April 9, 1932, editorial: "President Hoover is at last on the right road to an understanding of the nature and duration of the depression, the reason why it continues and the direction of the way out. Chairman McDuffie [D., Ala.] of the House economy committee recognizes this fact and its plain implication that neither House nor Senate can any longer engage in "passing the buck" for political ends. President Hoover is on the right road at last because he now grasps the immediate controlling factor prolonging the trade stagnation—the insupportable $13,000,000,000 cost of government. In a liquidating world this burden remains not only undiminished but relatively, and therefore actually, heavier than it ever was when we were prosperous."

So President Hoover, the *Journal* believed, was taking the right steps once more, after a questionable interim course. It thought one of his mistakes was the injection of government into the private sector in an effort to create jobs, an effort Treasury Secretary Andrew Mellon and other conservative Republicans had vigorously but unsuccessfully opposed. "Speaking of the responsibilities of the President and the Congress," the paper continued, "both must realize that public expenditures to create employment, in the present state of affairs, destroys more jobs than it creates. It cannot do otherwise so long as it sucks out of private business its lifeblood of working capital."

Meantime, the country's disenchantment with the financial establishment was complete. Wall Street came under investigation by the Senate Committee on Banking and Currency, headed by Republican Peter Norbeck of South Dakota, and so did several financial writers for New York newspapers, including two on *The Wall Street Journal* staff.

The first witness called to the Senate hearing was the debonair Richard Whitney, at that time president of the New York Stock Exchange, brother of a Morgan partner and a broker himself, who was at his elegant, arrogant best. Whitney contemptuously ignored the injunctions of Chairman Norbeck to stick to the issue, and instead lectured the Committee on the need to cut the pay of all government servants, including that of senators. This, said Whitney, should be the first step toward getting the federal house in order. In reply, Senator Smith W. Brookhart of Iowa told the witness that he regarded the New York Stock Exchange as a gambling hell that should be closed. There were more days of hearings conducted by a subcommittee. Ferdinand Pecora, a former New York prosecutor, questioned the witnesses as committee counsel. While the hearings were sulfurous under the guidance of the tough-minded Pecora, they turned up little new information. Several Wall Street brokers were accused of rigging the market in October 1929, but these accusations had been made and publicized previously, and those accused were not in violation of any law. Nor did any of the New York newspapers pay particular attention to charges made before Pecora's subcommittee by Mayor-elect Fiorello LaGuardia of New York that nine New York financial writers had received money or other favors for touting certain stocks in their newspapers during the Great Bull Market before October 1929.

LaGuardia had named men on nine newspapers, including four still being published, the *Daily News*, the *New York Post*, the *New York Times*, and *The Wall Street Journal*. One of the *Journal* men LaGuardia said was guilty of a violation of journalistic ethics was Richard Edmonson, who wrote the column "Abreast of the Market" prior to the time of the hearings. Oliver J. Gingold took it over shortly thereafter, and Edmonson continued on the staff as a general-assignment man. The other *Journal* man, William Gomber, according to Mayor-elect LaGuardia, accepted money while he was on the staff of *Financial America* (the name of the *Wall Street News* before 1925). Gomber transferred to the *Journal* when Dow, Jones & Company acquired the *Wall Street News* in June 1930. His column in the *Journal*, called "Broad Street Gossip," appeared for a few months prior to the hearings, then disappeared.

On June 27, 1932, Dow Jones & Company marked its fiftieth anniversary a few months early with a special 80-page edition of *The Wall Street Journal*, which also celebrated the opening of its new building. The structure of Indiana limestone and Vermont marble was a modest one, in keeping with the architectural design of its financial-district neighbors. While the building had a Broad Street address, its lobby also opened onto New Street. "The marble-lined corridor on the ground floor," said the paper, "while not a spacious thoroughfare from one street to the other, is a graceful solution to the architectural problem presented by the angle of the plat and its rise on the New Street side.

"News and editorial rooms, occupying all of the third floor, ventilated with conditioned air and equipped with improved lighting system and fixtures and Fenestra windows, are simply and pleasantly decorated with buff walls, white ceiling and brown trim . . . and are lined with sound-deadening celotex. Partitions are of steel. A feature of the building is the reception room on the fifth floor, furniture, fixtures and fireplace in early American style."

The paper boasted a little about its equipment, calling its new Hoe presses "the most improved models known to metropolitan journalism." The pressroom, opening onto loading docks, and the bulletin pressroom were on the ground floor, over basement rooms for newsprint storage, the Frigidaire plant, and the heating plant. The composing and stereotype rooms were on the second floor, and Ackell's automatic mailing machines were installed on a mezzanine floor. "The machines fold, wrap and address the mail edition," the paper said. The advertising department and library were on the fourth floor; business office, reception room, and offices of *Barron's* magazine on the fifth; on the sixth, circulation and purchasing departments; on the seventh were ticker, maintenance, and manufacturing departments.

"Topping these departments, which are devoted to the assemblage, publication and circulation of financial, industrial and related political news, opinion and statistics from all quarters of the world—by printed page and ticker—is the executive floor. There are no outside tenants except for U. Uhl & Co., druggists, on the Broad Street side of the first floor." In a page-one box, Hugh Bancroft, president, and Kenneth C. Hogate, vice-president and general manager, issued a birthday statement in which they called Dow Jones & Company a national institution. "Victories of America through the crises of fifty years, by their very repetition, vitalize confidence that the national difficulties of the present will surely fade," the statement said. It promised to continue "with fidelity and increasing facilities, constructively to present and to represent that which is desirable in American business and finance."

In promotional stories and advertisements during the remainder of the year, the paper grew almost strident in its achievement claims. "Dow Jones & Company maintains the largest financial news-gathering staff in the world—each man being an expert in his respective field—trained to ferret out all financial and industrial facts for the guidance of the trading and investing public." Advertisements seeking customers for the company wire services described the new, high-speed news tickers as capable of receiving 65 words a minute. Said a promotion-department news release in later years, "The high speed service was inaugurated in New York in 1931, and in Chicago in 1932. By 1936–37, the high speed Dow Jones news ticker, nicknamed 'The Broadtape,' was available in eleven American cities and in Montreal and Toronto, Canada. In 1939 the Russell Commodity Service, covering the provisions exchange, was incorporated into the Dow Jones service."

On July 6, 1932, the company accomplished a publicity feat, announcing that 275 of its news tickers were being installed in the various competition centers of the Tenth Olympiad, taking place in Los Angeles July 30 through

August 14. The system would report on the scattered Olympic events to the press and control center in Olympic Stadium, the company said. "No other Olympiad has had anything like it. . . . The system is separate and distinct from the well-known Dow Jones news wire system."

During the summer *The Wall Street Journal* grimly maintained its support of the Republican administration while calling for repeal of the Volstead Act and the Prohibition amendment. Hogate sent Washington Bureau Chief William Grimes to cover the Republican convention in Chicago in June, detached Editor Badger from *Barron's* to go to Washington, and moved up Cyril A. Player as interim editor of *Barron's*. Grimes wrote on convention eve, June 14, that the Republicans would adopt an anti-Prohibition plank. "The majority of the delegates favor it," Grimes said. "Left to itself, the convention will adopt an extreme anti-prohibition plank demanding repeal of the 18th amendment. There is even a chance that it will do so over the opposition of President Hoover and the administration forces. . . . The opinion is growing in Chicago that President Hoover is not strongly opposed to a set plank in the GOP platform."

Correspondent Grimes was mistaken. Following an angry floor fight, the Republicans voted to leave the Prohibition decision up to the states. *The Wall Street Journal* denounced this "straddle" plank. The Republicans nominated President Hoover and Vice-President Curtis on the first ballot. Two weeks later the Democrats, meeting in Chicago, called for repeal of the Eighteenth Amendment and nominated Governor Franklin D. Roosevelt for president and John Nance Garner of Texas as his running mate. *The Wall Street Journal* had no immediate comment on the respective tickets, but said on July 1 that the Democrats had the only honest plank on the Prohibition issue, which it previously labeled "the most important issue facing the nation." Then it added, "In many other respects the Democratic platform is the usual mixture of platitudes and evasions, though it is less offensive on the whole than the Republican platform."

On July 4 the *Journal* appeared prepared to sit out the election since it found both parties to be antibusiness. "No attempt to measure the relation between politics and business this year can ignore the low state to which the latter already has fallen as the campaign opens." But, by early fall, the paper seemed to warm up to the Republicans again, after inquiring sarcastically of its readers if they might care to consider Norman M. Thomas, the Socialist candidate, as an alternative.

Hogate sent Grimes on a tour of the country to test political sentiment. Hogate had been reprinting a series of "Dear George" letters written by Bernard Kilgore for the Pacific Coast edition, and since the columns dealing with financial subjects in a relaxed, easy style proved popular, he recalled

Kilgore to New York to cover the national scene from that vantage point. Robert Bottorff replaced him as news editor in San Francisco. Hogate was still searching for the man who could replace C. W. Barron.

Tom Woodlock was sent to London, where he promptly took up the *Journal's* feud with John Maynard Keynes on Keynes's own turf. The British economist sneered at Wall Street once again in London's revered *Economic Journal* while discussing the American political campaign. "Mr. Keynes, in referring to the 'seeming' recovery in Wall Street, notes that it is 'no more than a vivid illustration of the disadvantages of running a country's development and enterprise as a by-product of a Casino,' " Woodlock wrote. "This is a somewhat picturesque expression of a thought which President Roosevelt has elevated to a campaign issue." Woodlock then compared the evidence of pandemic gambling to be found in Great Britain, where, he said, "betting on the races is universal." He mentioned other gambling vices of the English, and also the Chinese for good measure, and concluded, "Now it is notable that in the United States none of these forms of gambling is widespread." Correspondent Charles Hargrove, meantime, covered the European scene capably for several months, but not in the C. W. Barron style.

Hogate's responsibilities and frustrations increased, and his family worried because he constantly overworked. Hugh Bancroft was ill much of the time. He increasingly retreated to his summer home at Cohasset, where he spent time with his hobbies, especially the forging of iron tools and ornaments in his workshop, and an occasional foray aboard his yacht, *Hourless*, which C. W. Barron in another derisive postmortem gesture willed him because Bancroft constantly insisted it was too expensive to operate. Hogate's name and title, vice-president and general manager, were now carried in the *Journal* masthead with Bancroft's. Hogate also acted as editor of the paper and as officer-in-charge of the Financial Press Companies of America. He made decisions on editorial policy as he pushed ahead with his ideas for editorial changes.

The paper continued to call for repeal of the Eighteenth Amendment, suggesting in an editorial on November 1 that the economy of the country as well as its morals would improve if Congress expedited repeal procedures immediately after the election, a *Journal* position that seemed to anticipate a Democratic victory. The *Journal* also revised an earlier position and now found the Hawley-Smoot tariff to be contributing to the continuing Depression, as 1,028 of the country's college economists had predicted when they petitioned President Hoover to veto it back in 1930. But Hoover had signed the measure, and now in 1932 Roosevelt also backed it. Thus the paper, finally deprived of a choice in the election, if it ever had one, said angrily on November 3: "Governor Roosevelt has unreservedly pledged himself to continue and extend the same impossible effort to afford tariff protection to export surplus producers which gave birth to the Hawley-Smoot Act and, worse, to the Agricultural Marketing Act and its $500,000,000 Farm Board folly. . . . At Madison Square Garden President Hoover pointed out that the protective tariff and its results upon our economic structure had become gradually embedded in our economic life, so much so that whole communities and even industries lean heavily upon them. That is why the cure of the tariff paralysis of international trade presents the stupendous difficulties it does."

In effect, the *Journal* sat out the election. On the day of voting, November 8, it achieved the zenith of editorial equivocation. "Has the political campaign been a check on business recovery?" it asked. "Will its outcome count heavily for or against the chance of that modest prosperity that would make all of us at least relatively contented? A simple yes or no to either question would be altogether too simple. No doubt it would be more nearly correct to answer 'yes and no.' " After waffling through several issues and categories of economic endeavor, the *Journal* closed by saying, "If then the political campaign has exerted only a mildly deterrent effect upon the progress of such business recovery as the year had brought, it must be concluded that its outcome can neither make nor break the country."

Franklin D. Roosevelt and John Nance Garner won with a plurality of 22,821,857 votes to Hoover's 15,761,841 and 884,781 for Socialist Norman Thomas. The electoral-college vote was 472 for Roosevelt and Garner to 59 for Hoover and Curtis. On November 10 the *Journal* congratulated President-elect Roosevelt and urged him to name his cabinet at the earliest possible moment and let the country know promptly how he intended to resolve the economic crisis. On December 10 it urged the lame-duck Congress to act swiftly and decisively on economic problems and to expedite a modification of the Volstead Act pending outright repeal. It assumed, however, that an extra session the following year would be inevitable. The paper suggested to President-elect Roosevelt that since the House and Senate were already heavily Democratic, Congress could move ahead during the short session with any plans he had in mind. Roosevelt, of course, ignored this suggestion.

Casey Hogate continued his own desperate search for solutions to Dow Jones and *Wall Street Journal* problems as the country awaited the inauguration of a new administration on March 4. The holding company, Financial Press Companies of America, was depleting its reserves; dividends were on a downward scale, falling from $3.50 per share in 1931 to 25 cents in 1938. Hugh Bancroft was in effect retired, though his name continued to appear as president in the *Journal's* masthead, just as Charles Dow's had after he left the paper. Hogate continued to run the entire company. There was trouble everywhere. The *Journal's* circulation was heading downward; the number of subscribers to news-ticker services decreased; advertising was down. The Pacific Coast edition was still in the red and already had lost more than half its paid circulation. The Boston and Philadelphia news bureaus could not repay their intercompany loans. *The Wall Street Journal's* constituency had turned cold since the 1929 crash and the Washington attacks on the stock exchanges. Hogate's efforts to make the paper viable appeared ineffectual; the more he tried, the worse things got. Yet he persisted, sure that the demoralization of the country and Wall Street was temporary and that *The Wall Street Journal* could help to find the way back. However, as demonstrated by the drab election posture of the *Journal*, finding the right answers wasn't easy.

Hogate sought to expand his Washington staff late in 1932, but he was equally pressed to upgrade the New York organization and to orient the San Francisco people to *Wall Street Journal* ways—and funds were short. His new writer from the West Coast, Bernard Kilgore, was a comfort. Hogate and Kilgore talked of columns, improved prose style, and better headlines much as Casey and Barron had chatted and exchanged memos a decade previously. After a few "Dear George" letters written in the East, Kilgore began a series of articles in what started as the C. W. Barron style but soon came out reading more like a Tom Woodlock essay. Then Kilgore turned to analytical reports that the *Journal* featured on page one with a copyright notice, indicating the esteem in which they were held by Hogate. Kilgore soon demonstrated that he had a crisp way of explaining national economic problems in language the layman could understand.

It was in the last of a series of articles on the money supply that the DePauw graduate, with less than three years' experience as a financial writer, proved his competence. He summarized his findings on November 5, 1932, dealing with problems that would claim the attention of monetarists for the next half century:

> The July, 1932 figures on the elements of basic credit in the United States . . . showed a truly enormous increase in the country's money supply. . . . A comparison of July averages with those for September shows the return of $244,000,000 monetary gold that left the country or was earmarked for foreign accounts during the disturbed months of late 1931 and early 1932. At the same time Treasury currency, adjusted, increased $55,000,000, largely representing the issue of new national bank notes under the Borah amendment to the Home Loan Bank Act of July. As confidence was restored to some extent at least in the banking structure, and as hoarding lessened, $140,000,000 of currency nominally "in circulation" came back into the banks.
>
> All of these changes tended to increase the all-important item of member banks' reserve balances, which, if used to their normal extent, determine the size of commercial bank deposits.

> However, as member banks' reserves swelled, they paid off about $180,000,000 of their borrowings at the Federal Reserve Banks. This reduced the Federal Reserve credit outstanding to just that extent. Hence the net increase in the Reserve balance was $266,000,000 or enough to support two and a half billion dollars or more in deposits.
>
> All these deposits were not in fact created, but it seems a logical assumption that they will be sooner or later. Excess reserves represent idle funds and earn nothing. The motive of profits normally impels banks and bankers to find customers for loans.

Bernard Kilgore had an upbeat approach that was neither pedantic nor patronizing. Yet, while Hogate appreciated the analytical skills of his young economic writer, he realized he really did not need another Tom Woodlock, however updated. Hogate assigned Kilgore to create an entirely new column, "Reading the News of the Day," in which he sought to provide general news of special interest to the businessman in a condensed and interpretative way. This was a departure from the hard financial news Kilgore had been presenting but, essentially, "Reading the News" retained a strong business slant. Many of the columns covered a wide range of general news, however, and Kilgore developed his own writing style, incisive, clear, and sometimes irreverent.

One of Kilgore's readers was a sometime gentleman farmer in Dutchess County. Although Hogate and Roosevelt had their summer places at opposite ends of the county, they continued to get together for friendly talks. Possibly Roosevelt told Hogate that he admired what Kilgore was doing, since, in *Journal* lore, FDR once said to him, "Kilgore understands gold." In any event, Roosevelt is on record as praising Barney Kilgore publicly on other occasions. When reporters complained to the President that they couldn't understand the budget, Roosevelt told them, "Read Kilgore in *The Wall Street Journal*, he understands it," according to an item in the *South Bend* (Indiana) *Tribune* that an Indiana friend sent to Kilgore, who did not neglect to pass it along to Hogate. Kilgore also used the item to gain a personal interview with President Roosevelt.

"I called up Steve Early, Mr. Roosevelt's secretary, and arranged for an appointment," Kilgore recalled for an unidentified interviewer, according to a memorandum in his files. "The President was in a serious but friendly mood and he talked very frankly. He even said I could write about his ideas as long as I didn't tie anything so closely to the White House that it would make trouble among the regular Washington correspondents.

"After I left, my head was buzzing with ideas and I sat down and wrote a piece about gold and silver money."

Franklin Delano Roosevelt was inaugurated on March 4, 1933. On March 5 the President proclaimed a nationwide bank holiday and embargoed gold export. He thus made unanimous for the 48 states the bank closings that had started when Governor W. A. Comstock of Michigan ordered state banks temporarily shut on February 14. New York became the twentieth state to close down its banks, doing so at 4:30 A.M. on Inauguration Day by proclamation of Governor Herbert H. Lehman; the New York Stock Exchange closed too.

President Roosevelt had also called a special session of Congress to deal with the bank crisis. It took Congress precisely eight hours on March 9 to pass the Emergency Banking Act, which handed almost dictatorial powers to the President. The *Journal* had been providing Roosevelt with unacknowledged advice since before the election and it gamely continued. Said its editorial on the day the President signed the Emergency Banking Act, giving him control over banking and foreign exchange and empowering him to issue his order forbidding the hoarding or exportation of gold: "Banks are being allowed to open for one-way operation. They are permitted to dole out strictly limited amounts of currency but are not allowed to resume elementary banking functions. It is of first importance to restore these at the earliest possible moment. Checks should be received for deposition but at present this is forbidden. It should be possible for depositors to draw checks upon their accounts, not cash withdrawal, but to make payments." The paper then explained why continued restrictions would have the effect of "keeping deposit money in a state of suspended animation. . . . That deposit money must be brought to life. . . . That is the first thing to do. This sort of resumption [that which was being allowed] is not resumption. 'The way,' Sherman said, 'to resume is to resume.' "

There was much, much more, of course. And in his column, "Reading the News of the Day," Bernard Kilgore advised the New York banks not to issue the bales of Clearing House scrip they were printing. In previous financial emergencies the New York banks used Clearing House certificates "largely as a means of settling inter-bank accounts," Kilgore explained. There was great danger in the certificate, or scrip plan, he believed. The scrip could be circulated at a discount and drive official government money into hiding unless it was backed by the government. In that case, Kilgore wrote, it would be equivalent to issuing real money quickly and without safeguards, endangering the nation's monetary system, a danger he had previously pointed out. "It would represent outright inflation if the supply of such scrip were to remain outstanding after normal bank credit were restored."

Kilgore's "Reading the News of the Day" had become a sophisticated interpretative column and an editorial column of opinion as well. It contributed intelligently to the discussion of the 1933 bank crisis, as did the *Journal* editorials. On March 13, in its lead editorial, the paper praised President Roosevelt's actions. "It would be hard to find a parallel in our history for the breath-taking events of the past week. It began with every bank in the country closed, a new President in office, a new Congress summoned in extra session. It ended with the new Congress organized, the President clothed with powers none of his predecessors possessed in time of peace, preparations complete for reopening, with safety, the larger banks and assisting or reorganizing others, a national legislature and people shocked into a new gravity of purpose by open discussion of threatened national bankruptcy and the means to avert it." The week signified an end to three years of drifting from bad to worse, the *Journal* declared. "It marked the end of the pathetic delusion that compromise with belligerent group interests could be so balanced with one another as to restore the well-being of all."

Never before in American history had every man and woman in the nation been so closely touched by economic adversity. The country had been paralyzed. Each adult found funds shut off with no prospect of restoration pending decisions of the new President. On March 12 President Roosevelt used the country's radio stations to broadcast his fireside chat of hope and confidence, thereby ending "that stage of the depression in which we imagined that we could avoid trouble by speaking of it only in whispers," said the *Journal*, which then added, "An end of a state of mind does not mean the end of conditions which produced and accompanied it. It does mean, however, that courage to face the inevitable may take the place of paralysis of fear, in this case unreasoning fear." And the editorial concluded: "For an explanation of the incredible change which has come over the face of things here in the United States in a single week we must look at the fact that the new Administration in Washington has superbly risen to the occasion. It and the country still have incalculable tasks to perform before they can afford so much as a pause for breath. But together they have a good beginning and there are times when a beginning is nearly everything."

The banking system was saved without proliferation of scrip as feared by Kilgore, although scrip was widely used around the country in this emergency. Congress in the following 100 days enacted laws creating the New Deal. The program to stimulate farm prices and to aid industry by restoring buying power among consumers was under way. The President disclosed to his staff that he intended to take the United States off the gold standard to restore commodity prices. "It was a wanton step" from the viewpoint of classical economic theory, wrote historian Arthur Schlesinger, and it aroused the business community against the Roosevelt administration and its New Deal. Even Lewis W. Douglas, the President's budget director, pronounced the move to be the "end of Western civilization," Schlesinger said. At that moment, recalled Raymond Moley, leader of the FDR brain trust, "hell broke loose."

Prime Minister Ramsay MacDonald of Great Britain was en route to Washington to discuss the world gold crisis at the time and, according to Schlesinger, he expected Roosevelt to beg England to return to gold. Instead, the historian wrote, "with one stroke he not only abolished the advantage which nations already off gold enjoyed over the United States in world markets, but reversed the bargaining position between America and Britain."

During the course of the banking holiday, the *Journal* on March 11 reported with satisfaction that "fears of a large issue of scrip or fiat money has proved groundless. . . . The Emergency Bank Act authorizes an ingenious method of providing secured circulating notes, under control of the Federal Reserve, which will be retired when the need is over." This was near the formula suggested in the Kilgore column. On March 16 the paper noted that the stock exchanges had opened free of price restrictions and that the market had responded "to the inestimable value of President Roosevelt's bold action to rescue the national credit by forcing drastic reduction of federal expenditure." Kilgore's column on April 6 predicted that the FDR moves would increase agricultural credit and tear down trade barriers. "This will result in a larger volume of business in general and should be of particular benefit to the farmer who depends to an important extent on markets outside the United States," he wrote. The *Journal* began publishing full lists of banks reopening "for your records," a unique service.

The abandonment of the gold standard on April 19 left the *Journal* editors dubious, however, especially since the action was accompanied by moves seen by them as precipitating "large scale inflation." The editors were beginning to perceive that President Roosevelt really had little hope of reducing government spending or of balancing the budget. Said the paper on May 7, "Just as the United States was the first nation to abandon gold voluntarily, it is now the first to deliberate publicly upon the expediency of debasing its currency in the absence of the traditional compelling reason thereto. For certainly the national budget could be balanced within a reasonable time without it. We are as a nation calmly discussing inflation 'as an instrument of national policy,' whereas heretofore it has always been begun stealthily by finance ministers desperate to conceal national bankruptcy from the people or from an armed enemy at the gates."

The *Journal's* enchantment with Franklin D. Roosevelt ended as it became increasingly evident that he was acting upon principles which the paper had criticized since it first encountered them in John Maynard Keynes's *Treatise on Money*, published in London in 1930. This work analyzed the American boom and bust, and blasted the idea that a capitalistic society automatically adjusted to economic crises. It was clear that the legislation pushed through Congress during the Hundred Days and in days thereafter would drastically change the economic power structure of the United States as well as its political orientation. Deficit finance frightened the editors even more than communism did. "There are Communists in America to be sure and it cannot be doubted that such party as they have is financed from Russia," the paper said in March. "If sensible citizens lose their heads about that, the first Communist objective will have been achieved." The *Journal* editors feared more the abandonment of a balanced budget and the regimentation of business and industry being attempted under the codes of competition of the National Recovery Administration (NRA).

Nevertheless, *The Wall Street Journal* posted the Blue Eagle of the NRA in its front-page flag, indicating that it subscribed to the publishing code, and it sent Bernard Kilgore, its new writing star, on a tour of New York State to report objectively on the NRA program even before most other businesses had acquired their Blue Eagle posters and flags.

Meantime, the paper both defended and attacked the New Deal in its editorials, saying it would wait to see about the NRA. The attacks were selective and consistent with past policy. The *Journal* had opposed the Tennessee Valley Authority Act (TVA), passed in May to maintain and operate the power plant at Muscle Shoals, Alabama, just as it had opposed government operation of Muscle Shoals immediately after World War I. On July 6 it backed the President, heartily approving his rejection of the currency-stabilization plan proposed by the gold-standard countries at the International Monetary and Economic Conference in London. "President Roosevelt is now applying to world affairs that 'realistic' treatment which European statesmen have been so prone to urge upon us," the *Journal* said. "His ultimatum to the economic conference bristles with realism that calls a spade a spade and unblushingly acknowledges national self-interest to be superior as a motivating force to hands-across-the-sea. . . . President Roosevelt has out-done the realists in realism." As a result of President Roosevelt's statement, the London conference ended in failure.

Kilgore's series on the NRA in New York State credited the mobilization of business, industry, and labor with beginning reasonably well in most areas. It was too early, Kilgore said, to determine whether the plan would actually create more jobs to help restore productivity and buying power. Kilgore's series was generally optimistic about most NRA goals being achieved. But in September the *Journal* declared in an editorial that the NRA was not working as well to achieve recovery as it should. It blamed the NRA bureaucracy, which insisted that businesses, forced to increase costs when they complied with NRA codes, should be required at the same time to hold down prices. This, the paper insisted, was not possible. And that was the kind of criticism

General Hugh Johnson, the NRA director, a blustering, hard-driving man who had succeeded in mobilizing production in World War I days, didn't care to tolerate.

General Johnson was even more exasperated by a special Kilgore report on the NRA written from Washington, which opened irreverently in the *Journal* on September 1:

> Washington—Donald Richberg, general counsel of the National Recovery Administration, has made another speech. His subject was "Freedom and Security under the NRA."
>
> After considerable talk along the usual "liberty in law" lines, Mr. Richberg got into the interpretation of the much-discussed Section 7(a) of the Recovery Act. As counsel for the NRA, Mr. Richberg feels that he has the right to offer such an interpretation, and as a lawyer with 30 years' experience in various fields, Mr. Richberg remarked: "I do not merely claim to have a balanced view, I admit it."
>
> And, having made this startling admission, Counsel Richberg proceeded to present his "balanced point of view."

Kilgore then quoted Richberg's interpretation of Section 7(a), which provided for collective bargaining, and his statement that Section 7(a) had not been included in the law "as an expression of a social idea, or as an attraction for labor support of the Act." Kilgore quoted lawyer Richberg further. "It would be indeed helpful in this time if persons who are mentally unable to accept the necessity and value of having a genuine and responsible labor organization for the self-protection of labor interests and the stabilization of industry would immigrate to some backward country where there are no free schools and where the level of common intelligence is very low, and would cease to clutter up progress in the United States with the rubbish of outworn ideas and dead philosophies."

Both Kilgore's style and substance infuriated General Johnson and his bureaucrats, who were especially outraged at having the precise words of one of their own used against them. When the Kilgore NRA series ended, having praised many facets of the NRA, General Johnson addressed the American Federation of Labor convention in Washington and referred to it in his own orotund style: "There are enemies of the NRA. Yesterday I heard a prominent Wall Street journal was going to conduct a survey of small employers for the purpose of demonstrating that the President's reemployment agreement was a failure. I know something about Wall Street. I used to work there. It has been much maligned and also properly criticized. But the idea of a Wall Street journal going out to demonstrate through the little fellow the failure of a great social regeneration is one of the grimmest ghastliest pieces of humor of all the queer flotsam of our daily work."

The Wall Street Journal, of course, reprinted General Johnson's remarks, saying it assumed their paper had been the target. It admitted having sent Kilgore on a survey of the NRA in New York State and said, "Some of Mr. Kilgore's dispatches told of satisfactory workings of the NRA, others indicated specific disturbances and disequilibrium." The paper declared that it was sending Kilgore out again, this time to the Pacific Coast, to write a series of business reports. The paper added: "Some of his articles may deal with the operations of the NRA. If so, successes and maladjustments will both be chronicled. Neither Mr. Kilgore nor any other writer for *The Wall Street Journal* is given instructions to 'find' any particular set of facts. *The Wall Street Journal's* editorial position is set forth on its editorial page and not in its news columns."

Shortly after the Johnson contretemps, Kilgore was invited to do a weekly radio report on the NBC national radio network. Hogate and Grimes approved, and Barney became an airways commentator.

On the morning of October 18, 1933, members of *The Wall Street Journal* staff read in the *New York Times* of the death of Hugh Bancroft, 53, in his home at Cohasset, news that reached the *Journal* office an hour after its own edition had gone to press. Said the *Times*, "Hugh Bancroft, lawyer and former publisher of the *Boston News Bureau* and *The Wall Street Journal*, died suddenly at 5:30 P.M. at his estate after a heart attack. Two years ago he retired. His health had been poor for several years." Bancroft's obituary filled a column in the *Times* and several pages of *The Wall Street Journal* on succeeding days as the paper published scores of tributes to the man who "under the guidance of Clarence Barron turned to the financial publishing business." Hogate and other staff members wrote their personal evaluations. Bancroft had taken the company into the twentieth century as a corporate structure and had prepared it for the future, his grateful associates said.

Funeral services were held at St. Stephen's Church in Cohasset, at 2:30 P.M. on Thursday, October 19. There were 45 financial and political leaders named as honorary pallbearers, and the members of the Boston, Philadelphia, and New York publications acted as ushers.

When Mrs. Jane W. W. Bancroft, director and chief owner of the companies managed by her late husband, met with Hogate and his wife after the funeral, she told him, "I want you to do what's best for the company. Don't you and the boys worry about dividends."

A meeting of the directors of the Financial Press Companies of America was held late that afternoon in the Bancroft home in Cohasset. Jane Bancroft and Hogate elected J. C. Hoskins to their board. After a formal tribute to their late president, Jane nominated K. C. Hogate for president, herself for vice-president, and Hoskins for secretary and treasurer. Mrs. Bancroft then cast roughly 90 percent of the votes for her ticket. Jane owned outright and controlled most of the shares of the Financial Press Companies of America, and the trust owned all shares of Dow Jones & Company, Inc.

Hogate had Jane's complete confidence. She let him know that she was prepared to make needed sacrifices to stabilize Dow Jones & Company as the center of strength and future growth, and she would give Hogate and his associates a completely free hand. On October 31 the *Journal* announced Hogate's election as president and said that Herbert B. Cole, managing editor of the *Boston News Bureau,* had been elected president of that subsidiary. The paper carried a brief, unsigned statement: "The death of Mr. Bancroft followed a severe illness of more than a year. Grieved as we are at his loss, it is a satisfaction to be able to state that the affairs of the businesses of which he was president are in excellent condition. His passing entails no change in the management and no substantial change in the ownership of the properties."

Chapter 13

The Changing World of Casey Hogate

Late in 1933 Casey Hogate, with his elite troops of Financial Press Companies of America and the staffs of Dow Jones & Company and *The Wall Street Journal,* was fighting a holding action against circulation and advertising erosion. He was eager to take the offensive, but his financial reserves were gone and he continued to have staffing problems. His *Journal* format changes failed to hold the line. While it was clear to many of his associates that general economic conditions impeded progress and made change unproductive, at least temporarily, there were others on his staff who simply opposed change. Hogate worried most about one genuine soft spot, the Pacific Coast edition, which, in exasperation, he sometimes called the western rathole. It might have become a total casualty except that Carl Miller, its president and chief executive, fought to keep it alive, and he had a convincing argument—without the edition, *The Wall Street Journal* could not possibly claim to be a national business newspaper. Miller was an able executive who would later make a fortune publishing California newspapers of his own. His managing editor, Robert Bottorff (formerly news editor), another DePauw University graduate who would become a top executive of *The Wall Street Journal,* was also very competent. But the time wasn't right for the Pacific Coast edition. Its paid circulation dropped under 1,000 by 1933. Yet Hogate ignored Bancroft's advice and his own judgment and poured a little more money into the western rathole.

When Hogate emerged as chief executive after the death of Bancroft, he continued to tolerate the Pacific Coast deficits. Jane Bancroft had given him her full support, and she shared Hogate's ambitions for a business newspaper of national scope. In 1970, Jane's daughter Jane Bancroft Cook, a Dow Jones director, recalled in a talk before a women's investment group the beginning of the Hogate regime. "When Kenneth C. Hogate succeeded my father, the word 'business' was added to the masthead of 'a financial newspaper.' This was the start of unbelievable expansion, now reaching people in every kind of business from the raising of dogs to the building of dams."

In Bancroft's final years he added Hogate's name to the paper's masthead. Now Casey went back to the style of C. W. Barron and early Bancroft, listing a single name in the masthead—Kenneth C. Hogate, President. There was to be no doubt about who was boss.

Casey Hogate's expansion program ran counter to the general retrenchment of the times. The redirection of the economy, which began with the launching of the New Deal in the spring of 1933, did not reflect a general forward thrust until 1939 war orders and U.S. rearmament provided a mighty stimulus. American farm exports also increased in the late 1930s. Hogate pushed ahead, but with caution. After boom and bust, the country was drastically changing, and Wall Street was especially affected. *The Wall Street Journal* needed to reflect the change; to provide for new needs; to recognize that financial control had shifted to Washington; to oppose, criticize, guide, and sometimes yield; but primarily to proceed in the forefront of change in its coverage of the news. The old order in Wall Street was over. During the Hundred Days Congress, business had been shackled as never before. The task of interpreting and explaining new laws and regulations, and merely listing them, had become a new big business. *The Wall Street Journal* fell heir to a part of the action and needed to handle its windfall intelligently.

Between March 9, 1933, when the Emergency Banking Act was passed, and June 16, when the Railroad Coordination Act became law, President Roosevelt sent 15 messages to Congress. The response was 14 major congressional acts, from the abandonment of gold and the abrogation of the gold clause in contracts to the Truth in Securities Act passed May 27 (to be followed by the Securities Act of 1934). All directly affected Wall Street. The *Journal* published texts of speeches, laws, and Supreme Court decisions. It sought to publicize, explain, interpret, justify, and selectively attack. The general press did its job, but the avalanche of legislation was too much for it. Hogate, with his specialized publications, undertook to cover it all.

Much of the Roosevelt legislation was accepted as necessary by the *Journal*. However, the President's abandonment of gold, his devaluation of the dollar, and his big-spending measures and repudiation of balanced-budget promises were never accepted. The paper feared deficit finance, the threat of inflation, and bureaucratic waste more than it feared the Great Depression. Some measures, such as the Railroad Coordination Act and the establishment of the Securities and Exchange Commission to regulate the securities markets, were warmly approved. Frequent editorial criticism of the administration was based on the merits of legislation, performance, and issues, not on personalities. Sherwin Badger, writing of his experience as editor of *Barron's* magazine during the early 1930s, recalled that Hogate sent a note to all staffs of the various Financial Press subsidiaries saying, "Criticize the President and the Administration whenever it seems proper, but never criticize him personally."

Badger, who left *Barron's* in 1936 to reenter the securities business, remembered a major problem Hogate faced as the new chief executive. "Here were publications which had supported Republican politics for years, and KCH understood that the New Deal innovations would be very hard to take." The policy of criticism and praise on merit disappointed rabid Republicans but was a simple formula that worked, Badger noted. Hogate made clear at all times that the policy of the paper was to be handled on the editorial pages. It was not possible, however, to entirely remove the human equation from reporting and commentary, especially for such veteran interpreters of the business and financial scene as Tom Woodlock, Oliver Gingold, and Henry Alloway. A new, feisty politician from Missouri who had risen from obscurity as a Jackson County commissioner in the 1934 elections and encountered Hogate's paper in Washington summarized a widespread view of it. "That *Wall Street Journal*," snapped Senator Harry S. Truman, "is the Republican Bible."

Casey Hogate, six feet two, three hundred pounds, and 36 years old when he became president of the Barron properties, had been in the executive ranks for ten years since C. W. Barron moved him into the managing editorship. Hogate added the duties and title of general manager before he was 30. Barron, in describing his young protégé, said a man had told him, "I once talked to Hogate for ten minutes and felt I knew him a lifetime." Casey was big, shaggy, genial. He wore his Phi Beta Kappa key on a gold chain across his ample chest, but he cared little for jewelry, fine clothing, or Barron's flamboyant life-style, though Hogate, too, was known to the headwaiters in the country's best restaurants.

Like Barron, Casey Hogate loved food and people, including those not his peers and not the source of news or influence. Cyril Player, who in 1936 became editor of *Barron's*, wrote of Hogate: "Some executives listen to their people's personal problems for business reasons, but Casey Hogate was interested in you as a person. He helped you whether the problem was office-related or not." Hogate was a soft-spoken, low-key man who rarely moved or acted quickly, never fired an employee, and never subjected anyone who worked for him to harassment. He remembered his own start as a printer's devil and carried in his pocket the printer's rule he had used in his father's Indiana newspaper shop. He was a Methodist, served on his suburban Scarsdale hometown board, and became mayor during World War II years. "I owe it to the place I call home," he said when asked to run.

Hogate was intensely patriotic and respectful of authority. When Franklin Roosevelt became president, Hogate carefully refrained from responding in kind to Roosevelt's chaffing, mocking humor. But on one occasion, their mutual friend Lowell Thomas recalled, Hogate did allow himself to become annoyed. That was when the Thomas-Hogate softball team, The Nine Old Men (a reference to FDR's Supreme Court packing plan), met the President's team on the Ogden Mills estate at Pawling, New York. Rexford Guy Tugwell, FDR's pitcher, served up a ball Casey liked, and he hit it out of the park, so that Harry Hopkins, another Roosevelt brain-truster, had to climb a fence to retrieve it. It should have been a home run, yet Casey Hogate managed to lumber only to first base. When Casey finally got around, the President called him over to rib him for his slowness. Hogate listened respectfully to his President and turned the jibes aside softly, but walking back he was heard to mutter, "Mr. President, that's the way it is for us businessmen these days—we have to hit a home run to get to first base."

Casey Hogate's changes in the *Journal* began before 1934 and generally were not costly, except the decisions to print the text of the President's speeches and many of the new laws and to publish the regulations of the new bureaus. His expansion of the news-ticker services, begun in 1927 with the first Dow Jones leased wire to San Francisco, extended also to Richmond, Virginia, and were improved in Boston and Washington that year. By the end of 1929 Dow Jones had taken over the Illinois Telegraph News Company in Chicago, launched the Pacific Coast edition, and added news tickers in Ohio, Baltimore, and northern New York. These added services, plus Ackell's improvement of communication equipment and the opening of the new building at 44 Broad Street, were needed as much as Bancroft's structural changes in the company before Hogate could really begin to plan the "national" business newspaper that existed only by proclamation in 1929.

Hogate desperately needed experienced newsmen, but they did not seem to be available. Financial journalism continued to be a highly specialized endeavor. Journalists generally didn't apply for work in Hogate's shop; they had to be recruited. Hogate's continuing need to find a writer who could succeed C. W. Barron could not be met. After experiments with various editorial styles, Bernard Kilgore had developed his own highly effective approach to the reporting of economic news, but he was no Barron. Hogate evidently recognized that Kilgore represented a new kind of financial journalism and was torn between having him work as a writer and making him an editor, and for a time, Kilgore appeared to serve as both. Hogate detached Edward Stein from his circulation-department duties and assigned him temporarily to Berlin. He sent a likely newcomer, H. E. Gronseth, to Detroit to report the efforts of the American auto industry to lead the nation in an economic comeback.

Washington news was a major concern of Hogate's. He had posted William Grimes, an experienced writer and editor, to Washington in the days when the bureau consisted of five employees, including bureau chief Grimes, a telegraph operator, and an office manager. "Even then," Grimes recalled, "there were periods between Congressional sessions when there wasn't much to do." The New Deal and the Great Depression changed that. "Up to that time," he wrote in the *Journal*, "the rest of the newspaper fraternity thought that *Wall Street Journal* reporters were a rather strange lot who covered places like the Federal Reserve Board and the Interstate Commerce Commission. Then, with the coming of the depression, business and financial news became important and all reporters began to look into those news sources."

Hogate authorized Grimes to build up his staff after sending a bright young man, Thomas W. Phelps, to his aid in 1932 and assigning Kilgore to various national news projects in New York or Washington, or to cross-country news tours of the kind Grimes previously made. Phelps soon began writing a "Washington Letter" in addition to general reporting. Hogate arranged for the publication in the *Journal* of Frank R. Kent's column, "The Great Game of Politics," which appeared in the *Baltimore Sun*. Kent, a critic of Roosevelt, was one of the best newsmen covering the Washington scene at the time. His column represented a departure from the *Journal* tradition of using only its own staff for any kind of reporting or commentary. It was well received by *Journal* readers and ran for years. Grimes's prize acquisition was made in 1933, when he hired William F. Kerby, a former summer reporter. Kerby had been working with Washington press services since his graduation summa cum laude from the University of Michigan, where he studied political science.

There were other newcomers in New York and Washington as well. Hogate signed on Buren H. McCormack, a DePauw University graduate, in the fall of 1931. Soon the names of N. S. Keith, John W. Broderick, and A. F. Flynn appeared as by-line writers. The paper no longer resembled the *Journal* of Charles Dow's period. Yet the changes were not dramatic; they occurred gradually. Hogate had added the word *business* to the masthead and the promotional advertising and he spoke of the *Journal* as a national newspaper, but he obviously was not thinking of a general circulation goal. As in the days of Charles Dow, Edward Jones, and Clarence Barron, *The Wall Street Journal* continued to be the paper for people who invested their money and engaged in business. Since there were relatively fewer such persons—the *Journal* regularly reported new lows in the number of shares sold and issues traded in Wall Street—circulation continued to decline despite the innovations.

Hogate's efforts were not limited to changes in the editorial and news-ticker divisions of Dow Jones. He also acquired two other DePauw University graduates, destined for his business departments. One was Robert McCleary Feemster, pint-sized, self-acknowledged genius who graduated from DePauw in 1930 after completing his studies in three and a half years rather than the usual four and who gave up plans to study law when Hogate offered him $30 a week to sell advertising. In later years, it was Feemster as the *Journal*'s director of advertising who designed the split-run system, which enabled an advertiser to buy either the full edition or a sectional pressrun, such as the Pacific Coast edition. This invention allowed the *Journal* and other national publications to vastly increase their advertising sales. Theodore E. Callis, also a 1930 graduate of DePauw, followed Feemster into the advertising department and eventually succeeded him as advertising director. Thus, in the early 1930s, Casey Hogate, with assistance from Grimes and Kilgore, gave *The Wall Street Journal* its future leaders—Bottorff, Callis, Feemster, Kilgore, and McCormack from DePauw University in Indiana like himself, and Grimes and Kerby with midwestern backgrounds.

In 1934 *The Wall Street Journal* continued its policy of judging New Deal legislation on its merits as seen from the paper's conservative view. But it was clear that President Roosevelt, after moves intended to rescue the economy with his New Deal, had become preoccupied with reformation of the economic system. The President's brain trust came from universities imbued with the ideas of John Maynard Keynes, which the *Journal* found no less odious because they were Americanized. When, late in 1933, Keynes himself undertook to directly influence Roosevelt by publishing an open letter to the President which appeared to suggest that economic recovery was certain if only the government would spend enough by borrowing more—"We owe it to ourselves" was the simplification of Keynes's advice—the *Journal* attacked the President's advisers, though not FDR himself. Even worse than Keynes, the paper said on January 2, was Nicholas Murray Butler, president of Columbia University, who also issued a statement "speaking as though the profit motive were today rampant and unchecked among all men, as though its subordination to service were the pressing need of the moment.

"What is this 'profit motive' which it is suddenly become fashionable to decry?" the paper asked. Then, of course, it answered in the context of the classical economics of Adam Smith. "The profit motive is simply the common aspiration of all men to better their material status through individual exertion. It takes root in self-interest and within limits it stands opposed to that other powerful mainspring of human conduct, the desire to promote the common good for the vicarious enjoyment of its satisfaction. . . . How many members of the Columbia University faculty have exerted themselves beyond the requirements of their inadequately salaried duties to make contributions to literature and the technological arts for which the world is glad to pay them?"

The following day the *Journal* conceded that President Roosevelt's devaluation of the dollar had been accompanied by signs of recovery, but it said it preferred not to inquire too closely whether these coeval events were entirely fortuitous. "The point worth noting is that the devaluation was fortunately timed," the paper said. In April the *Journal* reported an increase in retail trade and anticipated that this evidence of more money in the hands of the consumer would be accompanied by an increase in production. However, it added, there was at the moment no proof of a production increase. It blamed the "general uncertainty" for lack of investment in productive enterprise and accused Congress of being more irresponsible than the President, saying, "Passing over the experimentation of the New Deal, Congress chose to rebuff his [FDR's] leadership on the one issue intended to improve the government's credit [the independent offices appropriations bill]. Hardly anything that Congress could do would be more illogical."

Thus the paper appeared to believe in the spring of 1934 that President Roosevelt still intended to balance the budget when possible. It continued to reiterate its own position that the best way to stop deficit spending and the Depression and to avoid inflation was to stop increasing government spending, the antithesis of the spreading Keynesian philosophy. The *Journal* returned to the attack on April 3: "In only one field of action is the course and policy of government of supreme importance to economic recovery, namely the management of its own revenues and the resulting status of the national credit."

On April 4 the *Journal,* in a page-one editorial, called for passage of the Securities Exchange bill to establish the Securities and Exchange Commission. The Commission would have the power to regulate stock exchanges and limit bank credit for speculative purposes. This legislation complemented the registration and regulation provisions of the Securities Act of May 1933, which the paper also approved. "*The Wall Street Journal* has already endorsed the principles and essential provisions of the Robinson-Rayburn bill without reservation," it said. "It reaffirms and continues its support of the measure and repeats its earlier affirmation that not only the owners and users of investment capital but with them the investment bankers, whose fortune it is to bring these two interests face to face, should welcome the legislation." Not all newspaper publishers shared the *Journal's* approval of the bill. Eugene Meyer, former governor of the Federal Reserve Board and new publisher of the *Washington Post,* told the nation's editors assembled in Washington that week that the securities bill was one of those put forward by the New Deal ostensibly to regulate "while deceitfully establishing its powers for other purposes, i.e., control."

In May the *Journal* indicated that it was increasingly disenchanted with President Roosevelt and declared that the administration was surrendering to the silver producers and inflationists. "*The Wall Street Journal* cannot accept as true the current report that the President has privately agreed with Congressional members of the silver bloc," said the paper on May 19. "This newspaper refuses to believe that the United States has descended to such a level . . . that President Roosevelt has committed himself to a rotten currency." But the Silver Purchase Act of 1934 was passed by Congress and signed by the President, whose proclamation nationalizing silver was issued on August 9. Silver previously worth 50.01 cents an ounce was now priced at $1.29 in the government's paper money; confiscation of silver bullion in private hands was authorized for transfer to government vaults, where it would be held against insurance of more inflated currency.

The break between *The Wall Street Journal* and President Roosevelt was complete. Bernard Kilgore, writing from Washington on the New Deal, especially as it related to the NRA, said on May 22, "There is a tug of war between government and business which might be called Modified Laissez-Faire. Business has pulled to the Right, and government is pulling to the Left. To the Extreme Right lies the same old system of private monopoly now more familiarly known as Fascism. To the Left lies the same old system of government monopoly, now commonly called Collectivism." The economy was zigzagging, Kilgore wrote, and he was not sure that the middle road could ever become the national system. That, he concluded ominously, "as the editorial writers often say, remains to be seen." Hogate evidently felt his young writer had been a bit extreme, for two days later the paper's lead editorial presented the business-government confrontation in less threatening terms, calling the New Deal the "great experiment of substituting a controlled economy for depression-made chaos . . . which leaves the business community with a mixture of hope and fear." Some days later on July 1 the *Journal* reported that sales on the New York Stock Exchange had fallen to 380,000 shares for the five-hour session, the lowest mark in ten years.

Tom Woodlock, in his page-one column, had more than once accused President Roosevelt of following Keynes's economic theories, and he repeated his accusation. "What he is doing is precisely what Mr. Keynes thinks should be done," Woodlock wrote. "The administration policy is so closely following the ideas of Mr. Keynes in respect to currency devaluation, public expenditures and so forth, all directed to advancing commodity prices, that only extreme modesty can restrain him [Keynes] from appropriating no small credit to himself for leading us on the right path." Keynes, however, didn't appear to agree, and neither did the President. After they met at the White House, President Roosevelt told Frances Perkins, his secretary of labor, who had brought them together, "He left a whole rigamarole of figures. He must be a mathematician rather than a political scientist." Said Keynes to Miss Perkins: "I had supposed the President to be more literate, economically speaking."

In early September 1934 Casey Hogate began a series of changes that would ultimately result in the metamorphosis of *The Wall Street Journal* into a new kind of daily newspaper. Hogate himself evidently did not foresee precisely where the changes might lead, nor did he discern the need for a total transformation. In 1934 the company moved toward creating the logistical base required for improved communications and regional printing, largely through the efforts of Joseph Ackell, who turned to research on newspaper production. Ackell was able to broaden his research beyond the scope of news tickers and improved mailing devices, although basic work continued in those fields and resulted in an automatic transmitter for the news tickers in 1936 and a multiposting machine for record-keeping in 1937.

Hogate assigned Barney Kilgore to create a "What's News" column for page one of the *Journal,* and it appeared on September 4. A few days earlier he brought Grimes back to New York to become managing editor of the *Journal.* According to a typed memorandum in the Dow Jones archives, unsigned but bearing the notation "BK told me today," and dated July 21, 1955, Hogate and Grimes discussed the new column as soon as Grimes arrived from Washington and decided Kilgore should establish its format before going to Washington to succeed Grimes as bureau chief. "One of Hogate's ideas was that all of the news of the day could be put into a couple of paragraphs at the top of the column," said the "BK told me today" memo. Another memorandum, evidently of the same 1955 vintage and ascribing the information to George Shea, then news editor of the *Journal,* said, "B.K. wrote the first column and for several weeks thereafter and probably gave it its name."

Buren McCormack was also involved in the launching of "What's News" and wrote it when Kilgore departed for Washington. McCormack recalled that Hogate wanted all the day's news in a couple of paragraphs, "and there was a great deal of discussion and sweating trying to do it. But also, at least part of our efforts were to try to tell a particular story in a sentence or two and then spend the rest of the item interpreting it. But, whatever the effort, we couldn't make it work. I remember Kilgore saying, 'With that system, it would take three men and a boy to do this column.' "

But Kilgore did evolve a column exemplifying Hogate's basic ideas. It was finally decided, said one of the memos, that "it had to be just primarily a news summary with some relation of one news event with another." Later, a division was made between general and financial and business news. What was unique about Hogate's idea, so far as the *Journal* was concerned, was his desire to introduce general-interest news to the front page of a business paper. This Kilgore accomplished in succeeding days, but, because general-interest news that September 4 concerned a textile strike long anticipated, Kilgore's first column began with the kind of business news often found in the *Journal*'s coverage of strike developments:

> The first day of the long advertised textile strike brought the usual claims and counter claims from the contending forces.
>
> Union leaders claimed the walkout was unanimous in "numerous" southern mill towns.
>
> George Sloan, head of the Cotton Textile Institute, gave out figures showing that the tie-up amounted to only about 20%.
>
> In the New England centers general observance of the Labor Day holiday postponed the judgment on the effect of the strike.
>
> Future union operations in the South may increase the apparent effectiveness of the tie-up there, but at the present reading the labor leaders give the appearance of men who may have over-reached themselves.

The next item concerned the government's plans for financing subsistence factories for the unemployed. The third cited the omnipresent Professor Irving Fisher, showing his commodity price index up 1.2 points to 79.7, "the recovering high for the August 31 week." Professor Fisher favored a commodity dollar, one indexed to commodity prices. The column also reported New York's Mayor Fiorello LaGuardia in a Chicago Labor Day speech blaming industrial and business leaders for unemployment. World and Washington political news completed Kilgore's report.

Though the "What's News" column contained mostly economic news that first day, the element of general news exemplified the *Journal*'s recognition that its readers need not be given business and financial news exclusively. As Kilgore wrote the column during the following weeks to develop its form and to fix the format, he must have thought about applying such an approach to the *Journal*'s total news coverage. The "BK told me" memorandum, besides describing the inception of the "What's News" column in 1934, also mentioned the creation of a new front page for *The Wall Street Journal* in 1941. Kilgore himself evidently linked the two ideas, but it took six years from the time "What's News" began until Kilgore formulated his concept of *The Wall Street Journal* as a national newspaper of broader interest and could win the opportunity to implement his idea.

On that September 4 Casey Hogate took other important steps. He terminated the afternoon edition of *The Wall Street Journal,* which had begun life as an afternoon newspaper. He announced to his staff the appointment of William Grimes as managing editor to replace Cy Kissane, whom Grimes regarded as incompetent. (Hogate could never fire anyone. He demoted Kissane to writing a weekly newsletter.) Grimes was a quiet-spoken, somewhat acerbic and temperamental, distinguished-looking newsman who knew the New York and Washington financial and political scene, spoke cryptically, and pretended to be an enemy of change. Grimes did not especially want an executive job; he preferred the more reclusive life of an editorial writer or, given a second choice, of a writing bureau chief in Washington, but he was loyal to his paper and to Hogate.

The *Journal* accepted the Democratic victory in the November 8 congressional by-elections with considered equanimity. "President Roosevelt has every right to take deep satisfaction in the election returns," the paper said. "He has been given a vote of confidence so emphatic that the popular reaction to the party in power, which traditionally records itself in 'off-year' congressional elections, is this time almost obliterated." The paper impishly suggested, however, that deep down President Roosevelt might have preferred a lesser victory for the Democrats since a party with a smaller majority would have been easier for him to control.

Early in 1935 Hogate got the man he wanted into Washington as his bureau chief, Barney Kilgore. Kilgore at the time was only 26 years old, but he had bureau and executive experience in San Francisco and had been well trained in New York in Casey Hogate's ways. Thomas Phelps would soon return to New York to succeed Cyril Player as editor of *Barron's* magazine.

Economic conditions at Dow Jones and the *Journal* continued to be bad. Hogate was forced to cut his workers' wages and, at least in some divisions, to give them only "Scotch vacations"—a week or two off, but without pay. The dividend of Financial Press Companies of America declined to $1 a share in 1934–35. It would rise to $1.60 a share in 1937, then fall to 25 cents the next year. The Financial Press Companies were never in the red, but the 1938 net profit after payment of all federal taxes was a mere $23,000. Circulation, still unaudited, continued at the low of 28,000, from which it did not soon recover. Yet, despite difficulties and the curtailed budget, the 16 Dow Jones offices outside New York were maintained. Both the San Francisco and Philadelphia news bureaus were losing money, and publication of the

Philadelphia Financial Journal would cease on June 29, 1940. Hogate's name continued alone on the editorial-page masthead. He gave orders to William Grimes, to Frederick Korsmeyer, his chief editorial writer who for a time was unofficially called editor of the paper, and to Hoskins and Ackell. Memoranda indicate he dealt personally with his Detroit, San Francisco, and Washington bureau chiefs.

Grimes, the new managing editor, undertook to carry out further improvements in the *Journal* despite his reduced budget and his lack of sympathy for formal changes. Hourly averages of 70 stocks and a revised curb market report appeared late in 1934; Business and Finance departments were added to the "What's News" column early in 1935; and late in the year a weekly summary column, "Progress of the Week," was added. Set in two columns, this was printed in the Monday editions. Additions to the market report included an odd-lot listing, defaulted bond averages, and the ten most active stocks.

Grimes assigned to Kerby the duties of upgrading headlines to tell and sell the story and of tightening copyreading procedures, tasks Kerby executed with skill, as Kilgore observed from Washington. Kilgore sought whenever possible to get his own copy into Kerby's hands, which especially paid off when he developed his inside-Washington column in 1940. Kerby named it "Washington Wire" and played it on page one. Grimes changed staff procedures and press times and reorganized news coverage, but he generally opposed any content deviation. He objected to an unorthodox display of Kilgore's special column on the front page. "It belongs on the editorial page," he grumbled. But he finally agreed to allow Kilgore's first Washington column to appear on page one to "introduce it." Kerby kept "forgetting" to move "Washington Wire" inside. Kilgore was delighted and Grimes, getting a pleased response from the Washington bureau for a change, finally capitulated. "Washington Wire" stayed on page one.

Grimes, like Hogate, was an extremely hardworking man. He lived in Brooklyn Heights, ten minutes from the office, and, like Hogate, spent much of his time at the office. Occasionally, Grimes would head for his farm in Hopewell, New York, where he raised White Holland turkeys. A tight-lipped, short-tempered man who had little patience with trial-and-error experimentation, Grimes sometimes blew up with rage at what he regarded as incompetence or interference with his own tested editorial procedures, especially if perpetrated by persons outside the editorial department. Once, wrote Charles Stabler, who returned from San Francisco to learn more about the New York office, Grimes in an angry outburst threw his hat on the floor and jumped on it with both feet. Grimes let go outside the office as well. Once after a bad golf shot, he threw his bag into a tree, where it remained until recovered by his caddy, who had to borrow a ladder. Grimes's problems were numerous and corrosive. Stabler, for instance, was expected to return to the Pacific Coast edition after his New York training, but he soon took a job as financial editor of the *New York Herald-Tribune*.

When Bernard Kilgore arrived in Washington to take charge in early 1935, he found a staff of 13 at work, mostly new men recruited by Hogate and Grimes. William Kerby, however, a Grimes favorite among the recent college graduates, left to do public-relations work for the American Liberty League before Kilgore took over. (Kerby would rejoin the *Journal* as a copyreader in New York in 1936.) Ken Kramer, Kilgore's roommate in San Francisco when both were on the Pacific Coast edition, was the Washington bureau's news editor, who made assignments and edited copy for the news wires. The newest member of the staff was Vermont Connecticut Royster, a recent graduate of the University of North Carolina, whose first assignment was to take dictation from reporters on Washington beats and to aid Ken Kramer.

The *Journal*'s Washington office consisted of three rooms in the National Press Building. Biggest was the wire room, where copy was edited and transmitted to the Dow Jones news tickers or to the *Journal* in New York. A second room contained four typewriters, where reporters who didn't use a borrowed typewriter on one of the beats could work and *Journal* files could be inspected. The third room was a cubicle that Barney Kilgore used as his office, where he could write, keep accounts, and sign checks, as he was authorized to do that year by the board of directors, a function he was the first Washington bureau chief to possess. Hogate evidently intended to teach Kilgore to assume administrative responsibilities as early as possible.

When Barney could, he spent time in the wire room with co-workers talking shop or taking a hand in the game of coon can, a predecessor of gin rummy imported from Mexico that went on endlessly in the late afternoon. Their youthful boss was a good-looking man who closely resembled the popular screen star Buddy Rogers: he was about five feet ten, with brown hair and eyes, a man who spoke softly, smiled easily, and led one to quickly forget the nervous tic affecting the right side of his face. He liked his staff (although not always the quality of work they did) and they liked him. Kilgore was totally informal, relaxed, and affable, yet there was a tough resourcefulness, too, in his demeanor. Years later, after Kilgore became president of the company, William McSherry, who began as a secretary at the *Journal* and subsequently became director of news-department services, remembered his first sight of him. "B.K. came to my desk my first working day, sleeves rolled up, forearms like a blacksmith, collar and tie askew, warm smile and a firm handshake. I thought to myself, if I had the job of picking a president of Dow Jones out of a crowd, B.K. would be a most unlikely choice."

Most of the members of the Washington bureau staff soon knew that their boss was destined for something special. Some sensed that Barney was seething inside much of the time, anxious and impatient to implement his ideas for improving and broadening the news coverage and the paper. "The foxes of ambition are gnawing at Barney," one close acquaintance said. Yet this didn't appear to be true. Barney Kilgore was moving ahead faster than anyone else in the company. He had a prize job as bureau chief, he was showcased as a writer by his paper, and he was liked and respected by his men and his peers. But he did tangle with Managing Editor Grimes. Increasingly often, Kilgore sent Grimes notes on yellow memo paper criticizing the handling of Washington dispatches and suggesting specific improvements. His suggestions occasionally embraced the New York coverage as well, suggestions Grimes, who after all had been a Washington bureau chief himself and was already overloaded by Hogate, did not want. Sometimes the two men clashed by telephone, but not often. The *Journal* at the time couldn't afford needless long-distance calls. Sometimes Kilgore sent his suggestions to Casey Hogate, further irking Grimes when he learned of it.

On occasion, as Barney Kilgore slipped into the wire room to play a hand of cards, test the bottle of sipping whiskey, or talk a bit, young Vermont Royster studied him. Royster recalled his impressions some 40 years later:

> It was during this period—particularly when Barney was sitting around the card table—that I first began to get an inkling of some of the ideas he had for *The Wall Street Journal* of the future. Obviously the ideas weren't fully jelled. But he already had a concept that the news of business and economics was the one central area of news that was the same all over the country. . . . The businessmen of San Francisco needed the same business, economic and political news as the man in New York. Even at that time Barney thought that the San Francisco edition should be pretty much like the New York edition, but we knew it was not. . . . He also had the idea that we in Washington ought not to concentrate entirely upon what's called spot news, that is, just what happened today. That we ought to begin to write what Barney used to call situation stories. . . . You would take a situation such as the agricultural program that was being talked about by [Secretary of Agriculture] Henry Wallace and his advisors. You would sit down and write a situation piece in which you gave a lot of background, in which you tried to interpret the meaning—what effects would this program have if accomplished. You would try to put in the story what prospects it had of getting through Congress, that sort of thing. In other words, dealing with a current situation, but not just what happened yesterday. These efforts were primitive in terms of the *Journal* today. But it was another raw unformed beginning of what later became the "leader" concept of *The Wall Street Journal*.

A few such leader stories were written in the Washington bureau in the days when Kilgore was bureau chief, Royster remembered. In the beginning, a few were printed, but most were not.

In February 1935 the *Journal* was highly skeptical of the Federal Reserve Board's proposal to amend the Federal Reserve Law, which would place in the Board's hands through open-market operations the "power to control the expansion and contraction of bank credit and thus in a large measure to control the supply of money." Said the paper sarcastically: "There is no doubt the amendments are well designed to accomplish that purpose. . . . It is gratifying the country has so early been put upon notice as to what is afoot, for the acknowledged purpose contains implications of the most serious nature concerning the very lifeblood of the country's business. The power to control the country's credit supply is equivalent to the power to control the heart's action in the human body."

The *Journal* did not want such power given to the Federal Reserve Board, nor to any other commission "short of one as remote from politics as the Supreme Court." Later economic historians and economists formed a similar judgment of the Washington Federal Reserve Board of that era. But the legislation was approved. Wrote Milton and Rose Friedman in *Free to Choose*: "Since 1935 the [Federal Reserve] System has presided over—and greatly contributed to—a major recession in 1937–38, a wartime and immediate postwar inflation, and a roller coaster economy since, with alternate rises and falls in inflation and decreases and increases in unemployment."

But, while *The Wall Street Journal* thought that the Roosevelt administration had already debauched money and the economy by the Gold Reserve Act of 1934, followers of Keynes continued to think that FDR was not doing enough. Robert Lekachman, in his *Age of Keynes*, wrote ironically: "Indeed, the Roosevelt administration finally accepted the key public policy conclusion of Keynesian economics: deficits in time of unemployment are fine because they stimulate national income and employment. If deficits are beneficial, it follows that they should be large enough to do their job."

On April 5 the *Journal* charged that the entire nation was engaged in a vast waste of the people's money through the relief phases of the New Deal, especially the Works Progress Administration under Harry L. Hopkins and the Public Works Administration under Harold Ickes. "The United States of America, its people, its federal, state and local governments from coast to coast, its Democratic and Republican party wheelhorses, yea its statesmen, all are boondoggling," said the paper. A few days later it again attacked the government for wasting money on useless public-aid projects and asserted that government had become the enemy of business. "To put it bluntly . . . the majority of business leaders understand that their supplications to Washington are in vain." On May 29, 1935, the *Journal* was pleased to report that business had finally won an important victory over the National Recovery Administration: in *Schechter Poultry Corporation* v. *United States*, the Supreme Court ruled unanimously that the National Industrial Recovery Act (NIRA) was an unconstitutional delegation of legislative power. "It was a blanket indictment," the paper said. "Such assertions of extra-constitutional authority were anticipated." The page-one headline hailed the court's action: "Industry Cheered by NIRA Ruling."

But the *Journal* also accepted Roosevelt victories with good grace, as when the Court upheld the congressional resolution to exclude the gold clause from public contracts and the right of the Tennessee Valley Authority to dispose of surplus power. There were, however, other defeats for New Deal legislation: the provisions for oil-production control in the NIRA, the Frazier-Lemke Farm Bankruptcy Act, and the Agricultural Adjustment Act (AAA) were all ruled unconstitutional by the Supreme Court. The *Journal* applauded all but one of these decisions. When the AAA was voided in January 1936, *Journal* editors expressed regret since they feared the farmers would be hurt. "City dwellers, or certainly the more intelligent stratus thereof," Korsmeyer wrote in an editorial, "must concede that an equality of economic status between agriculture and industry is not only an abstract ideal of justice but would in the long run confer the maximum of well-being upon both of these two great segments of the population." The paper predicted that Congress "will earnestly strive to give 6,000,000 farmers an adequate substitute for the AAA. It will do so partly for reasons only too obvious in a campaign year, but there is always something more and better than politics behind 'farm relief.' Americans have never accepted the theory that Heaven has ordained that the tillers of the soil shall live at the mud-sills of civilization. . . . The farmer's demand for equality of opportunity, so far as can be vouchsafed him by the social organization, is not to be dismissed from anybody's reckoning."

The *Journal* repeatedly cautioned the government that it could not create capital out of thin air. The theme was repeated on February 1, 1936, after Congress passed the Soldiers' Bonus bill over the President's veto while at the same time omitting the appropriations clause. The paper said that the omission would create a deficit of more than $4 billion in 1937. Congress also reestablished the AAA, which the *Journal* favored, but in a manner sure to send the deficit even higher, so it worried about that too. "The Bonus and AAA decisions, not to mention minor factors, have thus raised again in acute form the question whether there is to be any control over spending and borrowing."

Yet *The Wall Street Journal* consistently supported the Roosevelt administration in its Wall Street legislation. While the paper insisted "there is no possibility of completely eliminating from investment the last residual factor of speculation," it continued to approve new SEC regulations. The proposal to segregate broker and dealer functions "is sound. . . . It has long been applied on the London Stock Exchange," the paper said on June 22. "The distinction between the specialist and odd-lot dealer also is sound.

. . . Not quite so clear is [the SEC's] conception of the floor trader's relation to the market." But the *Journal* advised the SEC to direct its attention to protecting the public by limiting margin trading rather than by creating rules excessively restricting traders. "Traders do not make the market." The paper was cold to another piece of New Deal legislation that spring—the Robinson-Patman Act covering regulation of chain stores. "The bill is a fine example of how to make work for lawyers," it said.

The *Journal* began warming to Governor Alfred M. Landon of Kansas as a presidential candidate from its first report on him, a story about his speech to the Attica High School graduating class in Kansas on May 19. "Alfred M. Landon may or may not occupy the White House," it conceded. "Quite apart from his political merits or fortunes is the fine quality of his address. . . . Governor Landon declared, in effect, that the gospel of those who would teach the rising generation to weep into their bean soup over the dirty deal the world is handing them is sheer nonsense."

Hogate and Grimes continued their remaking of the *Journal*, adding, removing, and revising columns, changing titles. Woodlock's column was renamed "Thinking Things Over," and Kilgore resumed his "Dear George" letters but dropped them when he was assigned to cover national politics, specifically to report on Landon's chances. Not good, Kilgore concluded. "Voters are on the fence and may stay on it," he wrote from Bucyrus, Ohio, in July. "The average voter can't tell you the difference between the Democratic and Republican platform on any one of the points on which they actually disagree." The "What's News" column went to two columns, then three. A "What's Ahead" column appeared, written by Frederick Korsmeyer.

In July the *Journal* declared that its advertising linage was up. "June 1936 compared with June 1935 UP 28%; 6 mos. 1936 compared with 6 mos. 1935 UP 17%." The big reason, the paper said, "is simply the fact that readers are intensely interested [in *The Wall Street Journal*]. Its daily content is so concentrated, its every page so important that 94% of its subscribers read it through. . . . Average reading time devoted to it is 29½ minutes a day." The statistics were "according to the findings of investigation by Ross Federal Research Agency." Dow Jones & Company, in other advertisements during the summer, announced a new service, DOW-VOX, a financial-news report providing market news by means of loudspeakers, using equipment furnished by the Teleregister Corporation.

Through the summer and fall, the paper worried about the planned economy of the New Deal moving the nation toward socialism. On October 28 it predicted the new Social Security plan would be in trouble, sooner or later. "It is conceivable that the Social Security Fund may become a pure convention of bookkeeping." The paper thought that the government might some day tap this reserve for its own purposes.

Barney Kilgore's campaign reports left no *Wall Street Journal* reader surprised by the Roosevelt and Garner landslide over Governor Landon and Frank Knox on November 3. The electoral-college result was 523 to 8. The paper had anticipated the result on November 2, indicating that the business community was prepared for it. "There is little tangible evidence that misgivings as to tomorrow's elections have seriously disturbed the calculations of the business man." On November 6 it was resigned to the voters' decision. "It is quite clear to them that President Roosevelt represented the best available embodiment of their aspirations for a social order reformed on more liberal lines within the American pattern. These are legitimate objectives not confined to any one class." Concerning widely published statements that the Republican party was dead, the *Journal* replied: "There have been five landslides in twenty years. Each time the losing party was declared dead, only to reappear in four years. The simple fact is that parties do not die as the result of defeats. They die from within when their hearts shrivel and no longer beat. There are 17,000,000 people in the country who do not believe the Republican party is dead." The editorial writer ignored the death of the Whig party after its defeat before the Civil War. He saw signs of public yearning for more conservative ways in returns repealing a chain-store tax in California and defeating public-power proposals in Washington and Oregon, propositions the *Journal* had opposed.

In January 1937 the *Journal* was pleased that President Roosevelt's budget message promised a reduction in the deficit, which the paper estimated at $438,979,000, leaving the total deficit for the fiscal year ending June 30 at $1,673,493,000. Such a prospect for 1937 was good, it said, and "much more interesting is the President's forecast of a 1938 budget balanced except for statutory debt retirement and a 1939 budget completely balanced."

But the *Journal* totally rejected President Roosevelt's call for an expansion and reform of the federal judiciary, i.e., the United States Supreme Court, "to conform to national needs." This became known as FDR's plan to pack the Supreme Court. Roosevelt's message to Congress recommending this astounding change was delivered on February 5, 1937, and the *Journal* responded with a brief, determined editorial on the 9th:

> It has not taken the country long to grasp the real purpose of the Administration's proposals for "reform" of the federal judiciary, despite the elaborate wrappings of the package. It is a simple issue that is raised—a plain question.
>
> Shall we change the rules of the game, or shall we change the present umpires for others whose decisions will suit the home team?
>
> The people of the United States can make any rules they please. They can at any time, if they desire, establish a monarchy, a dictatorship or an Oriental despotism by methods they themselves have used a score of times.

> Why then take the devious method of changing the rules by interpretation at the hands of umpires selected for that purpose?
>
> Would we tolerate the idea in football, baseball, golf, pugilism or any other human activity depending upon rules?
>
> If we would not, why should we tolerate it in the most important activity of all—government?
>
> The President's proposals invite us to do just that. Are we ready to do it?
>
> If not, now is the time to stop, look and listen.

By October the editors of the *Journal* had reason to fear that the Roosevelt administration no longer expected to balance the budget. The President responded to the recession of 1937–38 with the increased spending demanded by his liberal advisers, after first indicating he would go to the extreme of reducing the bureaucracy and cutting government pay. With new spending came new attacks on entrenched wealth. "It was typical that even when Roosevelt reverted to spending, he hedged his bet by requesting authorization from Congress of an investigation into the concentration of economic power in the United States," wrote Lekachman. The *Journal* on October 20 attacked such FDR concepts and demanded a balanced budget:

> Virtually all sections of the country, saving outright inflationists and radicals who hope for a general collapse of the economic system, are agreed that budget balance is a goal which must be reached within a reasonable period of time. President Roosevelt has held out hope that it can be reached, and has suggested that such a balance will be attained in the fiscal year of 1939.
>
> It is apparent that there are but two ways in which budget balance can be attained, if at all. One is by reduction in expenditure, the other by increase of revenue. President Roosevelt . . . places the blame in large part on the additional expenditures by Congress, which is certainly true, at least in part. But the statement overlooks the vital role played by a drop in internal revenues—there is little Congress can do about that.

The obvious solution, the *Journal* concluded, was to cut spending. The Keynesians, however, felt that increased spending wasn't enough.

After four years of economic recovery, business was slumping. President Roosevelt won a victory when the Supreme Court upheld the National Labor Relations Act by a five-four decision in April 1937, but he lost heavily when the Senate Judiciary Committee rejected his Supreme Court packing plan. Nonetheless, during the summer and fall of 1937, Americans began to turn from their concern about domestic problems, including the spread of strikes (especially those of the sit-down variety, which would total 4,471 before the year had ended), to renewed worries about the international situation.

Isolationism was prevalent. Congress had passed the Neutrality Act on

August 31, 1935, and extended it in the spring of 1937. Some critics of the President vowed that he would lead America into a war expected to erupt in Europe as Germany and Italy continued to act aggressively toward their neighbors, while in Spain Generalissimo Francisco Franco waged war against his countrymen, a war in which Germany, Italy, and the Soviet Union took sides. In the Far East, Japan broke through the Chinese Nationalist lines at Peking. The *Journal* insisted that the Neutrality Act—which, it was said, had been reluctantly signed by Roosevelt—reflected the mood of the country. The paper repeated this assertion when the President delivered his major foreign-policy speech at the dedication of the Outer Drive Bridge in Chicago on October 5, 1937. It would become known as the Quarantine Speech, since the President called for the quarantine of those nations guilty of violating treaties.

The *Journal* agreed with President Roosevelt that the people of the United States were against war as a policy of national aggrandizement, but it said it wanted no part of a quarantine policy either. "What avenue of escape do we then intend to seek?" the paper asked. "The President's use, in this connection, of the simile of a quarantine against epidemic disease is strongly suggestive of forcible measures against nations that wage aggressive warfare, declared or undeclared. Does anyone believe that public opinion in this country can be marshalled to support the United States in measures of international force?" The headline over the editorial read "We Could Muddle into War."

Early in January 1937 the *Journal* took note of consultations between the new Securities and Exchange Commission under Chairman William O. Douglas and the governing officials of the New York Stock Exchange. "They are likely to lead to the adoption of rules . . . dealing chiefly with trading by Exchange members on or off 'the floor' and with that by commission houses thereof for their own account," it said. Chairman Douglas had publicly criticized the New York Stock Exchange for ignoring the public interest, a charge made often by *The Wall Street Journal* since it first published such criticism during the panic of 1893.

At some time in the fall of 1937, Charles R. Gay, president of the New York Stock Exchange, talked with Casey Hogate about becoming a public member of a committee Gay proposed to form to make recommendations for reformation of the Exchange. Hogate agreed to serve. He believed, as Gay did, that a reconciliation with Washington was required, and he was aware that a Stock Exchange faction led by former Exchange President Richard Whitney would oppose Gay's efforts.

At various times during the year, the *Journal* reiterated its statement that new rules were required and hinted strongly that a study was in progress.

"There is no reason—or at least not much—to suppose that the governors of the New York Stock Exchange are heedless of the unavoidable limitations upon them," it said. Despite opposition by the Whitney camp to any concessions by the Exchange, or even acknowledgment that reform might be needed, President Gay announced on December 8 the formation of a committee to study "all aspects of a further development of organization and administration of the Exchange." Carle C. Conway, president of Continental Can Company, was named chairman. Members besides Hogate included Trowbridge Callaway, former president of the New York Better Business Bureau, vice-chairman; William McChesney Martin, Jr., secretary; and A. A. Berle, Jr., a founder of President Roosevelt's brain trust and a man close to SEC Chairman Douglas.

Following the completion of hearings and a series of special studies by the Conway Committee, Hogate joined in drafting the report that was submitted to President Gay in January 1938. Gay then appointed a Committee of Three to draw up proposed amendments based upon the recommendations of the Conway Committee. All of the suggestions would be submitted to the membership by amendments to be drafted by the Committee.

The Conway Committee report urged major changes, including a complete structural reorganization of the New York Stock Exchange, permanent inclusion of nonmembers on the governing board, and dispersal of board membership to outlying member companies, thus ending and precluding tight control by a Wall Street clique. The Committee proposed employment of a full-time salaried president who was not required to have a Wall Street background but who would have power to enforce Exchange rules.

The president of the Exchange, said the Committee, should upon election divest himself of all other business interests of every kind, should be adequately paid, and should devote full time to the task. "No restrictions should be placed upon the field from which the president may be chosen," said the report. The president would appoint committees, other than the executive committee, and all officers except the chairman and vice-chairman. He would hire personnel, set up the administrative machinery, and "he should be the point of contact with government agencies and the general public." The Committee recommended reduction in the number of standing committees and extensively discussed various technical problems of the Exchange.

The Committee declared that the New York Stock Exchange was little understood by the public. It indicated that its hearings showed the public to believe that the Exchange bought and sold stocks, which was untrue, and that it "has something to do with whether the market goes up or down, which, of course, is not the fact. . . . Even within financial circles there seems to be a considerable degree of misunderstanding," the report added. The Committee recognized that some government regulation of securities markets was required, but suggested that the Exchange could best police itself, and recommended that it do so.

The Conway report was well received by the public, government representatives, and the press, especially by *The Wall Street Journal*. It was said at the newspaper that Casey Hogate was being considered for first president of the reorganized Exchange. But Hogate had no intention of leaving the paper, and it is doubtful that the job was offered to him at the time. Although Chairman Douglas of the Securities and Exchange Commission welcomed the report, Whitney and his followers did not.

The Whitney faction appeared to be headed for defeat, and then events in the spring of 1938 made adoption of the Conway recommendations certain.

Chapter 14

Barney Kilgore Takes the Helm

In the week of March 7, 1938, Richard Whitney, the former president of the New York Stock Exchange whose callous arrogance in the Washington securities hearings seemed to symbolize for most Americans the Wall Street attitude toward government and public, fell from power. Whitney's demise provided Dow Jones with a newsbreak that rocked the Manhattan financial and stock-trading community and the country—and Whitney, like the aristocrat he professed to be, voluntarily handed it over to Hogate's organization in the camp of his enemies.

William F. Kerby recalled the event in his memoirs. He had returned to *The Wall Street Journal* in late 1936 and was on his way to becoming assistant managing editor in 1938. On the morning of March 8 he was wandering through the newsroom when he observed Edward Costenbader of the Dow Jones news-ticker service wildly beckoning to him.

Kerby hurried over to Costenbader's desk. "Get hold of Richard Whitney's office," Costenbader whispered, holding his hand over the telephone mouthpiece. "I've got a guy on the phone who claims to be Whitney."

Kerby knew what to do. It was a standard Dow Jones and *Wall Street Journal* procedure to prevent dissemination of false reports, which could be harmful and even disastrous. "I got Whitney's office," Kerby wrote, "identified myself, asked to talk to Mr. Whitney. 'Why,' his secretary replied, 'he's talking to Mr. Costenbader at Dow Jones right now.' I turned to Eddie. 'It's Whitney on your phone.'

"Eddie said, 'Thanks, Mr. Whitney,' hung up and bellowed to the teletype operator sitting beside him, 'Break! Break! Richard Whitney confesses to fraud.' "

Richard Whitney had given Costenbader some details and said he was leaving for the district attorney's office to turn himself in. Why he chose to confess first to Dow Jones no one could guess; possibly he wanted the news spread as fast and far as possible once his irrevocable decision was made.

The news stunned Wall Street. Within minutes it had been read on the floor of the Exchange and transmitted to the rest of the country and the world. The misfortunes of a brokerage house, even one as distinguished as Richard Whitney & Company, would no longer cause panic in Wall Street such as that following the failure of Grant & Ward in 1884, but there was a brief decline in the market. "The market taken completely by surprise, sold off following the announcement [on the floor]," reported the *Journal* on March 9. "The firm was suspended. . . . The Stock Exchange acted promptly in filing charges. . . . The public was not generally involved in the insolvency as the firm was bond broker chiefly for other brokers."

It was good news and bad news for those seeking to influence the New York Stock Exchange membership to adopt and implement the Conway Committee report. Although proof of the rumors concerning Whitney's fraudulent activities in the bond market meant his opposition to the Conway report would collapse, the Whitney scandal would also smear Wall Street badly. Whitney was an elegant, insolent man who exemplified in the public mind those qualities that made Wall Street hated by many people following the 1929 crash. In the beginning, Whitney's credentials as a responsible Wall Street leader had been impeccable, the kind of background all Wall Street and the country could esteem. Son of a Boston banker, brother of a Morgan partner, educated first at Groton and then at Harvard, where he rowed stroke oar, Richard Whitney represented the archetypical Wall Street broker and financier, though of a flamboyant variety characteristic of his time, like New York's Mayor Jimmy Walker.

In the years after the crash of 1929, President Roosevelt and his New Deal administration found men like Richard Whitney especially good targets in their assault on Wall Street. While *The Wall Street Journal* helped to fight the rearguard action in defense of the financial community and free enterprise, it did not condone Whitney's arrogant behavior or Wall Street's excesses.

The fall of Richard Whitney coincided with the high point of the New Deal attack. The Conway reform recommendations were swiftly adopted. By May 15 new rules to govern the New York Stock Exchange had been accepted by Chairman Douglas of the SEC. William McChesney Martin was elected the first paid, full-time president of the New York Stock Exchange. He began prompt and effective enforcement of the new rules, and he was strongly supported by

The Wall Street Journal. By April 1941 Martin had completed much of his reorganization. As a young, single man facing the draft, he resigned to enlist as a private in the Army. Hogate was asked to consider the job; however, being acutely aware of the problems ahead for his company and the *Journal,* he requested that his name be withdrawn from consideration.

Casey Hogate's problems were numerous and difficult, and as the Depression wore on they grew worse. Circulation declined for all of the company's publications, the *Journal* falling back to a low of 28,000 by 1938. There were declines also in the number of news-ticker clients, in advertising linage, and in profits. Hogate's drastic budget cuts, eliminating paid vacations and reducing wages, barely kept Dow Jones & Company and the Financial Press Companies of America out of the red. Mrs. Jane Bancroft had told Hogate to put the company's welfare ahead of dividend considerations, and this policy he sought to follow, but his editors considered themselves unduly constricted and were sometimes near revolt. Hogate was forced to cut expenses, but he also demanded better coverage of the glut of business news from Washington, despite reduced staff and curtailed newsprint. Managing Editor Grimes loyally sought to carry out his assignments. He revised formats to reduce paper usage, compressed charts, and eliminated illustrations. Editorials and news were typed on copy paper saved from pressroom wastepaper. While Hogate worked on Wall Street reforms, Grimes fine-tuned the news coverage and shaped up the staff.

The *Journal* generally supported securities legislation as well as the actions of the SEC, a policy warmly backed by President Charles Gay of the New York Stock Exchange and his successor, William Martin. They also saw the necessity for rapprochement between Wall Street and the Roosevelt administration. "Under the leadership of Charles Gay and William McChesney Martin," wrote Robert Sobel in his definitive *History of the New York Stock Exchange, 1935–1975*, "the New York Stock Exchange came to terms with the New Deal and the Depression." Hogate's contributions were made known publicly after his death in 1947 in letters to his widow from Joseph P. Kennedy, whom Roosevelt had named first chairman of the Securities and Exchange Commission; and also by his successor, William O. Douglas.

Throughout the period when the fate of the Conway Committee's work seemed in doubt, the *Journal* was preoccupied mostly with the domestic economy, steadily sharpening its tone of disapproval of the big government spending and deficits and added government regulations that became more oppressive to business. The paper also began turning away from President Roosevelt's foreign policy as his utterances increasingly suggested that he might expose the country to the threat of war.

"The nation's first concern is to stay safe and to keep out of war," the

Journal said in commenting on the President's defense message in January 1938. However, it continued to approve of his plans for building up the defense forces. On March 14 the paper said again, "Our problem is first, last and all the time to keep democracy safe. That job is none too easy as it is, but it would be impossible were we to be involved in a war like the last one. . . . Whether or not Europe is slipping into war, only time can tell. . . . We have had one experience with war to make the world safe for democracy, and that should be enough for us. . . . If we wait until another breaks out before preparing to stay out of it, we run the extreme risk of being caught up in it. Now is the best time for us to consider how we may best immunize ourselves against the danger."

The *Journal* approved some New Deal domestic policies, such as assistance to the unemployed, but wanted government action in any area to be limited, it said in an editorial on the unemployment problem. While conceding that government spending to create jobs might be temporarily needed, the editorial also insisted that "the only alternative to government spending is the resumption of normal industry." It recommended loans to business and relaxation of restrictions to allow the revival of business confidence, as well as spending for unemployment relief and work relief. It urged the government to "get going on both fronts. . . . The way to resume is to resume," it said once again. "The one great task of the Administration is to discover the cause that is keeping business paralyzed and to remove it." Thus, in a single editorial the *Journal* started out as a recognizable liberal and emerged a certified conservative. On March 24 it endorsed the suggestion of an old foe, Senator Robert F. Wagner, the New York Democrat who was chairman of the Senate Banking Committee and who proposed "an elaborate industrial credit system."

This was precisely what the *Journal* also wanted. "Does a country with millions of men unemployed, a country afflicted with an almost insupportable relief burden, a country which still holds to private enterprise as the keystone of its economic arch, need an expansion in the use of credit and in the volume of capital investment for productive purposes? Certainly it does. Nothing else is more essential to its emergence from the slough of industrial recession, to its escape from another 'major depression.' " The *Journal* wanted government credit for "qualified borrowers willing to accept the visible hazards of new venturing, confident enough of future legal and social conditions to bid for the use of capital."

Casey Hogate also continued to support ideas for further reform of the securities markets. The paper in August said of a new SEC proposal for further tightening of the rules: "Adoption by the Securities and Exchange Commission of additional rules for the New York Stock Exchange . . . carries out further the purpose of both to render Exchange regulation as nearly automatic and self-executing as it can be made . . .[and leaves] the policing of the public securities markets in the management of the exchanges subject to the alert supervision of the SEC. In formulating these rules . . . the SEC has been cautiously feeling its way, intent upon discharging its responsibility to the investing public without necessarily reducing the great usefulness of the securities market."

At the same time, the *Journal* again cautioned the government not to continue regulation of any part of the economy merely to seek reform rather than recovery. But it became increasingly clear that reform had become the goal of the New Deal.

On the eve of the Munich agreement, signed September 30, 1938, by England, France, Germany, and Italy and granting Czechoslovakia's Sudetenland to Germany, the *Journal* began publishing a series of antiwar editorials, saying at one point, "The mere thought of the United States participating in the holocaust is repugnant to us." It observed that the world press was calling upon President Roosevelt to use his prestige to stop impending war in Europe and declared, "This is precisely what he could not do. The failure of such a policy is being demonstrated at this moment in Europe." On October 7 the *Journal* saw grim significance in "Moscow's undisguised disapproval of events in Europe. If there is one thing that it suggests, it is deep disappointment that a general European war has been averted. . . . It is obvious that nothing would better suit the Red International than would such a war; such a troubling of the European waters would open a magnificent season for Communist fishing."

The *Journal* feared that war was on the way and increased its European coverage. Charles Hargrove and George V. Ormsby wrote not only from London but from many spots on the Continent, and stringers also provided reports of post-Munich maneuvers from the various European capitals. The paper sought to expand its Washington and domestic political and business coverage. Vermont C. Royster and George Bryant, Jr., were the leading by-liners from Washington. Kilgore covered the congressional by-election campaigns but, presumably for reasons of economy, traveled only through the eastern half of the country. The *Journal,* favoring Republicans as usual, was pleased when the party gained 8 seats in the Senate, raising its total to 15, and increased its House membership to 89 compared with 172 Democrats. In his election report Kilgore said the results indicated that "the GOP will be in a position to put up a real battle for the presidency in 1940."

On January 4, 1939, the *Journal* outlined its own legislative recommendations to Congress a day ahead of President Roosevelt. It acknowledged that "it was not mandating that body, but merely letting it know what the folks back home are thinking." The editors announced an eight-point program: (1) The national defense should have earnest but deliberate treatment ("We are strong enough to act deliberately"); (2) Useless but mischievous monetary powers should be allowed to expire ("Executive authority to alter the gold content of the dollar and to issue up to three billions in currency should go"); (3) Treasury silver purchases should cease altogether; (4) "Not more than $600,000,000 to carry the WPA to June 30 next" should be appropriated; (5) WPA grants should be limited to federal projects only; no more grants, only self-liquidating loans to local governments; (6) The Interstate Commerce Act should be amended to allow railroads to save themselves; (7) Additions should be made to the Wagner Act to clarify rights of the employer under the National Labor Relations Board rules; (8) The Agricultural Adjustment Act should be amended to eliminate crop loans to farmers and to develop genuine soil conservation. The various proposals were explained in detail in subsequent editorials.

On January 5 the *Journal* supported the foreign policy enunciated by President Roosevelt in his message to Congress, but with an exception. It conceded that although President Roosevelt appeared alarmist about the world situation, this was possibly part of his obligation to alert the country and Congress to defense needs. But, added the paper, when the President said that, in effect, "to save ourselves we must save all," he confused and alarmed *The Wall Street Journal.* So far as the President's domestic plans were concerned, the paper wanted none of them, and it asked, "Who was it who, only six short years ago, spoke the following words? 'Taxes are paid in the sweat of every man who labors because they are a burden on production and are paid through production. If those taxes are excessive, they are reflected in idle factories, in tax-sold farms and in hordes of hungry people tramping the streets and seeking jobs in vain.' "

During the spring the *Journal* evidently sought to create a contemporary version of the famed C. W. Barron's series of economic dispatches about a Europe moving toward war in 1914. Hargrove wrote from Berlin, Paris, London, and other European capitals, and Korsmeyer's editorials commented on the Hargrove dispatches. France, said the *Journal* on March 3, was living proof that repressive business policies were harmful and that a country could rebound when they were lifted. "From the time of the Great Depression . . . the movement in all countries toward business reform gained strength," the paper declared, but

> when it ran rampant—when reform became revolution as in Germany—the results were only too manifest. It was less conspicuous and violent, but was nevertheless the dominant political trend in France. . . . The result was the Leon Blum government, the imposition of drastic curbs on business and the continued plunge of France into depression. . . . The interesting thing about the course of

> events since that time [of the Blum regime] especially to the citizens of the United States, is the promptness with which the failure of that policy has been recognized. As Charles R. Hargrove's dispatch in *The Wall Street Journal* yesterday pointed out, there has been a considerable gain in French industrial activity. . . . Moreover, a gain in business confidence, as attested by the drop in interest rates, has been most marked.

But the paper found only moderate signs of improvement in the United States as the Roosevelt economic program increasingly appeared designed more for reform than for economic improvement. It did praise the appointment of William O. Douglas to the United States Supreme Court in March, lauding him for his excellent work with the Securities and Exchange Commission. It also noted that department-store sales were up 22 percent over the prior year in April and that automobile production held to slight gains over 1938, and indicated its belief in the future by expanding United Press service in its news report, announcing an enlargement of the Dow Jones Commodity News Service in April, and by acquiring *Investment News*. Thereafter, *Investment News* and *Wall Street News* were both included in the *Journal*'s editorial-page masthead.

In July 1939 the paper approved of the National Labor Relations Board's amendments to its rules benefiting employers—point 7 of the *Journal*'s January 4 message to Congress. It said there was hope that the usual summer business slump might be avoided, but the stock market continued to be dull, and grain-car loadings were down 20 percent. In late August the stock market was at first depressed and then moved up when news was published of the proposed nonaggression pact between Nazi Germany and Communist USSR. The paper on August 24 was by no means sure that the Hitler-Stalin pact, signed on the 23rd, would mean long-term peace, as the broad advance on the New York Stock Exchange seemed to indicate. "In view of the tissue-paper quality of treaties in the modern world, not to mention the somewhat devious record of Soviet and German diplomacy in particular, there is no assurance that the agreement means what it appears on its face," said the *Journal* with considerable prescience. "If the Nineteen-Thirties have taught nothing else, they have taught the bitter lesson that, in the Eastern Hemisphere today, *all* treaties are 'scraps of paper.' "

On September 1 Germany invaded Poland, and on September 3 Great Britain and France declared war on Germany. President Roosevelt addressed the nation by radio the following Sunday night, and the *Journal* said on September 5: "With vigor and with wisdom, President Roosevelt exercised in his radio address his high prerogative of leadership in forming public opinion on our relationship to a distant continent at war with itself. We seek a true neutrality, the foundation-stone of which is our abstention from the use of force to any other end than our own safety."

Two days later, the paper again urged absolute neutrality on the part of the United States. It recognized the difficulties in such a policy, however. "There are those among us who insist that neutrality can only mean our refusal to sell munitions, foodstuffs or raw materials to belligerents—or to neutrals for transshipment to belligerents. There are others—more numerous apparently—who assert that such refusal, because it would go far toward redressing the disbalance of sea power among the belligerents which antedated the war and was not of our making, is the practical equivalent of intervention and therefore the antithesis of neutrality." Thus, the editorial concluded, the controversy "could work lasting injury to our conception of the government of a free people without physically coming near our shores. One of our first obligations is to see that it does no such thing."

Management problems plagued Casey Hogate. Not the least of them were the continuing complaints of Washington bureau chiefs against his editors in New York. While still in Washington, Bill Grimes had been endlessly explosive about the inadequacies of Hogate's managing editor, Cy Kissane. Eventually, Hogate demoted Kissane, brought Grimes in as managing editor, and named Barney Kilgore chief of the Washington bureau. Soon he was receiving angry memoranda from Kilgore complaining of the narrow news vision under "Brother" Grimes. Kilgore did not criticize Grimes personally, but the strife between the Washington and New York editors continued. Casey Hogate was trying to concentrate on problems of the business and advertising departments. Instead, he felt compelled to keep close watch on the news and editorial pages as well. However he was doing it, Casey Hogate was unquestionably getting together an excellent young staff chosen almost entirely by himself.

Bill Grimes, called Henry by some associates, the seemingly calm man with the incandescent temper, was 47 and the veteran of that staff, a thoroughly competent editor, intensely loyal to Hogate. Barney Kilgore and Bill Kerby were 30; Buren McCormack was 31, as was Robert Bottorff, who had taken over as managing editor on the West Coast. Bob Feemster, advertising manager, was only 27; George Shea, news editor who became editor of *Barron's* in 1938, and Joe Ackell were in their early 30s. Only Shea and Ackell among the upcoming executives got their jobs unscreened by Casey Hogate. Ackell had simply walked in offering himself for secretarial work in the Barron era, and Shea, a Princeton graduate who was born in France and who received his early education abroad, was hired by Business Manager Joseph Cashman, also a Princeton graduate. The rest acquired their training or experience in the Midwest before coming to the *Journal,* most of them at DePauw University.

Bill Kerby, rising fast in the *Journal* hierarchy by 1938, recalled Hogate's personal interest in acquiring *Journal* personnel in his book, *A Proud Profession.* "In the spring of 1933 my former *Wall Street Journal* boss, Henry Grimes, called to say that Dow Jones was interested in giving me a job," Kerby wrote. "Kenneth C. Hogate, president of Dow Jones, was coming to Washington and wished to interview me." Kerby at the time was chief of the United Press staff, covering the House of Representatives, and was earning $45 a week. He had worked summers for the *Journal* while attending the University of Michigan. Grimes had wanted to hire Kerby full-time after he graduated but couldn't due to budget restrictions.

A few days after Grimes telephoned, Hogate found Kerby in the House press gallery, introduced himself, and chatted with him. At lunchtime Kerby recommended the House restaurant, where they attracted attention as they entered—Hogate over six feet and weighing 300 pounds, Kerby five feet seven and skinny. Both men were affable and outgoing, and they had numerous friends in the House, so they made slow progress to a table. There Hogate impressed Kerby with his zest for food. He ordered a seafood dish Kerby recommended. Kerby recalled it as "an enormous dish composed of creamed lobster, crab, oysters, shrimp and filet of sole, topped with a baked mashed potato cover and embellished with a full two ounces of Beluga caviar. . . . Casey ordered it; finished it; and ordered a second."

They then discussed the proffered job. Hogate pretended to be dismayed to learn that Kerby was born in the District of Columbia instead of the Midwest, but he jokingly suggested that the young man's education in Michigan might qualify him anyway. Hogate knew of course that Kerby was the son of a veteran Washington newsman, and he had a pocket full of news clippings written by Kerby that he obviously had read. His questions indicated that he had been well briefed by Grimes. Hogate then made his offer of $55 a week to join the *Journal*'s Washington staff. Kerby accepted.

Despite severe budget restrictions, Hogate not only expanded his newsgathering staff in 1938 but also added to the news-ticker service, acquiring General News Ticker, Inc., based in New York, from M. L. and W. H. Annenberg and A. F. Smuckler for $37,500, thereby insuring that the 1938 dividends could not be more than 25 cents a share. Hogate never ceased paying tribute to Mrs. Jane Bancroft when he made such decisions. "To her, Dow Jones is no mere commercial venture," Hogate told the staff on one occasion, "it is an institution of highest ideals which must be perpetuated and whose influence for good must ever be increased."

Late in 1938 Grimes made Kerby assistant managing editor, as Grimes himself assumed more of Hogate's editorial duties. Kerby has credited Grimes with most of the news department's organizational improvements since 1934, when Grimes took over from Kissane as managing editor. The paper at that time had been going to press with its morning edition at 6 P.M. When Hogate ended the evening edition on September 4, the day he announced Grimes's appointment as managing editor, Grimes decreed that 11:30 P.M. would be the closing time for the final, an order making night people of many of the staff members and converting the *Journal* literally overnight into a bona fide morning newspaper. "He also organized the first copydesk in the history of the *Journal,*" Kerby wrote. "He recruited first-class deskmen and, to the horror of the reportorial staff, gave them the authority to edit, rewrite (if necessary) and headline." Previously, a single copy editor had been assigned to check proofs for typographical errors.

Even after Grimes installed a full-scale copydesk of subeditors who read and corrected all stories to appear in the paper, Hogate himself also read and corrected every article in the early editions. He often rewrote story leads and the headlines over them. Hogate stayed late to accomplish these chores, and sometimes he sent down corrections already made by the copy editors checking the editions as Grimes required. This necessitated an elaborate system of cross-checking to avoid endless confusion in the composing room, but the text of the *Journal* did become more precise and accurate.

Casey Hogate also sided with Kerby to overrule Grimes, though probably not intentionally. "Charles Hargrove, the Paris bureau chief, had gone to Austria, anticipating a German invasion," Kerby recalled in his memoirs. "On March 12, 1938, the day after Hargrove arrived, Hitler's army marched into Austria. Tight outgoing censorship was clamped down. However, Hargrove, a British national, talked a friend in the embassy into including a brief and hurried dispatch in an outgoing diplomatic pouch. In this fashion, Hargrove's story reached Paris; was delivered by special messenger to our office; thence was urgently cabled to New York."

Kerby rewrote the cable, added background information and interpretative details, and scheduled the story for a lead position on page one. Grimes demurred. He wanted it condensed and carried as the lead item in the "What's News" summary. "Not the *Journal*'s type of story," Grimes was saying just as Hogate arrived for his daily visit to the newsroom.

Hogate picked up the story and read it with interest. "This is just the sort of thing we need more of," Hogate said. "You two are ganging up on me," Grimes complained. "Oh," said the unsuspecting publisher, "what were you going to do with it?" "Page one, column one," replied Grimes with a grin. "This was a real breakthrough," Kerby wrote, "a primitive prototype of the 'leader' type article which was to become the hallmark of *The Wall Street Journal.* It was the first time an offbeat story by *Journal* standards had been given top display.

"The next morning," Kerby concluded, "brought a phone call from Kilgore. 'How did you wangle that one past Brother Grimes?' "

Some associates of Hogate recalled that Casey helped to persuade Wendell Lewis Willkie, the Wall Street utilities lawyer and executive, to run for president on the Republican ticket in 1940. However, Hogate at no time made a public endorsement of Willkie. He knew Willkie but was friendlier with a rival candidate, his upstate neighbor Thomas E. Dewey, the small, sharp-eyed district attorney who obtained the indictment of Richard Whitney and was famed as a fighter of organized crime in New York. But Hogate did not publicly endorse Dewey either, for he had never permitted his personal friendships to be considered in editorial deliberations. So the Willkie boom was never especially aided by Hogate. It was launched by Russell Davenport, managing editor of *Fortune* magazine. He was assisted by book reviewer Rita Van Doren, Willkie's closest female friend and confidante. Wall Streeters for Willkie maintained a low profile.

Immediately after Willkie won the nomination over Tom Dewey and Ohio Senator Robert Taft at the Republican convention on June 27, the *Journal* confined itself to praising him for the objectives he listed in announcing his campaign plans. The paper especially liked his adherence to the "principles of national unity, defense, and the return of men to work. . . . He rightly put unity first. . . . The wedge of disunion has been driven more deeply into our common life in the last ten years than ever before in our history since the Civil War, our political struggles have threatened to split us into two groups with no common bond of purpose. That common bond must be strengthened. . . . Somehow our citizens must recover a basis for trust in each other's good faith and good will."

President Roosevelt was nominated for a third term on the first ballot at the Democratic convention in Chicago in July, as the *Journal* had unenthusiastically predicted. Henry A. Wallace of Iowa was his running mate. These developments were repugnant to the *Journal,* which assigned Bernard Kilgore to cover the Willkie campaign. Willkie's opening speech was a disaster, Kilgore reported, but he warmed to the candidate later, writing, "Mr. Willkie is seeking to show his contrasts with President Roosevelt. . . . What are these contrasts? (1) The New Deal is heading towards dictatorship. Willkie is heading towards a revitalization of individual enterprise. (2) The New Deal is headed towards bankruptcy. Willkie is headed towards prosperity. (3) The New Deal is headed towards war. Willkie is headed towards peace."

It was a confused and confusing campaign in which Senator Charles L. McNary of Oregon, Willkie's running mate, seemed a reluctant partner. On September 20 the *Journal* published its report on a George Gallup public-opinion poll indicating that Roosevelt and Wallace would carry 38 states. The paper did not attack President Roosevelt more than usual during the campaign and it came to his defense on what it regarded as one of the most important issues, national defense. "*The Wall Street Journal* does not question the President's firm purpose to create a national defense adequate to this time of world turmoil," it said on August 28. "Mistakes have been made, but they are errors of judgment, not of ultimate intention."

On October 23 the *Journal* declared that it was implacably against a third term. It criticized President Roosevelt for not making his position on the issues clear. On November 1 Kilgore reported that Willkie was believed to have a fifty-fifty chance of victory, but, he added, "the situation is confused." The *Journal* said in its November 2 editorial on the campaign: "If the tradition against the third term goes, one of the strongest safeguards of the free ballot will go with it."

On November 5, President Roosevelt was elected to his third term by a margin of more than 5 million popular votes. *Journal* editors displayed their petulance by barely recording the result on page one, saying merely at the bottom of the "What's News" column "Election results and analysis may be found on page 3." Two days later, Kilgore chided himself for a bad pre-election forecast. "I don't know why a lot of other people made mistakes," he wrote. "In my own case I was fooled by the noise." The *Journal* praised Willkie for effort, saying, "He carried on his shoulders the burden of campaign as no one since Lincoln has done."

Early in 1941 it appeared that the Financial Press Companies of America might hope to share in the industrial prosperity created by war orders from abroad and by America's defense requirements. Advertising linage improved as the prospering manufacturers took space in the paper to announce new war-related contracts or to keep their traditional image before the investing public. But circulation remained sluggish. *The Wall Street Journal* in 1941, with a circulation of 32,065, was near its 1938 low of 28,435, about half its unaudited high of 56,000 in 1930. *Barron's* magazine stood at 25,915 compared with 37,959 in 1939. The stock market continued in the doldrums. On March 11 the *Journal* answered a reader's question that must have been troubling many: "Why isn't big money buying stock?" The *Journal* restated the question:

> What fears keep big money from buying stock? How much or how little are those fears justified? Both questions are fundamental in that they may go to the root of the matter, namely, why is it that stock prices do not reflect earning capacity to the extent that they did in former days?
>
> The answer to the first question is not very difficult, for the general nature of the inhibiting apprehensions is pretty clear. They boil down to uncertainty about the future. In the first place there is a war which may without exaggeration be termed a world war. A war of such dimensions places a question mark against the future in respect to all concerned in it, either directly or indirectly, and would do so even had we been in a thoroughly stable state when the war opened.

> But in the second place, this was not the case. As everyone is well aware, we have been for nearly a decade in the process of extensive social, political and economic changes, affecting the position of private capital in the country's economy.

The disruptive changes caused by the New Deal did not require enumeration, the paper said. And, it concluded gloomily, "In addition to actual changes by way of reform, there was apprehension that those changes were mere forerunners to changes which might threaten the entire so-called capitalistic system."

Toward the end of 1940 Casey Hogate concluded that he could no longer blame general economic conditions for the failure of *The Wall Street Journal* to move ahead. Prosperity was returning; circulation was not. Barney Kilgore had been bombarding him with ideas for further improvement of the paper almost from the time he went to Washington. Hogate felt he needed Kilgore as a writer, but at long last he concluded that he needed him more as an editor and an executive. The training period was over. Kilgore was ready, as was the supporting staff. Bill Kerby was a highly capable assistant managing editor. A place could be found for Grimes where he could function most effectively. Buren McCormack had taken over the important banking and monetary editing job and was doing well, and Perry TeWalt had come in from Washington to write the "What's News" column. "What's News" was beyond doubt the paper's most popular feature, followed by Kilgore's "Washington Wire," Hogate believed. Kilgore had started both, and if two men could successively keep up the quality of "What's News" after Kilgore had established the format, successors ought to do the same with "Washington Wire," especially if Kerby edited it.

Early in 1941 Hogate and Grimes came to an understanding about the future. Perhaps both recalled that when Walter Barclay stepped aside for Hogate back in 1923, the action enabled Casey Hogate to make his first personal recruitment to the staff, hiring William Henry Grimes. Now Grimes agreed to move up to editor, though this position would be subject to some limitations. Kilgore would be brought in from Washington to become managing editor, and Hogate made it clear that Barney Kilgore would have a free hand.

When Grimes communicated this news to Kerby, he left no doubt about the untrammeled freedom Hogate had indicated Kilgore should receive. "He felt Barney should be free to pick his own team," Kerby wrote. "Grimes planned to transfer me to Washington eventually. However, for the next few months I would be on special reportorial assignment and pretty much free to develop my own story ideas. . . . I told Grimes I was delighted with Kilgore's selection . . . and would be happy when the time came to transfer to Washington."

Kilgore and Kerby felt alike about the *Journal,* they liked one another, and they worked well together. Yet Kerby was sincerely pleased with his new assignment, even though it could terminate his prospects for advancement in New York. Washington was home base for both Bill Kerby and his wife, Fanny. He was eager to do a special series of articles on what he considered to be major news, the burgeoning defense-oriented economy. "A series of trips into heavily industrialized areas along the Eastern seaboard produced material for a number of page one articles," he wrote in his memoirs. "To pacify Grimes, I contrived some sort of spot news lead for each, but I also tried to thoroughly background them and forecast future trends. Grimes thought they were fine, and my new boss-to-be dispatched applauding notes from Washington."

There was some consternation when Barney Kilgore appeared in the *Journal* newsroom early in February 1941. Barney was known as one prone to upset things, a man impatient with traditional operational methods. The fact that he also had a reputation for friendliness and a sweet temper didn't moderate the fear. It was believed in the New York office that Barney Kilgore didn't get on with Grimes, a fact probably much exaggerated, and was critical generally of the New York staff and its performance. He had been demanding in San Francisco, it was said, and he had imposed a new kind of discipline and high performance standards in Washington. Grimes was also demanding, but most of the New York writers and copyreaders believed they knew what he wanted. And there were the cynics who said that Barney Kilgore, despite his friendly ways, was most intent on making it to the top, over a few bodies if necessary. But his detractors conceded there were pluses. There was no denying that Barney Kilgore was a superlative writer who understood the problems of financial writing and editing. Even President Roosevelt had publicly praised his work. His Washington staff thought he was tough, yet fair. Bill Kerby swore by him. And he had, after all, worked in New York.

It didn't take Kilgore long to win over many of the suspicious and nervous newsmen to his personality. When he wandered through the office and the corridors in shirt-sleeves, greeting people with a warm handshake, calling out a name softly as he approached, he was too genuinely friendly for doubt. Kilgore liked people. He had quiet poise. His soft whistle as he wandered was pleasant and reassuring. He listened considerately and he remembered names. Even his nervous tic and occasional slight stutter were somewhat reassuring; Barney Kilgore had human problems like everybody else.

The second day on the job in New York, Kilgore came over to the desk where Kerby was typing one of his defense articles. "What's this I hear about you going to Washington?" Barney said. Kerby explained that Grimes planned to transfer him, that he and Fanny were pleased, and that she was packing.

"Tell Fanny to unpack," Kilgore said softly. "I need you here. I have Gene Duffield in Washington."

Kilgore was pleasant enough, and decent enough, but foreboding in the *Journal* newsroom was thick as a Fire Island fog when Casey Hogate sent down his notice to the staff on February 14, a St. Valentine's Day missive many of the staff thought singularly inappropriate:

> In a few days some changes will be effective in the newsroom about which I want the staff to be informed.
>
> W. H. Grimes will become Editor. Bernard Kilgore will become Managing Editor. Edward W. Costenbader will become Day Managing Editor in full charge of news ticker services. Eugene S. Duffield will become head of the Washington Bureau. William F. Kerby will take charge of some of the new features which are being developed for the first page of *The Wall Street Journal*.
>
> While this seems a sizable change, all the personalities are well and favorably known to the entire staff, and everyone affected, including even those more remotely affected, is in hearty approval.
>
> No changes of consequence—as a matter of fact, I know of none at this time—are contemplated elsewhere on the staff, and I am sure that these that have been made will be approved by the staff and will go into effect with your usual hearty cooperation.

Hogate obviously moved up the announcement after hearing that the proposed Kilgore changes might be resisted. He acted to check any counterattack. Actually, the staff members were more stunned than resistant. Most were convinced that they had been following the proper course in reporting business news. They had no wish to expand their horizons, and they could cite the views of former Managing Editor Grimes in support of the status quo. Hogate's announcement seemed merely to increase the dread, despite his good intentions and Kilgore's careful moves. There was no immediate hearty approval and none of the usual willing cooperation in the beginning.

Bill Kerby continued to write his special stories, and he collaborated with Eugene Duffield on another series. He was completing it when he was again approached by the new managing editor. "In addition to taking over the page one problem," Kilgore said, "I also want you to take charge of the paper on Sunday." Both proposals foreshadowed a revolutionary change in *Journal* procedures. For years the Monday paper had been put together on Saturdays, evidently because of the theory that business news stopped when the New York Stock Exchange closed. No newspaper known to Kilgore and Kerby at the time had an editor whose chief responsibility was to procure special materials for page one, as well as to supervise page-one editing and display.

"See what ideas the staff may have," Kilgore suggested. "Talk with people, make suggestions. Broaden the base of the news and take the best you can get for page one." Kilgore then explained that since he didn't want to publicly countermand Brother Grimes, he would not at once reinstate Kerby as assistant managing editor, but the specialized mission and his Sunday duties would give Kerby all the responsibility and authority he might require.

"You can choose your own assistant," Kilgore said.

"Fine," Kerby replied. "I choose McCormack. He's the best writer on the paper."

Kilgore nodded. The staff would have to learn a new writing style and they could learn best by good example. Kilgore himself intended to help Kerby and McCormack do the teaching.

The Kilgore regime was officially under way. Hesitant members of the staff were nudged and pushed. Some insisted they couldn't write the way Kilgore wanted, couldn't produce the headlines required, and one, Greg Green, a veteran copyreader, objected to Barney's demand for a brighter headline, refusing to redo one he had just written.

Said Kilgore quietly, "I'm sorry, but you either do as I say or find another job. And I mean now!"

"Okay," said Green, "I'm fired."

"You are," Kilgore replied. Veteran *Journal* newsmen remembered this as the only time in his long rule that Kilgore fired anyone out of hand. Open opposition to the Kilgore Revolution, as some called it, soon ended, though it was many months before the staff could adapt to meet the new writing and editing standards. In time it came to be understood that a statement about a company's financial position was no longer the mandatory lead to any business story appearing in *The Wall Street Journal.* Nor was it required that the lead tell the "who, what, why, and where" of a news report; it wasn't necessary to mention when at all unless the news reported didn't happen yesterday. Headlines were to tell the story and sell the news.

Kerby described Kilgore's principles of the requisite editorial approach: "Don't write banking stories for bankers. Write for the banks' customers. There are a hell of a lot more depositors than there are bankers. . . . For *The Wall Street Journal*, all news is national. The businessman in Portland, Oregon, and the businessman in Portland, Maine, need the same information. If it's important enough to run in any edition, it's important enough to run anywhere. It doesn't have to have happened today to be news. If a date is essential, use the exact date. Hook 'em with an intriguing, mystery lead and keep sinking in more hooks as you go." Kilgore waged unrelenting warfare on clichés, Kerby wrote. He cited an early Kilgore bulletin-board notice to his staff soon after he became president of Dow Jones in 1945: "If I read 'upcoming' in *The Wall Street Journal* once more, I'll be 'downcoming' and someone will be 'outgoing.' " And Kerby recalled another Kilgorism: "The easiest thing in the world for any reader to do is to stop reading." The trick was to grab interest and hold it.

There were complaints about the unorthodox new procedures, but Hogate and Grimes ignored them. They were ready to give Kilgore, Kerby, and McCormack a chance to demonstrate what their approach might do to win new readers. Kilgore himself set the example, patiently explaining and demonstrating his methods. He wanted the *Journal* to explore the entire news spectrum, with well-written, carefully edited news coverage, and to create its own kind of in-depth reporting. He was determined that facets of American life beyond economics and finance should be covered in *The Wall Street Journal*. The paper was no longer to be confined; it would have the freedom and technology to win general attention while retaining its homogeneous base.

Kilgore, Kerby, and McCormack translated the specialized trade terms used for years by *Journal* writers and editors into plain English the average reader could understand. "We wrote headlines that would sell the story," said Kerby. "We studied reader comprehension techniques and used them. We even brought in an outside lecturer, who appeared to impress our staff by demonstrating that the greatest of English writing could be understood by a 12-year-old. He impressed them even more, though, when he declared that page one of *The Wall Street Journal* had become the most readable front page in America."

Under Grimes, the editorial page also grew better. Felix Morley joined the group of distinguished editorial-page columnists that included Frank R. Kent, recruited earlier by Grimes, Tom Woodlock, Raymond Moley, and William Henry Chamberlain, another former liberal. Grimes would soon add the editorials of young Vermont Royster of the Washington staff. Grimes was not a foe of all change—he had made many changes in the *Journal* himself—but he firmly rejected any alteration in his editorial-page format. Yet even Grimes became unorthodox ideologically at least once after Kilgore took over. On April 9 he went to the extreme of rebutting a Frank Kent column in the paper by personally rejecting its prowar thesis in an open letter, a unique device for the editor to employ in *The Wall Street Journal*:

> Mr. Frank R. Kent
> Baltimore, Maryland
>
> Dear Frank:
>
> We are publishing today one of your contributions which contains a summary of the arguments for America becoming an active belligerent even though that course should involve violation of the constitutional provision that this nation can initiate war only by a majority vote of the people's elected representatives in Congress. You have understated rather than overstated the position of the group urging such a course. . . . What is it these people say? Isn't this the essence of it?
>
> Yes, we know that the great majority does not want war. We know it so well, we don't want Congress to vote on the matter. Anyway, that is not necessary. Regardless of how they got there, the American people are so far along the road to

war they cannot turn back. One more little shove and they are in. And they will go further in.

Frank, the thing is impractical to the point of insanity, and if it were practical, it would still be immoral.

Four-fifths of us don't want war. One-fifth does. Pretty soon the one-fifth plans to say to the four-fifths something like this: "Well whether you like it or not, you are in a war. So get about the business of fighting it."

It won't work. It never has. France tried it. Mussolini tried it. They drove luke-warm people to war. They met disaster.

A few have worked themselves into an emotion where they are ready to short-circuit democracy and to bypass the constitution at home, believing it to spread democracy abroad. . . . If we do that, have we the effrontery to tell them abroad that we are fighting, that men everywhere in this world may live according to their free choice? And if we have the effrontery to tell them, will they believe us?

Yours sincerely,
William H. Grimes, Editor

Chapter 15

The Kilgore Revolution

Page one of *The Wall Street Journal* changed steadily for the better under the ministrations of Barney Kilgore and his young marshals, Bill Kerby and Buren McCormack. The result reflected the indefatigable industry and dedication of the trio, who firmly believed that Kilgore had the right approach to financial journalism. It was heresy, of course, to insist that the right way to become a national business newspaper was to inject daily a broader assortment of news. But Casey Hogate believed that the young revolutionaries knew what *Wall Street Journal* readers wanted—a wide spectrum of news, presented under selling, persuasive headlines; news written in simple, readable style free of trade jargon; and coverage of business around the country. Hogate, his health steadily failing after a series of strokes, knew that, like Moses, he couldn't enter the promised land; nonetheless he decreed that the change must go on.

Robert Bottorff in San Francisco accepted the new faith, as did Eugene Duffield in Washington, and Vermont Royster on Grimes's editorial page. Some of those who refused the new doctrine, after inventorying the believers and noting that most came from DePauw University, went about the *Journal's* New York newsroom muttering maledictions on "that damn Methodist high school in Indiana." Their putative leader continued to be William Grimes, but even Grimes's grumbling about "needless change" was supportive; the madder Grimes got, the better his editorials read.

Some members of the staff professed to see no improvement in the paper, and the circulation figures did not at once reflect the correctness of Kilgore's policies. Circulation did rise to 35,395 by the end of 1942, however, and a year later it was 42,393. There were those who began to admit that Kilgore was right. Bob Feemster, shouting the praises of the new *Wall Street Journal* to the advertising community and whipping the circulation chariots to high speed, did more for Kilgore's ideas than most members of the news staff besides the true disciples. Circulation and advertising gains were small in the beginning, but they were gains ending years of decline, and they were steady.

Since "What's News" was surefire with the readers, according to the readership surveys Kilgore ordered, he naturally expanded it at the start of his rule. "What's News" went to three columns at the top of the front page. A two-column "Business and Finance" summary led off, followed by a two-column "Financial Diary." General news was presented in a third column, including a division called "World-Wide News." There were varying special reports in a fourth column. "Washington Wire" alternated with a new "Commodity Letter" and various other business-oriented reports. Most of the leader stories continued to be written by Kerby and McCormack. Staff members, urged to try, were rewarded with by-lines when they succeeded.

Some staffers continued to say privately that what was being run on page one wasn't news at all but frivolous feature fluff. The truth was that Kilgore was getting the kind of situation stories he had pioneered in Washington and Kerby had written even under the watchful Grimes in New York. They all had a news peg. Kerby continued to show the way with page-one articles on the nation's defense industry in April 1941. He often opened his stories with the one- or two-sentence paragraphs he recommended. Said Kerby's lead on April 4: "One year ago today American industry, at the call of President Roosevelt, entered upon the task of making this nation impregnable to foreign aggression. *The Wall Street Journal* now surveys the results of that effort."

The various Kerby series set a tone not only for the paper's writing style but also for its coverage of defense and war news. *The Wall Street Journal* led the country's press in reporting on the home front, a general news area it could cover superlatively well while continuing to cover business and economic developments.

In a column next to one of Kerby's articles on April 4, "Washington Wire" provided summary and "inside" reports on developments at home and abroad. The column also emphasized defense news and, additionally, hinted at upcoming international trends: "Washington fears German-Russian-Japanese 'encirclement' of the U.S. . . . Recent events [referring to the flight of Nazi Rudolf Hess from Germany to Scotland] may mean Axis-Russian partnership to partition the world, officials say. . . . Fight to break encirclement. . . . No war foreseen unless an 'incident' makes shooting popular."

The column continued in staccato style with materials provided and written by both Eugene Duffield and Kilgore: "Navy's 'patrol' work is danger-loaded. Torpedoing incident would not surprise some officers. First U.S. merchant ships will reach the Red Sea (now a Nazi war zone) by July-August."

The staccato style, the thesis lead, the code words of an insider, the format stating a situation to be examined, developed, and interpreted, were the final distillation of early Kilgore experiments in Washington. The summary column, later imitated by other newspapers and news magazines, quickly became a popular feature, presumably offering the esoteric side of the news, sometimes printed on tinted paper, leading off the format of popular magazines. The longer, in-depth situation articles also were copied by many. But Kilgore's insistence that news stories did not have to open with the who, what, why, when, and where of traditional reporting was a policy that did not catch on widely. Journalism schools continued to teach the established technique in their craft classes, and even *Journal* writers and editors found it hard to abandon routine beginnings.

Barney Kilgore and his aides were sure that their new approach to news would please *Wall Street Journal* readers and win new ones. "Write and edit the paper for the next 100,000 readers," Kilgore would tell them. However, although Bob Feemster was marvelously responsive to Kilgore's changes, the advertising community in New York was not, and Feemster was able to add advertising linage mostly because some businessmen found the changes refreshing and insisted on being represented in the paper. Even such businessmen, however, essentially wanted a good business newspaper, nothing more. Circulation and advertising gains were slow, and Kilgore, despite his outward calm, was sometimes discouraged. He even ordered further readership studies to help him determine whether another, less parochial name than *The Wall Street Journal* would drive home to potential readers the new quality of the paper. The first results tended to confirm his apprehensions, but Barney warily decided to delay any discussion of a change in name.

Editor Grimes asserted his power over the editorial page by refusing to permit any major format changes in that sacrosanct arena. Grimes continued the battle against profligate government spending and foreign involvement. Despite powerful East Coast sentiment in favor of the nations fighting Hitler and Mussolini, and the prowar attitude of much of the press (including the strongly interventionist posture of the *New York Herald-Tribune* and many leaders in Wall Street), *The Wall Street Journal* remained steadfastly antiwar. There was no doubt that many readers were disturbed by the paper's stand.

Their protests appeared in the expanded letters column, many demanding that the United States act at once to enter the war. Equally often the paper asserted, "We remain out of it," as it had in its editorial-page headline on April 1, 1940. A year later it responded to readers by answering the question, "Is it true that *The Wall Street Journal* is 'isolationist'?"

> We just don't know. The term "isolationist" was coined to describe the extreme opponents of American adhesion to the League of Nations. At that time there were those for the League, there were "mild reservationists," the "strong reservationists" and the "isolationists."
>
> After that an isolationist became a man who opposed the United States joining the World Court. Some wholly against the League looked kindly on the court.
>
> At the outbreak of the present war in Europe an isolationist became anyone who wanted to put an embargo on shipment of war materials to any warring nation. Later an isolationist was a man who did not want to extend aid to Great Britain. Recently he became a man who might be for aid to Great Britain, but who opposed its extension in a certain way. Now an isolationist seems to be a man who opposes getting together an army and a navy and sending them off to Europe to knock Mr. Hitler's block off.
>
> If we have guessed correctly at the present meaning, we are guilty because we don't want a shooting war.
>
> And what is the moral of all this? Obviously, we ought to quit thinking in labels for one thing.
>
> For another thing, it does not help clear thinking to invent words with a sinister meaning and then proceed to hurl them at people. Someone has said that you don't win arguments by impugning your opponent's ancestry.

During the summer and fall of 1941 the paper continued its antiwar position. It opposed all government efforts to commandeer business on the pretext that such control was needed for the defense effort, saying, "The country should not be delivered bound hand and foot to one man's keeping." In a series of articles, the *Journal* charged that enormous waste was occurring in the government's rearming activities, charges echoed on the House floor by Representative Marion Bennett of Missouri. The mistakes of the bureaucracy produced horrendous, though amusing results, the paper said on December 3, in quoting from Bennett's House presentation:

"During fourteen months and ten days preceding November 11, the War Department spent more than $8,000,000 for bar mosquito netting," the *Journal* said. "This would provide 30 yards for each of 1,500,000 soldiers and the purchasing is still going on." Bennett cited even more ridiculous figures, the paper noted: "77 million pairs of socks, 14 million pairs of khaki cotton trousers and 4 million pairs of herringbone twill trousers for officers; plus 5 million pairs of wool serge trousers for the navy, 14 million pairs of service shoes, 400,000 pairs of leather boots, 230,000 pairs of rubber boots and 6,992 pairs of ski boots." The *Journal* agreed with Bennett, who told the few colleagues who bothered to listen that it appeared the government was "really planning an expeditionary force of 10 million men." "General Marshall," the editorial added, "has testified before a Senate committee that the entire Western Hemisphere could be defended with approximately 1,720,000 men."

While the wastage of money for rearmament could be occasion for jocularity on the *Journal* editorial page, the disclosure by Washington bureau chief Duffield of extensive plans for recruiting men far beyond the number needed for defense was not. Duffield's series, published in August, was the basis for an editorial on December 6 in which the *Journal* charged again that President Roosevelt and his advisors had been contemplating a full-scale shooting war and were getting ready for it. "So, while the American people were allowed to believe that their government policy was still something described as 'short of war' and while those who dared to assert that an A.E.F. [American Expeditionary Force] was discussed or planned, risked contemptuous and often abusive denials, the real situation was that an all-out war was being officially discussed."

The paper's revival of Duffield's dispatches was triggered by a report in the *Chicago Tribune* and the *New York News* on December 4 asserting that a massive army of more than 10 million was planned, half of which would be sent to Europe in July 1943. The "plan" was later said to have been a hoax created by the British and fed by the Roosevelt administration to Senator Burton K. Wheeler of Montana, who opposed entering the war. The administration leaked the details to Senator Wheeler on the assumption he would release them to the press, which he did. It was rightly believed that publication of such information would deceive Germany into diverting troops from campaigns on the eastern front. The editorial was not misdirected. President Roosevelt's war policy had changed to almost the exact opposite of what had been advocated by the *Journal* over the years, which was "We remain out of it." But the December 6, 1941, editorial would be the paper's last demanding nonparticipation in Europe's second great war.

Barney Kilgore's decision to produce the Monday morning *Wall Street Journal* on Sunday instead of Saturday, thereby enabling it to become a truly fresh news edition, changed the life-styles of several members of the staff, including William Kerby, assistant managing editor responsible for the Monday paper. Kerby was on duty the afternoon of Sunday, December 7, 1941. Barney Kilgore came in about 3 P.M. to discuss the news outlook with him.

"A bit after 3 P.M., the bells began clanging on the entire battery of press association teletype machines," Kerby recalled in his memoirs. "The

Japanese had attacked Pearl Harbor. . . . I had just cleared the last of the page one articles for the first edition when Barney turned on me and said, 'Now write the lead piece.' It was 30 minutes before deadline.

"My effort was typed in paragraph takes and, with Casey Hogate reading over his shoulder, copyread by Kilgore." These "takes" were short bursts of copy that could be edited and sent to the printers as they were finished so that several printers could set the story in minimum time. Kerby drew on the defense series he had written for his material. His account would help set the theme of *Wall Street Journal* news reports throughout the war—coverage of the home front and the production forces that, in the end, would vitally contribute to Allied victory. Kerby's story ran under a page-wide, three-tiered banner headline, unique in the *Journal*'s history, and began:

> War with Japan means industrial revolution in the United States.
>
> The American productive machine will be reshaped with but one purpose—to produce the maximum of things needed to defeat the enemy.
>
> It will be a brutal process.
>
> It implies intense, almost fantastic stimulation for some industries; strict rationing for others; inevitable, complete liquidation for a few.
>
> War with Japan will be a war of great distances.
>
> Thus, certainly in its preliminary stages and probably for the duration, it will be a war of the sea and the air.
>
> This means unlimited quantities of ships and shells, bombers and bombs, oil, gasoline.
>
> Eventually, it also means an army dwarfing the present military establishment—5 million, 8 million. It's a guess. But that will come later.

On the extreme left of the page was Eugene Duffield's Washington story, also reading out of the banner headline. "Washington—The United States yesterday found itself fighting on two oceans," it began. "As the months ahead unfold, Americans will be fighting on three continents also. The war in Europe, Asia and Africa is reaching out to engulf the United States completely. This is the consensus in the nation's capital."

In column four was the *Journal*'s page-one editorial, "We Have a Duty." It was written by William Grimes and explained that routine editorial commentary on that issue had been discarded because "there is a stark, horrible reality that American territory has been attacked. Japan has declared a state of war exists between her and the United States. Every citizen has and knows his duty. It will be heavy for all. The sacrifices will be particularly heavy for the business and financial community of America. We say that the sacrifices will be made. The duty will be performed."

In the "What's News" column the writers sought to summarize business and trade repercussions, and in the "World-Wide" category to report breaking news, President Roosevelt's intention to address Congress on Monday, European reaction, the responses of President Roosevelt and Secretary of State Cordell Hull, and the progress of the war in Europe.

The Wall Street Journal responded magnificently to the greatest breaking news story in its history. It proved to itself and its readers that it was a broadly based daily newspaper, reaching beyond the specialized economic constituency of Wall Street, understanding its mission and able to execute it. The work of Hogate in experimentation and change, and of Kilgore in learning from Hogate's efforts and devising a new approach to news gathering and writing, paid off splendidly. That Monday's *Journal* was unique in the category of specialized journalism, and advanced beyond most of the general newspapers in its instant presentation of the significant interrelation of news events, their interpretation, and the projection of their significance. *The Wall Street Journal* of December 8, 1941, was the paper's supreme journalistic accomplishment up to that time. Kerby, under fire, demonstrated that the situation story was a matchless journalism technique, difficult to accomplish in a pressure situation but enormously effective. Duffield proved himself totally competent in the more orthodox journalism techniques as well. Kilgore, McCormack, and their associates put together a uniquely impressive front page for the paper in a short time, and the future of *The Wall Street Journal* was established.

The *Journal* wore proudly its Kilgore transformation on December 8, but Kilgore and his editors were desperate for writers ready to adhere to the new order, as evidenced by Kerby's recruitment of John O'Riley, secretary to deposed Managing Editor Cy Kissane, for the new page-one "Commodity Letter." "Kissane produced a feeble weekly imitation of the Kiplinger Letter," wrote Kerby, a kindly man but one addicted to telling the brutal truth. "I had the unenviable chore of editing this product. . . . One week I was astounded to receive a well-written, concise, and interesting version. The explanation—Kissane was home nursing a cold and his secretary had produced it." O'Riley, whom Kerby described as "a lanky ex-cowhand from Oklahoma who loved martinis and classical music," was a respected writer on economic subjects for the *Journal* and later an assistant managing editor. He also contributed to the page-one "Outlook" column until his retirement in 1977.

Bill Kerby was Kilgore's top editor and teacher-in-residence. His method was simple and direct. "Any reporter with a major story in hand was required to orally summarize it for me before attempting to put it on paper," Kerby wrote. "At first, the odds were astronomical that the version coming from his typewriter would bear little or no resemblance to the story as he had told it to me." Kerby would then catechize the reporter, who would be urged to reassort his facts and try again. Kerby, like Kilgore, had aphorisms and rules, at least one a bulletin-board classic the staff remembered: "From today on there will be virtually no virtuallys used in *The Wall Street Journal*."

Frank Dezendorf came quickly into the Kilgore fold and wrote many of the page-one stories. Joseph Guilfoyle, who would become editor of the Dow Jones news-ticker service, was excellent both on rewrite and as a writing reporter. Kilgore and Kerby depended heavily on ten *Journal* copy editors to convert traditional reporting copy into the new prose. The outbreak of war opened the way for employment of newcomers, and Kerby and his aides searched newspapers and journalism schools for talent, especially young women, but hired no one as a financial-reporting specialist. It had become more important to determine simply whether the newcomer could write a tight, readable story. The new editors banned from the paper such technical argot as "arbitrage," "the Bombay straddle," "prime rate," and "gray goods" unless explained. Most new staff members found they could get along well in plain English.

The new *Journal* editors also believed in doing things in a big, dramatic way on occasion. On December 17, 1941, the paper called for price controls as a wartime measure, a shocking departure from its traditional editorial position. "The question of limits on wages and the prices of farm products and other goods has become a simple one," the paper said. "Will price regulation of any degree of severity contribute to our war effort? Will it help to sustain the morale of the fifty million or more who must sustain themselves to equip, clothe and nourish our fighting forces? . . . We believe a thorough-going price control will serve these ends." So did the administration and Congress. On the first day of price controls, Kerby assigned 50 staff members to go shopping for a designated market basket of groceries in 12 cities. "My shoppers reported what they were charged and checked prices against the official Office of Price Administration ceilings," Kerby recalled. "It was a blockbuster."

Some of the country's newspapers sought to pay the new *Journal* the compliment of imitation, especially its "What's News" column, the world-news summary, and situation stories. Nevertheless, the paper was having problems. Most people still regarded *The Wall Street Journal* as a parochial financial paper. In addition, transportation problems, newsprint rationing, a rise in costs, and the elimination of circulation promotion because of those and other factors prevented the paper from pressing the sale of its new look to the wider public for which it was intended. There was no way at the time for the quality of the Pacific Coast edition to equal that of the New York paper, and no possibility to gain the ultimate Hogate-Kilgore-Kerby goal—a national publication—so long as the war continued. Yet circulation grew from 35,395 in 1942 to 64,400 in 1946.

Kilgore and Kerby directed the news coverage of the *Journal*, Grimes and Korsmeyer wrote editorials, and Grimes kept his hand in with the rest of the paper. So did Hogate. He acquired the Associated Press service, even though the AP organization of general newspapers refused to recognize the *Journal* as a general newspaper. "Dow Jones became sort of a distant relative," Kerby recalled. "Under the initial agreement with the AP, Dow Jones was not permitted to designate Associated Press dispatches with the AP logotype, so the term 'World-Wide News' was employed to cover the compacted Associated Press reports used in the 'What's News' column. Under the arrangement, the Dow Jones ticker service also carried AP bulletins, and the AP was free to use Dow Jones and *Journal* material. The *Journal* could use no more than 500 words from AP daily. It also acquired the Reuters business and financial report in addition to United Press. From these various sources, and some staff coverage, it distilled its war news. But, generally, the *Journal*'s coverage of the war was on the production front."

The final page-one format evolved gradually. Kerby was the editor. Kilgore carefully read galley proofs and the finished page and made endless suggestions. Kilgore, Kerby, and McCormack met daily to discuss shortcomings and assignment ideas. Soon other top editors joined the morning story conference. "Kilgore would come armed with a marked up copy of the paper," Kerby recalled. "We would first critique ourselves on the current issue and then turn to the generation of story ideas. In the early days 95 percent of the story ideas originated with Kilgore, Kerby, and McCormack and very little came spontaneously from the staff. Generally, we had more ideas than reporters to execute them. We tried to think ahead of the news. For example, someone had the idea that aluminum was getting scarce—what would that scarcity mean to industry and consumers? We predicted that aluminum would soon be placed on government allocation and that certain consumer goods made of aluminum would become scarce or unobtainable. This would do certain things to certain companies . . . changing their product lines, etc. That was the type of thinking we did." The morning meetings were as earthy and informal as the gathering around the cracker barrel in an Indiana country store, and they came to be called the kaffeeklatsch. They were jovial and relaxed, but always highly purposeful and highly productive.

Early in January 1942 the *Journal* said in an editorial that all phases of American industry "will be deeply submerged in a wartime economy." The editors recognized the need for controls in wartime and saw their own mission as forwarding the smooth transmission of the financial and industrial communities into a wartime economy. The war itself, of course, was national news, and Washington continued to be the major source of news beyond Wall Street.

"War Output to Take 75% to 85% of Nation's Plant Capacity" said a headline on a brace of Washington stories by W. C. Bryant on January 5,

1942. Nearly all the stories in the 80-page first-of-the-year special edition were related to the war on the home front. "Army and Navy Want 4,000 Planes a Month by November" another headline disclosed. "Civilian Use of Wool Slashed This Quarter, More Cuts on the Way" said still another. There were new special columns designed to aid business in adjusting to its role in the war. One was called "Machine Tools and Arms, a Dow Jones Survey for Investors," which detailed the wartime goals of business for stock buyers; another column was called "Defense News, A Daily Checklist of Developments Affecting Business." A news story predicted that trolley cars would return to popularity when auto tires wore thin and gas was rationed. There were special reports on shipbuilding, airplane manufacturing, industrial retooling. Kerby and Duffield wrote a special series on the wartime economy and the adjustments business was making. "War in Europe, Asia, Africa and on the seven seas will determine the kind of life Americans will lead in the years ahead," said the preface. "This series of articles seeks to picture a national economy shaped for the sort of war that must be waged."

Journal editorials attacked those who opposed the war. "Of course we remember the theory of our old self-styled liberals about the inspiration for wars," the paper said on June 4, 1942. "Anyone who made a piece of ammunition bigger than a shotgun shell was a 'merchant of death.' 'Big Business' was always plotting a war. If Big Business did not plot boldly enough, why the 'international financiers' prodded the Big Businessmen. Yes, you must remember."

The *Journal* editor said that he personally knew many big businessmen and never found any of them before the war plotting anything more than how to break 100 on the golf course. The editorial declared that *The Wall Street Journal* did not believe anyone should profit from the war. "Excess profits, meaning war profits, should be subject to final determination as an average for the whole duration, or for at least three years." Contractors should not be allowed to keep excessive profits, but neither should the war effort be impeded by intense quibbling over profits. The paper frequently recalled its editorial of January 2, 1942: "Production, production, production! More airplanes, tanks, guns, ships and yet more; a war bill of fifty-six billion dollars a year, heavy taxes for all and sacrifices to the bare essentials of life; those were the high points of President Roosevelt's State of the Union address to Congress. . . . We think we know the country's response. . . . 'Okey, Mr. President, let's go.' "

During the war years the *Journal* began hiring women because of a loss of newsmen to the draft. Barney Kilgore suggested writing to the deans of leading journalism schools for the locations of bright women students who had gone into journalism. Once candidates for jobs were located, Kerby wrote them letters. "About eight acceptances came back," Kerby recalled, and these women were hired. "I have never worked with a more efficient, dedicated group," said Kerby. "One recruit became make-up editor. . . . She was absolutely great, and she had those printers terrorized. Those gals were all successful. Only two remained with us after the war, however, Betty Donnelly and Alice Estil. None left for other professional jobs, but for family reasons."

The wartime *Journal* specialized on reports of industrial reorganization, Washington economic news, and financial, tax, and budget problems of the war economy, but much attention also was given to the consumer. The paper published regulations of the War Production Board, relating them to consumer products and constantly urging the public to conserve. At the same time it pointed out that the American public fared better in wartime than did people in other countries. "Most of the outside world would like to trade places with us at the dinner table," wrote Charles B. Frazier, opening an article on the U.S. food supply. "They envy our war menus." He predicted that America would eat well no matter how long the war lasted.

The paper published a drawing of a men's suit that would lose its cuffs, vest, patch pockets, and pleats to save wool. "Drawing shows a 'Victory Suit,' " the caption read. "Saving wool won't result in freakish garments." The paper commended the War Production Board. The suits were sufficiently in style, it explained, to obviate the outmoding of existing clothes. Had that been done, the effect of saving wool would have been lost. But the editors were skeptical about the Board's plans for women's wear. "The W.P.B. is composed of courageous, patriotic and high-minded men. At this time we wish to remark only that we wish them all the luck in the world."

The editors of the *Journal* understood that wool had to be saved, that gasoline was in short supply, and that the Allies must be supplied with food. Yet it warned the government against too much rationing. "Rationing is not a weapon to combat inflation," it said on May 15, "and any attempt in such a way will bring any number of dislocations, influencing inflation. . . . There is, for instance, a plentiful supply of wheat. Let us suppose that, nevertheless, we attempt to ration bread and cereals made from wheat. The wheat raiser has been encouraged to produce. Either rationing takes away part of his market or else it is a foolish and unnecessary interference with the usual processes of commerce." Despite the war, the paper concluded, the government could best control inflation by curtailing unnecessary government spending. Rationing any consumer product when there was an adequate supply "would not be accepted. It would be resented as an absurdity and flouted."

The *Journal* itself had to operate with a wartime ration of newsprint, and Bill Kerby concluded that it was a "useful editing tool." He reviewed a month's issues of the pre-ration period, reediting all the stories of substantial length. "I then . . . arrived at the average number of columns per day needed to present tightly edited news in adequate fashion," he recalled in his memoirs. "I issued a ukase to the copydesk. From now on the *Journal* would contain no more than 54 columns (nine pages) of news content. The only individual with the authority to vary from this formula was the managing editor personally. . . . The results were startling. The *Journal* became a much better edited, more concise, meatier newspaper."

Thereafter, the size of the *Journal* was determined by adding the day's advertising quota to the news quota. The printers knew in advance how much type to set. Production costs went down. Much advertising was sold on a time-option basis and could be held for another day if that would save the need to enlarge the paper. The new system of making up the paper continued after the war and is still in use, although the standard allocation of space for news has been greatly expanded.

By December 1942 Casey Hogate was forced to admit that he could no longer carry the burdens of management alone. After suffering a stroke, he often could not come to the office for extended periods. Hogate had assumed Hugh Bancroft's duties in addition to his own ten years previously and relinquished only a few to Joe Ackell. He decided to name Ackell general manager since Ackell was running the production department, where many of the wartime problems existed. Hogate felt there were excellent managers in the editorial department, and advertising and promotion were in good hands under Feemster. But his editor, William Grimes, objected strongly to Ackell's advancement. An editorial man had run *The Wall Street Journal* since the days of Dow and Jones, and Grimes wanted to keep it that way. (Grimes presumably had forgotten or ignored the fact that Hugh Bancroft once was president of Dow Jones & Company and thus ran the *Journal*, but Bancroft did have some editorial experience in Boston.) Grimes didn't want the job for himself; he preferred his work with the editorial page. But, he suggested, there was an obvious possibility—Hogate's own protégé, Barney Kilgore. Hogate was unconvinced. Grimes talked with Kilgore and said he would talk with Kerby.

"One night I received a phone call at home from an agitated Henry Grimes," Kerby wrote. Grimes outlined Hogate's plan. "Said Grimes in effect: If they appoint Ackell, I'm going to resign, and I think Barney will, too. What will you do?" "I'll quit, too," Kerby told Grimes.

Grimes declared that he would call Jack Richardson, Boston attorney and business adviser to Jane Bancroft, to tell him of the resignation threats and to recommend Kilgore for the job. "There are, I know, other and less dramatic versions of how Barney Kilgore became top man in Dow Jones," Kerby wrote, "but this is the way Grimes reported it and the way I'm convinced it was. Whether Grimes actually used the threat of an exodus of the company's top three news executives, I do not know."

Later that night Grimes invited Kerby to his home in Brooklyn Heights. Kilgore had already arrived. Grimes then said, "Barney's in as general manager. I stay as editor and keep an eye on all news operations and you are managing editor of *The Wall Street Journal*. Who do you want as assistant managing editor?" Kerby chose Buren McCormack. The appointments were announced to the staff on December 30, 1942.

The *Journal* continued to be the focus of Vice-President and General Manager Kilgore's attention. Kerby conducted the morning editorial meetings, which Barney Kilgore attended whenever he could. Kerby continued to personally teach others, including the art of composing the "A-heds" he had invented for the page-one feature stories. The subjects of the A-heds often symbolized the new relaxed *Journal* style: "The New Poor—Mr. A. Was Too Busy to Live Expensively; Now He Hasn't the Money" headlined a story dealing with the plight of wartime executives. Said other A-heds: "Fifth Avenue—Its Luxury Shops Doing Good Business Despite Salary Ceilings, Taxes"; "Home-Grown Hemp—U.S. Revives Industry of Colonial Days to Assure Supply in War"; "Christmas Mail—Many 1942 Cards Will Arrive in 1943, Postal Heads Ponder 'Deadline.' " The stories were fascinating, illuminating, and significant, but the paper could have gone to press without them, especially since there was a paper shortage. However, the editors found that *Wall Street Journal* readers loved them.

On January 4, 1943, the leader story was on industrial production going to war, and the two-column leading news story at the upper right of page one described the higher living standards America would enjoy when the war ended. It was one of the Kilgore "situationers," beginning, "The flood tide of the scientific revolution, which has been creeping up the beaches of industry for a decade, has been whipped into a tidal wave by the winds of war. . . . More new ideas have been pushed into use in the past year than in the preceding five years of peace."

Journal executives and editors were thinking about the future and counseled their readers to do the same. "If private industry expects to survive the post-war years as private industry," the paper said on January 5, "it must do its own planning to meet the contingencies of that time. We are going to have—already have, in fact—a welter of plans from self-appointed authorities on the general welfare, each of which is based on the theory that the government must control the national economy throughout the new emergency that is to come with peace." The *Journal*, however, indicated that it did not see peace coming soon.

The war had changed the life-style of Americans drastically, and Hogate and Kilgore expected the country would never be the same, even if government bureaucrats were thwarted in their postwar plans. They sought to determine the effect of wartime conditions on the "new" *Wall Street Journal* readership. Kilgore ordered a readership study by Roy Eastman to measure the reader traffic through the paper, not only in New York but also in Chicago, St. Louis, Milwaukee, and Providence, where the *Journal* had made gains following its recent changes. Kilgore gave Hogate the final result of the Eastman study on May 5, 1943.

"What's News" was still the best-read feature in the *Journal,* Eastman found. Its readership was 100 percent. "Our best inside feature now is the War & Business checklist," Kilgore said in a letter to Hogate, who was away ill. "The war summary still rates very high even though most of these subscribers get their papers at least one day late. The page one columns and the leader stories are pulling high averages in readership." The editors were somewhat surprised to learn that the survey showed the "Business Checklist" column slightly ahead of "Washington Wire."

Kilgore thought it especially significant that one out of ten subscribers was reading the *Journal* in lieu of a regular morning newspaper. Eastman found a "high percentage of enthusiasm reflected in an equally high 'intention to renew' figure." The chief complaint was late delivery. "That, of course, for the time being is something we can't do much about." Kilgore indicated he had discussed the problem with Leslie Davis, his circulation promotion man, and Davis agreed that as long as the war continued, they could not get the paper to subscribers on the day of publication in all areas "we would consider early morning delivery territory."

"Then, too," Kilgore added, "another interesting thing is that most of these subscribers now consider *The Wall Street Journal* as a business newspaper, or a business-financial combination paper. . . . As might be expected in cities as far away as these, a good many subscribers said they got their market quotations elsewhere and *The Wall Street Journal* could leave them out as far as they were concerned. Obviously, we can't do any such thing, but it apparently does show that people will buy the paper even though they can't get it early enough to use the daily quotations in it."

Few newspaper editors at the time paid attention to reader-traffic studies, which they regarded as a tool of the advertising department. Those who even looked at such studies generally rationalized the results to indicate they were editing the paper correctly. Barney Kilgore, no longer an editor, nevertheless concluded that it was the new content of the *Journal* that was pleasing readers and improving circulation, a conclusion obviously fully justified. "In general," he told Hogate, "the report indicates we are on the right track and everybody is happy about it, and I know you will be, too. Brother Grimes maintains that the figures on the editorial page are far too high, but I think he is secretly pleased about it, as well he might be."

Kilgore visited the Pacific Coast edition plant in San Francisco to study the problems there in January and again in August of 1943. In a report to Hogate from New York early in February, he referred to the draft of a letter he planned to send Carl Miller, president of the operation, in which he offered Miller alternatives: "The PCE either ought to be closed down or our whole organization ought to unite—with you—on a real effort to improve the situation. As of today, the facts in favor of continuing appear to outweigh the facts in favor of discontinuing."

Kilgore planned to tell Miller that he understood Miller was eager to cooperate, but the problem bluntly stated was:

> Editorially, the PCE is out of gear with the New York Edition. We are, in effect, publishing two distinct papers rather than two editions of one newspaper. The additional elements which a Pacific Coast Edition should properly possess today overshadow the basic elements which a long process of sweat and trial and error has established as the philosophy formula of the "new" *Wall Street Journal*. In our opinion, the PCE is making some of the same mistakes we made here and is (as much our fault as anybody's) some years behind the NYE.
>
> As we see it here, *The Wall Street Journal* must serve a function between that of the trade journals and the regular daily press. That's difficult to define, let alone serve. And yet we think we have arrived at a successful way of doing it. We think PCE is on a different track.

Kilgore then explained that the New York edition put individual company stories inside the paper in order to keep page one for news of wider interest. The New York edition "depends on no local assortment of spot stories to support it—because it has no locality big enough to support it. Such being the case, the WSJ literally had to invent a front page. This was a long process in which KCH [Hogate] invented some things and laid the whole foundation, Grimes invented others, and, in some small way and with the assistance of able and energetic staff men including Bill Kerby, I invented a few myself. The details on all this are manifold, but when Deac [Hendee] comes East, he will find Kerby and me full of the subject, and we will both be delighted to put before him all the things about editorial formula we think we have uncovered."

Thus, the alternative for Carl Miller was to send Editor Deac Hendee east for training and to improve collaboration. Also, Kilgore told Hogate, they could send Leslie Davis of circulation and Bob Feemster of advertising to the West Coast to help find ways to coordinate those phases of the publishing problem with New York. The development of editorial cooperation would be left to Hendee and Kerby, while Kilgore and Miller would concentrate on the transcontinental communications problems. Kilgore indicated that a joint study of production problems would have to be made and suggested that Joe Ackell could take charge of that phase.

Kilgore had zeroed in on the main obstacle to genuine cooperation between New York and San Francisco: lack of communication. The company was in part at fault, and the exchanges he contemplated would correct that situation. The New York edition was finally showing healthy circulation gains, rising to 42,393 by the end of 1943. San Francisco's editors and writers needed to learn New York ways. But even more important would be the development of technology to permit complete duplication of the New York edition in San Francisco. The application of the *Journal*'s successful journalistic formula on a national scale required communications and printing technologies that were not being used or were only beginning to exist.

In August Barney wrote optimistically to Hogate of his latest visit to the San Francisco plant. Deac Hendee, he said, had returned "full of enthusiasm for the general philosophy of news presentation and treatment which we have found successful in the territory served by the New York Edition. At the same time his personal contact gave New York some idea of PCE problems. As one result, I believe our news department in New York now feels a definite responsibility for seeing to it that PCE gets the material it needs to get out a good paper. . . . You probably have observed that as one result the Pacific Coast Edition now looks a great deal more like the New York Edition." Kilgore added that Leslie Davis was completing his study of West Coast circulation problems, and Feemster was attempting to devise a way to sell advertising. If the PCE problems were solved, Kilgore concluded, he felt the total circulation of the *Journal* could soon reach 50,000.

In New York, Managing Editor Kerby carried on with editorial experiments and taught the new journalism, sometimes writing major stories himself. In his book on life at *The Wall Street Journal,* Kerby related the occasion when Sydney B. Self, who wrote many of the new-product reports, came up with a prospective major story.

> Late one afternoon he ambled up to my desk and in a matter-of-fact way said, "I think I could be on to one of the best news stories I ever had." What he was "on to" was ironclad confirmation that Du Pont scientists had invented what later came to be known as nylon, then code-named Product X. Among other things, it quickly preempted the largest and most profitable markets for natural silk. . . .
>
> With Syd sitting beside me and feeding me information and ideas, I wrote the page one article on Product X. Syd was a greatly talented and highly respected reporter in his specialty, but neither nature nor Princeton University had vested him with the ability to translate his information into written English easily comprehensible to the layman.
>
> The ticker editors went into a frenzy the next morning when they read *The Wall Street Journal*'s front page. Here was a story which devastated prices in raw

> silk futures, then one of the most important and volatile of commodity markets. . . . The ticker editors found it hard to believe I hadn't known anything about Syd's scoop until well after trading had ended for the day.

Reporters and editors of the *Journal* had been required for years to serve both the paper and the news tickers on breaking news stories. But they wanted to hold back exclusive stories for by-line treatment, especially after Kilgore and Kerby had upgraded the front page. This argument was logical; if it was exclusive, it couldn't have been breaking news. Barney Kilgore solved the problem of two masters for the news staff by making Kerby executive editor in December 1945 with both the *Journal* and the ticker organizations under his jurisdiction.

Sydney Self did his work well, and his stories about new products were important fare in the *Journal*. One such story, published March 3, 1943, ran under the paper's new "interest hook" style of headline: "A New Plastic / It Can Stand 500 Degrees Heat and May Be Used in Liquid Form Like Oil / Includes a Mineral Element (Silicon) for First Time—Has Many War Uses." Self demonstrated that he knew the Kerby axiom "There is nothing wrong with a one-sentence paragraph." The story began:

> A new kind of plastic is being made.
>
> For the first time organic chemicals that have been used to make these synthetic materials have been wedded with an inorganic mineral—silicon. That is something plastics chemists have dreamed about for a decade.
>
> The result is a plastic that will do a lot of things other plastics couldn't. As a solid, for instance, the melting point is close to 500 degrees Fahrenheit, far above that of other plastic. This means it can be used on electrical connections where extreme heat may develop.

The story said the new plastic was developed in the laboratories of Corning Glass Company and Dow Chemical Company, and a jointly owned subsidiary, Dow-Corning Corporation, had been formed to produce it. It was the beginning of electric circuitry miniaturization, making possible computers and controls in space satellites, which the *Journal* would one day use to speedily transmit images of its pages to a nationwide network of printing plants. Arrival of the silicon chip and transistor would enable the paper to complete the Kilgore Revolution in the production area and would transform communications for the country as a whole. The *Journal* carefully followed that story.

Even before the war ended, the *Journal* was concerned with the economic outlook for the postwar years. The paper at first did not appear to be unusually disturbed that John Maynard Keynes might dominate the efforts by free-world economists to create a world bank and to provide for world currency stabilization. Nor was the *Journal* unduly upset that President Roosevelt sought a fourth term, although it did point out that even in wartime national leaders were not indispensable, suggesting that Winston Churchill was meeting difficulties in England.

On February 28, 1944, the paper discussed the obligation of Congress to oppose "usurpation" by the President, but having said that, it added it was talking about the peacetime ahead. The *Journal* wanted wartime restrictions on business and finance lifted as swiftly as possible once peace came. It feared the New Dealers would seek to maintain their hold by insisting on regulating the transition from a wartime to a peacetime economy but appeared resigned to Roosevelt. On April 19 its new columnist Raymond Moley, a former Roosevelt brain-truster, discussed "The Men Around Dewey," saying that Dewey would have a difficult campaign if he again sought the presidency as expected.

In July the *Journal* announced that it was taking a dim view of the deliberations taking place as world economists met at Bretton Woods, New Hampshire. The conference was being covered by its special correspondent, V. I. Neal, attached to its Washington staff. The paper wanted government control of world economies no more than at home. "It has been a weakness of the post-war financial plans put forward by the Treasury and their opposite numbers in Great Britain that they went far beyond what they are purported to be," it said on July 5. "In the name of stabilization, Lord Keynes proposed world economic control. The American Treasury proposed a plan which hardly concealed its intention to induce Congress to allow some unnamed group of experts to be a World Lady Bountiful. . . . These plans have been modified, but the absurdities have never been removed."

On November 6, after printing a few editorials during the presidential campaign that indicated it was not happy with either Governor Dewey or President Roosevelt, the *Journal* published a page-one statement: "The first concern of Americans is to win the war. . . . This newspaper is devoted largely to economic news." However, it was not on economic grounds that it was insisting that the country should get ready for peace by insuring a transition back to individual responsibility as smoothly as possible. "We are not arguing against regulatory laws as a whole," the paper explained. "We have them and we will have more." But the paper did not want a continuation of the restrictions of wartime. Yet it knew many would remain if the Democrats won again. It was resigned. On November 8, after yet another Roosevelt victory, the *Journal* said, "The fact is the folks back home are asking for the very thing they all agree must be prevented."

Chapter 16

The Kilgore Years

The Kilgore Revolution had endured four years by 1945, and circulation passed the 50,000 level Barney Kilgore envisioned. Dividends of the Financial Press Companies of America had risen to $2.50 for each of the 166,250 shares in 1943. Although they fell to $1.70 a share the following year on the way to $1 in 1945, the outlook for *The Wall Street Journal* nevertheless seemed good. Circulation momentum had been achieved. Bob Feemster and Ted Callis of the advertising department found it possible to sell added linage in both the New York and Pacific Coast editions thanks to Feemster's ingenious split-run rate schedule. By 1946 dividends were back to $2 a share and would thereafter grow steadily.

Casey Hogate had served as an executive for almost 20 years, and during much of that time *The Wall Street Journal* and other company publications had fought against adversity. Hogate was weary and ill. Early in April he instructed Barney Kilgore to prepare for the time when he would assume the duties of chief executive. On April 13 Kilgore, in his capacity as vice-president and general manager, issued a memorandum to the executive and administrative personnel:

"Effective April 18, 1945, Mr. Grimes, Mr. Feemster, Mr. Ackell and Mr. Hoskins are appointed members of a new Executive Committee of the Financial Press Companies of America. This committee will function largely through Dow Jones & Co., as a central operating staff for the Publisher's office. It will function as a group and also with new individual responsibilities." Kilgore's memorandum named William Henry Grimes, then *Journal* editor, as editorial director of all FPCA publishing activities; Robert Feemster, advertising manager, as assistant general manager in charge of sales; Joseph Ackell in production as assistant general manager in charge of operations; and J. C. Hoskins, secretary and treasurer, as fiscal adviser of "this new central organization." In addition, Kilgore appointed Leslie Davis, his close adviser on circulation and research problems, special assistant to the publisher. Kilgore made it clear that members of the Executive Committee would be advisers. They would not make final decisions on policy affecting divisions of the company "nor issue orders towards implementation of policy."

Casey Hogate's health continued to deteriorate. He consulted his executives and the members of the Barron-Bancroft family, who owned most of the FPCA stock, mostly by telephone now. On November 6, 1945, Bernard Kilgore was made president of FPCA and Dow Jones & Company; Kenneth C. Hogate was elected chairman of the board. Kilgore disclosed to the board that Hogate did not expect to be able to assume other than advisory duties. He made it clear that he felt he was merely standing in for Casey, nonetheless, and wanted no publicity on the change.

Barney Kilgore became chief executive officer, but until a few weeks before Casey Hogate's death in February 1947, he served as Hogate's surrogate. In 1966, when he was praised in a story in *California Publisher* for his leadership of the company since 1945, he sent a note to Edward Cony of the *Journal*'s news staff "correcting" it:

> In 1945 I was elected president but this was almost a state secret. We did not want to announce that Casey had given up hope of coming back to work. Because of this rather unusual state, almost nothing "dates" from 1945. I cannot personally remember anything about this particular promotion except feeling awfully sorry for Casey. . . . Actually, while the process of shifting towards a new basis covered a good many years and some trials and errors, my own biggest contribution to the change, the appearance of "leader" stories on the front page, occurred when I was managing editor.
>
> This was in 1941. I wasn't managing editor very long, really, because Casey Hogate was stricken, and I became VP and general manager in 1942. I took this job mostly because I was sure that if somebody else got it, it would quite likely upset what we were trying to do with the paper. . . . Even at this late date, these things are not easy to explain and time would only be wasted trying to do so. I would have credit for news accomplishment as managing editor (an honorable title) rather than as president.

Hogate had suffered a stroke but he could advise and consult with Barney Kilgore and others by telephone, and they were fortunate to have an experienced management team in place. During the next several months Kilgore's group worked well together. Grimes acted mostly as an adviser in the area of general news, with Executive Editor Kerby actually directing the news operations.

Grimes devoted himself primarily to writing editorials and editing the editorial page. In May 1947 he won for the *Journal* its first Pulitzer Prize, one of journalism's highest awards, for the general excellence of his editorials in 1946. The particular editorial that caught the attention of the judges was not indicated, but some *Journal* editors thought it was "Apathetic and Pathetic," a foreign-policy commentary that appeared on March 7, 1946. In it Grimes deplored the loss of freedom under totalitarian governments, referring specifically to Russia, Argentina, and Spain. Some believed, however, that Grimes thought his two-sentence editorial on Henry A. Wallace was the best of that year. President Truman had demanded the resignation of his liberal secretary of commerce on September 20, and *New Republic*, the liberal magazine the *Journal* detested as much as it did Wallace, soon announced that he would join its staff as editor. Said the Grimes editorial, "Henry Wallace has become editor of the *New Republic*. We suggest that it serves both right." Characteristically, Editor Grimes shared his Pulitzer Prize honors with Frederick Korsmeyer, the paper's veteran editorial writer.

As the editor who established policy, Grimes was tough, puritanical, and uncompromising. Vermont Royster, the young staff writer Grimes brought in from Washington to assist on the editorial page, soon clashed with him. Richard Cooke, the staff drama reviewer, had reviewed a Broadway play that dealt with homosexuality on the same day that a book reviewer reported on a book about adultery and free love, Royster recalled. Royster was at the time handling editorial page makeup, among other duties.

"Grimes came dashing up with proofs of the reviews, his glasses on his forehead, his eyes flashing fire," Royster remembered. "It was about 4:30 P.M., and the page was about to close. 'Kill that Cooke theater review,' Grimes cried. 'Kill that book review.' " Royster protested. "I told him that Cooke was reviewing a Broadway play that was likely to be a hit," Royster said. "I told him, 'We can't help it if it's about homosexuality. Both authors are saying that everyone has a right to do his own thing.' " Grimes waved him down. " 'It's not fit reading for the readers of *The Wall Street Journal*,' he said. So, he killed all the stuff. It was too late to substitute, so we had to jump page-one news stories into the editorial page to fill it."

Early in 1946 Laurence Lombard, a slight, soft-spoken, sandy-haired Boston lawyer who had served as counsel with the War Production Board in Washington, returned home to resume his private practice. He was about to join a new firm, Hemenway & Barnes, when he was contacted by a prospective client who had been referred by mutual friends. She was Mrs. Jessie Cox, wife of William C. Cox, one of Jane Bancroft's two daughters and a trustee of Financial Press Companies of America. Mrs. Cox, her sister, Jane, and their mother were concerned about the family business, FPCA, and its subsidiary, Dow Jones, she told Lombard. The chairman, K. C. Hogate, was seriously ill, and there was a young new president, Bernard Kilgore, whom she had barely met. The owners maintained contact with the company mostly by telephone. The trustees of FPCA met infrequently, the directors of Dow Jones hardly at all.

Lombard agreed to look into the company's affairs. He soon recommended creating a board of directors to supplant the trustees and proposed an ultimate reorganization of the trust and subsidiary companies. Lombard suggested that the board of directors should have at least two outside directors—individuals not directly involved in the company's day-to-day business—and should meet at least once a month. He found that the *Boston News Bureau* was losing money and advised that it be dissolved, with *The Wall Street Journal* taking over the circulation lists.

Mrs. Jessie Cox and her sister arranged a meeting between Lombard and Jane Bancroft. "It would be a mistake to put Kilgore in as trustee immediately, if at all, since he is president of the company," Lombard said. "It would take away their [the board's] control if they became unhappy with the job Kilgore was doing." Lombard again urged that the company in which Mrs. Bancroft and her children had a fortune invested should operate as a corporation rather than as a trust.

Mrs. Bancroft agreed with Lombard's analysis and plan. She asked her own lawyer to withdraw both as her attorney and as a trustee of the Financial Press Companies of America. He agreed to do so. Lombard then undertook to convince Hogate. Lombard recalled that "Mr. Hogate, due to a stroke, was at home, and very much reduced in activity, but mentally functioning." He and Mrs. Hogate owned 15,000 shares of FPCA stock, and Lombard spoke to them jointly. "Both were opposed to my idea," Lombard remembered, "but they asked whom I would recommend as an outside director." Lombard proposed Harold Boeschenstein, president of Owens Corning Fiberglas Company of Toledo, Ohio, a War Production Board executive who had been in charge of the paper and pulp division, including newspapers. Lombard had served as counsel for Boeschenstein at the Board, and Casey Hogate, who seemed to know everybody, knew Boeschenstein and admired him. That helped. Lombard agreed to Mrs. Bancroft's suggestion that he become the second outside director if the new board should be constituted. Then Hogate agreed that the Lombard plan should be adopted.

Although he was not especially happy with corporate developments, Kilgore cooperated with Lombard in setting up the new board, pending creation of a new corporate structure. Kilgore let it be known that he doubted whether non-newspaper people knew much about publishing a newspaper, but in time he would assure Lombard that outside help was most valuable. He in particular followed Lombard's advice. On April 5, 1947, the *Boston News Bureau* said, "We regret to announce that this will be the last issue of the *Boston News Bureau* as a separate publication." *The Wall Street Journal* took over circulation of the paper C. W. Barron established 60 years previously, and on June 18 the *Boston News Bureau* ticker-service staff was absorbed by the New England News Bureau, established by Dow Jones.

Since Barney Kilgore was willing to accept outside directors, Lombard also was ready to compromise. At the annual meeting of the FPCA in April 1947, the trustees elected included Bernard Kilgore, Mrs. Jane W. W. Bancroft, Laurence M. Lombard, Harold Boeschenstein, and William C. Cox. Kilgore was president; Guy Bancroft, brother of Hugh, vice-president; and J. C. Hoskins, treasurer. On December 14, 1948, when Hoskins retired, William F. Kerby replaced him as treasurer.

During 1946, the *Journal* was able to duplicate at considerable cost a number of its New York edition pages in California on a day-to-day basis, although the pattern was not exact. Deac Hendee, Bob Bottorff, and their staff knew what the editors in New York wanted; dispatches by leased wire usually arrived on schedule; and Feemster was able to supply advertising on a split-run as well as national basis. On April 1, 1946, advertising was removed from the front page of the paper, a sign of strength. By the end of the year, circulation stood at 64,400, the Pacific Coast edition contributing more than 11,000 paid subscribers.

Barney Kilgore worried nonetheless. Though he and his staff had totally revised the paper from front to back, even moving the market quotations from the back to an inside page, he feared they had not done enough. They added a dozen regular features, beginning with "Commodity Letter" and "Tax Report," started on successive days in April 1941, through "London Cable," "Business Milestones," "Who's News," and various service features that covered all possible facets of financial and business reporting. The format seemed successful. Feemster liked it, and Feemster had the responsibility of selling both circulation and advertising. He demonstrated his approval of Kilgore's front pages by reproducing them as advertisements in the other New York newspapers on the same day they appeared in the *Journal*, a much admired promotional coup.

Kilgore searched for weaknesses but found no major fault with *The Wall Street Journal*. The *Journal* appeared ready to become a truly national newspaper, and the time was right. Never had American business, industry, and finance had a more fascinating story for the newspaper to report. World War II, ending with victory in Europe on May 8, 1945, and the surrender of Japan on August 14, destroyed or depleted competitive industries and farms in Europe and Asia, and Europe's financial dominance was ended. America, supplier of products and money that had been important to victory, was uniquely prepared for peacetime leadership in the new order of economic affairs.

And in America it was *The Wall Street Journal* that was uniquely prepared to report and interpret on a daily basis the nation's new role as leader in world business and politics. Many industrial plants abroad had been demolished by the war, especially in Germany and Japan. Although postwar surveys would show that strategic bombing by both the Allies and the Germans did not have the devastating effect on war production that had been assumed during the war, it did wreck factories, removing them from commercial competition with America. And what the bombs didn't destroy in Germany, the Russians dismantled and hauled home. The American production system soon dominated world trade and became vastly profitable, until Europe and Japan rebuilt with American aid and created their superior, highly efficient, plants.

America wasn't worried about foreign competition and political reorganization immediately after the war. The people clamored for demobilization and a return to normal life. The *Journal* summed it up in a sentence: "What Americans want is to get into their new automobiles and drive someplace." The focus of news had indeed shifted to the civilian economy. What would Detroit's assembly lines turn out? What about General Electric's new refrigerators with automatic icemakers? Would prefab houses help end the housing shortage? What would the quick-frozen-food industry offer? Not to mention television, tape recorders, drive-in movies, and automated bowling alleys? The *Journal*, which had been reporting on new products throughout the war, was now the publication best qualified to cover the new consumer news of peacetime. Prospering manufacturers were eager to use the *Journal*'s columns and could afford to do so.

The paid circulation of *The Wall Street Journal* would pass 76,000 in 1947, yet Barney Kilgore continued to be anxious. He confided to Casey Hogate that he had heard criticism of the paper's name. "Wall Street" was too parochial for an aspiring national newspaper. And suppose there was a financial crash similar to that of 1929? People had hated the name of Wall Street then, and Kilgore was sure this angry emotion had rubbed off on *The Wall Street Journal* and caused circulation losses. A prewar survey had indicated that perhaps a change in name was in order. Kilgore and Hogate agreed that a new survey should be conducted to provide a clearer reading on the public attitude. In February 1947 Kilgore wrote Hogate, referring to the survey, done by the "Benson polling organization of Princeton":

> Benson and his associates are very definitely of the opinion that the name, *The Wall Street Journal*, is a handicap to our growth. . . . They cheerfully admit, however, that they are uninhibited in this respect by any consideration of the property value of the present name. They look at it only from the point of view of public reaction. . . . I am inclined to think that we perhaps have a double problem. One angle is the term "Wall Street" in our name which ties us close to a specific segment of the financial field and may make our future progress unduly dependent upon the prevailing view of the stock market.
>
> We do, of course, cover the stock market, and I believe that the broader we make our coverage, the better financial newspaper we are. At the same time, the increasing proportion of our readership is non-financial—at least in the sense that it is not directly related to stocks and bonds. The second angle of our problem is the fact that our present name does not always convey the idea of daily publication. Of course, the word "journal" means daily, but through usage has been watered down [he cited *Ladies' Home Journal* and *Farm Journal*, monthly magazines]. On these grounds I think we would be well advised to think in terms of broadest possible meaning. . . . Not many of the names I have been able to think of fit. . . . One idea that I had was "World's Work," which is a title that I think is probably available for use. The name you mention, "Financial America," may still, to most people, convey the more restrictive meaning of stocks and bonds. One suggestion Bill Grimes has made, "The National Journal." To me, this sounds a bit more like a sub-title rather than a main title. I had a notion the other night that perhaps "North American Journal" would sound a little bit more euphonious. . . . Perhaps the name, "Business Day," would not be too bad.

Hogate's reply is not on record. Fortunately, nothing was done.

Bob Feemster and Joe Ackell, unworried about implications of the paper's name, were moving ahead with their approach for publishing and selling it. Barney Kilgore wrote Carl Miller in San Francisco instructing him to drop his practice of publishing special-advertising editions, since Feemster's split-run system was producing adequate linage. "We have a feeling that every special edition the PCE runs may cost our organization as a whole more revenue than it produces on the Coast," Kilgore said. Kilgore wasn't especially fond of Feemster, the flamboyant director of sales whose pugnacious style and supercilious manner were attributed by some to an inferiority complex because he was short but by most to an insufferable egotism; however, he respected Feemster's ability. Kilgore was drawn to Joe Ackell, reclusive and efficient, and sought to have Joe teach him the mysteries of microwave communication.

Ackell and Feemster, despite an extreme difference in temperaments, worked well together. They cooperated in the area of news tickers, a service the Feemster-supervised staff sold. By 1946 they had created a truly national news-ticker service, controlled from New York, the necessary preliminary to possible transmission of news simultaneously to several regional newspaper editions.

Joe Ackell himself was credited with many of the technological improvements. "Numerous patents have been granted and assigned to Dow Jones for various machines and techniques developed by its engineers," he said when he became business manager in August 1948. "They developed the automatic transmitters for tickers, the 5 hole standard transmitter in 1936, with refinements later; the multiposting machine for circulation servicing which went into use on the *Barron's* list in 1947. They also developed mechanical equipment for preparation for the D.J. averages chart." Actually, Ackell himself led the way in all developments, but he preferred to let others take the bows. When he decided, as business manager, that the famous Dow Jones messenger-delivered bulletin service should end in November 1948, he allowed Bob Feemster to issue the necessary order. The final messenger bulletins, started by Dow Jones in November 1882, went out on November 30, sixty-six years later.

In the spring of 1947 Kilgore directed Ackell to make plans for opening another publishing plant somewhere in Texas. Laurence Lombard had proposed a Southwest edition of the paper, his studies of FPCA and Dow Jones having convinced him that regional editions indeed represented the wave of the future. Kilgore was delighted to have his suggestion. Dallas was chosen as the site and Kerby was directed to create an editorial team. John O'Riley, Kerby's first selection, turned down the job of news manager. "I worked like hell to get out of that damned country," said O'Riley, who was from Oklahoma. Maurice Farrell, Jr., was chosen. Farrell, Kerby wrote in his memoirs, was an able, young reporter with good news contacts in the oil industry. "What I didn't realize when I picked Farrell," Kerby added, "was that I was picking a man who would, of sheer necessity, also have to function as production manager, business manager, circulation director, and, for a time, advertising production manager."

Dallas seemed destined for disaster from the start. Kerby went there a month before scheduled start-up time. "I found our building was weeks behind schedule. Except for the press, equipment deliveries were badly, almost fatally, delayed. . . . We had no office furniture; only temporary flooring in the office areas; no ceilings; no partitions; no air conditioning." And worst of all, no plumbing. Kerby arranged for toilet facilities in a neighboring building. Nevertheless, the Southwest edition went to press on May 3, 1948, only an hour and a half late. Stanley Marcus, head of the famed Neiman-Marcus department store, pressed the starter button. Kerby called Kilgore to report that they had made it. The next morning he and Farrell learned that the entire air shipment of papers for the Denver area never got off the ground. Joe Ackell had subcontracted the printing, and this created many problems. The fledgling edition was bombarded with reader complaints. "Droves of subscribers who had been transferred to the Dallas edition demanded that they be shifted back to the New York printing, despite the delayed delivery. . . . Neiman-Marcus, our biggest account, canceled its entire schedule," Kerby wrote. Nevertheless, the paper was covering another section of the country from its own regional publishing plant.

In New York, *The Wall Street Journal* provided some details in a news story announcing the start of the Dallas edition. "Like its regional counterpart on the Pacific Coast, it will serve a group of important, thriving states that cannot be reached from *The Wall Street Journal*'s original printing plant in New York City with the speed that modern business life requires of a daily publication. . . . The principal objective of all three editions will remain that of providing news and interpretative material that go to make up a national business newspaper."

On February 12, 1947, *The Wall Street Journal* reported the death of Kenneth C. Hogate, 49, chairman of Dow Jones & Company, at the Palm Springs Hospital in California early the morning of the 11th. He had suffered a cerebral hemorrhage on February 1. There were columns of words on Casey Hogate in the *Journal* and much in newspapers around the world. Grimes wrote the paper's editorial tribute to its leader, which spoke not only of his accomplishments in journalism, but also of the regard in which he was held among those who worked with him and knew him best.

Said the *Boston News Bureau*, "He was a big man in every sense—physically, mentally, spiritually." The *New York Times* praised Hogate as a journalist and for his work with the Conway Committee, as did the *New York Herald-Tribune* and other metropolitan papers. Said the *London Times*, "As president of *The Wall Street Journal* since 1933, he was the leading figure in financial journalism on the American continent. Under his direction, *The Wall Street Journal* sought to discover and foretell coming events from current trends of the market, not only changes in the market itself but also what was likely to happen in home and international affairs."

The name of Bernard Kilgore, president, thereafter led *The Wall Street Journal* editorial masthead, with William H. Grimes, editor, also sharing publicly the responsibility for the paper. The men around Barney Kilgore, then 39 years old, said in later years that they considered him a genius, as did his secretaries. Editor Grimes, as well as most of the copyreaders and reporters, noted for their cynicism, saw Barney Kilgore as someone special. "A genius, but not infallible" was the consensus. He was definitely modest and low-key. He was intensely honest but he could be devious. Barney Kilgore would become the most admired and loved executive in the *Journal*'s history before death ended his career prematurely in 1967.

Leslie Bernard Kilgore was born in Albany, Indiana, November 9, 1908. His father, Tecumseh Kilgore, was a teacher and later a school superintendent. Barney, who detested the name Leslie and never used it unless legally required, spent much of his childhood in South Bend, Indiana. While attending DePauw University at Greencastle, Indiana, he met Mary Lou Throop, daughter of a Greencastle dentist, and married her in 1938. When Kilgore was called to New York in 1941 to become *Journal* managing editor, they lived for a time in the city, but then settled in a big house on Pretty Brook Road outside Princeton, New Jersey, where they reared their three children. Barney's hobbies changed every few weeks, varying from photography to building model trains, and he liked golf but rarely had time for it. He became an elder in the Presbyterian church, a director of Princeton Municipal Improvement, Inc., and owner and publisher of the *Princeton Packet*, the state's oldest newspaper, and several other weeklies, which he operated during his association with Dow Jones.

Kilgore's position as chief executive of Dow Jones did not in the slightest change his life-style as far as his associates could observe. He arrived at his penthouse office on the eighth floor of 44 Broad Street at 9:35 A.M. every business day after commuting from Princeton. The train ride gave him time to thoroughly read and mark up *The Wall Street Journal* and to tear up various other New York and Washington newspapers, thus providing him with a wad of clippings and notes by the time he reached New York. Frequently, Barney would horrify Mary Lou by ripping apart a book he wished to read so that he could conveniently carry the pages or sections he required that day. There was no point in toting the entire volume, he rationalized.

Kilgore's office routine varied little from the time he became president and has been described by William McSherry, his secretary from 1957 through Kilgore's final illness. When McSherry first came to the job as substitute secretary, he was told by Arthur Lissner, his predecessor, what to expect. "When B. K. entered the office, he would give me the marked *Wall Street Journal* to call the printing people on production errors," McSherry said. "Meantime, he would riffle through the mail. Dictation started promptly at 9:45 A.M. and ended about 10:10 A.M. Five additional minutes to outline what he wanted, and B. K. was off to the kaffeeklatsch clutching a marked copy of the paper."

By that time Kilgore, a dark-eyed, bushy-haired, youthful man, was generally in shirt-sleeves with his tie loose, collar open, and sleeves rolled. He departed the eighth-floor executive suite by stairs to visit aides he wanted to see en route to the third-floor newsroom. When Barney entered Kerby's kaffeeklatsch, he slid unobtrusively into his chair and listened to the discussion, banter, and laughter until Kerby's glance told him his observations were expected. His comment was always brief and precise but also understanding of errors and generous with compliments. He didn't mind being interrupted by a question or even dissent. "Kilgore had been a first-rate reporter, and he knew the value of when to listen and when to shut up," wrote John F. Bridge, himself a *Journal* reporter and later editor of the famous *Journal* front page.

Back in his office for the afternoon, Kilgore "attacked correspondence, speeches and problems like a newsman zeroing in on hard news," wrote McSherry in appraisal of his boss. "He got it done correctly and fast. His working rule was to have mail from morning answered by lunchtime and the afternoon mail signed and posted before he left the office. He didn't take kindly to delay. The second week on the job in his office [as a substitute for Lissner, who was ill], I got bogged down and didn't get the afternoon letters transcribed and typed before he left for the day. The next day he protested vigorously when I put them on the desk for his signature."

McSherry thus learned that whatever Kilgore assigned had to be done that day. If he became overloaded, he was authorized to get help. Kilgore refused to work from files. "He seemed to remember what a correspondent had written previously, or what the news had been," said McSherry. "I would always check him against the files and never found him to be wrong." Kilgore had rules for his own conduct. One was never to show anger in a letter. "He'd dictate his displeasure," McSherry recalled. "I'd translate my notes, B. K. would put the writing away in a drawer; couple of days later, he'd redo it and laugh at his original expression of indignation." McSherry became Kilgore's administrative assistant and eventually had his own secretary. "I was proud of that," McSherry said. "He didn't care to pass out titles."

"B. K. never changed," McSherry said, "even when he became a millionaire as Dow Jones stock went to $2,000 a share. He was very careful with money and was modest in his life-style. Probably his greatest asset was being able to move among ordinary working people, such as pasting up a page of copy, operating a teletype machine, changing the block of a motor on his Ford. He was accepted by people as their own because he was good at what they did." In college Kilgore ran everything, his friends said, and he was into everything at Dow Jones, but in a way that didn't irk the person whose domain he entered. "Barney was simply trying to learn things," a friend explained. Kilgore's trusted lieutenant was Bill Kerby, McSherry said. "Kilgore liked the way Kerby ran the paper."

And, as Kerby himself remembers, Barney liked the way Kerby made martinis, which they consumed while they talked over the day's work in

Kerby's office. Most days Kilgore left his office early, at 4:20 P.M. or so, but often that was merely the start of a new day. Conferences with lawyers and board members, a look into the newsroom, martinis with Kerby and Ted Callis of the advertising department, then dinner meetings, a night on the town with Mary Lou, or home to her and their children at Pretty Brook Road.

Barney liked to go out on the town. "When B. K. and Mary Lou moved to their summer home at Twin Lakes [Pennsylvania]," McSherry recalled, "B. K. would come to the office early Tuesday morning and work Tuesday and Wednesday until bedtime. When Thursday night came around, he was ready for some rest and relaxation, and he would hunt up a crony or two; usually Ted Callis would be one of them. I went to the Gaslight Club with him several times. He played piano and entertained the customers and really enjoyed himself. Off to Twin Lakes on Friday, and the next Tuesday, a replay of the week."

Although Kilgore had the frugal small-town background he often referred to, he had never been poor. His father was superintendent of schools at South Bend, Indiana, and the family was moderately well-to-do. It seemed that Barney always had a way of getting what he wanted. As a Boy Scout in South Bend, he was determined to win a Scout birdhouse-construction contest and did. He invented an owlhouse category, talked the committee into including it, and submitted the only entry.

Kilgore disliked arrogance in other people and was totally free of it himself. Lindley H. Clark, who became page-one editor of the *Journal*, recalled that when he first arrived in New York to become a copyreader in the *Journal* newsroom, he observed Barney Kilgore, the Dow Jones president, in shirtsleeves and with tie loose, enter the newsroom and approach a stack of newspapers just off the press. Another new hand, who did not know Kilgore, was in charge of the stack of papers. "May I take one?" Barney asked. "No, we hardly have enough for our own use," the new hand said. "Oh, I'm sorry," Kilgore responded, and wandered away. He went down two flights to the pressroom and got a copy there.

Unlike Casey Hogate, Barney Kilgore was an executive who could delegate responsibility. He was also expert in motivating and maneuvering his staff. Kilgore was admittedly not fond of Robert Feemster, his pompous assistant general manager in charge of sales who loved cowboy boots and big Texas hats, which he sometimes wore to the office. Feemster was sure that he deserved a higher position than Kilgore appeared to envision for him, and he undertook to convey his dissatisfaction to Kilgore. Barney always held his temper. Once when an employee confronted Kilgore in the presence of Buren McCormack and hotly criticized him, he kept his cool, though McCormack was furious. "Forget it," Kilgore said as the placated worker finally walked away. "In my job I can't afford to get mad. He needed to sound off." So did Feemster, evidently, but Kilgore did not always forgive everybody.

At the August 2, 1948, meeting of the Executive Committee, Kilgore presided and demonstrated his mastery of the art of executive maneuver by neatly submerging Feemster in a bureaucratic morass while he made Kerby a vice-president and Joe Ackell business manager, a promotion Feemster coveted—and he did it with Feemster's enthusiastic approval. As the meeting opened, Kilgore announced that he wished to nominate Bob Feemster for an important new position, chairman of the Executive Committee, a job Kilgore was creating. He described the proposed duties: "To call meetings of the Executive Committee upon the chairman's own motion or upon request of any member of the committee; to prepare agenda for such meetings, including in such agenda any material submitted by other members of the committee; to keep on file material for use of the committee, either individually or as a group; to prepare reports on matters discussed by the committee; to prepare recommendations for action provided such recommendations are unanimously agreed to by all members of the committee."

"Mr. Feemster was thereupon elected to that position," said the report of the meeting, evidently dictated by Kilgore himself. "Mr. Kilgore stated that it would be the policy of management to permit Mr. Feemster to use the title of Chairman of the Executive Committee publicly in addition to his present title as assistant general manager in charge of sales. It was stated that while his executive functions would be unchanged except as outlined above, the recognition of his place as a key executive would undoubtedly prove useful to the organization."

Kilgore then suggested that since Joe Ackell's title was not really descriptive of his work, he should be named business manager. Thus Kilgore mollified Feemster, who continued to do excellent work and to cooperate with Business Manager Ackell. Feemster bore his new title proudly. Kilgore's accomplishment was the kind that might have been expected of the solemn little boy who once induced a birdhouse-contest committee to create an owl-house category.

During the 1948 presidential campaign, President Truman, the Democratic nominee for reelection, received laughter and applause in the country with his occasional references to *The Wall Street Journal* as the Republican Bible. "I can think of no greater authority on the Republicans and what they believe than this same *Wall Street Journal*," said the President in discussing the agricultural-price-support program before a crowd at McAlester, Oklahoma, on a sweltering September day. "That is the Republican Bible. . . . They use half their editorial columns giving me hell because I am for the people."

The *Journal* editors felt obliged on October 1 to take note of what the President said. They did not object to the scriptural allusion but plaintively dissented from President Truman's exaggeration of the paper's criticism. "In our comments in these columns," the *Journal* replied, "we try to state what we believe to be sound economic principles. Whenever Mr. Truman adopts, or advocates, government policies which seem to us to depart from those principles, we point out what we believe to be the fallacies involved. Whenever Governor Dewey, the Republican candidate, has acted similarly, we have been critical of him. And we shall continue to be critical of both candidates under the circumstances.

"If President Truman is a consistent reader of this newspaper—as we certainly hope he is—he must be aware of the fact that our loyalties are to the economic and governmental principles in which we believe and not to any political party. We regret he chooses to distort this newspaper's position."

The President was, of course, engaging in political hyperbole to some extent. The *Journal* had criticized him and also praised him over the years. It recalled its opinion of January 22, 1946, when it said of his presidential message, "We sincerely wish that our comment could be less critical. Mr. Truman has served his country sincerely and has to his credit some accomplishments for which he deserves gratitude, notably that of inducing early surrender by Japan. By refusing to follow the 'unconditional surrender policy' to its remorseless conclusion, Mr. Truman saved thousands of lives and avoided duplication of the chaotic condition which has made the German occupation such a difficult task." Its criticism of Truman's domestic policy had been mild. "Mr. Truman's requests for government activities are by no means niggardly. He is by no means a disciple of Coolidge economy. His fiscal policies do exhibit a better sense of financial order than we have had in Washington in some years."

The *Journal*, however, had not thought well of some economic policy-makers, especially Secretary of Commerce Henry Wallace, with whom the President himself grew disenchanted and eventually asked to resign, and Chester Bowles, wartime director of the Office of Price Administration. Of Bowles's policies, the paper said on February 12, 1946: "That set of more or less unintelligible rules which Washington has been pleased to call a stabilization policy having met its inevitable failure, a new policy is soon to be announced. We mean no disrespect for Mr. Snyder [John W. Snyder, director of the Office of War Mobilization and Reconversion, with whom Bowles had been having a policy debate in which both threatened to resign their posts] when we say that whether or not they stay in Washington is a very minor matter. If they differ, it may very well be that both are wrong. The important thing is not to keep them happy, but to find and adopt measures to speed up production and get goods into the hands of the people who want and need them badly."

President Truman's foreign-aid program received a promise of support from the *Journal*, providing it could be carried out "without clamping controls on the domestic economy." The paper strongly supported President Truman's March 12, 1947, speech to Congress enunciating the Truman Doctrine. The story itself was covered in a way that must have pleased Kilgore. The "Washington Wire" provided inside background: "Block Russia now or later, Marshall [secretary of state] told Truman. A Moscow-to-Washington phone call sparked the President's bold words. . . . Secretary Marshall in Moscow attending the Conference of Foreign Ministers 'figured the odds: Give Moscow a free reign now and face a sure clash later. . . . Palestine is the next worry. The hard-pressed British want out.' " The following day, the *Journal* provided another of the Kerby surveys, created by sending most of the paper's reporters and correspondents around the country to determine what people were saying about the new Truman Doctrine, which would provide aid to Turkey and Greece to block USSR-backed regimes. "The American people were talking yesterday as if they would back up President Truman's new foreign policy," the survey said. The paper's editorial on March 13, 1947, was hard-hitting:

> The many, of whom this newspaper was one, who have criticized American foreign policy as fuzzy and indecisive and statements of policy often lacking in candor, will lodge no such complaints against President Truman's address to Congress yesterday. In proposing a vast expansion of this nation's role in world affairs, Mr. Truman "let go with both barrels."
>
> The President said in clear, blunt language that Soviet Russia has seized upon post-war chaos to impose upon helpless people totalitarian regimes which those people do not like; that in the process the Russians have broken solemn international agreements. The United States is fed up with such business. He proposed that this nation notify the world that it intends to put a stop to it. He proposes to start with Turkey and Greece.

The *Journal* indicated it was quite aware of the obligations the United States would assume and the sacrifices that would be required: "Probably at least a part of expectations of tax reductions will go out the window." It concluded that President Truman had met the requirements of world leadership. "We hope that the discussion [of his policy] will remain at the high level at which he pitched it."

Although the *Journal* endorsed Truman's plan for aid to Greece and Turkey, it initially looked askance at the proposal made by Secretary of State George Marshall in a speech at Harvard University on June 5, 1947. Marshall urged the nations of Europe to outline a program for their economic recovery in which the United States could effectively participate. In commenting on the speech, the paper said Marshall was too vague, and concluded that what the secretary wanted was for Europe to get its house in better economic order.

When England called for European leaders to meet in Paris in July to consider Marshall's proposal, the *Journal* provided some specific ideas for their guidance.

First of all, the nations needed to reform their financial and trade practices, the paper declared on June 16. "The mere admission by governments that their currency evaluations are fictitious would not constitute internal reforms of much consequence," it warned. A few days later it softened its conditions. "We have no intention of saying that a ravaged continent with its productive plant partly wrecked and its money supply chaotic can find any course which will bring recovery overnight. What we do mean is that the European nations must reconsider courses they have chosen [so that] recovery can be stimulated by American goods and services." The *Journal* accused English socialists of scuttling banking and trade practices that in the past earned American dollars, citing the copper and cotton markets, which England led in prewar days. "They were a source of income just as much as physical exports," it explained.

Meantime *Pravda*, the newspaper of the Soviet Communist party, was denouncing Marshall's proposal as an extension of the Truman Doctrine. For once *The Wall Street Journal* agreed with *Pravda*. "Soviet Russia is intent on blocking Secretary Marshall's proposal," it added. "We think that it is quite possible that the Soviet government, contrary to its intention, is in fact promoting the cooperation among all the European states which Mr. Marshall has been urging. . . . We think it is decidedly encouraging that . . . the actual work of the conference so far promises to effect economic integration of the Continent. If that integration begins by drawing together only the western European states, it will have served an immensely useful purpose."

Thereafter the *Journal* supported the Marshall Plan. Congress approved the program in 1948, and over the next four years more than $12 billion in aid was extended to 16 European nations.

Although *The Wall Street Journal* had not devoted half its columns to giving Harry Truman hell, as he so picturesquely claimed, there was no doubt in the 1948 campaign that it wanted Governor Tom Dewey of New York to win, and it didn't doubt he would. In approving of a Dewey foreign-policy statement on October 3 in which the Republican candidate said the U.S. foreign-aid program should not be "just for relief, but to help prod European nations toward union," the *Journal* said, "This newspaper welcomes that statement from a man who is very likely to be President after next January 20." Two weeks later, it had Governor Dewey almost elected: "There are good reasons why Governor Dewey has taken what was a party policy (American unity), used it as a campaign policy, and promised with every mark of sincerity to make it national policy when he becomes president." And, on October 19: "Political prognosticators and polls tell us that the election will send Governor Dewey to the White House by a thumping majority."

On November 2 President Truman was elected by 24,105,695 votes to 21,969,170 for Governor Dewey, with Governor J. Strom Thurmond of South Carolina—running on a states'-rights ticket created by Democrats from 13 states who bolted the Democratic convention—getting 1,169,021. The popular vote translated into 303 electoral votes for President Truman to 189 for Dewey.

Said the paper on November 4: "Barring those few who were in adulthood at the time of Abraham Lincoln's election, we think that no man now living witnessed a political news event greater than the election of President Truman on Tuesday." It described the President's problems, the three-way Democratic party split, and the unanimity of the polls. "By all tests of political sentiment, Governor Dewey was an easy victor," it said. "President Truman made the kind of campaign to which American voters are accustomed. He slugged at his opponent. He told what he intended to do, and he identified the interest and emotions of the voters with his program. Governor Dewey did none of these things." Both the House and the Senate remained Democratic. On December 16, after recovering from shock, the *Journal* told the Republicans in Congress that they had better try to figure out soon what happened and to change their ways. "It begins to look like the Republican Party was mortally wounded. Some day it may back up to a looking glass and see where it was hit in the rear while fleeing from a principle."

Chapter 17

How the West Was Won

Late in 1949 it was clear that Barney Kilgore's formula for the *Journal* was working and would continue to work extremely well. The subscription price increased from $18 to $20 a year on January 2, 1948, and from 7 to 10 cents a copy; the rising circulation sales graph never faltered. Total circulation reached 129,878 in 1948 and it would pass 145,000 copies by the end of 1949, more than triple the 42,393 total in 1943, the second full year of the Kilgore Revolution. The Pacific Coast edition, greatly improved, would contribute 21,970 in 1950, while the new Southwest edition, coming up fast, would be near 16,000. President Kilgore had won the complete confidence of the "family"—Jane Bancroft and her daughters, the majority stock owners, and their adviser, Laurence Lombard. Kilgore and Lombard worked closely that autumn, giving attention to attorney Lombard's recommendation that Financial Press Companies of America, a trust, should be reorganized once more, this time as a modern corporation under the laws of the state of Delaware to be named Dow Jones & Company (Delaware law gave corporations greater freedom for expansion and diversification).

The studies were well advanced when Kilgore came up with one of his inspired ideas for increasing collaboration between owners and management: Why not dramatize to the directors the new national status of *The Wall Street Journal* and present the new reorganization plan at a special session in San Francisco? They could meet with the staff of the Pacific Coast edition and some West

Coast advertisers and opinion-makers, and they could dedicate the new presses that were being installed at San Francisco. Bill Kerby took charge of general logistics for the trip, and Carl Miller, president of the Pacific Coast operation, set up a welcome for the Dow Jones directors and executives.

Kerby chartered a private railroad car, which was hitched to the end of a Century Limited out of New York. The trip was a joyous one, despite the fact that Jane Bancroft, director and matriarch of the Bancroft family, was forced at the last minute to remain at home in Boston due to an illness. Kerby found it necessary to replenish his liquor supplies in Chicago. Director William Cox, husband of Jessie, celebrating his forty-third birthday for 26 straight hours as the Dow Jones safari passed through three time zones en route to the West Coast, kept his companions awake and entertained while they again depleted Kerby's stock of viands and beverages.

There was work done en route, too. Lombard explained the details of the reorganization proposal. He and Kilgore spent hours drafting a plan for an employees' profit-sharing fund that Mrs. Bancroft had approved in principle back in Boston. Lombard and Kilgore also talked about a possible Midwest edition some day, with Chicago as a likely publication site. The trip was highly successful: Carl Miller prepared splendid entertainment, the delegates met San Francisco's financial and political leaders, and new twin flatbed presses were dedicated. These had been intended for an edition of the Army newspaper, *Stars and Stripes*, in the Pacific combat areas but were purchased as war surplus by an alert Joe Ackell after Japan surrendered.

On the return trip, Kilgore and Lombard completed work on the Dow Jones Profit Sharing Pension Fund. Mrs. Bancroft told them that the family, which owned about 80 percent of FPCA stock and all Dow Jones shares at the time, would pay the full cost. To their knowledge it was a uniquely liberal plan, since company contributions would be unusually large, the percentage increasing as profits rose. Also, employees would be permitted to take their vested interest with them, should they leave Dow Jones. By the time the expedition returned to New York and Boston, the pension and profit-sharing plan was fully drafted. Immediately after the trip, on November 25, Lombard, Guy Bancroft, and Richard Cole, former president of the Boston News Bureau, filed articles of incorporation for Dow Jones & Company, Inc., with the Delaware secretary of state. The first meeting of the directors of the new corporation, which would supersede both the Financial Press Companies of America and Dow Jones & Company, Inc., of New York, took place in Boston on December 2, 1949, enabling Mrs. Jane Bancroft to be present.

The meeting participants included shareholders in the FPCA owning 156,270 of the total 170,000 shares. Of this number the Bancroft family and trusts owned 135,000 shares and the Kenneth C. Hogate estate held 12,500; Frank M. Simmons, new head of the Boston properties, 600; Richard Cole and J. C. Hoskins, 500 each; Bernard Kilgore, B. F. Griffin, William Devlin, and Carl Miller, 300 each; George Shea, 225; Joseph Ackell and William Grimes, 200 each; Oliver Gingold, 125; Fred Korsmeyer and H. C. Weitzmann, 100 each; and Edward Costenbader, 50. All were employees or former employees of Dow Jones or the Boston News Bureau. According to company lore, the biggest employee block of FPCA stock had once been owned by Edward Stein, former reporter, Berlin correspondent, and circulation manager, who bought $75,000 worth of shares in the mid-1930s to enable the company to meet its payroll. Then, some months later, Stein sold them at a small profit. However, there is no record, other than 1,760 shares Stein held in 1930, of such ownership in the existing corporate records. Stein, who might have become a multimillionaire, died in moderate circumstances a decade later.

On December 21, 1949, Jane Bancroft died in her home in Boston. The daughter of Jessie Barron and the adopted daughter of C. W. Barron, Jane represented the last family link to the era of Barron, Charles Dow, Edward Jones, and Charles Bergstresser. Jane had been a strong leader in Dow Jones and *Wall Street Journal* business affairs, though, unlike her mother, she declined to directly influence any *Journal* editorial decisions. She backed Casey Hogate when he was making his difficult personnel and business moves to keep the company alive during the Depression.

"The company is Mrs. Jane Bancroft's family," Hogate told the employees. It was Jane Bancroft to whom her daughters appealed when they wanted to bring in their lawyer, Laurence Lombard, to become a company director. It was Jane who signaled acceptance of the compromise worked out by Lombard and Kilgore that brought in outside directors and permitted Barney, president of the company, to become a director and important stockholder. Jane's last act during her final illness had been to create the employee profit-sharing pension plan and to approve the reorganization of Dow Jones.

Now, in December 1949, President Kilgore asked Lombard to write a message of appreciation and eulogy about Jane Bancroft to be directed primarily to Dow Jones employees. "She was a wonderful woman," Lombard wrote. "She had always regarded Dow Jones employees as her 'family,' and her decisions in the business had always held the employees' interest uppermost. . . . With the foresight that one would expect, Mrs. Bancroft has taken the necessary steps to make sure that her death would not impair the stability of the business nor alter the policies for which her father, her husband, and she had successively stood."

Lombard then added that Mrs. Bancroft left all her stock to members of her family and "the undersigned as trustee for the benefit of her family." Thus, "except for Mrs. Bancroft, the same persons will continue [to direct the company] in the future, and I am authorized to say that no change whatsoever is contemplated in the policies or in the operations of the Dow Jones enterprises."

Two changes in the board of directors did occur within the next few weeks, however, to maintain the family line on the board. Richard B. Cole resigned. His place and Jane Bancroft's were filled by Jane's daughter Mrs. Jane Cook and by William Cox. The granddaughters, who remembered well their colorful stepgrandfather, C. W. Barron, said their policy for the company could be described in a sentence: "Just keep on running it as grandpa would have done."

There would be no change in the board of directors for the next 15 years, except the addition of James N. White, a Boston investment counselor and Harvard graduate, whom Lombard sponsored for the board. In 1966 Kilgore, after learning that his own illness was terminal, paid tribute to the outside directors introduced by the Bancrofts and Lombard, saying, "Their contributions have been of inestimable value to management."

Before the end of 1949 Treasurer William Kerby drafted the new Dow Jones management chart: Kilgore, president and chief executive officer; Grimes, editor of the *Journal* and member of the Executive Committee in charge of all news and editorial operations; Kerby, treasurer and executive editor of the *Journal* and Dow Jones News Services; Ackell, business manager and member of the Executive Committee in charge of factory and other production operations; Feemster, chairman of the Executive Committee and member in charge of sales; McCormack, managing editor of the *Journal*; Costenbader, managing editor of Dow Jones News Services; and Callis, advertising manager of the *Journal*. Thus Kilgore loyalists, led by Kerby, moved up.

Kerby's chart of the company's activities included Dow Jones News Service (United States); Dow Jones Commodity News Service; Dow Jones Canadian News Service; *The Wall Street Journal*, with editions in New York, Dallas, and San Francisco; and *Barron's* magazine.

Kerby's management list did not include the new editor of *Barron's*, John Davenport, appointed in November 1949. He was a Yale University graduate who had been a member of the board of editors of *Fortune* magazine. He succeeded George Shea, who returned to the *Journal* as financial editor. The financial problems of *Barron's* continued. In November 1954 Davenport resigned to return to *Fortune* magazine. Kerby, urged by Kilgore to "make it or kill it," named Robert Bleiberg editor. Bleiberg, a graduate in economics from Columbia who earned his master's in business administration at New York University, had joined *Barron's* as associate editor in 1946. He and Kerby agreed to turn *Barron's* into a "magazine for money managers." Kerby closed down *Barron's* press in Boston and took the printing to the *Journal*'s facility at Chicopee, Massachusetts. The new editorial formula worked. By 1955 *Barron's* circulation went to 62,669 from a low of 25,915 in 1941.

Advertising linage in 1955 increased to 493,265 lines. By 1973 *Barron's* was also printed at Riverside, California.

Kilgore expanded the responsibilities of wizened, hard-bitten William Grimes despite the fact that his editorial page underwent the least change during the Kilgore Revolution. Although editorial content improved under Grimes, he steadfastly maintained past policies and altered the format not at all. *Journal* editorials continued to be staunchly conservative, pro-Republican, and, under Grimes, somewhat more acerbic and parochial than under Woodlock or Hamilton. Kilgore delegated authority and left policy to Grimes and Korsmeyer, but Lombard gently nudged Grimes into taking several European trips to broaden his perspective. This ploy succeeded. Grimes appeared more relaxed after his trips away, his editorials crisper and more urbane. Also, his assistant, Vermont Royster, contributed more and more to the writing in addition to making up the editorial page.

The *Journal* continued to be a stern but fair critic of President Truman, saying on January 5, 1950, that the President had mellowed in his State of the Union message, an improvement the paper welcomed. "We are glad, and we believe that generally the country will be glad, that Mr. Truman recognizes that those who differ with him may be quite as unselfish and patriotic as himself." The *Journal* emphasized, however, that the President's change for the better was in style, not substance. "Politely, but firmly, Mr. Truman insists on his big-government welfare state program. With equal politeness, we hope that the program will continue to be resisted."

Bill Grimes was on course ideologically so far as Barney Kilgore and the directors were concerned, but in June 1950, when Grimes was on one of those European trips recommended by Lombard, Kilgore and Kerby, assisted by Royster, completed the typographical phase of the Kilgore Revolution by redesigning Grimes's editorial page. Henceforth, all editorials would be set in two columns, indented measure, and the paper's editorial masthead, which by definition ("the top of a mast," a nautical term) belonged at the upper left of the page in an orthodox publication, was relegated to the right-hand bottom, a profanation and defilement that Grimes learned about after he returned to New York.

The changes were completed as the month ended, and, by modern typographical standards and ordinary canons of art, they were beautiful. William Henry Chamberlain's column would run under a two-column head, as would contributed columns and reviews. Some of the new two-column heads on the editorial page read remarkably like the sometimes irreverent A-heds introduced by Kilgore and Kerby on page one. Readers' letters were provided with a two-column headline and more space. Cartoons and drawings were introduced, with a cartoon implanted into the "Pepper and Salt" humor column, again under a two-column head, where it was thus guaranteed to appear each day. The new editorial page was clean, visually cheerful, easy to read, and would endure in essentially the same form into 1982.

When Bill Grimes got back, a small bundle of fury, he stormed and protested, but Kilgore and Kerby were accustomed to that, and they firmly believed that Grimes really did not oppose the change in his heart. After all, he had introduced many changes himself, and Kilgore and Kerby revered him as a friend and mentor. Such considerations, of course, did not make the slightest difference to Bill Grimes, but he bowed to the changes and thereafter referred to the editorial page as "Kerby's goddam picture page" whenever Kerby was around.

The lead editorial on July 3, 1950, made no mention of the revised format but proceeded at once to disapprove of President Truman's June 30 order that sent ground forces from Japan to Korea to repel invaders crossing the 38th parallel from the north to attack South Korea and that sent the Navy to blockade Korea. The *Journal* wanted no further American involvement abroad, but since the country had been presented with a fait accompli, it believed the American forces should have all the support needed for a quick victory and withdrawal. It assumed that the Soviet Union was backing the North Korean Communists and thus concluded that no quick victory would be possible without an immediate all-out effort.

As usual, the paper asserted its right to second-guess the President, even on foreign policy: "There is in this country an apparently dominant idea that one ought not to criticize in the matter of foreign affairs and particularly when foreign affairs are in a critical state," the *Journal* conceded. "We can think of no idea which has done greater damage. . . . If there had been a check when Mr. Roosevelt and his advisors were dealing with the Russians in setting up post-war settlements, if there had been some discussion of Yalta, for instance, if the minority had been allowed even to know what was taking place, there might today have been no Korean crisis."

The paper praised President Truman's choice of General Douglas MacArthur as commander in chief of American forces in Korea and even accepted the fact that they would be under the United Nations flag, but it warned again on July 13 that the Russians would obstruct any quick settlement. "It ought not to be necessary to warn. Watch out for deals with the Russians. Certainly all our experience has shown the futility and dangers of accords with the Soviets. . . . If, by some miracle, the Russians would agree to persuade the North Koreans to go back above the 38th parallel, that would be welcome news indeed, that is, it would be welcome news if the withdrawal took place. . . . When the Russians say they will do something, it doesn't mean they will do it."

In November the *Journal* published a special series of articles on possible war with Red China as a result of the American presence in Korea. The series was written from Washington by Ray Cromley, who in World War II served as an American liaison officer with the Chinese Communist Army. It carried a "precede"—a brief introduction set off from the story—saying, "This article is not intended to imply that there will be a war with Red China." In an editorial, however, the paper warned that intervention in Korea by Red China "could mean that the United States may be forced to choose between the alternative of interminable border war, which will keep a number of troops tied up, or a first magnitude war against China itself, which certainly could promise no ending for a long, long time." The United States could have avoided it all by staying out of Korea, the paper continued. "Thus the United States put itself in a position where the next fateful decision—whether there will be a big war or a little war—was left to our enemies."

It became increasingly clear that the dilemma the paper had described would come to pass. On December 4 it spoke of the threatened extension of the war and directed its fire at the true enemy. "Most surely the American people do not want to fight anyone whatsoever. Nor do we believe that a general world war is inevitable. . . . But if there must be a war, then it should be fought with Russia, the inspiration and the brains of world aggression. It would be silly to fight China or any other Russian satellite. Undoubtedly that suggestion will shock some of our readers," said the *Journal* with an excess of understatement, "but we think logic will support it."

Barney Kilgore and his executives and editors of *The Wall Street Journal* were concerned with more than Korea, President Truman's efforts to regulate the internal economy, the implementation of the Marshall Plan, and the improving stock market during the summer and fall of 1950. Seeking a way to launch a Midwest edition of the *Journal,* Kilgore reportedly discussed with officials of the *Chicago Daily News,* an afternoon paper, the possibility of publishing such an edition on *Daily News* presses. But in May, Bill Kerby provided Kilgore with an alternative Barney was quick to seize.

Kerby's close friend Hollis K. Thayer, a partner in the New York brokerage firm of Dominick and Dominick, wished to know if Dow Jones would be interested in purchasing the *New York Journal of Commerce* and the *Chicago Journal of Commerce* from the Ridder Publishing Company. The Dominick firm had been engaged to find a buyer. "My first question was whether it was an all-or-none package," Kerby recalled. "I thought Dow Jones might have an interest in the Chicago paper, but the *New York Journal of Commerce* was too specialized a trade publication to be marriageable with *The Wall Street Journal.* He replied that he thought the Ridders would consider such an offer."

Kerby told Thayer that he would check with Barney Kilgore and report back. He reached Kilgore at his home in Princeton that night; Barney was enthusiastic. *The Wall Street Journal* was selling about 25,000 copies in the midwestern states at that time, mostly sent by air at high cost. The *Chicago*

Journal of Commerce, founded by Knowlton L. Ames in 1920, had been sold in 1947 to the Ridder brothers, publishers of a group of newspapers. John D. Ames, editor and publisher at the time of the sale, remained under the Ridders and would be interested in staying. The Chicago publication had a circulation of 31,413. Kilgore instructed Kerby to continue negotiating with Thayer and the Ridders while he undertook getting a favorable vote from the directors. In December, after months of work, Bill Kerby presented the proposed acquisition to the board. The cost was $1.5 million.

Laurence Lombard, who had urged the move for a Southwest edition and discussed a possible Midwest edition with Kilgore months previously, hesitated because of the large amount of capital involved. Kerby urged that "we would be buying the Midwest franchise and a clear field nationally." Kerby also pointed out that the purchase of the Chicago newspaper would include its contracts for newsprint, a condition so important that he had insisted on its inclusion in the sales contract. Lombard was satisfied, and the directors unanimously approved the purchase.

The proposed deal was not well received among some members of *The Wall Street Journal* staff, especially Editor Bill Grimes. Grimes and some others in the news department thought that enormous losses would be incurred, thus endangering the entire company. Kilgore and Kerby were trying to expand too fast, they believed. A few days later, as Kerby was leaving his office with a check for $1,500,000 to purchase the *Chicago Journal of Commerce,* he found Editor Grimes "waiting around the corner." Grimes was seething. "Bill," he said in a voice taut with anger, "I want you to stop by the newsroom on your way out. Those people are all your friends. Many you hired. You know their wives and children. Then think to yourself, 'I'm on my way to ruin Dow Jones and put all these people out of work.' "

Kerby went on, shaken but sure that Dow Jones was making the right move. He might have recalled one of Barney Kilgore's axioms: "Listen to everybody, take an interest in what they say, but do the job your way." Or another: "There never is a good time to do anything. So you do it when you have a chance."

During the final week of December 1950, Bill Kerby led to Chicago the task force of *Wall Street Journal* editors and production and advertising men who would take over the *Journal of Commerce.* Kerby brought Joe Ackell to work with Al Shuman, the production manager for the *Journal of Commerce* who would continue in his job. Buren McCormack would supervise the news operations, assisted by Bob Bottorff, who was being shifted from San Francisco to become managing editor in Chicago. Robert Feemster would supervise the reorganization and coordination of advertising and circulation. Kerby was in charge of the transition staff and would give special attention to personnel problems and the impact of the Dow Jones takeover on the Chicago and Midwest business community. Kerby brought with him from New York the

The man who would realize Casey Hogate's dream of making *The Wall Street Journal* the country's only truly national daily was Bernard Kilgore. A gifted yet unassuming man, Kilgore remained a shirt-sleeved editor even after becoming the *Journal*'s highest-ranking executive. Said the paper at his death, "If you ask what he did, you need only to look at this newspaper you are reading."

Weather Forecast

THE WALL STREET JOURNAL.

Copyright, 1941, by Dow, Jones & Co., Inc.

VOL. CXVIII. NO. 135 — NEW YORK, MONDAY, DECEMBER 8, 1941 — SEVEN CEN

War With Japan—

U. S. Industry's Sole Objective: Arms Production Speedu
Congress Prepares To Act; Tax Bill Will Be Rushed;
N. Y. Stock Exchange To Open As Usual Today, Says Schrar

Washington Sees Fight on 2 Oceans And 3 Continents

Expects Half the National Income Allocated to Army, Navy — Labor Registration

More Curbs on Vital Materials

By Eugene S. Duffield

What's News—

Business and Finance

TRADE REPERCUSSIONS of the outbreak of hostilities between Japan and the United States swept over the nation's entire economy. Industrially, this development meant reshaping of the productive machine to assure maximum output for the enemy's defeat. Congressional leaders prepared to start work immediately on a new tax program to supply the sinews of war. The U. S. Treasury halted all financial, commercial transactions with Japan.

World-Wide

Japan Attacks Hawaii, Damage and Loss of Life Reported Heavy; Japan Declares War on U. S., England

Roosevelt to Address Congress Today

Tokyo Envoy Delivers Reply to U. S.; Hull: "Infamous," Filled With Lies

Reds Claim Gains on All Fronts

British, Axis Tanks in Major Battle

We Have a Duty

[An Editorial]

The business and financial discussion which customarily appears on this page in Monday morning's issue of The Wall Street Journal was written Saturday evening and given to the compositors yesterday. As the galley proof reached the editorial room, press association wires carried the flash that the Japanese had attacked Hawaii.

In that moment, the events of last week seemed suddenly to have been removed to some remote era of antiquity. The things that business and finance discussed last week seem now to have no relation to tomorrow nor to the many days to come after tomorrow.

There is a stark, horrible reality that American territory has been attacked. Japan has declared a state of war exists between her and the United States.

Every citizen has and knows his duty. It will be heavy for all. The sacrifices will be particularly heavy for the business and financial community of America.

We say that the sacrifices will be made. The duty will be performed.

New, Stiffer Levies Now Are Imminent

Will Fall on Firms, Individuals Alike Based on How Much Must Traffic Bear

By Fred Warner Neal

All Consumption Curb Due To Be Stiffened; Scarcity List Will Grow

Vast Supplies of Ships and Shells, Bombs a Bombers, Oil and Gasoline Will Be Essenti Outline Already Visible

By William F. Kerby

Market Officials Expect No Trouble

But Will Be On Hand Early to Study Situation — SEC to Meet This Morning

By B. H. McCormack

U.S. Well Stocked With Far Eastern Commodities, But Curbs Will Tighten

By John O'Riley

Kilgore's efforts to change the appearance and content of the *Journal* came together in the December 8, 1941, issue, a successful blend of analytical and comprehensive coverage of the Japanese attack on Pearl Harbor.

Above: The Dow Jones news-ticker newsroom about 1940. In the foreground is Ed Costenbader, whom Richard Whitney, president of the New York Stock Exchange, phoned in 1938 to confess to fraud. **Below:** The *Journal* newsroom about 1950, the copy desk in the background. Sam Lesch sits at the national news desk in right foreground.

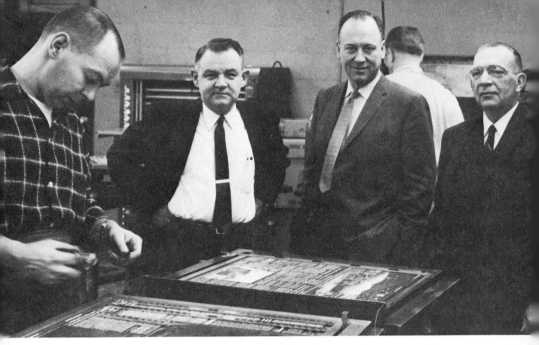

From right: William Kerby, Barney Kilgore, and Vermont Royster are on hand as a printer makes up pages in the composing room of the Washington plant, probably as the first issue of the *National Observer* (February 4, 1962) went to press.

"What did you expect a financial wizard to look like?"

Left: Since 1950 panel cartoons have graced the "Pepper and Salt" corner of the editorial page, a change instituted by Kilgore, Kerby, and Royster while Editor Bill Grimes was away in Europe. **Opposite page:** Buren McCormack (center) inspects a first-off *Journal* as it comes off the press. A key figure in the Kilgore Revolution, McCormack was later named executive vice-president and a Dow Jones director.

William F. Kerby (left), Kilgore's right-hand man, succeeded to the Dow Jones-*Journal* helm in 1966 and presided over Dow Jones's entry into satellite communications. Vermont Connecticut Royster (right), shown here in 1953. A Southern gentleman well versed in the classics, Royster followed Grimes as editor and as writer of the famous column "Thinking Things Over."

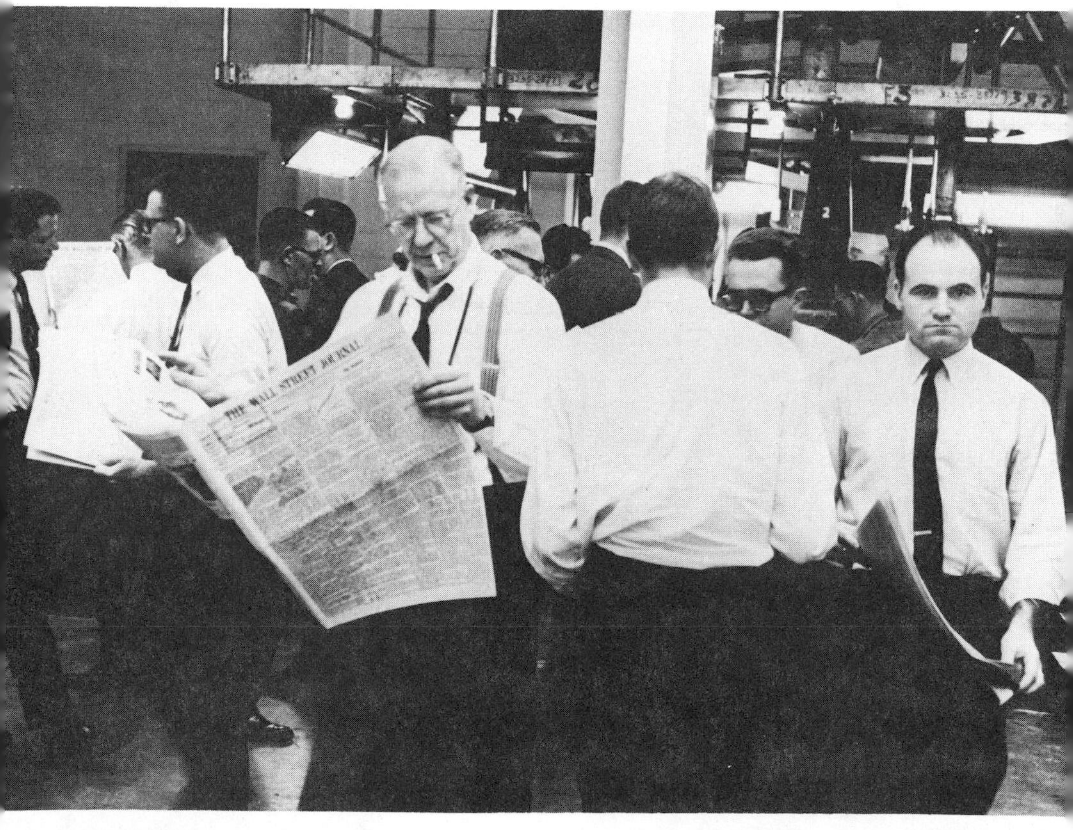

Warren H. Phillips (top left), Dow Jones president and chief executive officer since 1975, served as a correspondent in Europe and was Kerby's chosen successor. Peter R. Kann (bottom left), associate publisher of the *Journal*, won a Pulitzer in 1972 as a correspondent in Asia. Ray Shaw (top right), former director of development, was elected president and chief operating officer of Dow Jones in 1979. The *Journal*'s editor is now Robert L. Bartley (bottom right), who initiated the paper's op-ed page and won a Pulitzer for his editorials in 1980.

Wall Street, 1980, with a view of the facade of the New York Stock Exchange, 11 Wall Street, from Federal Hall. A bronze plaque in the wall of the building marks the birthplace of *The Wall Street Journal* at 15 Wall Street. (Courtesy New York Stock Exchange)

The trading floor of the New York Stock Exchange, showing the new look of the "Big Board." Video screen–equipped trading posts were installed early in 1980 to help brokers handle an increasingly heavy volume of sales. An electronic system provides quotations, transmits orders, and records sales. (Courtesy New York Stock Exchange)

new page-one logotype, *The Chicago Journal of Commerce Edition of The Wall Street Journal*.

The new owners were taking no chances. From past experience they remembered that angry subscribers to the Dallas edition at first demanded to be put back on the New York subscription list of *The Wall Street Journal*, even if it meant getting the news a day late. And in Texas, the New York paper had not supplanted a local business paper, as it was doing in Chicago. Chauvinistic Chicagoans, with a long history of disdain for New York, might be even harder to please. Thus the decision was made to retain the *Chicago Journal of Commerce* name for as long as necessary. "One of our fears," Kerby wrote years later, "was that the Chicago business community would deeply resent the disappearance of its local business publication."

On the last night of the year, the New Yorkers gave themselves a sedate New Year's Eve party with Shuman, the sole *Journal of Commerce* man included. The party broke up promptly at midnight. A few hours later Kerby and his group entered the headquarters of their newest acquisition, a beat-up red brick building at 12 Grand Avenue on the Near North Side of Chicago. Kerby himself carried the well-wrapped logotype that would lead off the page-one layout of the newly merged newspaper that night, bearing the dateline January 2, 1951.

The members of the New York crew who had not previously visited the Grand Avenue building found the physical setup nauseatingly dismal. The floors sagged and the typesetting equipment was old, jury-rigged with wire and wood supports, and oddly scattered over the composing-room floor. Al Shuman explained the strange placement of the linotype machines. "Simple. They have to rest on floor beams; otherwise they'd fall into the basement." Ackell clucked sadly to Kerby as they inspected the place. Kerby assured him that the people back home were aware of the situation and that he would have full support in seeking out a new printing facility. It didn't take Joe Ackell long to solve that problem once publication was well under way. By February he had found space at 650 Washington Street and was completing installation of a used Octuple press bought from the *Baltimore Sun*. The new press was running by February 13, as were Dow Jones–built mailing machines capable of folding, wrapping, and addressing 11,000 papers an hour.

By February 13 the entire format of the Midwest edition had been revised to conform to other *Journal* editions. Joe Ackell praised the work of Al Shuman and his men, who kept things going at Grand Avenue "by devoted nursing and ingenious in-house repairs," Kerby wrote. There was one problem, however, that neither Ackell nor Shuman could solve. The *Journal*'s composing room was on the second floor, across the alley from the rooms of a hotel much used by prostitutes. The *Journal* was a morning paper, and both the printers and occupants of the whorehouse worked mostly at night. The shades were rarely drawn, and the printers regarded time to observe the diversions in the windows as part of their fringe benefits, and refused to relinquish it.

Kerby, Ackell, and Feemster sought to retain as many of the *Journal of Commerce* workers as possible, but there was a sizable exodus from the editorial department. The special approach to *Wall Street Journal* writing and editing style proved as difficult for the staff in Chicago as it had for the New York staff years before. "The axe fell hard," wrote Ray Vicker, a Chicagoan who mastered the Kilgore style in a hurry and would become a distinguished *Journal* foreign correspondent. "For weeks the top brass of D. J. remained in Chicago working from about 8 A.M. to midnight," Vicker remembered. "I can still see Kilgore in his shirt sleeves [Kilgore arrived later] studying a galley proof, Kerby running up the stairs like a copyboy from the print shop to the news room, McCormack trying to convince a pressman he knew all about presses. For weeks these guys were getting out the paper, having themselves a ball as they were doing fundamental things that hadn't occupied their attention in years."

The New York executives realized that the Chicago edition had to be the best New York could create or the Kilgore Revolution would not advance to become truly national. San Francisco and Dallas were not real precedents. The New York brass taught the remaining Chicago people their kind of journalism, and in Ray Vicker's opinion, they learned a few things, too. "They brought in the New York influence, with a certain scorn of provincialism, a strong belief in sophistication and much more concern for the way things are written; and they brought in their belief that Washington is the pole around which the world revolves. They learned something from the Chicago influence which believes in the invincibility of American industry and business, the wastefulness of governments and the inefficiency of everything having to do with government. They also learned something about the provinces, enabling them to have a really national slant."

Robert Bottorff, an experienced, hard-nosed financial newsman, took over in Chicago when the New Yorkers departed. Bottorff was an excellent choice for the task of staff reorganization, and his assistant, John A. McWethy, would become known throughout the Dow Jones organization as a teacher of the new journalism and a recruiter of fine talent. In later years Chicago people widely and capably staffed Dow Jones operations and were known as graduates of "the McWethy School of Journalism."

Hogate had hired McWethy during the war years and sent him to Cleveland after training on the *Journal*'s New York staff. By 1945 McWethy was made bureau chief in Chicago. He joined the *Journal*'s Midwest edition staff as assistant managing editor at the start of the new operations in January 1951 and became managing editor in 1957. In February 1971 McWethy was severely injured in an automobile accident, and it was feared he would never walk nor work again. But eight months later he was back on the job, a quadriplegic but able to assume his duties as a result of his courage and determination and the aid he received at Chicago's famed Rehabilitation Institute. In 1977 McWethy retired to live in Arizona.

On January 2, 1951, The *Chicago Journal of Commerce Edition of The Wall Street Journal* bowed on schedule. All four editions of *The Wall Street Journal* that day carried a lead editorial entitled "A Newspaper's Philosophy," written and signed by William H. Grimes. To salute the edition Grimes wrote:

> The new publishers of the *Chicago Journal of Commerce* will not change its basic character. It will remain a business newspaper. There will be changes in makeup and the presentation of the news. We cannot forecast what they will be for they will be determined largely by the wishes and the suggestions of readers.
>
> What we can tell you now—indeed what we think is due you—is an account of the principles and standards which guide us in the making of a business philosophy.
>
> A business newspaper must be two things at one and the same time. It must be specialized. Yet the interests and activities of its editors must be as diverse as the American landscape. The editors are specialists in the way a medical diagnostician has a certain function, but to perform that function he must have an accurate and detailed knowledge of human anatomy. Just so the business editor must have access to all the news. His specialty is selection and treatment.

The editorial ran for several hundred words, many of them meant to demolish myths about business editors and newspapers. Grimes then discussed businessmen and "Big Business"; he saw in them a common denominator, or mutuality of interests.

> We think that so far as information wants is concerned business is universal. The information on which the great automobile manufacturer acts is the same information which influences a man who buys trucks. If retail trade in New York booms or slumps, there is a man in San Francisco who wants to know the whys and wherefores.
>
> It does not pay to be too certain about anything, but we think we have pretty strong evidence that business is a national community. We publish *The Wall Street Journal* in New York and we publish it also in Dallas and in San Francisco. Each of those editions is essentially the same newspaper. The readers seem to like it that way.
>
> It was said that a national newspaper is impossible in the United States because the country is too vast; that the mere problem of distribution would be insuperable. We do have a national circulation. We have been printing in three cities. Now we have added a fourth, and that is something to which we have long looked forward. We can now deliver to most parts of the country on the date of publication.

In his concluding paragraphs, Grimes pointed out that the readers included all kinds of people, not just businessmen. "They like a publication which presents the meaningful news and news interpretation of the day, which presents them without bias, which omits the fires, the assaults and the murders. . . . On our editorial page we make no pretense of walking down the middle of the road. Our comments and interpretations are made from a definite point of view. We oppose all infringements on individual rights whether they stem from attempts at private monopoly, labor union monopoly or from an over-growing government. We are not much interested in labels, but if we were to choose one, we would say that we are radical. Just as radical as the Christian doctrine."

The day's editorials covered general subjects also. The *Journal* happily summarized 1950 as a year "of unprecedented prosperity. The statistics look wonderful. The wage earners' incomes are at record levels and so, too, are business profits. That mystic figure 'the gross national product,' which is supposed to measure everything, is fantastic. Anywhere you look for the statistics of prosperity, you can find them." But, of course, "the trouble is these statistics don't tell very much. They all measure something against the yardstick of the dollar and the dollar has become a rubber yardstick that gives you a different reading every time you look at it."

The *Journal* also pointed out that its new Midwest edition would cover 14 states with a combined population of 48.5 million. By June 1950, as a result of the Chicago expansion, the total circulation of *The Wall Street Journal* would reach 148,241.

The Chicago newspapers and the country's daily press ignored the *Journal*'s Chicago expansion move, but the news magazines *Newsweek* and *Time* both took notice. *Newsweek* on January 8 published an Ed Wergeles portrait of Barney Kilgore with a story and interview on the Chicago venture. Kilgore was characterized as "the brilliant 42-year-old publisher who has pushed *The Wall Street Journal* to its present eminence in covering the news on a national level" and was quoted as declaging that Chicago changes in format would not be accelerated. "Only through very slow change, its new publisher promised, would it ever become a mirror of the most successful business-paper format of them all—*The Wall Street Journal.*"

Time magazine also used the Chicago scene as the occasion for again summarizing Kilgore achievements at *The Wall Street Journal,* concluding, "Ten years ago it was a worthy but dull financial sheet. He turned the W.S.J. into one of the best U.S. newspapers."

Two young staff members of *The Wall Street Journal* who would find their way to the top of the increasingly acclaimed news staff moved up that fateful summer and fall of 1950. Warren H. Phillips, who would become chairman and chief executive, was named chief of the paper's London bureau. Vermont Royster, destined to become editor, was tapped for permanent assignment in New York by Editor Grimes. Grimes had requested Royster from the

Washington bureau on a temporary basis, but by mid-1950 he knew he had found the future editor of the editorial page, despite the fact that he and "Roy" argued occasionally over policy.

Royster lost one round during the Truman-Dewey campaign in 1948. He had written a column suggesting that Governor Dewey might lose the election. Although the column was scheduled for the editorial page, Grimes killed it, saying it would make the *Journal* look silly. "After the election, I used to tell him, 'Damn it, Mr. Grimes, you cost me a Pulitzer Prize,' " Royster remembered. " 'I would have won for being the only reporter who saw Harry Truman had a chance!' "

Vermont Connecticut Royster, born in North Carolina in 1913, was descended from Colonial settlers in Tidewater Virginia, a great-great-grandfather serving as an overseer of the famed Byrd plantations. Vermont Royster was named for a grandfather who thought his progeny could best be distinguished from each other if designated by names of states. Royster's father was a lawyer and former teacher of Greek and Latin at the University of North Carolina. By the time Royster enrolled in the university, where his father was then teaching law, he had been well tutored in classical languages and had prepped at Webb School in Tennessee. He majored in English literature and history while continuing his language studies. When Bill Grimes discovered him, Royster already possessed the most graceful writing style in the English essay tradition of any *Journal* writer, with the possible exception of Thomas Woodlock. Grimes concentrated on teaching Royster journalistic techniques.

Young Royster, a Southern gentleman and former naval officer who served as a commander of destroyer escort vessels in World War II in both the Atlantic and the Pacific, had an almost perfect background for editorial writing. After Grimes schooled him in pragmatic method, Grimes initiated a new policy for the *Journal* by sending Royster out as an editorial-page representative to cover the congressional elections of 1950.

Royster's reports on what appeared to be a hopeless and dull campaign by Everett McKinley Dirksen to win a U.S. Senate seat by ousting incumbent Democratic Senator Scott Lucas in an intensely Democratic year provided *Wall Street Journal* readers with some of the best political reportage they would find. Royster caught Dirksen in the hot, dusty cornfields and ripening orchards of southern Illinois in October and followed the curly-haired political "evangelist" into the sweltering town of Vienna, Illinois:

> The crowd was mostly in shirtsleeves and galluses. They had come from all over Johnson County to eat catfish, to talk and to listen. The men had come from the field in the early afternoon, for many were not shaven, and nearly all were in their working clothes. The women were aproned, for they had to fry the fish and set the long tables inside the big frame meeting hall, but beneath the aprons they wore bright print dresses, mindful of the festivities. The passel of children were in

> T-shirts or simple pinafores, save for one youngster in a white shirt and his Sunday suit.
>
> The evangelist came, appropriately, in a rush and a cloud of dust. Beside his own car, there were two carloads of followers and the inevitable pickup truck equipped to take his voice and spread it around the countryside. Spread it loud and spread it far was what he asked. Everett McKinley Dirksen had come to wrestle with a live devil . . . and he wanted the countryside to pay attention.

Of Dirksen's style, Royster commented, "Bing Crosby could not have been more suavely folksy . . . Billy Sunday more astute at playing on emotions. . . . While the hour wore on (Dirksen had his coat off now), it grew clear that the spirit had come upon Gideon, and his trumpet blew louder. The people saw . . . the devils with whom he wrestled, and they could see too that they were strong devils because his tie was slipped away from his collar and his hair grew ruffled as he wrestled."

Dirksen had blown a lone trumpet, Royster said in his coverage of the Illinois campaign, but it was loud enough to bring down Senator Scott Lucas. Dirksen thereafter would charm the U.S. senators with his silvery tones, and Vermont Royster, having charmed Bill Grimes with his own style, would write distinguished editorials, become senior associate editor of the *Journal* on June 6, 1951, and win the Pulitzer Prize on May 3, 1953, for the general excellence of his 1952 editorials. The citation read, "for distinguished editorial writing . . . the test of excellence being clearness of style, moral purpose, sound reasoning, and power to influence public opinion." It was the paper's second Pulitzer, the first being won by Royster's boss, Bill Grimes.

In the summer of 1947 Bill Kerby hired a future reporter, correspondent, and editor freshly graduated cum laude from Queens College, New York. He was Warren Henry Phillips, born in New York City and educated in the city's public schools. The son of a World War I aerial gunner and Manhattan clothing manufacturer, Phillips would become the first native New Yorker to attain the top Dow Jones position as chairman and chief executive officer. Like Barney Kilgore, Phillips applied to the Columbia University Graduate School of Journalism after receiving his B.A. degree but was denied admission. And like Vermont Royster, Phillips was refused a job by every other daily newspaper in New York before he applied to the *Journal.* Kerby really had nothing available when Phillips applied, but he liked the cut of the tall, soft-spoken graduate, and gave him a job double-checking galley proofs.

Phillips first worked under the guidance of Betty Donnelly, a Syracuse University journalism graduate who had been hired by Barney Kilgore as a copyreader in the war years and was reading page-one copy, and Samuel C. Lesch, the paper's national news editor and later managing editor of the Dow Jones News Service. Lesch was famed as a teacher of Dow Jones news personnel. Phillips became a rewrite man under Lesch and soon wrote the *Journal*'s leading column, "What's News." It was Phillips's ambition to become a foreign correspondent, but the paper had no such opening, so he departed the staff in February 1949 to take a job with the Army newspaper, *Stars and Stripes,* based near Frankfurt, Germany.

Soon, at the suggestion of Managing Editor Henry Gemmill, Phillips was sending page-one leader stories back to the *Journal* on a free-lance basis. Late in 1949 Joseph E. Evans, foreign editor of the paper, gave Phillips a full-time job as correspondent in Germany. He covered the lifting of the Berlin blockade, the end of the military government, and the establishment at Bonn of the first freely elected German government, under Konrad Adenauer. Then he was sent to London in January 1950 to help cover the British election in which Clement Attlee defeated Winston Churchill. Phillips worked with George Ormsby, former teacher in the London School of Economics and veteran chief of the *Journal*'s London bureau.

Following Ormsby's death from a heart attack the same year, Phillips became chief of the bureau. Albert E. Jeffcoat was sent out from New York to aid him. Phillips was 24 and Jeffcoat was about the same age. They were relatively inexperienced as foreign correspondents—Jeffcoat had only a year in New York as a reporter—but both knew something of special *Journal* requirements. They searched for the offbeat page-one stories needed and wrote a "London Cable" column modeled after Kilgore's "Washington Wire." It was created mostly by culling news from the London and continental newspapers. At the same time there was also a great deal of news about the British economic crisis and progress of the Marshall Plan to be reported. The London office also was responsible for the opening of the London market, the first dispatch on the Dow Jones wire to New York each morning. That was mostly handled by Frank Linge, an English veteran in the office.

In London Phillips wrote a series of editorial-page articles on the Marshall Plan, collaborating on some of them with Charles R. Hargrove, the paper's veteran Paris correspondent. He shocked some people by reporting on August 15, 1950, that Marshall Plan officials doubted the plan would ward off inflation in Europe, nor did they believe it would solve the mounting economic problems in England. Britain had the largest balance in hand of any Marshall Plan country, Phillips wrote, and added, "but if this money is now to be used to finance additional government spending in the form of armaments, Britain might just as well print and put into circulation an additional $585 million in pound notes [the amount of its counterpart funds under the Marshall Plan]. It would be no more of an invitation to inflation."

Phillips continued to report on England's postwar rearmament, as well as covering stories in France, Spain, Italy, Greece, and Turkey. In a series of articles, he and Jeffcoat followed the efforts of Churchill's new Tory government to assault the national industrial complex created by the Clement Attlee Labor government, a tougher job than Churchill and his followers had anticipated, they wrote. By 1951, Phillips foresaw increasing chances for success of the Marshall Plan in England, but he warned that the prop which the Marshall Plan had given to the British economy could be rudely removed because another prop, "British Socialism," was being substituted. "The short run outlook holds the seeds of economic crisis," Phillips predicted. "At best the British will be getting by on day-to-day expedients. In the long run—it is a grim reckoning—not recovery that awaits them. The high cost of Socialism is sapping the country's competitive strength, as will be seen on the day a buyer's market returns to world trade." It was a remarkably prescient view.

At the end of 1951 Phillips transferred to New York to become foreign editor. Returning home with him was Mrs. Barbara Phillips, formerly Barbara Ann Thomas of Cape Charles, Virginia, whom Warren married in London earlier that year. Jeffcoat took over the London bureau. On September 7, 1954, Jeffcoat won a worldwide scoop for the *Journal* on the Ford Motor Company's plan to go public. The home office alerted Jeffcoat to the possibility of an important Ford story and instructed him to find Henry Ford II, who was believed to be in Paris. Jeffcoat found Ford at the bar of the Ritz Hotel in Paris and got the story. A year later Jeffcoat joined the Ford Motor Company in organizing its first company stockholder relations department.

Warren Phillips continued his interest in foreign-news coverage, as foreign editor, as news editor, and again as managing editor, first in Chicago and then in New York in 1957. Phillips was managing editor when the *Journal*'s star writer, Henry Gemmill, went to London to beef up foreign coverage in 1958. Later, when Henry Gemmill moved to Washington as bureau chief, Phillips assigned another star, Ray Vicker, then the paper's roving foreign correspondent, to London to take charge. Philip Geyelin went out as Vicker's assistant.

Phillips wanted top men in London and Washington, but London office accommodations were definitely on the modest side, according to Vicker. "We were on a third floor [just off Fleet Street] in a tiny corner office with room for three desks, two news tickers and one filing cabinet," Vicker recalled. "When a drawer of the filing cabinet was open, it would block Frank Linge's access to his desk." Ray Vicker, the paper's most widely traveled and best-known foreign-news writer, would become European news editor in 1960, and in 1980 senior national correspondent based in San Francisco after 20 years abroad.

In January 1951 the *Journal*'s lead editorial called for a foreign-policy debate by the presidential candidates, saying that "a workable foreign policy can be forged only in the heat of debate." It chose Senator Robert Taft, the Ohio Republican, as its champion in the contest. "The purpose is to construct a foreign policy that will be workable within American strength and which will look toward peace. Senator Taft has made a most important contribution."

Senator Taft had declared "that the people of the United States were ready to accept limited war, but not inevitable war."

Even in supporting Taft, the *Journal* was wary, saying, "Limited wars do not stay limited wars." Senator Taft would not use ground forces in Asia, and the *Journal* agreed with that: "One cannot forget that this country intervened in Korea with the declared intention of not using ground forces." The paper attacked President Truman's domestic policies once again. "The government planners," it said, "have come up with a new anti-inflation proposal, more government spending. If this sounds like economic nonsense, it is."

Bill Grimes, the frail, feisty editor, and his assistant, Vermont Royster, not much bigger but more complacent and loaded with southern charm, could agree on lambasting Truman's domestic policies, but they did not agree on Korea. Grimes favored Truman's policy generally until April 11, when President Truman relieved General MacArthur of all Far Eastern commands in their dispute over Korean war policy. Editor Grimes was dismayed and strongly supported the general, while Royster insisted that although MacArthur had the right to tactical control of his forces, he had overstepped his powers in seeking to make national policy. The President was right in removing the general, he concluded. Grimes finally bowed to the thinking of his ex-Navy officer after Royster agreed to present both viewpoints, but Grimes promised grimly that they would be swamped with angry letters from both sides. He was right.

On April 12 Royster's editorial on MacArthur began: "The situation which brought about the dismissal of General MacArthur ought never to have arisen." The United States should have stayed out of Korea in the first place, the editorial contended, warning the Republican right not to go all out for the general. "It seems to us that it would be stupid for the Republicans to do as some of them seem to threaten, which is to attach themselves as the tail to General MacArthur's kite without first considering where that kite is to be flown." The following day, the *Journal* declared that the United States should not get into a war with Red China for the benefit of MacArthur's good name, but it added that President Truman's policy, proposing no alternative toward a drift to the same place, didn't make sense either.

"The mail came in by bags full," Royster remembered in later years. "Everybody was angry, those pro-Truman and those pro-MacArthur." It was Royster's duty to read the letters and respond. "I learned a lot by reading those letters," Royster said. "I learned of the great diversity of *Wall Street Journal* readers. The letters came from all over the country, from those in every field of economic endeavor and from women readers, teachers, politicians and retired persons. I learned to understand the kind of readership we had."

By September 1951 the *Journal* itself was considering alternatives. Editor Grimes assigned himself to go to Paris to talk to General Dwight D.

Eisenhower, NATO commander. Grimes wrote on October 2 that it would be months before Eisenhower would make up his mind, but he added that Ike might become available for the presidency. "The reason he can't speak out now is that he has a job to do that only he can do." Weeks later the *Journal* reported that Eisenhower would not leave his present post in Europe to seek the presidential nomination, but it editorialized, "If the Republican Party drafts him, he will run for the presidency"—a nice distinction.

The *Journal* thought that President Truman also would run. While it said on January 28, 1952, that Washington correspondents "seem more and more inclined to the view that President Truman will not be a candidate for the nomination this year," the *Journal* wasn't buying it. It thought that Truman was playing coy politics (Eisenhower evidently was not). Said the *Journal* about Truman, "When one sees a fowl which waddles when it walks but swims gracefully and gives out a quacking call, one is justified in thinking he has seen a duck."

The Wall Street Journal firmly supported General Eisenhower for president by the time of the Republican convention in Chicago in July. There had been stories, editorials, and a profile from Paris written by Edward Hughes and Jeffcoat that didn't tell readers much about Ike's political views. On July 1 the paper examined the question of whether Dwight D. Eisenhower was a conservative. "Mr. Eisenhower understands the meaning of the term conservative," it said. "One of that philosophy neither opposes progress nor does he sit up at night plotting how a few people can grind the majority under their heels. He wants to build on what experience has proved good."

Dwight Eisenhower himself said, "I don't mind what they call me. I remember my mother conserved things in the fall—not the cockleburs and sunflowers, but the good things out of the garden."

The *Journal* urged the Republican platform builders to make domestic policy the main campaign issue rather than foreign policy. It reminded the delegates that in 1948 they formed a closed corporation for hard-liners and reached a new high in bickering: "If the Republicans have not learned their lesson and if they repeat their mistakes, the result can hardly be different." But the Republicans, nominating Eisenhower on the first ballot, could do no wrong with such a candidate. Senator Taft sulked for a while and then came out for Ike. The *Journal* backed the nominees, Ike and Senator Richard M. Nixon of California for vice-president from the start. "Many Americans have thought of Mr. Eisenhower as their president because he seems to express and embody that for which their hearts hunger," the paper said soon after the convention. "Dwight D. Eisenhower has only to remain Dwight D. Eisenhower, and he has little to fear from his enemies." It was an almost perfect analysis of the situation.

Albert Clark, W. C. Bryant, Alan L. Otten, and Philip Geyelin covered the campaign after the Democrats nominated former Governor Adlai Stevenson of Illinois for president and Senator John Sparkman of Alabama as his running mate to appease the South. They reported in a round-up story on October 23 that Eisenhower had a better than even chance of becoming the next president. The *Journal* remained faithful to Charles Dow's policy of not endorsing a presidential candidate by name, but it did say on election eve that "Mr. Eisenhower himself has dominated the Republican campaign to the extent that President Truman for a time dominated the Democratic [1948] campaign." Eisenhower actually did much better, winning by a popular margin of 5.5 million votes compared with Truman's victory margin of 2.2 million in 1948.

On May 3, 1953, as President Eisenhower's administration was under way, the *Journal* predicted that Ike would prove to be one of the great presidents. He demonstrated during the campaign that he would not be pushed, it said, and it did not believe he could be pushed into an unwise course by Congress. "On the one side the President is under pressure to maintain military expenditures. On the other side there is pressure to reduce these expenditures and to cut taxes. . . . Mr. Eisenhower is resisting a hasty decision in any direction. . . . Whether President Eisenhower will solve the military and financial problems he faces to the country's satisfaction, this newspaper will not attempt to predict. Along the way he very likely will do things that displease some people—including this newspaper—but if one thing is clearer than another about the President at this stage of his administration, it is that trying to push Mr. Eisenhower is a bootless effort."

On January 4, 1952, the *Journal*'s leader story, written by Eugene J. Smith, described a highly significant development in the printing industry. "A mechanical marvel is fomenting a revolution in the business of publishing newspapers and magazines. . . . This wonder-worker is the Teletypesetter—TTS for short. It is a device for helping to turn words on paper into words in type. It does the job in about half the usual time. Unlike the conventional typesetting apparatus, it can be operated from a place thousands of miles from the scene of the typesetting—as far away as a wire can reach."

Joseph J. Ackell of *The Wall Street Journal* knew as much as any man in the world about automated typesetters. He had rejected other developments as inadequate and had been experimenting with his own model, which, like the others, required a printer using a keyboard to punch each news item into coded perforations in a paper tape. Then, by Ackell's system, the tape was "read" electrically, and the electric impulses activated the typesetting machines automatically at any number of distant locations. Ackell's device could be attached to almost any typesetting machine. On December 16, 1952,

Barney Kilgore announced that Ackell's Electro-Typesetter, an improvement over the TTS, would be ready for service within a year.

In 1935 Ackell had founded the Dow Jones Engineering Laboratories, and he ran the division thereafter. His first lab was a windowless room on West Thirtieth Street; next he moved to a small suite at 44 Broad Street; and in 1951 the labs occupied the entire sixteenth floor at 100 Sixth Avenue. There in 1952 he built his own model of an automated typesetter. In the spring of that year he invited Bill Kerby to his laboratory to see it. Kerby wrote of his first view: "A maze of electronic tubes and other gadgetry was mounted on a series of long tables. From them ran an electrical connection to another Rube Goldberg-ish contraption, which in turn was connected with a standard linecasting machine. The whole apparatus occupied a room some 20 feet square. But it worked. The next step, Joe explained, was to condense all his apparatus into a commercial model. . . . 'I have the machine,' said Joe. 'Now, what do we do with it?' "

Kilgore, Kerby, and Ackell agreed that no more should be attempted initially than the production of the full stock-market quotations by means of Ackell's Electro-Typesetter. "Quotations generated by the Associated Press arrived by narrow gummed tape," Kerby said. "This was sorted and pasted on sheets by a sizable corps of quotations clerks." The Associated Press agreed to furnish full market quotations for use by Dow Jones provided Dow Jones paid AP's full costs, since Dow Jones would initially be the only user.

Then it was up to Ackell to get the printers to agree to work with the automated machines. New York union officials refused to even discuss the proposal. Ackell and Kerby approached national representatives of the International Typographical Union, including President Woodruff Randolph. Ackell told the union representatives that Dow Jones felt compelled to use the new equipment. "We will use it with or without the union. We much prefer to work with union journeymen," he said. Kerby conceded that the *Journal* would obviously employ fewer printers in each existing *Journal* plant, but added "that we would find it economic to open additional plants in new locations and thus our overall national employment would be increased." This evidently impressed the national officers who were doing the negotiating. On June 26, 1953, the Electro-Typesetter was used for the first time to set stock and bond quotations for the Eastern edition.

Barney Kilgore and his aides were elated. They felt that before too long the entire contents of the *Journal* would be set automatically by Joe Ackell's machines, which Dow Jones would manufacture. There would be a national network of automatic typesetting and, for the first time, it would be feasible to produce *Journal*s identical in editorial content and quality anywhere in the United States.

Chapter 18

Years of Pride and Glory

The Wall Street Journal was 65 years old in 1954, the year it came of age as *the* national business newspaper. May 1954 was especially significant for the *Journal,* ranking only after July 1889, when the paper began, and December 1941, when the Barney Kilgore changes merged triumphantly in the Pearl Harbor edition. In May the *Journal* jolted its readers by its strong support of the United States Supreme Court decision in *Brown* v. *Board of Education,* the landmark civil-rights ruling that would change the nation. Its editorial served notice that the *Journal* could not be pegged as an immutable conservative, and it brought an avalanche of angry mail from readers.

That same month the publisher and editors rocked the newspaper and advertising community by their resolute stand in the face of a challenge by America's most powerful corporation. That steadfast defense of editorial integrity, advertising men said years later, won the paper recognition of incalculable value. Also in May, Joe Ackell's Electro-Typesetter set the entire Eastern edition of the *Journal* and the stock and bond quotations of the Pacific Coast edition. Kilgore's vision of simultaneous duplicate editions across the country was about to be realized. It was a month of decision, wild fears, and ultimate success on editorial, advertising, and production fronts.

The year began quietly enough, with excellent prospects. President Kilgore told the directors at the annual spring meeting that the outlook was good for earnings and circulation to soar to new highs. They did. In 1954 Dow Jones & Company would pay out $546,000 in dividends at a rate of $3.50 a share, and the burgeoning circulation would pass 295,000. During the year, growth would compel the company to take over the building at 38–40 Broad Street, adjacent to its 42–44 Broad Street premises.

That spring *Journal* advertising linage soared, too. Robert M. Feemster was selling just about everything around Dow Jones that wasn't nailed down as he dashed about the country singing the praises of Kilgore's editorial accomplishments. "We have to make it a good newspaper to come up to Feemster's claims," one editorial cynic said, and he was right.

"Dow Jones has a serious responsibility to everyone who looks to it for dependable economic news," Feemster, speaking as chairman of the Executive Committee of *The Wall Street Journal,* told the Newcomen Society of New York on April 27, 1954. "More than that, Dow Jones has a responsibility to the American way of life. Much of the basic struggle between statism and democracy is on the economic level. One of our most important weapons in the struggle is economic truth—objective, factual economic news—constantly available to our nation. This responsibility has been accepted by the men and women of Dow Jones." No *Journal* editorialist ever said it better.

Feemster also expounded his pragmatic views of the *Journal* and Dow Jones. "It has been suggested for many years that *The Wall Street Journal* is a 'working tool' for men who want help to keep getting ahead in business," he said, referring to his own slogan for the paper. "People who read *The Wall Street Journal* are not the ordinary kind; each one is a person with ambition . . . [who] constantly strives to find a better way to work and live. *The Wall Street Journal* fits perfectly into his life."

Feemster's contributions to the *Journal* were vital to the success of Kilgore's drive for national circulation through regional publication. Major advertisers could use and pay for the full run of the paper if they desired national coverage. Advertisers content with regional circulation could select the region and pay less, a privilege not previously available to advertisers in national publications. At the same time, recognizing the unique characteristic of the *Journal,* its elitist, affluent readership, Feemster positioned his advertising campaigns not against the local daily newspapers but against the country's national mass-circulation magazines. Although this was a tough market for the *Journal* to crack, it was the proper one and the one most rewarding.

Feemster also invented and developed other inducements and appeals to the advertiser that resembled those of an aggressive daily newspaper. He established a classified display area for companies seeking skilled workers at executive and supervisory levels. Soon the paper was attracting pages of such linage, and large metropolitan newspapers entered into vigorous competition for it. There was a "Real Estate Corner" of classified display, and also a section of miscellaneous advertising, classified by the nature of appeal. This was grouped under "The Mart" heading and it, too, swiftly swelled. In April 1953 the *Journal* was running 18 pages, packed with advertising, and by the next April it was often 22 or 24 pages. The real-estate corner had become a full page; later, such advertising would fill as many as ten pages. (In August 1954 the Saturday issue of the paper was dropped without a loss of linage.)

By 1954 the paper's advertising content was glamorized with beautiful women, some wearing the new nylon nighties sold by Lord & Taylor, others displaying jewelry or selling perfumes. Generally, however, any "body contact" advertising was barred from the *Journal*. When the paper started, ointments and unguents and patent medicines were widely advertised in most newspapers, but *The Wall Street Journal* accepted none of it. Perfume, however, was not judged to be "body contact" since the connotations were pleasant. Airlines, auto makers, travel agents, luxury hotels, and makers of costly goods of all kinds presented their wares to the affluent *Journal* readers, many slanting their appeals to women. The consumer advertisers were in addition to the traditional *Journal* space buyers—the bankers, investment houses and brokerage firms, insurance firms, and businesses of every sort seeking to establish an image or to maintain one among the influential clientele.

On February 26, 1954, Joseph James Ackell, trim, balding, bespectacled, presided over the chattering Intertypes in the *Journal*'s San Francisco plant as they were set into operation by a signal from New York. The eastern control center was at last setting stocks and bonds for San Francisco and New York simultaneously. By May all four regional plants would receive the quotations from New York while Ackell's Electro-Typesetter also set the editorial content of the Eastern edition. Ackell's long, lonely sessions in the laboratory had finally paid off. Despite its essential crudeness—the Electro-Typesetter was operated by electrically activating mechanical fingers that pressed the keys controlling the typesetting machines—Ackell's invention met the fine tolerance needs of a financial newspaper known for its complete and accurate stock and bond lists. Sending the complete news report would be merely a matter of providing the needed number of "Ackell's mixers," as Dow Jones people called them.

When Barney Kilgore first announced in 1952 that Ackell had at last perfected his invention and that Dow Jones would manufacture it, he had praised it as a major breakthrough. Ackell, however, was much more conservative. "It represents the application to newspaper publishing of the automatic controls that so many industries now use for purely mechanical tasks," he explained. "The Electro-Typesetter is so simple and compact that a unit can be unplugged from a typesetting machine and a spare plugged in. The whole operation is about as complicated as changing a couple of electric light bulbs."

But in March 1954, *Western Printer & Lithographer* magazine of Los Angeles described Ackell's invention as a marvel of automation. The control principle was really a simple one, as Ackell indicated. The perforated tape produced by Ackell's machine functioned in much the same way as the perforations in a player-piano roll played a tune. Joe Ackell had found a way to convert words into electrical impulses via tape. The pattern could then be sent electronically a thousand miles or so to punch another similar tape in San Francisco, Dallas, or Chicago. Any number of such tapes could be punched simultaneously to operate any number of machines. They, in turn, cast on signal a line of lead type, which was put together with other such lines to create a newspaper page. This page of type, plus halftones and etchings if pictures were to be included, would be used to create a molded matrix into which hot lead was poured to make the curved stereotype plates to be locked onto a rotary printing press. Still slow and expensive, the process was a big step forward toward the remote-control publication of identical newspaper editions. But it wasn't the final solution.

On May 17, 1954, the United States Supreme Court, in *Brown* v. *Board of Education*, handed down its momentous decision unanimously declaring that segregation in the public schools must end. The opinion rejected the separate-but-equal doctrine in the Court's *Plessy* v. *Ferguson* decision on May 18, 1896.

Implementation of the Court's decision was delayed for a year to enable the country to get ready for it, but the associate editor Vermont Royster, born, reared, and educated in the South, was among those who immediately perceived the total significance of the ruling and who correctly anticipated some of its implications. Royster told his astounded superior, Editor William Grimes, that *The Wall Street Journal* should immediately endorse the opinion of the Court and call for compliance without reservation. Readers everywhere, and businessmen especially, needed to know the full implications and to recognize that the decision had been inevitable.

Grimes's conservatism was rugged and honest. He was certain that the ruling would shake up the country, and Royster agreed with that. Grimes did not think that the nation, especially the South, could possibly accept the ruling in the foreseeable future, and there Royster disagreed. The two bantam editorial writers had argued long and hard previously, but this time, Grimes gave in rather soon. He warned that the glut of mail would exceed that of the MacArthur affair and promised Royster that he would have the privilege of reading it. Then he instructed his young editor to go ahead. Royster took into account some of Grimes's fears and what he thought was "the foreseeable reaction."

On May 20, 1954, under the headline "Society and the Law," Royster wrote in his editorial, "The Supreme Court decision in the segregation cases was an inevitable one. If it had not come at this session, or from this court, still it would have come. The justices have not so much made history as followed it."

Royster explained major points of the decision and indicated that the Court had put off to another day its implementation, "so it is clear that while the days of segregation . . . are coming to an end, the end will not come immediately." He predicted the decision would be "unsatisfactory to extremists" on both sides.

> The Supreme Court's procedure is indeed unusual. But once the decision was made, there is much to recommend the Court's approach to carrying it out. There is certainly no simple way to put an end to an old order before society is ready to create a new one.
>
> The philosophy of racial distinction under the law could not have forever survived, in any event, because it does not comport with the majority view of the equity of government. Yet it does not comport either with the equity of government to require the people of a large region to tear down overnight the whole social structure which, though we are apt to forget it today, is rooted in ancient social necessity. . . .
>
> There is a burden upon the Southern states to accept the principle of the Court and to work diligently toward a method of living with it. Of this burden we shall doubtless hear much, for the voices calling it to the South's attention will be very loud. But there is also an equal burden upon the rest of the country to recognize that this is not a change to be wrought by instant coercion upon a minority section of the country without consequences as bad as the ills it seeks to cure. . . . [There is] an honest conviction on the part of Southerners that their children will be injured by submergence in a culture that has not had time fully to mature. The quality of forbearance is not strained.

The hell that Bill Grimes had predicted broke loose. "This plea for forbearance was not heeded even by our readers," Royster wrote years later. "Once more we were inundated by letters. The Court's decision proved as controversial as the MacArthur firing." Many but not all of the readers were angry, Royster said. Some understood the editorial's sympathy for the South; a few agreed with all its points. "*Wall Street Journal* readers," Royster was again reminded, "were not all of one mind."

A year later when the Court issued its second decision, placing the U.S. district courts in charge of the desegregation procedure, the *Journal* called the arrangement "a wise one." The problems were local, and "the judges of the lower Federal Courts are far better fitted to determine justly the problems the Supreme Court admonished them to pay attention to," the paper said. But it foresaw grave difficulties. "The problems of administration, transportation, personnel, physical conditions of school plants, revision of school districts and attendance areas—all mentioned specifically by Chief Justice Warren—are very different and cannot be settled by a specific rule from Washington nor will they be settled overnight."

Later in that turbulent May 1954 the *Journal* was involved in another controversy, one that caused the cancellation of $250,000 in advertising, by Bill Kerby's estimate. On the 28th the paper published a number of photographs and drawings of the 1955 models of various automobile manufacturers, together with appropriate data and a story on the new models for the fall. General Motors Corporation, insisting that the exclusive story, by John D. Williams, the *Journal*'s Detroit bureau manager, revealed trade secrets of great value, withdrew all news contacts and advertising from *The Wall Street Journal*, an action promptly followed by many subsidiaries and affiliates of the company. The *Journal* said that the pictures and information were given freely to its correspondent, though not, of course, officially, and that they constituted news.

Henry Gemmill, managing editor through 1954, and John Williams, in interviews with John Bridge years later, denied that any data or pictures of new car models were stolen. Having read a series of reports by Ray Vicker on the activities of automotive-industry suppliers the prior year, Williams decided, with an assist from Vicker, to go to such sources for advance information on the new models. He was welcomed and spent several weeks talking with people who had to know in advance what the new cars would be like. He knew he had a good story: Designs had been frozen because of steel shortages during the Korean conflict, and Americans were eager to know what the rumored 1955 changes would be like.

"I could feel a new competition had returned," Williams told Bridge. "Buyers were going to be able to go out and pick and choose again the kind of car they wanted. So all the forces were going forward toward a year when the new models would be a big story. I was sent to Detroit to get news. So I worked hard, got my material together, and got lucky. Someone offered me pictures. The pictures that made it all controversial were a Dodge sedan and a Chevrolet sedan. Then there was a rough sketch of a Ford and two silhouettes."

Henry Gemmill played the pictures big, which added to the shock effect since the *Journal* didn't ordinarily use pictures except in advertising. During the long Memorial Day weekend after May 28, the paper did not publish. There was little reaction in Detroit, Williams remembered, probably because most auto executives were out of town. "I was certainly happy to have my story on page one," Williams said. "Even when the roof fell in, I was still happy—someone had read my story."

Managing Editor Gemmill, on being shown the story and art from Williams and operating under the *Journal*'s "fairness doctrine," sought to reach appropriate automobile executives for comment through his New York staff. He also asked Williams to see whom he could find in Detroit. "I did call before publication of the pictures," Williams remembered, "but nobody wanted to see them, except a press representative of General Motors. I went to the General Motors headquarters on Grand Avenue. The press relations man came out of his office to see me and looked at the picture I showed him. When I asked him to comment on its accuracy, he declined rather tersely and returned to his office."

When the roof did cave in, Williams said, he was called to the Chrysler offices and "very thoroughly bawled out" by L. L. Colbert, Chrysler's president, who told him that he "had put a dagger into the hearts of the dealers." (That fall, however, the dealers had their best year in a decade.) Williams insisted he had simply reported the news, the position taken by Gemmill, Kerby, and Kilgore. Gemmill's news judgment, in the opinion of Kerby and Kilgore, was superb, but Kilgore wasn't sure the paper was on sound legal ground in publishing one sketch, that of a 1955 model Chevrolet, without permission. "General Motors, in particular, was outraged," Kerby said in his memoirs. "It canceled all advertising in the *Journal* and barred *Journal* newsmen from access to GM news. Then telegrams began arriving from General Motors subsidiaries and affiliates, also canceling all advertising. More than $250,000 in annual business was lost overnight, an enormous sum for the *Journal* in those days." Thus General Motors placed itself on shaky ground.

Kerby arranged for added General Motors news coverage from Associated Press. "Otherwise," he wrote, "we kept things in low key. But the word spread like wildfire. Nationwide, the press, and many public figures, rallied to the support of the *Journal*. GM had made an enormous public relations error." The *Journal* acknowledged the flood of angry letters from "readers in the auto industry" and published many of them. In an editorial, the *Journal* was sympathetic, but it declared that "new models are always news."

The editorial declared it never had and never would submit to censorship. "A newspaper exists only to provide information to its readers," it said. "It has no other reason for being. It provides that service only so long as it diligently seeks out what is happening and reports it as accurately and clearly as it can. This is particularly so of a newspaper that concentrates on business news. . . . In the end the truth about what is happening is the only thing that is of value to anybody. And when a newspaper begins to suppress news, whether at the behest of its advertisers or on pleas from special segments of business, it will soon cease to be of any service either to its advertisers or to business because it will soon cease to have readers."

By mid-June, Kerby wrote, "The news blackout was quietly lifted, with no quid pro quo from the *Journal*." With this major victory Barney Kilgore suggested to Harlow H. Curtice, president of General Motors, that the time had come for peace. Curtice agreed, and Kilgore went to Detroit for a meeting with him on July 7. In September there was a New York luncheon meeting of General Motors and Dow Jones executives and newsmen, and a peace arrangement was declared permanent. That fall General Motors Corporation and the various subsidiaries resumed advertising in the paper.

"*The Wall Street Journal* benefited enormously from that encounter," said Donald A. Macdonald, vice-chairman of Dow Jones & Company, years later. "We demonstrated our integrity, and the response from our readers and advertisers and the public was magnificent. Our future was assured."

Despite the success of *The Wall Street Journal,* life as a chief executive was not easy for Barney Kilgore. He wanted to stay an editor. He visited the kaffeeklatsch as often as he could to participate in the discussions and to make suggestions. Kilgore was comfortable when Bill Kerby was his managing editor in the paper's day-to-day operations, but always he needed Kerby's help elsewhere. So he created the job of executive editor to put Kerby in charge of all news operations, including the Dow Jones wire services. Kerby was named to the new job in December 1945. A month later Buren McCormack became managing editor. McCormack was a loyal member of the team, a meticulous reader of copy and proofs who could please even Barney Kilgore with his "nit-picking," as some of the staff called it. Despite his merits, McCormack never quite satisfied Kilgore as managing editor, though he served four years in that demanding position. In April 1950 Kilgore made McCormack senior associate editor in charge of editorials under Grimes, a move that was a near disaster. Neither Grimes nor Vermont Royster wanted McCormack, and Royster entertained outside job offers until Kilgore gave him a raise and indicated he had other plans for McCormack.

Henry Gemmill, who, thought Kilgore, was the best news writer on the staff, had been named managing editor in 1950, and in June 1951, Kilgore made Kerby vice-president of Dow Jones. McCormack succeeded him as executive editor. Kilgore secretly gave Kerby a note reading "When I am away, Bill Kerby is in charge," instructing Kerby to use it only if he "couldn't manage any other way." It was generally known among the staff that Kilgore was grooming Kerby as his successor, but he explained to Kerby that he didn't wish to bruise "the sensitive egos" of other executives.

Buren McCormack still wasn't positioned for the most effective use of his talents. He had succeeded Kerby as treasurer in 1955 and in January 1956,

Kilgore appointed him business manager of the *Journal* while naming Joe Ackell general manager of the division of development and planning. Kilgore seemed increasingly dissatisfied with Ackell's research and development after his accomplishment of composing the entire edition of the paper with his Electro-Typesetter in May 1954.

That same month the *Journal* had disclosed that Mergenthaler Linotype Company had developed a new typesetting machine that would further revolutionize printing by using a photographic typesetting technique in an offset printing process. Ackell had agreed with Kilgore that he should investigate the possibilities of facsimile printing and the new photocomposition process, but when little progress was reported from the Dow Jones labs by the end of 1955, Kilgore turned to his new business manager, McCormack. He had heard a lecture in Washington about the newspaper of the future, including facsimile reproduction, offset printing, light-pencil editing, and similar futuristic gear, and he asked McCormack to keep track of such experiments worldwide. At the same time, McCormack was empowered to reorganize the production department. Both assignments to Buren McCormack would pay off well.

Director Laurence Lombard also worked on a special assignment from Kilgore, to study current operations and future opportunities. He praised the *Journal*, saying it was expanding fast enough. He predicted a circulation of 1 million and agreed with Kilgore's position that the paper shouldn't expect to get bigger than 32 pages, which was "the right size for us," Kilgore said. Lombard also was satisfied with the Dow Jones wire services, except that he felt they should provide more services "in the investment trust area. We must be alert to capitalize on this trend."

He urged further improvement in the format of *Barron's* magazine, indicating that he and Kilgore had discussed this problem previously. "Perhaps we are aiming too high when we talk about the *London Economist*," Lombard wrote. "I would like to see *Barron's* a better and bigger operation, as a more important part of our picture, and [I would] like to have all three prongs of our operation, namely *The Wall Street Journal*, the ticker service, and *Barron's*, profitable." Could *Barron's* appeal to a wider readership? Lombard wondered. He suggested that there was a shortage of top talent in the company and warned that "skimping on talent to make more money for the stockholders would not pay off long range."

Yet at the same time, Lombard declared that the company "should pay dividends of $6 a year, and more if earnings justify it." He urged incentive pay "for top talent interested in bringing share earnings up to $6 or $9 or $10 a year." Barney Kilgore got the message. In 1955 Dow Jones dividends went to $6 a share. The executives were further shifted about to provide more of them with varied experience.

The *Journal*, meanwhile, continued to do well. There had been excellent stories under Henry Gemmill as managing editor, and the editorial features of the *Journal* had been expanded to include a new column, "Financing Business"; a listing of the ten most active stocks; a "Table of Rallies," which included highs and lows for the year; a department called "How Companies Are Doing," later enlarged to "A Digest of Earnings Reports"; and the introduction of Frederic Banberry's drawings in "America at Work." But Gemmill disliked administrative work and wanted to go back to reporting and writing, so he was detached to become a roving correspondent. On December 1, 1954, Kilgore called in Bob Bottorff from Chicago to take over as managing editor, a move that sent the rising young Warren Phillips to Chicago as managing editor of the Midwest edition.

Bottorff drove hard on the news-coverage front. The paper was bright, thorough, and interesting. Vermont Royster, senior associate editor since June 1951, was increasingly in charge of the editorial page. He held steady on a conservative editorial course, but the editorials were shorter and sharper and often glinted with sardonic humor. Kilgore liked what the paper was doing, especially with its circulation, which at the end of 1955 totaled 365,000.

Robert Feemster continued to be a magnificent salesman of the *Journal* in both advertising and circulation areas. Feemster's promotions and slogans were unquestionably helping to bring in even more readers. Kilgore disliked Feemster's flamboyant ways as much as ever but he also recognized and appreciated Feemster's skills and his sound analysis of their problems and opportunities. In his public appearances, Feemster made good use of his title of chairman of the Executive Committee, bestowed by Kilgore, and if he sometimes made it sound like chairman of Dow Jones & Company, Kilgore forgave him. The little man needed all the prestige he could amass to carry out his difficult job. Sometimes, Bill Kerby recalled, Kilgore met businessmen who said they knew his boss, Bob Feemster. Kilgore did not correct them. He was satisfied that Feemster was doing a good job and that his friend Ted Callis, whom he elevated to director of advertising in 1955, was Feemster's able backup man.

Barney Kilgore gave a few talks about the *Journal* himself. Whether addressing the staff or outsiders, he always emphasized that *The Wall Street Journal* was a business newspaper. He warned against change merely for change's sake. "Just changing things around with no fundamental purpose is silly," he declared in discussing his famous front page. When he was asked whether newspapers ought to "play down" bad news, Kilgore replied, "There is no really bad news. It is misinformation and ignorance which causes trouble." Later, talking about freedom of the press, he said, "Freedom of the press has nothing to do with the quality of the press. . . . Quality is a matter of opinion." On newspapers generally: "The fish market wraps fish in paper. We wrap news in paper. The content is what counts, not the wrapper."

Kilgore made it clear that he did not regard the *Journal* as the source of great stock-market prescience, nor was it a "tip sheet." "I'm not a stock-market expert," he said. "I don't think there are many stock-market experts." Answering a question about the role of the *Journal* in forecasting market behavior, he replied, "There is no such role. . . . It would be an exercise in futility." Kilgore's recipe for a newspaper: "Paper, ink, brains."

Bob Bottorff and his editors were careful to restrain some of the reporters and copy editors who wanted to further "broaden the paper." They heeded Kilgore's injunction to remember that it was essentially a business newspaper. Barney always added, of course, that almost everybody was in business, "the business of making a living." Even the A-heds almost always had a business slant. During the height of the 1955 World Series fever, when the New York Yankees and Brooklyn Dodgers were engaged in a subway contest for the world championship, *The Wall Street Journal* told its readers what businesses some of the stars were in, including those not even in the Series. Stan Musial, the St. Louis Cardinals' batting champion and the National League's highest-paid player ($85,000), was, quite logically, a bank director; Bob Feller, a pitcher for the Cleveland Indians, operated his own ranch in Texas as well as the family farm near Van Meter, Iowa. The story started on page one under the A-hed: "The World Series / Ends Today. The Ball Players / Are Still in Business." (Brooklyn won the Series 4–3.)

The paper's editorials pounded away in 1955 at government spending and the growing national debt, but agreed that the increase in congressmen's salaries to $22,500 a year was justified if it helped to provide the country with better representatives. The raise brought the pay of congressmen to the household median of that for *Wall Street Journal* subscribers, according to one of Feemster's surveys. But the paper continued to attack deficit spending, blaming most of the problems on neo-Keynesians, as Vermont Royster called them; he believed that John Maynard Keynes initially had stated some truths about government-spending programs, while his later disciples carried his big-spending remedies to harmful extremes. Nevertheless, the paper whacked the master himself on January 3, 1956, in asserting that the country could be facing ultimate ruination from the deficit-spending policies it attributed to Lord Keynes.

"For more than a generation we as a people have been content to live by borrowing from the future," the *Journal* said. "Like a man devouring the patrimony of his sons, we have piled up our debts to buy prosperity on credit." It praised two leading Republican opponents of big spending, Senator Barry Goldwater of Arizona and Representative Thomas B. Curtis of Missouri, and two Democrats, Senator Paul Douglas of Illinois and Representative Wilbur Mills of Arkansas, for possessing good economic sense but it didn't expect them to be heard in an election year. Then the paper observed dourly, "In the long run, true enough, we shall all be dead, as Lord Keynes once reminded us. Perhaps then the present generation can continue to eat, drink and be merry without giving thought to the reckoning."

On January 24, 1956, the *Journal* again spoke of this debt, concluding sadly, "When a family—or a Government—finds its future obligations piling up at a faster rate than its current bills, or its income, then it raises a question about its husbandry." On March 27 it bitterly condemned a further $4.9 billion foreign-aid request by the Eisenhower administration, saying that the liberals who favored such giveaways were never satisfied and asked only "Whether it [the plan] is bold and imaginative, . . . that is, expensive enough."

After the Republican convention in August, which again nominated Dwight Eisenhower and Richard Nixon, the *Journal* accepted the verdict equably, saying on August 23 of Nixon, whom it had profiled the previous day: "Mr. Nixon is a controversial figure. But it is hard to put one's finger on exactly what it is that some people find objectionable in him. He is, without question, a tough opponent in debate or in a campaign; it is not surprising that the Democrats do not care for Mr. Nixon. But it is also a fact that of the people who talked loudly of wanting to see Mr. Nixon dumped, the great majority were people who also want to see Mr. Eisenhower dumped. Mr. Nixon's name was on the list Mr. Eisenhower turned over to the convention leaders in 1952 of men acceptable to him. . . . Since that time, Mr. Nixon certainly has grown in stature. . . . It is no wonder that Mr. Eisenhower refused to dump him, and it is no wonder that the delegates endorsed him."

During the campaign the *Journal* attacked Adlai Stevenson, the Democratic candidate, for proposing the same deficit-spending route for the government that the paper had long opposed.

> His basic approach is summed up in the sentence, "We have to use the Government's power as a balance wheel to help keep the economy stable." This isn't a new view; it is simply Keynes in simple language.
>
> There is, of course, one practical difficulty in all this. In times of recession the Government can cut taxes, increase spending, and make up the difference without a public outcry. . . . It is when they try to shut off the pump that governments come a-cropper. Since the Korean War we have had the biggest boom of our history, but Government spending is at its biggest peace-time level. So are taxes. And even very mild restraints of this Administration have caused political balking. . . . So in the real world "compensatory spending" is a one-way street. It never had led any place but to inflation.
>
> But that's only part of the trouble. Even if Mr. Stevenson could establish a dictatorial Government so that his economic planners could safely ignore the political pressures, there is the little matter of deciding how to manipulate the

> levers. . . . It wasn't so long ago that the prevailing judgment of the economic planners was that this country had passed the peak of growth. What sort of an economy would we have had in 1956 if the economic planners in 1936 had actually had the power to freeze the economy at that year's stability?
>
> Perhaps using taxes to "balance" things would keep the economy stable. But it would be the kind of stability the tax manipulators decide we ought to have, a stability achieved when things never change nor grow.

As usual the *Journal* did not urge by name a vote for President Eisenhower. It greeted the election news on November 7 with equanimity—Eisenhower and Nixon won by a plurality of more than 9 million and an electoral vote of 457 to 73. Nevertheless, it warned, "We need not think that the complexities of our political affairs, both at home and abroad, have been magically resolved by the voters' decision."

Early in 1957 Kilgore and Kerby made another change in the *Journal* management team, looking toward a final lineup that would become effective in 1958. Warren Phillips, managing editor in Chicago, was called to New York in March 1957 to take over the post of managing editor from Bottorff, who would take the restored executive editor job. Ray Vicker, the brilliant reporter and writer from the *Chicago Journal of Commerce* who, as a *Journal* foreign correspondent, would appraise in taut terms the world's business and political leaders, provided his estimate of Phillips and Bottorff in his Chicago years:

> Phillips was a sharp contrast to the blunt, sometimes abrasive Bottorff. Phillips used persuasion rather than a charge forward to attain his ends. To some he may have seemed cold and unemotional. Actually, he is a warm person, but he likes to hide his emotion behind an inscrutable wall, probably feeling that the fellow who keeps his mouth shut has less chance of saying the wrong thing than has the garrulous backslapper. One cannot conceive of Phillips ever developing into a backslapper.
>
> Bottorff may have been just the man for taking a new newspaper [the Chicago edition] and shaping it into another edition of *The Wall Street Journal*, knocking heads together in the process. Phillips was better for analyzing long-term editorial goals. Before long, working under Phillips, one got the impression that one was working for *The Wall Street Journal*, not the Chicago edition of *The Wall Street Journal*. Phillips paid much closer attention to detail. He liked to have the lines of authority leading to his hands. Still, he encouraged originality and was quick to see stories which became fixtures in the *WSJ*.

In Phillips, who was born and educated in New York, and gained reporting experience in Europe and the Middle East and administrative experience in the London bureau and as managing editor of the Chicago edition, the *Journal* had its most broadly trained news executive. The managing editorship in New York was again in the hands of a man on whom Kilgore and

Kerby could depend for instant good judgment under pressure, a man who was an excellent motivator and director of personnel. Phillips, 30 at the time, would hold that post on the firing line for eight and a half years before moving up, the longest tenure of any Kilgore-era managing editor.

At the same time, Royster was moving rapidly on the equally sensitive editorial-policy front. In months Kilgore would complete his management team and make his selections relatively final by publishing them in the paper's masthead, the first time *Journal* executives would be so acknowledged in more than 30 years. The masthead that appeared on August 5, 1958, confirmed a lineup actually at work some months before: Kilgore, president and chief executive; William F. Kerby, vice-president and editorial director; Buren McCormack, business manager; Robert Bottorff, executive editor; Vermont Royster, editor; William H. Grimes, vice-president and contributing editor. Former Editor Grimes had retired to live in Florida following a heart attack. Hugh Bancroft had also included his advertising managers; Kilgore did not.

Although their names were omitted from the *Journal* masthead, Assistant General Manager Robert Feemster and Advertising Director Theodore Callis, aided by a newcomer, Donald A. Macdonald, were doing a superlative job for the paper. *Journal* advertising would total nearly 20 million lines in 1958. A prior high had been 5,734,317 lines in 1930. Linage had fallen to 1,731,353 in 1938, but, following the 1941 changes, had climbed to nearly 2 million in 1942, and then to more than 10 million lines in 1951. These gains were made against constantly increasing rates as circulation grew. Macdonald, a cum laude graduate of New York University in 1948 who earned a master of business administration degree from the NYU Graduate School of Business in 1950, had joined the *Journal* staff as an advertising salesman in 1953; by 1958 he had become eastern advertising manager.

Bob Feemster and his associates conducted what were perhaps the most effective advertising promotion and circulation campaigns of any newspaper or magazine in the country. Feemster introduced the highly effective slogan "The men who get ahead read *The Wall Street Journal*" and similar phrases appealing to self-interest. In 1957 the advertising and promotion attack, replete with persuasive sales statistics, was concentrated on New York: "Since 1946 *Wall Street Journal* circulation has grown 539%, but advertising cost-per-thousand has dropped 52%. . . . You reach more top executives in *The Wall Street Journal* than with any other publication. This fact is proved again and again through research."

The advertisements explained the four editions of the paper, urging potential space buyers to write or telephone for details on purchasing linage in one or all four editions. All editions, said the ads, would possess the same superior editorial content. Feemster had a slogan for that, too: "Same Day,

Same News Over the USA." Feemster's ads were excellent, well laid-out typographically, provocatively written, and liberally surrounded by that white space Feemster recommended to his clients. Some were illustrated with drawings by Frederic Banberry.

On Sunday, October 6, 1957, Managing Editor Phillips and his staff were getting together the Monday paper. The USSR had released the news that its satellite Sputnik had successfully gone into earth orbit on October 4. It was a news event of inestimable consequence, Phillips realized, as he put his staff to work on a round-up story. The handling of Sputnik that day and in the days to follow was somewhat reminiscent of the *Journal's* treatment of Pearl Harbor in that the consequences flowing from the news event were explored and woven into the leading story. Phillips saw many and grave consequences ahead, as his reporters and writers sought to evaluate this herald of the space age in terms of American power, the armaments race, future foreign relations between the superpowers, and world economic consequences.

The launching of the Russian satellite didn't match Pearl Harbor in its sudden intensity, but Phillips and his staff made clear its meaning to the average American. The second major story of the day was from Henry Gemmill and Joseph Guilfoyle, the team Phillips had sent to Little Rock, Arkansas, after President Eisenhower dispatched troops there to obtain compliance with federal court orders to integrate Central High School and to stop subsequent disturbances. Gemmill and Guilfoyle probed the economic nuances of the story in depth, and it was handled from that viewpoint on successive days. Four years later *Newsweek* magazine, reviewing the progress of the *Journal* in American journalism, marked the Little Rock stories as the start of a new pattern in reporting sociopolitical events. "While other reporters bored in on obvious, tumultuous events of the school closing, *Journal* hands searched out the economic repercussions. Economics proved to be the key ending the crisis."

Warren Phillips would remember that particular Sunday. He felt then that journalistic responsibilities had drastically changed in the turbulent wake of Sputnik and civil-rights disturbances. There would be need for special teams and experienced writers capable of reporting in depth the significance of social change, its possible economic consequences, and its meaning for the future. Civil rights would be a national story requiring constant, objective, comprehensive reportage. Space developments would have to be recounted by writers familiar with science, sociology, and geopolitics. Communications, medicine, education, world armaments, and world affairs would be affected and would produce momentous news on a continuing basis. The American life-style would change.

The Wall Street Journal would have to again broaden its base, Phillips concluded. Business people's main workday interest might be business, but their interests did not stop at business. The same in-depth, interpretative-reporting techniques the *Journal* used to illuminate the world of business would have to be applied to covering business people's health, their children's education, and the social forces shaping the society in which they lived.

The *Journal* had no easy solution for complex world problems, but the editors were determined to provide their readers with as much factual information as they could find and present intelligently. That included covering the Sputnik political, economic, and social fallout from its American, Canadian, and European bureaus. It also included the development of more specialists to cover complex scientific advancements, and nationwide coverage of civil-rights developments. The expanding editorial staff extended its reach over the changing technological, social, and political scene. Its garnering of still another Pulitzer Prize by staff member Ed Cony, announced in 1961, was the paper's first for news coverage and was followed by two more in the same category within three years.

Under Vermont Royster the *Journal's* editorial page won widespread favor for its acute analysis, its incisive style, its urbane humor. Royster managed to attend the kaffeeklatsch on most days to hear what other editors had to report, including their insights on the significance of news events. Usually Kerby or Kilgore or both were present. Royster listened, made his own comments, sometimes heard criticism of an editorial, then walked away to think about the next day's commentary and to discuss ideas with his assistants. The makeup of Royster's staff varied but for some years included Joseph Evans, who would succeed him. Together they made policy.

"I knew the thinking of the kaffeeklatsch," Royster said in discussing his procedure. "I made my own judgments in consultation with other editorial writers. The owners of the company and the chief executives mostly got the word with the regular readers when the *Journal* hit the streets. Of course, no member of the Socialist Workers Party or its equivalent is appointed chief of the editorial page in the first place." *Newsweek* described Royster's policy as "conservative (admires Senator Goldwater), but mulishly independent (thinks Goldwater unrealistic)."

The paper also demonstrated its capability for covering, on a massive scale, the activities of an uncooperative, powerful company that insisted its business was a private matter despite the fact that it was about to go public. *Journal* editors felt that the public was entitled to specific, detailed, and complete information about the Great Atlantic & Pacific Tea Company in the fall of 1958. When company officers refused the *Journal* information, Warren Phillips assigned 26 reporters around the country to dig it out. It appeared in a series published in December, probably the most complete, comprehensive, and analytical profile of a company ever to be published for the general public, the editors believed. "A&P management has declined to supply information," the paper said. "Our 26 reporters have gathered information from scores of other well-informed sources around the nation."

The series chronicled John Hartford's business techniques that had made A&P nationally powerful in the grocery-merchandising business, "now modern after 99 years of slumber," and detailed stock ownership by members of the Hartford family and Hartford Foundation. Said the concluding article, "A&P's retailing triumphs, it must be admitted, are very much A. and very little P."

The *Journal* maintained its intense interest in politics and keen concern about the investment community. It continued also to be angry to the point of exasperation at the Republicans for what it regarded as stupid politics. On November 6, 1958, in discussing the by-elections in which the Democrats increased their control of both Houses, the paper was again openly indignant: "There is no use mincing words. The Republican Party has simply disintegrated, and the wreckage is strewn across three thousand miles of countryside." This, despite the fact that Nelson Rockefeller in New York State managed to win the governorship.

On December 19, 1958, emphasizing its careful watch over Wall Street, the *Journal* again raised the specter of overspeculation. The Dow Jones Index had risen from 436.89 in February 1957 to 572.38 on December 18, 1958, an increase of nearly one third; the paper urged caution. It conceded that business earnings were up but said, "By no stretch of the imagination can the improvement in business be equated to the increase in stock market prices. The ratio of present stock prices to business earnings is high, [and] that large and amorphous body, the public, may be correctly foreseeing such a further improvement in business as to justify the present high stock prices. That has happened before. Still, that is speculation. On the part of some people it may be a carefully thought out assessment of future prospects. It is speculation, nonetheless. It is, we suppose, a killjoy thought. But no drug company has yet found the pill that will arrest the speculative fever, once it is in full flush, until it has run its appointed course. The only cure is to avoid infection."

The *Journal* did not cease to fight deficit spending and inflation, whether the Truman or Eisenhower administration espoused it. It said on February 24, 1959, in reiterating its position, "This newspaper does not believe that some higher economic law requires the Government to end up in the black every year, year in and year out. In times of war or other catastrophe it would be all but impossible. Even in calmer times a case can be made for running a deficit once in a while for special purposes."

But the *Journal* objected strongly "to 23 deficit years out of the last 28 years." Even the Eisenhower administration ended eight years with nearly $17 million of deficit, the paper pointed out, though it held Congress even more to blame. It referred to the Keynesian thinking during Franklin Roosevelt's administration, when it had been necessary to spend beyond tax revenues to get the country started again, but then cited the fallacy of continuing such a policy: "Thanks to the remarkable intellectual attrition [of neo-Keynesian economists], we have the half-dollar dollar and the rocketing public debt, export troubles, a poor government bond market, and the Treasury's economic difficulties. . . . The spendthrift politicians have made the budget battle the most urgent of our time."

It was an example of *Journal* consistency and Vermont Royster's editorial technique of first giving a few points to his opponents and then taking away the ostensible advantage. The editorial exemplified Royster's belief that "Lord Keynes was sometimes right" but that his latter-day followers were wrecking the country.

In August 1959 the *Journal* once more backed its old friend William McChesney Martin, chairman of the Federal Reserve Board, who refused to allow reserve banks to support the government's long-term bonds. The editorialist who reviewed the situation wrote, "Large sums of money are now tied up in government bonds because, if the holders sell them now, years ahead of the maturity date, they will have to sell them below face value. If the Reserve Board would offer to buy these bonds at higher prices—as the proposed Congressional Resolution asks it to do—then this would make more money available. . . . Mr. Martin does not think it wise to again charge up the engine of inflation."

The Wall Street Journal, of course, fervently agreed with Martin. But the government would continue piling up debts, inflating its own bond prices, printing money, spending excessively, and devaluing its currency until the national debt approached an astronomical total of 1 trillion dollars.

The achievements of *The Wall Street Journal* under Kilgore leadership in appealing to the country's intellectuals as well as the business community were effectively described by John Brooks, author of books on Wall Street and the stock market, in the March 1959 issue of *Harper's* magazine. Brooks wrote in sprightly prose under a fetching title, "*The Wall Street Journal* Woos the Eggheads." "The paper's growth is the outstanding phenomenon in American daily journalism during the past two decades," he told his elitist readers.

Referring to the paper's reader surveys, Brooks noted that nine tenths of the readers were men, four fifths of them in the prime of life (between the ages of 25 and 64); that more than a fourth were the directors of at least one company; nearly a fourth were owners or presidents of a business; and more than half had a net worth of $75,000. The author proclaimed the figures to be "a rather awe-inspiring picture of power and influence." He said buyers of the paper numbered above 570,000 in 1958, "making the paper they cleave to so lovingly each morning on their commuting platforms probably the eighth, and certainly at least the ninth, ranking daily newspaper in circulation in the United States."

Brooks then came up with his own comparatives, which must have excited the admiration of Bob Feemster and his promotion people: the *Journal's* circulation had doubled in five years, almost quadrupled in ten years, and in 17 years had multiplied almost 17 times!

> Furthermore, while getting rich, the *Journal* has broadened its cultural horizons to an exemplary degree. Whether the broadening brought success or vice versa is an open question, but it is a fact that in transferring itself from a straightforward stock and bond sheet into the relatively civilized organ it is now, the paper has picked up support from a most unlikely quarter. It has become the intellectual's pet down-towner. Just as it has been fashionable in certain circles to call the lowbrow, tabloid *New York News* "the best edited paper in New York," so in approximately the same circles it has now become the thing to pronounce *The Wall Street Journal* as one's favorite breakfast reading. In some cases this may be merely an effort to shock or a reflection of wistful egghead dreams of economic glory.

Brooks covered the history of the paper, calling Clarence W. Barron "the celebrated financial pundit and Wall Street character," detailed the recent opening of the *Journal's* new Washington publishing plant (1955), and went on to the paper's promotional efforts: "The *Journal* probably advertises itself more often and more spectacularly than any other American daily." He reviewed some promotional ads. "Read the *Journal* and you will make more money" was a somewhat crass theme, Brooks thought; "Don't give up the ship in 1958" was too patronizing to its business executive readers; but he liked a *Journal* advertisement aimed at the advertising agencies: "Confessions of a Lady Space Buyer," which, he said, "was appropriately coy." Then he added, "To a critic who might have complained that, in seeking not to be a bore, the *Journal* had become a showoff, it could reply that every businessman, even in Wall Street, knows you sometimes have to play the fool or not clinch the deal."

The article didn't give Feemster credit as the paper's preeminent promoter, but Feemster's name led the list of DePauw University graduates on the *Journal* staff. In stating his wonder at the large number of DePauw people (he missed K. C. Hogate, who was first and brought in most of the others), Brooks said, "The secret of DePauw—which has no journalism school—is something that many publishers who continually comb their more celebrated alma maters for young talent would undoubtedly like to know."

Brooks found much to admire in the *Journal* editorials: "Whether you like them or not, [they] have an air of integrity, consistency, and intransigence. Naturally, numerous dedicated readers are severely critical of them." He interviewed Vermont Royster, "whose name sounds like a Saturday night square dance," and quoted him: "Basically, we are for minimum government. We believe that the primary reason for government is to provide police power—to keep me from knocking you over the head. In foreign affairs, we don't think the United States can run the world, or even the Western world." Brooks said the *Journal* was proud of its editorial stands against Eisenhower's order of troops to Lebanon, against Northwest public-power proposals, and in favor of right-to-work laws. Brooks interviewed Barney Kilgore, who told him that while Wall Street was no longer a descriptive name, "we keep it because it works."

The *Journal* accepted the wash of praise with decent modesty and took in stride the sour notes, too, predictably supplied by *Time* magazine. "Measured by the tastes and habits of the ordinary newspaper reader, *The Wall Street Journal* front page is agonizingly dull," said *Time* on October 12, 1959. "For determinedly conservative makeup, the *Journal's* front page—six solid columns of type unrelieved by a picture—has no rival among U.S. metropolitan dailies. Its stories can hardly be called sensational: a looming shortage in milk bottles, potholes in the Inter-American highway, a slump in the price of dried fruit, a rise in individual assets—to cite a few of the subjects that rated Page One play last week."

But *Time* admitted that the *Journal's* readers were far from ordinary, reciting once again Feemster's surveys. "The *Journal* has more readers living in California than in New York, and the subscribers live in virtually all the 3,944 counties in the continental U.S." The chances were, *Time* added, that the *Journal* reader owned stocks and that he also lived in "that community to which President Kilgore staked a grandiloquent claim—'everyone who is engaged in making a living or is interested in how other people make a living.' " *Time* ranked the *Journal* as one of the top ten, and gave it the encomium of "the country's only real contender for the title of national daily."

Chapter 19

"Truly a National Newspaper"

Prospects never seemed brighter for *The Wall Street Journal* as the 1960s began, yet the editors surveying the national scene were glum in their year-end review. Nor did they glow perceptibly on January 3, 1960, when Senator John F. Kennedy of Massachusetts announced that he would seek the Democratic nomination for president of the United States. Vermont Royster, the paper's editor, and Joe Evans, his editorial-page assistant, had served in Washington, and they knew and liked Senator Kennedy. But they were aware that he was currently consorting with such persons as Chester Bowles, "hero of the liberal left"; John Kenneth Galbraith, an admitted "aggressive evangelist for the Keynesian system in its standard form"; Arthur M. Schlesinger, Jr., a historian and a liberal; and the *New Republic* crowd. They feared Kennedy had been infected with neo-Keynesian virus and would come down with deficit-spending fever. They were also, of course, acquainted with Vice-President Richard Nixon, who disclosed his candidacy for the Republican nomination six days later. While their enthusiasm for Nixon was faint, the *Journal* editors believed him to be immune to the Keynesian malady, as well as a proven conservative. Nixon would undoubtedly get such support as the *Journal* gave to anybody.

Barney Kilgore was heavily occupied with long-range corporate problems: an approaching breakthrough on the facsimile-publishing front, where Buren McCormack was reporting progress; a new national weekly publication; and a plan to take

Dow Jones printing activities completely out of New York City. Kilgore was satisfied to allow Vermont Royster to make editorial policy as Grimes had done before him, while Kerby and Bottorff monitored the activities of the editors in the news department. Editor Royster attended the morning coffee sessions, where he heard the views of Kilgore, Kerby, and news-staff executives. Evans, who also wrote editorials, was former foreign editor of the paper, and John Bridge, a Navy veteran like Royster, had edited copy for page one before being assigned to Royster's staff to edit editorial-page features. All three were well steeped in *Journal* policy and discipline.

Kilgore definitely wasn't bothered by Vermont Royster's making policy as independently as it had ever been done. On one occasion late in 1958, shortly after taking over from Bill Grimes as editor, Royster offered an editorial critical of President Eisenhower to Barney Kilgore for comment. "I laid it on his desk," Royster recalled. "He picked up the copy, handed it back to me and said, 'I'll read it in the paper tomorrow.' " Royster liked intellectuals and some evidences of liberalism, as did Senator Kennedy, but his editorial changes were mostly gradual and subtle, and the *Journal* continued on its generally conservative course. Like Hogate and Grimes, Royster backed the economic policies of William McChesney Martin, chairman of the Federal Reserve Board. He continued to criticize Eisenhower's policies from time to time, and he supported additional segregation and other civil-rights orders issuing from the Supreme Court. There was occasional flak from some of the Dow Jones directors and some of the *Journal* staff members; however, Kilgore, Kerby, and Grimes liked Royster's style and substance. Royster sometimes felt he was under criticism in some quarters because he wasn't liberal enough, and he would accept luncheon and dinner engagements to explain his beliefs. On one occasion when he and his wife were dining with Mrs. Jessie Bancroft Cox and her husband, director Bill Cox, Royster outlined some of his views and problems, especially problems with two of the "outside" directors. "Don't pay any attention to them," Jessie told him. "They're just hired hands."

Senator Kennedy's defeat of Adlai Stevenson for the Democratic nomination at Los Angeles in July was easy enough for the *Journal* to take, although Kennedy was yet to be tested. "A very impressive man determined to make his mark, though still uncertain how," Royster had written of Kennedy in his notebook. Nor was he quite sure of the political philosophy of Senator Lyndon B. Johnson of Texas, Kennedy's running mate, but the choice was understandable. Vice-President Nixon of California was highly acceptable as Kennedy's opponent, especially since he was bracketed with another good Massachusetts man, Henry Cabot Lodge, Jr., U.S. ambassador to the United Nations. But the campaign aroused neither enthusiasm nor excitement on the *Journal*'s editorial page.

The acid test for both presidential candidates continued to be economics, and on November 1, the *Journal* disclosed what all of its readers already knew—that Kennedy had flunked. "Senator Kennedy makes a good diagnosis of what ails the dollar," the editorial said. "Strangely enough, though, the cure he prescribes is more of what ails it."

The next day the paper discussed Nixon, floundering a bit in an assessment of his personal courage and his attempt to come up with a position on inflation. "The American people," the editorial lamely concluded, "ought not to forget that Mr. Nixon offers a different road from that strewn with promises redeemable only in profligacy. Nor let a brief campaign obscure those qualities that he has displayed in a long and remarkable career."

When the election was over, the *Journal* said somewhat sourly on November 9, "Rarely have two candidates talked so much and said so little. . . . With some notable exceptions, neither candidate treated the public as intelligent people willing and anxious to hear a candidate take notice of an issue of the day, explore it, reason his way to a conclusion and then support it with arguments." On November 10, after further lucubration, the paper added, "The voters have made one thing quite clear in this election. They have given the mandate to nobody." The complete but uncanvassed returns were in by then, Kennedy's 34,226,731 total representing an apparent victory margin of fewer than 120,000 votes, the closest election in 72 years. The Democrats, however, retained control of both Houses, and the *Journal* predicted that the country was in for more trouble with the big spenders. It congratulated Senator Kennedy and wished him well.

Shortly before President-elect Kennedy took office on January 20 and after he indicated his intention to make his brother Robert attorney general, an idea the *Journal* blasted, Kennedy invited the editor of *The Wall Street Journal* to lunch. They met in New York's Carlyle Hotel, Vermont Royster recalled in a tribute to the late President Kennedy written some years later. "The staid Carlyle was pretty much bedlam," he wrote. "The doorman, reception desk and two flustered ladies at the elevator were obviously overwhelmed by the reporters, photographers, Secret Service agents, and political hangers-on that filled the lobby. Upstairs, confusion was compounded. In the suite of the President-elect two meetings were going on in different rooms with much bustling back and forth. No one seemed to know that the Senator had made a journalistic luncheon date. In fact, no one had bothered to order lunch at all."

Editor Royster suggested steak, medium rare with mushrooms, to a young woman who seemed to be working in the suite, and it was ordered. Then the two former naval officers sat down, one tall, spare and reserved, his jaw somewhat taut and bulging, his eyes glinting with the fire of combat; the other short, a little plump, and relaxed although he was aware that a bawling-out was forthcoming. He was right. Kennedy made it clear that he was damned irritated by that critical editorial "about my brother." Then the President-elect softened his voice and they talked man to man.

"He complained about being 'too busy to think,' " Royster wrote. "He professed puzzlement at fears among some in the business community that he was, as he put it, 'fiscally irresponsible'—and perhaps the journalist could help him change that image?

> He explained that the Eisenhower budget, due a few days later, would be balanced, but that it would be a "phony balance" because it depended on a postal rate increase and a hike in the gasoline tax. As President himself, he said, he would indorse the Eisenhower revenue requests, but Congress probably wouldn't grant them. Eisenhower, indeed, seemed much on the President-elect's mind. In commenting on the Southeast Asian crisis (it was Laos that winter), for example, he said quite frankly he hoped it would come to an end before he took over. The decision would have to be unpleasant, he commented, and "I don't have the confidence of the people the way Eisenhower does."
>
> So it went—on Cuba, on the farm problem, on domestic economics, on the foreign balance of payments. He appeared to be a young man suddenly appalled by the complexities of the job he had won, and yet so engaging in his uncertainties as to stir instinctive sympathy.

There were other meetings with President Kennedy, the tension growing as Vermont Royster wrote about the disaster of inflation, and as the President listened to advisers such as John Kenneth Galbraith, whose *Affluent Society,* a kind of guide to big government spending, became widely influential. The *Journal* reviewed the history of American deficit spending and inflation since the Roosevelt era in a series of January 1961 editorials. It found that the United States was possibly the world's foremost victim of "inflation's deceptive lure." Many other nations, it said, "have gone in for balanced budgets and improved tax structures, and they have otherwise taken care against artificially cheap money." The *Journal* did not name them. "When we have all this childish talk of what the Government is going to do for the economy," it said, referring to Kennedy's utterances, "we ought to remember not only the profound immorality of inflation but also the practical question of its effectiveness." On January 30, while saying it knew that the problems facing the new President were numerous and grave, the paper added, "But we would feel more reassured if we were sure that this Administration, in its haste to deal with things that are wrong, will not upset the things that are right."

At one meeting of some of the country's leading editors, Press Secretary Pierre Salinger, who was abundantly aware of Kennedy's opinion of *Wall Street Journal* editorials, was astonished and appalled when the President, looking around the room to invite questions, called on "Mr. Royster." Vermont Royster promptly rose to assail the President with one of those "acerbic questions" Kennedy especially detested.

"Why did you do it?" Salinger asked after the meeting, according to Tom Wicker of the *New York Times,* to whom Salinger related the incident.

"Well," said the President with a rueful grin, "the little bastard is the only one in there whose name I know."

But the *Journal* was not always unkind to President Kennedy. Following the Cuban Bay of Pigs disaster in April 1961, the paper held the President's advisers to blame, although President Kennedy blamed himself. On January 2, 1962, after adoption by Congress of the President's Alliance for Progress program for aid to Latin American republics, the confrontation with Premier Khrushchev of the USSR in Vienna, and the President's meeting with British Prime Minister Harold Macmillan in the Bahamas—all foreign-policy failures in the opinion of the *Journal*—it said, "History will likely forgive Mr. Kennedy his disaster in Cuba if, in the end, his civilization and his country are preserved." The President could be great, the editorial declared, if he could deal effectively with domestic problems. "He can keep his popularity in the Gallup poll or lose it by his skill with labor, farmers and businessmen; the future will measure only what he did to the economic world in which they work." The *Journal* thought the President was learning the hard way. "All the easy promises for spending money, which came to him so easily the first months in office, have now begun to haunt him."

Business at Dow Jones & Company continued to be good. Circulation of the *Journal* passed 784,000 at the end of 1961, and the value of Dow Jones stock was estimated at $235 million, "more than the stock of any other publishing company in the world," according to *Newsweek. Investor's Reader,* distributed by Merrill Lynch, Pierce, Fenner & Smith, published in its August 1961 issue an impressive analysis of Dow Jones's 1960 financial achievements: Total revenues of $47,678,000 were more than five times the $9,094,000 of 1950 and 15 times the $3,126,000 of 1940; earnings in 1960 were $6,369,000 or $40.77 on the 156,220 shares outstanding, as compared with $169,000 on 169,000 shares in 1940. "Only a handful of shares are traded publicly," the survey stated, "but they have zoomed from about $100 a share ten years ago to $1,425 bid, $1,525 asked. Circulation of *The Wall Street Journal* has risen from 29,000 in 1940 to 166,000 in 1950 and 707,000 by the end of 1960."

President Barney Kilgore himself continued to be a man much in the news. He accepted many invitations to speak and an award from the Columbia University Graduate School of Journalism, which once declined to admit him as a student. When Buren McCormack was elected president of Sigma Delta Chi, the national journalism society, Barney Kilgore took office as treasurer. He received awards for distinguished service to journalism from the University of Missouri in 1960, and from Colby College, Syracuse University, and the University of Kansas in 1961–62. He also added to his string of New Jersey weekly newspapers.

Despite his burden of corporate responsibilities and outside civic and educational activities, Kilgore found time to attend some morning kaffeeklatsches, but he usually dashed away before the discussion had ceased. At 52, Barney was a brawny, square-jawed man whose dark, bushy hair was beginning to thin a bit. Outsiders who interviewed him usually mentioned his mild, guarded manner of speaking and his "driving restlessness." The coffee sessions continued to be relaxed, but in the opinion of many who saw him, Barney Kilgore was not.

A *Newsweek* report on the *Journal* in November 1961 predicted that the paper would pass 800,000 in circulation and said that *Barron's* stood at more than 139,000. It also disclosed that Dow Jones & Company would soon publish a new newspaper of national circulation. "Christened the *National Observer* and due to be printed in Washington early next year, the projected weekly will be the nation's first national Sunday paper," *Newsweek* said. The article quoted from Kilgore's announcement to *The Wall Street Journal* staff: "The flow of news is already big. We don't need more people telling us what has happened as much as we need people who can put events together and explain them. . . . It will not be a weekly *Wall Street Journal*. It won't compete with existing Sunday papers, but with news magazines."

In his presentation to the Dow Jones directors, Barney Kilgore had not suggested that he intended to position the *National Observer* against national news magazines. He said his mass-circulation newspaper would recycle Dow Jones and *Journal* news materials. The treatment of raw news would be somewhat along the lines of the *Journal* but without the heavy business slant. Kilgore wanted the newspaper to be directed at young people, he indicated. It would capture the television generation, the young who had never formed the daily newspaper habit.

Kilgore's prestige was such that his idea was approved by the company directors, though some of them had reservations. Bill Kerby wrote in his memoirs that at the time he would rather Dow Jones considered the acquisition of a chain of small daily newspapers, a step he later took as the company's chief executive. But he loyally supported Kilgore's ideas. Laurence Lombard still preferred his own proposal to restructure *Barron's* magazine. However, there was no real opposition to Kilgore's project among the directors, Lombard recalled. Buren McCormack enthusiastically advocated it. Only Robert Feemster, the director of sales, who would be responsible for both circulation and advertising revenues, was openly opposed. He warned that the proposed *National Observer* "would lack appeal to advertisers" since there was "no defined audience" for the publication.

Kilgore evidently won acceptance of his plan not only because of his splendid record with the *Journal* but also for his emphasis on recycling the news. Feemster saw the fallacy in Kilgore's approach, however. Not only would the new paper fail to lure the younger generation from television, it couldn't snatch an adequate share of the advertising going into television's ample maw. In the new age of television, such established weekly magazines as *The Saturday Evening Post*, *Look*, and *Life* would crash under the weight of rising costs and lack of advertising revenue.

But Feemster and his staff entered into the *National Observer* project with determination once the decision was made. Ted Callis was given the job of organizing an advertising staff. He named Quentin de Maria from the Dow Jones advertising department as manager, and solicited salesmen from company offices around the country. Kerby recommended a top *Journal* newsman, William Giles, as editor, and Don Carter, formerly of the *Atlanta Journal*, as managing editor. Carter had been running the Newspaper Fund, a foundation Dow Jones created in 1958 to encourage young people's interest in journalism careers. Buren McCormack was directly in charge of *Observer* circulation sales. Thus Kilgore had the best people the *Journal* could provide to help insure the success of the *Observer*, among them some of his close friends.

The debut of Barney Kilgore's *National Observer* on February 4, 1962, became international news even before it occurred, such was Kilgore's reputation for wizardry in the publishing field. Even the staid *Economist* of London took notice of the impending event in its February 3 issue:

> This weekend the Dow Jones Company's new Sunday newspaper, the *National Observer*, makes its first appearance. The decision of the publishers of *The Wall Street Journal* to establish their new publication in Washington rather than in New York may have been influenced by the widely-felt need for a strong conservative voice in the nation's capital. But the location—like the project itself—can also be seen simply as a further example of the realistic attitude toward the business of journalism that has made the *Journal* itself an extraordinary success—both professionally and financially—in an era of fading newspapers. One reason for the *Journal*'s success was, in fact, its early recognition of Washington as a news center needed for competent reporting of the proliferating activities of the federal government. Today it often devotes more of its news space to material from Washington than to that from the nation's financial capital, New York, and a far greater proportion than any other periodical, including the *New York Times*.
>
> Its thorough coverage of Washington is only one facet, however, of the *Journal*'s excellent reporting of business and finance, to which its attention is mainly directed. Its original, detailed and independent coverage contrasts sharply with most metropolitan newspapers whose financial pages tend to be superficial, uniform and subservient to the interests of corporate advertisers. Together with the

> *New York Times* and a very few other newspapers, the *Journal* offers some positive evidence against the attitude, which is alarmingly present in the American press, that "good journalism is not good business." And only the *Journal* has been able to turn to its advantage that central fact of economic life which has decimated the press: the arrival of mass marketing and the revolution it has caused in advertising.

The *Economist* was wrong on some counts: the American press had not been "decimated," not by any definition or statistic; in fact, advertising linage in the daily press had increased with the arrival of mass marketing. But it was true that some daily newspapers had been subservient to business interests at times, and others, like the *Journal*, had fought against certain firms who were among their advertisers. It was also true that some weekly American magazines had suffered from an advertising revolution created by the proliferating electronic media, and the *National Observer* would prove to be one of them. The *National Observer* was superbly written and edited, highly readable, and well accepted by its peers, and it would win loyal followers. But Bob Feemster had seen the fatal flaw. The *Observer* could not develop a well-defined constituency. Advertising, Feemster knew, and many of his associates would discover, could be sold consistently only into a publication serving a readership able to buy what the advertisers desired to sell.

The *Economist* was also mistaken in assuming that Kilgore's *Observer* was intended to become a national political newspaper. But it was right in its assessment of the *Journal*'s success formula. Hogate and Grimes had made the paper outstanding in its coverage of Washington news, a policy followed by Kilgore, Kerby, and Phillips while they continued to broaden the paper's news base. It correctly attributed the paper's essential appeal to the economic self-interest of its readers, and forecast with considerable accuracy that "in the near future it will become the country's second-largest daily newspaper, surpassed only by the two million copies a day of the *New York Daily News*." By 1979 the *Journal*, with 1,768,000 circulation, passed the *News*, which had declined in circulation, and became first in circulation. In 1981 it totaled more than 2 million subscribers and buyers.

In reciting the history of *The Wall Street Journal* in its full-page profile, the *Economist* went on:

> While the paper is conservative and pro-business, it has kept its columns relatively and surprisingly independent. . . . Editorially, the *Journal* espouses a simon-pure (sometimes simple simon-pure) doctrine of laissez-faire that leads it to depart from the orthodox conservative line by advocating, for instance, absolutely free trade between nations and abandonment of all fair trade laws (for the maintenance of minimum prices). It continues to be suspicious of politicians, regardless of whether they were Republicans or Democrats, and it was noticeably cool to both Mr. Eisenhower and Mr. Nixon during their campaigns for the presidency.

One little known fact which may help to explain how a paper called *The Wall Street Journal* can be independent is that its controlling editorial group is largely composed of Midwesterners—most of them, in fact, graduates of a very small college, DePauw University in Greencastle, Indiana.

Kilgore, Kerby, and McCormack for years had been closely following the progress of scientists in experiments with semiconductors, lasers, and facsimile and offset printing. Some essentials had been in use or well known for a number of years. Small boys learned something of semiconductors when, shortly after World War I, they began building crude radio receivers using a galena crystal and a "cat whisker" that could find a sensitive point of the crystal to receive broadcast signals. The crystal converted alternating current to direct current, activating receiving equipment that could amplify the received energy and convert it to sound. In 1956 Dr. William Shockley, John Bardeen, and Walter Brattain of Bell Telephone Laboratories received the Nobel Prize for developing the transistor, which would revolutionize communications. Around the same time, Dr. T. H. Maiman of Hughes Aircraft Company built the first laser, which could propel pellets of light along optic-fiber conductors. The laser, among many other capabilities, could scan a photograph or newsprint page, read the images, and convert them to electrical energy for transmission. Thus, by the 1960s, facsimile pages of newspapers could be transmitted by coaxial cables and microwave transmitters for reproduction and printing at points hundreds or thousands of miles distant.

Buren McCormack, as business manager, followed facsimile experiments in Japan and Europe. He was especially impressed with developments at the *Manchester Guardian* and Muirhead, Ltd., of Beckenham, Kent, England. The experiments of *Asahi Shimbun* in Tokyo and the *Manchester Guardian* were duplicated and advanced by Dow Jones engineers in the United States. Dow Jones, meantime, had obtained land for a printing plant at Riverside, California, 60 miles east of Los Angeles. It would be the first daily newspaper plant in the United States to be designed for facsimile printing. The Riverside site was selected for various reasons. Southern California circulation required chartered airplanes to carry the papers from San Francisco, and weather, especially fog, often delayed the flights, causing readers to miss the paper for a day or longer. In addition, there was an opportunity for the *Journal* to increase its circulation. And Joe Ackell, who was superintending the production developments in California, had induced the Pacific Telephone & Telegraph Company, a subsidiary of American Telephone & Telegraph Company, to cooperate by charging a low experimental tariff of $15,000 a month to cover transmission costs. The experimental rate could be approved by the State of California since the transmission lines would be entirely within the state. George W. Flynn, a young printer from Elizabethtown, Illinois, who studied publication management at the University of Illinois and had joined the Dow Jones production department in 1956, serving as assistant production manager in Washington, Dallas, and Chicago, was put in charge of facsimile printing experiments early in 1961. In 1962 he was made production manager of the new *Journal* facility in Riverside. The facsimile plant went into operation on May 28, 1962.

The printing process for the Riverside edition began with transmissions from the San Francisco plant. There page proofs of the *Journal*, wrapped on a rotating cylinder, were scanned by an incandescent light source that "read" the page. Type images were converted into electrical energy and sent via coaxial cable to microwave transmitters on a chain of towers spaced 30 to 35 miles apart along a 392-mile route to Riverside. There a parabolic disc, a small microwave antenna, picked up the signal and recorded it on photographic film, which could be used to duplicate the San Francisco page exactly on zinc photoengraved plates. These plates were used to print the Riverside edition.

President Kilgore, announcing the publishing feat, said it was the first use of facsimile printing by remote control on a commercial basis in America. "The paper is an exact duplicate of the San Francisco printing," he declared. "*The Wall Street Journal* has been constantly trying to improve printing facilities to keep up with growth. On January 1, 1954, there were 278,000 subscribers; current circulation now exceeds 837,000. The new facilities provide better service to our subscribers and make possible day-of-publication delivery. . . . This is truly a national newspaper."

Later that year a New York City printers' strike shut down most of the city's newspapers for 114 days before ending on March 31, 1963. The *Journal* published during the strike, but Kilgore announced on April 2 that *The Wall Street Journal* would close printing operations in New York on July 1. The *New York Times* attributed the move to high publishing costs in New York and said the *New York Journal of Commerce* was making a similar move. Buren McCormack insisted that the decision had nothing to do with the printers' strike; the move had in fact been planned for a number of years.

The New York metropolitan-area circulation of the *Journal* was handled from the Chicopee plant after July 1, with other eastern plants taking over other sectors of eastern circulation. Eventually, a new publishing plant to serve the New York area would be built at South Brunswick, New Jersey. The *Journal*'s New York printing operations ended after 74 years.

Microwave transmission of facsimile pages was not the final solution to the *Journal*'s publishing problems, however. McCormack and his aides sought offset printing equipment that could accommodate long, high-speed pressruns. McCormack, Dow Jones production engineers, and *Journal* editors also watched closely the development of new transmission techniques by means of satellites by AT&T and the new government-backed Communications Satellite Corporation (COMSAT). On July 10, 1962, as Telstar I was launched, AT&T, which paid NASA for the launch costs, announced plans for a new, "synchronous" satellite (its orbit speed would match the earth's rotation speed) to be launched the following year. Such a satellite would be put into orbit exactly 22,300 miles above the equator. Since it would orbit the earth at the same speed as the earth turned, it could be said to be "parked," or in a fixed position. To a person on earth, it would always appear stationary. This provided maximum performance capability as a communications receiver and sender.

The paper carried several stories on COMSAT, a part public, part private enterprise created to develop telecommunications on an international basis. Stock in the corporation was sold to the public. COMSAT built satellites, arranged launchings, and initiated and managed the International Telecommunications Satellite Organization (INTELSAT), designed to control international space communications. The purpose was to establish a system in competition with AT&T since the government feared a monopoly.

The *Journal* gave President Kennedy's domestic policy mixed reviews during 1962. It approved of his reduction of tariffs, characterized his forced rollback of the steel industry's price increases in April as "the use of naked force," opposed the President's silver demonetization order, and attacked his general-aid-to-education message, challenging his assertion that fears of federal control where federal money was offered were unfounded. "The right question [for citizens to ask] is not whether huge Federal aid leads to Federal control, but what kind of Federal control," it said on February 7. The editorial listed examples of creeping federal control in education and urged the restoration of local regulation. "There is no certainty the Federal standards are the right ones," the *Journal* said. "The nation is better off with an infinite variety and experimentation that comes when localities can operate without interference. . . . An examination of the Administration's own proposals suggests that the fears of Federal control cannot be brushed aside as baseless. They are well founded because they are grounded in the nature of tightly-centralized government."

President Kennedy was reading *The Wall Street Journal* less and disliking it more. He found Royster's editorials increasingly exasperating, perhaps because they portrayed him as zealously pushing centralized government, contrary to the states' rights philosophy of his party, and furthering inflation, an evil the President insisted he was fighting. Even seemingly harmless asides from the White House brought scornful appraisal. When the President said the government would have to "find" jobs for the unemployed, the *Journal* upbraided him. What was wrong, the paper asserted, was Kennedy's implication that automated tools were putting people out of work. Not so. "Tools, whether wheelbarrows or automated factories, are not the creators of surplus labor. . . . Automated ditch-diggers are unnecessary, and therefore unborn, until there are no longer enough men to dig economically the number of ditches society needs to have dug. . . . There's no way the government can 'find' new jobs unless it leaves the economy free to grow and create them." It was the kind of patronizing lecture the President especially disliked.

When, in January 1963, the Cuban missile crisis was declared over and President Kennedy was preparing to send his tax-cutting proposal to Congress, the *Journal* ended a brief spate of all-out support and began sniping again. Kennedy's tax plan, it reported, would encompass a three-year $13.6 billion tax-reduction schedule, but the paper was neither pleased nor appeased.

> Everybody—well nearly everybody—seems to agree that taxes are too much with us. And that we should lighten the burden to get the country going again. On this point it is hard to tell a liberal from a conservative without a score card.
>
> In fact, the liberals are telling us we don't even have to worry about Government deficit. The tax cut will spur savings, pump new capital into business, set the wheels humming. Thus the Government will get more revenues from lower taxes. . . . And so it might. Still, we wonder if the people, and particularly the liberal politicians, are ready to recognize the kind of taxes that are true constrictions on savings, capital accumulation and economic progress. To admit them and remove them would require the abandonment of a whole generation of liberal shibboleths.

The *Journal* believed, of course, that the liberal Kennedy administration had no intention of removing such constrictions on the formation of capital as "heavy death duties, high rates on high income, the capital gains levy." These taxes did not come accidentally, the paper said. "They came in obedience to the sociological doctrine that the 'rich' should be leveled and the political belief that it's profitable to 'soak the rich.' The rich, of course, are anyone who earns more than you do." President Kennedy had, in fact, taken refuge among the neo-Keynesians, who concluded that, as economist Robert Lekachman put it, "public spending would not only stimulate the economy but would also feed the starved public services and do something to rectify the social imbalance between public and private spending."

President Kennedy, despite his own statements on "the myths about our public debt" (which, he said, was not actually growing relative to the growth of the gross national product), proposed a tax plan more conservative than the *Journal* had anticipated, though some critics insisted it was nevertheless Keynesian. Although Congress would amend it, the proposed Kennedy plan liberalized plant depreciation, reduced income-tax progression, and promised control of federal spending. The *Journal* consequently grew a bit friendlier to President Kennedy when details became known, although it still opposed his dispatch of advisers to Vietnam. "The war is going badly for the South Vietnamese forces and their U.S. military advisors," it said, pointing out that the 12,000 Americans could advise, but not command. "Is this a practical military approach?" it asked. "Nobody wants a full commitment of U.S. fighting men, but to win a stalemate in Korea, the U.S. did have to fight along with the South Koreans and the U.S. was in charge. Elsewhere we have deterred Communist aggression with the implicit threat of nuclear retaliation. The Vietnam business by contrast looks like a military mishmash. . . . Perhaps we should all realize that there are certain things the U.S., for all its military power, cannot do. One is to reshape the nature of peoples of radically different conditions and values."

On November 22, 1963, while riding in a motorcade in Dallas, Texas, President Kennedy was shot to death by a sniper. *The Wall Street Journal* on November 25 paid tribute to the martyred President. It admitted that "we have differed with him on the role of government, yet all who knew him even slightly, as we did, could sense his statesmanship and see what an engaging and thoughtful man he was. All the harder then, to believe that this man, with his gentle jibes, his Frostian wisdom and his Lockean skepticism, has been so brutally cut down by a sniper's bullet, his darting intelligence stilled forever."

On the same day the *Journal* wished President Lyndon B. Johnson well and said that he brought to his task a quality of experience in government and a lifetime experience in politics that would be much needed by the country. "We are, right now, a nation almost equally divided on many great issues. We made our choice at the last election only by a hair's breadth, and it was from this division among the people, deep and sincere, that grew many of President Kennedy's great difficulties. That the nation is now one in sorrow and outrage does not alter the fact that, as a nation, we are still undecided about the shape of the national society and about the means of molding it."

President Kilgore, preoccupied with corporate responsibilities and the *National Observer*, left day-to-day Dow Jones operations "pretty much to me," Bill Kerby wrote. Bob Bottorff, executive editor, was directly in charge of the *Journal*'s news department; Editor Vermont Royster directed the editorial page and also wrote "Thinking Things Over," the column once written by Thomas Woodlock and later by Bill Grimes. Buren McCormack handled daily production and circulation problems in addition to his studies of technological developments. In December 1962 Bob Feemster resigned and went to Florida to look after a hotel property he had acquired. Ted Callis succeeded him as general sales manager. Donald A. Macdonald became advertising director of the *Journal*, *Barron's*, and the *National Observer*, succeeding Callis. A short time later, on January 14, 1963, Bob Feemster was killed in a private plane crash near Fort Pierce, Florida.

On May 22, 1963, the directors of Dow Jones voted to increase the number of common shares to 3,500,000, each existing share being split ten to one. There would be other splits in this period: an increase to 7 million shares on March 3, 1964; to 9 million shares on August 17, 1966; and to 18 million shares on November 19, 1969. After the May 1963 split, there was an immediate secondary offering of 103,500 shares (shares in the hands of individual stockholders willing to sell) at $112 a share. This offering was promptly oversubscribed.

By the end of 1964 Dow Jones said it had news-ticker clients in 676 U.S. cities in 48 of the 50 states, and "through redistribution contracts with press associations, Dow Jones reports reach nearly every daily newspaper and sizable radio and television station in the Free World." The news, or broad-tape, tickers operated by Dow Jones from New York were fed information by *Journal* reporters on breaking stories, as they had been since the service started in 1897; the Canadian Dow Jones tickers received news from Montreal. The broad-tape tickers were leased at a rate of roughly $180 a month after an increase on June 1, 1963. By 1964 *The Wall Street Journal* provided the bulk of Dow Jones's revenue, followed by the news-ticker service and *Barron's*.

Barney Kilgore and his associates were cheered by a Goldman Sachs & Company analysis that indicated good progress was being made by the *National Observer* and the company. Noting that circulation of the *Observer* was 330,630 in 1964 (on its way to 414,298 a year later), the report said, "We understand the subscription renewal rate has been excellent. Management, and many potential advertisers as well, considered the *Observer* 'in business' when circulation passed 300,000 and will regard it as a major publication when 500,000 is reached." *The Wall Street Journal* circulation was 805,849, said the analysis issued in August. "First half earnings [of Dow Jones in 1964] were up sharply despite a heavy concentration of promotional expenses for the *Observer* and the *Journal*, as well as the computerization program at Chicopee. We expect a strong second half."

At some time in 1964 Kilgore recruited Bradford Mills of New York Securities, financial consultants, as an outside adviser for the Dow Jones diversification program. On November 1, 1965, Mills provided President Kilgore and the directors with a two-volume study plus exhibits. The analysis of Dow Jones activities was generally favorable. It especially praised the installation of an IBM 360 computer at South Brunswick "to assist in internal communications and processing. . . . In two years Dow Jones will have the capability of retrieving, storing and disseminating information with a trained staff of programmers." A number of activities for the computer in investment and banking were suggested.

The consultant urged a further investment of $1,500,000 with Scantlin Electronics for research and development (Dow Jones had previously invested $1 million) but was cold to Barney Kilgore's proposal of a student edition of the *National Observer*. Instead, the study urged extending the *Journal*'s Educational Service Bureau, which in 1964 supplied educational materials and *Journal*s at special rates to more than 3,500 professors and their students in 940 colleges. Ten years later Dow Jones would estimate that 22,000 college professors were using the *Journal* in their classrooms, and it was noted that 2,000 high school teachers "make use of the *National Observer* as an educational tool."

The study was enthusiastic about a book-publishing alliance for Dow Jones. New York Securities studied 15 companies in the trade and college-textbook publishing fields. They recommended the latter as having greatest growth potential and Richard D. Irwin, Inc., the Homewood, Illinois, textbook publisher, as an especially good acquisition prospect. Richard D. Irwin founded his own company in a one-room Chicago office in 1933 to specialize in publishing and distributing books on business and economics. The company grew and in 1951 moved to Homewood.

Kilgore and his associates acted swiftly on the book-publishing recommendation. On September 28, 1966, the paper announced that the directors of Dow Jones and Richard D. Irwin had approved a merger. Problems developed, however, so the association became less formal, and the actual merger did not take place until 1975, when Richard D. Irwin, Inc., became a wholly owned subsidiary of Dow Jones & Company. That year Irwin had 709 book titles in print plus new or revised titles scheduled for the year. Irwin operations included Dow Jones/Irwin Books, hardcover business books (a previous joint venture with Dow Jones); Dorsey Press, social-science textbooks; and Learning Systems Company, producers of Programmed Learning Aids for colleges and graduate schools. Irwin subsidiaries included Business Publications, Inc. (Dallas), hardcover business books; Irwin-Dorsey International (London); and Irwin-Dorsey, Ltd (Ontario, Canada).

The acquisition study seeking other fields "most congenial to Dow Jones" covered selected trade journals; newspapers in Texas and the Southeast; radio and television stations; paper; printing; expansion of electronics, computer, and information-retrieval services; and an expanded communications network. The numbered copies of the study given to the directors were well-thumbed at a section labeled "production facilities which can be used when not in operation to produce additional newspapers and trade journals."

A proposal immediately and unanimously rejected, however, suggested that Dow Jones produce a Sunday financial supplement to be sold to metropolitan newspapers for distribution in their Sunday editions. Syndicated supplements such as *This Week* and *Parade* were highly profitable to their publishers at the time but *Wall Street Journal* executives had no intention of going into competition with themselves.

In February 1965 Dow Jones & Company, Inc., moved its corporate headquarters and its news, editorial, and advertising-production departments to 30 Broad Street, a 47-story building that then became known as the Wall Street Journal Building. All divisions at 44 Broad Street and elsewhere in New York—including *Journal* and *Observer* advertising-sales and promotion departments, Dow Jones News Service sales and service departments, and *Barron's*, which moved from 50 Broadway—made the transfer. Bill Kerby, executive vice-president, said that the 44 Broad Street building would be sold. "For the first time in years, it has been possible to bring together all New York City operations under a single roof," Kerby declared. It was a symbolic move, full of nostalgia, he noted, for it meant a final physical break with the past.

In May 1965 Kerby and Buren McCormack, general manager, were made directors of Dow Jones & Company. The board increased to nine with the addition of another outside director, Carl J. Gilbert, chairman of the board of the Gillette Company. Editor Royster, General Sales Manager Callis, and Executive Editor Bottorff were elected vice-presidents, and Business Manager John J. McCarthy was named treasurer.

Stock-market news turned better in 1964 after the Kennedy tax bill, signed into law by President Johnson, spurred the economy. "The vanguard, at least, of the army of small investors 'burned' in 1962 is beginning to edge back," said the *Journal* on March 15. "Ever since the 1962 break drove away most 'public' investors, price gains have been powered largely by institutions such as mutual funds. But now there are crowds in the board rooms." Brokers were saying that buyers were interested in blue chips, the paper said, and there were no "wild-eyed speculators such as were active in 1961."

The editors were far from pleased with the general business outlook, however. "Far too many economists and politicians seem to believe that rising prices are [either] an unavoidable consequence or a prior condition of satisfactory economic growth. . . . The idea of growth-through-inflation certainly offers an attractive simplicity. If the government will only put enough money into the hands of the consumers and investors, the reasoning runs, the demand for everything will expand, the unemployment problem will disappear, and the nation will grow more prosperous." But the paper insisted that what the government then started, it couldn't or wouldn't stop. The total

American economy was consequently crippled by big spending, big debt, and devaluation. When the government bought goods, in the *Journal*'s view, it simply took away the public's ability to buy or to invest. The increase in the gross national product meant little when measured by a "rubber" dollar, the paper insisted, especially since government was one of the big buyers. The GNP stood at $103 billion in 1929, sank to $56 billion in 1933, and then in 1961 rose to a whopping $614.4 billion. But the problems of unemployment had not been corrected, except in wartime, and the national debt became ominously oppressive.

Trying to modernize America by devaluing or overexpanding its supply of money wouldn't work either, the *Journal* said. "That is an old notion. . . . Even the ancient kings sooner or later found out how ruinous it is to start shaving a little gold or silver from their coins." The paper praised Chairman Martin of the Federal Reserve for his conservative advice and actions, saying, "It is a good thing there is at least one Mr. Martin in the government." Yet it had little real hope that Martin alone could prevail: "Lasting correctives like monetary and fiscal restraint are not to the liking of the Johnson administration; they are anathema to the AFL-CIO which has such proprietary feelings about the administration."

On March 11, 1965, the paper condemned many Republicans as well as Democrats for going along with President Johnson's plan to authorize the Great Society spending program while the Vietnam War continued without paying for either currently. The Republicans, the paper said, were offering a school-aid plan that would outspend Johnson's spendthrift ideas, and it predicted that the GOP medicare plan would do the same thing. "The public welfare," cried the editorialist in some desperation, "must embrace more than raiding the Treasury, or worse, financing 'benefits' with an inflation injurious to the people."

The *Journal*'s news coverage in the mid-1960s continued to win added circulation, compliments, and awards. Subscribers and buyers totaled 1,002,835 by the end of 1966. Its fourth Pulitzer Prize went to Norman "Mike" Miller, Washington bureau chief in 1964, for general reporting. Miller followed an ordinary bankruptcy action filed in a Newark, New Jersey, court on November 3, 1963, against a relatively unknown company until it became a national scandal. In a bizarre swindle, Allied Crude Vegetable Oil Refining Corporation borrowed nearly $150 million on fake receipts for "salad" oil allegedly held in company storage tanks. Most of the oil was missing when the company filed for bankruptcy. A dozen other firms also went down. The story was incredibly complex and difficult to follow, but Miller and his associates on the *Journal* "reconstructed" what happened. The series made clear that Anthony "Tino" DeAngelis, former president of Allied, masterminded the hoax. DeAngelis was convicted and sentenced to 20 years in prison.

The following year, Louis Kohlmeier of the Washington bureau received the Pulitzer for national reporting for his two-part series detailing how President Johnson's wife, Lady Bird, parlayed a $417,500 investment in 1943 into a multimillion-dollar Texas broadcasting business. In 1967 Stanley Penn, a writer in the New York bureau specializing in investigative work, and Monroe "Bud" Karmin, based in Washington, won the Pulitzer Prize for a series of articles on the probable link between the "Bay Street Boys," a white-power group that controlled the Bahamian government, and Bahamas gambling and organized criminals in the United States. "They documented the rise of Wallace Groves, a Wall Street financier who had served a prison term for mail fraud, to the dominant position in Bahamian commercial development with the help of 'The Bay Street Boys,' " said the citation. As a result of the exposé, the government fell; native politicians, led by Lynden O. Pindling, took over.

In the summer of 1965 Barney Kilgore visited his wife, Mary Lou, in Princeton Hospital, where she was undergoing tests, and unexpectedly became a victim of severe stomach pain. The preliminary diagnosis indicated an obstruction, so Kilgore remained in the hospital for tests and treatment. A week later, after Mary Lou signed herself out, Barney Kilgore underwent surgery. It was a long and difficult operation, the doctors told Mary Lou and Bill McSherry, Kilgore's secretary and assistant at *The Wall Street Journal*. But they were advised that "B.K.'s full recovery was indicated. We were given every reason to believe that he would be back in action shortly," McSherry recalled.

Barney Kilgore, of course, was eager to get back, but he soon had a satisfactory command post established in the hospital. He was in touch with Bill Kerby by telephone every day, and McSherry came regularly to the hospital bringing mail, messages, good wishes, and corporate matters requiring his attention and signature. Kilgore was cheerful and optimistic. After his release from the hospital, he and Mary Lou went to Palm Springs, where he could rest and relax. Barney kept in touch with Kerby and McSherry by telephone. He also spoke frequently with Laurence Lombard.

"I suspect that the day-to-day decisions were being made by Kerby alone," McSherry said years later. "They discussed longer range problems, but Kerby was the man at the wheel of the Dow Jones empire."

McSherry was right. Bill Kerby, executive vice-president, was in charge. Kerby told the story in his memoirs:

> "I have cancer, but I am going to live my life as though I didn't."
>
> This from Barney Kilgore to me one morning in 1965.
>
> He added that he planned to retire as chief executive officer in the spring of the following year. . . . He would be chairman of the board, but would make his office in our new building near Princeton. "You will have a clear field." . . . I

found it impossible to accept the fact that this virile, energetic man, the inspired architect of the modern *Wall Street Journal* and my close friend for 35 years, was telling me he had a terminal illness.

The rest of the conversation is a blur.

Late in the fall of 1965 Kilgore returned to duty, spending two days a week in New York and three days at South Brunswick. McSherry served as his secretary and assistant at both bases. "I would drive from New York with matters to be handled by him," McSherry wrote years later. "He would dictate and instruct. Hand-delivery by courier kept delays minimal." Jim Borgia, who was one of the regular couriers handling service between South Brunswick and New York, carried most of Kilgore's messages. The president joked, sometimes told a story, and the cheerful young Italian didn't suspect the boss was ill.

On January 7, 1966, Kilgore issued a statement to the Dow Jones staff:

> At the time of the annual stockholders' meeting on March 15, I expect to retire as President of the Company and to become Chairman of the Board.
>
> This is not a sudden decision. I have been President for more than 20 years and for the last 15 months or so, in consultation with other directors of the company, I have been at work on appropriate recommendations whereby our management team could be expanded and responsibilities more broadly shared.
>
> I will formally propose to the Board of Directors that William F. Kerby be elected President, Buren McCormack as Executive Vice President, and Robert Bottorff, already a Vice President, be designated as General Manager. This will, in turn, increase the scope of the work of other officers and executives.

Barney Kilgore and Bill Kerby worked together in New York on details of the power transfer. During periods of remission, Kilgore seemingly regained all past vigor and zest for work. But there were dark periods, and Barney knew that the verdict of the doctors was immutable and final. He instructed McSherry to separate his personal files in the New York office and turn the others over to Bill Kerby. "All credit cards were returned as well as business club memberships," Bill McSherry remembered. At home, Barney tried not to let Mary Lou and the children know about his bad times. "He never talked about his illness," she told John Bridge years later, "never." But Mary Lou, of course, knew what the doctors diagnosed.

Barney Kilgore, Lombard, and Robert S. Potter of Dow Jones's legal counsel were busy those weeks arranging Kilgore's retirement, including a negotiated settlement of a retirement contract Kilgore signed in December 1946. The *Journal* published on February 21, 1966, details of the proposal under which President Kilgore would receive a lump-sum payment of $3,503,678 "to buy out his rights" under the old agreement. Kilgore would have received, under this agreement, an amount based on the earnings of 150,000 shares of Dow Jones stock for as long as he might live, with his widow receiving an amount based on the earnings on 75,000 common shares for as long as she lived. Dow Jones stock earned $2.07 a share in 1965.

"The company stated," the story in the *Journal* said, "that it is impossible to place a definite valuation on the benefits" of the 1946 contract. It suggested that if Bernard Kilgore lived out a normal life expectancy of 18 years, and Mrs. Kilgore 24 years, the company would pay out $6 million. The settlement worked out by the lawyers was thus considered advantageous to the company, compared with the amount that would have been paid if the 1946 agreement had been allowed to stand. (Actually, the amount involved on the old contract basis would have turned out to be much higher as a result of a great increase in Dow Jones earnings in subsequent years.) In addition to the lump-sum settlement, the *Journal* said, President Kilgore would be named chairman of the board on his retirement and would receive a consulting contract paying $25,000 a year for five years.

There were objections to the settlement by a shareholder who threatened legal action to stop it, but Lombard and Manly Fleischman, special counsel to the company for this purpose, assured the directors and the stockholders that the proposed settlement was a desirable compromise. Since the Bancroft sisters, Mrs. Jane Cook and Mrs. Jessie Cox, and other family members controlled 3,826,270 of the 4,670,322 shares, the Kilgore settlement was approved by an overwhelming stockholder vote. The threatened lawsuit was never pressed.

Barney Kilgore presented his resignation at the directors' meeting on March 15 and was elected chairman of the board. William F. Kerby was elected president and chief executive officer of Dow Jones & Company. Kerby's new team soon appeared in the *Journal*'s masthead. In addition to Kilgore and Kerby himself, Buren H. McCormack was made executive vice-president; Robert Bottorff, vice-president and general manager; and Vermont Royster, vice-president and editor. Warren Phillips had been named executive editor in 1965. Not included in the masthead, under traditional company policy, were John McCarthy, business manager and treasurer; Theodore Callis, vice-president and general sales manager; and Edward R. Cony, who succeeded Phillips as managing editor.

Kilgore's consulting contract provided that he would deal primarily but not exclusively with editorial techniques and that he would undertake special studies of the subsidiaries. Barney went to work as a consultant with characteristic enthusiasm. In addition to his stated duties, he looked into a possible merger with the Gannett newspaper group, but the deal did not jell, a keen disappointment to him, according to McSherry. Kilgore continued to send story ideas to the *Journal* and advise the staff of the *Observer*, but his health deteriorated, and he had to take several vacations. Sometimes, in periods of renewed energy, he seemed himself again. In January 1967 *The Wall Street*

Journal completed its first offset printing plant at Highland, Illinois, near St. Louis. There was Barney Kilgore, joining other executives from New York, helping to unpack equipment. William Satterfield, newly recruited into the Dow Jones production department and later to become production manager at Orlando, worked near Kilgore. Although he was a newcomer, Satterfield recognized the chairman of the board.

"He was in his shirt-sleeves, knocking open boxes and removing hardware," Satterfield recalled. "He worked like the rest of us. One of our printers who didn't know who he was asked Mr. Kilgore what he did regularly for the company. Barney pointed to the masthead of a copy of the *Journal* he had with him. 'That's me,' he said."

By autumn 1967 illness kept Barney home, although he continued to study company publications, to consult by telephone, and to dictate to McSherry. One published article on his influence on *The Wall Street Journal* especially absorbed him. It was written by Phillips for the October issue of the *Bulletin of the American Society of Newspaper Editors*. There had been many discussions, at meetings and in print, of Barney Kilgore's work and ideas, but he never commented on any of them except to say that his credit should be limited to the development of "leader" stories for the *Journal*. When questioned, he covered his contributions with quips and aphorisms. A book he edited with Henry Gemmill included nothing of Kilgore's writings and philosophy about journalism.

However, Kilgore was impressed by Phillips's description of *The Wall Street Journal*'s approach to reporting and writing, which included an appraisal and analysis of Kilgore's work, and he sent a note to the author with copies to Kerby, Bottorff, Royster, and McCormack. He indicated the frail state of his health by saying, "My chances these days of writing things for the paper, even for the file, are pretty limited, so I thought I'd send you a copy of this." "This" was Kilgore's dictated statement on Phillips's article:

> It was not an especially startling statement in any way, but it pleased me greatly to read something that I myself might have written 25 years or even longer ago. Insofar as my participation in making news policy is concerned, my role is apparently still meaningful, although it has been inactive in the sense of holding the highest news executive job on the newspaper, as Warren Phillips does today. It means to me that the staff must still understand quite clearly what we are trying to do even though we do not always succeed.
>
> What is *The Wall Street Journal* anyhow? The most significant thing to me about it is that it is a newspaper and not a trade paper. It has more to do with the *Pittsburgh Post-Gazette* than it does with *Iron Age* [a trade paper]. It serves a community which is not geographic, except in a national sense, but includes so many different fields and interests and shapes and sizes that its community behaves more like a city than it does any occupation or interest. . . .
>
> A good many *Wall Street Journal* readers, even today, do not fully understand

> the basic nature of the publication. . . . In any event, it doesn't make any difference to them as long as it serves their purposes adequately, but the basic definition of any publication is of utmost importance to its editors. And, while it doesn't make a great deal of difference to anyone else, it makes a great deal of difference to me as to what Warren H. Phillips, executive editor, says even in what appears to be a rather casual or routine discussion of his purpose.

Kilgore, in his note, distilled the essence of Phillips's article, which covered the technique and philosophy behind the *Journal*'s news-gathering, writing, and editing, and cited examples. Concluding the essay, Phillips said they were "handing down and building on techniques pioneered over a quarter of a century by Barney Kilgore.

> Kilgore, more than any other, broadened the concept of what constitutes news of importance to *Journal* readers. It also was he who developed the Page One leader story which, while dealing with current events, was not tied down by yesterday's developments. This permitted the staff to dig into a situation over a period of several days or even weeks, then write about it with care and clarity and give the reader a comprehensive report.
>
> The heavy editing that these reports undergo, and the multiple duties of our reporters, produce irritations from time to time. But they are overshadowed by the enthusiasm and staff esprit that seem to thrive on challenge to each man to produce the best he can give, to meet standards in which he can take deep pride.
>
> We fall short of the standards we set for ourselves as often as we attain them, of course. The battle . . . may never be won. But a lot of enthusiasm is being poured into the fight.

Barney Kilgore had been reassured by the Phillips article that the ideas he shared with Kerby, McCormack, and Royster were being carried on by a new generation, and he was pleased. He must have been pleased, also, if he happened to see in his reading a little item in a book by Gerald Carson, *The Polite Americans*, which was popular that fall. Noting the practices of elitist Americans in the 1960s, Carson wrote, "In the higher circles, weight watching has become as important an ingredient of success as reading *The Wall Street Journal*."

Kilgore continued to work at home a few more weeks. McSherry was with him most working days, taking down memos and suggestions for the *Journal* and his *National Observer*. He was gravely concerned about the future of the latter publication. "I saw him five days before his death," McSherry recalled. "Although he was having blood tests taken, he sat in his living room with a pile of papers he went through one by one. I left him four hours later with enough work to keep busy for a week."

One of the last visitors from the office Kilgore saw was his friend William Kerby, and his thoughts were with the *Observer*. "His last words as he lay dying in his Princeton home," Kerby wrote, "were, 'Bill, will my baby make it?' "

On November 14, 1967, shortly before midnight, McSherry heard on the radio that Bernard Kilgore had died at home near Princeton. The Associated Press carried the dispatch early on the morning of the 15th; *The Wall Street Journal* and other morning newspapers around the world published the news and obituary on November 16. The story of Barney Kilgore in the *Journal* was handled in a uniquely fitting way. It appeared in column four, the space until then exclusively reserved for one-of-a-kind special stories Kilgore invented for the paper's first page, under the equivalent of the A-hed, designed by Bill Kerby. The account, running four and a half columns, was simply written. The *New York Times*, too, paid journalistic tribute to Kilgore by the way it handled the story of his death that same day. Under the Associated Press announcement, the *Times* story began, " 'Financial people are nice people and all that,' Bernard Kilgore once said, 'but there aren't enough of them to make this newspaper go.' "

The *Journal*'s obituary credited Kilgore with bringing the earnings of Dow Jones & Company from $211,201 in 1945 to more than $13 million in 1966, which was important to Barney, the paper said, "because he was convinced that only a sound financial structure could support good journalistic enterprises. . . . But he never forgot the purpose of his business management and never ceased himself to be a shirt-sleeved newspaperman."

The lead editorial recounted Barney Kilgore's great achievement of bringing the circulation of the *Journal* from "around 33,000 to more than one million, seeing it published in eight plants scattered across the country and grown rich in resources and prestige as the country's first national newspaper." The editorial spoke of Barney Kilgore's personal qualities:

> He was, strangely enough for a dynamic leader, the gentlest of men. There were those who have worked with him a lifetime and who bear witness to his stubbornness with an idea, who have never seen him lose his temper or make those flamboyant gestures which make for legends. By the nature of his work—from reporter to prominent publisher—he walked with the peers of his time, and he was known and respected by all. Yet he always walked with them shyly, just as he was shy with those who worked with him.
>
> Somehow among those gifts given him was the boon of self-containment, if not always self-content. There was a demon in him about what he wanted to create; his pride in his newspaper was as great as that of a composer for his symphony, and so was his jealousy for it. Yet he had not the slightest need for self-aggrandizement or personal publicity to nourish an uncertain ego.
>
> Thus his work is more famous than himself. If you ask what he did, you need only to look at this newspaper you are reading.

Chapter 20

Dow Jones and the *Journal* Go International

The close and enduring partnership of Barney Kilgore and Bill Kerby assured a smooth transition of power at Dow Jones and the *Journal* even before Kerby became chief executive in March 1966. The management team they created in the days of the Kilgore Revolution 25 years previously was still in place and working well together. From the time Barney first disclosed his terminal illness to his friend and became even more a man in a hurry, Kerby served as chief operating officer of the company, loyally carrying out Kilgore policy, sometimes smoothing the way among company directors for his impatient president. After Barney Kilgore's death, Kerby and the team maintained momentum. Buren McCormack served well in specialized production areas and as Kerby's confidant. Ted Callis, director of sales, pushed the *Journal*'s circulation to 1,218,935 in 1968, and up another 40,000 the year following as the economy boomed. Vermont Royster, directing *Journal* editorial policy; Robert Bottorff, vice-president and general manager; and Executive Editor Warren Phillips, in charge of news operations, were all Kilgore-era veterans.

Bill Kerby inherited an experienced management team; he also inherited problems. The very success of *The Wall Street Journal* had become a problem in Kilgore's view, a belief shared by Kerby. The *Journal* earned 94 percent of all Dow Jones profits in 1968. That put too much dependence on a single publication having as its basic mission coverage of economic news, even though it had become a national business newspaper. In 1969 Dow Jones & Company had the most profitable year in its history up to that time, according to *Fortune*, which rated its earnings record as the best of any American newspaper. Nonetheless, President Kerby was as much in a hurry to broaden the Dow Jones business base as he had been to broaden the news base of the paper in the 1940s. While he contemplated a diversification program, however, there were day-to-day problems to be solved. Since the paper's circulation was increasing, Kerby boosted advertising rates on January 1, 1967, and the years following.

The increased income from a bigger *Journal* and higher advertising rates could be used in part to pay for plant expansion; for an investment of $3,245,712 in Scantlin Electronics, Inc.; to cover *National Observer* losses; to provide for the faster news-ticker machines Kerby was determined to have; and to pay for Kerby's own special project, the purchase of a number of small-city daily newspapers as part of his acquisition plan. In July 1966 Kerby had prompted Dow Jones to file with the Federal Communications Commission a statement of the company's interest in using a domestic communications satellite "at appropriate tariffs," saying "this would encourage Dow Jones to expand its utilization of facsimile transmission to more plants to give subscribers faster and better service." Despite its early application, Dow Jones didn't get its earth-station license until six years later.

In August 1969 President Kerby was delighted to learn that a Harris public-opinion survey, commissioned by the advertising department of *Time* magazine, showed *The Wall Street Journal* to be "the most trusted newspaper" in the country, while the *National Observer* tied with the *New York Times* for second place. Kerby made effective use of its findings in speeches and statements. He was elated by the survey's conclusions, he said, but he felt humble, too. "It is an oft-noted truism that the loneliest job in the world is that of chief executive officer," he wrote years later. "This is the lot of the chief executive of any sizable company. If the business is publishing, it is an added burden. And, in my case, there was the burden of knowing I was the person ultimately accountable for every word printed by 'America's most trusted newspaper, *The Wall Street Journal*.' "

Kerby may have been awed by his responsibilities and the mighty influence attributed to his newspaper, but he never forgot its primary mission, which made that influence possible. "*The Wall Street Journal*," Kerby once said, "always touches our reader's most important nerve, his pocketbook nerve."

Then Kerby's job grew even lonelier. Buren McCormack—"my tower of strength," Kerby called him—was ill for many months before dying on February 28, 1972. Vermont Royster, editor and senior vice-president, had a carcinoma diagnosis and, after major surgery, requested retirement in

January 1971. Fortunately, Royster recovered, resumed his column, "Thinking Things Over," and became a director of Dow Jones. But he remained in Chapel Hill, North Carolina, as editor emeritus of the *Journal*, while serving as professor of journalism and public affairs at the University of North Carolina. In 1970 Ted Callis and Bob Bottorff retired. Harold Boeschenstein, who, with Lombard, was Kerby's close confidant on the board of directors, died in 1972. It was a time of retirement for a number of longtime veterans, among them Richard Platt Cooke, a Princeton graduate who joined the *Journal* in 1927 and had been transportation editor and drama critic of the paper since 1938.

Bill Kerby had to bring up new executives fast. Early in his regime, his chief aide had been Warren Phillips, the brilliant young editor who by 1971 was vice-president of Dow Jones and editorial director of all company publications. Another rising executive was Donald Macdonald, a tough, craggy, hard-driving advertising man. "Bring him on fast; he's got brass balls," Kilgore advised. Macdonald would be in the forefront of the company's foreign ventures, especially in Asia. Joseph Evans ran the editorial page after Royster departed, but Evans himself was in poor health. He and Royster in 1964 had recruited for their editorial page Robert L. Bartley, a graduate of Chicago Managing Editor John McWethy's "School of Journalism," after he contributed some articles and book reviews they liked and printed, and Bartley had been assigned to write editorials and articles from Washington, as Royster had done. Born in Marshall, Minnesota, Bartley received his B.S. degree from Iowa State University of Science and Technology and his M.S. in political science from the University of Wisconsin.

Warren Phillips repeatedly demonstrated his ability as a general executive to Kerby, including his performance in a Dow Jones negotiations project in 1965. Sales Manager Albert Anastasia of the Dow Jones news-ticker service was urging the company to sell its service in England. Kerby, Callis, and Bottorff liked the proposal and expanded the concept to all Europe. They approached American representatives of Reuters, the British news service that handled a limited amount of Dow Jones dispatches to some British clients. Reuters's American representatives appeared interested, and London executives of Reuters came to New York to talk, but when Kerby went to England for a meeting, they rejected the idea. The reason, Kerby learned later, was that Reuters planned to enter the U.S. market itself, expanding its own financial service in competition with Dow Jones.

It was a discouraging turn, but United Press International (UPI), an American news service strong in Europe, approached Dow Jones some months later with its own suggestion of a joint effort abroad. Kerby assigned Phillips, then executive editor, to negotiate with UPI. When the latter was slow to move after initial advances, Phillips talked with executives of Associated Press (AP), the leading American news service. Soon Phillips and Kerby had a deal. AP would handle sales and service as well as the communications network, while Dow Jones was responsible for world business news. In the next several years, the new partnership acquired clients in 40 countries. "Not only was this a profitable and successful venture in itself, but it has peripheral benefits for Dow Jones," Kerby wrote. The extensive network of AP–Dow Jones bureaus supplemented the *Journal*'s own foreign offices, and these news resources were also available to the domestic Dow Jones news service.

The Associated Press–Dow Jones News Service took off first in the Far East. Stan Swinton, representing AP, negotiated the first big contract, with Kyodo News Service of Japan, in 1968, and Swinton and Phillips went to Tokyo to sign the contract. Dow Jones & Company had entered its international-service phase. Japan soon was second to America in buying Dow Jones news. By 1968, AP–Dow Jones had customers in seven countries. Shortly thereafter, competition with Dow Jones in the United States increased as Reuters expanded its American activities. For some time Kerby had been urging the Dow Jones technical division under Ackell to provide a faster news-ticker machine, but modernized equipment wasn't forthcoming. When Reuters arrived with new high-speed equipment and an American partner, General Telephone & Electronics Corporation, Kerby turned to Production Manager George Flynn, who had taken over some of Ackell's duties, to "find superior telegraphic printers at any cost."

Flynn recommended General Electric machines, which had been developed for computer printouts and could be modified for the Dow Jones broad-tape. They were capable of speeds of 300 words a minute. Kerby told Flynn to go ahead. "The cost was high, and the impact on Dow Jones News Service earnings was traumatic," Kerby wrote. The service went into the red, but it withstood the Reuters challenge.

Meantime, Kerby engaged in discussions with Paul Miller, chairman of the Gannett newspaper group, who suggested that the two companies might consider an alliance after "a trial marriage." The talks resulted in Dow Jones's purchase of Gannett stock, but when practical difficulties developed, merger talks were dropped and Dow Jones sold its stock at a nice profit. Kerby remained determined to take the company into the general-newspaper field. His studies of Gannett holdings confirmed his belief that general daily newspapers in small cities and suburbs had excellent growth potential.

In the spring of 1968 he found the opening he had wished for. Kerby discussed his interest in small-city papers with his close friend James Ottaway, Sr., owner of a chain of such papers in the Northeast, suggesting that Ottaway might let him know when he had a buying opportunity outside his own interest. "How about a group?" was Ottaway's prompt answer. "How about the Ottaway papers?"

Warren Phillips joined the discussions with James Ottaway, Sr., and his son, James, Jr. There was a problem of price, as far as the Ottaways were concerned, and some opposition at Dow Jones; Buren McCormack called the proposed purchase "small potatoes." In May 1970 an agreement and plan of merger was entered into, and on July 30 the merger took place. Ottaway Newspapers, Inc., including nine dailies and three Sunday newspapers, became a subsidiary of Dow Jones & Company, which agreed to pay $36 million in Dow Jones stock, 24 times the projected 1970 Ottaway earnings of $1.5 million. The Ottaway group would grow to 20 daily newspapers in 1981, with James, Sr., as a Dow Jones director, and later his son directing the acquisition program. James Ottaway, Jr., would also become a vice-president of Dow Jones & Company. In 1980, Ottaway group earnings totaled $8,659,000 compared with $1,724,000 in 1970.

By mid-1971, Kerby's editorial management team of the future was in place. Warren Phillips assumed more corporate responsibilities. Edward R. Cony, executive editor, aided Phillips with news department management. Frederick Taylor, a graduate of the University of Oregon who had served in Detroit and Washington and had been assistant managing editor of the Pacific Coast edition, was made managing editor in August 1970. Sterling E. (Jim) Soderlind, a Rhodes scholar at Oxford University in England after his graduation from the University of Montana, and a former page-one editor and managing editor, was named economics editor; he was later drafted by Phillips to assist him in long-range planning for the company.

Also coming up fast was Ray Shaw, who would be named director of development in 1972. Shaw, born in Oklahoma, started reporting for the *Oklahoma City Times* while attending the University of Oklahoma. After working for AP, Shaw joined *The Wall Street Journal* as a page-one rewrite man and served as manager of the Southwest edition. When AP–Dow Jones was organized in 1966, Shaw became managing editor of the service. He was made assistant general manager of Dow Jones in 1971 and later was given duties as chairman of Dow Jones–Bunker Ramo News Retrieval Service created that year.

It was a period of expansion and change also for the Dow Jones board of directors, new members including in 1969 J. Paul Austin, chairman, the Coca-Cola Company, and attorney Bob Potter; in 1970, Vermont Royster, James Ottaway, Sr., James Q. Riordan, senior vice-president, Mobil Oil Corporation, and Bert S. Cross, chairman, Minnesota Mining & Manufacturing Company; and in 1971, William McChesney Martin, Jr., former chairman of the Federal Reserve Board. Charles A. Meyer, vice-president of corporate planning, Sears, Roebuck & Company, named to the board in 1967, had returned to the board after a tour of duty with the State Department. Earlier in 1967, Mrs. Jessie Cox had joined Mrs. Jane B. Cook and Laurence Lombard as representatives of the Bancroft family and trusts.

There were major editorial changes also during this period. After the death of Joseph Evans of a sudden heart attack in 1972, Robert Bartley succeeded him as editor of the editorial page, on his way to becoming editor of *The Wall Street Journal* on January 1, 1979.

Managing Editor Taylor would become executive editor of the paper in 1977. He would be succeeded by Laurence G. O'Donnell, a Brooklyn boy who earned his A.B. in history from College of the Holy Cross in Worcester, Massachusetts, and joined the *Journal* in 1958. O'Donnell worked in the Detroit bureau and as an assistant managing editor in New York before succeeding to the managing editorship.

In August 1971 the *Journal* was profiled in *Fortune* magazine under the somewhat provocative title "One Story *The Wall Street Journal* Won't Print." "As a business enterprise, the *Journal* is indeed a powerhouse," said the article by Carol J. Loomis.

> After thirty years of vigorous growth, it has swept past almost all other U.S. newspapers in daily circulation. At its current level of 1,300,000, it is surpassed only by the *New York Daily News*, whose weekday circulation is 2,100,000, and is well ahead of the third-ranking *Los Angeles Times*, which is around the one-million level. And neither of these competitors can claim—indeed, no other daily U.S. publication can seriously claim—that it is a national daily. . . . Its subscribers constitute what might be thought of as a city of businessmen, inhabited at latest count by 173,390 presidents, 112,320 vice presidents, and so on right down to 2,640 cashiers and assistant cashiers.
>
> Finally, the *Journal* is splendidly profitable. A fat 80 percent of the paper's circulation comes from subscribers, most of whom seem to renew automatically, as if the $35 annual cost were small change (or were being paid, as it often is, by the subscriber's employer). Newsstand sales . . . boomed during most of the 1960's. So did advertising revenues, to the point that the *Journal* in 1969 became physically unable to accommodate, in the forty-page editions to which it was limited, all the advertising placed with it. Lately, admittedly, the *Journal* has not suffered any such problems. With Wall Street in a panic last year and with advertising expenditures in general down sharply, the *Journal* and Dow Jones experienced what Kerby has described as a "difficult" year.

Fortune listed some of Kerby's "difficulties," and then noted that Dow Jones & Company had earned a profit nonetheless. "The *Journal* is the main reason Dow Jones does so well," it said.

> The paper's revenues last year were $90 million, almost two-thirds of which were from advertising, the remainder from circulation. Dow Jones does not divulge the *Journal*'s profits, but their magnitude can be estimated. . . . A reasonable estimate is that, in that difficult year of 1970, the *Journal* made about $14 million after taxes, which means that it had a profit margin of about 15.5 percent. In 1969, its best year ever, it probably made at least $17 million on revenues of $99

million, for a profit margin above 17 percent. No other major newspaper appears to have done as well in either year. The closest contender was probably the *Los Angeles Times*, which earned an estimated $13 million on revenues of $156 million in 1970. The *New York Times*, whose revenues of about $210 million topped all other newspapers, netted only about $9 million. The *Journal* is probably the most profitable newspaper in the country.

In New York some reporters grumbled about the tight Dow Jones discipline, its code of conduct, the strict editing, and the conservative posture of the paper. A few liberals and malcontents continued to journey from New York to Washington from time to time to participate in protest demonstrations, especially those against the Vietnam War. One, A. Kent MacDougall, wrote many page-one leaders on the press, and was a specialist in one-sentence openers: "Spice is the life of *Variety*" began his article on *Variety*, the show-business publication; "Dying is no laughing matter" opened a story on newspaper obituaries. In December 1971 MacDougall informed Managing Editor Frederick Taylor that he planned to resign from the *Journal* and then used the Dow Jones leased wire network to inform the various bureaus that "On January 7, after ten years and three months of DJ peonage, I will be free at last, free at last, great gawd almighty, free at last. Rgds, MacDougall, NY."

That Friday Taylor summoned MacDougall to his office, gave him dismissal pay, and ordered him from the premises. The following October, MacDougall wrote one of his press profiles for *More*, a New York journalism magazine, detailing his servitude at the *Journal* and airing his grievances: "The weekly pay of a beginning journeyman reporter of $335 was only $5 more than a two-inch advertisement in the paper; the company union was ineffectual; the paper studied the South Bronx slum in detail, but not the big corporations." The *Washington Journalism Review*, taking a look at *The Wall Street Journal* in its July/August 1980 issue, said that outside criticism of the paper "is spotty." All it uncovered were MacDougall's piece in *More* and "a wrist slap" from the *Columbia Journalism Review* "for the *Journal*'s practice of crediting a staff reporter with stories that were little more than corporate press releases." The *Washington Journalism Review* quoted MacDougall as charging that the *Journal* was "conservative pro-business" and didn't become angered by "unjust wars, unnecessary famines, environmental rape, even unwise governmental regulation of business." Then it added, "Such complaints have not seemed to dent the paper's reputation as one of the best in the country."

The union MacDougall complained about, the Independent Association of Publishers' Employees, had been organized by company men, including Kerby, then a copyreader, and McCormack, a reporter, back in 1938. George Kennedy, president in 1979, summarized its history in the *I.A.P.E. National*

Newsletter that year: "This union was formed over 40 years ago by a group of concerned Dow Jones employees . . . to deal with management as a united front and a single voice of all employees. At the time, raises were either non-existent or extended only to a minority of employees. Job security was unheard of. . . . I am not describing Dow Jones itself as much as the times. The first organization was called Dow Jones Employees Association. By 1979 the association represented 1,300 employees. The current contract speaks for itself. The best in the newspaper industry."

President Kerby's main problem was the inability to deliver 1,300,000 *Journals* from nine publishing plants to subscribers on the day of publication—Kilgore's dream. The publishing plant for the Southeast was in Maryland, hundreds of miles from Florida. Even where day-of-publication delivery was possible, problems arose. The Cleveland plant sent its Two-Star edition, 23,000 copies, by early mail truck to Detroit, but it couldn't carry the late news reports. These appeared in the Three Star, 15,000 copies, which didn't always make that night's last mail to Detroit.

Bill Kerby was working on both the Florida and Cleveland problems. They'd be solved by the construction of an earth-satellite printing plant in Orlando, Florida, the world's first, and the creation of an alternate delivery service to get the *Journal* to subscribers on the morning of publication when the post office couldn't do it. But the problem of gripes about the *Journal*'s demands for breaking news-ticker stories as well as reports for the paper, Dow Jones discipline, and tight editing, Kerby didn't intend to correct. He assigned such concerns to Warren Phillips and his editors but frequently made his own views clear in office memoranda, in public statements, and in his memoirs: "The News Service is crucial to the quality of *The Wall Street Journal*. The ticker's demands for fast, accurate coverage of the whole spectrum of business and financial news are the whip and the spur which keep the reporting staff functioning at peak performance."

Kerby also worried about "advocacy journalism," which he regarded as dishonest reporting. He wrote:

> Many of the worst journalistic sins were committed by young reporters in well-meant efforts to "enliven" news reports. . . . I knew the *Journal* had good, experienced editors. I knew that, as the news staff went through its necessary rapid expansion, the training process was as thorough as feasible. But still I would read *The Wall Street Journal* each morning with apprehension. . . . Eventually I felt reasonably comfortable that the tendency toward advocacy journalism had been pretty well quashed, with the able aid and the continuing vigilance of the *Journal*'s editors. The more flagrant offenders (without exception talented writers) became uncomfortable and with some encouragement, drifted away to other and more congenial employment.
>
> The editorial page was never a problem. Under the able direction of Vermont Royster and his talented successors, the late Joseph Evans and Robert Bartley, it

> just got better and better. . . . I am often asked how closely I, as the *Journal's* publisher, watched over the editorial page. My answer: "When you are blessed with a first-class editor and one whose basic philosophy is kindred to yours, there is no need to play policeman."

It was the publisher's job, however, to enunciate high-level corporate policy and to shield the editors from unusual outside pressure. When President Johnson's White House staff sought to get Dow Jones to change the Dow Jones Industrials to reflect an economic picture that the President thought represented conditions more accurately, President-Publisher Kerby stepped in with a firm "No." The New York Stock Exchange started its own market index, an expanded and, some said, more representative list.

By the end of 1971 Dow Jones took another step into the computerized future by joining with Bunker Ramo, Inc., an Illinois-based computer-service company, to form the Dow Jones-Bunker Ramo News Retrieval Service, Inc., providing wholesalers and users such as banks and brokerage houses access to a data bank of news and information from the *Journal*, *Barron's*, Dow Jones news services, and some selected stories from the *New York Times*. The new joint project was immediately successful. In 1979 Dow Jones purchased Bunker Ramo's 50 percent interest.

Kerby and Phillips also attempted to close the one rent remaining in the company's corporate fabric: the *National Observer* continued to show large financial losses. Henry Gemmill, former *Journal* managing editor and chief of the Washington bureau, was assigned in 1971 to join John Bridge, formerly Royster's prized editor of editorial-page features, at the *Observer*. Gemmill became editor and Bridge managing editor, with full authority to revise the format and editorial approach as needed to make it go. Don Macdonald, senior vice-president and director of sales, undertook a drive to boost advertising and circulation revenues. Circulation continued to gain, but advertising did not.

In 1972 Kerby moved the entire New York corporate, news, and sales organization once again, this time to a 34-story building at 22 Cortlandt Street, where Dow Jones leased four floors. The space was ample. It would become the headquarters of one of the world's most sophisticated communications systems operated outside government and the television, telegraph, and telephone companies. Yet 22 Cortlandt Street was also one of the most understated corporate headquarters of any major American business. Dow Jones & Company began in a basement behind a soda fountain at 15 Wall Street in 1882. Ninety years later, the entrance to Dow Jones was flanked by a Woolworth store, the Little Essex Deli, and the Majestic Pizza Parlor, all eager neighbors who welcomed Dow Jones a bit more warmly than had Henry Danielson, the soda-water man, years earlier.

Cortlandt Street, a block long running from Broadway to Church Street, is about a quarter of a mile from Wall Street and has Wall Street kinds of neighbors, too, the East River Savings Bank on the corner and a branch of Manufacturers Hanover Trust and Merrill Lynch, Pierce, Fenner & Smith offices across the street. It is a convenient address in lower Manhattan, and historic, also, not far from the twin World Trade Center towers, which, at 1,350 feet and 110 stories, comprise New York's tallest buildings. To the east Cortlandt Street joins Maiden Lane, where the Dutch girls once carried the family laundry to the neighborhood creek. Oloff Cortlandt, a Dutch soldier, came to New York in 1637, stayed on to amass a fortune as a brewer, and served as burgomaster from 1655 to 1665. The street was named for him.

The Wall Street Journal criticized President Kennedy's Vietnam policy from the start. It didn't want America involved in further foreign adventures, and it believed that sending military advisers followed by a limited number of troops was unwise both in concept and execution. The *Journal* favored the policy expounded by George Kennan, formerly of the State Department, proposing containment of communism, but it asked on various occasions, "Is this the time and is Asia the place for a confrontation?" Nevertheless, President Kennedy, counseled by his special military adviser, former Army Chief of Staff Maxwell Taylor, announced a policy of fighting "brush fire" wars after the Bay of Pigs disaster and the President's clash with Khrushchev in Vienna. To the *Journal*'s dismay, Vietnam was chosen for an early test.

Once America became involved, the *Journal*'s editorials continued to be critical while moving toward support of the war effort. On May 25–26, 1967, explaining Vietnam in its political context, the paper reluctantly approved of the Johnson administration's policy: "In both national policy and political tactics we think the Administration's least unfavorable course is more or less the current one, unless there is a sudden shift in the context of the war. . . . The full-scale U.S. commitment is only two years old, after all. . . . Though it may be sad to say, the best course may be to hang on and hope."

The following day the paper devoted much of its editorial to criticizing "doves," especially those Republicans who "rather carelessly tend to imply their party could end the war by negotiation. It is true that a change of administration conceivably could become an occasion for negotiation, and it may be true that the present Administration is so tightly locked into its present positions it cannot end the war by negotiation or otherwise.

"The last two Democratic Administrations have slipped into the Vietnamese war more by inadvertence than through conscious policy. They apparently gave no consideration to whether South Vietnam was the proper place for an anti-Communist stand in Asia. . . . To point this out forcefully is not necessarily to argue we should withdraw now, and it is unfortunate that the Republicans allowed their recent staff white paper to be taken that way."

It was a dilemma that frustrated most Americans. The United States couldn't win the war and couldn't get out. "This piecemeal approach," the *Journal* said earlier, "intensifies the war without moving it closer to decision." The May 26 editorial ended with advice: "The Republicans should not claim a panacea for the war; voters know this is not true. Rather, they should stress that the recent management of the war should be replaced and perhaps needs to be replaced to end the war."

Certainly, American strategies were not working. The North Vietnamese Army could retreat to sanctuary in Cambodia and Laos when pressed. The Viet Cong infiltrated the South, melting away into jungles and across rice paddies when the South Vietnamese and their American allies appeared, and tunneled under American bases near Saigon to live, fight, and attack behind the lines. President Johnson ordered bombing raids to punish the North for a reported raid on American ships in the Gulf of Tonkin in August 1964, yet by 1968—as such air attacks continued from Thailand, the Seventh Fleet, and even Guam—the North merely appeared stronger.

Increasingly dismayed by such events, the *Journal* at last impressively demonstrated its growing dissatisfaction and its conviction that the United States must change policy, publishing on January 9, 1968, a strong statement against the war by a former Kennedy adviser with whom in the past it inevitably disagreed. John Kenneth Galbraith, then professor of economics at Harvard, urged the American industrial and business community to defend its own interests by demanding withdrawal from Vietnam. "What is often considered conservatism in the business and financial community is more often public cowardice in asserting clear and even overriding interest," Galbraith wrote. He was concerned about the status of the American dollar, which had been worsened by the war. "Now it can no longer be doubted that the American business and financial community faces a disaster of most compelling proportions. The fruits of a great and strenuous private effort and of the most carefully considered public policy extending over the last several decades are about to be extinguished. This is a wholly avoidable disaster."

The astonishing appearance of such an essay in the *Journal*, even though it swiped at Johnson administration spending policies as much as at the war, obviously demanded an explanation. The *Journal* declared it did not mean to endorse all of Galbraith's views. "John Kenneth Galbraith urges businessmen to end the Vietnam war," the editorial began. "Dr. Galbraith is right when he says the U.S. economy is in serious trouble, trouble to which Vietnam has contributed." The paper added that while it agreed with Galbraith's general position on the war, it did not believe that the United States "can now lightly pick up and go home." However, it approved a move toward disengagement and peace. "Businessmen do have the obligation to encourage an acceptable peace. But an obligation, it also seems to us, to press for policies that will make it possible for peace to contribute to sound economic progress and prosperity."

On February 15, 1968, after the Tet offensive, which menaced even the American embassy in Saigon, *The Wall Street Journal* published the first of two editorials calling upon America to end its Vietnam involvement. "Three years after the big U.S. buildup [of American forces in Vietnam] it seems we hold, in a truly secure sense, practically nothing," the paper said. On February 23 the *Journal* took the final step, demanding that the United States pull out. The people, it declared, must "prepare for the bitter taste of a defeat beyond America's power to prevent." Written jointly by Royster and Evans, the editorial was picked up by the press wire services and widely distributed and reprinted. It said in part:

> We think the American people should be getting ready to accept, if they haven't already, the prospect that the whole Vietnam effort may be doomed; it may be falling apart beneath our feet. The actual military situation may be making academic the philosophical arguments for the intervention in the first place.
>
> Hanoi is believed to have relatively large numbers of troops still uncommitted in North Vietnam. The Communists appear to be getting ample supplies of weapons from the Soviet Union and Red China. As long as the arms keep coming in and there are Vietnamese Communists to use them, you would suppose they could keep up the struggle more or less indefinitely. . . . Meantime, the present South Vietnamese government, never very impressive, looks worse and worse. . . .
>
> This is a government and a nation in chaos: how long can it go on? The failing, it should be stressed, is not in U.S. will or valor, but basically in something lacking in Vietnam itself.

The editorial credited the United States with commendable objectives in initially going to the assistance of South Vietnam. "The U.S. went in to keep South Vietnam out of Communist hands." But it was failing to do that. "The U.S. also went in to demonstrate to Communist China that it couldn't get away with it." The cause had been lost. The editorial acknowledged that withdrawal "will be a disaster. It will be a stunning blow to the U.S. and the West in the larger struggle with international communism. At home it will be a traumatic experience to have lost a war in which thousands of Americans have died in vain." But, to stay on in the circumstances would bring even worse disaster, the paper warned. "President Johnson seems more firmly committed to Vietnam than ever. . . . We believe the Administration is duty-bound to recognize that no battle and no war is worth any price, no matter how ruinous, and that in the case of Vietnam it may be failing for the simple reason that the whole place and cause is collapsing from within."

Antiwar protests in the United States increased, and some *Journal* staffers in New York went to Washington to march in demonstrations against the war. When they called upon Dow Jones to suspend operation of the news-ticker service for one minute as an antiwar protest, however, they were curtly refused. The exploitation of *Journal* news columns or Dow Jones news services for political goals or personal gain was, of course, prohibited by long-standing Dow Jones policy. Later Warren Phillips would codify the rules in a paper called "Conflicts of Interest Policy." Using the news wire for propaganda purposes was an offense too obvious to even require mention, but a strict limit was placed upon Dow Jones employee conduct beyond ordinary rules of good conduct in business. Employees could not serve on boards or as officers of any other company devoted to profit making. They could not accept gifts, entertainment, or reimbursement of expenses "of more than nominal value or that exceeds customary courtesies . . . nor should they offer any material, equipment, or services to any company or person in a position to make or influence any business or governmental decision affecting Dow Jones."

Employees should not use, directly or indirectly, for personal financial gain, any information about Dow Jones "gained in Dow Jones employment, or any 'inside information' gained from corporations while covering news or arranging for the publication of advertising." No employee should act on any news obtained from a staff position "before it is available to the general public." No employee was to become "indebted to brokers or to any other group we cover" or to advertisers. "While we do not want to penalize our staff members by suggesting that they not buy stocks or make other investments, we reiterate that it is not good enough to be incorruptible and act with honest motives. It is equally important to use good judgment and conduct one's outside activities so that no one—management, our editors, an SEC investigator with power of subpoena, or political critic of the company—has any grounds for even raising the suspicion that an employee misused a position with the company."

The *Journal* liked President Johnson's domestic policies no better than his conduct of the war in Vietnam. "The case for the President's tax increases is weak from every angle," it said on January 4, 1967, and added that while the President added a surcharge on corporate and most individual income taxes, he was paying neither for the war nor for his increased domestic expenditures but instead had deepened the deficit by $2 billion in two years. "He made no mention of reducing non-defense spending," the paper complained. "If it really was to finance a war, even a confused and confusing war, the taxpayer would not mind so much. But it is an affront to the American people to have to pay so much for political greed."

The evils of deficits and massive government spending were to be the *Journal*'s counterpoint to its criticism of war policy as the Ninetieth Congress came and departed, leaving to the nation President Johnson's Great Society. The predicted deficits were added to deficits, and the paper said grimly a year later that the harvest would be inflation and economic disaster. On January 23, 1968, it expressed some satisfaction that the administration at last conceded inflation had become a problem. "For years the Administration's theorists have been saying that all those budget deficits are nothing to worry about; now at long last some of them are getting a little concerned. It's not that the Government finally recognizes that the deficits, financed through the banking system, have been putting upward pressures under prices. The official line still is that inflation is chiefly, if not solely, the fault of errant businessmen and labor leaders. . . . Deficits can at times be embarrassing in upper reaches of Government. But when it comes to the pain, that's reserved for the common people." The *Journal* wanted its readers to know that it did not oppose all social progress, however, only "welfare gone wild." It attacked the "inexcusable chaos and incompetence of the administration and disbursing" of Great Society largess. "What is wanted is not obliteration of all Federal aid, but ways to make it effective and worthy of a free society."

The *Journal*'s anti-Johnson editorials did appear restrained in the summer of 1968 and presented a somewhat sanguine approach to the American future, despite campus revolt, the emergence of the underground counterculture to mock tradition and conservatism, the threat of war with China over Vietnam, and the agony of Vietnam itself. The editors saw a light of hope ahead; they believed that conservatism was arising again in America, despite considerable evidence to the contrary.

In the summer of 1968, Vermont Royster and Alan Otten, chief of the Washington bureau, led a *Journal* delegation to Miami Beach to witness the restoration of Richard M. Nixon as the Republican candidate for president, and to wonder at his choice of Governor Spiro Agnew of Maryland for vice-president. The *Journal* would stir those ashes later, coming up with the first story on Agnew's past that helped to speed his departure from government. But for the moment the paper was satisfied. "By all the portents this should be the year of Republicans, unless Richard Nixon himself should throw away the election," it said on August 9. "And while that certainly can happen, it certainly need not happen. . . . We think the monumental discontent with the Johnson Administration is indeed a large part of current political feeling. There is also a growing trend in the country toward the re-establishment of traditional values—call it a conservative mood for a lack of a better term—and it has been growing for years."

The *Journal* correctly, if somewhat prematurely, called the turn that tumultuous summer. In various editorials, it said the country wanted a return to law and order, and the reassertion of individual and local community values in the face of "dehumanizing technology tied to enormous, impersonal government." Even liberals, it asserted without specific citation, recognized "the all but total failure of liberal policies during the 34 years in which those policies have been dominant. . . . The whole liberal dream—that you could radically improve, even remake, human nature by sufficient Government spending and paternalism—lies broken in decaying cities, spiritual malaise, racial tensions, and unremitting violence."

The paper advised Nixon that the country was ready and eager to arise from national prostration, and declared, "It would be a massive misreading of the national mood for the GOP nominee to take the old-style liberal approach of pinning unquestioning faith in the competence of government to heal the country's ills. The voters won't buy it anymore. . . . When the liberals themselves preach decentralization—getting away from reliance on government that has demonstrated its incompetence, it would be inappropriate for Republicans to turn into the party of Big Government."

Candidate Nixon felt able to read the public mood for himself. After Vice-President Hubert Humphrey's nomination as the Democratic presidential candidate, with the accompanying turmoil and division created by Senator Eugene McCarthy's "children's crusade" and the defection of the South to George Wallace's American Independent Party, Nixon found it prudent to say very little of substance about anything during the course of the campaign. He won by the squeaking plurality of less than 500,000 votes among some 65 million, garnering 302 electoral college votes to 191 for Humphrey and 45 for Wallace. Said the *Journal* on November 7: "Finally it's settled; clearly enough Richard Nixon will be the next President of the United States. Yet it is equally clear that the American people have not yet settled in their collective mind on what they really want. . . . It becomes impossible to read any definitive mandate into this election. Especially so against the background of this political year, a year of wrenching development. Candidates like Eugene McCarthy and George Wallace rose to surprising momentary prominence. Primary outcomes and public opinion polls shifted mercurially. The only certainty was uncertainty."

The paper suggested that the real mood of the country could be discerned by adding together the votes for Nixon and those for Wallace, which it thought would signify that the country was fed up with "the record of the past few years." It hoped "Mr. Nixon will move away from the approach that has failed in these years and toward its historical alternative, common-sense conservatism. In this, he will follow the only instruction the voters have given him—some sort of mandate for some kind of change."

Late in December the *Journal* saw the difficulties ahead for a Vietnam peace, recognizing that the problem of disengagement of forces would be a formidable one. It summarized the views of Henry A. Kissinger, the Harvard University professor scheduled to become President Nixon's national security adviser, on the peace talks under way between South Vietnam and the Viet Cong in Paris. Kissinger, the paper said, "provided a certain ring of realism.

He is in fact quite unhopeful that the United States will be able to negotiate an agreement settling the political future of Vietnam. He would shunt that illusory goal aside and concentrate on negotiating a reduction of their [the United States and North Vietnam] respective parts in the hostilities."

This reduction remained President Nixon's goal a year later, while the war protesters continued to demonstrate. The *Journal* defended the President's efforts toward an American withdrawal short of total surrender. "Last year at the Democratic convention," it pointed out on November 5, 1969, "the doves mobbed the streets in favor of a platform plank calling for 'phased withdrawal.' The President has given them that. A precipitate withdrawal, which the President rejected, would be so costly, in both world stability and the stability of American society, that even antiwar spokesmen rejected it." The paper was satisfied for the moment that American troop levels had dropped and American casualties were fewer. It counseled the unheeding protesters and the country to give the President more time to find the way to peace.

Peter R. Kann, covering the war in Vietnam for the *Journal*, wrote from Saigon two days later: "The war drags on. President Nixon has ruled out any quick withdrawal, and the enemy attacks seem to be increasing once again. No progress is reported in Paris. But if there is no progress at the peace table, is there at least progress on the battlefield? . . . There isn't a clear answer. Progress is measured here in many ways. The Air Force computes the tonnage of bomb loads dropped. The Army tots up bodies. Pacification planners neatly categorize hamlets on computerized evaluation charts. Psychological warriors conduct mini-Gallup polls among taxi drivers. Embassy officers sip tea with Saigon legislators and seek to divine their Delphic utterances."

Kann undertook to find out what was going on in company with two fellow correspondents. They traveled in a 1954 Volkswagen through the Mekong Delta area, and then by sampan, motor launch, and helicopter, visiting battle areas along the Cambodian and Laotian borders. Kann's conclusion: "Vietnam seems to defy analysis. The war remains a kaleidoscopic conflict over a splintered society in a fragmented nation, and the bits of Vietnam one man sees probably are no more typical—and no less valid—than the fragments perceived by another."

Kann, a 1964 Harvard graduate who had joined the *Journal* staff after serving a summer internship, remained in Asia for some years. He won a Pulitzer Prize in 1972 for his coverage of the India-Pakistan war in 1971 and his reports on the birth of the independent nation of Bangladesh. Diplomatic correspondent Robert Keatley also covered Vietnam for the *Journal*. In a dispatch from Leuong Quoi, the first American base to be abandoned, he described the problems of Nixon's efforts to withdraw American troops. "The process has barely begun; only 25,000 of the 540,000 American troops in the country have been recalled. But some estimates predict 250,000 or more men will be gone by 1971. . . . It's generally agreed that ARVN [Army of the Republic of Vietnam] and its supplemental supply forces have shown vast improvement, thanks to better equipment and training and some gains in leadership. . . . However, the Communists have more punch than they've shown in recent months, and ARVN's new abilities haven't been tested. The situation is delicate. If we start throwing our stuff out of Vietnam in a hurry, there could be real trouble; things could really collapse."

There remained the United States and the rest of the world to cover. Ray Vicker worked Israel and the Middle East those years, sending in some of the best-informed reports on the coming oil crisis. Felix Kessler was writing from London. Art Sears, Jr., and Donald Moffitt researched and wrote articles on the proliferation of urban ghettos in early 1969, pointing out that Johnson's Great Society millions merely appeared to make things worse. Albert R. Hunt took the high road, describing the country's leading ski resorts. Mary Bralove chronicled the curious mores of the nation's hippies, including some who could be found in Wall Street; Thomas B. Carter profiled some conservative heroes, among them Samuel Ichiye Hayakawa, acting president of San Francisco State College who chose to do battle with student protesters and later won election to the Senate. Frank J. Prial discussed the problems of bird-watchers under one of the famed A-heds, and Alfred L. Malabre, Jr., John A. Prestbo, Richard E. Rustin, and others did what some people thought the *Journal* did exclusively—they wrote about business in Wall Street. Everett Groseclose analyzed the administration's tax-revision proposals in a series of articles, and Alan Otten, soon to become chief of the *Journal*'s London bureau, analyzed President Nixon, saying perceptively, "It's a bit possible that Mr. Nixon may be a bit more liberal than most believed."

The *Journal* remained faithful to Nixon, asserting early in 1969, "He has already credibly started to calm some of the turbulence that has recently marred national discourse." And in January 1970, reviewing his first year, it praised both his domestic and foreign policies, saying of the latter: "It seems to us that the Nixon Administration is assembling a foreign policy that is reasonably coherent and appropriately restrained. It cannot cure a strife-darkened world, but it is aimed at a safer and saner one. . . . One of the intriguing parts is [its] interest in creating a basis for getting along with Communist China in the future."

In 1970 William McChesney Martin, the *Journal*'s longtime hero whom Galbraith dubbed "that impeccable conservative," retired from the chairmanship of the Federal Reserve Board. Bill Kerby welcomed him to the Dow Jones board of directors, and President Nixon accepted his loss equably. Like presidents before him and after him, Nixon found it hard to accept the independence of Federal Reserve chairmen. He named his good friend Arthur Burns to the job, only to discover that Burns, too, was somewhat inflexible. Burns generally agreed with Martin's description of the duties of the

Federal Reserve. "We're the people," Martin said, "who take away the punch bowl just when the party is getting good." But Dr. Burns could be malleable. "Times change, old rules must change," he told the President.

As Otten wrote in the *Journal*, President Nixon was a bit more liberal than most people thought, and a growing economic crisis changed him further. On January 4, 1971, after a formal interview, Nixon told Howard K. Smith of the ABC network, "I am now a Keynesian in economics." It was like a Christian Crusader saying "I think Mohammed is right," Smith thought. The shock waves were limited, though, because the President's disclosure wasn't widely disseminated at the time. Later that year, in meeting the new economic challenge, Nixon demonstrated just how much his economic views changed.

The nation seemed about to witness a rerun of the 1895 gold crisis but on a vaster, mind-boggling scale. Ever since 1895 the United States had enjoyed a favorable balance of trade as a producer of food and raw materials, including gold, beyond domestic needs, and had acquired its own store of the mystical yellow metal used in trade. In 1933 President Roosevelt took the United States off the gold standard, confounding America's European allies, especially England. The nation's gold stores increased. But, as C. W. Barron foresaw in *The Wall Street Journal*, difficult economic problems could accrue to an exporting nation in a world best nourished by free trade, particularly if the lesser nations were crushed, as Germany was in 1918. "If you get all the marbles," Hjalmar Schacht, Germany's financial wizard, later explained, "we'll have to get a new game." But it was poker, not marbles, and in July 1944 America, with altruistic intentions, actually raised the stakes. It invited its friends to the Bretton Woods economic conference, and there it was agreed that all the world's currencies, including that of Japan and Germany if they wished to join, would be pegged to the American dollar, which in turn was riveted to U.S. stores of gold bullion at $35 an ounce.

For the next 25 years, the American dollar was supreme in the world. Industrial competition had been crushed in World War II. Not until the early 1960s did Japan and Germany, with new, sophisticated plants replacing those destroyed by bombs and shells, rise to challenge American industry, which had retained obsolete plants and grown fat and somewhat slovenly in the period of competitive lull. The Bretton Woods gold agreement was no longer effective, as American inflation raged and productivity lagged. Imports, from Asian radios and color television sets to Germany's efficient and inexpensive Volkswagens, poured into the United States, ending the favorable trade balance long before the Organization of Petroleum Exporting Countries oil cartel shattered it. By April 1971 Maurice Stans, secretary of commerce, warned that the United States would have a trade deficit for the entire year. The attack on the dollar was under way. Holders of dollars abroad rushed to redeem them in gold at $35 an ounce. American gold stores fell from a peak of $25 billion to $10.5 billion by July 1971.

President Nixon faced a gold crisis in August. This time there was no J. P. Morgan to organize the rescue. On Friday, August 13, Nixon called his top economic advisers to Camp David, and on Sunday evening, August 15, he addressed the country on the decisions made in the emergency meetings that weekend. America would stop redeeming its dollars in gold. There would be an immediate 90-day freeze on wages, prices, and rents. The President also proposed a $4.7 billion cut in government spending, an income-tax reduction for individuals and businesses, and a 10 percent tax on imports. The drastic action was needed to check inflation and to protect the dollar, Nixon said. He would say later that he had to act swiftly to save the dollar "or there would have been no dollar left to save."

This decision stunned the nation, wrote historian Theodore H. White in *The Making of the President 1972*. "This was not simply a rupture with all past Republican philosophy, the businessman's ethic which held that a free play of market forces brought, over the long run, the greatest good to the greatest number of people. It was a rupture with American economic history."

The Wall Street Journal shocked most of its readers by holding with the President and even accepting the wage-price freeze as temporarily necessary. "President Nixon's 90-day wage-price freeze, while no remedy for the underlying causes of inflation, should at least provide a breathing spell in which the country can make a renewed effort to deal with those causes," it said on August 18. The paper blamed the nation's ills mostly on the low state of American productivity. "The American economy is vast and complex. It can and does accomplish an enormous amount of work every day. But that work must be done by people. Continued improvement in national well-being is dependent upon the performance of every individual."

The paper asserted with some heat that George Meany, president of the AFL-CIO, who had been calling for price and income controls, was already dragging his feet and complaining that the wage freeze was unfair to organized labor. "All of which suggests that Mr. Meany wasn't so in favor of a freeze in the first place," it said, blaming the labor-wage contracts for "playing no small role in keeping the inflation spiral going."

Many readers of the *Journal*, in business and labor alike, wrote angry letters to the paper. By August 26 the *Journal* feared the temporary freeze wouldn't help much and reminded its readers that the President "in his historic August 15 statement" restated his opposition to any "formal wage-price freeze." It dourly noted, however, that "he has already accepted something of a philosophic jolt by opting for any freeze at all." The *Journal*'s own support for wage-price controls was definitely temporary. On September 17 the paper replied to readers "who appear to think we don't appreciate the merits of the gold standard" with a memorable description of the kind of gold standard the *Journal* was at that time supporting:

> First, perhaps, we should make sure that we all agree on what we're talking about. A gold standard would mean that a nation's currency would be convertible into gold at a standard rate, both by other nations and by the first nation's citizens. If the gold standard were to be truly international, moreover, every major nation would have to be on it.
>
> That sort of gold standard, of course, hasn't existed anywhere since the early 1930s. Since then the U.S. dollar has had a tie to gold, and other currencies have had a tie to the dollar; what was called a "gold exchange" standard really could more accurately be described as a dollar standard.
>
> Whatever it was called, it didn't prevent a breakdown. So probably it's understandable that a great many people now are nostalgic about the way things were.
>
> How were they? Well, it is true that a full gold standard, as long as it was allowed to exist, did exert considerable discipline on a nation's financial affairs. If citizens or foreign countries grew nervous about a nation's monetary or fiscal policies, they could start exchanging a nation's money for its gold—and thus deplete that nation's ability to print more money.
>
> As a short-run assurance of stability, this arrangement is hard to beat. If a government can resist its own citizens' pressure for more government spending or for more expansive monetary policy, the nation is likely to continue along the path of financial rectitude.

Gold had shortcomings, too, said the editorial, written by Lindley Clark. One was that if the miners couldn't keep up with the world's growing economies, the supply of money would rise less swiftly than the amount of work money is supposed to do. Deflation would result. Even deflation could be healthful, the paper explained, if it could be managed. But generally prices couldn't be cut back sufficiently fast. People lost jobs, businesses failed. America, which produced relatively little gold, could do better without it if the country demonstrated the self-discipline needed to manage its money well. "To key the money supply to business activity, the supply could be increased when the average prices fall, decreased when they rise; the goal should be relative price stability.

"With stable prices, citizens would have the opportunity to exchange their currency for useful products and services, not ornamental gold. If a well-managed system were established and allowed to function for some years, there would in time be less interest in gold."

Thus *The Wall Street Journal* embarked on a course reflecting a blend of ideas from the monetarists, whose high priests would be Milton Friedman of the University of Chicago, winner of the Nobel Prize in economics in 1976, and Karl Brunner of the University of Rochester and the University of Bern. It also restated the old *Journal* editorial stands for free trade and against neo-Keynesian economics and deficit spending. Support for President Nixon's wage and price policy was highly transitory, and so, it would turn out, was the paper's position on gold.

In the fall of 1972 *The Wall Street Journal* published a series of ten articles on China by Warren Phillips, its editorial director and executive vice-president. The paper had shown intense interest in China since American newsmen were readmitted, sending correspondent Robert Keatley there first in 1971 and again in 1972 with President Nixon. Phillips traveled with a party of American editors, stopping in Tokyo and Hong Kong before and after the China visit. His mission in Asia was not only to evaluate political and economic developments in China but to survey the Asian scene for possible *Journal* and Dow Jones expansion efforts. The Phillips news reports and those written earlier by Keatley were combined in a book, *China: Behind the Mask*, published in 1973. It detailed what the two writers had seen and how they interpreted China's new posture toward the West.

"The Chinese were candid in answering our skeptical questions," Phillips wrote. "They made no effort to prevent us from talking to students, workers, farmers and housewives whom we selected at random. . . . We saw much of the bad side—the poverty, the pervasive totalitarianism—as well as the good." Phillips came back convinced that Dow Jones should look thoroughly into possibilities for establishing a Dow Jones base in the Far East.

As the Phillips articles were appearing in October, the *Journal* was showing somewhat desultory interest in the current presidential campaign in which President Nixon's bid for a second term was being contested by Senator George McGovern of South Dakota, the Democratic nominee. The *Journal* continued to be firm in its support of the President but without real enthusiasm. It approved of his decisive action in the gold crisis and understood the delay in getting a Vietnam peace. On November 9 the paper hailed the President's reelection as "a landslide," which it definitely was, Nixon gaining 47,169,911 votes to 29,170,383 for McGovern, a margin of almost 18 million. Much of the press, most of the liberals, and many of the intellectuals (McGovern carried the big university towns) opposed Nixon, but, as Theodore White pointed out, the President had "the people out there." They wanted peace but not at any price. Said the *Journal*: "It will be fascinating to see how the President's critics react to the rebuff he has given them. We have previously remarked on their attempt to shift fire from Mr. Nixon to the American people. We may now be told that the American people are killers, racists and moral degenerates. Indeed, there were hints of that among the television commentators Tuesday night. . . . In the wake of the President's landslide there may be reason to hope that his critics will learn enough from their defeat to reassess their posture."

The *Journal* itself, however, had not been completely happy with President Nixon during the campaign. "We have the wage-price controls despite the President's doleful wartime experience in the Office of Price Administration," it complained on November 3. "We have *de facto* racial quotas in government programs; we have huge budget deficits. We have a revenue-sharing program just as state and local budgets are moving into surplus and the federal budget is threatened with a still deeper deficit." But the editorial added on the plus side: "Inflation has not raged and has been brought under control despite the deficits, thanks to the Federal Reserve and its credit crunch. Finally, in the last few months, the Administration has begun to speak against reckless spending."

In November 1972 Bill Kerby recommended to the board of directors that Warren Phillips be elected president of Dow Jones & Company. It was done unanimously. Kerby himself was named chairman, and he remained chief executive. Chairman Kerby had been on the line every day, responsible both for day-to-day operations and many policy decisions, since Barney Kilgore made him executive vice-president in 1961. He had taken Dow Jones to new highs in revenues, paying for the vast expansion program out of earnings, and accumulating in reserve $33 million in cash and marketable securities. President Phillips was also named chief operating officer. The Kerby-Phillips management lineup was a tested team looking into the computer space-age future and ready for ventures beyond America's shores. It included Don Macdonald, senior vice-president; Ed Cony, vice-president and executive editor; George Flynn, vice-president/operations; Ray Shaw, director of development; John McCarthy, vice-president/finance; William L. Dunn, an economics graduate of Drake University who was formerly of the production department, business manager; Bill Giles, former *Observer* editor, director of management programs; Frederick G. Harris, comptroller; Fred Hetzel, treasurer; and Edgar Roll, circulation manager.

The team would take the company to historic new highs in most of its endeavors in 1973: advertising, $109,809,278, an increase of more than $13 million over the prior year; circulation, news services, and other revenues, $70,564,376, up over $4 million. Profits for the year totaled $22.3 million, up 17.3 percent. But there were problems, too. Increases in newsprint and mailing costs and a weak securities market limited the rise in revenues for the refurbished news-ticker service. The *Journal* began publishing "Listed Securities Options," a new service soon requiring almost a page of newsprint to cover options markets, another added cost. The *National Observer* continued to report losses.

Dow Jones executives again looked closely at possibilities in Southeast Asia after Warren Phillips's visit there. Dow Jones and the *Journal* had achieved an excellent presence in the Far East when the AP–Dow Jones News Service signed its first big contract with Japan's Kyodo News Service. Donald Macdonald in 1972 led a small delegation to the Far East to look into the possibility of a *Wall Street Journal* edition. They returned convinced that such a newspaper was needed, but Macdonald saw no immediate possibility of selling the advertising to sustain it. Macdonald had been tough. "I was the one who in effect killed the *Asian Journal* in 1972 because there was no money for advertising anywhere in Asia at that time," he recalled. "But we made some friends there. And we saw the need. What we didn't have was any capability of selling advertising there or around the world, so we came up with the Dow Jones International Marketing Service concept."

In the next several months Macdonald and his associates signed 28 publications around the world, among them *Le Monde* in Paris, *Die Welt* in Germany, the *Toronto Globe and Mail*, and the *Sydney* (Australia) *Herald*, leading newspapers in their nations, to participate in an international marketing service. Commissions on this advertising representation business reduced Dow Jones's costs of fielding a large sales force around the world that could at the same time work on behalf of Dow Jones publications. Macdonald, accompanied by Cony, then went back to Hong Kong and Tokyo to take another look at the possibilities there. While in Tokyo, Macdonald arranged with *Nihon Keizai Shimbun*, Japan's national economic newspaper, to establish a Japanese advertising sales company. "Dow Jones International Marketing Service was now in place around the world," said Macdonald. "We had the capability of an international advertising representation in effect selling for an *Asian Wall Street Journal*."

Dow Jones's first publishing venture in Asia came with the purchase in 1973 of 40 percent (later increased to 49 percent) of the *Far Eastern Economic Review*, published in English in Hong Kong. "Dow Jones will be an active partner and not a passive investor," Chairman Kerby said in announcing the purchase. The remaining 51 percent of the *Economic Review* was owned by the South China Morning Post, Ltd. In 1975 Dow Jones bought a 10 percent interest in the *Morning Post*, also published in English in Hong Kong, for about $4.9 million. In 1976 President Phillips reported that the *Economic Review* had more than doubled its 1973 circulation of 17,000, and advertising revenues were up 123 percent. In 1979 Dow Jones purchased an additional 6 percent interest in the *Morning Post*, giving it a 16 percent interest in Hong Kong's leading English-language newspaper, with a total ownership of 5,200,000 shares costing about $12 million. The *Post* in turn would become one of four Asian partners in an upcoming Dow Jones venture. Warren Phillips became a director on the board of the *Morning Post* and later resigned, to be succeeded by Macdonald.

The Asian Wall Street Journal bowed as a new edition of *The Wall Street Journal* in Hong Kong on September 1, 1976. "Dow Jones raised a few eyebrows and got a smattering of polite 'ah, so's' when we announced plans to start our first overseas publication," Ray Shaw, Macdonald's close associate on the project, recalled. "We had collected some far-sighted Asian partners, and we set out to conquer Asia." The presses on which the Asian edition was printed were owned by Dow Jones's partner, the South China Morning Post, Ltd. The other partners were the *Nihon Keizai Shimbun* of Tokyo, the *Straits Times* of Singapore, and the *New Straits Times* of Malaysia. Each partner was responsible for distributing the *Journal* in its respective area. "Our aim is to be as useful to Asian businessmen as we are to their counterparts in the United States," said President Phillips in announcing the new paper.

The Asian Wall Street Journal resembled its New York parent in appearance. Peter Kann was its first publisher and editor. Initially, much of the news in the paper arrived from the New York offices of the *Journal*. Kann soon turned the Hong Kong edition into an indigenous publication, giving increased emphasis to Asia while also printing New York market reports, major news stories, and features from *The Wall Street Journal*. "I'm trying to protect the losses on the goddam thing," Macdonald said, "and Kann is raising the budget! In less than one year he changed the original concept and made it a truly Asian *Journal* with over 65 percent of the news from Asia. And once we even went into the black for five minutes." (The Hong Kong edition in 1981 was still operating at a loss, though a small one.) Macdonald would go on to supervise Asian operations as president of the Dow Jones International Group reporting to Phillips, and Kann was on his way to a high place in the company hierarchy.

Chapter 21

Microchips and Macroeconomics

While Dow Jones corporate officials looked into overseas expansion possibilities, *The Wall Street Journal*, like most other newspapers, ran late in pursuit of a major political news story. The June 17, 1972, break-in at the Watergate apartments complex down the street from the new Kennedy Center in Washington appeared to be a local police item in the beginning. Even when it became evident that the purpose was to rob and electronically bug Democratic national headquarters, the caper appeared too sophomoric to interest the Washington bureaus of leading out-of-town newspapers. "I and our people in Washington frankly couldn't figure out what the hell was going on," Fred Taylor of the *Journal* recalled. "We assumed that the White House wasn't as stupid as it appeared to be, which was absolutely wrong. By the time we realized that this was really true, we were way behind on the story and never caught up."

With regard to the *Journal*'s news coverage, the frank-speaking Taylor said: "I think we did an adequate job in the waning days of the Nixon administration, but this was not one of our better efforts."

From the beginning, the editorial page held to an easily defensible position: no final judgment until all the facts were in. Until almost the end, *Journal* editors believed proof was lacking that the President was himself involved. As more and more became known about the Watergate affair, from the break-in trials held before Judge John J. Sirica and the investigations of Senator Sam J. Ervin's Select

Committee on Presidential Campaign Activities, the *Journal* toughened its position to say that the President was responsible for the actions of his aides, even if he had not authorized their misguided conduct, and that he should have helped expose them.

After James W. McCord, Jr., a convicted conspirator, revealed he had been talking to Senate investigators and had promised to disclose all he knew about the Watergate bugging, the paper conceded on March 27, 1973: "Ultimately, President Nixon is responsible. It is up to the President to make sure his subordinates will be disciplined, that high standards will be maintained. President Eisenhower, after all, fired his chief of staff over a vicuna coat. But in this far uglier affair President Nixon has been unwilling to call to task any member of his official family. That is a job that needs to be done. If the President will not do it himself, we can only offer our best wishes to Judge Sirica and Senator Ervin in their attempts to do it for him."

While the *Journal*'s editorials continued to call for convincing evidence, there were scores of reports, interpretations, and analyses through the spring and summer written by Vermont Royster, Alan Otten, Washington bureau chief, and staff members Albert Hunt, Norman Miller, John Pierson, and Fred L. Zimmerman. Not much in the way of new facts and details was provided by the *Journal*. Unrelated to Watergate was Jerry Landauer's exposé of certain of Vice-President Spiro Agnew's activities while governor of Maryland. A Department of Justice investigation and further disclosures of misconduct eventually forced Agnew's resignation of his office in October. Gerald R. Ford was sworn in as vice-president.

When the President's closest aides, H. R. Haldeman and John Ehrlichman, resigned because they were directly linked with covering up facts about the Watergate break-in, the paper said on May 9: "Now . . . an inexorable momentum carried us to the question of Mr. Nixon himself. It is a moment to recognize that toppling the most exalted White House aide is one thing, and toppling the President is quite another. . . .When you damage the President, you also risk damaging the nation. We should not balk at such a thing, but we first must know what we are doing." The paper called for a court review of the evidence. "The worst outcome of the Watergate episode that we can conceive," it said, "is an impeachment effort that does not succeed, that leaves half the nation feeling that the President can get away with crime and the other half feeling he was the victim of an over-reaching and political assault by his long-standing enemies."

The Wall Street Journal became increasingly critical of the President as more evidence came in. After John Dean, recently dismissed as White House counsel, began appearing before the Ervin Committee's televised hearings, the paper said, "The President will have to bear no little blame simply for bringing into the White House the parade of flawed personages we are watching on television." The "What's News" column summarized Dean's testimony on June 26: "Nixon ordered Watergate cover-up but didn't know what he was doing."

On July 16, it was revealed publicly that since spring 1971 the President had been secretly recording conversations in the Oval Office and in his Executive Office Building office. During the next several weeks the *Journal* agonized with the nation as the Justice Department's special Watergate prosecutor attempted to obtain the tapes. When President Nixon refused to surrender the controversial tapes, insisting that the principle of executive privilege was involved, the paper agreed with him. Yet, when Nixon did consent to give up the tapes, on October 23, it was pleased, saying, "We have not been among those crying for the President's scalp and claiming he was defying a court order, but we are nonetheless happy that he decided yesterday to comply with the court order."

On November 1, 1973, Vermont Royster brought up the possibility of President Nixon's impeachment. "What happens to Richard Nixon personally in all this turmoil is not of great consequence to the country. What happens to the country is of great consequence to everybody." Royster noted the clamor for an impeachment trial was increasing, but he insisted there was no easy way out for Congress and the country. He pointed out that President Nixon might resign, which, he conceded, would be unprecedented. But the paper's editorials did not call for impeachment or resignation. On December 19, however, the *Journal* declared that White House power had grown too strong and too arrogant "and must be curbed in future. . . . It would not do to absolve Mr. Nixon of considerable blame. But the real lesson would seem to be that it is not the imperial presidency that we face. Rather, it is overgrown Government in its entirety." On December 28 the paper reviewed the year coming to a close. "The decade-long horror of Vietnam was at last ended," it said. But it spoke sorrowfully of Nixon. "He won one of the major electoral mandates in American history. . . . He had a chance to bring the American people together. Instead, 1973 has become the year of Watergate."

Watergate dominated 1974 as well. In February, the House of Representatives authorized its Judiciary Committee to begin an impeachment inquiry. In April, in response to a Judiciary Committee subpoena, the President released 1,308 pages of edited tape transcripts; the contents were widely viewed by press and public as reflecting unfavorably on the President. The House Judiciary Committee concluded its deliberations in July by voting three articles of impeachment.

After the August 5 release of official transcripts of still more Nixon tapes, the *Wall Street Journal*'s editors at last concluded that sufficient evidence was in. "We believe that the new Oval Office transcripts released Monday provide ample evidence for President Nixon's impeachment, conviction and removal from office," they wrote on August 7. "Indeed, it seems to us, as it apparently seems to Mr. Nixon's former supporters on the House Judiciary Committee, that the evidence is now clear enough that the nation can now take this momentous step in a spirit approaching unity."

On August 9, 1974, President Nixon resigned. His valedictory to the nation, the *Journal* declared on August 12, was the best speech of his career. "He has managed to confound his critics once more. Mr. Nixon's plea to the people made two points. With regard to his career, much has been attempted and much accomplished—the end of the Vietnam war, the opening of Russia and China, the hope of building foundations to peace in the future. In regard to Watergate, mistakes have been made." Many would not accept the ex-President's defense, the paper conceded. "For our part we do not know our own minds on the final judgment of Richard M. Nixon."

President Gerald R. Ford, the nation's thirty-eighth, "would inherit a delicate and excruciating task," the paper said. "Many vice presidents have ascended to the presidency, but of them all only Andrew Johnson faced problems comparable to Mr. Ford's. . . . It is a task for which no man can fully prepare, and Mr. Ford has not been in a position to make any open preparations whatever. Yet, in the wake of Watergate, he is fortified by the great feeling of relief in the nation."

William F. Kerby turned over his job as chief executive to Warren Phillips in March 1975. Kerby, who then had been with Dow Jones & Company for some 42 years, remained chairman of the board. The transfer of power proceeded smoothly, as it had in the Hogate and Kilgore eras.

President Phillips, quiet and seemingly shy, described as "a slim dapper man with a precise, professional manner" by *Media & Advertising*, was, as Ray Vicker noted back in Chicago, a man who knew how to organize his forces and get things done. He was a saltwater sailor and a tennis buff, a man more aloof than Bill Kerby and more addicted to organizational detail, but an equally dedicated newsman who appeared almost mystical about the goals of Dow Jones and the *Journal*. "Dow Jones's reason for existing, and the motivation behind everything we do, is to strengthen our publications and news wires for our society," he wrote for the company's employee publication in 1972. "This may seem so self-evident as to be trite, but that doesn't make it any less true."

Phillips, his associates knew, was disciplined, tough, and well organized. Although he delegated authority as Kilgore and Kerby had done, Phillips soon made it abundantly clear that, as publisher of *The Wall Street Journal*, he was ultimately responsible for its policy and image, as well as for its financial health. Years later, when a question was raised concerning the reputed autonomy of *Journal* editors, Phillips responded:

> As Chief Executive and Publisher, I not only have the authority, but because our paper is different in that we have had journalists in the past in the publisher or chief executive role, I feel, and Kerby and Kilgore felt, that we are sufficiently experienced that we can make decisions as to the direction of the paper and enforce them without any concern about our own credentials or our ability to make the right judgments. Kilgore used restraint, and I have used restraint in exercising editorial authority on a day-to-day basis. Our method is to choose capable editors and delegate considerable responsibility to them. We join in making policy, but when it comes to whether policy and direction stay on course, I don't think there is any question of editors' independence; it exists and has existed so long as we continue in the direction we feel the paper should move. Should the paper not move in that direction, changes would be made.

Phillips warmly praised Robert Bartley, who had been named editor of the *Journal* in 1979 (the title had been allowed to lapse since Royster's retirement), and then cited an early example of the cooperative efforts of the publisher and editors in making a major change in the editorial-page format. Rarely in the past had outsiders contributed regularly to the page, with the exception of Frank Kent, the *Baltimore Sun* columnist. But late in 1975, at the suggestion of Phillips "to increase the diversity of opinion on the page," Bartley formed a board of contributors composed of distinguished persons who would write for the paper regularly. Bartley was enthusiastic about the idea and found his writers mostly among scholars at the country's leading universities, some holding views at sharp variance with *Journal* editorial policy.

"The editorial page has been greatly improved under Bartley," Phillips said. "He recruited the members of the Board of Contributors, and it is because he chose so well that this feature has added strength to the paper. There are new features and columns and a new op-ed page [the page opposite the editorial page], all ideas originated by Bob and his colleagues. In the editorial columns themselves, Bob Bartley is responsible for putting our editorial page in the forefront of economic and political thought in the country and making it more of a force and a respected forum than ever in the past."

The news columns, Phillips said, were and would remain totally free of bias and slant. "If we are to perform our function of informing the public, we must have the trust and confidence of our readers, without which we have nothing, neither journalistic nor economic success. We can only retain that trust if we are accurate and fair and are perceived to be unbiased in our news columns. And over the years we have had a very clear separation between what appears in our editorial columns and the independent professional reporting that appears in the news columns. We are very conscious of the need to earn and re-earn the trust of our readers every day of the year."

The first article by a member of the board of contributors appeared early in 1976, the nation's bicentennial year, when Arthur Schlesinger, Jr., professor of humanities, City University of New York, winner of Pulitzers for history and biography, wrote on the need of a nation to understand its history. Irving Kristol, professor of social thought at New York University Graduate School of Business, also widened the scope of the editorial page with his choice of subjects, though most contributors stayed close to their specialties of business and economics, in which fields they were all professors. The board also would include Martin Feldstein of Harvard University, who became president of the National Bureau of Economic Research in 1977; Walter Heller of the University of Minnesota, former chairman of the Council of Economic Advisers under Presidents Kennedy and Johnson; Herbert Stein of the University of Virginia, former chairman of the Council of Economic Advisers under Presidents Nixon and Ford; Paul McCracken, professor of business administration at the University of Michigan and former chairman of the Council of Economic Advisers under President Nixon. On March 20, 1981, Charles L. Schultze, senior fellow of the Brookings Institution and former chairman of the Council of Economic Advisers under President Carter, joined the group.

These noted contributors attracted other leading writers in support or dissent, and the *Journal*'s editorial pages glowed. The paper also featured its own distinguished staff commentators: Vermont Royster, former editor of the paper; Norman Miller, Pulitzer winner whose regular column was called "Perspective on Politics"; Lindley Clark, who received his M.A. in economics from the University of Chicago and wrote "Speaking of Business" as the paper's economics editor; and a new staff member, Suzanne Garment, former member of the Yale University faculty whose Washington column was called "Capital Chronicle." There were also reviews, essays, and dissertations on various topics, including sports, by various members of the *Journal* staff.

The year 1975 was one of spectacular progress for Dow Jones and the *Journal*. Facsimile publication via a satellite orbiting the earth was scheduled for November at the Orlando facility, which had recently gone into operation as a facsimile printing plant in anticipation of the new technology. Orlando, the *Journal*'s tenth printing facility, would become the first newspaper-printing plant in the world to use a satellite-communications system.

The development had been a long time in preparation. "I commissioned a little engineering group in California to see if they could come up with improvements in the technology," said George Flynn in recalling some early problems. "They developed data compression [a kind of space-age shorthand that greatly reduced sending and receiving time]. We used it experimentally for our microwave transmissions. A year or so after COMSAT launched the first communications satellite we began talking to them about using our data compression technology for facsimile via satellite." William Dunn, a graduate of Drake University who joined the Dow Jones production department in 1961 and became production manager at Chicopee in 1965, worked with Flynn on the satellite project.

Dow Jones and COMSAT conducted experiments in the laboratories of Communications Satellite Corporation at Clarksburg, Maryland. Signals transmitted to INTELSAT IV over the Atlantic 22,000 miles away were received back in the laboratory in about six minutes. Data compression had greatly sped the process of sending and receiving the large volume of material required to produce a newspaper. Then, in tests conducted by Bill Dunn and Bill Harmer, production manager at Orlando, the Orlando plant received for printing from the Chicopee sending station an entire *Wall Street Journal* edition from a satellite parked over the equator. "Bill Dunn really brought us into actual satellite transmission," Flynn said. The *Journal* was ready to enter the satellite age.

Toward 7 P.M. on the evening of November 19, 1975, Dunn, Harmer, and their production crews prepared to welcome aboard officials and directors of Dow Jones & Company who had been meeting in Orlando earlier that day. The Orlando plant, with its new dish-shaped parabolic antenna endlessly eyeing the southwest quadrant, where Westar II was parked, is set in a clump of pines hidden in a cul-de-sac off Presidents Drive, Orlando Central Park, south of the city. The antenna, a large gray soup bowl with a stamen-like amplifier in the center, seemed a kind of Henry Moore sculpture celebrating modernity. Its black *"The Wall Street Journal."* legend marked the end of the long experimental trail for the *Journal*'s engineers. The flat, severe building was a modest one, but the sophisticated communications and printing equipment was at that moment the world's most advanced.

As the visitors filed in, the newspaper was about to receive from Westar II, riding in orbit 22,300 miles over the equator, a signal to start facsimile production of the *Journal* as edited in New York and composed and laid out in the plant at Chicopee. Earlier that evening Dunn, Harmer, and James H. Peters, the young, red-bearded satellite-operations supervisor, had again checked out final details.

Signals sent from Chicopee at a power of six gigahertz (six billion cycles per second) would go into space much like a television or microwave transmission, Peters explained to his visitors. The sending antenna in Chicopee was aimed at one of the transponders on Westar II, space *The Wall Street Journal* leased through American Satellite Corporation from Western Union. The transponders were the equivalent of channel selectors on a television set, except that a transponder could receive several different signals on the same antenna simultaneously. Chicopee, using an 11-meter antenna, transmitted to Westar on channel 7. Since the satellite was in motion over the equator at earth speed, the *Journal*'s fixed antenna continued to focus on it with slight tuning from its control shack. Westar itself needed only occasional nudging now and then from earth to keep it in its proper orbit.

"Westar uses energy from its solar-powered batteries to step up the microwave energy received from Chicopee," Peters explained. "It is extremely weak after traveling about 24,000 miles from Chicopee to the satellite." In Massachusetts, a laser beam in the sending apparatus scanned the photographic positive of a *Journal* page, compressed what it "read" into bits of data that, converted into electromagnetic energy, were sent into space. Then at Orlando another laser beam reported to the receiving drum—like two spools of thread nearly 1,300 miles apart being unwound and wound simultaneously.

When the laser in Orlando had exposed the negative to the images it was receiving from Massachusetts, a *Wall Street Journal* page was developed and printed much as an ordinary photographic negative would be processed. The satellite signals would provide *Journal* pages at greatly reduced cost. Microwave expense had been about $74,000 a month. The cost of the new satellite transmission would average $2,000 a month in 1975. Printers then transferred the page image to thin aluminum sheets coated with a light-sensitive silver emulsion, which recorded dark images as collections of tiny dots, leaving smooth, bare aluminum to represent the white space. The image would hold the oil-base ink used for printing while a water spray kept the bare aluminum free of ink. The underlying principle of the offset printing process is the old truism: oil and water don't mix.

The aluminum plates were affixed to the fast new Goss offset presses, ink fountains and water jets were set, and the press crew retreated to its "quiet room," where the rheostats and other press controls were situated. Soon *The Wall Street Journal* of November 20, 1975, Eastern edition, Orlando, was issuing from the automatic folders at a rate of 70,000 an hour en route to waiting trucks, the first newspaper edition in the world to be published by satellite transmission.

Dow Jones was producing papers for day-of-publication delivery at acceptable cost anywhere readership justified in the United States. There were new problems, however. Rising postal costs and late delivery in some areas led the circulation division, under Vice-President John McCarthy, to introduce and push expansion of its alternate delivery system. By the end of 1977, 160,000 copies of the *Journal* (or 12 percent of total subscribers) were being delivered to individual subscribers through the Dow Jones system. Ray Shaw, reporting on the system, predicted that in the 1980s 40 percent of the *Journal*'s subscriber copies would be delivered by Dow Jones "less expensively through alternate delivery than through the mails." (At the end of September 1981 alternate delivery to individual subscribers had increased to 408,000 copies at a cost of 12.6 cents per copy, compared with a post-office charge of 14 cents per copy.) The company also undertook to control its newsprint costs and to assure adequate supplies by purchasing a 39.9 percent interest in a new Canadian newsprint mill at Rivière-du-Loup, Quebec, and also a 30 percent interest in another new mill near Richmond, Virginia.

On June 13, 1976, Dow Jones & Company became listed on the New York Stock Exchange. That year Dow Jones increased revenues by 15.6 percent, Chairman Kerby and President Phillips reported, followed in 1977 by another 15.4 percent revenue increase.

The Wall Street Journal soared to a new circulation high of 1,509,251 in 1977, while *Barron's* and the Ottaway papers remained nearly even. But the *National Observer*'s problems increased with cumulative losses totaling $16.2 million after 15 years of existence. On June 30 Warren Phillips went to Washington to tell the staff of the *Observer* that the July 2 issue would be its last. The paper had devoted readers and an excellent reputation with press critics and the public, but, as Robert Feemster had foreseen many years earlier, a difficult advertising position. Phillips praised the staff while saying the losses could no longer be sustained.

Expansion and change went on. The Chicopee and Palo Alto plants had gone to cold-type printing in 1975, and others would follow. The Canadian newsprint mill was proving profitable. Work started on three new satellite printing facilities: one near Seattle, one near Denver, and one in Naperville, Illinois, not far from Chicago. *The Asian Wall Street Journal* doubled its circulation and gained added advertising support. *Barron's* reported advertising gains, and Phillips announced that it would expand its international and Washington coverage during 1978. The format was revised, coverage of investment news increased, and graphics improved, as Robert Bleiberg, editor, Bernard T. Flanagan, advertising director, and Alan Abelson, managing editor, took advantage of new opportunities to move ahead. In 1977 *The Wall Street Journal* received the Sigma Delta Chi Distinguished Service Award for a series of articles exposing corporate payoffs in the United States and abroad. The series led Congress to pass in late 1977 the Foreign Corrupt Practices Act prohibiting such activity.

In March 1978 William Kerby withdrew completely from day-to-day active duty and took an advisory position as chairman of the Executive Committee. Warren Phillips was named chairman, continuing as president and chief executive officer. The South Brunswick plant began receiving *Journal* pages via satellite that spring, and in July Chairman Phillips was at the new Federal Way plant near Seattle to start the printing of *Journals* for northwestern states, as well as western Canada. The papers were produced from full-page facsimile transmission by satellite from Palo Alto. A short time later the Denver plant began operations, also receiving from California via satellite. That same month, Executive Vice-President Ray Shaw announced the appointment of William Cox, Jr., to the newly created position of director of advertiser relations for Dow Jones. Cox, grandson of Jane and Hugh Bancroft and son of William and Jessie Cox, continued the family association with the company.

During 1978 Dow Jones acquired *Book Digest* magazine, a monthly publication presenting excerpts from various new books, including bestselling fiction and works on politics, science, social trends, travel, and the arts. *Book Digest* sold over a million copies by subscription, but after the magazine failed to become profitable in the following years, Dow Jones in 1981 cut circulation back to 400,000 copies. It hoped that a new sales formula, appealing to a more elite, affluent readership, would improve the publication's advertising position.

The year 1979 saw Warren Phillips well on the way to reorganizing Dow Jones & Company and effecting changes in the *Journal*. In March Phillips recommended that the directors elect Ray Shaw president, chief operating officer, and a director. Don Macdonald became vice-chairman and a director. Other new directors who joined the board in 1976 included William Cox, Jr.; William M. Agee, chairman of Bendix Corporation; Davis W. Gregg, president of The American College. Richard D. Wood, chairman of Eli Lilly & Company, joined in 1978. (In January 1981 Martha S. Griffiths, great-granddaughter of Jessie Barron, would be added as another family board member, succeeding Jessie Cox, who retired.)

On January 30, 1980, Phillips presented his plan for reorganization of Dow Jones & Company to the board, a plan created in consultation with his new executive team as part of a long-range program. Seven management groups with authority divided largely along product lines would replace the vertical structure that had previously been a hallmark of the management pattern. "We are streamlining our management structure to organize the company more effectively for growth," Phillips said. He listed the seven groups: *The Wall Street Journal*, Magazines, International, Ottaway Newspapers, Irwin Books, Information Services, and Operating Services. "Two of the groups are not as self-defining as the others," he said. "The Information Services Group will include Dow Jones news wire, broadcast, computerized information retrieval services and future ventures involving delivery of information via some of the newer electronic systems ranging from home computers to cable TV. Operating Services will include printing plants, satellite, computer, engineering, in-plant communications and distribution activities that serve publishing operations and are too large and complex to be included under the supervision of any one publication."

All seven management groups would report directly to President Shaw day to day, and through him to Phillips. Vice-Chairman Macdonald was named president of the Magazine and International groups. Senior Vice-President Flynn was assigned to work with and supervise the Ottaway newspapers and Richard D. Irwin book subsidiaries, as well as the company's partly owned newsprint mills and other operations; he was given the title of president of the Affiliated Companies Group. Vice-President Dunn was named president of the Information Services Group and the Operating Services Group. Vice-President Kann was made associate publisher of *The Wall Street Journal*. Vice-President Cony was assigned to work with Macdonald and other executives on international publications and on the editorial aspects of *Barron's* and Dow Jones news services. Fred Harris, named vice-president/finance in October 1977, would advise all divisions and Phillips on financial analysis, acquisitions, and related activities. Harris earned his M.B.A. from Ohio State University in 1948 and joined Dow Jones as chief accountant in 1956. By the end of 1979 the *Journal* had reached a new circulation high of 1,768,000, and circulation revenues for all Dow Jones publications had increased 23.8 percent over 1978 to a total of $117,622,000.

There had been changes in the editorial department preceding Phillips's 1980 reorganization. Frederick Taylor became executive editor, with Larry O'Donnell succeeding him as managing editor. Under the Phillips plan, Peter Kann, the newsman he brought back from Asia as his assistant in the spring of 1979, was assigned to supervise the news operations of the paper, as well as its business side. Taylor and O'Donnell would report to Kann, and Bartley would work with him on administration of the editorial page. Clearly, both Bartley and Kann rated exceptionally high with the Dow Jones chief executive officer. They assumed lead roles in the new Phillips approach to management of the paper.

Bob Bartley's thrust in the editorial-policy area had been winning wide attention. Politically, the paper continued on its traditional course, though some readers regarded the policy as bearing to the right. Bartley himself described it as "neo-conservative." He and colleagues George Melloan, deputy editor, and Tom Bray, a news-department veteran and former editorial-page feature editor who had been made associate editor, would restate the paper's economic policy in more advanced terms. Bartley campaigned for and obtained added space for his special editorial features, the op-ed page among them. He recruited brilliant young writers: Paul Craig Roberts, who earned his Ph.D. in economics at the University of Virginia and had been working with New York Congressman Jack Kemp in Washington, helping him to draft proposed income-tax reduction legislation; Jude Wanniski, formerly a reporter for the *National Observer*; and Susan Lee, a former Columbia University faculty member who joined Suzanne Garment, the former Yale professor, in writing special reports. Seth Lipsky, from *The Asian Wall Street Journal*, was named an associate editor.

Almost from the start of the Ford administration, the *Journal* quarreled with the President's economic policies. In February it declared the U.S. economy to be in dreadful shape. Sarcastically, the paper congratulated President Ford on the fact that Congress wasn't following the recommendations in his State of the Union address, saying things might have been worse if it did. "Even Mr. Ford's own people now privately admit that [his] tax rebate idea was a blunder," it said. The *Journal* didn't expect too much from Congress either. It anticipated an increase in investment-tax credit, which would be good, but demanded more—a tax cut across the board. "As distasteful as the idea may seem to liberals," the paper said, "a cut in the corporate tax rate is the most effective way to put the unemployed back to work. . . . We are not saying that the tax cuts should be concentrated on savings. If we did so, we'd be guilty of looking only at the supply problem and not the demand problem. Rather, we're saying that personal taxes should be cut across the board, and that so far as 'benefits' go to business, they should be through corporate tax reductions, not investment tax credits."

This supply-side statement reflected the *Journal*'s growing preoccupation with an economic concept almost as revolutionary as Barney Kilgore's new approach to business news. Editor Bartley and his writers on economics, Wanniski and Melloan, would propel it to adoption, with modifications, by the Reagan administration in 1981. But the supply-side concept, though newly named and given a new, pragmatic thrust by *Journal* writers, wasn't new in theory. It was a long-accepted precept in classical economics stated by the Frenchman Jean Baptiste Say in the early nineteenth century and known as Say's law: Supply creates its own demand. Say asserted that the sum of wages, profits, and rents in the production of a good would be sufficient to buy it.

The theory, promulgated in Say's campaign against the high tariffs of his era, had been accepted for years by *Journal* editors, but economists in general, and liberal politicians in particular, agreed that John Maynard Keynes had demolished Say's ideas when he published his *General Theory of Employment, Interest, and Money* in 1936. Keynes said then that the amount of demand is limited "by what the community will choose to spend on consumption when it is fully employed . . . [by] the propensity to consume." At the time Keynes was acting as doctor to an economically sick world stricken by unemployment. His pump-priming remedy as prescribed by President Franklin Roosevelt in the United States had been credited with bringing the nation out of its economic slump.

But *Journal* editors in the Vermont Royster period argued that while Keynes's ideas may have been effective in an emergency, they had been perverted by the neo-Keynesians in the next half century into wasteful government spending on a seemingly permanent basis. This policy would create a trillion-dollar deficit, resulting in diminished investment in productive facilities, high taxes, high interest rates, soaring inflation, and continuing unemployment.

Robert Bartley and his editors regarded Keynes's theories as mostly an intellectual exercise. They argued a "crowding out" theory in their debate on Keynesian ideas. "It [the government] borrows the money it uses to prime the pump, taking with one hand and giving with the other. How can this stimulate the economy?" they asked. "The government 'crowds out' funds which otherwise would go into productive investment and jobs." Said Editor Bartley, "This seemed to me to undo the Keynesian consensus and to clear the way for supply-side thinking. . . . Keynes's pump-priming ideas may have been a valiant intellectual effort in the emergency. In our view, tax reduction was needed to check the ensuing 'stagflation' [a combination of economic stagnation and inflation]." Bartley, Wanniski, and Melloan, in their *Journal* editorials in the mid-1970s, called for a new approach to the nation's economic ills. Herbert Stein, the conservative economist, adviser to presidents and a member of the paper's board of contributors, somewhat derisively dubbed the policy "supply-side fiscalism."

Jude Wanniski, the *National Observer* columnist drafted by Bartley to the *Journal* editorial staff, was an intense, talkative young man who relentlessly pursued ideas, then snared and shared them with evangelistic zeal. Son of a Pennsylvania coal miner who moved to Brooklyn in 1942, when Jude was 4, Wanniski probed for knowledge from Flatbush Avenue to Fairbanks, Alaska, during his journalism career, and earned B.A. and M.S. degrees from the University of California in Los Angeles before joining the *Observer*. In Washington, Wanniski found the economic ideology he knew he had been seeking. He met and came to admire Arthur Laffer, a University of Chicago maverick who had become chief economist for President Nixon's Office of Management and Budget. Through Laffer, Wanniski met Robert Mundell, the Canadian economist then teaching at Columbia University who came to Washington in May 1974 to address a conference on global inflation. Mundell, described by Laffer as "the greatest living economist," shocked many in his audience by declaring that a $10 billion tax reduction was needed to stop the stagflation left by Nixon administration policies. The administration of President Ford was arguing for a tax increase.

Wanniski was converted to Mundell's ideas and impressed by Laffer's graphic demonstration of the benefits of Mundell's tax-cut proposal with his Laffer's Curve. This curve charted a new tax law of diminishing returns, to become better known to his contemporaries than Say's law. Too great a tax increase actually decreases returns to the government by driving money out of productive investment and into untaxed or unproductive shelters, Laffer and Mundell asserted. They also demanded a return to the gold standard. Wanniski and Laffer discussed the Mundell theories intensively. After Wanniski joined the editorial-page staff of the *Journal* in New York and Laffer returned to the University of Chicago, they continued to talk by telephone almost daily, reviewing news events in light of their new economic theories.

Wanniski undertook to convert Editor Bartley and Deputy Editor Melloan. Initially, Wanniski got nowhere. He did, however, publish an article, "The Mundell-Laffer Hypothesis—A New View of the World Economy," in the spring 1975 issue of *Public Interest*, a publication edited by Professor Irving Kristol, who would become a member of the *Journal*'s board of contributors. In his 1974 book on macroeconomics, *The Way the World Works*, Wanniski would say of Lord Keynes that he "argues the benefits and magic of public debt."

The conversion of Bob Bartley, the editorial staff of *The Wall Street Journal*, and eventually the Reagan administration to supply-side economic theories (sometimes called Reaganomics) has been detailed by Washington columnists Rowland Evans and Robert Novak in their book *The Reagan Revolution*, published in 1981; by Dan Morgan in the *Washington Post* on February 15, 1981; and in the *Journal* in a story by staff writer Paul Blustein appearing on October 8 the same year. Convincing the staff wasn't easy.

"When Bartley, a protege of retired editor Vermont Royster, set out building a young, conservative staff of his own . . . he brought in Wanniski," Morgan wrote in the *Post* under the title "Selling 'Supply-Side' in the *Journal*." "Bartley, a cool, precise intellectual, contrasted with Wanniski, the garrulous son of a Pennsylvania coal miner . . . but in several important respects they were well suited to work well together."

Not in the beginning, Blustein observed in his report in the *Journal*: "The conversion of Robert Bartley was a gradual process." Wanniski, said Evans and Novak, was a registered Democrat who had voted for Kennedy and Johnson. "He became totally converted" to the Laffer and Mundell economic views, "but he could not yet [in 1974] convert *Wall Street Journal* editorial policy to the heresy of tax reduction and inflation." In December 1974, however, Bartley gave Wanniski an okay to write a long editorial-page article on Mundell and his plan for combining tax cuts with a policy of extremely tight money. "Nobody understood what he was talking about," Bartley told Morgan, but Bartley himself began reading Mundell. Soon he, Wanniski, and Melloan were all writing on supply-side economics in its many manifestations, and economists and political observers joined the fray. "As Bartley and Wanniski were venturing these ideas on the economic front," Morgan said in the *Post*, "the [editorial] page was becoming a sort of national bulletin board for political and military commentary by the network of conservative and neo-conservative intellectuals and out-of-power policymakers. But it was on economic matters that Bartley's page played its most activist role, in publicizing and popularizing theories that still seemed extreme to people grounded in orthodox economics."

Jude Wanniski's signed articles in the *Journal* attracted the attention of Congressman Jack Kemp, a Republican and former quarterback for the Buffalo Bills who was elected in 1970 in a predominantly Democratic congressional district. (*Journal* writer Paul Craig Roberts had been Kemp's economic adviser.) Kemp wrote to Wanniski, who, on his next trip to Washington, called on the congressman. Kemp had introduced a complicated tax bill to benefit business, and Wanniski volunteered to tell him what was wrong with it. The two discussed Kemp's desire to aid the economy the rest of that afternoon and later that evening in Kemp's Maryland home. Kemp was converted to the teaching of Mundell and Laffer, Evans and Novak wrote. And Wanniski was converted to Kemp.

With Delaware Senator William Roth, a Republican, Kemp introduced the Kemp-Roth bill calling for a 30 percent across-the-board reduction in marginal income-tax rates over a three-year period, a time provision insisted upon by Roth. The tax-cut idea was presented to Ronald Reagan of California sometime in 1976. Reagan, who was preparing for his contest with President Ford for the Republican nomination, didn't formally endorse a tax-cut policy in the 1976 campaign, but he had studied the writings of economist Say himself in his Eureka (Illinois) College economics courses; he read *The Wall Street Journal* and he was friendly to supply-side ideas.

Robert Bartley directed an editorial campaign powerfully supportive of supply-side theories during the President Carter years, and Wanniski even attempted to personally sell the idea to President-elect Carter's staff when it assembled in Atlanta. Such enthusiasm for individual political activity led Wanniski eventually to resign from the paper rather than curtail his deepening political involvement, since campaigning for candidates or parties violated the *Journal*'s code for its staff. Wanniski became a consultant and participated in the successful push for an across-the-board income-tax cut.

Meanwhile, Bartley continued to advocate the supply-side philosophy, and at the same time wrote incisive, pragmatic editorials on day-to-day realities that won him the Pulitzer Prize for editorials in 1980, the eighth to be received by a member of the *Journal* staff. They dealt with various topics: the possible impact of the Chappaquiddick accident on Senator Ted Kennedy's prospects in the Democratic primaries; the repercussions of President Carter's handling of the Iranian hostage crisis; General Motors' partial acceptance of wage-price controls; Chrysler's appeal for government aid.

In an evaluation of the leadership qualities of presidential primary candidates, Bartley wrote: "In the case of Senator Kennedy . . . so far as we can see, he has never led anything except maybe a regatta off Hyannis. . . . He has spent 16 years in the Senate championing such perennial losing causes as national health insurance and various anti-trust brainstorms. While this, of course, endears him to the left, it also leaves his legislative career devoid of substantive accomplishment."

On Senator John Connally of Texas seeking the Republican nomination: "Mr. Connally, by contrast, has a proven record as a leader. As Treasury Secretary, he led us into wage-price controls and the devaluation of the dollar. It can, of course, be argued that these particular steps were more or less inevitable given the economic and especially the political realities of August 1971, but the episode did show that Mr. Connally is a man who steps in with both feet."

On President Jimmy Carter: " 'I will never tell you a lie,' was Jimmy Carter's winning slogan in the last presidential campaign, so neatly capturing the voters' desire for a new face from outside Washington. . . . We would hope that this time the voters also look to see what's behind the slogan, if anything. . . . Mr. Carter has been a weak leader because, far from being out in front of the people, he has had to be led, kicking and screaming, to go in the directions that the nation needs to go and wants to go."

The *Journal*'s favorable opinions of Governor Ronald Reagan were well known to the paper's readers. As candidate Reagan developed his economic program, including a three-year, across-the-board income-tax cut, the paper, of course, expressed approval. Many supply-siders contributed to the *Journal* during the course of the 1980 primaries and campaigns, among them Arthur Laffer, Representative Kemp, David A. Stockman, Norman Ture (later to become undersecretary for tax and economic affairs), businessman-scholar Lewis Lehrman, and George Gilder, whose *Wealth and Poverty* would become a kind of guidebook for the incoming administration. But there were opposition contributors too, among them Herbert Stein, described as a conservative Keynesian; the monetarist Milton Friedman, Nobel laureate in economics; Walter Heller, who accused the *Journal* of overstating liberal positions "to use them for a punching bag"; and historian Arthur Schlesinger, Jr. Later, David S. Broder, the *Washington Post* writer whose column was syndicated, would give the paper high marks for its input to the Reagan economic administration. "*The Wall Street Journal*," he wrote, "is the most powerful journalistic advocate of Reagan's economic program."

The *Journal* was for Governor Reagan from the start. After his nomination in Detroit as the Republican candidate for president, the paper said of his economic policy: "It is essentially a modest proposal. . . . Mr. Reagan has, in short, spelled out a prudent, gradual, responsible re-ordering of economic priorities, not much different from the kind of thing Republicans have always offered. The question is not whether it is sound enough economically, but whether it is bold enough politically."

Lively debates filled the editorial pages of the *Journal* as President Carter defended his administration in the campaign with Governor Reagan in the fall of 1980. Ultra-Keynesians, as Theodore White called them, attacked Reagan supply-side economists, whose advocates responded in the contributor columns; and the paper's excellent readers' letters received more space to accommodate this and other discussion. But there wasn't much doubt in the editors' minds that Reagan was going to win. The *Journal* meanwhile pleaded with Chairman Paul Volcker of the Federal Reserve Board to hold the line on inflation, denounced the proposed government loan to Chrysler Corporation, and criticized President Carter's arrangement to win release of the American hostages from Iran because it was obtained under duress.

The *Journal* called President-elect Reagan's victory a landslide and a mandate, conclusions promptly challenged by contributing historian Schlesinger, who declared, "It is hard to see how 1980, when Reagan got a bare 51 percent against a candidate who stood for nothing but himself, represented a test of anything." But the *Journal* was convinced of the genuine turn to conservatism it had predicted back in the 1972 campaign and was well satisfied with the election results. "It looks more and more like the historic event that will change the contours of both major parties for the coming generation," the paper said on November 13. "A new electoral pattern emerged in the election, although ironically obscured by the extent of the Republican sweep. It means that Northern liberals like Teddy Kennedy and Walter Mondale face greatly diminished prospects as presidential candidates."

The paper's editorials, which early in the spring advised the Federal Reserve to get on with fighting inflation and abandon attempts to fine-tune the economy, now urged Congress to get on with tax cuts. In addition to editorials, the paper published essays by Paul Craig Roberts, who had left the *Journal* to become assistant secretary of the treasury for economic policy; Peter F. Drucker, professor of social science at Claremont Graduate School; and its own Lindley Clark, lambasting Keynesians and explaining how the Reagan tax cut would help restore the American economy. "Once people catch on to the supply-side, they will realize that old categories of personal versus business tax cuts don't make any sense," wrote Roberts. "The proposed reduction in personal income tax rates is a business tax cut, too." Said Drucker: "The Keynesian panacea is essentially management of consumer demand, the creation of purchasing power through government spending. The monetarist cure-all involves keeping the money supply on an even keel. For supply-side economists, cutting tax rates will simultaneously increase consumption, increase investment, and *increase* total taxes."

The *Journal* strongly supported Reagan as a candidate and as President. "Obviously we shared many of the ideas and goals on which Mr. Reagan campaigned, but we fretted endlessly over whether his administration would have the strength, determination and intellectual coherence to make those ideas prevail—or, more to the point, to insure them a fair test," the paper said on February 10, 1981. "We feel better now."

That was three weeks after the inauguration. The *Journal* would continue to give President Reagan support, but it became dissatisfied with his White House team in later months and sometimes accused Reagan himself of forgetting campaign promises. The editors watched for apostasy by the President or his chiefs, especially Budget Director David A. Stockman, who soon proved himself guilty of heretical departure from the tenets of supply-side economics.

The *Journal* remained loyal to supply-side principles, supporting the tax cuts it said were needed to restore the economy and emphasizing the gold-standard side of the theory. "With these supply-side economists, then, tax reduction and gold have always been complementary twins," it said on October 13, 1981, after publishing articles by well-known economists, politicians, and businessmen on all sides of the gold problem. That same day the editorial page carried an essay by Arthur Laffer and associate Charles W. Kadlec urging the return to gold.

A few days earlier, the *Journal* had published Robert Mundell's similar "powerful argument for the gold standard." Said the paper, "Those who profess themselves smitten with surprise that some supply-siders find the return to gold an urgent priority either haven't been doing their homework or are a bit disingenuous. As a supply-side prescription, gold is old."

The supply-side economic position was neither accepted nor approved by all *Journal* readers, however. Some in Wall Street and the conservative community strongly dissented. One of them, syndicated columnist Kevin Phillips, calling himself a Republican conservative in his column on November 29, sneered at the *Journal*'s "fatuous paeans" to supply-side theories. "More than any other segment of the American media," fumed Phillips, "the editorial page of *The Wall Street Journal* has undercut the conservative future."

The *Journal* remained steadfast in its support of the administration in other areas. "President Reagan's four-point plan for arms reduction goes a long way toward restoring some sanity to what had become a badly bent process," it said on November 19 after the President presented his START (Strategic Arms Reduction Talks) proposal. But it criticized his "mild response" to the martial-law crisis in Poland, and his entertaining ideas of tax increases, and it cracked down on his administration for "slipshod management in the White House." On January 20, 1982, it remarked:

> Simply put, Ronald Reagan has a mammoth management problem. . . . He has failed in the task of creating a management structure to make the organization execute the policies he prefers. . . . The leading example of Mr. Reagan's problem is the ongoing spectacle of tax policy. Over the last six weeks we have read a series of accounts: David Stockman wants to raise taxes (having failed to control the deficit by cutting the budget), but the President says no. Most of the President's advisers want to raise taxes, but the President hasn't decided. The merits of the policies aside, what kind of a management organization is this?

Tax reduction had been the President's central economic initiative, the paper reminded its readers. The policy being tried had not been given a chance to work, yet Reagan's highest officials were pressuring him to back away. "They ought to be pressuring the government to find ways to make that policy work. It is ludicrous to believe that these possibilities have been exhausted."

Paul Craig Roberts, who had written persuasively on supply-side for the *Journal*, was leaving his government job, said another editorial that day. Roberts was not being fired or driven from his post but was taking "an uncommonly attractive academic post, the William E. Simon chair in political economy at Georgetown University." This departure should provide another warning sign: "When a President loses competent loyalists and retains officials who are uncertain or equivocal in their commitment to his program, it is but one more sign that he needs to have a fresh look at the management structure he has put together."

Monetarist Milton Friedman was less severe on the President. The supply-side economists were expecting too much, he told columnist William F. Buckley, Jr. The Kemp-Roth bill, he said, "just isn't going to yield high enough revenues to beat the deficit. That's one reason some of them are now shifting their emphasis to the need for the gold standard." Buckley then asked if Friedman meant that supply-side doesn't work. "Heavens no, of course it works," Friedman told him. "But what President Reagan should have done is what for political reasons he couldn't do, which is bring down a top tax of 25 percent."

So supply-siders and monetarists were on the same side, and when President Reagan, in his State of the Union speech to Congress on January 26, 1982, gave a firm no to a tax increase, *The Wall Street Journal* praised him warmly. "He raised his presidential stature a notch or two by demonstrating that an unholy coalition of putative friends and avowed enemies had not driven him out of his anti-tax position," the paper declared. And it praised President Reagan's New Federalism policy, too, saying "he recaptured the public policy agenda, at least for the time, by proposing a bold and plausible restructuring of federal and state responsibilities for social programs. After a full year, his economic policy and his presidency have survived, and to some degree prevailed, which is saying a lot when you look at the record of his recent predecessors."

Vermont Royster in his column on February 3 lauded the President for rare courage, "the courage of a political leader who in the face of much criticism and of sure opposition, of possible defeat, will state his views on his country's need and say here I stand, win or lose; I will not equivocate, I will not yield, I will not retreat. . . . In that speech he did not withdraw one inch from the policies he promised when he sought office or from those he proposed a year ago. On the contrary, he reiterated them and dared ask the nation to take further steps to implement them."

Meantime, the *Journal* published Friedman's article critical of the Federal Reserve interest-rate policy. "My complaint about monetary policy is not that it has been persistently 'too tight' or persistently 'too easy,' " he wrote, "but that it has alternated erratically between the one and the other." The Federal Reserve System, not forces outside its control, was responsible for "the yo-yo pattern of monetary control," Friedman declared.

The *Journal* responded to Friedman's attack on Paul Volcker and the Federal Reserve Board with an editorial entitled "Paul the Navigator" on February 2. Paul, chosen by Jimmy to captain the U.S.S. *Dollar*, may have been a fine skipper, the scenario suggested, but he was given a faulty compass—the M-1, the Federal Reserve formula for controlling the money supply, along with formulas M-1B and M-2. These compasses didn't always point the same way at once. The *Journal* advised Paul the Navigator, who had been "retained" by the new management, to throw away the compasses and give up his zigzag course.

Thus, in 1982, the President, the monetarists, the supply-siders, and the *Journal* appeared to be on line and firing when ready.

In the spring and summer of 1980 *Newsweek* and *Time* again reviewed the remarkable progress of *The Wall Street Journal*. Said *Newsweek* on April 21, "After it became the country's largest paper late last year, it kept right on growing, adding another 159,000 copies in less than three months to reach average sales of 1,927,000 early in March, straining its printing and delivery capacity. 'We can't get enough newsprint,' says Publisher Warren Phillips." The paper also had to turn down advertising, *Newsweek* reported.

Newsweek attributed the *Journal*'s current popularity to the intense interest in such ongoing business stories as inflation and the energy crunch, as well as to an increase of the base readership of affluent persons in the country between the ages of 35 and 54. "The *Journal* has built its editorial reputation on its thoughtful political analyses, its sophisticated interpretation of business and economic news, its eye for social trends, its company profiles and its whimsical 'off-lead' pieces covering everything from the last door-to-door milkman to the increase in assaults among airline passengers."

Time took its fresh look at the *Journal* on July 7, again calling it "the nation's truly national daily." *Time* marveled at the *Journal*'s circulation and at the advertisers standing in line to pay $43,000 a page for a full-run advertisement. It called the *Journal*'s typography "gray" and quoted Executive Editor Taylor: "The paper speaks in a calm voice, no matter how bad, how great or how exciting the news is." Front-Page Editor Glynn Mapes said, "We want graphics that add information to a story, not just decorate." "Throughout the 1950s and the 1960s, many of the *Journal*'s front page stories focused on social change," *Time* said. "But as economic and energy problems grew, and as other papers stepped up their coverage of business news, the *Journal* began concentrating more and more on its original franchise." *Time* praised the *Journal*'s Washington news staff as one of the nation's top three, along with the *New York Times* and the *Los Angeles Times*, citing for good work James M. Perry and Albert Hunt (politics); Dennis Farney (Congress); Richard J. Levine (economics); Kenneth H. Bacon (defense); and Karen Elliott House (foreign affairs).

A compliment that must have especially pleased *Journal* editors appeared in Harrison E. Salisbury's book *Without Fear or Favor*, published in 1980. In describing the changing *New York Times*, Salisbury noted that it was the dream of its late Publisher Orvil Dryfoos for his *Times* to become "a truly national paper on the pattern of *The Wall Street Journal*, where it would be able with electronics, automation, photo composition, push-button layout and makeup to produce editions that would serve other regions of the country, not just the Northeast triangle."

George N. Gordon, chairman of the communications department at Hofstra University, also rated the *Journal* a national newspaper, calling it "eccentric." "It covers only the news it wishes to cover," wrote Gordon in his book *The Communications Revolution*. "It seems to open its pages to unorthodox ideas of every kind."

The *Journal*'s new two-section paper with vast new expansion potential appeared on June 23, 1980, adding 10 percent to news space and providing more room for advertising. Months in preparation, created by Warren Phillips and his editors, the new edition provided a second front page, attractively composed, in a modular, horizontal makeup that provided display space for special features and columns. Inside was more room for international news and special business interests, which had previously received less attention. The second section, which would run 16 to 20 pages, reserved pages two and three for foreign news. Market news, quotations, data, regular features such as "Digest of Earnings Reports," and advertising filled the rest of the section.

The editorial department of the *Journal* continued its expansion, opening domestic news bureaus in Denver and Houston, and foreign bureaus in Bonn, Paris, and Peking, for a total of 26. The paper's advertising linage was up 9.1 percent in 1980 over the prior year. Between 1971 and 1976 ad linage grew 27 percent; during the 1971–80 period, it grew 88 percent. Cost per page for run of paper advertising increased from $19,003.20 per page at the national open rate in 1970 to $48,804.48 per page in January 1981. The price would be $56,121 for a national full-run page by 1982, $62,621 if the international editions were included.

Chairman Warren Phillips's 1980 annual report was upbeat as usual. Revenues totaled $530,700,000 compared with the previous high of $440,929,000 in 1979. Net income was $58,900,000 representing $3.79 net per share; dividends per share, $1.60. Printing plants were under way or scheduled at Des Moines, Iowa (the company's fourteenth, completed in

December 1981); Sharon, Pennsylvania; Bowling Green, Ohio; La Grange, Georgia; Charlotte, North Carolina; and Beaumont, Texas. The circulation of *The Wall Street Journal* reached 1,930,400, heading for 2 million in 1981. *Barron's* stood at 264,000 and showed its tenth successive year of advertising-linage increase. The Ottaway papers passed 500,000, and *The Asian Wall Street Journal* reported circulation up 14.3 percent. Richard D. Irwin, Inc., had expanded its college-textbook business to include textbooks for use by companies in development and training programs. *Book Digest* magazine was redesigned for the elitist reader under a new editor, Raymond Sokolov, a graduate of Harvard and Oxford University. It bowed in its new dress in November 1981, "a fitting companion to *The Wall Street Journal* and *Barron's*," the promotion advertising said.

Following a two-for-one stock split in the spring of 1981, there were 5,704 Dow Jones stockholders owning 32,220,042 shares out of 50 million authorized. The preponderance of the shares were owned in Massachusetts, of course, home state of the Bancroft-Barron family and the various Bancroft trusts. Among them were 784 shareholders reported in Massachusetts, 813 in New York State, and 516 in Illinois. There were shareholders in ten foreign countries, including 32 owners of 114,276 shares in Canada, 12 with 5,670 shares in the United Kingdom, one owning 500 shares in Saudi Arabia, and eight owning 3,230 shares in Hong Kong.

In April 1981 the *Wall Street Transcript*, a financial weekly established in 1963, awarded Warren H. Phillips with its gold medal after its staff and some 60 media specialists and financial analysts around the country had chosen him "the best chief executive in the publishing industry." Phillips had formidable competition for the honor: Robert F. Erburu, chief executive of the Times Mirror Company in Los Angeles, publisher of the *Los Angeles Times* and other newspapers, and owner of publishing subsidiaries, was in second place; Allen H. Neuharth, chairman, president, and chief executive officer of Gannett Company, owner of America's largest chain of daily newspapers, placed third. Said the *Transcript* in announcing its winners:

> We select Phillips for the gold award for these reasons: He has been aggressive in experimenting with new concepts for the distribution of information and has generally been ahead of his competitors in taking advantage of technological advances. Dow Jones is in the forefront in experimenting with the electronic transmission of information directly to customers. . . . He has improved *The Wall Street Journal* by adding a second section and increasing the depth of its news coverage, and it has the largest circulation of any newspaper in the country. . . . Earnings rose from $1.67 a share in 1975 when Phillips became C.E.O. to $3.79 a share last year.

Phillips obviously had no intention of resting on past achievements. He described plans for electronic publishing in 1982, Dow Jones's centennial year, including participation in cable television systems. "These moves into electronic publishing will not replace or diminish in any way the *Journal*, the Ottaway newspapers, *Barron's* or our other publications," he said. "We see cable TV as a supplementary source of information, just as news wire services, new retrieval services, and broadcasting are today. . . . Newspapers can be read whenever and wherever the reader wants, whether on planes, trains or buses, in the office or living room, on a park bench or at the beach. They can be clipped and shared. They can be browsed without knowing what you will find that will interest you. The electronic services don't have this serendipity advantage, the joy and usefulness of coming across the unexpected. This and the very great talents of our own staffs assure a long and prosperous life for newspapers in the decades ahead and reinforce our commitment to them."

At the same time, the strong Dow Jones commitment to electronic communications and journalism was again demonstrated in October 1981 when the company announced with Boston-based Continental Cablevision, Inc., an agreement to invest $80 million to acquire a 24.5 percent interest in the cable television firm. In late 1981 Continental was the thirteenth-largest multiple-cable-system operator in the United States, serving 410,000 subscribers in ten states, and it had interests in other cable systems. Separately, Dow Jones, in a partnership arrangement, was building a cable television system in Princeton, New Jersey.

Meanwhile, Dow Jones continued to expand its own electronic information distribution systems, often called data-base publishing. In November 1981 the Dow Jones News/Retrieval Service, an interactive, or two-way, information-distribution system, reached 28,000 users by means of various terminals, including personal computers and cable television. New data bases were being added at a rapid rate. The retrieval service allowed clients to call up on video screens or printers such information as historical stock-market quotations, a daily summary of *The Wall Street Journal*, and up-to-the-minute business and financial news during the working day.

In 1981 Dow Jones also began a new cable television program, "*The Wall Street Journal* Evening News," which reached 8 million homes via the USA Network, first organized in 1977 to cover Madison Square Garden sports events and later expanded to become an entertainment and education cable network.

In February 1982, Chairman Phillips reported Dow Jones's 1981 profit up 21 percent to $71.4 million, or $2.28 a share. The improvement occurred despite a third-quarter write-down of $9.4 million from the book value of *Book Digest*. Revenue in 1981 reached $641 million, also up 21 percent, compared with the 1980 total of $530.7 million. The increase, said Phillips, was largely due to strong gains in advertising and circulation at *The Wall Street Journal*. Most other operations posted higher 1981 results.

Dow Jones Chairman Phillips, in public statements, staff memos, and annual reports, continued to concentrate on ethical and almost mystical goals, though he might state them in pragmatic terms. "Strategic and non-strategic issues are inextricably linked together," he told a company management group in May 1981. "If we don't deal successfully with such issues as training our people well, encouraging them in the development of their careers, organizing ourselves with a minimum of bureaucracy, for cooperation and coordination among ourselves, then we'll stand little chance of achieving our strategic objectives or anything else for that matter. Our first strategic objective is to serve the public well. It starts with our public trust function which is to inform, to educate. It covers quality in our editorial content. It extends to quality of service to our customers, and it goes beyond that, right down to courtesy, to suppressing any outcropping of arrogance."

Phillips continued this theme in his 1982 message to *Journal* readers, opening the Dow Jones centennial year:

> Through the years, the chief goal of the *Journal* and Dow Jones has never been to be the biggest, but rather to be the best in the business news field—to excel in the quality and usefulness of the information and service provided to you. Our purpose has been to serve readers and our society well. As Dow Jones enters its centennial year we are moved to pause and reflect with you on what the company and the *Journal* may have achieved.
>
> We like to think that to the extent we have made business news understandable, even popularized it in some respects, we have made knowledge of how our economy works more widely accessible. We have tried to take business issues out of the world of the arcane and esoteric, strip them of their mysteries and enable any of us to understand what was going on.
>
> We like to think that more readily available knowledge and awareness, in turn, opened up more opportunities for advancement to employees and employers, entrepreneurs and professionals, young and old. Perhaps, by making accurate information widely available and by spreading understanding, *The Wall Street Journal* and Dow Jones's other publications have played some part in the unprecedented growth of American business and the American economy in many of our readers' lives. We would like to think so.

Notes and Acknowledgments

Charles Dow, Edward Jones, and Charles Bergstresser may have been too preoccupied with day-to-day reporting to keep enduring records. Almost none for the years before 1900 have been found. This situation isn't unusual among American newsmen and businessmen of that era. Kenneth Wiggins Porter, author of *John Jacob Astor, Business Man*, deplores the loss of boxes of early Astor data "for want of a small cartage fee" when Astor moved his quarters. In his biography of John D. Rockefeller, Allan Nevins complains that his subject was inconsiderately careless of early company records. Dow Jones & Company also moved frequently in the beginning. Unlike Adolph Ochs, who wrote home to Knoxville, Tennessee, of his early struggles with his *New York Times*, or Joseph Medill, who described to his wife, Katherine, his problems with the *Chicago Tribune*, Dow and Jones appear to have written nothing of a personal nature to anyone; only Bergstresser, reporting his retirement travels to his daughter, Ethel, has left a few words concerning the Dow Jones beginning.

The early days have been recounted in some detail, however, by associates of the Dow Jones & Company founding partners. Thomas Woodlock, editor of *The Wall Street Journal* after Dow, left a considerable record in his columns over a number of years. John W. Barney, brought to New York by Dow from the *Providence Journal*, where he had worked with Dow and Jones, later became president of Dow Jones & Company and provided useful information in his memoirs, published in the *Providence Journal* in 1904. William Peter Hamilton, also an editor of *The Wall Street Journal*, provides a brief but useful biography of Charles Dow in *The Stock Market Barometer*, his book on the Dow Theory published in 1922. Other biographical data on Dow appear in early books by Benton W. Davis, Samuel Nelson, and Sereno Pratt (who followed Woodlock as editor), and in recent books dealing with the Dow Theory by George W. Bishop, Jr., and Harold M. Finley. Bishop has given us the most complete biography of Charles Dow, including some of Dow's early newspaper articles from the *Providence Journal*. Finley has written an excellent appreciation of the Dow Theory in *Everybody's Guide to the Stock Market*. The books cited here and in the text are listed in the Bibliography. The best summary of the first 20 years of Dow Jones & Company activity can be found in *The Wall Street Journal*'s fiftieth anniversary issue, published on June 27, 1932, to which Woodlock, Henry Alloway, and other veterans made extensive contributions.

Information on Dow Jones & Company is widely scattered. I am grateful to Dow Jones and *Wall Street Journal* personnel who aided me in a difficult search, as well as to the always helpful staffs of various libraries. I was especially aided by Bruce Levy and Dorothy Vero of the Dow Jones reference department; and by William McSherry, former secretary and assistant to Barney Kilgore and now manager of news-department services, and Robert Werner, former secretary to William F. Kerby, who between them provided memoranda, letters, and records relating to the Kilgore, Hogate, and Barron eras. Notes written by Louis M. Atherton, William P. Tidwell, Edward M. Stein, and Arthur Lissner when they were secretaries to C. W. Barron and other top executives proved highly useful. Arthur Lissner became secretary and assistant to Kilgore; Edward Stein became circulation manager of the *Journal* in the Kilgore era. Mrs. Claire R. French, librarian of the Sterling Library, Oneco, Connecticut, and Mrs. Cathy Nurmi of the Sterling Historical Society were most helpful in the search for Charles Dow data in the town where Dow was born. Ruth Gallup and her sister, Mrs. Julia Geist, whose parents and grandparents were neighbors of the Dows on Ekonk Hill, Connecticut, also provided information on Charles Dow and his parents.

Staffs of the following New York libraries have been very helpful: Dow Jones Library, Lottie Lindberg, librarian; New York Stock Exchange Library, Jean Taber, librarian, and Deborah Gardner, archivist; Pierpont Morgan Library; New York Public Library, one of the country's best research institutions; New York Historical Society; United Nations Library; and Brooklyn Public Library. Other libraries have also assisted me, including the Library of Congress, Washington, D.C.; George F. Baker Business Library, Harvard University, Cambridge, Massachusetts, which has the C. W. Barron scrapbooks and the files of the *Boston News Bureau* (1887–1947); Yale University Library, New Haven, Connecticut, where the original copies of most editions of *The Wall Street Journal* may be found; Babson College Library, Wellesley, Massachusetts; John D. Rockefeller, Jr., Library and Athenaeum Library, Brown University, Providence, Rhode Island; David Bishop Skillman Library, Lafayette College, Easton, Pennsylvania; Sterling Public Library, Oneco, Connecticut; Orange County Library, Orlando, Florida; Hudson Library, Highlands, North Carolina; and Macon County Library, Franklin, North Carolina.

C. W. Barron left a diary meticulously recording the first days of his Boston News Bureau. While he left no detailed record of what transpired when he purchased Dow Jones & Company in 1902, other than the minutes of his Boston company and those of the Dow Jones & Company joint-stock association, he dictated thousands of notes, letters, and memos in his lifetime. Pound and Moore, in their brief biography of Barron written as a foreword to their first book, *They Told Barron*, estimated that they reviewed 2 million words. None of these, however, tell precisely how it happened that Barron named Mrs. Jessie Waldron Barron, his wife and former landlady, to be his surrogate in the management of Dow Jones & Company and *The Wall Street Journal* from 1902 until he assumed active management in 1912. However, Barron indicates in the material published in two volumes by Pound and Moore that he rarely had direct contact with *The Wall Street Journal* staff.

The account of the transition of Dow Jones & Company to the Barrons can be reconstructed from the memoranda left by Barron's secretaries and the Dow Jones corporate records. Also, the manuscript biography of Barron by William L. Moise, a Wall Street banker who was acquainted with the publisher, has proved extremely helpful, though Moise did not have access to some memos and records. The Moise manuscript in the Dow Jones Archives provides an excellent account of Barron's early life, using in part Barron's autobiography of his early years and material obtained through research and interviews. Jessie Barron's management of Dow Jones and the *Journal* for a decade is borne out by Dow Jones corporate records. They also tend to support the story of Tidwell, Lissner, and others that Mrs. Barron's mining stock, which she considered valueless until Barron was able to sell it for her, provided the funds that, with Barron's 63 personal notes, enabled them to buy Dow Jones & Company.

The Wall Street Journal itself is, of course, the source of much of the information for this book. I have benefited also from the personal recollections of several company officials, directors, and workers. They have been extremely cooperative in participating in interviews and in guiding me to sources and data.

I am grateful to William F. Kerby, former Dow Jones & Company chairman, chief executive, and publisher of *The Wall Street Journal*, and present chairman of the board of trustees, New College Foundation of the University of South Florida, who has given me much guidance and help, including advance access to his excellent memoirs, *A Proud Profession*, published in 1981. Since Chairman Kerby knew K. C. Hogate, William Grimes, and others of an earlier era, and was the closest associate and eventual successor of Barney Kilgore, his recollections and writings have been of great help to me in checking and organizing my material.

Similarly, other busy executives have given me their full cooperation and help: Warren H. Phillips, chairman of the board, chief executive of Dow Jones, and publisher of the *Journal*; Ray Shaw, president of Dow Jones & Company; Vermont Royster, former editor of the *Journal* and now professor of journalism and public affairs at the University of North Carolina; Donald A. Macdonald, vice-chairman and president of the Dow Jones Magazine Group and the International Group; and Sterling E. Soderlind, vice-president/planning.

Others I have interviewed include Dow Jones directors Jane Bancroft Cook, Laurence Lombard, and Robert S. Potter, and the following Dow Jones and *Wall Street Journal* staff members: George W. Flynn, senior vice-president; Robert L. Bartley, editor; Peter R. Kann, vice-president and associate publisher of the *Journal*; vice-presidents Edward R. Cony and William L. Dunn; Frederick Taylor, executive editor; Laurence G. O'Donnell, managing editor of the *Journal*; Everett H. Groseclose, manager of the Dow Jones news services; Daniel Hinton, national news production manager; Larry Armour, public relations and corporate affairs; Robert McGilvray and Edward Behr, Washington bureau; Frederic G. Sibley, director of special projects, advertising; and Thomas G. Sullivan, director of special projects, treasurer's department, who helped me especially with research into corporate records.

I found particularly helpful my interviews with George Flynn, president of the Affiliated Companies Group, and William Dunn, president of the Information Services Group and the Operating Services Group, concerning the early developments in satellite communications of Dow Jones and the *Journal*. I'm also grateful for the demonstrations and explanations provided by William Satterfield, production manager, and Jim Peters, satellite-operations supervisor at the Orlando, Florida, plant, and to Michael Clark, production manager, and Larry Wolf, satellite-operations supervisor at the Seattle, Washington, facility.

I owe a debt to Ray Vicker, one of the *Journal*'s leading writers and foreign correspondents, who patiently provided me with information and insights, in person and in fascinating letters. I also drew heavily on the series of interviews conducted by John F. Bridge, former editor of editorial-page features for *The Wall Street Journal* and former managing editor of the *National Observer*, with staff members of the *Journal* and, in two cases, their widows. Some 40 of these valuable interviews are available in the Dow Jones Archives, and I have quoted and used information from the following: Joseph J. Ackell; Betty Donnelly Angelini; Mary Lou Kilgore, widow of Bernard Kilgore, now Mary Lou Berlman; Robert Bottorff; Theodore Callis; Lindley Clark; Jessie Bancroft Cox; Maurice "Larry" Farrell; Henry Gemmill; Ellis Haller; Anna Hogate, widow of K. C. Hogate, now Anna Hogate Hamlet; Sam Lesch; John McWethy; Norman C. Miller; John O'Riley; Alan Otten; Vermont Royster; George Shea; Ray Vicker; and John Williams.

I am particularly indebted to Harold Finley, Chicago investment manager, chairman of the board of Lincoln Memorial University, and author of books on stock-market and investment practices, who has guided me on my difficult way through the Dow Theory and the arcane lore of Wall Street. I am grateful to Hugh Lalor, formerly of the Miami business community, for background on Florida in the fabulous 1920s; Larry Armour, corporate affairs manager, Dow Jones & Company; Leonard E. Doherty, assistant to the vice-president/finance, Dow Jones; and Anne Ruggiero for assistance in my interviews and research work in New York and Princeton, New Jersey.

I owe much to the editors of Rand McNally & Company. A newspaper history is replete with unique problems since newspapers are involved in so many widely varied activities at the same time; those of Dow Jones, pioneering new kinds of technology as well as journalism, proved particularly difficult for me. I especially appreciate the interest of Elliott H. McCleary, senior editor, and the achievement of Peggy Leith Anderson, who shaped up my prior newspaper history, and who, ably assisted by Deborah Jacobs, has done it once again.

Finally, without the help and understanding of Martha Wendt, and the dedicated assistance of Susan M. Chin, who aided with the research and expertly discharged the responsibilities of manuscript preparation, I could not have met the challenges of this task.

LLOYD WENDT
SARASOTA

Selected Bibliography

Adams, Henry. *The Education of Henry Adams*. New York: Time, Inc., 1964.

Adams, James Truslow, et al., eds. *Album of American History*. 4 vols. New York: Scribner's, 1944–48.

Allen, Frederick Lewis. *Only Yesterday: An Informal History of the 1920s*. New York: Harper & Row, 1931.

Andrews, Wayne, ed. *Concise Dictionary of American History*. New York: Scribner's, 1962.

Barron, Clarence W. *The Boston Stock Exchange*. Boston: Hunt & Bell, 1893.

———. *Financial Affairs*. (Columns from *Boston Transcript*, Vols. 1-6, Baker Library, Harvard University, Mass.)

Baruch, Bernard M. *My Own Story*. New York: Henry Holt & Company, 1957.

———. *The Public Years*. New York: Holt, Rinehart & Winston, 1960.

Beard, Charles A., and Beard, Mary R. *New Basic History of the United States*. Garden City, N.Y.: Doubleday, 1968.

Berger, Meyer. *The Story of The New York Times*. New York: Simon & Schuster, 1951.

Bishop, George W., Jr. *Charles H. Dow and the Dow Theory*. New York: Appleton-Century-Crofts, 1960.

———. *Charles H. Dow, Economist*. Princeton, N.J.: Dow Jones Books, 1967.

Brooks, John. *Once in Galconda*. New York: Harper & Row, 1969.

———. *The Seven Fat Years*. New York: Harper & Row, 1958.

Byrnes, Garrett D., and Spilman, Charles H. *The Providence Journal, 150 Years*. Providence, R.I.: Providence Journal Company, 1980.

Cabel, Phillip. *From Crash to the Blitz, 1929–1939*. New York: New York Times Company, 1969.

Carson, Gerald. *The Polite Americans*. New York: William Morrow, 1966.

Clark, Lindley H., Jr. *The Secret Tax*. Princeton, N.J.: Dow Jones Books, 1976.

Clews, Henry. *Fifty Years in Wall Street*. New York: J. S. Ogilvie Publishing Company, 1908.

Comier, Frank. *Wall Street's Shady Side*. Washington, D.C.: Public Affairs Press, 1962.

Crockett, Albert Stevens. *Peacocks on Parade: A Narrative of a Unique Period in American Social History and its Most Colorful Figures*. New York: Sears, 1931.

Daniels, Jonathan. *The Time Between the Wars*. Garden City, N.Y.: Doubleday, 1966.

Davis, Benton W. *Dow 1000: The Exponential Secret of the Great Bull Market*. New York: Womrath, 1923.

de Conde, Alexander. *A History of American Foreign Policy*. 2nd ed. New York: Scribner's, 1971.

Dictionary of American History. 7 vols. and index. 3rd rev. ed. New York: Scribner's, 1928–1974.

Dow, Charles H. *History of Steam Navigation between Providence and New York*. Providence, R.I.: William Turner & Company, 1877.

———. *Newport, the City by the Sea*. Providence, R.I.: John E. Sanborn, 1880.

Dow, Robert Pierce. *The Book of Dow*. Rutland, Vt.: The Tuttle Company, 1929.

Eames, Francis L. *The New York Stock Exchange*. New York: G. K. Hall, 1894.

Eckenrode, H. J., and Wight, P. W. *E. H. Harriman: The Little Giant of Wall Street*. New York: Greenberg, 1933.

Ellis, Edward Robb. *The Epic of New York City*. New York: Coward-McCann, 1966.

Evans, Rowland, and Novak, Robert. *The Reagan Revolution*. New York: E. P. Dutton, 1981.

Farrell, Maurice L., ed. *The Dow Jones Averages, 1885–1970*. New York: Dow Jones Books, 1972.

Faulkner, Harold Underwood. *American Economic History*. Rev. ed. New York: Harper, 1931.

———. *American Economic History*. 8th ed. New York: Harper, 1960.

Finley, Harold M. *Everybody's Guide to the Stock Market*. Chicago: Henry Regnery, 1956.

Fisher, Irving. *The Stock Market Crash—and After*. New York: Macmillan, 1930.

Friedman, Milton, and Schwartz, Anna J. *A Monetary History of the United States, 1867–1960*. Princeton, N.J.: Princeton University Press, 1963.

Friedman, Milton, and Friedman, Rose. *Free to Choose: A Personal Statement*. New York: Harcourt, Brace & Jovanovich, 1980.
Galbraith, John K. *The Affluent Society*. 2nd rev. ed. Boston: Houghton Mifflin, 1969.
———. *Economics and the Public Purpose*. Boston: Houghton Mifflin, 1973.
———. *The Great Crash, 1929*. Boston: Houghton Mifflin, 1955.
———. *The Industrial State*. Boston: Houghton Mifflin, 1967.
Gardner, John W., ed. *President John F. Kennedy: To Turn the Tide*. New York: Harper & Brothers, 1962.
Gilder, George. *Wealth and Poverty*. New York: Basic Books, Inc., 1981.
Half a Century with The Providence Journal. Providence, R.I.: Providence Journal Publishing Company, 1904.
Hamilton, William Peter. *The Stock Market Barometer*. New York: Harper, 1922.
Harris, Seymour E. *Twenty Years of Federal Reserve Policy*. Cambridge, Mass.: Harvard University Press, 1933.
Hendrick, Burton J. *The Age of Big Business: A Chronicle of the Captains of Industry*. New Haven, Conn.: Yale University, 1919.
Hungerford, Edward. *Men and Iron*. New York: Thomas Y. Crowell Company, 1938.
Josephson, Matthew. *The Robber Barons: The Great American Capitalists, 1861–1901*. New York: Harcourt, Brace, 1934.
Kerby, William F. *A Proud Profession: Memoirs of a* Wall Street Journal *Reporter, Editor, and Publisher*. Homewood, Ill.: Dow Jones-Irwin, 1981.
Keynes, John Maynard. *The General Theory of Employment, Interest, and Money*. New York: Harcourt, Brace, 1935.
Kogan, Herman, and Wendt, Lloyd. *Bet a Million! The Story of John W. Gates*. Indianapolis: Bobbs-Merrill, 1953.
Lekachman, Robert. *The Age of Keynes*. New York: Random House, 1966.
Lyons, Eugene. *Herbert Hoover: A Biography*. New York: Doubleday, 1964.
MacDougall, A. Kent. *The Press, A Critical Look from the Inside*. Princeton, N.J.: Dow Jones Books, 1972.
Medbury, James K. *Men and Mysteries of Wall Street*. Wells, Vt.: Fraser Publishing Company, 1876.
Miller, Norman C. *The Great Salad Oil Swindle*. London: Victor Gollancz, 1966.
Moise, W. S. J. Barron manuscripts. New York: Dow Jones Archives.
Morison, Samuel Eliot, and Commager, Henry Steele. *The Growth of the American Republic*. 2 vols. 4th rev. ed. New York: Oxford, 1950.
Morrison, Elling E., ed. *The Letters of Theodore Roosevelt*. Cambridge, Mass.: Harvard University Press, 1952.
Moscow, Warren. *Roosevelt and Willkie*. Englewood Cliffs, N.J.: Prentice-Hall, 1968.
Nelson, Samuel Armstrong. *The ABC of Stock Speculation,* Vol. 5 of Nelson's Wall Street Library. New York: S. A. Nelson, 1900.
Nevins, Allan. *Grover Cleveland: A Study in Courage*. New York: Dodd, Mead, 1932.
———. *John D. Rockefeller*. 2 vols. New York: Charles Scribner's Sons, 1940.
Noyes, Alexander Dana. *Forty Years of American Finance*. New York: G. P. Putnam's Sons, 1898.
———. *The Market Place: Reminiscences of a Financial Editor*. Boston: Little, 1938.
Pecora, Ferdinand. *Wall Street Under Oath*. New York: Simon & Schuster, 1937.
Phillips, Warren H., and Keatley, Robert. *China: Behind the Mask*. Princeton, N.J.: Dow Jones Books, 1973.
Pound, Arthur, and Moore, Samuel Taylor. *More They Told Barron*. New York: Harper & Brothers, 1931.
———. *They Told Barron*. New York: Harper & Brothers, 1930.
Pratt, Sereno S. *The Work of Wall Street*. New York: D. Appleton & Company, 1921.
Prestbo, John A. *This Abundant Land*. Princeton, N.J.: Dow Jones Books, 1968–73.
Preston, Charles, ed. *The Best of The Wall Street Journal*. Chicopee, Mass.: Dow Jones Books, 1973–74.
———. *The New World of The Wall Street Journal*. New York: Simon & Schuster, 1963.
———. *The World of The Wall Street Journal*. New York: Simon & Schuster, 1959.

Rhea, Robert. *The Dow Theory*. New York: *Barron's*, 1932.
Rider, Fremont, ed. *Rider's New York City*. New York: Macmillan, 1924.
Roberts, Charles. *LBJ's Inner Circle*. New York: Delacorte Press, 1965.
Roberts, Edwin A., Jr. *The Stock Market*. New York: Franklin Watts, 1965.
Rosenboon, Eugene H., and Eckes, Alfred E., Jr. *A History of Presidential Elections*. New York: Macmillan, 1957.
Royster, Vermont. *A Pride of Prejudices*. New York: Alfred A. Knopf, 1967.
Satterlee, Herbert L. *J. Pierpont Morgan: An Intimate Portrait*. 2 vols. New York: Macmillan, 1940.
Schlesinger, Arthur M., Jr. *The Age of Roosevelt, The Crisis of the Old Order, 1919–1933*. Boston: Houghton Mifflin, 1957.
———. *The Coming of the New Deal*. Boston: Houghton Mifflin, 1959.
———. *The Imperial Presidency*. Boston: Houghton Mifflin, 1973.
———. *A Thousand Days: John F. Kennedy in the White House*. Boston: Houghton Mifflin, 1965.
Securities and Exchange Commission. *In the Matter of Richard Whitney*. Washington, D.C.: Library of Congress, 1938.
Senate Committee on Banking and Currency, *Stock Exchange Practices,* Vols. 1-6. Washington, D.C.: Library of Congress, 1932.
Sherwood, Robert. *Roosevelt and Hopkins, An Intimate History*. New York: Harper & Brothers, 1948.
Simonds, William Adams. *Edison, His Life, His Work, His Genius*. Indianapolis: Bobbs-Merrill, 1934.
Sloan, Harold D., and Zurcher, Arnold. *Dictionary of Economics*. 5th ed. New York: Barnes & Noble, 1970.
Smith, E. V. *The City of New York*. Riverside, Conn.: Chatham Press, 1789.
Smith, Howard R. *Economic History of the United States*. New York: Ronald Press, 1955.
Sobel, Robert. *The Big Board*. New York: Free Press, 1965.
———. *The Great Bull Market: Wall Street in the 1920s*. New York: Norton, 1968.
———. *A History of the New York Stock Exchange, 1935–1975*. New York: Weybright and Talley, 1975.
———. *Panic on Wall Street*. New York: Macmillan, 1968.
Sparling, Earl. *Mystery Men of Wall Street: The Powers Behind the Market*. New York: Greenberg, 1930.
Stedman, Edmund C. *The New York Stock Exchange*. New York: Stock Exchange Historical Company, 1905.
Sterling in Retrospect. Sterling, Conn.: Sterling Bicentennial Committee, 1976.
Sullivan, Mark. *Our Times: The United States, 1900–1925,* Vol. 1, *The Turn of the Century, 1900–1904*. New York: Scribner's, 1926.
Talese, Gay. *The Kingdom and the Power*. New York: World Publishing Company, 1969.
Teblou, Charleton W. *A History of Florida*. Coral Gables, Fla.: University of Miami Press, 1971.
Thompson, Slason. *A Short History of American Railways, Covering Ten Decades*. New York: D. Appleton-Century, 1925.
Van Antwerp, William C. *The Stock Exchange from Within*. Garden City, N.Y.: Doubleday, Page, 1914.
Veblen, Thorstein. *The Theory of the Leisure Class*. New York: Modern Library, 1934.
Villard, Oswald G. *Early History of Wall Street, 1653–1789*. New York: G. P. Putnam's Sons, 1897.
Wanniski, Jude. *The Way the World Works*. New York: Simon & Schuster, 1978.
Warren, Harris Gaylord. *Herbert Hoover and the Great Depression*. New York: Oxford University Press, 1959.
White, Theodore H. *The Making of the President 1972*. New York: Atheneum Publishers, 1973.
Wickwire, Arthur M. *The Wicked Deeds of Wall Street*. New York: New Castle Press, 1933.
Wilson, Woodrow. *The Public Papers of Woodrow Wilson*. 3 vols. Edited by Ray Stannard Baker and William E. Dodd. New York: Harper, 1927.
Winkler, John K. *Morgan the Magnificent*. New York: Vanguard Press, 1930.
Wyckoff, Peter. *Wall Street and the Stock Markets*. Philadelphia, Pa.: Chilton, 1922.

Index